Bed & Breakfast

Where to Stay Guide 2006

visitscotland.com
0845 22 55 121

Scotland is split into eight tourist areas. You will find accommodation listed alphabetically by location within each of these areas. There is an index at the back of this book of all associated accommodation operators in VisitScotland's Quality Assurance Schemes which may also help you.

Introduction

Accommodation

Appendix

More Accommodation

Welcome to Scotland

Bed & Breakfast

A bed and breakfast is perfect for a short holiday – an escape to the country, a city break in Edinburgh or Glasgow, or a place to unwind after a day's travel or business. It's also the ideal accommodation for stopping on a touring holiday to take in the history and scenery that make Scotland famous.

There's a wide range of bed and breakfasts to choose from around the country, wherever you may travel – whether it be a farmhouse in a highland glen, a croft on a remote Scottish island, or in the heart of Scotland's buzzing city-life.

Friendly, hospitable and always economical, the bed and breakfast is one of the best ways you can get to know Scotland – and the Scots. The family home atmosphere, where the owner's touch makes all the difference, offers good food, comfortable surroundings, together with local knowledge, advice and information. It's a great combination, offering good value for money.

Welcoming doors – to suit every taste – are awaiting you, so start making your choices now from the hundreds available in this book!

Using This Book

Bed & Breakfast

Where to Stay...?
Over 1800 answers to the age-old question!

Revised annually, this is the most comprehensive guide to serviced accommodation in Scotland.

Every property in the guide has been graded by VisitScotland Quality Advisors.
See page vi for details.

How to find accommodation
This book has been split into eight areas of Scotland:

The map on page xix shows these areas. Within each area section you will find accommodation listed alphabetically by location.

Alternatively there is an index at the back of this book listing alphabetically the accommodation locations in Scotland.

More Accommodation
There is also a complete directory of all VisitScotland Quality Assured Serviced Establishments on page 251.

Using This Book

Bed & Breakfast

Learn to use the symbols in each entry – they will contain a mine of information! There is a key to symbols on the back flap.

Naturally, it is always advisable to confirm with the establishment that a particular facility is still available.

Prices in this guide are quoted per person and represent the minimum and maximum charges expected to apply to most rooms in the establishment. They include VAT at the appropriate rate and service charges where applicable.

The prices of accommodation, services and facilities are supplied to us by the accommodation operators and were, to the best of our knowledge, correct at the time of going to press. However, prices can change at any time during the lifetime of the publication, and you should check again when you book.

Bookings can be made direct to the establishment, through local Tourist Information Centres, through a travel agent or through **Scotland's National Booking and Information Centre –** Tel: 0845 22 55 121. or, from outside the UK: +44 (0)1506 832121

A £3 booking fee applies to telephone bookings through the National Booking Centre.

The prices stated are inclusive of a 10% agency commission where applicable.

Remember, when you accept accommodation by telephone or in writing, you are entering a legally binding contract which must be fulfilled on both sides. Should you fail to take up accommodation, you may not only forfeit any deposit already paid, but may also have to compensate the establishment if the accommodation cannot be re-let.

Using This Book

Bed & Breakfast

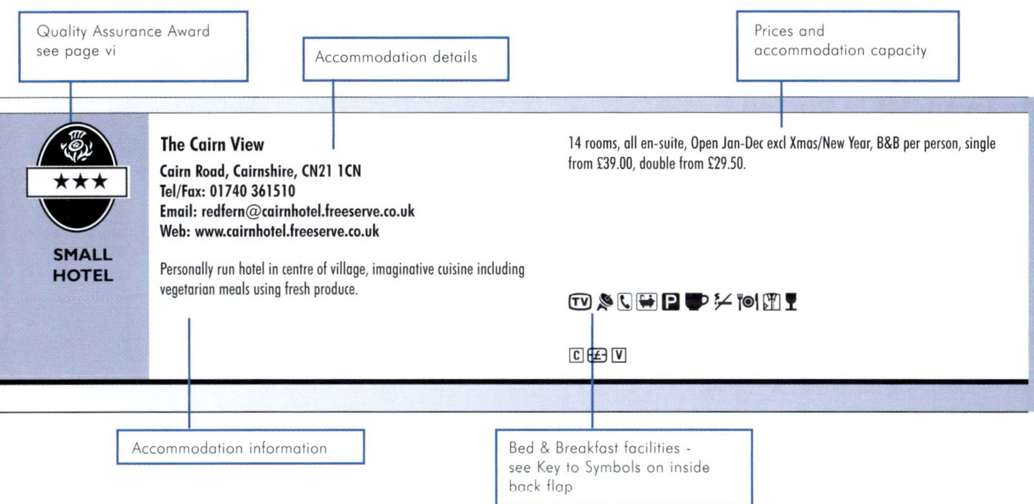

Disclaimer

VisitScotland has published this guide in good faith to reflect information submitted to it by the proprietors of the premises listed who have paid for their entries to be included. Although VisitScotland has taken reasonable steps to confirm the information contained in the guide at the time of going to press, it cannot guarantee that the information published is and remains accurate.

Accordingly, VisitScotland recommends that all information is checked with the proprietor of the premises prior to booking to ensure that the accommodation, its price and all other aspects of the premises are satisfactory.

VisitScotland accepts no responsibility for any error or misrepresentation contained in the guide and excludes all liability for loss or damage caused by any reliance placed on the information contained in the guide. VisitScotland also cannot accept any liability for loss caused by the bankruptcy, or liquidation, or insolvency, or cessation of trade of any company, firm or individual contained in this guide.

Signs You Need To Know

Quality Grading

Follow the stars and you won't be disappointed when you get to the inn.

The VisitScotland Star System is a world-first. Quality is what determines our star awards, not a checklist of facilities. We've made your priorities our priorities.

Quality makes or breaks a visit. This is why the most important aspects of your stay; the warmth of welcome, efficiency and friendliness of service, the quality of the food and the cleanliness and condition of the furnishings, fittings and decor earn VisitScotland Stars, not the size of the accommodation or the range of available facilities.

This easy to understand system tells you at a glance the quality standard of all types and sizes of accommodation from the smallest B&B and self-catering cottage to the largest countryside and city centre hotels.

Quality Assurance awards correct at end September 2005

Look out for this distinctive sign of Quality Assured Accommodation.

VisitScotland star grading schemes take the guesswork out of arranging a holiday in Scotland. Branded under the Scottish Tourist Board label, the schemes are impartial, reliable and easy to understand.

Signs You Need To Know

Quality Grading

The standards you can expect:

★★★★★   Exceptional
★★★★   Excellent
★★★   Very good
★★   Good
★   Fair and Acceptable

A trained VisitScotland Quality Advisor grades each property every year to give you the reassurance that you can choose accommodation of the quality standard you want.

To help you further in your choice the VisitScotland System also tells you the type of accommodation and the range of facilities and services available.

Please turn over for details.

For further information call into any Tourist Information Centre, or contact VisitScotland.

More details available from:

Quality and Standards Department
VisitScotland
Thistle House
Beechwood Park North
INVERNESS
IV2 3ED

Tel: **01463 723040**
Fax: **01463 717244**
Email: **qa@visitscotland.com**

If you have a complaint about your accommodation, make it known to the management as soon as possible so that they can take action to investigate and resolve the problem. You should not feel reluctant to complain if you are dissatisfied with some aspect of your accommodation. Indeed, it is always the best policy to draw attention to the problem on the spot. Proprietors and their staff want you to return and for you to recommend what they provide to your friends. If you let them know what displeases you at the time they have an opportunity to put matters right. However, if you do have a problem with one of our Quality Assured properties which has not been resolved by the proprietor, please contact us at the above address.

Signs You Need To Know

Quality Grading

Accommodation Types:

Self Catering

A house, cottage, apartment, chalet or similar accommodation which is let normally on a weekly basis to individuals where facilities are provided to cater for yourselves.

Serviced Apartments

Serviced apartments are essentially self catering apartments where services such as a cleaning service is available and meals and drinks may be available. Meals and drinks would normally be provided to each apartment or in a restaurant and/or bar which is on site.

Guest House

A guest house is usually a commercial business and will normally have a minimum of 4 letting bedrooms, of which some will have ensuite or private facilities. Breakfast will be available and evening meals may be provided.

B&B

Accommodation offering bed and breakfast, usually in a private house. B&B's will normally accommodate no more than 6 guests, and may or may not serve an evening meal.

Hotel

A hotel will normally have a minimum of 20 letting bedrooms, of which the majority will have ensuite or private bathroom facilities. A hotel will normally have a drinks licence (may be a restricted licence) and will serve breakfast, dinner and normally lunch.

Small Hotel

A small hotel will normally have a maximum of 20 letting bedrooms and a minimum of 6. The majority of the bedrooms will have ensuite or private facilities. A small hotel will be licenced (may be a restricted licence) and will serve breakfast, dinner and normally lunch. It will normally be run by owner(s) and reflect their style and personal input.

International Resort Hotel

A hotel achieving a 5 Star quality award which owns and offers a range of leisure and sporting facilities including an 18 hole golf course, swimming and leisure centre and country pursuits.

Lodge

Primarily purpose-built overnight accommodation, often situated close to a major road or in a city centre. Reception hours may be restricted and payment may be required on check in. There may be associated restaurant facilities.

Inn

Bed and breakfast accommodation provided within a traditional inn or pub environment. A restaurant and bar will be open to non-residents and will provide restaurant or bar food at lunchtime and in the evening.

Restaurant with Rooms

In a restaurant with rooms, the restaurant is the most significant part of the business. It is usually open to non-residents. Accommodation is available, and breakfast is usually provided.

Campus Accommodation

Campus accommodation is provided by colleges and universities for their students and is made available - with meals - for individuals, families or groups at certain times of the year. These typically include the main Summer holiday period as well as Easter and Christmas.

Signs You Need To Know

Quality Grading

Serviced Accommodation: Facility and Service Symbols

TV in bedrooms

Satellite/cable TV

Tea/coffee making facilities in bedrooms

Telephone in bedrooms

Hairdryer in bedrooms

Evening meal available

Room service

Restaurant

Leisure facilities

Indoor swimming pool

Laundry service

Porterage

Lounge

TV Lounge

Full alcohol drinks licence

Restricted alcohol drinks licence

Non-smoking establishment

Smoking restricted

Payphone provided

Washbasin in bedrooms

Ensuite bath and/or shower for all bedrooms

Ensuite bath and/or shower for some bedrooms

Private bath and/or shower for all bedrooms

Private bath and/or shower for some bedrooms

Private parking

Limited parking

No TV

For a Quality Destination

You not only want to be sure of the standard of accommodation you choose to stay in, whichever type it may be, you want to be sure you make the most of your time.

VisitScotland not only grades every type of accommodation every year, but also a wide range of visitor attractions every second year to grade the standard of customer care provided for visitors.

The grading scheme for visitor attractions provides you with the assurance that an attraction has been assessed for the condition and standard of the facilities and services provided – the warmth of welcome, efficiency of service, level of cleanliness, standard of visitor interpretation and of the toilets, restaurant and shop, if provided.

A large world famous castle, or small local museum can attain high grades if their services for the visitor are of a high standard.

The Standards You Can Expect:

★★★★★ Exceptional
★★★★ Excellent
★★★ Very good
★★ Good
★ Fair and Acceptable

In addition to the star grades, every attraction is categorised under one of the following types to help give the visitor an indication of the type of experience on offer:

Visitor Attraction
Castle
Historic Attraction
Museum
Tour
Garden
Activity Centre
Tourist Shop
Leisure Centre
Arts Venue
Historic House
Garden Centre

Look for the VisitScotland/Scottish Tourist Board sign of quality:

Signs You Need To Know

Mobility Needs

Visitors with particular mobility needs must be able to be secure in the knowledge that suitable accommodation is available to match these requirements. Advance knowledge of accessible entrances, bedrooms and facilities is important to enable visitors to enjoy their stay.

Along with the quality awards which apply to all the establishments in this, and every VisitScotland guide, we operate a national accessibility scheme. By inspecting establishments to set criteria, we can identify and promote places that meet the requirements of visitors with mobility needs.

The three categories of accessibility – drawn up in close consultation with specialist organisations are:

 Unassisted wheelchair access for residents

 Assisted wheelchair access for residents

 Access for residents with mobility difficulties

Look out for these symbols in establishments, in advertising and brochures. They assure you that entrances, ramps, passageways, doors, restaurant facilities, bathrooms and toilets, as well as kitchens in self catering properties, have been inspected with reference to the needs of wheelchair users, and those with mobility difficulties. Write or telephone for details of the standards in each category – address on page vii.

For more information about travel, specialist organisations who can provide information and a list of all the Scottish accommodation which has had the access inspection, get in touch with our **National Information and Booking Line on:**
0845 22 55 121 or e-mail: info@visitscotland.com
(or ask at a Tourist Information Centre) for the VisitScotland booklet "Accessible Scotland".

A £3 booking fee applies to telephone bookings of accommodation.

Tourism for All
The Hawkins Suite
Enham Place
Enham Alamein
Andover
Hampshire SP11 6JS

Tel: **0845 124 9971**
Fax: **0845 124 9972**
Minicom: **0845 124 9976**
Email: **info@holidaycare.org**
Web: **www.tourismforall.org.uk**
In addition, a referral service to put enquirers in touch with local disability advice centres is:

Update
27 Beaverhall Road
Edinburgh
EH7 4JE

Tel: **0131 558 5200**
Fax: **0131 558 5201**
Minicom: **0131 558 5202**
Email: **info@update.org.uk**
Web: **www.update.org.uk**

Signs You Need To Know

Quality Grading

Over 1000 quality assured accommodation providers are offering an extra warm welcome for visitors who are cycling or walking for all, or part, of their holiday in Scotland.

As well as having had the quality of the welcome, service, food and comfort assessed by VisitScotland, they will be able to offer the following:-

★ hot drink on arrival
★ packed lunch/flask filling option
★ late evening meal option
★ early breakfast option
★ drying facilities for wet clothes
★ local walking and/or cycling information
★ daily weather forecast
★ local public transport information
★ secure, lockable, covered area for bike storage
★ details of local cycle specialists

Walkers Welcome Scheme

Cyclists Welcome Scheme

Look out for the logos in this guide and other accommodation listings.

Green Tourism

In response to the increasing need for businesses throughout the world to operate in an environmentally friendly way, VisitScotland has developed the Green Tourism Business Scheme.

Where tourism businesses are taking steps to reduce waste and pollution, to recycle and to be efficient with resources they are credited in this Scheme with a "Green Award". In our assessment of the degree of environmental good practice the business is demonstrating they are awarded one of the following;

Bronze award   BRONZE

for achieving a good level

Silver award   SILVER

for achieving a very good level

Gold award   GOLD

for achieving an excellent level

Signs You Need To Know

Eat Scotland

Eating out in Scotland... the choice is yours... but where?

Perhaps you feel like dining in a beautiful restaurant, with first-class ingredients carefully prepared by talented chefs. Or you might be looking for something quicker, simpler. You might be on holiday, or maybe you live in Scotland and you like to eat out now and then. Where do you turn for advice?

VisitScotland has come up with the answer. To help you choose, there is now a consistent, reliable, authoritative and, most important of all, comprehensive guide to quality eating in Scotland.

EatScotland is the new food quality assurance scheme for Scotland and of course only places offering good quality food can participate in the scheme. Hundreds of restaurants, tea rooms, coffee shops, pubs, self-service restaurants and takeaways across the length and breadth of Scotland have already been assessed, ensuring these businesses meet EatScotland's rigorous standards, not only in terms of good quality food, but also ambience, cleanliness and service.

The new website, www.eatscotland.com, will be your definitive guide to great places to eat and drink in Scotland. This site will provide you with everything you need to know to get the best out of Scotland's larder.

Haggis and whisky might hold the position of "most recognised" traditional Scottish fare, and maybe porridge. Why not add to the list Cullen Skink, Arbroath smokies, clapshot, cranachan, clootie dumpling and howtowdie wi' droppit eggs… discover the tastes that match such romantic and ancient names.

Even if you don't go for traditional fare, you'll find eating out in Scotland an experience in itself.

Scotland's quality produce is a source of inspiration for many enterprising chefs with our world famous beef, venison, grouse, seafood, cakes, fruit and vegetables

and the number of world-class restaurants has increased dramatically over the last few years.

Restaurant design has moved with the times and there are some stunning new eating places around the country, from glass walled restaurants on the banks of a river to rooftop eyries with stunning views. You can have afternoon tea in an ancient castle steeped in dramatic legend, or sip your café latte in the cool sophistication of the 21st century.

The choice is yours, and EatScotland is there to help, no matter whether you are looking for a first-class gourmet dinner, a humble fish supper or a nice, refreshing cup of tea.

So look out for the EatScotland logo of food and drink outlets throughout the country and log onto the website at www.eatscotland.com

Traveller's Tips

Getting Around

Scotland is a small country and travel is easy. There are direct air links with UK cities, Europe and North America. There is also an internal air network bringing the islands of the North and West within easy reach.

Scotland's rail network not only includes excellent cross-border services but also a good internal network. All major towns are linked by rail and there are also links to the western seaboard at Mallaig (for ferry connections from Skye and the Outer Hebrides) and to Aberdeen, Thurso and Wick for ferries to Orkney and Shetland.

All the usual discount cards are valid but there are also FirstScotRail Rovers (multi journey tickets allowing you to save on rail fares) and the Freedom of Scotland Travelpass, a combined rail and ferry pass allowing unlimited travel on Caledonian MacBrayne ferry services to the islands and all of the rail network. In addition Travelpass also offers discounts on bus services.

Cross-border rail services are available from all major centres, for example: Birmingham, Carlisle, Crewe, Manchester, Newcastle, Penzance, Peterborough, Preston, Plymouth, York and many others.

There are frequent rail departures from Kings Cross and Euston stations to Edinburgh and Glasgow. The journey time from Kings Cross to Edinburgh is around 4.5 hours and from Euston to Glasgow around 5 hours.

Coach connections include express services to Scotland from all over the UK; local bus companies in Scotland offer explorer tickets and discount cards. Postbuses (normally minibuses) take passengers on over 130 rural routes throughout Scotland.

Ferries to and around the islands are regular and reliable, most ferries carry vehicles, although some travelling to smaller islands convey only passengers.

Contact **Scotland's National Booking and Information Line – Tel: 0845 22 55 121,** or any Tourist Information Centre, for details of travel and transport.

Traveller's Tips

Getting Around

Many visitors choose to see Scotland by road – distances are short and driving on the quiet roads of the Highlands is a new and different experience. In remoter areas, some roads are still single track, and passing places must be used. When vehicles approach from different directions, the car nearest to a passing place must stop in or opposite it. Please do not use passing places to park in!

Speed limits on Scottish roads:
Dual carriageways 70mph/112kph;
single carriageways 60mph/96kph;
built-up areas 30mph/48kph.

The driver and front-seat passenger in a car must wear seatbelts; rear seatbelts, if fitted, must be used. Small children and babies must at all times be restrained in a child seat or carrier.

Traveller's Tips

Getting Around

Opening Times

Public holidays: Christmas and New Year's Day are holidays in Scotland, taken by almost everyone. Scottish banks, and many offices close. Scottish towns also take Spring and Autumn holidays which may vary from place to place, but are usually on a Monday.

Banking hours: In general, banks open Monday to Friday, 0930 to 1700, with some closing later on a Thursday. Banks in cities, particularly in or near the main shopping centres, may be open at weekends. Cash machines in hundreds of branches allow you to withdraw cash outside banking hours, using the appropriate cards.

Pubs and restaurants: Pubs and restaurants are allowed to serve alcoholic drinks between 1100 hours and 2300 hours Monday through to Saturday; Sundays 1230 hours until 1430 hours then again from 1830 hours until 2300 hours.

Residents in hotels may have drinks served at any time, subject to the proprietors discretion.

Extended licensing hours are subject to local council applications.

Telephone codes

If you are calling from abroad, first dial your own country's international access code (usually 00, but do please check). Next, dial the UK code, 44, then the area code except for the first 0, then the remainder of the number as normal.

Bring your pet

The Pet Travel Scheme (PETS) means you are able to bring your dog or cat into the United Kingdom from certain countries and territories without it first having to go into Quarantine, provided the rules of the scheme are met. PETS only operates on certain air, rail and sea routes and your own government should be able to provide you with details. Alternatively you may wish to obtain detailed information from:

Department of Environment Food and Rural Affairs
1a Page Street
London
SW1P 4PQ

Tel: **0870 241 1710**
Fax: **0207 904 6834**
E-mail:
pets.helpline@defra.gsi.gov.uk
Web:
www.defra.gov.uk/animalh/ quarantine

Scotland on the net

Visit our web site at:
visitscotland.com

"VisitScotland is committed to ensuring that our natural environment, upon which our tourism is so dependent, is safeguarded for future generations to enjoy."

Prize Draw

The perfect companion to your holiday.

February Draw

Entries must be received before 1st February 2006

May Draw

Entries must be received before 1st May 2006

September Draw

Entries must be received before 1st September 2006

**Fill in the form overleaf
to have the opportunity of winning
this great prize.**

Prize Draw

Send Entries to VisitScotland, Where To Stay Prize Draw, Ocean Point One, 94 Ocean Drive, Edinburgh EH6 6JH

Title: Mr, Mrs, Miss, Ms

Name:

Address:

Postcode:

Home telephone number:

E-mail address

Date of Birth dd/mm/yy

Data Protection:

We'd like to keep you informed of special offers from VisitScotland/visitscotland.com
Would you like to receive these?

Yes, by post ☐   Yes, by e-mail ☐   Both No ☐

In future VisitScotland may wish to contact you for research purposes. Is this okay?

Yes ☐   No ☐

From time to time we permit other tourism organisations to write to you about their products or services. Would you like to receive these?

Yes, by post ☐   Yes, by e-mail ☐   Both No ☐

Are you interested in any of the following activities?

Adventure Sports	☐	Festive Breaks	☐	Island Hopping	☐	Trekking & Riding	☐
Archeology	☐	Field Sports	☐	Mountain Biking	☐	Visiting Gardens	☐
City Breaks	☐	Fishing	☐	Off-road Driving	☐	Walking	☐
Romantic Breaks	☐	Cruising	☐	Food & Drink	☐	Sailing	☐
Watersports	☐	Culture	☐	Geneology	☐	Shopping	☐
Wildlife Watching	☐	Cycling	☐	Golf	☐	Snowsports	☐
Winter Breaks	☐	Events	☐	Hiking	☐	Spring Breaks	☐
Family Attractions	☐	Historic Sites	☐	Touring	☐		

Other (please state)

Prize draw rules:

1. Closing date for entry into the free prize draws are as follows: February Prize Draw entries must be received by the 1st February 2006; May Prize Draw entries must be received by the 1st May 2006; September Prize Draw entries must be received by the 1st September 2006.
2. Only one entry per household.
3. Employees of VisitScotland, visitscotland.com, their agencies and immediate families are not eligible to enter.
4. The winners will be notified by post as follows: February Draw winner by 15th February 2006; May Draw winner by 15th May 2006; and September Draw winner by 15th September 2006.
5. The winners' names will be available after the dates above (15th February, 15th May and 15th September 2006) by applying in writing enclosing a stamped, self-addressed envelope and writing to: VisitScotland Where To Stay Prize Draw, Ocean Point One, 94 Ocean Drive, Edinburgh EH6 6JH within 6 weeks of the closing date.
6. Prizes are non-transferable and no cash alternative will be offered.
7. All entrants must be UK residents and aged 18 or over.
8. The prize is a beautiful hamper full of wonderful delights to make your holiday or party that little bit special.
9. The promoter of this prize draw is VisitScotland. The promoter's decision is final and no correspondence will be entered into.
10. In the event of unforseen circumstances the Promoter reserves the right to offer an alternative prize of equal or greater value. Entry implies acceptance of rules.
11. Entries must not be sent through agents or third parties. Any such entries will be invalid.

Maps

Scotland's Tourist Areas

Accommodation

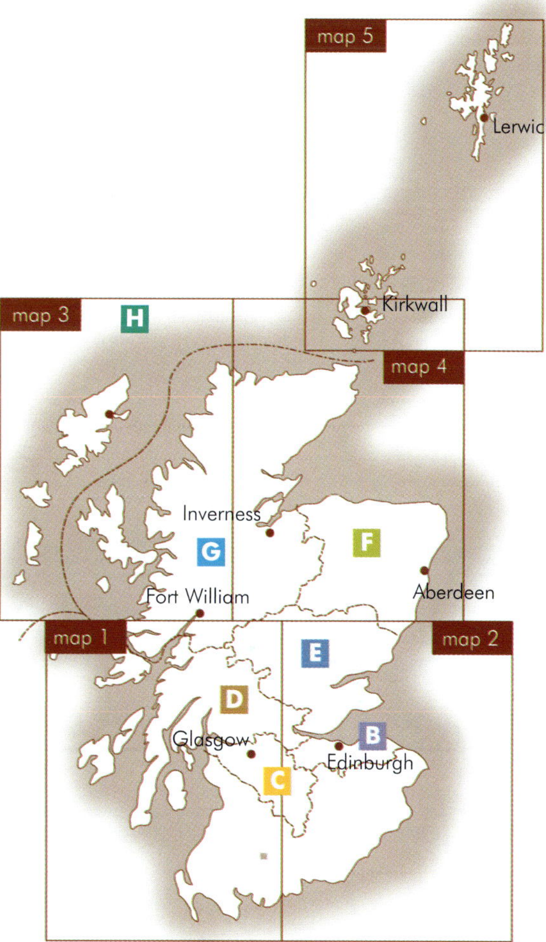

Map 1

COLL
Arinagour
Scarinish
TIREE
Tobermory
Calgary
Dervaig
Strontian
Glencoe
Loch Leven
Ballachulish
Kinloch Rannocl
G
Lochaline
Salen
Appin
Fishnish
Craignure
Connel
Ardchattan
Killin
MULL
Oban
Dalmally
Crianlarich
Lochearnhead
Balquhidder
Isle of Iona
Pennyghael
Kinlochspelve
IONA
Lochbuie
Strathyre
Fionnphort
Bunessan
Inveraray
Cairndow
Inversnaid
Brig o'Turk
Callande
Craobh Haven
Ardfern
Strachur
Tarbet
Port of Menteith
Arrochar
Aberfoyle
H
G
F
Lochgoilhead
Loch Lomond
Balmaha
MAP 1
E
MAP 2
Luss
Drymen
Fintry
D
Scalasaig
COLONSAY
Crinan
Balloch
C
A
Helensburgh
Alexandria
JURA
Lochgilphead
D
Dunoon
Greenock
Milngav
Rhubodach
Colintraive
Gourock
Port Askaig
Feolin
Portavadie
Wemyss Bay
Paisley
ISLAY
Ballygrant
Tarbert
Rothesay
Ascog
Largs
GLASGOW
Kennacraig
Cumbrae
Fairlie
Lochwinnoch
Port Charlotte
(winter only)
BUTE
CUMBRAE
Millport
Beith
Claonaig
Kilchattan Bay
Lochranza
Ardminish
Tayinloan
Corrie
Ardrossan
Kilwinning
Kilmarnock
Port Ellen
Lagavulin
ARRAN
Brodick
Irvine
Carradale
Troon
Symington
Mauchline
ATLANTIC
Blackwaterfoot
Firth of Clyde
Prestwick
OCEAN
Whiting Bay
Ayr
Dunure
Girvan
Ballycastle
Ballantrae
Car ferries and terminals:
Brodick
Ardrossan
Cairnryan
Newton Stewart
Gatehouse of Fleet
Scale 1:1 300 000
Stranraer
Glenluce
Wigtown
0   10   20 miles
© Collins Bartholomew Ltd 2005
Larne
Luce Bay
Sorbie
Port William
Whithorn
These maps show locations of establishments appearing in the Main Advertising Section of this guide. For route planning and touring please use a current road atlas.
BELFAST
To Douglas, Isle of Man
To Liverpool

Map 2

A B C D E F G H
1 2 3 4 5 6 7 8 9 10 11 12
NORTH SEA
Pitlochry
Kirriemuir
Forfar
Letham
Aberfeldy
Alyth
Glamis
Dunkeld
Blairgowrie
Birnam
Bankfoot
Arbroath
Methven
Monifieth
Carnoustie
Scone
Dundee
Broughty Ferry
Perth
Tayport
Firth of Tay
Leuchars
Comrie
Crieff
St Andrews
Forgandenny
Strathkinness
Auchterarder
Abernethy
Auchtermuchty
Kingsbarns
Dunshalt
Ceres
Crail
Milnathort
Markinch
Anstruther
Dunblane
Kinross
Lundin
Blairlogie
Links
Tillicoultry
Ballingry
Leven
Coaltown
of Wemyss
Stirling
Kirkcaldy
Dunfermline
Cowdenbeath
Inverkeithing
Culross
Burntisland
Firth of Forth
Limekilns
Dalgety Bay
Gullane
North Berwick
Rosyth
North Queensferry
South Queensferry
Port Seton
East
Linton
Dunbar
Falkirk
Linlithgow
EDINBURGH
Tranent
Winchburgh
Musselburgh
Haddington
Cockburnspath
Dechmont
Broxburn
Dalkeith
St Abbs
Airdrie
Livingston
East Calder
Lasswade
Coldingham
Eyemouth
Blackburn
Gorebridge
Chirnside
Motherwell
Penicuik
Berwick-upon-Tweed
Hamilton
To Zeebrugge
West
Linton
Lauder
Lanark
Peebles
Biggar
Broughton
Innerleithen
Galashiels
Kelso
Melrose
Yetholm
Selkirk
St Boswells
Ancrum
Crawford
Jedburgh
Hawick
Moffat
Thornhill
Langholm
Lochmaben
Lockerbie
Canonbie
Dumfries
Ecclefechan
Newcastle
upon Tyne
Gretna Green
Gretna
Sunderland
Castle
Douglas
Dalbeattie
Carlisle
Kippford
Twynholm
Auchencairn
Kirkcudbright
Solway Firth
Middlesbrough

Map 3

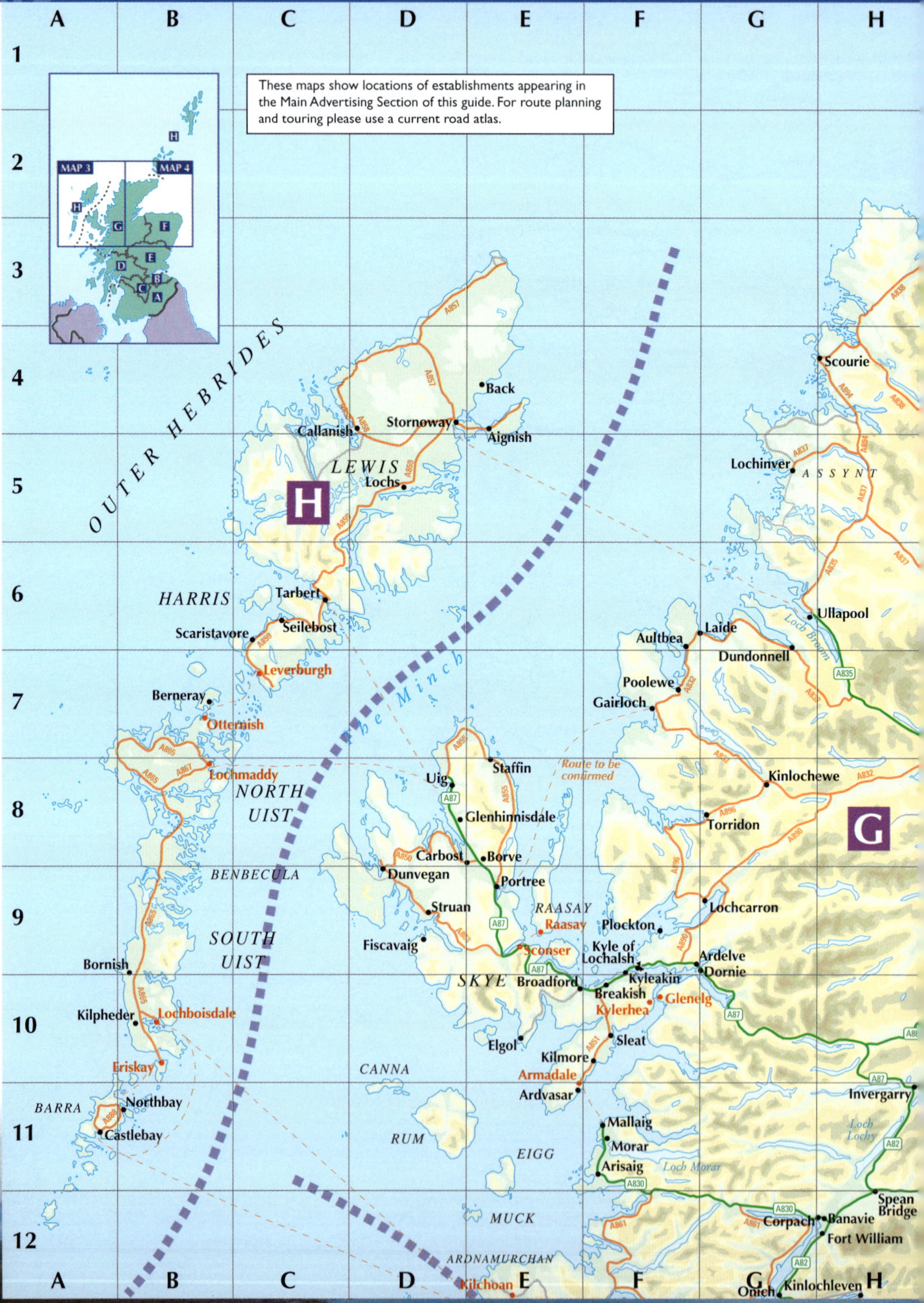
These maps show locations of establishments appearing in the Main Advertising Section of this guide. For route planning and touring please use a current road atlas.
MAP 3
MAP 4
OUTER HEBRIDES
LEWIS
HARRIS
NORTH UIST
BENBECULA
SOUTH UIST
BARRA
SKYE
RAASAY
CANNA
RUM
EIGG
MUCK
ARDNAMURCHAN
ASSYNT
The Minch
Route to be confirmed
Loch Broom
Loch Morar
Loch Lochy
Back
Stornoway
Aignish
Callanish
Lochs
Tarbert
Seilebost
Scaristavore
Leverburgh
Berneray
Otternish
Lochmaddy
Bornish
Kilpheder
Lochboisdale
Eriskay
Northbay
Castlebay
Uig
Staffin
Glenhinnisdale
Carbost
Borve
Dunvegan
Portree
Struan
Fiscavaig
Raasay
Sconser
Broadford
Elgol
Kilmore
Armadale
Ardvasar
Sleat
Breakish
Kyleakin
Kylerhea
Glenelg
Kyle of Lochalsh
Plockton
Lochcarron
Ardelve
Dornie
Torridon
Kinlochewe
Gairloch
Poolewe
Aultbea
Laide
Dundonnell
Ullapool
Lochinver
Scourie
Invergarry
Mallaig
Morar
Arisaig
Spean Bridge
Banavie
Corpach
Fort William
Kilchoan
Onich
Kinlochleven
H
G
A B C D E F G H
1 2 3 4 5 6 7 8 9 10 11 12

Map 4

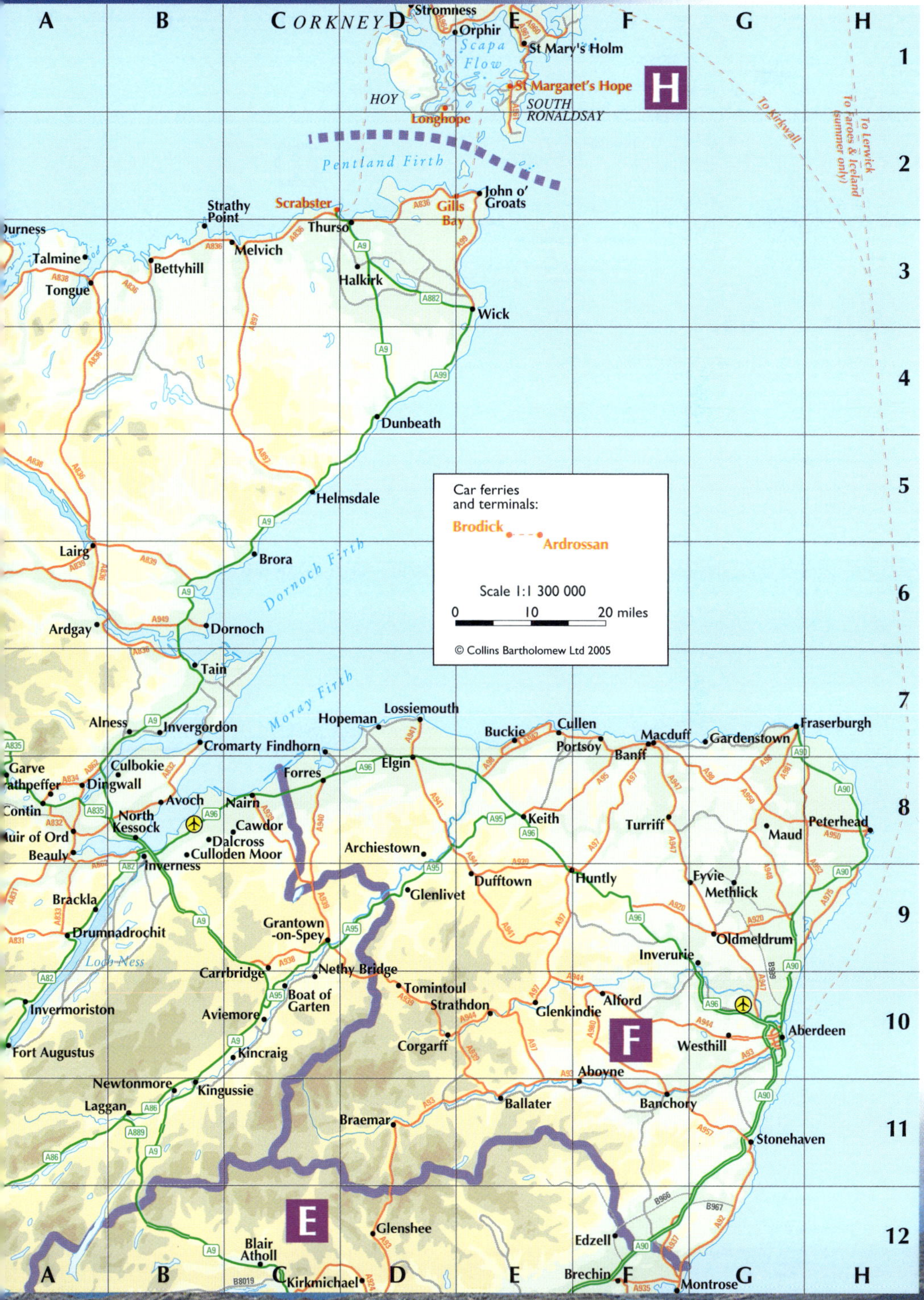
ORKNEY
Stromness
Orphir
Scapa Flow
St Mary's Holm
St Margaret's Hope
HOY
SOUTH RONALDSAY
Longhope
Pentland Firth
To Kirkwall
To Lerwick
To Faroes & Iceland (summer only)
John o' Groats
Gills Bay
Scrabster
Strathy Point
Thurso
Durness
Melvich
Talmine
Bettyhill
Tongue
Halkirk
Wick
Dunbeath
Helmsdale
Lairg
Brora
Dornoch Firth
Ardgay
Dornoch
Tain
Moray Firth
Car ferries and terminals:
Brodick
Ardrossan
Scale 1:1 300 000
0
10
20 miles
© Collins Bartholomew Ltd 2005
Alness
Invergordon
Cromarty
Findhorn
Hopeman
Lossiemouth
Buckie
Cullen
Portsoy
Macduff
Banff
Gardenstown
Fraserburgh
Garve
Culbokie
Dingwall
Forres
Elgin
Avoch
Nairn
North Kessock
Cawdor
Dalcross
Culloden Moor
Inverness
Keith
Turriff
Maud
Peterhead
Archiestown
Beauly
Brackla
Drumnadrochit
Loch Ness
Glenlivet
Dufftown
Huntly
Fyvie
Methlick
Grantown -on-Spey
Oldmeldrum
Inverurie
Carrbridge
Nethy Bridge
Tomintoul
Boat of Garten
Strathdon
Alford
Glenkindie
Invermoriston
Aviemore
Aberdeen
Westhill
Fort Augustus
Kincraig
Corgarff
Aboyne
Newtonmore
Kingussie
Ballater
Banchory
Laggan
Braemar
Stonehaven
Glenshee
Edzell
Blair Atholl
Kirkmichael
Brechin
Montrose
E
F
H

Map 5

MAP 5
H

A B C D E F G H
1
2
3
4
5
6
7
8
9
10
11
12

Car ferries
and terminals:
Brodick   Ardrossan

Scale 1:1 300 000
0   10   20 miles

© Collins Bartholomew Ltd 2005

These maps show locations of establishments appearing in
the Main Advertising Section of this guide. For route planning
and touring please use a current road atlas.

H
UNST
Island of Unst
Gutcher   Belmont
YELL
Oddsta
FETLAR
Ulsta
OUT SKERRIES
Toft
SHETLAND
Brae   Vidlin
Laxo   Symbister
To Faroes & Iceland
(summer only)
BRESSAY
Lerwick
FOULA
Trondra
To Norway
(summer only)
A970
A971
A968
FAIR ISLE
WESTRAY
NORTH
RONALDSAY
SANDAY
ROUSAY
EDAY
To Aberdeen
H
Birsay
Evie
STRONSAY
Rendall
Sandwick
Shapinsay
SHAPINSAY
Harray
Kirkwall
Stromness
ORKNEY
Orphir   St Mary's
Holm
Scapa
Flow
To Aberdeen

Bed &
Breakfast

Where to Stay Guide 2006

visitscotland.com
0845 22 55 121

South of Scotland: Ayrshire and Arran, Dumfries and Galloway, Scottish Borders

Scotland starts here in the south: rolling hills, legends of Scottish independence, and golf courses by the name of Troon, Turnberry and Prestwick. But it gets better…

Turnberry Championship Golf Course

You're spoilt for choice in these regions. Sports, castle spotting, sandy beaches, quaint villages, gardens, poets, fishing – the list goes on. The Borders, essentially Scotland's Deep South, is a place where Scottish armies 'negotiated' independence with England. Robert the Bruce and William Wallace won battles here, and Smailholm tower, near Kelso, is an example of the square towers that defended the Borders in the 16th century.

Beautiful scars remain in the Abbey ruins of Dryburgh, Jedburgh, Kelso and especially Melrose, where Robert the Bruce's heart is allegedly buried. Finding fish in the nearby Tweed River is easier. Try your hand at fly-fishing and hook yourself Scotland's finest salmon or trout. For insight into different worlds, visit The Edwardian mansion of Manderston and Georgian house of Mellerstain. Or walk in the Eildon Hills starting at Melrose and see romantic Scotland through the eyes of famous poet, Sir Walter Scott. More exciting, Glentress mountain biking in Peebles was recently voted the UK's best mountain biking route, providing tracks from mild to manic. To the east lie rich farmlands, ending abruptly in the cliffs of St Abbs, a must for birdwatchers.

Villages are dotted along the Solway Firth, but for gravitas, Caerlaverock Castle owns the coast. Look overhead and trace the flight of oyster-catchers to the nearby Wildfowl and Wetlands trust centre. Dumfries is a bustling market town with the warmth of red-sandstone houses. The 20 bookshops of Wigtown, plus an annual literary festival in September, make this Scotland's National Book Town.

South of Scotland:

South of Scotland: Ayrshire and Arran, Dumfries and Galloway, Scottish Borders

Any moment now… cast a line in the River Tweed

South of Scotland:

South of Scotland: Ayrshire and Arran, Dumfries and Galloway, Scottish Borders

Melrose Abbey. A plaque marks the spot where Robert The Bruce's heart is allegedly buried.

Ayrshire rings with the name of Robert Burns, Scotland's star poet who, among other things, gave the English-speaking world that well known tune, *Auld Lang Syne*. There are related sites throughout the region, but Alloway is home to the Burns National heritage Park and a cracking folklore festival in May. It's easy to see other reasons for visiting, sandy beaches have made Ayr the leading family seaside resort on the Firth of Clyde. Largs has similar appeal, plus a chance to rub shoulders with Vikings at the Vikingar! Centre.

Culzean castle is arguably the finest castle in these parts. Lashings of tapestries, paintings and French windows are in a castellated mansion overlooking the Isle of Arran. Don't stop there – an hour's sail will take you to a place of quiet beaches, mountains, and drams at the Isle of Arran Distillery. Not to mention the seven golf courses.

As you can guess, the golf is bliss, not just at Championship greats but with scores of smaller clubs too. There's also 400 miles of the National Cycle network.

And you can always go for walk along the 212 mile coast-to-coast Southern Upland Way.

Events

South of Scotland: Ayrshire and Arran, Dumfries and Galloway, Scottish Borders

8 APRIL
MELROSE SEVENS
Traditional rugby competition with teams of seven players.
Tel: 01896 822993
www.melrose7s.com

21-22 APRIL
SCOTTISH GRAND NATIONAL, Ayr
The highlight of the Scottish horseracing year.
Tel: 01292 264179
www.ayr-racecourse.co.uk

12-14 MAY
NEWTON STEWART WALKING FESTIVAL, Ayrshire
Tel: 01671 403676
www.newtonstewartwalkfest.co.uk

20-29 MAY
BURNS AN' A' THAT, Ayrshire
A celebration of life and contemporary Scottish culture.
Tel: 01292 678100
www.burnsfestival.com

26 MAY-4 JUNE
DUMFRIES AND GALLOWAY ARTS FESTIVAL
Multi arts festival featuring music, dance, theatre and literature.
Tel: 01387 260447
www.dgartsfestival.org.uk

16 JUNE
SELKIRK COMMON RIDING
The battle of Flodden in commemorated with the casting of colours in the market place and the traditional riding of the marches.
Tel: 01750 21954

21-22 JULY
WICKERMAN FESTIVAL, Nr Kirkcudbright
Scotland's alternative music, dance and arts festival.
Tel: 01738 449430
www.thewickermanfestival.co.uk

5 AUGUST
BRODICK HIGHLAND GAMES, Isle of Arran
Traditional Highland games with pipe bands, athletic events and highland dancing.
Tel: 01770 302290

18 AUGUST-29 OCTOBER
GAELFORCE 2006
Arts festival celebrating Celtic culture.
Tel: 01387 262084
www.gaelforcefestival.co.uk

Cars and horses share the backroads of Peebles.

22 SEPTEMBER-1 OCTOBER
WIGTOWN BOOKTOWN FESTIVAL
A celebration of books and literature in Scotland's national book town.
Tel: 01988 402036
www.wigtown-booktown.co.uk

** denotes provisional date, event details are subject to change please check before travelling*

South of Scotland: Ayrshire and Arran, Dumfries and Galloway, Scottish Borders

Please refer to the maps on pages xix-xxiv for the locations of establishments appearing in the main advertising section of this guide.

Finding out more...

For practical advice, ideas and information about exploring Scotland and to book your accommodation:

Tel: 0845 22 55 121*
or if calling from outside the UK: +44 (0) 1506 832121

Email: info@visitscotland.com
Web: www.visitscotland.com

* A £3 booking fee applies to telephone bookings of accommodation.

Tourist Information Centres

South of Scotland: Ayrshire and Arran, Dumfries and Galloway, Scottish Borders

Ayrshire and Arran

Ayr
22 Sandgate
Tel: (0845) 22 55 121
Jan – Dec

Brodick
The Pier, Isle of Arran
Tel: (0845) 22 55 121
Jan – Dec

Largs
The Railway Station
Main St
Tel: (0845) 22 55 121
Apr – Oct

Dumfries and Galloway

Castle Douglas
Markethill Car Park
Tel: (01556) 502611
Easter – Oct

Dumfries
64 Whitesands
Tel: (01387) 253862
Jan – Dec

Gatehouse of Fleet
Car Park
Tel: (01557) 814212
Easter – Oct

Gretna Green
Gretna Gateway
Tel: (01461) 337834
Easter – Oct

Kirkcudbright
Harbour Square
Tel: (01557) 330494
Easter – Oct (restricted winter opening)

Moffat
Unit 1, Ladyknowe
Tel: (01683) 220620
Easter – Oct

Newton Stewart
Dashwood Square
Tel: (01671) 402431
Easter – Oct

Stranraer
28 Harbour Street
Tel: (01776) 702595
Jan – Dec

Scottish Borders

Eyemouth
Auld Kirk, Manse Road
Tel: (0870) 6080404
Easter – Oct

Hawick
Drumlanrig's Tower
Tel: (0870) 608 0404
Apr – Oct

Jedburgh
Murray's Green
Tel: (0870) 608 0404
Jan – Dec

Kelso
Town House, The Square
Tel: (0870) 608 0404
Jan – Dec

Melrose
Abbey House, Abbey Street
Tel: (0870) 608 0404
Jan – Dec

Peebles
High Street
Tel: (0870) 608 0404
Jan – Dec

Selkirk
Halliwell's House
Tel: (0870) 608 0404
Apr – Oct

Blackwaterfoot, Isle of Arran

Map Ref: 1E7

★★★

B&B

The Greannan

Blackwaterfoot, Shiskine, Isle of Arran, KA27 8HB
Tel/Fax:01770 860200
Email:susanthegreannan@hotmail.com
Web:www.thegreannan.co.uk

Comfortable recently refurbished family home set in elevated position
with magnificent views over countryside and sea to Irish Coast. Half a
mile from Blackwaterfoot. En-suite rooms all with colour TV and
hospitality tray. Garden with picnic benches for guest use. A perfect,
peaceful place to stay and enjoy the old world charm of this lovely island.
Quality self catering apartments also available. Credit Cards Accepted.

5 rooms, all en-suite, Open Jan-Dec, B&B per person, single from £22.50,
double from £22.50.

Brodick, Isle of Arran

Map Ref: 1F7

★★★

GUEST HOUSE

Glencloy Farm Guest House

Glen Cloy Road, Brodick, Isle of Arran, KA27 8DA
Tel:01770 302351
Email:glencloyfarm@aol.com
Web:www.SmoothHound.co.uk/hotels/glencloy

A Farmhouse full of character set in a peaceful glen with views of hills and
sea. A good base for exploring all that Arran has to offer. You will receive a
very warm family welcome from Neil, Caroline and their chicks, a real home
from home. Our 5 rooms are comfortable and individual with TV/Video and
access to a video library. Breakfast is served in our cosy drawing room with
some of the freshest eggs you will have eaten.

5 rooms, some en-suite, Open Jan-Dec, B&B pppn, single £27.00-35.00,
double £25.00-40.00.

★★

SMALL HOTEL

Ormidale Hotel

Brodick, Isle of Arran, KA27 8BY
Tel:01770 302293 Fax:01770 302098
Email:reception@ormidale-hotel.co.uk
Web:www.ormidale-hotel.co.uk

Family run Victorian Hotel built in the 1800s, set in mature woodland by
the golf course. Home cooked meals for the family served in the
conservatory. CAMRA approved. Good pub atmosphere.

7 rooms, all en-suite, Open Apr-Sep, B&B per person, single from £34.00, double
from £34.00.

Ayr

Map Ref: 1G7

★★

GUEST HOUSE

Belmont Guest House

15 Park Circus, Ayr, KA7 2DJ
Tel:01292 265588   Fax:01292 290303
Email:belmontguesthouse@btinternet.com
Web:www.belmontguesthouse.co.uk

Victorian townhouse in a quiet tree lined conservation area, within easy
walking distance of town centre. Ground-floor bedrooms, all with ensuite
facilities. Guest lounge with extensive book collection. On street and
private car parking. Credit/Debit cards are accepted.

5 rooms, all en-suite, Open Jan-Dec excl Xmas/New Year, B&B per person, single
from £28.00, double /twin from £26.00, family from £26.00.

Important: Prices stated are estimates and may be subject to amendments

Ayr	Map Ref: 1G7

★★★★

B&B

Deanbank

44 Ashgrove Street, Ayr, KA7 3BG
Tel:01292 263745
Email:deanbankayr@hotmail.com

Semi-detached late Victorian town house in quiet residential street within easy walking distance of town centre and seafront. Deanbank offers a quality breakfast including home baking. Ideal holiday base for golfing, riverwalks and exploring Burns Country.

2 rooms, both ensuite/or shower, Open Jan-Dec excl Xmas/New Year, B&B per person, single from £30.00, double from £25.00.

★★★

B&B

The Dunn Thing

13 Park Circus, Ayr, KA7 2DJ
Tel/Fax:01292 284531
Email:Sheiladunn13@aol.com
Web:www.thedunnthing.co.uk

The Dunn Thing offers a warm welcome and a cup of tea on arrival to all our guests. This is a Victorian town house close to the town centre and sea front, situated in quiet area of Ayr. Free pick-up can be arranged from Prestwick Airport or Ayr Train or Bus Station. Euros now accepted. Credit cards taken.

3 rooms, all en-suite, Open Jan-Dec, B&B per person, single from £24.00, double from £22.00, room only single from £20.00, room only double from £40.00.

★★★

B&B

Garth Madryn

71 Maybole Road, Ayr, KA7 4TB
Tel:01292 443346
Email:emackie@garthmadryn.fsnet.co.uk

Easy access to International golf courses and town centre. Near to Rozelle and Belleisle Parks and the Burns National Heritage Park. Situated close to Burns by Bike cycle route and main cycle route through Ayr. Close to Brig O'Doon Hotel - ideal for overnight wedding guests. Cyclists welcome.

2 rooms, all en-suite, Open Jan-Dec, B&B per person, single from £22.00, double from £20.00.

★★★

B&B

Jacmar Guest House

23 Dalblair Road, Ayr, KA7 1UF
Tel:01292 264798
Email:mail@dgambles.fsnet.co.uk

A high quality, friendly B&B in central location. Ideally situated for all local interests and attractions. Local amenities offer an excellent selection of shops, bars, restaurants and golf courses right on your doorstep. All rooms are tastefully decorated and well appointed with TV, hospitality tray and hairdryer. 5 mins walk from both bus and rail stations, 15 mins from Prestwick Airport.

4 rooms, some en-suite, Open Jan-Dec excl Xmas/New Year, B&B per person, single from £22.50, double from £22.50.

★★

GUEST HOUSE

Kilkerran Guest House

15 Prestwick Road, Ayr, KA8 8LD
Tel:01292 266477
Email:margaret@kilkerran-gh.demon.co.uk
Web:www.kilkerran-gh.demon.co.uk

Family run guest house on main road from Ayr to Prestwick airport. Two minutes drive from town centre and convenient for Burns country. Television lounge with satellite TV. Some annexe accommodation.

9 rooms, some en-suite, Open Jan-Dec, B&B per person, single from £20.00, double from £20.00.

VAT is shown at 17.5%: changes in this rate may affect prices.

Key to symbols is on back flap.

by Ayr

Map Ref: 1G7

★★★

B&B

Fisherton Farm B&B
Dunure, Ayr, KA7 4LF
Tel/Fax:01292 500223
Email:lesleywilcox@hotmail.com

Traditional stone-built farmhouse on working mixed farm, with extensive sea views to Arran. 5 miles from Ayr and convenient for Prestwick Airport. Ground floor accommodation available. Central base for exploring Burns Country, places of historical interest, golfing, fishing and walking.

3 rooms, all en-suite, Open Jan-Dec excl Xmas, B&B per person, single from £25.00, double from £22.50.

Ballantrae, Ayrshire

Map Ref: 1F9

★★★

B&B

Mrs Georgina McKinley
Laggan Farm, Ballantrae, Ayrshire, KA26 0JZ
Tel:01465 831402
Email:jandr@lagganfm.freeserve.co.uk

Dairy farm with large comfortable farmhouse 0.5 miles south of Ballantrae on the Ayrshire coast. Guests have their own dining room and sitting room with colour tv. Tea/coffee making facilities plus home baking is available in the dining room in the evening. Ideal base for touring, golfing, woodland walks and fishing by arrangement.

2 rooms, some en-suite, Open May-Oct, B&B per person, single from £20.00, double from £19.00.

Beith, Ayrshire

Map Ref: 1G6

SHOTTS FARM
BEITH, AYRSHIRE KA15 1LB
TEL: 01505 502273
E.MAIL: shotts.farm@btinternet.com
Comfortable friendly accommodation is offered on this 200-acre dairy farm. Situated between the A736 and A737, its location is ideal for golf courses, country parks, shopping centres and the ferries to Arran and Millport. Breakfast has something for all appetites, try our home-baked bread, scones and local farm produce. Contact- Mrs Jane Gillan
STB ★★★   AA ★★★

★★★

B&B

Farmhouse Bed & Breakfast
Shotts Farm, Beith, Ayrshire, KA15 1LB
Tel/Fax:01505 502273

Family run farmhouse accommodation on a 200 acre dairy farm. Ideal base for Burns country, Arran and cultural Glasgow. Guests can enjoy a welcome cup of tea and homebaking on arrival and try our homemade bread and scones at breakfast time. We only use free range eggs in our varied and generous breakfasts.

3 rooms, some en-suite, Open Jan-Dec, B&B per person, single from £18.00, double from £18.00.

Canonbie, Dumfriesshire

Map Ref: 2D9

★★★

B&B

Four Oaks
Canonbie, Dumfriesshire, DG14 0TF
Tel:01387 371329

Well appointed comfortable rooms in this family B&B. Ensuite bedrooms, with televisions, private parking and garden where guests can sit and relax. Plenty of walking in this beautiful area. Eating places in the near vicinity - plenty of variety.

2 rooms, all en-suite, Open Jan-Dec excl Xmas/New Year, B&B per person, from £22.00-24.00.

Important: Prices stated are estimates and may be subject to amendments

Castle Douglas, Kirkcudbrightshire   Map Ref: 2A10

**Craigadam, Near Castle Douglas DG7 3HU
Tel/Fax: 01556 650233
e.mail: inquiry@craigadam.com
Web: www.craigadam.com**
Craigadam, near Castle Douglas is an elegant country house within an organic working farm. Antique furnishings, log fires and friendly atmosphere. Relax in our elegant drawing room and enjoy the views across Galloway. All the bedrooms are ensuite. Dine in our oak panelled dining room where we specialise in venison, duck, salmon and sweets, not for the calorie conscious! Extensive wine list and honesty bar. Enjoy a game of billiards after dinner, catch a trout on our hill loch and have it for breakfast. All home-cooking using local produce.
Booking via establishment only.
AA ◆◆◆◆◆ RAC ◆◆◆◆◆ ⊛

★★★★

B&B

Craigadam
Castle Douglas, Dumfries & Galloway, DG7 3HU
Tel/Fax:01556 650233
Email:inquiry@craigadam.com
Web:www.craigadam.com
18th century farmhouse with panoramic views of surrounding countryside. An ideal base for golfing, walking, fishing. All bedrooms are ensuite. There is a billiard room for after dinner entertainment. Come home in the evening to comfort, super food and good Scottish hospitality. We specialise in local produce including venison, pheasant, salmon. There is a trout loch on the estate. Booking via establishment only.

7 rooms, all en-suite, Open Jan-Dec excl Xmas/New Year, B&B per person, single from £50.00, double from £38.00.

---

nr Castle Douglas, Kirkcudbrightshire   Map Ref: 2A10

★★★

GUEST HOUSE

Airds Farm
Crossmichael, Castle Douglas, Kirkcudbrightshire DG7 3BG
Tel:01556 670418
Email:enquiries@airds.com
Web:www.airds.com
Superb views over Loch Ken and the picturesque village and church of Crossmichael will delight visitors to this traditional farmhouse. Lovers of nature will enjoy walking through the wooded glen and pastures nearby or relaxing in the conservatory. Gardens, castles and other attractions are within easy reach, fishing, boating and watersports are available on the loch. A warm welcome, in a comfortable and relaxing home. Booking via establishment only.

4 rooms, some en-suite, Open Jan-Dec, B&B per person, single from £26.00, double from £22.00.

VAT is shown at 17.5%: changes in this rate may affect prices. | *Key to symbols is on back flap.*

Coldingham, Berwickshire   Map Ref: 2F5

DUNLAVEROCK HOUSE

COLDINGHAM BAY, EYEMOUTH, BERWICKSHIRE, TD14 5PA
TEL: 01890 771450 FAX: 01890 771103
E-MAIL: info@dunlaverock.com
WEBSITE: www.dunlaverock.com
Spectacularly located, Edwardian house in peaceful location overlooking and
with garden access to Coldingham sands and seashore.
Many walks through the St. Abbs National Nature Reserve, Sea Fishing Trips
and nearby Golf Courses. Licensed.

★★★

**GUEST
HOUSE**

Dunlaverock House
Coldingham Bay, Berwickshire, TD14 5PA
Tel:018907 71450 Fax:018907 71103
Email:info@dunlaverock.com
Web:www.dunlaverock.com

Find peace and comfort in our beautiful villa. Spectacularly situated over
sandy beach and rocky coastline. Large, comfortable ensuite bedrooms
and delicious award winning food.

6 rooms, Open Mar-Jan excl Xmas/New Year, B&B per person, single from £40.00,
double from £30.00.

Millport, Isle of Cumbrae   Map Ref: 1F6

★★

B&B

Cirmhor
35 West Bay, Millport, Isle of Cumbrae, KA28 0HA
Tel:01475 530723

On the edge of Millport with views to the Wee Cumbrae and Portencross.
Ideal for walking, birdwatching & cycling. Attractive conservatory and
garden available for guests. Packed lunches available.

2 rooms, B&B per person, single from £20.00, double from £20.00.

Dumfries   Map Ref: 2B9

★★★

B&B

Craignair B&B
5 Newall Terrace, Dumfries, DG1 1LN
Tel:01387 251796

Family run Bed & Breakfast in traditional, semi-detached sandstone
house in quiet residential area close to town centre. All bedrooms are
ensuite. Guest lounge. Close to main line station. Secure private parking.

3 rooms, all en-suite, Open Feb-Nov, B&B per person, double from £24.00.

★★★

B&B

The Haven
1 Kenmure Terrace, Dumfries, DG2 7QX
Tel:01387 251281
Email:havenbandb@aol.com
Web:www.thehavenbandb.co.uk

Guests are assured of a warm welcome at The Haven B&B by owners
Stewart and Caroline Cochrane and their family. The Haven is a
delightful Victorian sandstone villa, recently refurbished and newly
redecorated throughout. Situated beside the River Nith with views over
the suspension bridge and Dumfries. Non-smoking.

3 rooms, Open Jan-Dec, B&B per person single from £25.00, twin from £20.00.

Important: Prices stated are estimates and may be subject to amendments

Dumfries

Map Ref: 2B9

★★★

B&B

Low Kirkbride Farmhouse Bed&Breakfast
Low Kirkbride, Auldgirth, Dumfries, DG2 0SP
Tel/Fax:01387 820258
Email:lowkirkbride@btinternet.com
Web:www.lowkirkbridefarm.com

Warm, comfortable farmhouse set in beautiful countryside, lovely views from every room and all rooms en-suite. Family room in new steading conversion. Friendly atmosphere. Superb breakfasts and tasty aga home baking. Evening meals by arrangement. Attractive garden, own walking leaflet. Working beef and sheep farm. Pedigree herd of Belted Galloways. Walking, golfing, fishing, wildlife. 10 miles north of Dumfries. www.lowkirkbridefarm.com

3 rooms, all ensuite, Open Jan-Dec, B&B per person, single from £25.00, double from £22.00, family from £20.00.

Wallamhill House B&B

Kirkton, Dumfries DG1 1SL Tel: 01387 248249
e.mail: wallamhill@aol.com Web: www.wallamhill.co.uk
Large modern country house with 2 acres of landscaped garden, nestling in the Nith Valley yet only 5 minutes from Dumfries. Lovely views from front and rear of house. Beautifully appointed spacious en-suite bedrooms. All ground floor. A special experience, come and relax. Small health suite with sauna and steam room. Safe private parking. AA ♦♦♦♦♦

★★★★

B&B

Wallamhill House B&B
Kirkton, Dumfries, DG1 1SL
Tel/Fax:01387 248249
Email:wallamhill@aol.com
Web:www.wallamhill.co.uk

Spacious house in quiet countryside, beautiful views of Nith Valley. 2 miles from Dumfries town centre, safe parking. All rooms ground floor level, spacious, with ensuite shower rooms. Ideal and luxurious base to explore Dumfries and Galloway. Small health suite with steam shower and sauna. Evening meals by arrangement.

3 rooms, all en-suite, Open Jan-Dec excl Xmas/New Year, B&B per person, single from £28.00, double from £25.00.

Ecclefechan, Dumfriesshire

Map Ref: 2C9

★

B&B

Carlyle House
Main Street, Ecclefechan, Lockerbie, Dumfriesshire
DG11 3DG
Tel/Fax:01576 300322

Comfortable family accommodation convenient for M74. Children and pets welcome. Opposite Carlyle's birthplace.

3 rooms, Open Jan-Dec excl Xmas/New Year, B&B per person, from £17.00 single or double.

Galashiels, Selkirkshire

Map Ref: 2D6

★★★

B&B

Ettrickvale
33 Abbotsford Road, Galashiels, TD1 3HW
Tel:01896 755224
Email:ettrickvale@aol.com

Comfortable family run semi-detached bungalow with garden, recently refurbished. By A7. On outskirts of town but only a short walk from local amenities. All accommodation on ground floor. Evening meals by arrangement. Ensuite facilities available.

3 rooms, some en-suite, Open Jan-Dec excl Xmas/New Year, B&B per person, single from £20.00, double from £20.00.

Girvan, Ayrshire — Map Ref: 1F8

B&B

Hawkhill Farm
Old Dailly, Girvan, Ayrshire, KA26 9RD
Tel:01465 871232
Email:isobel@hawkhillfarm.co.uk
Web:www.hawkhillfarm.co.uk

Farmhouse B & B with that little bit extra! Former 17th Century Coaching Inn with spacious well-furnished rooms, warm welcome and home baking. Near Culzean Castle, Burns Country, Golf, Walking, Restaurants, Ferries and more. Find out in our brochure, or visit our website. Which Good Bed & Breakfast recommended. Dogs by arrangement.Total Non Smoking.

3 rooms, some en-suite, Open Mar-Oct, B&B per person, single from £40.00, double from £27.50.

Glenluce, Wigtownshire — Map Ref: 1G10

B&B

Tha Butchach
New Luce, Newton Stewart, Wigtownshire, DG8 0AW
Tel:01581 600217
Email:peter.tuckfield1@btinternet.com
Web:www.thabutchach.co.uk

Comfortable accommodation provided at this family run B&B in picturesque village of New Luce. Two ensuite bedrooms plus one with private facilities, tea-trays and TV's. Clothes washing and drying facilities available. Walkers and cyclists welcome. Evening meals available by prior arrangement.

3 rooms, 2 en-suite, 1 private, Open all year, B&B per person, single from £24.00, double from £24.00, BB & Eve.Meal from £34.00.

Gretna, Dumfriesshire — Map Ref: 2C10

B&B

Thistlewood
Rigg, Gretna, Dumfriesshire, DG16 5JQ
Tel:01461 337810
Email:rodandcelia@aol.com
Web:www.warmanbie.co.uk/thistle.htm

Rural surroundings. Gretna two miles. Only five minutes from main tourist routes. Comfortable cosy bedrooms (one four-poster). Patio garden for guest use. Off-road parking. Ensuite bedroom. Evening meals by arrangement. Dinner, Bed & Breakfast.

3 rooms, some en-suite, Open Jan-Dec excl Xmas/New Year, B&B per person, single from £25.00, double from £22.50.

Gretna Green, Dumfriesshire — Map Ref: 2C10

Barrasgate House
AA

Millhill, Gretna Green DG16 5HU
Tel: 01461 337577 Fax: 01461 339932
e.mail: info@barrasgate.co.uk Web: www.barrasgate.co.uk

Five minutes from M74/M6/M7, surrounded by country views and broadleaf woodland. En suite bedrooms. Barrasgate bears the family Crest of The Grahams of Netherby Hall; their roots dating back to the 1600s. Ideal for exploring Carlisle's 12th century Castle and Cathedral, Hadrian's Wall & Solway coast with its beautiful scenery and beaches. A special discount on midweek breaks which can include supper.

B&B

Barrasgate House
Millhill, Gretna Green, DG16 5HU
Tel:01461 337577 Fax:01461 339932
Email:info@barrasgate.co.uk
Web:www.barrasgate.co.uk

Former farmhouse surrounded by woodland in a quiet, secluded location, yet close to the M6/M74 and only 2 miles from Gretna. Credit card facility.

4 rooms, all en-suite, Open Jan-Dec, B&B per person, single from £25.00, double from £22.50, BB & Eve.Meal from £32.50.

Important: Prices stated are estimates and may be subject to amendments

Hawick, Roxburghshire

Map Ref: 2D7

★★★

B&B

Wiltonburn Farm

Hawick, Scottish Borders, TD9 7LL
Tel:01450 372414/07711 321226
Email:sheila@wiltonburnfarm.co.uk
Web:www.wiltonburnfarm.co.uk

You will be warmly welcomed and cared for on our lovely hill farm, within 2 miles from Hawick. Our cashmere knitwear shop will make your stay more pleasurable. Farmstay member. Welcome Host.

3 rooms, some en-suite, Open Jan-Dec excl Xmas, B&B per person, single from £30.00, double from £25.00.

Innerleithen, Peeblesshire

Map Ref: 2C6

★★

B&B

The Old Schoolhouse

Traquair, Innerleithen, Peeblesshire, EH44 6PL
Tel:01896 830425/07986 682426 Fax:01896 830425
Email:caird@old-schoolhouse.ndo.co.uk
Web:www.old-schoolhouse.ndo.co.uk

A former traditional village school house recently modernised to provide all the creature comforts in a traditional setting. A lovely detached house of character with comfortable bedrooms and warm guest sitting room. Open views of fields with sheep grazing, cherry trees and forested hills. Log fires and home cooking with evening meals by arrangement. Innerleithen close by and Southern Upland Way 50 mts.

3 rooms, Open Jan-Dec excl Xmas/New Year, B&B per person, single from £22.00, double from £20.00.

Jedburgh, Roxburghshire

Map Ref: 2E7

★★★★

B&B

Froylehurst

The Friars, Jedburgh, Roxburghshire, TD8 6BN
Tel/Fax:01835 862477

Detached Victorian house (retaining many original features) with large garden and private parking. Spacious rooms. Overlooking town, 2 minutes walk from the centre.

4 rooms, Open Mar-Nov, B&B per person, single from £22.00, double from £22.00.

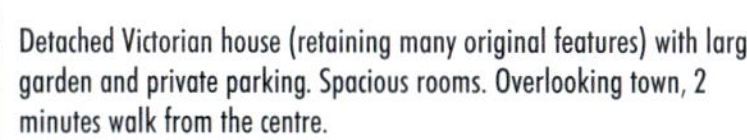

VAT is shown at 17.5%: changes in this rate may affect prices.

Key to symbols is on back flap.

Jedburgh, Roxburghshire

Map Ref: 2E7

B&B

Hundalee House

Jedburgh, Roxburghshire, TD8 6PA
Tel/Fax:01835 863011
Email:sheila.whittaker@btinternet.com
Web:www.accommodation-scotland.org

Historic, early 17c house set in 15 acres of secluded gardens and
woodlands. Jedburgh 1 mile. Two rooms with four poster beds.

4 rooms, all en-suite, Open Mar-Oct, B&B per person, single from £30.00, double
from £22.00.

Riverview

Newmill Farm, Jedburgh TD8 6TH
Tel: 01835 862145/864607
e.mail: liz.kinghorn@amserve.net
Web: http://mysite.freeserve.com/riverviewbandb

A warm welcome in spacious en-suite accommodation awaits you at Riverview.
Enjoy country views while being only 2 miles from Jedburgh. Complimentary lift
to and from Jedburgh for walkers and those wishing to wine and dine. Extensive
breakfast menu. Full details including photographs of all rooms on website.

B&B

Riverview

Newmill Farm, Jedburgh, TD8 6TH
Tel:01835 862145/864607
Email:liz.kinghorn@amserve.net
Web:http://mysite.freeserve.com/riverviewbandb

Modern villa on quiet country road in rolling Scottish Borders Farmland.
Overlooking the river Jed. Large residents lounge with balcony. Free
trout fishing available for guests. Spacious car park area. Jedburgh 2
miles. Kelso 8 miles. Close to St Cuthberts Way (Grid ref NT659227).

3 rooms, all en-suite, Open Apr-Oct, B&B per person, single from £25.00, double
from £18.00.

THE SPINNEY

Langlee, Jedburgh, Roxburghshire TD8 6PB
Tel: 01835 863525
e.mail: thespinney@btinternet.com   Web: www.thespinney-jedburgh.co.uk

*Set in mature gardens, bordering woodland and open countryside The Spinney
offers accommodation of the highest standard. The en-suite bedrooms have many
extra touches to make your stay more comfortable. There is a varied menu at
breakfast which is served in the elegant dining room at separate tables.*

B&B

The Spinney

Langlee, Jedburgh, Roxburghshire, TD8 6PB
Tel:01835 863525
Email:Thespinney@btinternet.com
Web:www.thespinney-jedburgh.co.uk

Set in six acres of garden, woodland and fields, The Spinney enjoys an
excellent location in the heart of the countryside, only 2 miles south of
Jedburgh on the A68. Rich in history, visit abbeys, castles and gardens
with many outdoor pursuits including walking trails, golf and fishing.
Self catering lodges also available.

3 rooms, some en-suite, Open Mar-Nov, B&B per person, double £25.00-27.00.

SOUTH OF SCOTLAND

Jedburgh, Roxburghshire

Map Ref: 2E7

GUEST HOUSE

Willow Court

The Friars, Jedburgh, Roxburghshire, TD8 6BN
Tel:01835 863702
Email:mike@willowcourtjedburgh.co.uk
Web:www.willowcourtjedburgh.co.uk

Set in 2 acres of grounds close to town centre, with excellent views. Peaceful setting, yet close to all amenities including Abbey, Castle and a good selection of restaurants. All rooms are ensuite. Most rooms are on the ground floor.

3 rooms, all en-suite, Open Jan-Dec, B&B per person, single from £36.00, double from £23.00.

Kelso, Roxburghshire

Map Ref: 2E6

B&B

Craignethan House

Jedburgh Road, Kelso, Roxburghshire, TD5 8AZ
Tel:01573 224818

Experience a warm Scottish welcome at this delightful detached house overlooking the town and the river Tweed, with panoramic views of Floors Castle and surrounding countryside. Ground floor bedroom. Ample off street parking adjoining the house.

3 rooms, Open Jan-Dec, B&B per person, single from £26.00, double from £23.00.

Kilmarnock, Ayrshire

Map Ref: 1G6

B&B

Tamarind Bed & Breakfast

24 Arran Avenue, Kilmarnock, Ayrshire, KA3 1TP
Tel:01563 571788   Fax:01563 533515
Email:info@bedandbreakfastonline.co.uk
Web:www.bedandbreakfastonline.co.uk

Ranch style bungalow in residential area. Convenient base for touring, and centrally situated for Ayrshire's many golf courses.

4 rooms, all en-suite, Open Jan-Dec excl Xmas/New Year, B&B per person, single from £35.00, double from £22.50.

West Tannacrieff Bed & Breakfast

Fenwick, by Kilmarnock, Ayrshire, KA3 6AZ
Tel:01560 600258   Fax:01560 600914
Email:westtannacrieff@btopenworld.com
Web:www.smoothhound.co.uk/hotels/westtannacrieff.html

West Tannacrieff is a working dairy farm with a new high quality purpose built bed and breakfast unit with all modern amenities. Large spacious bedrooms all tastefully decorated. All rooms are en-suite with televisions and tea/coffee making facilities. Large parking area and garden. Enjoy breakfast made with Scottish and local produce with homemade breads and preserves. Homebaking also available with tea/coffee making facilities.

3 rooms, all en-suite, Open Jan-Dec excl Xmas/New Year, B&B per person, single from £22.50, double from £20.00.

B&B

Kilwinning, Ayrshire

Map Ref: 1G6

B&B

Blairholme

45 Byres Road, Kilwinning, KA13 6JU
Tel:01294 552023
Email:pcullinane@tiscali.co.uk

Turn of the century, semi detached bungalow, close to railway station. Ideal location for touring, golfing and walking. Ideally situated for ferries (Irish and Arran), airports (Glasgow and Prestwick) - within area of Dalry, Irvine and Ardrossan.

2 rooms, Open Jan-Dec excl Xmas/New Year, B&B per person, single from £25.00, double from £20.00.

VAT is shown at 17.5%: changes in this rate may affect prices.

Key to symbols is on back flap.

Kirkcudbright

Map Ref: 2A10

★★★★

B&B

Baytree House
110 High Street, Kirkcudbright
Dumfries & Galloway, DG6 4JQ
Tel/Fax:01557 330824
Email:jackie@baytreekirkcudbright.co.uk
Web:www.baytreehouse.net

A glass of sherry awaits you at this recently restored Georgian town house with a magnificent drawing room. Baytree is situated in the quiet conservation area of Old High Street in the artist's town of Kirkcudbright.

3 rooms, all en-suite, Open Jan-Dec, B&B per person, single from £40.00, double £30.00-35.00.

Largs, Ayrshire

Map Ref: 1F5

★★★★

B&B

Broom Lodge
5 Broomfield Place, Largs, Ayrshire, KA30 8DR
Tel:01475 674290
Email:broomlodge@aol.com
Web:www.broom-lodge.co.uk

Set overlooking the bay of Largs towards Cumbrae with commanding views of the ferries and yachts. Close to town with its shops, restaurants and pubs. All rooms ensuite or private facilities. 2 single rooms on first floor.

4 rooms, some en-suite, Open Jan-Dec, B&B per person, single from £25.00, double from £25.00.

★★★

B&B

The Old Rectory
Aubery Crescent, Largs, Ayrshire, KA30 8PR
Tel:01475 674405
Email:ashrona@aol.com
Web:www.OldrectoryLargs.co.uk

A warm welcome at this family home situated on the sea front with views over Cumbrae to Arran. A five minute stroll along the promenade into town. Large garden with private parking area. Spacious residents lounge with separate dining room and good sized bedrooms makes for a comfortable and relaxing stay.

2 rooms, all en-suite, Open Jan-Dec, B&B per person, single from £30.00, double from £25.00.

Lauder, Berwickshire

Map Ref: 2D6

★★★★

**SMALL
HOTEL**

The Lodge, Carfraemill
Lauder, Berwickshire, TD2 6RA
Tel:01578 750750   Fax:01578 750751
Email:enquiries@carfraemill.co.uk
Web:www.carfraemill.co.uk

A former coaching Inn offering friendly hospitality and bistro/restaurant meals. Situated in rural Lauderdale at the junction of the A697/A68. Ideally situated for both Edinburgh and the Borders. Experienced in weddings, business meetings and corporate hospitality.

10 rooms, all en-suite, Open Jan-Dec, B&B per person, single from £60.00, double £40.00-45.00 per person.

Lochmaben, Dumfriesshire

Map Ref: 2B9

★★★

B&B

Ardbeg Cottage
19 Castle Street, Lochmaben, DG11 1NY
Tel/Fax:01387 811855

Small friendly B&B on quiet street near village centre. Warm comfortable en-suite bedrooms and lounge/diner, all on ground floor. One bedroom has twin beds, and the other can be arranged with either twin beds or a super king-sized double bed. Evening meals and packed lunches are available given prior notice, also vegetarian dishes. As well as the usual basic facilities there are aids for guests with walking difficulites, drying room, cycle storage and a paved garden. Non smoking. No pets.

2 rooms, all en-suite, Open Jan-Dec, B&B per person, single from £22.00, double from £22.00, BB & Eve.Meal from £32.00.

Important: Prices stated are estimates and may be subject to amendments

Mauchline, Ayrshire | Map Ref: 1H7

B&B
★★★

Ardwell Bed & Breakfast
103 Loudoun Street, Mauchline, by Ayr, KA5 5BH
Tel:01290 552987
Email:ardwell@zetnet.co.uk
Web:www.ardwell.zetnet.co.uk

Ardwell is a detached house situated in the historic village of Mauchline, it is convenient for Glasgow & Prestwick Airports. It is located near the village centre within easy walking distance of shops and eating establishments. Both rooms are en-suite and extremely comfortable. Ardwell prides itself on its hospitality and the standard of the breakfasts and home cooking. Mauchline has access to Scotland's scenic West Coast.

2 rooms, all en-suite, Open Jan-Dec, B&B per person, single from £19.00, double from £17.00.

B&B
★★

Treborane
Dykefield Farm, Mauchline, Ayrshire, KA5 6EY
Tel:01290 550328

Bed and breakfast accommodation in cottage on working farm in the heart of Burns Country. Friendly atmosphere, evening meal and ensuite bedroom. 1 mile from the village of Mauchline. 20 mins to the centre of Ayr town.

2 rooms, some en-suite, Open Jan-Dec, B&B per person, single from £15.00, double from £15.00, BB & Eve.Meal from £20.00.

Melrose, Roxburghshire | Map Ref: 2D6

**GUEST
HOUSE**
★★★

Braidwood Bed and Breakfast
Buccleuch Street, Melrose, Roxburghshire, TD6 9LD
Tel:01896 822488 Fax:01896 822148
Email:enquiries@braidwoodmelrose.co.uk
Web:www.braidwoodmelrose.co.uk

Friendly welcome in attractive listed town house only a stones throw from Melrose Abbey and Priorwood Gardens. Strictly non-smoking.

4 rooms, some en-suite, Open Jan-Dec, B&B per person, single from £30.00, double from £25.00.

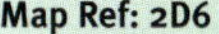

**GUEST
HOUSE**
★★★

Dunfermline House
Buccleuch Street, Melrose, Roxburghshire, TD6 9LB
Tel:01896 822411
Email:dunfermline-house@virgin.net
Web:www.dunfermlinehouse.co.uk

Overlooking Melrose Abbey. A highly respected and well established guest house offering very high standards. All rooms (except one) with en-suite facilities, the single room has a private bathroom. Traditional Scottish breakfasts. Non-smoking house.

5 rooms, some en-suite, Open Jan-Dec, B&B per person, single from £25.00, double from £25.00.

---

by Melrose, Roxburghshire | Map Ref: 2D6

B&B
★★★★

Fauhope House
Gattonside, Melrose, Roxburghshire, TD6 9LU
Tel:01896 823184/822245
Email:fauhope@bordernet.co.uk

Elegant Edwardian house in extensive grounds overlooking River Tweed, Melrose Abbey and the Eildon Hills - ten minutes walk to Melrose over Georgian footbridge.

3 rooms, all en-suite, Open Jan-Dec excl Xmas/New Year, B&B per person, single from £45.00, double from £35.00.

VAT is shown at 17.5%: changes in this rate may affect prices.

Key to symbols is on back flap.

Moffat, Dumfriesshire

Map Ref: 2B8

★★

GUEST HOUSE

Barnhill Springs Country Guest House
Moffat, Dumfries & Galloway, DG10 9QS
Tel:01683 220580

Barnhill Springs is an early Victorian country house standing in its own grounds overlooking upper Annandale. It is a quiet family run guest house situated ½ a mile from the A74/M at the Moffat junction no.15. Barnhill Springs is ideally situated as a centre for touring Southern Scotland, for walking and cycling on the Southern Upland Way or for a relaxing overnight stop for holiday makers heading North or South. AA 3 Diamonds.

5 rooms, Open Jan-Dec, B&B per person, single from £25.00, double from £25.00, BB & Eve.Meal from £41.00.

★★★

GUEST HOUSE

Hartfell House
Hartfell Crescent, Moffat, Dumfriesshire, DG10 9AL
Tel:01683 220153
Email:enquiries@hartfellhouse.co.uk
Web:www.hartfellhouse.co.uk

An elegant Victorian family run guest house with spacious, comfortable rooms in a quiet location only four minutes walk from High Street.

7 rooms, all en-suite, Open Mar-Dec excl Xmas, B&B per person, single from £30.00, double from £27.50.

★★★

GUEST HOUSE

Limetree House
Eastgate, Moffat, Dumfriesshire, DG10 9AE
Tel:01683 220001
Email:info@limetreehouse.co.uk
Web:www.limetreehouse.co.uk

Friendly hosts, beautifully decorated rooms and wonderful breakfasts offer a truly memorable experience at Limetree House. Secure storage for bicycles and motorbikes.

6 rooms, all en-suite, Open Jan-Dec excl Xmas, B&B per person, single from £29.00, double from £24.00.

★★

B&B

Lochhouse Farm Retreat Centre
Lochhouse Farm, Beattock, Moffat, Dumfriesshire, DG10 9SG
Tel:01683 300451
Email:bookings@lochhousefarm.com
Web:www.lochhousefarm.com

Time out and space apart is assured at this family run B&B. A relaxed atmosphere where guests can enjoy peace and quiet. Near to the pretty town of Moffat where there is a variety of activities available. Excellent walking area for novice and experienced walkers. We are on the Southern Upland Way. Pets welcome by arrangement.

2 rooms, 1 en-suite, Open Jan-Dec excl Xmas/New Year, B&B per person, single from £20.00, double from £18.00.

★★★

B&B

Morag
19 Old Carlisle Road, Moffat, Dumfriesshire, DG10 9QJ
Tel:01683 220690
Email:morag_moffat44@btopenworld.com

A warm welcome is assured at this family run Victorian house located within quiet suburbs ½ mile from Moffat town centre. It is an excellent base for exploring the Moffat Water Valley and the Galloway countryside to the west. Southern Upland way ½ mile. Homecooking with our own free range eggs. Evening meals by arrangement. Non-smoking. Ensuite facilities available.

3 rooms, some en-suite, Open Jan-Dec excl Xmas/New Year, B&B per person, single from £23.00, double from £21.00.

Important: Prices stated are estimates and may be subject to amendments

Moffat, Dumfriesshire   Map Ref: 2B8

★★★★

B&B

Queensberry House
12 Beechgrove, Moffat, Dumfriesshire, DG10 9RS
Tel:01683 220538
Email:queensberryhouse@amserve.net

3 rooms, all en-suite, Open Jan-Dec excl Xmas/New Year, B&B per person, single from £30.00, double from £25.00.

A warm welcome is guaranteed at this well appointed Victorian house in a quiet area opposite the bowling green and within a few minutes walk from town centre. All accommodation on ground floor.

★★★

GUEST HOUSE

Seamore Guest House
Academy Road, Moffat, Dumfriesshire, DG10 9HW
Tel:01683 220404
Email:allanseamorehouse@btinternet.com
Web:www.seamorehouse.co.uk

5 rooms, all en-suite, Open Jan-Dec, B&B per person, single from £25.00, double from £22.50. Master suite now available.

Seamore House is an attractive listed Victorian guest house offering comfort and quality at an affordable price. Ideal base for Walking, Golf, Fishing or just relaxing. Glasgow, Edinburgh & Carlisle are all less than 1 hour drive.

WOODHEAD FARM
OLD CARLISLE ROAD, MOFFAT, DUMFRIESSHIRE DG10 9LU
Tel/Fax: 01683 220225
e.mail: sylvia@woodhead4.freeserve.co.uk

Luxuriously appointed farm house set in 100 acres of rolling countryside, two miles from the beautiful spa town of Moffat. All bedrooms are en suite with panoramic views. Breakfast is served in our conservatory overlooking mature garden and hills. Murray and Sylvia extend a warm welcome to their peaceful home. Ample safe parking.

★★★★

B&B

Woodhead
Old Carlisle Road, Moffat, Dumfriesshire, DG10 9LU
Tel/Fax:01683 220225
Email:sylvia@woodhead4.freeserve.co.uk

3 rooms, all en-suite, Open Jan-Dec, B&B per person, single £40.00, twin/double with shower £30.00, deluxe twin with bath £32.50.

Luxuriously furnished farmhouse situated on 100 acres of pasture. All bedrooms have panoramic views of the surrounding, very peaceful countryside. Breakfast served in conservatory overlooking mature garden. Ample safe parking. Just 2 miles from spa town of Moffat.

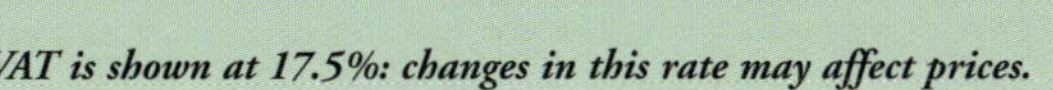

VAT is shown at 17.5%: changes in this rate may affect prices. | *Key to symbols is on back flap.*

Benera Bed & Breakfast

Benera, Corsbie Road, Newton Stewart, Wigtownshire DG8 6JD

Tel: 01671 403443 e.mail: ethel_prise@hotmail.com

Friendly and quiet modern bungalow with panoramic views of Galloway Hills. Ideal base for touring, golfing, fishing, cycling and walking.

★★★

B&B

Benera Bed and Breakfast

Corsbie Road, Newton Stewart, Wigtownshire, DG8 6JD
Tel:01671 403443
Email:ethel_prise@hotmail.com

Modern bungalow peacefully situated on the edge of the town with superb views of the Galloway Hills. Ideal location for golfing, fishing, walking, cycling and bird watching as well as exploring this scenic corner of Scotland.

2 rooms, some en-suite, Open Apr-Oct, B&B per person, single from £27.00, double from £23.00.

Flowerbank Guest House

Millcroft Road, Minnigaff, Newton Stewart, Wigtownshire DG8 6PJ
Tel: 01671 402629
e.mail: enquiries@flowerbankgh.com Web: www.flowerbankgh.com

Mick and Di Reynolds warmly invite you to stay at Flowerbank, a charming 18th century house set in an acre of grounds where the River Cree runs alongside our stunning landscaped garden.

★★★

GUEST
HOUSE

Flowerbank Guest House

Millcroft Road, Minnigaff, Newton Stewart, DG8 6PJ
Tel:01671 402629
Web:www.flowerbankgh.com

Detatched 18th Century stone house set in one acre of wooded garden on the banks of the River Cree. Situated in a quiet and pretty village yet within easy walking distance of the bustling market town of Newton Stewart. Totally non-smoking.

5 rooms, most en-suite, Open Mar-Nov, B&B per person, double from £24.00, BB & Eve.Meal from £35.00.

Peebles | Map Ref: 2C6

DROCHIL CASTLE FARMHOUSE

**Contact: Mrs A Black, Drochil Castle Farm, By Peebles
West Linton, Peeblesshire EH46 7DD
Tel/Fax: 01721 752249
e.mail: annblack@drochilcastle.co.uk
Website: www.drochilcastle.co.uk**

Spacious and comfortable accommodation awaits you at Drochil Castle Farm. Log fires in the lounge. Afternoon tea and cakes to greet you on arrival. Stunning views and tranquility is yours. Peebles and West Linton a mere 10 minutes drive. Edinburgh 30 minutes. Childrens outside play area. Large garden and private parking.

★★★★

B&B

Drochil Castle B&B

by Romano Bridge, by Peebles, EH46 7DD
Tel/Fax:01721 752249
Email:AnnBlack@drochilcastle.co.uk
Web:www.drochilcastle.co.uk

A warm welcome awaits you at this traditional working beef and sheep farm. Set amongst rolling Borders hills with fine views down the Lyne & Tweed Valley. Located beside the ruins of the 16th century Drochil Castle.

4 rooms, some en-suite, Open Jan-Dec excl Xmas, B&B per person, single £22.00-26.00, double £22.00-26.00.

★★★

B&B

Lyne Farmhouse

Lyne Farm, Peebles, EH45 8NR
Tel/Fax:01721 740255
Email:lynefarmhouse@btinternet.com
Web:www.lynefarm.co.uk

Large Victorian farmhouse of character on working farm with uninterrupted open views over Stobo Valley and surrounding countryside. 4 miles (10 mins) from the Royal Burgh of Peebles on A72. Usually 45 mins by car to Edinburgh City Centre. Evening meals by prior arrangement.

3 rooms, Open Jan-Dec, B&B per person, single from £25.00, double from £24.00, BB & Eve.Meal from £35.00.

★★★

B&B

Winkston Farmhouse Bed & Breakfast

Edinburgh Road, Peebles, EH45 8PH
Tel:01721 721264 Fax:01721 730365
Email:holidayatwinkston@btinternet.com
Web:www.winkstonholidays.co.uk

Welcoming & pleasant country house 2 miles from Peebles. Very centrally situated for good local amenities and touring lovely Border countryside and Edinburgh.

3 rooms, some en-suite, Open Jan-Dec excl Xmas/New Year, B&B per person, double from £20.00.

St Abbs, Berwickshire | Map Ref: 2F5

★★★

B&B

Murrayfield

7 Murrayfield, St Abbs, Berwickshire, TD14 5PP
Tel:01890 771468 Mobile 07719 703796

Former fisherman's cottage in quiet village, close to beach, harbour and nature reserve. Both rooms comfortably furnished, one ensuite and one with wash-hand basin. Lounge available for guests' use with TV. On street parking available.

2 rooms, some en-suite, Open Jan-Dec, B&B per person, single from £25.00, double £19.00-21.50.

VAT is shown at 17.5%: changes in this rate may affect prices. | *Key to symbols is on back flap.*

St Boswells, Roxburghshire

Map Ref: 2D7

★★★

B&B

Mainhill

Charlesfield Road, St Boswells, Roxburghshire, TD6 0HG
Tel:01835 823788

2 rooms, Open Jan-Dec, B&B per person, single from £27.00, double from £22.00.

Traditional Georgian House set well away from the road in its own spacious grounds. Peaceful and relaxing atmosphere. Good touring base. 1 mile from St Boswells.

Selkirk

Map Ref: 2D7

★★★

B&B

Dinsburn

1 Shawpark Road, Selkirk, TD7 4DS
Tel:01750 20375 mobile 07790 728001
Email:moama2000@aol.com

3 rooms, some en-suite, Open Jan-Dec, B&B per person, single from £25.00, double from £22.00, BB & Eve.Meal from £32.00.

Semi-detached, sandstone Victorian house in residential area on east side of town centre. Next to bowling green. Well appointed ensuites and furnishings.

★★

B&B

Mrs J F Mackenzie

Ivy Bank, Hillside Terrace, Selkirk, TD7 2LT
Tel:01750 21470/21270 Fax:01750 21270
Email:janet@aol.com
Web:www.ivy-bank-bed-and-breakfast.co.uk

2 rooms, some en-suite, Open Apr-Nov, B&B per person, single from £20.00, double from £20.00.

Detached stone built villa situated in own grounds with beautiful views over the Linglie Hills. Central for touring the Borders and Edinburgh. Private parking.

Sorbie, Wigtownshire

Map Ref: 1H11

★★★

B&B

East Culkae Farm House

Sorbie, Newton Stewart, Wigtownshire, DG8 8AS
Tel:01988 850214
Web:www.ewetoyou.co.uk

3 rooms, all en-suite, Open Feb-Oct, B&B per person, single from £30.00, double :- one night £25.00 pp, two nights £24.00 pp, three or more £23.50 pp.

Set in it's own grounds of 123 acres this restored farmhouse B&B is offering very comfortable accommodation with modern ensuites and an attractive guests TV lounge. One bedroom is on the ground floor and is ideal for the less-abled. Well situated for nearby tourist attractions and beaches. Self Catering in caravan available.

Important: Prices stated are estimates and may be subject to amendments

East Challoch Farmhouse
DUNRAGIT, STRANRAER, WIGTOWNSHIRE DG9 8PY
TEL: 01581 400391
A warm welcome awaits at our farmhouse set in open countryside with beautiful views over Luce Bay. Our bedrooms are tastefully decorated with C.H., colour TV, tea/coffee facilities and all ensuite bathrooms. Delicious home cooked dinners available on request. Ideal for golf, fishing and exploring gardens in unspoilt S.W. Scotland.

★★★

B&B

East Challoch Farmhouse

Dunragit, Stranraer, Wigtownshire, DG9 8PY
Tel:01581 400391

A warm welcome awaits you at our family run traditional farmhouse with views over Luce Bay. Spacious double, twin rooms or single with ensuite facilities. All rooms with TVs and tea trays. Comfortable lounge for guests' use. Evening meal available by prior arrangement. Feel free to use our well established garden. Only 7 miles from Stranraer. Pony trekking, golf course within 1 mile.

3 rooms, all en-suite, Open Jan-Dec excl Xmas/New Year, B&B per person, single from £26.00, double from £21.00.

★★

B&B

Jerviswood

Linton Bank Drive, West Linton, Peeblesshire, EH46 7DT
Tel/Fax:01968 660429

Comfortable modern home with attractive garden, located in picturesque historic village with excellent eating places all within easy walking distance. Within easy reach of Edinburgh and Scottish Borders. Ideal centre for walking, touring and golfing.

3 rooms, Open Jan-Dec excl Xmas/New Year, B&B per person, single from £21.00, double from £18.00.

★★★

B&B

The Meadows B&B

4 Robinsland Drive, West Linton, Peeblesshire, EH46 7JD
Tel:01968 661798
Email:mbthain@ntlworld.com
Web:www.themeadowsbandb.co.uk

West Linton is a small village on the A702, the main Carlisle-Edinburgh road. 15 minutes from the Edinburgh city by-pass. Convenient for touring Central Scotland and The Borders or as a stop over on the way north. Good pub and restaurant 5 minutes walk in the village.

3 rooms, Open Jan-Dec, B&B per person single from £22.50, double from 20.00.

★★

B&B

Rowallan

Mountain Cross, West Linton, Peeblesshire, EH46 7DF
Tel:01968 660329
Email:carolinecottam@aol.com

Situated on A701, 10 miles to Peebles, 20 miles south of Edinburgh. Comfortable modern bungalow with fine views in charming rural area. Private parking in front of the house and all bedrooms and bath/shower rooms on ground floor. Ideal base for walking, cycling or fishing. Evening meals by prior arrangement.

3 rooms, Open Jan-Dec, B&B per person twin from 20.00, double from £20.00, family from £20.00. Room only twin from £40.00, double from £40.00, family from £60.00.

Welcome to Scotland

Edinburgh and Lothians

Why do visitors travel thousands of miles to walk The Royal Mile? If one street has this effect on people, imagine what the whole city can do…

Climb the Scott Monument to see Edinburgh from a bird's view.

Everybody knows the name. Edinburgh is larger than life, offering more than you can fit into one holiday. It's also a city that continues to influence the world, which is remarkable when you consider it has a population of just half a million.

This is a city for time travel – just take The Royal Mile. At the southern end is the pomp and splendour of Holyrood House, official residence for the Royal Family in Scotland. A short walk will take you to the new Scottish Parliament, a bold architectural nod to the future of government. Then step back five billion years to see how the planet was created at Dynamic Earth, an interactive science museum. At the top of the hill is a castle - the castle. Once a royal palace and then a military fortress, Edinburgh Castle is still imposing, but not discouraging to a million visitors every year.

Head down the cobbled streets behind the castle, or try a walking tour of the old cemetery if you dare. Are you prepared for the MacKenzie Poltergeist? You're less likely to bump into witches and grave robbers today, just friendly locals who inhabit the bars and clubs nestled by The Old Town. And there's no shortage of them. Edinburgh has 700 bars in total. Many are located in the New Town, an elegant legacy of the

Edinburgh and Lothians

Street performers during Edinburgh's Fringe Festival in August.

The Union Canal, Ratho.

1800s when the city achieved new wealth and status, and Scots colonised distant lands. Princes Street combines Georgian facades with high fashion, much to the delight of shoppers. But for the priceless, you have to visit the museums and galleries. A weighty collection of Scottish and European masters is on display at The National Gallery of Scotland. Thousands of everyday objects, costumes and machines relive the country's evolution at the Museum of Scotland, adjoining the Royal Museum.

Above all, Edinburgh has a knack for turning traditions on their head. That's why you'll find comedians like, 'The Giant Pineapple Boys' hamming it up at the Fringe Festival.

A different reality lies a few miles away. From the summit of Arthur's Seat, Edinburgh's ex-volcano, you can see the hills and coastline of the Lothians. Nature reserves, sandy beaches and seaside resorts beckon.

Don't miss seeing the finest medieval stone carving in Scotland at Rosslyn Chapel, also rumoured to be the last resting place for the Holy Grail. If castle visiting is on the agenda visit the wildly romantic Dirleton Castle in East Lothian, and the dramatic ruins of Tantallon Castle with its views to Bass Rock. A bracing walk along the beaches in East Lothian is another treat, just 30 minutes from the city. Climbers will have a field day at Ratho Adventure Centre, which is simply the world's largest indoor climbing area with 2.4 square kilometres of artificial terrain.

Events

Edinburgh and Lothians

1 JANUARY
LOONY DOOK
On the first day of every year a brave few leap into the freezing cold water of the Firth of Forth at South Queensferry.
www.hogmanay.net

30 APRIL
BELTANE FIRE FESTIVAL
A celebration of summer's arrival.
Tel: 0131 228 5353
www.beltane.org

2-4 JUNE
GARDENING SCOTLAND
The biggest gardening and outdoor living show in Scotland.
Tel: 0131 333 0969
www.gardeningscotland.com

22-25 JUNE
ROYAL HIGHLAND SHOW
The highlight of the Scottish country calendar.
Tel: 0131 335 6200
www.rhass.org.uk

4-26 AUGUST
EDINBURGH MILITARY TATTOO
The capital's annual military extravaganza featuring a unique blend of music, dance, drama and pageantry set against the dramatic backdrop of Edinburgh Castle.
Tel: 08707 555 1188
www.edintattoo.co.uk

6-28 AUGUST
EDINBURGH FESTIVAL FRINGE
The largest arts festival in the world showcasing comedy, theatre and music.
Tel: 0131 226 0026
www.edfringe.com

12-28 AUGUST
EDINBURGH INTERNATIONAL BOOK FESTIVAL
This prestigious literary festival includes readings, author interviews and discussions.
Tel: 0131 228 5444
www.edbookfest.co.uk

13 AUGUST-2 SEPTEMBER
EDINBURGH INTERNATIONAL FESTIVAL
One of the world's most prestigious arts festivals offering the very best in international opera, theatre, music and dance.
Tel: 0131 473 2001
www.eif.co.uk

23-25 SEPTMEBER
BELHAVEN BEST TRADITIONAL MUSIC FESTIVAL, Dunbar
Popular music festival with concerts, sessions and dancing.
Tel: 01368 863301
dtmf.dunbar.org.uk

24 NOVEMBER-24 DECEMBER
EDINBURGH'S CHRISTMAS
Edinburgh's Christmas opens with the annual Christmas lights switch-on and includes many festive events including the Edinburgh Wheel, ice skating and the Christmas market.
Tel: 0131 529 4310
www.edinburghschristmas.co.uk

** denotes provisional date, event details are subject to change please check before travelling.*

Edinburgh and Lothians

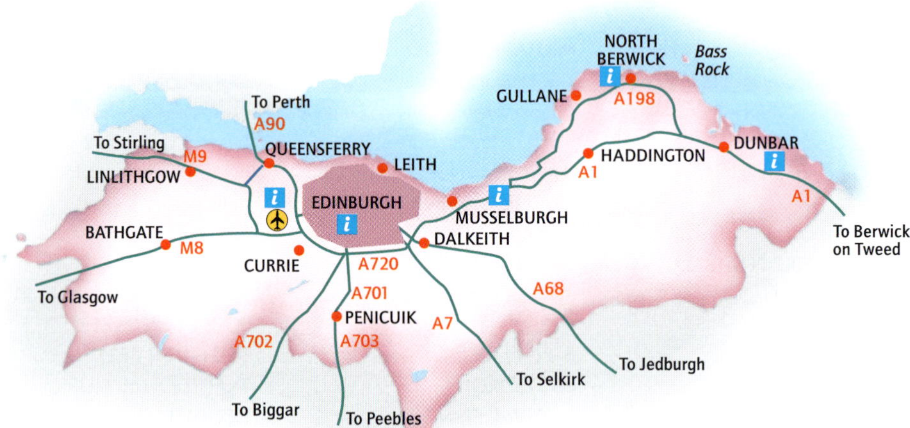

Please refer to the maps on pages xix-xxiv for the locations of establishments appearing in the main advertising section of this guide.

Finding out more...

For practical advice, ideas and information about exploring Scotland and to book your accommodation:

Tel: 0845 22 55 121*
or if calling from outside the UK: +44 (0) 1506 832121

Email: info@visitscotland.com
Web: www.visitscotland.com

* A £3 booking fee applies to telephone bookings of accommodation.

Tourist Information Centres

Edinburgh and Lothians

Edinburgh and Lothians

Dunbar
143A High Street
Tel: (0845) 22 55 121
Apr – Oct

Edinburgh
Edinburgh & Scotland
Information Centre
3 Princes Street
Tel: (0845) 22 55 121
Jan – Dec

Edinburgh Airport
Main Concourse
Tel: (0845) 22 55 121
Jan – Dec

Linlithgow
Burgh Halls
The Cross
Tel: (0845) 22 55 121
April – Oct

Newtongrange
Scottish Mining Museum
Tel: (0845) 22 55 121
Easter – Oct

North Berwick
Quality Street
Tel: (0845) 22 55 121
Jan – Dec

Old Craighall
Old Craighall Service Area (A1)
Tel: (0845) 22 55 121
Apr – Oct

Blackburn, West Lothian | Map Ref: 2B5

CRUACHAN BED & BREAKFAST

78 EAST MAIN STREET, BLACKBURN, WEST LOTHIAN EH47 7QS
Tel: 01506 655221 Fax: 01506 652395
e.mail: cruachan.bb@virgin.net Web: www.cruachan.co.uk

A relaxed and friendly base is provided at Cruachan from which to explore central Scotland. Hosts Kenneth and Jacqueline ensure you receive the utmost in quality of service, meticulously presented accommodation and of course a full Scottish breakfast. They look forward to having the pleasure of your company.

★★★

B&B

Cruachan Bed & Breakfast

78 East Main Street, Blackburn, West Lothian EH47 7QS
Tel:01506 655221   Fax:01506 652395
Email:cruachan.bb@virgin.net
Web:www.cruachan.co.uk

Located on A705 in Blackburn. Cruachan is 1.5 miles from junction 4 of M8 allowing easy access to road links for Edinburgh and Glasgow, or enjoy the benefit of a 30 minute rail journey to Edinburgh from nearby Bathgate. An ideal central location for your visit to Scotland.

4 rooms, 3 en-suite, 1 priv.facilities, Open Jan-Dec, B&B per person, single from £30.00, double from £25.00.

Broxburn, West Lothian | Map Ref: 2B5

BANKHEAD FARMHOUSE B&B

Bankhead Farm, Dechmont, Broxburn, West Lothian EH52 6NB
Tel: 01506 811209 Fax: 01506 811815
e.mail: Bankheadbb@aol.com Web: www.bankheadfarm.com

Perfectly placed for exploring Edinburgh and Scotland. Bankhead has 7 modern ensuite bedrooms in traditional farmhouse building. Panoramic views of local hills and over the Forth to Fife, yet close to 3 historic towns and less than 20 minutes from Edinburgh Airport. Easy access to main Scottish routes. Car essential.

★★★★

**GUEST
HOUSE**

Bankhead Farm

Dechmont, Broxburn, West Lothian, EH52 6NB
Tel:01506 811209 Fax:01506 811815
Email:bankheadbb@aol.com
Web:www.bankheadfarm.com

Perfectly placed for Edinburgh and airport. Stay in a traditional farmhouse with modern en-suite bedrooms. Panoramic views of Scottish countryside.

7 rooms, all en-suite, Open Jan-Dec excl Xmas, B&B per person, single from £40.00, double from £35.00.

Accommodation made easy

call: 0845 22 55 121 £3 booking fee applies to telephone bookings

info@visitscotland.com

Visit*Scotland*.com

Important: Prices stated are estimates and may be subject to amendments

Dalkeith, Midlothian

Map Ref: 2C5

GUEST HOUSE

The Guesthouse@Eskbank
Rathan, 45 Eskbank Road, Eskbank, Dalkeith EH22 3BH
Tel/Fax:0131 663 3291
Email:guesthouse@eskbank.scot.cc
Web:www.eskbank.guest.scot.cc

Award winning B&B with tranquil child-secure walled garden, croquet lawn and private parking. Set in the leafy Eskbank conservation area. Excellent park & ride base for Edinburgh. Low fat 'Highland' breakfasts and vegetarian option.

6 rooms, all en-suite, Open Feb-Dec excl Xmas, B&B per person, single from £35.00, double from £35.00.

Dunbar, East Lothian

Map Ref: 2E4

GUEST HOUSE

Springfield Guest House
Belhaven Road, Dunbar, East Lothian, EH42 1NH
Tel:01368 862502
Email:smeed@tesco.net

An elegant 19c villa with attractive garden. Family run with home-cooking. Ground floor room with private bathrooms available. Ideal base for golfing and touring East Lothian, Edinburgh and the Borders.

5 rooms, Open Jan-Nov excl Xmas/New Year, B&B per person, single from £25.00, double from £22.00.

East Calder, West Lothian

Map Ref: 2B5

ASHCROFT FARMHOUSE

EAST CALDER, NEAR EDINBURGH EH53 0ET
Tel: 01506 881810 Fax: 01506 884327
e.mail:scottashcroft7@aol.com
Web: www.ashcroftfarmhouse.com

Enjoy true Scottish hospitality in our ranch-style farmhouse set in award winning gardens, enjoying lovely views over surrounding countryside. 10m City Centre, 5m Airport, Ingliston, A720, M8/M9, Livingston. Regular bus/train nearby to Edinburgh, so no parking problems. Choice of delicious breakfasts using local produce including home-made sausage. Ideal base for touring. All rooms on ground floor, including romantic four poster bedroom. Rooms are attractively furnished in antique pine with co-ordinating fabrics. Elizabeth was West Lothian 'Businesswoman of the Year 2004' and Runner-up AA Landlady of the Year Awards 2005.

AA/RAC ◆◆◆◆◆ No Smoking or pets indoors, sorry.

GUEST HOUSE

Ashcroft Farmhouse
East Calder, Nr Edinburgh, EH53 0ET
Tel:01506 881810 Fax:01506 884327
Email:scottashcroft7@aol.com
Web:www.ashcroftfarmhouse.com

A warm Scottish welcome awaits you. Runner-up AA Landlady of the Year Awards 2005. Award winning landscaped gardens. Superior Guest House accommodation. Bus/train Edinburgh city centre 10 miles; airport 5 miles; M8/M9/A720 5 miles. Superb choice of breakfasts. AA & RAC 5 Diamonds.

6 rooms, all en-suite, Open Jan-Dec, B&B per person, single from £45.00, double from £32.00.

VAT is shown at 17.5%: changes in this rate may affect prices.

Key to symbols is on back flap.

East Calder, West Lothian   Map Ref: 2B5

Overshiel Farm
EAST CALDER, near Edinburgh EH53 0HT
Telephone: 01506 880469
e.mail: enquiries@overshielfarm.com
Web: www.overshielfarm.com
PEACEFUL COUNTRY SETTING, 6 MILES WEST OF
EDINBURGH. EASY ACCESS INTO CITY CENTRE BY CAR, BUS
OR TRAIN (STATION 1.5 MILES). ALL ROOMS HAVE COLOUR
TV PLUS TEA/COFFEE-MAKING FACILITIES. SAFE PARKING.

B&B

Overshiel Farm

East Calder, West Lothian, EH53 0HT
Tel:01506 880469
Email:enquiries@overshielfarm.com
Web:www.overshielfarm.com

Stone built farmhouse set in large garden and surrounded by arable
farmland. 5 miles (8kms) from Edinburgh Airport. Easy access to M8 and
M9. Non-smoking establishment. Wide range of eating places within
short drive.

3 rooms, some en-suite, Open Jan-Dec, B&B per person, single £30.00-40.00,
double £20.00-27.50.

WHITECROFT
7 RAW HOLDINGS, EAST CALDER, WEST LOTHIAN EH53 0ET
Tel: 01506 882494 Fax: 01506 882598
e.mail: Lornascot@aol.com Web: www.whitecroftbandb.co.uk
Douglas and Lorna extend a warm Scottish welcome with all rooms
on ground level. Whitecroft is surrounded by farmland yet only
10 miles from city centre. Airport 5 miles. Safe private parking.
A full hearty Scottish breakfast is served using local produce.
There are restaurants in the area providing evening meals.

B&B

Whitecroft B&B

East Calder, West Lothian, EH53 0ET
Tel:01506 882494   Fax:01506 882598
Email:lornascot@aol.com
Web:www.whitecroftbandb.co.uk

Family bungalow on 5 acre small holding adjacent to Almondell Country
Park. On main bus route to Edinburgh (20 mins) and 5 minutes drive to
Livingston. Private parking. Ground floor accommodation. No Smoking.

3 rooms, all en-suite, Open Jan-Dec, B&B per person, single from £35.00, double
from £26.00.

Edinburgh   Map Ref: 2C5

GUEST HOUSE

Aaron Guest House

16 Hartington Gardens, Edinburgh, EH10 4LD
Tel:0131 229 6459 Fax:0131 228 5807
Email:info@aaronguesthouse.co.uk
Web:www.aaronguesthouse.co.uk

Quiet 18th Century home with private car parking within walking
distance of Edinburgh City Centre. Come and enjoy our hospitality.

8 rooms, all en-suite, Open Jan-Dec, B&B per person, single from £30.00, double
from £20.00.

Important: Prices stated are estimates and may be subject to amendments

Map Ref: 2C5

Abcorn Guest House
4 Mayfield Gardens, Edinburgh EH9 2BU
Tel: 0131 667 6548 Fax: 0131 667 9969
e.mail: sales@abcorn.co.uk Web: www.abcorn.co.uk
The Abcorn is a family run guest house in a detached Victorian villa, near to the city centre, with a private car park. All our rooms are ensuite and also have colour TV and tea/coffee-making facilities.

GUEST HOUSE

Abcorn Guest House
4 Mayfield Gardens, Edinburgh, EH9 2BU
Tel:0131 667 6548   Fax:0131 667 9969
Email:sales@abcorn.co.uk
Web:www.abcorn.co.uk

Personally managed by the owners Jimmy and Marjorie Kellacher, this detached guest house is centrally located, on a frequent bus route to the city centre. Ample private parking. Ground floor accommodation available.

7 rooms, all en-suite, Open Jan-Dec excl Xmas, B&B per person, single £28.00-42.00, double £28.00-42.00.

GUEST HOUSE

Adria Hotel
11-12 Royal Terrace, Edinburgh, EH7 5AB
Tel:0131 556 7875   Fax:0131 558 7782
Email:manager@adriahotel.co.uk
Web:www.adriahotel.co.uk

Friendly family run private hotel in quiet Georgian terrace. Spacious bedrooms. A pleasant short walk to Princes Street, Waverley Train Station and bus terminal. Totally non-smoking.

23 rooms, some en-suite, Open Feb-Nov, B&B per person, single from £30.00, double from £25.00.

Edinburgh
Map Ref: 2C5

AEON-KIRKLANDS GUEST HOUSE
128 Old Dalkeith Road, Edinburgh EH16 4SD
Tel: 0131 664 2755 Fax: 0131 621 0866
email: dot@baigan.freeserve.co.uk
Web: www.aeon-kirklands.co.uk

Aeon-Kirklands is a 200 year old former coach house. It is a family owned Guest House and personally run by the owners Ted and Dot Baigan. All rooms are fully ensuite with colour TV, hairdryers and hospitality tray, we also have a large car park. We are the nearest guest house to the new Royal Infirmary which is a few minutes walk away and close to the city centre and all tourist attractions. Ideally situated for the city bypass and Edinburgh Airport. A warm welcome awaits.

GUEST
HOUSE

Aeon-Kirklands Guest House
128 Old Dalkeith Road, Edinburgh, EH16 4SD
Tel:0131 664 2755 Fax:0131 621 0866
Email:dot@baigan.freeserve.co.uk
Web:www.aeon-kirklands.co.uk

Ideal base for sightseeing many of this city's historic attractions. Some ground floor en suite annexe accommodation. On main bus route to city centre. Close to Craigmillar Castle. Within walking distance of Royal Edinburgh Infirmary.

9 rooms, all ensuite, Open Jan-Dec, B&B per person, single from £35.00, double from £22.50. Family room available.

B&B

Mrs Linda J Allan
10 Baberton Mains Rise, Edinburgh, EH14 3HG
Tel:0131 442 3619
Email:LJA_bandb_edin@hotmail.com
Web:www.linjallan.pwp.blueyonder.co.uk

Family home in quiet residential area. Unrestricted parking. Frequent bus service to Princes Street. Convenient for Golf Courses and Heriot Watt University.

1 room, Open May-Oct, B&B per person, single £20.00-36.00, double £16.00-18.00.

Important: Prices stated are estimates and may be subject to amendments

Map Ref: 2C5

Allt-nan-Craobh

28 Cammo Road, Edinburgh EH4 8AP

Tel: 0131 339 3613

A VERY WARM WELCOME AWAITS OUR GUESTS IN OUR COMFORTABLE, TASTEFULLY FURNISHED VILLA. SET IN AN ATTRACTIVE PEACEFUL GARDEN WHICH IS SITUATED IN A QUIET, WOODED AREA ONLY FOUR MILES FROM THE TOWN CENTRE. CLOSE TO EDINBURGH AIRPORT, BY-PASS AND THE NORTH. EASY AND SAFE PARKING. EXCELLENT BUS SERVICE. NON-SMOKING.

★★★★

B&B

Allt-nan-Craobh

28 Cammo Road, Edinburgh, EH4 8AP
Tel:0131 339 3613

2 rooms, Open all year, B&B per person, single from £25.00, double from £22.00.

A warm welcome awaits you at this family home in quiet residential area with easy access to Queensferry Rd and Airport. Ideal base for touring Edinburgh and surrounding countryside. Ample, free on-street parking. Open all year round.

ARDEN GUEST HOUSE

126 OLD DALKEITH ROAD, EDINBURGH EH16 4SD

Tel: 0131 664 3985   Fax: 0131 621 0866

e.mail: dot@baigan.freeserve.co.uk   Web: www.ardenedinburgh.co.uk

Family run Guest House on main A7, minutes from City Centre, Airport, City Bypass and walking distance to new Edinburgh Royal Infirmary. Full ensuite rooms with cable TV, tea/coffee facilities, hairdryer and telephone. Furnished to a high standard throughout. A warm welcome and home comforts at an affordable price.

PRIVATE PARKING.

★★★

GUEST HOUSE

Arden Guest House

126 Old Dalkeith Road, Edinburgh, EH16 4SD
Tel:0131 664 3985   Fax:0131 621 0866
Email:dot@baigan.freeserve.co.uk
Web:www.ardenedinburgh.co.uk

19 rooms, all en-suite, Open Jan-Dec, B&B per person, single from £25.00, double from £20.00.

Privately owned guest house, all rooms ensuite with ground floor level accommodation. On main A7 road, situated on south side of city 10 minutes from city centre. Ideal base for business guests. Off-street parking. Easy access to all amenities. Walking distance from the New Royal Infirmary.

Ardenlee Guest House

9 Eyre Place, Edinburgh EH3 5ES
Tel: 0131 556 2838
e.mail: info@ardenlee.co.uk Web: www.ardenlee.co.uk

Beautiful Grade 'B' listed Victorian town house in the very centre of Edinburgh (off Dundas Street). Only half a mile from Princes Street and within easy walking distance of all main attractions, train and bus stations. Family run offering a warm welcome, spacious comfortable rooms and a fully cooked breakfast.

GUEST HOUSE

Ardenlee Guest House
9 Eyre Place, Edinburgh, EH3 5ES
Tel:0131 556 2838 Fax:0131 557 0937
Email:info@ardenlee.co.uk
Web:www.ardenlee.co.uk

Personally run terraced guest house, in New Town approximately 0.5 mile (1km) from Princes Street and city centre. Ideal touring base. Non-smoking house. Variety of shops and restaurants nearby. Most rooms en-suite.

9 rooms, some en-suite, Open Jan-Dec, B&B per person, single from £27.50, double from £27.50.

B&B

Aros House
1 Salisbury House, Edinburgh, EH9 1SL
Tel:0131 667 1585
Email:aros.house@virgin.net
Web:http://freespace.virgin.net/aros.house

Georgian House on first floor, family home 1 mile S of city centre with excellent bus service. Qualified tour guide.

2 rooms, all en-suite, Open Feb-Nov, B&B per person, double/twin £24.00-30.00.

B&B

Ascot Garden
154 Glasgow Road, Edinburgh, EH12 8LS
Tel/Fax:0131 339 2092

A warm Scottish welcome awaits you in this family home situated on the main Edinburgh to Glasgow A8 road. Close to the city by-pass and all major routes north and south. Short drive from Edinburgh Airport. Directly opposite Marriot Hotel.

2 rooms, all en-suite, Open Jan-Dec, B&B per person, single from £25.00, double from £25.00 pp.

Accommodation made easy

call: 0845 22 55 121 £3 booking fee applies to telephone bookings

info@visitscotland.com

VisitScotland.com

Important: Prices stated are estimates and may be subject to amendments

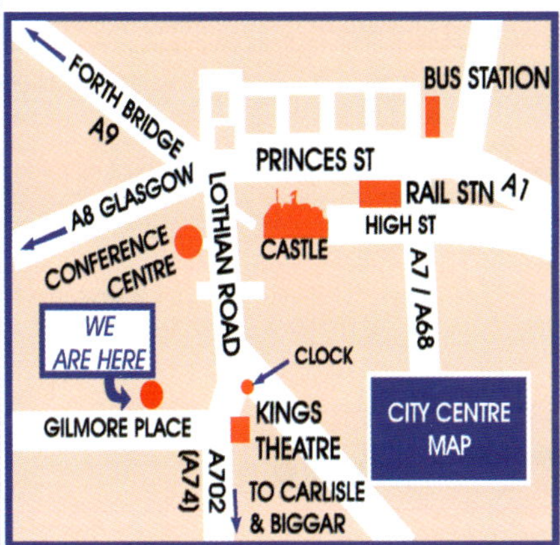

CENTRAL EDINBURGH
AVERON GUEST HOUSE

Built in 1770 as a farmhouse, charming, centrally situated Georgian period house offers a high standard of accommodation at favourable terms.

- Full cooked breakfast •
- All credit cards accepted •
- 10 minutes' walk to Princes Street and Castle •
- STB ★ • AA Listed • RAC Listed •
- PRIVATE CAR PARK •

44 Gilmore Place, Central Edinburgh EH3 9NQ
Tel: 0131 229 9932
e.mail: info@averon.co.uk Web: www.averon.co.uk

Averon Guest House
44 Gilmore Place, Edinburgh, EH3 9NQ
Tel:0131 229 9932
Email:info@averon.co.uk
Web:www.averon.co.uk

Central location with private car park to rear. 10 minute walk to Princes Street and Castle. Near Kings Theatre and Conference Centre. Many rooms on ground floor.

10 rooms, some en-suite, Open Jan-Dec, B&B per person, single from £26.00, double from £22.00.

Beresford Hotel
32 Coates Gardens, Edinburgh, EH12 5LE
Tel:0131 337 0850
Email:bookings@beresford-edinburgh.com
Web:www.beresford-edinburgh.com

Family run establishment close to city centre and Haymarket station. Most rooms en-suite. Children very welcome.

12 rooms, 10 en-suite, Open Jan-Dec, B&B per person, single from £30.00, double from £22.50.

VAT is shown at 17.5%: changes in this rate may affect prices.   *Key to symbols is on back flap.*

Bield Bed and Breakfast

3 Orchard Brae West, Edinburgh EH4 2EW
Tel: 0131 332 5119
e.mail: bieldltd@hotmail.com Web: www.bieldbedandbreakfast.com

This delightful bungalow is located in a quiet cul-de-sac and is
only 10 minutes walk from the city centre. A family run business offering
superb facilities for our guests. Ample private parking. You are assured of a
friendly welcome and a comfortable, relaxing stay in central Edinburgh.
Family room available with private bathroom.

★★★

B&B

Bield Bed & Breakfast

3 Orchard Brae West, Edinburgh, Midlothian, EH4 2EW
Tel:0131 332 5119
Email:bieldltd@hotmail.com

3 rooms, 2 en-suite, Open Jan-Dec, B&B per person, single £35.00-40.00, double
£25.00-35.00, family £25.00-35.00, discounts for children.

Commfortable Bed & Breakfast accommodation located within 10 - 15
minutes walk from Princes Street.

★

**GUEST
HOUSE**

Blossom House

8 Minto Street, Edinburgh, EH9 1RG
Tel:0131 667 5353   Fax:0131 667 2813
Email:blossom_house@hotmail.com
Web:www.blossomguesthouse.co.uk

7 rooms, some en-suite, Open Jan-Dec, B&B per person, single from £25.00,
double from £20.00.

Comfortable, family run guest house. City centre within walking distance.
Excellent bus service. Private car park. Close to Commonwealth pool and
Royal College of Surgeons.

BONNINGTON GUEST HOUSE

202 Ferry Road, Edinburgh EH6 4NW
Tel/Fax: 0131 554 7610
e.mail: bonningtongh@btinternet.com
web: www.bonnington-guest-house-edinburgh.co.uk

A comfortable early Victorian house (built 1840), personally run,
where a friendly and warm welcome awaits guests. Situated in
residential area of town on main bus routes. Private car parking.

**AWAITING
INSPECTION**

Bonnington Guest House

202 Ferry Road, Edinburgh, EH6 4NW
Tel/Fax:0131 554 7610
Email:bonningtongh@btinternet.com
Web:www.bonnington-guest-house-edinburgh.co.uk

6 rooms, some en-suite, Open Jan-Dec, B&B per person, single from £35.00,
double from £28.00.

Important: Prices stated are estimates and may be subject to amendments

Karen Bridges B&B

56 East Claremont Street
Edinburgh EH7 4JR
Tel: 0131 478 4463
E.mail:
enquiriesandbookings@karenbridges.co.uk
Web: www.karenbridges.co.uk

We will welcome you to this elegant bed and breakfast situated in the New Town close to Botanic Gardens, the Playhouse Theatre and the city centre. Close to Omni Centre and friendly Broughton Street. 15 minutes walk to Princes Street. Totally non-smoking. No parking restrictions. All rooms en-suite.
Credit cards accepted

★★★★

B&B

Mr Semlali
56 East Claremont Street, Edinburgh, EH7 4JR
Tel: 0131 478 4463
Email:enquiriesandbookings@karenbridges.co.uk
Web: www.karenbridges.co.uk

Comfortable B&B, furnished to a high standard, within easy reach of city centre. 10 minutes walk to Princes Street and main attractions.

2 rooms, all en-suite. Open Jan-Dec. B&B per person per night: single £20.00-50.00, double £20.00-40.00, family £20.00-40.00.

BRIGGEND GUEST HOUSE

19 Old Dalkeith Road, Edinburgh, EH16 4TE
Tel: 0131 258 0810 Fax: 0131 620 2873
email: reservations@briggend.com Web: www.briggend.com
Briggend is a small family run Guest House. All rooms en-suite with cable TV, tea & coffee, hairdryers. Private parking. All rooms are ground level. We are minutes from Edinburgh City Centre and within walking distance of new Edinburgh Royal Infirmary.

★★★

**GUEST
HOUSE**

Briggend Guest House
19 Old Dalkeith Road, Edinburgh, EH16 4TE
Tel:0131 258 0810 Fax:0131 620 2873
Email:reservations@briggend.com
Web:www.briggend.com

Recently extended traditional cottage, now providing 4 ensuite bedrooms, all on ground level, on south side of city with very easy access to main routes, the new Edinburgh Royal Infirmary, Universities and many of the city's attractions. Also on main bus route.

4 rooms, all ensuite, Open Jan-Dec, B&B per person per night, single from £35.00, double from £22.50. Family room available.

VAT is shown at 17.5%: changes in this rate may affect prices.

Key to symbols is on back flap.

B

Edinburgh   Map Ref: 2C5

BRODIES GUEST HOUSE

22 East Claremont Street, Edinburgh EH7 4JP
Telephone: 0131 556 4032   *Fax*: 0131 556 9739
e.mail: info@brodiesguesthouse.co.uk   Web: www.brodiesguesthouse.co.uk
**A warm Scottish welcome awaits you at our Victorian town house
set in a landscaped cobbled street only 5-10 minutes walk from
the city centre. Princes Street, bus/rail stations, Botanic Gardens,
Castle, Dynamic Earth, Britannia and Playhouse are close by.
Many extras provided. Full Scottish breakfasts a speciality.**

★★★

**GUEST
HOUSE**

Brodies Guest House
22 East Claremont Street, Edinburgh, EH7 4JP
Tel:0131 556 4032   Fax:0131 556 9739
Email:info@brodiesguesthouse.co.uk
Web:www.brodiesguesthouse.co.uk

Small, friendly, family run Victorian town house in a cobbled street
within ½ mile of Princes Street. Convenient for bus/railway station,
Playhouse Theatre, pubs and restaurants nearby. Scottish breakfasts a
speciality.

6 rooms, some en-suite, Open Feb-Dec excl Xmas, B&B per person, single from
£29.00, double from £29.00.

BURNS GUEST HOUSE

67 Gilmore Place, Edinburgh EH3 9NU
Tel: 0131 229 1669   Fax: 0131 229 9225
e.mail: burnsbandb@talk21.com   Web: www.burnsguesthouse.co.uk
Popular homely B&B in city centre close to Princes Street, Castle, E.I.C.C.,
tourist attractions, theatres, pubs, restaurants. Comfortable en-suite rooms.
Good breakfasts. Parking - some secure spaces. No-smoking, no pets.
Access with your own keys. B&B from £25 - £35 pppn.
Visa/Master Cards accepted. Open all year.
Contact Mrs Burns as above.

★★★

**GUEST
HOUSE**

Burns Guest House
67 Gilmore Place, Edinburgh, EH3 9NU
Tel:0131 229 1669   Fax:0131 229 9225
Email:burnsbandb@talk21.com
Web:www.burnsguesthouse.co.uk

Charming pre-Victorian terraced house, personally run by Mrs Burns.
Close to city centre, tourist attractions, Kings Theatre, E.I.C.C and local
restaurants. 3 ensuite. Non-smoking.

4 rooms, 3 en-suite, Open Jan-Dec excl Xmas/New Year, B&B per person, single
from £25.00, double from £25.00.

★★

**GUEST
HOUSE**

Caravel Guest House
30 London Street, Edinburgh, EH3 6NA
Tel:0131 556 4444   Fax:0131 557 3615
Email:caravelguest@hotmail.com
Web:www.caravelhouse.co.uk

A warm welcome at this guest house with spacious, en-suite bedrooms.
This Georgian house is situated in the heart of Edinburgh's New Town
only a short distance from Princes Street and close to Waverley Station
and the bus station.

11 rooms, some en-suite, Open Jan-Dec, B&B per person, single from £30.00,
double from £25.00.

Edinburgh

Map Ref: 2C5

Castle Park Guest House

75 Gilmore Place, Edinburgh EH3 9NU
Tel: 0131 229 1215 Fax: 0131 229 1223
e.mail: castlepark@btconnect.com

Family run close to Kings Theatre and city centre conference centre.
Always a warm welcome awaits you.
All bedrooms have colour TV, Sky, tea and coffee.
Central heating. Full Scottish breakfast. Children welcome.
Special prices. Street parking. £20.00–£25.00 pppn.

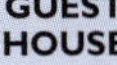

GUEST HOUSE

Castle Park Guest House
75 Gilmore Place, Edinburgh, EH3 9NU
Tel:0131 229 1215   Fax:0131 229 1223
Email:castlepark@btconnect.com

Family run guest house close to city centre. Convenient for Kings Theatre and Conference Hall. A variety of local restaurants and bistros. Children welcome.

9 rooms, some en-suite, Open Jan-Dec excl Xmas/New Year, B&B per person, single from £20.00, double from £25.00.

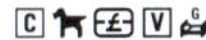

GUEST HOUSE

Charleston House Guest House
38 Minto Street, Edinburgh, EH9 2BS
Tel:0131 667 6589   Fax:0131 668 3800
Email:joan_wightman@hotmail.com
Web:www.charleston-house.co.uk

Traditional Georgian family home with many original features - circa 1826. Awarded prestigious Bronze Green Tourism plaque. Only 1- 1.5 miles from city centre. Excellent bus route, very frequent service. Within easy walking distance of various restaurants.

5 rooms, some en-suite, Open Jan-Dec excl Xmas, B&B per person, single from £25.00, double from £20.00.

B&B

The Conifers
56 Pilrig Street, Edinburgh, EH6 5AS
Tel:0131 554 5162
Email:liz@conifersguesthouse.com
Web:www.conifersguesthouse.com

Friendly family home, within walking distance to city centre and Playhouse Theatre. Unrestricted parking. Non Smoking.

4 rooms, some en-suite, Open Jan-Dec, B&B per person, single from £25.00-40.00, double/twin/family from £25.00-40.00 pp.

B&B

Corner House
1 Greenbank Place, Edinburgh, EH10 6EW
Tel:0131 447 1077
Email:keith.t@lineone.net

Comfortable accommodation in this family home situated in Edinburgh. Very convenient for the city centre and also bus routes. Spacious rooms and free street parking. Convenient for Napier University, Braid Hills Hotel and Golf Course. Excellent local shops and amenities close by.

3 rooms, Open Jan-Dec, B&B per person, £20.00-26.00.

CRAIGMORE B&B

20 Craigs Road, Edinburgh EH12 8EL
Tel/Fax: 0131 339 4225
e.mail: raemac@fourstaredinburgh.com
Web: www.fourstaredinburgh.com

Discover the history, culture and fun of our capital city Edinburgh from Craigmore Bed & Breakfast. Leave your car parked by us and relax using the convenient public transport. We are near the airport and main trunk roads to the South, West and North.

★★★★

B&B

Craigmore Bed & Breakfast

20 Craigs Road, Edinburgh, EH12 8EL
Tel/Fax:0131 339 4225
Email:raemac@fourstaredinburgh.com
Web:www.fourstaredinburgh.com

Lovely home with secluded garden situated between airport and city centre with frequent bus service to both. A friendly welcome assured. Restricted off-street parking. Bedrooms fully ensuite.

2 rooms, all ensuite, Open Jan-Dec, B&B per person, single from £31.00, double from £26.00. Room Only per room, single from £35.00, double from £52.00.

★★★

GUEST HOUSE

Crioch Guest House

23 East Hermitage Place, Leith Links, Edinburgh EH6 8AD
Tel/Fax:0131 554 5494
Email:welcome@crioch.com
Web:www.crioch.com

Set on a frequent bus route to the city centre, Crioch overlooks the leafy park of Leith Links. All rooms have ensuite shower or private bathroom, TV, radio alarm and welcome tray. You can choose from continental or full cooked breakfast. Free parking and the frequent bus service leaves you to enjoy Edinburgh's sights on foot, and a short stroll takes you to Leith's fine cafes, bars and restaurants.

6 rooms, some en-suite, Open Jan-Dec, B&B per person, single from £25.00, double from £22.50.

★

B&B

Mr & Mrs T Divine

116 Greenbank Crescent, Edinburgh, EH10 5SZ
Tel:0131 447 9454
Email:mary@greenbnk.fsnet.co.uk
Web:www.greenbank.i12.com

Family home in quiet residential area with easy access to city centre and bypass. On main bus routes. Private parking off road.

2 rooms, Open Mar-Oct, B&B per person, single from £20.00.

★★

B&B

Doocote House

15 Moat Street, Edinburgh, EH14 1PE
Tel:0131 443 5455

Well established traditional B&B. Approx 2 miles (3kms) from city centre. Unrestricted street parking. Kitchen available for guests.

3 rooms, Open Mar-Oct, B&B from £22.00 per person.

Map Ref: 2C5

★★★★

GUEST HOUSE

Ellesmere Guest House
11 Glengyle Terrace, Edinburgh, EH3 9LN
Tel:0131 229 4823
Email:celia@edinburghbandb.co.uk
Web:www.edinburghbandb.co.uk

City centre Victorian terraced house in quiet location overlooking Bruntsfield Links. Kings Theatre, Conference Centre and all amenities within walking distance. All rooms en suite. Full Scottish Breakfast is served and a warm welcome is extended to all guests.

4 rooms, all en-suite, Open Jan-Dec, B&B per person, single from £35.00, double from £35.00.

Falcon Crest

70 South Trinity Road Edinburgh EH5 3NX
Tel/Fax: 0131 552 5294
Email: manager@falconcrest.co.uk   Web: www.falconcrest.co.uk
A friendly welcome awaits at our family run guest house in a quiet residential Victorian terrace. Located between the Royal Botanic Gardens, Newhaven Harbour and Granton Marina.
Ten minutes by frequent bus service from the city centre. Good road links. Private parking. Special diets by prior request.

★

GUEST HOUSE

Falcon Crest Guest House
70 South Trinity Road, Edinburgh, EH5 3NX
Tel/Fax:0131 552 5294
Email:manager@falconcrest.co.uk
Web:www.falconcrest.co.uk

Victorian terraced family home in attractive residential area, near main bus route to city centre. Free on street parking.

6 rooms, some en-suite, (1 single, 2 twin, 2 double, 1 family), from £18.00 Single, double from £18.00.

VAT is shown at 17.5%: changes in this rate may affect prices.

Key to symbols is on back flap.

Ellesmere House
11 Glengyle Terrace,
EDINBURGH
Tel: 0131 229 4823   EH3 9LN   Fax: 0131 229 5285
e.mail: celia@edinburghbandb.co.uk Web: www.edinburghbandb.co.uk
"Your home away from home"
Ellesmere House is situated in an
enviable location overlooking
"Bruntsfield Links" in the CENTRE
of Edinburgh, within easy walking
distance of most places of interest.
The International Conference Centre,
theatres and various good restaurants
are very close by. Rooms are all ensuite and are tastefully furnished and decorated
to a very high standard and many extras added with your comfort in mind.
For honeymooners or that special anniversary there is a four-poster bed available.
Start the day with our delicious full Scottish breakfast.
Prices from £35, all rooms ensuite. Excellent value and competitive prices.

Personally run by Cecilia & Tommy Leishman who extend a
very warm welcome to all of their guests.

Four Seasons Guest House

47 Minto Street, Edinburgh EH9 2BR
Tel: 0131 667 2963
e.mail: thefourseasons@edinburgh-guesthouses.net

Very well situated near city centre, University Royal Colleges of Surgeons and Physicians, Queen Hall and Festival Theatre. Commonwealth Pool, Holyrood Palace. Ensuite facilities. Family room with facilities, relaxed homely comfort. Frequent bus services. Private car park.

GUEST HOUSE

Four Seasons Guest House

47 Minto Street, Newington, Edinburgh, EH9 2BR
Tel:0131 667 2963
Email:thefourseasons@edinburgh-guesthouses.net

Situated on main bus route, with frequent service to city centre. Some ensuite facilities and small private car park. Easy walking distance to many restaurants, cinema and swimming pool. Some accommodation on ground floor level.

7 rooms, some en-suite, Open Jan-Dec, B&B per person, single from £22.50, double from £22.50.

GUEST HOUSE

Gifford House

103 Dalkeith Road, Edinburgh, EH16 5AJ
Tel/Fax:0131 667 4688
Email:giffordhotel@btinternet.com
Web:www.giffordhousehotel.co.uk

A well appointed Victorian stone built house situated on one of the main routes into Edinburgh. Close to Holyrood Park and Arthur's Seat and only 300 metres from Royal Commonwealth Swimming Pool. Regular bus services to all city amenities. Well positioned for conference centre.

7 rooms, all en-suite, Open Jan-Dec excl Xmas, B&B per person, single £35.00-75.00, double from £30.00-55.00.

GUEST HOUSE

Gildun Guest House

9 Spence Street, Edinburgh, EH16 5AG
Tel:0131 667 1368   Fax:0131 668 4989
Email:gildun.edin@btinternet.com
Web:www.gildun.co.uk

A warm and friendly run guest house recently refurbished to an excellent standard situated in cul de sac with private parking. Close to Commonwealth Pool and bus route to city centre. Cameron Toll Shopping Centre nearby and situated near University Halls of Residence. A variety of eating establishments within walking distance.

8 rooms, some en-suite, Open Jan-Dec, B&B per person, single from £24.00, double from £24.00.

VAT is shown at 17.5%: changes in this rate may affect prices.   *Key to symbols is on back flap.*

GLENDEVON
50 GLASGOW ROAD, EDINBURGH EH12 8HN
Tel/Fax: 0131 539 0491   e.mail: simpson-glendevon@fsmail.net
Web: www.simpson-glendevon.co.uk

A warm welcome awaits visitors at 'Glendevon'. A detached bungalow with attractive garden, open outlook and private parking. On good bus route to city centre and 3 miles from airport. All rooms centrally heated and tastefully furnished with W.H.B., tea/coffee making facilities and colour TV. Residents lounge available. Non-smoking.

★★★

B&B

Glendevon
50 Glasgow Road, Edinburgh, EH12 8HN
Tel/Fax:0131 539 0491
Email:simpson-glendevon@fsmail.net
Web:www.simpson-glendevon.co.uk

1930's family bungalow on major bus route to city centre and 3 miles from the Airport. Private parking. Some ground floor accommodation. Non-smoking.

3 rooms, Open Apr-Oct, B&B per person, single/double £25.00-30.00.

★★

B&B

Glenfarrer House
36 Farrer Terrace, Edinburgh, EH7 6SG
Tel/Fax:0131 669 1265
Email:betty@glenfarrer.fslife.co.uk

Family run chalet bungalow in quiet residential area, east of city centre. Main bus route to city centre nearby. Homely atmosphere.

4 rooms, some en-suite, Open Apr-Oct, B&B per person, single from £18.00, double from £22.50.

★★

HOTEL

Herald House Hotel
70 Grove Street, Edinburgh, EH3 8AP
Tel:0131 228 2323   Fax:0131 228 3101
Email:info@heraldhousehotel.co.uk
Web:www.heraldhousehotel.co.uk

A friendly hotel located in a quite area of the city yet only 15 minutes walk from the centre's main attractions (Princes Street and Edinburgh Castle). All 45 bedrooms have en-suite shower room and there is a breakfast room and brasserie/bar serving drinks and snacks including Internet access. Staff are very helpful and to start the day a full breakfast is served and included in the price.

45 rooms, all en-suite, Open Jan-Dec, B&B from £25.00 pppn sharing.

Important: Prices stated are estimates and may be subject to amendments

HERIOT-WATT UNIVERSITY

Riccarton, Edinburgh EH14 4AS
Tel: 0131 451 3669 Fax: 0131 451 3199
e.mail: reservations@eccscotland.com
Web: www.eccscotland.com

Set in parkland, just six miles from the city centre, Heriot-Watt University offers comfortable and cost competitive year round accommodation. There are 165 rooms available throughout the year in addition to the student accommodation available during vacation. Rooms are serviced daily and all year round rooms have en-suite shower and toilet, television, telephone and tea/coffee facilities. On site amenities include restaurants, bar, shop, hairdressers and sport centre. Situated a short distance from the airport, with excellent access to major road networks and ample onsite free car parking, the University offers an ideal base for Edinburgh and the surrounding area.

CAMPUS ACCOMMODATION

Heriot-Watt University

Riccarton, Edinburgh, EH14 4AS
Tel:0131 451 3669 Fax:0131 451 3199
Email:reservations@eccscotland.com
Web:www.eccscotland.com

Situated in 370 acre picturesque campus of Heriot Watt University. 6 miles (10kms) west of city centre, 3 miles (5kms) from Edinburgh airport.

1626 rooms, 1161 en-suite, 465 standard/study, Open Jan-Dec excl Xmas/New Year, B&B per person, single from £37.50, double from £27.50.

B&B

Hopetoun

15 Mayfield Road, Edinburgh, EH9 2NG
Tel:0131 667 7691 Fax:0131 466 1691
Email:hopetoun@aol.com
Web:www.hopetoun.com

Completely non-smoking, small, friendly bed and breakfast on the south side of the city, 1.5 miles (2.5kms) from Princes Street. Close to Edinburgh University and city by-pass. Guests are encouraged to make use of the owners wide knowledge of what the city has to offer.

2 rooms, some en-suite, Open Jan-Dec, B&B per person, double from £25.00.

INGLENEUK

31 DRUMBRAE NORTH, EDINBURGH EH4 8AT
Tel/Fax: 0131 317 1743
e.mail: ingleneukbnb@btinternet.com
Web: www.ingleneukbandb.co.uk

Stuart and Lynda Ritchie invite you to visit their comfortable home situated in a quiet residential area. The accommodation comprises
• double bedroom with en suite shower/toilet and private conservatory
• twin/family unit comprising twin bedded room with seating and breakfasting area, double bedroom and shower/toilet.
All rooms have private entrances and overlook a landscaped garden. Breakfast is served to your room in the morning. Free off street parking.
4 miles from City Centre. 3 miles from Airport. Good bus service. Close to Forth Bridge.

★★★

B&B

Ingleneuk
31 Drumbrae North, Edinburgh, EH4 8AT
Tel/Fax:0131 317 1743
Email:ingleneukbnb@btinternet.com
Web:www.ingleneukbandb.co.uk

On the west side of town, convenient for the Forth Bridge and the airport, this cottage styled B&B backs onto a landscaped garden alive with birds and squirrels. Both rooms have their own private entrance, one is a family suite suitable for four persons, the other with private conservatory. Enjoy a relaxed breakfast, served in the comfort of your own room.

2 rooms, all en-suite, Open Jan-Dec, B&B per person, single from £30.00, double from £25.00.

International Guest House

37 MAYFIELD GARDENS, EDINBURGH EH9 2BX
Tel: 0131 667 2511 Fax: 0131 667 1112
e.mail: intergh1@yahoo.co.uk
Web: www.accommodation-edinburgh.com
SCOTTISH TOURIST BOARD ★★★★
"One of the best Guest Houses in town."
"International reputation for quality – service – comfort"
- Well-appointed bedrooms all with ensuite facilities
- Colour TVs, tea/coffee-making facilities/direct dial telephone
- Short distance from city centre
- Realistic rates from £25 Bed & Breakfast
- Own keys for all day access
- Warm and friendly atmosphere
- Some private parking

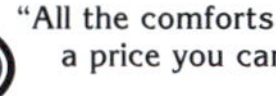

"All the comforts of home at a price you can afford"

★★★★

GUEST HOUSE

International Guest House
37 Mayfield Gardens, Edinburgh, EH9 2BX
Tel:0131 667 2511   Fax:0131 667 1112
Email:intergh1@yahoo.co.uk
Web:www.accommodation-edinburgh.com

Stone built Victorian house in residential area with regular bus service to city centre. All rooms have ensuite facilities. Some private parking and on-street parking. Ground floor room available for persons with limited mobility.

9 rooms, all en-suite, Open Jan-Dec, B&B per person, single from £30.00, double from £25.00.

★★★

B&B

Lindenlea
6 St Marks Place, Portobello, Edinburgh, EH15 2PY
Tel:0131 669 6490
Email:betty@lindenlea6.freeserve.co.uk

Traditional stone-built Victorian villa set in quiet residential area within Portobello. All local amenities nearby with only a short distance to the beach, promenade and historic Victorian baths. Free on street parking with frequent bus services on the doorstep. Ideal base for enjoying the city's attractions and exploring the coastline of East Lothian.

3 rooms, all en-suite, Open Jan-Dec, B&B per person, single £22.00-30.00, double £22.00-30.00.

★★★★

GUEST HOUSE

Mackenzie Guest House
2 East Hermitage Place, Edinburgh, EH6 8AA
Tel:0131 554 3763 Fax:0131 554 0853
Email:info@mackenzieguesthouse.co.uk
Web:www.mackenzieguesthouse.co.uk

A warm welcome awaits you at the Mackenzie Guest House, set in an excellent location overlooking Leith Links and only a 10-15 minute ride from the City Centre. Leith Waterfront with its Bars & Restaurants, Ocean Terminal & the Royal Yacht Britannia are all within walking distance.

5 rooms, some en-suite, Open Jan-Dec, B&B per person, single from £25.00-50.00, double/twin from £24.00-45.00.

VAT is shown at 17.5%: changes in this rate may affect prices.

Key to symbols is on back flap.

Edinburgh

Map Ref: 2C5

★★★

B&B

McCrae's B & B
44 East Claremont Street, Edinburgh, EH7 4JR
Tel/Fax:0131 556 2610
Email:mccraes.bandb@lineone.net
Web:http://website.lineone.net/~mccraes.bandb

Comfortable accommodation in the Victorian part of the New Town, conveniently located, within a pleasant walk to city centre. Unrestricted on-street parking. Bedrooms are all on ground floor level.

3 rooms, all en-suite, Open Jan-Dec, B&B per person, single from £28.00, double from £25.00.

★★★

GUEST HOUSE

Priestville Guest House
10 Priestfield Road, Edinburgh, EH16 5HJ
Tel/Fax:0131 667 2435
Email:priestville@hotmail.com
Web:www.priestville.com

Friendly Scottish Hospitality in Victorian Townhouse, quiet residential area. 20 minute walk to city centre. Excellent bus service. Full fry, Smoked Salmon or Haggis for breakfast. Close to Commonwealth Pool, Holyrood Park and Golf Course. Broadband and wireless Internet access and Parking Available.

6 rooms, some en-suite, Open Jan-Dec, B&B per person, single from £25.00, double from £20.00.

★★★

B&B

Pringles Ingle
26 Morningside Park, Edinburgh, EH10 5HB
Tel:0131 447 5847
Email:migpringle@emailwise.co.uk
Web:www.pringlesingle.com

Traditional terraced villa, unrestricted on-street parking with shops, restaurants, cinema and a theatre locally. By the Royal Edinburgh Hospital and Napier University. On main bus route to city centre. Continental style breakfast, home made bread and preserves a speciality.

2 rooms, one en-suite, Open Jan-Dec, B&B per person, single from £30.00, double from £25.00.

St. Margaret's

13 Corstorphine High Street, Edinburgh EH12 7SU
Tel: 0131 334 7317 Fax: 0131 334 7317
e.mail: CHRISTINE861@aol.com
A warm welcome awaits you at this small friendly newly refurbished main door flat. 10 minutes from city centre and 10 minutes from Edinburgh Airport. Excellent bus service. Many restaurants nearby. Parking. Non smoking house.
Price £25 per person sharing double room. £30 for single.

★★★★

B&B

St Margarets
13 Corstorphine High Street, Edinburgh, Midlothian, EH12 7SU
Tel/Fax:0131 334 7317
Email:christine861@aol.com

Newly refurbished ground floor accommodation with en-suite facilities. Well appointed bedroom with TV/DVD player. Experience the atmosphere of the old 17th century village of Corstorphine. Situated equal distance from Edinburgh Airport and City Centre, (both 3 miles away). Non - smoking.

1 room, en-suite, Open Jan-Dec, B&B per person, single from £30.00, double from £25.00.

Important: Prices stated are estimates and may be subject to amendments

Edinburgh

Map Ref: 2C5

★

GUEST HOUSE

Sakura House
18 West Preston Street, Edinburgh, EH8 9PU
Tel/Fax:0131 668 1204

6 rooms, some en-suite, Open Jan-Dec, B&B per person, single from £18.00, double from £18.00.

Victorian house in central location, close to castle and shopping centre. Numerous good restaurants and pubs in immediate vicinity. On main bus route. Video recorders in bedroom and a selection of videos for guests use. Single guests welcome.

Salisbury Guest House

45 SALISBURY ROAD, EDINBURGH EH16 5AA
Tel/Fax: **0131 667 1264** *e.mail:* **brenda-wright@btconnect.com**
Web: **www.salisburyguesthouse.co.uk**
Comfortable en-suite accommodation in superb central location. Personal service in "home from home". Close to university, Castle, Royal Mile, Holyrood Park and train station. Private car parking. Non smoking throughout. *Contact: Brenda or William Wright for further details.*

★★★

GUEST HOUSE

Salisbury Guest House
45 Salisbury Road, Edinburgh, EH16 5AA
Tel/Fax:0131 667 1264
Email:brenda-wright@btconnect.com
Web:www.salisburyguesthouse.co.uk

8 rooms, some en-suite, Open Feb-Dec excl Xmas/New Year, B&B per person, single from £29.00, double from £25.00.

Georgian Listed building in quiet conservation area, 1 mile (2kms) from city centre. Ensuite and private facilities. Private car park. Non-smoking house.

★★★★

GUEST HOUSE

Sandaig Guest House
5 East Hermitage Place, Leith Links, Edinburgh EH6 8AA
Tel:0131 554 7357   Fax:0131 467 6389
Email:info@sandaigguesthouse.co.uk
Web:www.sandaigguesthouse.co.uk

8 rooms, all en-suite, Open Jan-Dec, B&B per person, single from £35.00, double from £30.00.

Marina and Derek personally welcome you to their delightful Victorian terraced villa overlooking historic Leith Links. Unrestricted street parking. Variety of restaurants nearby or frequent bus service to Princes Street with all its amenities. Totally non-smoking house.

VAT is shown at 17.5%: changes in this rate may affect prices.

Key to symbols is on back flap.

Map Ref: 2C5

SANDEMAN HOUSE

33 COLINTON ROAD, EDINBURGH EH10 5DR
Tel/Fax: 0131 447 8080 e.mail: joycesandeman@freezone.co.uk
Web: www.sandemanhouse.co.uk

A charming non-smoking Victorian Home. (circa 1860) Centrally located. Beautifully restored. All bedrooms with private/en-suite bathrooms, T.V/Radio, tea/coffee making facilities. Wonderful breakfasts. Unrestricted parking. On major bus routes, theatres, restaurants and specialist shops minutes walk away. Most credit cards accepted. Open all year.

★★★★

B&B

Sandeman House
33 Colinton Road, Edinburgh, EH10 5DR
Tel/Fax:0131 447 8080
Email:joycesandeman@freezone.co.uk
Web:www.sandemanhouse.co.uk

Victorian non-smoking listed house centrally situated. All comforts thoughtfully presented with wonderful breakfasts, extensive choice. Wide range of individual shops and eating places within short walking distance.

3 rooms, some en-suite, Open Jan-Dec, B&B per person, single from £45.00, double from £30.00.

★★★

GUEST HOUSE

Smiths' Guest House
77 Mayfield Road, Edinburgh, EH9 3AA
Tel:0131 667 2524   Fax:0131 668 4455
Email:mail@smithsgh.com
Web:www.smithsgh.com

Victorian town house, recently refurbished. Near to city centre.

7 rooms, all en-suite, Open Jan-Dec, B&B per person, single from £18.00, double from £18.00.

STEWARTS BED & BREAKFAST

21 Hillview, Queensferry Road, Edinburgh EH4 2AF
Tel: 0131 539 7033
e.mail: ann@amayo.fslife.co.uk Web: www.stewartsbandb.co.uk

Attractive Edwardian terraced villa just
10 minutes from Edinburgh city centre.
Bus services pass the door. Friendly welcome in a
relaxed family home with comfortable rooms.
Free on street parking.

★★★

B&B

Stewarts B&B
21 Hillview, Queensferry Road, Edinburgh, EH4 2AF
Tel:0131 539 7033
Email:ann@amayo.fslife.co.uk
Web:www.stewartsbandb.co.uk

Attractive Edwardian terrace villa just 10 minutes from Edinburgh city centre. Near airport and bypass. Bus services pass door. Friendly welcome in a relaxed family home with comfortable rooms.

3 rooms, all en-suite, Open Jan-Dec, B&B per person, single from £25.00, double from £22.00.

Important: Prices stated are estimates and may be subject to amendments

Villa Nina House

39 LEAMINGTON TERRACE, EDINBURGH EH10 4JS
Tel/Fax: 0131 229 2644
E.mail: villanina@tiscali.co.uk Web: www.villanina.co.uk

Comfortable accommodation in central Edinburgh, within walking distance of Princes Street. Fully cooked breakfast. Part en-suite. Member of STB, GHA.
Bed and Breakfast from £20.00 per person.

★★

**GUEST
HOUSE**

Villa Nina Guest House
39 Leamington Terrace, Edinburgh, EH10 4JS
Tel/Fax:0131 229 2644
Email:villanina@tiscali.co.uk
Web:www.villanina.co.uk

Terraced house. Convenient for the city centre. Near Kings Theatre, the Castle, conference centre and shops. Showers in bedrooms.

3 rooms, Open Feb-Nov, B&B per person, single from £25.00, double from £20.00.

Faussetthill House

20 Main Street, Gullane EH31 2DR
Tel: 01620 842396 Fax: 01620 842396
e.mail: faussetthill@talk21.com

A delightful Edwardian house in well tended gardens. Immaculately maintained, the house is both comfortable and inviting. The well proportioned bedrooms are tastefully decorated and a first floor lounge with TV and well stocked bookshelves. Full Scottish breakfast is served in the attractive dining room.

★★★★

B&B

Faussetthill House
20 Main Street, Gullane, East Lothian, EH31 2DR
Tel/Fax:01620 842396
Email:faussetthill@talk21.com

Detached Edwardian house lovingly restored and redecorated throughout. Retaining many of its period features, well tended garden and private parking. Edinburgh 30 minutes by car. Sandy beaches and several golf courses nearby. Non-smoking.

3 rooms, en-suite, Open Apr-Oct, B&B per person, single £48.00-50.00, double £34.00-36.00.

VAT is shown at 17.5%: changes in this rate may affect prices.

Key to symbols is on back flap.

Gullane, East Lothian   Map Ref: 2D4

JADINI GARDEN
Goose Green, Gullane, East Lothian EH31 2BA
Tel: 01620 843343   Fax: 01620 843453
e.mail: marychase@jadini.com   Web: www.jadini.com

Located in the quiet coastal village of Gullane 30 minutes drive from Edinburgh. Jadini Garden is 2 minutes walk from the 3 famous golf courses and beautiful sandy beaches. Quiet secluded walled garden for the use of guests. Private parking. French, German and Spanish spoken.

★★★

B&B

Jadini Garden
Goose Green, Gullane, East Lothian, EH31 2BA
Tel:01620 843343 Fax:01620 843453
Email:marychase@jadini.com
Web:www.jadini.com

Family home located in a secluded walled garden, on the road to the beach. Only a few minutes walk from Gullane's three famous public golf courses and a half hour drive from Edinburgh city centre. Comfortable rooms, garden facilities for the use of guests and private parking. French, Spanish and German spoken.

3 rooms, some en-suite, Open Mar-Dec, B&B per person, single from £28.00, double from £22.00.

Haddington, East Lothian   Map Ref: 2D4

★★★★

B&B

Carfrae Farmhouse
near Garvald, Haddington, East Lothian, EH41 4LP
Tel:01620 830242   Fax:01620 830320
Email:enquiry@carfraefarmhouse.com
Web:www.carfraefarmhouse.com

19c listed farmhouse on a working farm with open aspect overlooking the walled garden. Furnished to a high standard. Edinburgh, the Borders and many golf courses within easy reach. Extremely peaceful location. All rooms have private or en suite facilities.

3 rooms, 2 en-suite, Open Apr-Oct, B&B per person, single £25.00-50.00, double £27.00-35.00.

★★★★

B&B

Eaglescairnie Mains
by Gifford, Haddington, East Lothian, EH41 4HN
Tel/Fax:01620 810491
Email:williams.eagles@btinternet.com
Web:www.eaglescairnie.com

Beautiful house in quiet rural situation, on working mixed farm. Winner of National Conservation Awards. Farm walks with wonderful views. 4 miles (6kms) from Haddington, 30 mins drive from Edinburgh.

3 rooms, all en-suite, Open Jan-Dec excl Xmas, B&B per person, single from £35.00, double from £30.00.

★★

B&B

Fieldfare B&B
Upper Bolton Farm, Haddington, East Lothian, EH41 4HW
Tel:01620 810346

Large Victorian cottage of character, set in rural location with open views over the picturesque East Lothian countryside. Only a half-hour drive from Edinburgh and 20 mins drive to the sandy coastline. Private wing available. Plenty private parking.

5 rooms, Open Jan-Dec excl New Year, B&B per person, single from £22.00, double from £20.00.

Linlithgow, West Lothian

Map Ref: 2B4

★★

GUEST HOUSE

Aran House
Woodcockdale Farm, Lanark Road, Linlithgow
West Lothian, EH49 6QE
Tel/Fax:01506 842088
Email:sheona@aranhouse.co.uk
Web:www.aranhouse.co.uk

Look no further for a modern farmhouse on a working farm in rural area yet with easy access to Edinburgh, Glasgow and the Lothians. Edinburgh and Glasgow airports within easy reach. Full fire certificate held. Ground floor rooms. Don't delay - phone today.

3 rooms, some en-suite, Open Jan-Dec, B&B per person, single from £20.00, double from £20.00.

AWAITING INSPECTION

Mrs Janet Gray
26 Cameron Knowe, Philipstoun, Linlithgow, EH49 6RL
Tel/Fax: 01506 834284

2 rooms. Open Jan-Dec. B&B per person, single from £25.00, double from £30.00. Room only per night, single from £25.00, double from £50.00.

★★★★

B&B

Strawberry Bank House
13 Avon Place, Strawberry Bank, Linlithgow
West Lothian, EH49 6BL
Tel/Fax:01506 848372
Email:gillian@strawberrybank-scotland.co.uk
Web:www.strawberrybank-scotland.co.uk

A fully modernised and comfortable B&B with all rooms ensuite. Decorated and furnished to a high standard. A non-smoking establishment. Historic Linlithgow Palace is in the view of the house and the canal behind. Edinburgh is in easy driving distance.

3 rooms, all en-suite, Open Jan-Dec, B&B per person, single from £25.00, double from £25.00.

Thornton
Edinburgh Road, Linlithgow, West Lothian EH49 6AA
Tel: 01506 844693
e.mail: inglisthornton@hotmail.com   Web: www.thornton-scotland.co.uk

Relaxed, friendly family home with ground floor accommodation. Located only 5 minutes walk along canal towpath from town centre and Linlithgow Palace (birthplace of Mary Queen of Scots). Excellent choice of pubs and restaurants. Visit historic houses and the unique Falkirk boatlifting wheel. Frequent trains to Edinburgh, Glasgow, Stirling.

★★★★

B&B

Thornton
Edinburgh Road, Linlithgow, West Lothian, EH49 6AA
Tel:01506 844693
Email:inglisthornton@hotmail.com
Web:www.thornton-scotland.co.uk

Comfortable, non-smoking family run Victorian house with original features retained. Large garden, private parking. 1km from railway station and town centre and 20 mins by train to Edinburgh. Rosyth Ferry Terminal easily accessible. Award winning breakfasts. Early booking advisable.

2 rooms, all en-suite, Open Mar-mid Dec, B&B per person, single from £30.00, double from £28.00.

VAT is shown at 17.5%: changes in this rate may affect prices.

Key to symbols is on back flap.

Mid Calder, West Lothian   Map Ref: 2B5

REDCRAIG BED AND BREAKFAST

Redcraig, Mid Calder, Livingston EH53 0JT
Tel/Fax: 01506 884249 e.mail: jcampbelljack@aol.com
Web: www.redcraigbedandbreakfast.co.uk

Redcraig is in a countryside location 20 minutes drive to the west of Edinburgh. Ideally located as only minutes from main road networks for Edinburgh, Glasgow, Stirling and the north. Edinburgh airport 10 minutes drive. Kirknewton railway station 1 mile away. All rooms are of a high standard. Ample parking.

★★★

B&B

Redcraig Bed and Breakfast
Mid Calder, Livingston, EH53 0JT
Tel/Fax:01506 884249
Email:jcampbelljack@aol.com
Web:www.redcraigbedandbreakfast.co.uk

A warm friendly welcome is assured at our family home. Rooms are of a high standard and tastefully decorated throughout. Non-smoking establishment.

3 rooms, all en-suite, Open Jan-Dec, B&B per person, single from £32.00, double from £25.00.

Musselburgh, East Lothian   Map Ref: 2C5

Mrs Elizabeth Aitken ★★ B&B

18 WOODSIDE GARDENS, MUSSELBURGH, EAST LOTHIAN EH21 7LJ
Telephone: 0131 665 3170/3344

Well-appointed bungalow within 6 miles of Edinburgh in quiet suburb with private parking. Excellent bus/train service to city. Two minutes from oldest golf course in world and race course. Easy access to beaches and beautiful countryside.

All rooms hot and cold water, colour TV and tea/coffee. Private parking.

★★

B&B

Mrs Elizabeth Aitken
18 Woodside Gardens, Musselburgh, East Lothian, EH21 7LJ
Tel:0131 665 3170/3344

Detached bungalow in quiet residential area, close to Musselburgh Racecourse and golf course. Private parking. 7 - 8 miles from Princes Street, Edinburgh. Close to sandy beaches and river walks.

4 rooms, Open Jan-Dec, B&B per person, single from £19.00, double from £19.00.

North Berwick, East Lothian   Map Ref: 2D4

★★★★

B&B

The Glebe House
4 Law Road, North Berwick, East Lothian, EH39 4PL
Tel:01620 892608 Fax:01620 893588 Mob:07973 965814
Email:gwenscott@glebehouse-nb.co.uk
Web:www.glebehouse-nb.co.uk

Former Georgian manse (1780) furnished in period style and set in own grounds above North Berwick, with views of the sea and Berwick Law. Four poster bed available. 2 minutes walk to sandy beach and town centre. Numerous golf courses. ½ hour by car or train to Edinburgh city centre. All rooms en-suite or private facilities.

3 rooms, two en-suite, one priv.facilities, Open Jan-Dec excl Xmas/New Year, B&B per person, double £35.00-45.00.

Important: Prices stated are estimates and may be subject to amendments

Penicuik, Midlothian

Map Ref: 2C5

★★★
B&B

Braidwood Farm
Penicuik, Midlothian, EH26 9LP
Tel:01968 679959   Fax:01968 679805
Email:info@braidwoodfarm.co.uk
Web:www.braidwoodfarm.co.uk

Braidwood is an attractive modern farmhouse set in 240 acres on the edge of the Pentland hills only 10 miles from Edinburgh. Ideal base for visitors to both Edinburgh and the Borders. No children please.

4 rooms, all en-suite, Open Apr-Oct, B&B per person, single from £30.00, double from £30.00.

South Queensferry, West Lothian

Map Ref: 2B4

★★★
B&B

Mr D & Mrs H Maclean
98 Provost Milne Grove, South Queensferry
West Lothian, EH30 9PL
Tel/Fax:0131 331 1893
Email:hazelmaclean@aol.com

In residential estate, semi-detached modern house close to local shops and amenities. Two minutes drive to Forth Road Bridge and access to Scotland's motorway system. Suitable base for touring Kingdom of Fife, historic Dunfermline and Edinburgh. Interesting sea-front with many restaurants and a view of the famous bridges. Street parking.

2 rooms, Open Jan-Dec, B&B per person, single from £22.50, double from £35.00.

PRIORY LODGE
8 The Loan, South Queensferry EH30 9NS
Tel/Fax: 0131 331 4345
e.mail: calmyn@aol.com
Web: www.queensferry.com

A warm welcome is extended for guests old and new to this delightful purpose built guest house. Conveniently situated just off the cobbled high street in the picturesque village of South Queensferry which sits between the two famous bridges on the south side of the River Forth.

The attractive bedrooms are maintained to a high standard and are comfortably furnished in antique pine. There is also a cosy guest room where free internet access is available. Visitors are welcome to use the modern kitchen facilities. A hearty Scottish breakfast is served at individual tables. The guest house is totally non-smoking.

★★★★
**GUEST
HOUSE**

Priory Lodge
8 The Loan, South Queensferry, West Lothian EH30 9NS
Tel:0131 331 4345   Fax:0131 331 4345
Email:calmyn@aol.com
Web:www.queensferry.com

Traditional Scottish hospitality in this friendly family run guest house located in the picturesque village of South Queensferry. Edinburgh city centre 7 miles: Airport / Royal Highland Exhibition grounds 3 miles. Priory Lodge is within walking distance of the village shops, variety of eating establishments, Forth Bridges and Dalmeny train station. Internet access available. Non-smoking establishment.

5 rooms, all en-suite, Open Jan-Dec excl Xmas, B&B per person, single from £50.00, double from £30.00.

VAT is shown at 17.5%: changes in this rate may affect prices.

Key to symbols is on back flap.

Tranent, East Lothian Map Ref: 2D5

★★★★

B&B

Schiehallion

1 Edinburgh Road, Tranent, East Lothian, EH33 1BA
Tel:01875 611224
Email:catherine@schiehallion.fsbusiness.co.uk
Recently refurbished to an excellent standard, Schiehallion Bed &
Breakfast is new to Tranent (previously in Haddington). A detached
house of character with spacious en-suite rooms and ample secure
private parking to the rear. Ideally situated just off the A1 and close to
both Edinburgh, North Berwick and Haddington. Railway stations
(Wallyford/Prestonpans/Longniddry) less than 5 minutes by car. TV's and
DVD players in both rooms as well as the use of the owners lounge.

2 rooms, all en-suite, Open Jan-Dec, B&B per person, single from £35.00, double
from £25.00.

Welcome to Scotland

Greater Glasgow and Clyde Valley

Ever since James Watts invented the steam engine, Glasgow has led a revolution. There was industry, then architecture, and now style. Join the cause…

Explore Glasgow by night – in your party shoes

Glasgow is a tour de force of character. The friendliness of locals is infectious, whether in a bar or simply asking for directions. They love their city, and they want you to love it too.

At first glance, Glasgow is an exciting fusion of style. From the rooftops you can see the Gothic, Art Nouveau, post-modern, and Victorian buildings vying for attention. When Britannia ruled the waves, this city exploded with new ideas, technology, and wealth. That attitude has shaped the streets, including George Square, home to the neoclassical façade and rich marble of Glasgow City Chambers.

Walk through Merchant City to see old Victorian warehouses restored as homes with edge. The West End is student bohemia set against terraces, sandstone mansions and galleries. Straddling the streets, Glasgow Cathedral is one of the few Gothic churches to have remained intact over the centuries. But for the definitive 'Glasgow Style', you have to visit the Glasgow School of Art, where Charles Rennie Mackintosh threw the book at art establishment. Critics said he led the 'Spook school', but Mackintosh blended Celtic with Japanese influences to create Art Nouveau and iconic high-backed chairs.

It's a style of passion, or obsession, which can be seen in more than 20 galleries. Essential places include the Burrell Collection, where a man's life is expressed through 8000 pieces of art from every corner of the world.

Greater Glasgow and Clyde Valley

Princes Square Shopping Centre, Glasgow

Greater Glasgow and Clyde Valley

The Clyde weaves through the gentle farmlands of South Lanarkshire.

Or the sumptuous European masters of Kelvingrove Art Gallery and Museum.

Glasgow has elevated another pastime to the status of 'art'. Shopping. Experience the A-list of designer garb in malls resembling palaces or galleries. Princes Square is style central; Argyll Arcade is Paris indoors; St Enoch Complex is a glass juggernaut; and The Italian Centre of Merchant City boasts Ralph Lauren, Armani, Versace and Boss.

But the streets really sizzle with local charm and quirkiness. This is where you can find Doctor Who's TARDIS, a time machine in the shape of a Police Box, turned into a coffee stall. Follow the tongue-in-cheek from 'Where The Monkey Sleeps' café to 'King Tut's Wah Wah Hut' music club. King Tut's and Barrowland Ballroom are where you're also likely to see the next big thing – Radiohead and Oasis had early gigs there. Clubbers can get their fix of edgy sounds at The Arches and Sub Club.

Discerners of the classics can breathe easy. The city is home to Scottish Opera, Scottish Ballet and the Royal Scottish National Orchestra.

Leave the city behind for Renfrewshire's gentle hills, or the Inverclyde coastline. Take a trip aboard the Waverley, the world's last sea-going steamer. You can also visit New Lanark – an immaculately preserved mill town and a World Heritage Site in its own right.

Paisley, home of the Paisley Pattern, is just a short journey from the city and the whole story of the distinctive design is told in the town's Museum and Art Gallery. Paisley Abbey, dating back to 1163, with its inspiring stained glass and 10th Century cross, is also well worth a visit.

Greater Glasgow and Clyde Valley

11-29 JANUARY
CELTIC CONNECTIONS
Celebration of Celtic music.
Tel: 0141 353 8000
www.celticconnections.com

16-26 FEBRUARY
GLASGOW WORLD FILM FESTIVAL
Showcase of movies from around the world.
Tel: 0141 332 6535
www.glasgowfilmfestival.org.uk

9-25 MARCH
GLASGOW COMEDY FESTIVAL
Festival featuring stand-up, cabaret and theatre.
Tel: 0141 552 2070
www.glasgowcomedyfestival.com

19 APRIL-1 MAY
GLASGOW INTERNATIONAL
Colourful festival of contemporary art.
www.glasgowinternational.org

3 JUNE
SHOTTS HIGHLAND GAMES
Traditional Highland games.
Tel: 01501 823560
www.shottshighlandgames.org.uk

8 JUNE
LANIMER CELEBRATIONS, Lanark
100 year old traditional procession through the town of Lanark culminating with the crowning of the Lanimer Queen.
Tel: 01555 663251
www.lanarklanimers.co.uk

9-26 JUNE
WEST END FESTIVAL
A varied festival of music, dance, theatre, comedy and much more.
Tel: 0141 341 0844
www.westendfestival.co.uk

23 JUNE-2 JULY
ROYAL BANK GLASGOW JAZZ FESTIVAL
Annual international jazz festival with a whole host of big name acts and local talent.
Tel: 0141 552 3552
www.jazzfest.co.uk

15-16 JULY
GLASGOW RIVER FESTIVAL
Rollicking family entertainment on the Clyde River and shore.
Tel: 0871 700 0685
www.glasgowriverfestival.co.uk

12 AUGUST
WORLD PIPE BAND CHAMPIONSHIP
Pipe bands from all over the world compete for the prestigious title.
Tel: 0141 221 5414
www.rspba.co.uk

7-13 AUGUST
PIPING LIVE!
A sizzling international piping event of the highest calibre.
Tel: 0141 353 0220
www.pipingfestival.co.uk

31 DECEMBER
GLASGOW'S HOGMANAY
Join the celebrations and take in the New Year with live music and entertainment.
Tel: 0141 204 4480
www.glasgowshogmanay.org.uk

** denotes provisional date, event details are subject to change please check before travelling*

Greater Glasgow and Clyde Valley

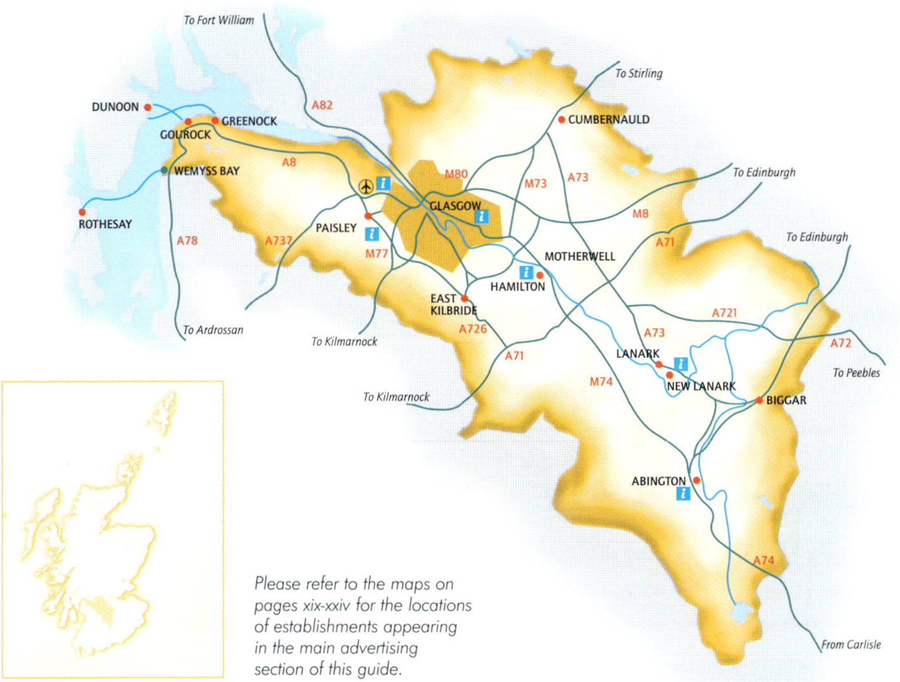

Please refer to the maps on pages xix-xxiv for the locations of establishments appearing in the main advertising section of this guide.

Finding out more...

For practical advice, ideas and information about exploring Scotland and to book your accommodation:

Tel: 0845 22 55 121*
or if calling from outside the UK: +44 (0) 1506 832121

Email: info@visitscotland.com
Web: www.visitscotland.com

* A £3 booking fee applies to telephone bookings of accommodation.

Tourist Information Centres

Greater Glasgow and Clyde Valley

Greater Glasgow and Clyde Valley

Abington
Welcome Break Service Area
Junction 13, M74
Tel: (01864) 502436
Jan-Dec

Biggar
155 High Street,
Tel: (01899) 221066
Easter-Sep

Glasgow
11 George Square
Tel: (0141) 204 4400
Jan-Dec

Glasgow Airport
Tourist Information Desk
Tel: (0141) 848 4440
Jan-Dec

Hamilton
Road Chef Services
M74 Northbound
Tel: (01698) 285590
Jan-Dec

Lanark
Horsemarket, Ladyacre Road
Tel: (01555) 661661
Jan-Dec

Paisley
9a Gilmour Street
Tel: (0141) 889 0711
Jan-Dec

Biggar, Lanarkshire

Map Ref: 2B6

LINDSAYLANDS HOUSE
BIGGAR, LANARKSHIRE ML12 6NR
TELEPHONE: 01899 220033/221221 FAX: 01899 221009
E.MAIL: ELSPETH@LINDSAYLANDS.CO.UK WEB: WWW.LINDSAYLANDS.CO.UK

THIS LOVELY LISTED COUNTRY HOUSE IS SET IN ITS OWN GROUNDS SURROUNDED BY 94 ACRES OF ITS OWN FARMLAND. SITUATED OFF MAIN ROAD 1 MILE WEST OF BIGGAR. 3 LARGE BEDROOMS WITH PRIVATE FACILITIES, GUEST LOUNGE AND DINING ROOM. IDEAL BASE FOR TOURING GLASGOW, EDINBURGH, BORDERS OR JUST RELAXING. PRICES FROM £28 PER PERSON, PER NIGHT.

★★★★

B&B

Lindsaylands House

Biggar, Lanarkshire, ML12 6NR
Tel:01899 220033 Fax:01899 221009
Email:elspeth@lindsaylands.co.uk
Web:www.lindsaylands.co.uk

Attractive country house William Leiper architecture. Set in 6 acres of garden, amidst lovely countryside with views to Border Hills. Hard tennis court and croquet lawn. Ideal base for touring Edinburgh, Glasgow and Scottish Borders.

3 rooms, some en-suite, Open Mar-Nov, B&B per person, single from £35.00, double from £28.00, BB & Eve.Meal from £43.50.

---

by Biggar, Lanarkshire

Map Ref: 2B6

★★★

B&B

Walston Mansion Farmhouse

Walston, Carnwath, Lanarkshire, ML11 8NF
Tel:01899 810334 Fax:01899 810338
Email:kirby-walstonmansion@talk21.com
Web:www.walstonmansion.co.uk

19c stone built farmhouse on a working farm situated on the edge of a small village in the shadow of the Pentland Hills. 5 miles from Biggar, 24 miles from Edinburgh, 30 miles from Glasgow and 16 miles from Peebles, an ideal holiday centre. Home cooking using home produced meat and organic vegetables. Delicious fresh bread made daily on premises. Evening meal provided by prior arrangement.

3 rooms, some en-suite, Open Jan-Dec, B&B per person, single £20.00-23.00, double £18.00-20.00, BB & Eve.Meal from £28.00-30.00.

Glasgow

Map Ref: 1H5

ADELAIDES
209 Bath Street, Glasgow G2 4HZ
Tel: 0141 248 4970 Fax: 0141 226 4247
e.mail: info@adelaides.freeserve.co.uk Web: www.adelaides.co.uk

Part of stunning Baptist Church restoration. City centre guest house, centrally heated modern rooms, most ensuite, non-smoking, families welcome. Colour TV, complimentary tea and coffee in all rooms. Most of Glasgow's main attractions e.g. shops, theatres, museums of this revitalised city are within 10 minutes walk.

★★

GUEST HOUSE

Adelaides

209 Bath Street, Glasgow, G2 4HZ
Tel:0141 248 4970 Fax:0141 226 4247
Email:info@adelaides.freeserve.co.uk
Web:www.adelaides.co.uk

Adelaide's is an unusual conversion of an 1877 church. The Guest House formed from some of the ancilliary accommodation comprises 8 individual rooms. Breakfast available. Centrally located near the Kings Theatre, 10 min walk from the main shopping and entertainment areas, on bus routes to most of Glasgow's tourist attractions and has a wide variety of restaurants in the vicinity. Parking nearby.

8 rooms, some en-suite, Open Jan-Dec excl Xmas/New Year, B&B per person, single from £45.00, double from £30.00.

VAT is shown at 17.5%: changes in this rate may affect prices.

Key to symbols is on back flap.

Glasgow

Map Ref: 1H5

★★

**GUEST
HOUSE**

Alison Guest House
26 Circus Drive, Glasgow, G31 2JH
Tel/Fax:0141 556 1431
Email:circusdrive@aol.com

7 rooms, 3 ensuite, Open Jan-Dec, B&B per person, single from £22.00, double from £17.50. 3 Family en-suite rooms available.

Victorian semi-villa in quiet residential area of East End yet only 15 minutes walk from city centre, 10 minutes walk from Cathedral, Royal Infirmary, Strathclyde University Campus. One ground floor room. Limited access to kitchen available for takeaway's for evening dining. Ideally situated for Celtic Park.

THE BELGRAVE GUEST HOUSE
2 BELGRAVE TERRACE, HILLHEAD, GLASGOW G12 8JD
*Tel: 0141 337 1850 Fax: 0141 337 1741
e.mail: belgraveglasgow@aol.com
Web: www.belgraveguesthouse.co.uk*
Situated in the heart of the West End, about 5 minutes' walk from galleries,
it is fitted and furnished to a very high standard. Ensuite available. Television, tea/coffee facilities in
every room. Private car park also available. Two minutes from underground station and minutes
from the city centre. DVDs in all rooms. Free internet.

★★

**GUEST
HOUSE**

Belgrave Guest House
2 Belgrave Terrace, Hillhead, Glasgow, G12 8JD
Tel:0141 337 1850   Fax:0141 337 1741
Email:belgraveglasgow@aol.com
Web:www.belgraveguesthouse.co.uk

11 rooms, Open Jan-Dec, B&B per person, single from £25.00, double from £20.00.

Refurbished guest house, in the West End. Convenient for Botanic Gardens, other local attractions and amenities. 5 minute walk from two tube stations. Many restaurants, cafes and bus a few minutes walk away. Small private car-park to rear. Ensuite rooms available.

★★★

HOTEL

Bewleys Hotel
110 Bath Street, Glasgow, G2 2EN
Tel:0845 234 5959/0141 353 0800   Fax:0141 353 0900
Email:gla@bewleyshotels.com
Web:www.bewleyshotels.com

103 rooms, all en-suite, Open Jan-Dec excl Xmas, from £69.00 Room Only.

Contemporary, relaxed and informal that is the ethos of the Bewley's Hotel Glasgow. The rooms, which have been designed with both the tourist and business traveller in mind, are spacious and the top two floors have large windows with spectacular views over the City. Loop bar and restaurant provides a relaxed, informal dining experience. Food is served throughout the day.

★

HOTEL

Buchanan Hotel
185 Buchanan Street, Glasgow, G1 2JY
Tel:0141 332 7284 Fax:0141 333 0635
Email:salesbuchanan@strathmorehotels.com
Web:www.strathmorehotels.com

60 rooms, all en-suite, Open Jan-Dec, B&B per person, single from £35.00, double from £39.00, BB & Eve.Meal from £45.00.

City centre hotel near to Queen Street Station and Buchanan Street Bus Station. Ideally situated for shopping, Royal Concert Hall and major theatres.

Glasgow

Map Ref: 1H5

★★

B&B

East Rogerton Lodge
Markethill Road, East Kilbride, G74 4NZ
Tel/Fax:01355 263176
Email:christine.mclearvy@ntlworld.com

Comfortable, ground floor accommodation in this friendly, family home set in an attractive rural location only 1 mile from the original village of East Kilbride, 6 Miles from Glasgow and with easy access to all major routes. Entry door 1st on the right hand side.

3 rooms, Open Jan-Dec excl Xmas/New Year, B&B per person from £20.00 double/twin.

★★

GUEST HOUSE

The Georgian House
29 Buckingham Terrace, Great Western Road
Hillhead, Glasgow, G12 8ED
Tel:0141 339 0008   Email:thegeorgianhouse@yahoo.com
Web:www.georgianhousehotel.com

Restored Georgian townhouse, retaining many original features, set in the heart of the vibrant West End on the road to Loch Lomond. Close to Botanic Gardens, University of Glasgow, BBC, SECC and many other local attractions as well as a range of cafes and restaurants to suit all tastes. Comfortable rooms of varying sizes all with private or en suite facilities. Private parking.

15 rooms, some en-suite, Open Jan-Dec, B&B per person, single from £25.00, double from £25.00 per person.

★★★

GUEST HOUSE

The Heritage Hotel
4-5 Alfred Terrace, Glasgow, G12 8RF
Tel/Fax:0141 339 6955
Email:bookings@heritagehotel.fsbusiness.co.uk

Privately owned hotel, close to Botanic Garden, University, SECC and the major hospitals. Short walk to Underground.

27 rooms, all en-suite, Open Jan-Dec excl Xmas, B&B per person, single from £35.00, double from £27.50, family from £25.00.

★★

GUEST HOUSE

Lomond Hotel
6 Buckingham Terrace, Great Western Road, Glasgow G12 8EB
Tel:0141 339 2339 Fax:0141 339 0477
Email:info@lomondhotel.co.uk
Web:www.lomondhotel.co.uk

Victorian terraced house in the West End. Close to the BBC, Botanical Gardens and Glasgow University. On main bus routes to city centre and five minutes walk from underground, restaurants and shops.

17 rooms, some en-suite, Open Jan-Dec, B&B per person, single from £24.00, double from £21.00.

Glasgow
Map Ref: 1H5

University of Strathclyde
Residence and Catering Services
50 Richmond St., Glasgow G1 1XP
Tel: 0141-553 4148 Fax: 0141-553 4149
e.mail: rescat@mis.strath.ac.uk Web: www.rescat.strath.ac.uk

Strathclyde University offers a range of attractive accommodation in Glasgow city centre at affordable prices. En-suite and standard single rooms are located in the modern campus village adjacent to the Lord Todd bar/restaurant.

★

CAMPUS ACCOMMODATION

University of Strathclyde
Residence and Catering Services,
50 Richmond Street, Glasgow, G1 1XP
Tel:0141 553 4148 Fax:0141 553 4149
Email:rescat@mis.strath.ac.uk
Web:www.rescat.strath.ac.uk

Modern, purpose-built halls of residence on city centre campus. Attractive bar/restaurant on site. Ideal centre for exploring the city.

600 rooms, including 300 en-suite, Open Jun-Sep, B&B per person, single from £21.25, double from £22.00.

Glasgow, Milngavie
Map Ref: 1H5

Tambowie Farm
Tambowie Farm, Milngavie, Glasgow, G62 7HD
Tel: 0141 956 1583 Fax: 0141 955 1424
e.mail:irenegraham@amserve.com
Web: www.tambowiefarm.co.uk

Tambowie is a very attractive, spacious and beautifully appointed farmhouse situated in splendid countryside 1 mile from Milngavie and Bearsden. Enjoying outstanding views of the Campsie Hills and Clyde Valley. Golf courses and walking trails from our doorstep and a whisky distillery nearby. Easy access by car or train to Glasgow city centre 20 mins, Glasgow International Airport 20 mins by car. Many excellent local pubs and restaurants catering for every taste.

★★★

B&B

Tambowie Farm
Milngavie, Glasgow, G62 7HD
Tel:0141 956 1583 Fax:0141 955 1424
Email:irenegraham@amserve.com
Web:www.tambowiefarm.co.uk

Very attractive, spacious and beautifully appointed farmhouse in a superb rural setting enjoying panoramic views of the Campsie Hills and beyond. Situated one mile from Milngavie and Bearsden, 20 minutes drive from the city centre and Glasgow International Airport and a one hour drive from Edinburgh. It is an excellent base for touring, walking and relaxing. Easy access to the city for business purposes.

4 rooms, some en-suite, Open Jan-Dec excl Xmas, B&B per person, single from £30.00, double from £25.00.

Greenock, Renfrewshire
Map Ref: 1G5

★★

B&B

Denholm Bed & Breakfast
22 Denholm Street, Greenock, PA16 8RJ
Tel:01475 781319
Email:dannychundoo@hotmail.com

Semi detached house in quiet suburb yet close to restaurants, shops and waterfront area. Down the hill from Greenock golf club. 5 minute walk from station with its fast train service to Glasgow City Centre. Ideal base for Dunoon and Rothesay ferries. Loch Lomond under an hour's drive. Unmetered street parking available. French & Hindi spoken.

2 rooms, all en-suite, Open Jan-Dec, B&B per person, single from £25.00, double from £25.00.

Important: Prices stated are estimates and may be subject to amendments

Lanark
Map Ref: 2A6

Jerviswood Mains Farm
LANARK ML11 7RL   Telephone: 01555 663987
e.mail: jerviswoodmains@aol.com Web: www.jerviswoodmains.com
★★★★ B&B
Good hospitality is offered in this early 19th-century traditional farmhouse, 1 mile from Lanark on the A706, heading northwards. We are near a trout and deer farm and provide good food in a relaxed atmosphere. We combine old world charm with modern amenities. The unique 1758 industrial village of New Lanark, now a World Heritage Site, and many places of historical interest are nearby, equidistant between Glasgow and Edinburgh. This is an excellent touring base.

★★★★
B&B

Jerviswood Mains Farm
Cleghorn, Lanark, ML11 7RL
Tel:01555 663987
Email:jerviswoodmains@aol.com
Web:www.jerviswoodmains.com

A warm welcome awaits you at this early 19c stone built farmhouse of considerable character, 1 mile (2 kms) north of the historic market town of Lanark. Less than one hour's drive from both Glasgow and Edinburgh, is an excellent base for touring Scotland. Ample private parking.

3 rooms, Open Jan-Dec excl Xmas/New Year, B&B per person, single from £30.00, double from £25.00.

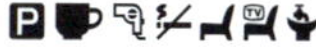

C V

Lesmahagow, Lanarkshire
Map Ref: 2A6

★★
B&B

Dykecroft
Dykecroft Farm, Kirkmuirhill, Lesmahagow, ML11 0JQ
Tel/Fax:01555 892226

Modern farmhouse bungalow in rural situation 20 miles (32kms) south of Glasgow and airport. An hour's drive from Edinburgh, Stirling, Ayr and Loch Lomond, only 2 miles from the M74. Pub/Restaurant 1 mile. Ample private parking. Fishing and sports nearby.

3 rooms, Open Jan-Dec, B&B per person, single from £24.00, double from £21.00.

C 🐕 W V

Lochwinnoch, Renfrewshire
Map Ref: 1G5

EAST LOCHHEAD COUNTRY HOUSE & COTTAGES
LARGS ROAD, LOCHWINNOCH PA12 4DX TEL/FAX: 01505 842610
E.MAIL: admin@eastlochhead.co.uk WEB: www.eastlochhead.co.uk
Janet Anderson guarantees you a warm welcome at award winning East Lochhead where you will find every home comfort. 2 acres of beautiful gardens overlooking Barr Loch and Renfrewshire hills. Cycle track passes the house. Good base for sightseeing. Glasgow airport 15 mins, Prestwick 30 mins. Taste of Scotland home cooking awaits you.

★★★★
B&B

East Lochhead Country House & Cottages
Largs Road, Lochwinnoch, PA12 4DX
Tel/Fax:01505 842610
Email:admin@eastlochhead.co.uk
Web:www.eastlochhead.co.uk

Spacious Victorian country house overlooking Barr Loch. Easy access to Glasgow and Prestwick Airports and motorway network. Convenient for Ayrshire Coast, Burns Country, Loch Lomond and Glasgow. Evening meals available and breakfasts a speciality. All rooms en-suite.

3 rooms, all en-suite, Open Jan-Dec, B&B per person, single from £45.00, double from £37.50, BB & Eve.Meal from £60.00.

C 🐕 £ W V

VAT is shown at 17.5%: changes in this rate may affect prices.

| *Key to symbols is on back flap.* |

Motherwell, Lanarkshire | Map Ref: 2A5

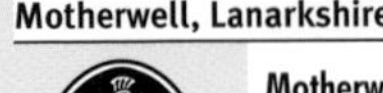

**CAMPUS
ACCOMMODATION**

Motherwell College - Stewart Halls of Residence
Dalzell Drive, Motherwell, Lanarkshire, ML1 2DD
Tel:01698 261890   Fax:01698 232527/232600
Email:m.col@motherwell.co.uk
Web:www.motherwell.ac.uk

On college campus and all on one level. Close to Strathclyde Park and
M8/M74 motorway link for Glasgow and Edinburgh.

52 rooms, Open Jan-Dec excl Xmas/New Year, B&B per person, single from £20.00.

Welcome to Scotland

West Highlands and Islands, Loch Lomond, Stirling and Trossachs

Between the Lowlands and the Highlands is an area of startling personality - or multiple personalities. Romantic, epic, and quirky, prepare to be charmed...

The Falkirk Wheel is unique for being the world's only rotating boat lift.

The endless list of things to do is a reflection of the landscape and people. Spanning the full width of the country, from Falkirk to the far-flung islands in the west, the area is a range of colourful personalities.

As a gateway to the mountainous north, Stirling is the cradle of independence and Scotland's newest city. The famous castle, once the hallowed throne of Scottish Kings, sits loftily above the Old Town. Visible from a nearby hill, the William Wallace monument pays homage to Scotland's first freedom-fighter. Or feel your skin crawl at Bannockburn, an outlying battleground where brutal fighting secured 300 years of freedom.

Behind the medieval stone is a kinetic city driven by students and young professionals. Why don't you join the throng at Cambio, Pivo or Best Bar None? And when the night closes in, go clubbing at The Beat, Fubar, or The Yard. Connoisseurs of fine dining will savour the flavours and impeccable service of Hermanns.

Continuing west from Stirling, hopeless romantics will be seduced by the sparkling beauty of Loch Lomond. Scotland's largest loch offers plenty of cruising options, and is part of a National Park extending into the Trossachs. The postcard towns of Callander and Aberfoyle provide easy access to an area rendered in hills, woods and wild glens. Ever had romantic thoughts about cattle rustlers? The heroic exploits of Rob Roy MacGregor, clan chief and wrongly accused outlaw, were immortalised by romantic poet, Sir Walter Scott. Delve into his legend at the Rob Roy Visitor Centre, Callander.

The 'bristly country' of Scott's poetry inspires walking, whether meandering through hills on a lazy

West Highland and Islands
Loch Lomond, Stirling and Trossachs

Loch Lomond

West Highland and Islands
Loch Lomond, Stirling and Trossachs

A tiny island with a big role. Iona introduced Scotland to Christianity.

picnic, or hiking the entire West Highland Way – that's a cool 95 miles. Spice up your holiday with some high-octane fun at Croft na Caber, at Kenmore on Loch Tay. Take your pick of jet skiing, canoeing, and quad biking.

Continue west and happen across a land of giants. Enclosed by dense, towering forests, the Cowal Peninsula has a primal majesty. Closer to monoliths than trees, the redwoods of Benmore Botanic Gardens elicit awe. Let your imagination go wild - in true pagan style - among the prehistoric stone circles at

Kilmartin, near Lochgilphead. The Scots arrived here from Ireland in the 6th century, putting an end to iffy rituals and uniting scattered tribes into the first kingdom. Escape to sandy beaches and island fantasies farther down Kintyre peninsula. It's just a short ferry ride to one of the outlying islands: Gigha, Jura, Islay or Colonsay. Islay abounds in whisky, crafting a variety of distinct malts from its seven distilleries. Jura is defiantly minimal, opting for space to soothe the senses.

Heading further north, Mull attracts birdwatchers eager for a glimpse of the re-introduced white-tailed sea eagle. And children of all ages will recognise Tobermory's brightly-painted houses from the popular children's programme, 'Balamory'.

Neighbouring Iona is a tiny island with a far-reaching influence on Christianity. A burial place of Scottish Kings, Iona expresses the beauty of faith through Celtic crosses and sturdy chapels. And Oban is a popular coastal resort providing easy access to Mull and Iona.

Events

West Highlands and Islands, Loch Lomond, Stirling and Trossachs

15-22 APRIL
WALKISLAY, Islay and Jura
The routes allow you to visit local historical sites and appreciate the abundance of wildlife, you might even spot a golden eagle or the odd otter as well as the fantastic views across to Mull and Arran.
Tel: 01496 850382
www.walkislay.co.uk

27 APRIL-1 MAY
ISLE OF BUTE JAZZ FESTIVAL
The big names of jazz flock to this small island for a festival of dazzling music.
Tel: 01700 502151
www.butejazz.com

MAY-4 JUNE
ISLAY FESTIVAL OF MALT AND MUSIC
Whisky and song come together in this joyous collaboration.
www.feisile.org

27-28 MAY
LOCH FYNE FOOD FAIR
A feast of West-Coast seafood and quality local produce.
Tel: 01499 600264
www.loch-fyne.com

6-9 JULY
BARCLAYS SCOTTISH OPEN, Loch Lomond
Major PGA European Tour golf tournament.
Tel: 01436 655555
www.lochlomond.com

28-30 JULY
LOMOND FOLK FESTIVAL
A unique weekend of high quality traditional and folk music including concerts, ceilidh, workshops, open sessions, competitions, craft fair and street entertainment.
Tel: 01389 603278
www.lomondfolkfestival.com

29-30 JULY
WORLD CHAMPIONSHIP HIGHLAND GAMES, Callander
Traditional Highland games and Highland dancing competitions.
Tel: 01877 330919

23-24 AUGUST
ARGYLLSHIRE GATHERING, Oban
Traditional Highland games and Highland dancing.
Tel: 01631 562671
www.obangames.com

24-26 AUGUST
COWAL HIGHLAND GATHERING, Dunoon
One of the largest and most spectacular Highland games in the world featuring Highland dancing and pipe band championships.
Tel: 01369 703206
www.cowalgathering.com

13-15 OCTOBER
TUNNOCK'S TOUR OF MULL CAR RALLY
High-octane thrills on the Isle of Mull.
www.2300club.org

13-21 OCTOBER
THE ROYAL NATIONAL MOD IN DUNOON
The premier festival of Gaelic arts and culture.
Tel: 01463 709705
www.the-mod.co.uk

** denotes provisional date, event details are subject to change please check before travelling*

West Highlands and Islands, Loch Lomond, Stirling and Trossachs

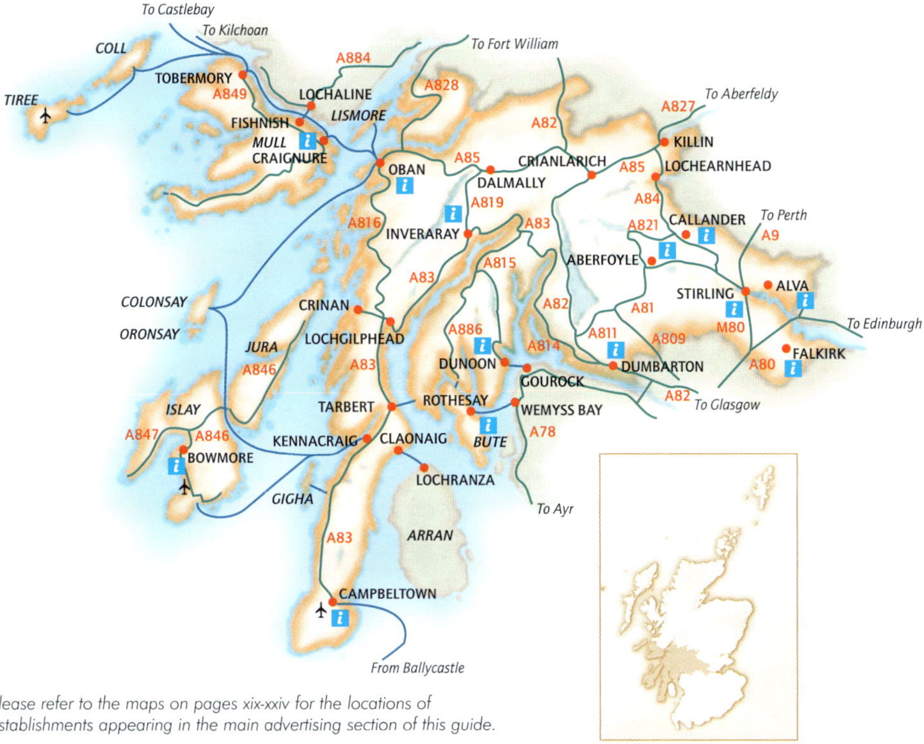

Please refer to the maps on pages xix-xxiv for the locations of establishments appearing in the main advertising section of this guide.

Finding out more...

For practical advice, ideas and information about exploring Scotland and to book your accommodation:

Tel: 0845 22 55 121*
or if calling from outside the UK: +44 (0) 1506 832121

Email: info@visitscotland.com
Web: www.visitscotland.com

* A £3 booking fee applies to telephone bookings of accommodation.

Tourist Information Centres

West Highlands and Islands, Loch Lomond, Stirling and Trossachs

Aberfoyle
Trossachs Discovery Centre
Main Street
Tel: (08707) 200604
Jan – Dec

Alva
Mill Trail Visitor Centre
Tel: (08707) 200605
Jan-Dec

Ardgartan
Arrochar
Tel: (08707) 200606
Apr-Oct

Balloch
The Old Station Building
Tel: (08707) 200607
Apr-Oct

Bo'ness
Seaview Car Park
Tel: (08707) 200608
May-Sep

Bowmore
Isle of Islay
Tel: (08707) 200617
Jan-Dec

Callander
Rob Roy and Trossachs
Visitor Centre, Ancaster Square
Tel: (08707) 200628
Mar-Dec
Jan and Feb weekends only

Campbeltown
Mackinnon House
The Pier, Argyll
Tel: (08707) 200609
Jan-Dec

Craignure
The Pier, Isle of Mull
Tel: (08707) 200610
Jan-Dec

Drymen
Drymen Library, The Square
Tel: (08707) 200611
May-Sep

Dumbarton
Milton, A82 Northbound
Tel: (08707) 200612
Jan-Dec

Dunblane
Stirling Road
Tel: (08707) 200613
May-Sep

Dunoon
7 Alexandra Parade, Argyll
Tel: (08707) 200629
Jan-Dec

Falkirk
2-4 Glebe Street
Tel: (08707) 200614
Jan-Dec

Helensburgh
The Clock Tower
Tel: (08707) 200615
Apr-Oct

Inveraray
Front Street, Argyll
Tel: (08707) 200616
Jan-Dec

Killin
Breadalbane Folklore Centre
Tel: (08707) 200627
Mar-Oct Feb weekends only

Lochgilphead
Lochnell Street, Argyll
Tel: (08707) 200618
Apr-Oct

Loch Lomond
Loch Lomond Gateway Centre
Loch Lomond Shores, Balloch
Tel: (08707) 200631
Jan – Dec

Oban
Argyll Square, Argyll
Tel: (08707) 200630
Jan-Dec

Rothesay
Discovery Centre, Winter
Gardens, Isle of Bute
Tel: (08707) 200619
Jan-Dec

Stirling
41 Dumbarton Road
Tel: (08707) 200620
Jan-Dec

Stirling
Royal Burgh of Stirling
Visitor Centre
Castle Esplanade
Tel: (08707) 200622
Jan-Dec

Stirling
Pirnhall Motorway Service Area
Junction 9, M9
Tel: (08707) 200621
Apr-Oct

Tarbert, Loch Fyne
Harbour Street
Argyll
Tel: (08707) 200624
Apr-Oct

Tarbet-Loch Lomond
Main Street
Tel: (08707) 200623
Apr-Oct

Tobermory
The Pier, Isle of Mull
Tel: (08707) 200625
Apr-Oct

Tyndrum
Main Street
Tel: (08707) 200626
Apr-Oct

Aberfoyle, Stirlingshire

Map Ref: 1H3

CREAG-ARD HOUSE

ABERFOYLE, STIRLING FK8 3TQ Tel/Fax: 01877 382297

e.mail: cara@creag-ardhouse.co.uk Web: www.creag-ardhouse.co.uk

Nestling in three acres of beautiful gardens, this lovely Victorian house enjoys some of the most magnificent scenery in Scotland; overlooking Loch Ard, stunning views of Ben Lomond. Own trout fishing, boat hire available. Perfect for touring the Trossachs, walking, cycling or relaxing in a lovely country house.

★★★★

**GUEST
HOUSE**

Creag-Ard House
Aberfoyle, Stirling, FK8 3TQ
Tel/Fax:01877 382297
Email:cara@creag-ardhouse.co.uk
Web:www.creag-ardhouse.co.uk

Welcoming Guest House with superb views over Loch Ard 3kms from the centre of Aberfoyle Village in the heart of the Trossachs. A haven of peace and tranquility. Delicious breakfast with homebaking.

6 rooms, all en-suite, Open Mar-Oct, B&B per person, single from £45.00, double from £32.00.

Alexandria, Loch Lomond

Map Ref: 1G4

★★★★

B&B

Sheildaig Farm
Upper Stoney Mollen Road, Alexandria, G83 8QY
Tel:01389 752459   Fax:01389 753695
Email:sheildaigfarm@talk21.com
Web:www.sheildaigfarm.co.uk

Totally refurbished farm courtyard buildings in secluded setting. Conveniently situated for touring Loch Lomond and the Trossachs. Easy access to A82 and Glasgow Airport. 5 minutes from Balloch station with its service into Glasgow city centre.

3 rooms, all en-suite, Open Jan-Dec, B&B per person, single from £50.00, double from £30.00.

Appin, Argyll

Map Ref: 1E1

LOCHSIDE COTTAGE - APPIN

Fasnacloich, Appin, Argyll PA38 4BJ Tel/Fax: 01631 730216
e.mail: broadbent@lochsidecottage.fsnet.co.uk
Web: www.lochsidecottage.fsnet.co.uk

Total peace on the shore of Loch Baile mhic Chailen, in an idyllic glen of outstanding beauty. There are many walks from the cottage garden, or alternatively visit Fort William, Glencoe and Oban, from where you can board a steamer to explore the Western Isles — a pleasant way of ensuring a happy, relaxing holiday, away from the hurly-burly of modern life.

★★★★

B&B

Lochside Cottage
Fasnacloich, by Appin, Argyll, PA38 4BJ
Tel/Fax:01631 730216
Email:broadbent@lochsidecottage.fsnet.co.uk
Web:www.lochsidecottage.fsnet.co.uk

The friendly atmosphere of the Broadbents' home welcomes you at the end of the day. Delicious home cooked dinner, a log fire and the certainty of a perfect night's sleep in an attractive and comfortable ensuite bedroom, all contribute to an unforgettable holiday at Lochside Cottage.

3 rooms, 2 en-suite, Open Jan-Dec excl Xmas/New Year, B&B per person, single from £32.00, double from £32.00. Dinner £25.00.

Arrochar, Argyll
Map Ref: 1G3

FERRY COTTAGE
Ardmay, Arrochar, Argyll & Bute G83 7AH
Tel: 01301 702428 Fax: 01301 702729
e.mail: info@ferrycottage.com
Web: www.ferrycottage.com

Quietly situated at the gateway to the Highlands and in Loch Lomond National Park, the freshness of our non-smoking establishment is appreciated by smokers and non-smokers alike. In our centrally heated ensuite bedrooms, facilities include tea, coffee, toiletries and hairdryers – attention to detail alongside a warm welcome ensure a perfect stay.
With panoramic views across Loch Long towards the Cobbler and the Arrochar Alps this is the idyllic location for touring and hill-walking.
Loch Lomond is close by. For peace of mind we have a fire certificate and off-road parking. Payment by credit card is welcome (small fee applicable). Winter Breaks min 3 nights Oct-Apr.
NON SMOKING ESTABLISHMENT.

Ferry Cottage
Ardmay, Arrochar, Argyll & Bute, G83 7AH
Tel:01301 702428   Fax:01301 702729
Email:info@ferrycottage.com
Web:www.ferrycottage.com

B&B

Refurbished 200 year old house with attractive bedrooms and ensuite shower-rooms. Scenic views across Loch Long. Major credit cards accepted. Private parking. Evening meals available & packed lunches. 5 minutes drive from Loch Lomond.

3 rooms, all en-suite, Open Jan-Dec excl Xmas/New Year, B&B per person, double £25.00-34.00.

Balloch, Dunbartonshire
Map Ref: 1G4

Aird House
1 Ben Lomond Walk, Balloch, G83 8RJ
Tel:01389 754464 Fax:01389 732903

B&B

Enjoy excellent Scottish hospitality at this newly built modern villa set on the main A811 Stirling Road in Balloch. Small colourful garden at front. Ideal base for exploring Loch Lomond and Scotland's National Park. Non-smoking.

2 rooms, some en-suite, Open Jan-Dec, B&B per person, single £25.00-30.00, double/twin from £22.00-25.00.

Oakvale B&B
Drymen Road, Balloch, Dunbartonshire, G83 8JY
Tel:01389 751615
Email:oakvalebb@blueyonder.co.uk

B&B

Extended 1940's bungalow near country park. 5 mins walk to Loch Lomond, cruises, restaurants and pubs.

3 rooms, all en-suite, Open Jan-Dec, B&B per person, single from £25.00, double from £20.00.

Important: Prices stated are estimates and may be subject to amendments

Balloch, Dunbartonshire
Map Ref: 1G4

GUEST HOUSE

Woodvale B&B
Drymen Road, Balloch, Dunbartonshire, G83 8HT
Tel:01389 755771
Email:woodvale@blueyonder.co.uk

Comfortable family home close to the centre of Balloch. Ideal base for your stay in Scotland, as many places of interest are only a comfortable drive away. The picturesque village of Balloch offers a variety of restaurants and bars, all within a short walk of your accommodation. After enjoying the local scenery you will be able to relax in your comfortable rooms. You will waken refreshed and ready to enjoy a hearty Scottish breakfast.

3 rooms, some en-suite, Open Jan-Dec, B&B per person, single £35.00-55.00, double £23.00-27.50.

by Balloch, Dunbartonshire
Map Ref: 1G4

B&B

Braeburn Cottage
Auchencarroch Farm, by Balloch, Dunbartonshire G83 9LU
Tel:01389 710998/078036 82715
Email:braeburn@bigfoot.com
Web:www.braeburncottage.co.uk

New bungalow on family run working farm. Four miles above Balloch overlooking hills and glens around Loch Lomond across its large landscaped gardens. Ideally placed for touring Stirling, Loch Lomond or taking the train to Glasgow for shopping, restaurants & galleries. Glasgow Airport 30 minutes.

2 rooms, all en-suite, Open Jan-Dec, B&B per person, single from £20.00, double from £18.00.

Balmaha, Stirlingshire
Map Ref: 1G4

B&B

Dunleen, Mrs K MacFadyen
Milton of Buchanan, Balmaha, by Drymen, Glasgow, G63 OJE
Tel:01360 870274

Comfortable modern ranch style home situated in secluded, lovely garden with a trout burn on its border that is overlooked by the guest lounge. Situated on east side of Loch Lomond close to the West Highland Way, Rowardennan and Ben Lomond. The closest Munro is within 8 miles. 'Which' guide recommended.

2 rooms, Open May-Oct, B&B per person, double from £23.00.

nr Bo'ness, West Lothian
Map Ref: 2B4

B&B

Bomains Farm
Linlithgow, West Lothian, EH49 7RQ
Tel:01506 822188
Email:buntykirk@tiscali.co.uk
Web:www.bomains.co.uk

A warm welcome to this family home. Rural but central location. Excellent views over the River Forth. Ideally located for motorways, Glasgow and Edinburgh. Gateway to the Highlands.

3 rooms, all en-suite, Open Jan-Dec, B&B per person, single from £30.00, double from £25.00, BB & Eve.Meal from £39.00.

Brig O'Turk, Perthshire
Map Ref: 1H3

B&B

Burnt Inn House
Brig O'Turk, Callander, Perthshire, FK17 8HT
Tel:01877 376212 Fax:01877 339209
Email:burntinnhouse@aol.com
Web:www.burntinnhouse.co.uk

Former Coach House dating back to the 1850's now recently refurbished family home offering comfortable en-suite accommodation. Set in the midst of the Trossachs with views to Ben Venue & Queen Elizabeth Forest Park. Enjoy breakfast in our traditional farmhouse kitchen, complete with welcoming Aga.

3 rooms, all en-suite, Open Jan-Dec excl Xmas/New Year, B&B per person, single from £25.00, double from £25.00.

VAT is shown at 17.5%: changes in this rate may affect prices.

Key to symbols is on back flap.

Ascog, Isle of Bute

Map Ref: 1F5

★★★★

B&B

Ascog Farm B&B
Ascog, Isle of Bute, PA20 9LL
Tel:01700 503372
Email:johnandirene@ascogfarm.fsnet.co.uk

A well appointed sympathetically restored 200-year-old farmhouse in a peaceful setting. Log fires and friendly welcome, come and be spoilt. The farmhouse is decorated with the traditional principles of Feng Shui harmonising with nature.

4 rooms, 1 double, 3 single. Open Jan-Nov excl New Year, B&B per person, single from £20.00, double from £20.00.

Callander, Perthshire

Map Ref: 1H3

★★★

B&B

Almardon
Leny Road, Callander, Perthshire, FK17 8AJ
Tel:01877 331597
Email:almardon@btinternet.com

Enjoy a relaxing stay in our spacious bungalow at the west end of town. Adjacent to Meadows Park and River Teith yet only minutes from shopping area and other amenities. Comfortable en-suite bedrooms with tea/coffee facilities, colour T.V, radio/alarm, hairdryer and iron. Ample parking within own grounds. Callander is so centrally situated, it makes an ideal base for touring the Central Highlands,walking,climbing and cycling.

3 rooms, all en-suite, Open Feb-Dec excl Xmas/New Year, B&B per person, double from £23.00.

★★★★

GUEST HOUSE

Brook Linn
Leny Feus, Callander, Stirlingshire, FK17 8AU
Tel/Fax:01877 330103
Email:derek@blinn.freeserve.co.uk
Web:www.brooklinn-scotland.co.uk

Comfortable, quiet family run Victorian house set in two acres of gardens with magnificent views. Short distance from town centre and all facilities. Non-smoking.

6 rooms, all en-suite, Open Easter-Oct, B&B per person, single from £25.00, double from £25.00.

DUNMOR HOUSE
Leny Road, Callander FK17 8AL
Tel: 01877 330756
email: reservations@dunmorhouse.co.uk
Web: www.dunmorhouse.co.uk
Discover Dunmor House nestling underneath Callander Crags in the Trossachs benefiting from a central location in Scotlands first national park. Enjoy quality en-suite accommodation at affordable prices with exceptional service and attention throughout. Be tempted to stay longer and take advantage of our special 2 night and long stay rates.
Book yours now!!

★★★★

GUEST HOUSE

Dunmor House
Leny Road, Callander, FK17 8AL
Tel:01877 330756
Email:reservations@dunmorhouse.co.uk
Web:www.dunmorhouse.co.uk

Victorian villa, antique pieces. Three minutes from centre, private parking. Peaceful location under crags, lovely walks. Pets welcome. Only 15 minutes from Stirling in Trossachs where there is so much to see that one night will not be enough!

4 rooms, all en-suite, Open Feb-Nov, B&B per person, single from £30.00, double from £30.00.

Important: Prices stated are estimates and may be subject to amendments

Callander, Perthshire

Map Ref: 1H3

RIVERVIEW GUEST HOUSE

Leny Road, Callander FK17 8AL
TEL: 01877 330635 FAX: 01877 339386
E.MAIL: drew@visitcallander.co.uk
WEB: www.visitcallander.co.uk
Detached stone-built Victorian house in own grounds with private parking. Convenient for town centre, leisure complex and local restaurants. An ideal location for walking, cycling and motoring holidays. Cycle storage available. All rooms en-suite with TV and tea making. Good home cooking.
B&B from £24 pppn. Discount for long stays.

★★★

**GUEST
HOUSE**

Riverview Guest House
Leny Road, Callander, Perthshire, FK17 8AL
Tel:01877 330635   Fax:01877 339386
Email:drew@visitcallander.co.uk
Web:www.visitcallander.co.uk

Detached stone built Victorian house set in its own garden with private parking. Close to town centre, leisure complex and local amenities. Within easy walking distance of pleasant riverside park and cycle track. Ideal base for exploring the beautiful Trossachs.

5 rooms, all en-suite, Open Mar-Nov, B&B per person, single from £24.00, double from £25.00.

★★★★

B&B

Westerton
Leny Road, Callander, Perthshire, FK17 8AJ
Tel/Fax:01877 330147
Email:westerton.callander@tiscali.co.uk
Web:www.westerton.co.uk

Beautifully restored Victorian house set in gardens on the banks of the River Leny offering an excellent standard of quality accommodation. Relax in style and comfort in elegant rooms furnished in period style with views of the Trossachs hills. The perfect base to explore the walking, cycling and touring opportunities. Relaxed and friendly atmosphere.

2 rooms, all en-suite, Open Feb-Nov, B&B per person, double from £30.00.

Connel, Argyll

Map Ref: 1E2

★

B&B

Rosebank
Connel, by Oban, Argyll, PA37 1PA
Tel:01631 710316

A warm welcome is to be expected into this family home in the heart of Connel village, close to hotels, post office and local shops. Railway station 100 metres walk. Oban 6 miles (9 km). Pets welcome.

3 rooms, Open Easter-Oct, B&B per person, single from £18.00, double from £17.00.

VAT is shown at 17.5%: changes in this rate may affect prices.

Key to symbols is on back flap.

Craobh Haven, by Lochgilphead, Argyll   Map Ref: 1E3

Lunga Estate

Craobh Haven, Argyll PA31 8QR
Telephone: 01852 500237 Fax: 01631 572248
e.mail: colin@lunga.com Web: www.lunga.com
Lunga, a 17th-century mansion overlooking Firth of Lorne and
Sound of Jura, home to the MacDougalls for over 300 years, who
offer comfortable rooms for Bed and Breakfast and self-catering flats
or cottages. Join us for our famous candle-lit dinners and share the
facilities of this beautiful 3,000-acre coastal estate.

★★

B&B

Lunga
Craobh Haven, Argyll, PA31 8QR
Tel:01852 500237 Fax:01631 572248
Email:colin@lunga.com
Web:www.lunga.com

5 rooms, Open Jan-Dec, B&B per person, single from £20.00, double from £19.00,
Eve.Meal from £18.00.

Crianlarich, Perthshire   Map Ref: 1G2

★★

INN

Ben More Lodge Hotel
Crianlarich, Perthshire, FK20 8QP
Tel:01838 300210 Fax:01838 300218
Email:info@ben-more.co.uk
Web:www.ben-more.co.uk

Pine lodges of a high standard with restaurant and bar adjacent. Ideal
base for touring, hillwalking and fishing.

11 rooms, all en-suite, Open Feb-Dec excl Xmas, B&B per person, single from
£42.00, double from £26.00.

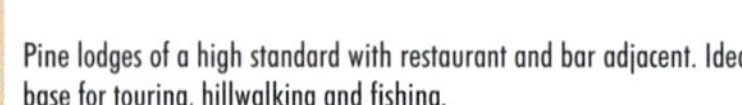

★★

**SMALL
HOTEL**

Suie Lodge Hotel
Luib, Glen Dochart, Crianlarich, Perthshire FK20 8QT
Tel:01567 820417 Fax:01567 820040
Email:suielodge@btinternet.com
Web:www.suielodge.co.uk

Family run hotel in former Shooting Lodge, in scenic Glendochart.
Offering a relaxed atmosphere, comfortable bedrooms. Many en-suite.
Good Scottish food. Excellent centre for touring.

10 rooms, some en-suite, Open Jan-Dec, B&B per person, single from £25.00,
double from £27.50.

Dalmally, Argyll   Map Ref: 1F2

★★★

B&B

Craigroyston
Monument Hill, Dalmally, Argyll, PA33 1AA
Tel:01838 200234
Email:b&b@craigroyston.com
Web:www.craigroyston.com

A stone built Edwardian villa on the edge of the quiet village of Dalmally.
Three comfortable first-floor rooms and ample parking. Guests are welcome
to use the conservatory and good sized gardens. There is grand walking,
cycling and fishing in the area or you can just relax. Dalmally is an ideal
base for touring in the Oban - Inveraray - Glencoe area. Fine home-cooked
meals are offered and a friendly welcome is assured.

3 rooms, some en-suite, Open Jan-Dec excl Xmas/New Year, B&B per person, single
from £20.00, double from £22.00.

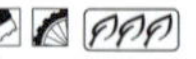

Important: Prices stated are estimates and may be subject to amendments

Dalmally, Argyll — Map Ref: 1F2

★★★

B&B

Strathorchy
Dalmally, Argyll, PA33 1AE
Tel/Fax:01838 200373
Email:strathorchy@loch-awe.com

Recently built traditional style house in countryside setting beside No 1 tee on golf course. Good base for touring Argyll, the glens and islands. Close to the beautiful Kilchurn Castle at the head of Loch Awe. Walkers and cyclists welcome. Ideal base for Munro Baggers with 5 in the surrounding area. Loch fishing nearby.

3 rooms, some en-suite, Open Jan-Dec excl Xmas/New Year, B&B per person, single from £20.00, double from £18.00.

Drymen, Stirlingshire — Map Ref: 1H4

**AWAITING
INSPECTION**

Elmbank B&B
10 Stirling Road, Drymen, Stirlingshire, G63 0BN
Tel:01360 661016/07977 756226
Web:www.elmbank-drymen.com

4 rooms, Open all year, B&B per person, single from £18.00, double from £18.00.

Dunblane, Perthshire — Map Ref: 2A3

★★★

B&B

Mrs Jean MacGregor
Ciar Mohr, Auchinlay Road, Dunblane, Perthshire, FK15 9JS
Tel:01786 823371

Modern spacious family home set on the banks of the river Allan, overlooking the park. Set in a peaceful and quiet location on the outskirts of Dunblane within close proximity of the town centre and rail station. Ideal base for touring central Scotland.

2 rooms, Open Jan-Dec, B&B per person, single from £25.00, double from £20.00.

Helensburgh, Argyll — Map Ref: 1G4

★★★

B&B

Bonniebrae
80 Sinclair Street, Helensburgh, Dunbartonshire, G84 8TU
Tel:01436 671469
Email:kbonniebrae@aol.com

Traditional stonebuilt cottage, two minutes walk from centre of town with its shops and restaurants. Private garden and off road parking. 4 miles from Loch Lomond. 40 minutes via Erskine Bridge to Glasgow Airport.

2 rooms, all en-suite, Open Jan-Dec, B&B per person, single from £25.00, double from £23.00.

★★★★

**GUEST
HOUSE**

Sinclair House
91/93 Sinclair Street, Helensburgh, Argyll & Bute G84 8TR
Tel:0800 1646301
Email:bookings@sinclairhouse.com
Web:www.sinclairhouse.com

Sinclair House is located in Helensburgh town centre with views over the Clyde Estuary from the upper rooms. As such, we are close to numerous restaurants, bars, shops and Helensburgh Central Railway Station. We like to spoil our guests providing mini-fridges, free wireless internet access, freeview receivers and DVD players in all rooms with over 400 free DVD movies available. See our website for full details.

4 rooms, all en-suite, Open Jan-Dec, B&B per person, single from £50.00, double from £25.00.

VAT is shown at 17.5%: changes in this rate may affect prices.

Key to symbols is on back flap.

Inveraray, Argyll | Map Ref: 1F3

★★★
B&B

10 Argyll Court
Inveraray, Argyll, PA32 8UT
Tel:01499 302273
Email:anne.macpherson1@virgin.net
Web:www.inveraryaccommodation.com

Small terrace house in a quiet court off the main road, with views over Loch Fyne and the Cowal Hills. Five minutes walk to the town centre. This part of Argyll is steeped in history with magnificent scenery and is an ideal base for taking day trips.

2 rooms, all en-suite, Open Jan-Dec excl Xmas/New Year, B&B per person, single from £30.00, double from £25.00.

★★★
B&B

Creag Dhubh
Inveraray, Argyll, PA32 8XT
Tel:01499 302430
Email:stay@creagdhubh.com
Web:www.creagdhudh.com

Family run traditional granite Victorian detached house set in own grounds with lovely panoramic views across Loch Fyne to the Cowal Peninsula. Within 5 minute walk of the town centre of historic Inveraray.

5 rooms, all en-suite, Open Jan-Nov, B&B per person, single from £27.00, double from £23.00.

Iona, Isle of, Argyll | Map Ref: 1B2

★★
B&B

Finlay Ross Ltd
Martyr's Bay, Isle of Iona, Argyll, PA76 6SP
Tel:01681 700357   Fax:01681 700562
Email:bandb@finlayrossiona.co.uk
Web:www.finlayrossiona.co.uk

Purpose built rooms some with television all on one level and convenient for the ferry. Buffet styled continental breakfast served. Also cottage annexe with TV lounge.

13 rooms, some en-suite, Open Jan-Dec, B&B per person, single from £28.00, double from £25.00.

Port Ellen, Isle of Islay, Argyll | Map Ref: 1C6

Glenmachrie Country Guest House

Glenmachrie, Port Ellen, Isle of Islay, Argyll, PA42 7AQ
Telephone: 01496 302560 Fax: 01496 302560
e.mail: glenmachrie@lineone.net
Web: www.glenmachrie.com
Best Breakfast in Scotland Award 2005 from Aga Rayburn and British Cereals. Which? Hotel Best Island Hideaway in Britain. Superb en-suite bedrooms. Birdwatching, horseback riding and distillery tours personally arranged for you. Next to famous Machrie Links golf course. Free fly fishing on own private river. Highland hospitality; wonderful memories.

★★★★
GUEST HOUSE

Glenmachrie Country House
Glenmachrie, Port Ellen, Isle of Islay, Argyll PA42 7AQ
Tel/Fax:01496 302560
Email:glenmachrie@lineone.net
Web:www.glenmachrie.com

Farmhouse in quiet location, fine views westwards across Laggan Bay towards the Rhinns. Family run farm using the best of Islay's larder. Private fishing for wild brown trout.

5 rooms, all en-suite, Open Jan-Dec.

Important: Prices stated are estimates and may be subject to amendments

Port Ellen, Isle of Islay, Argyll   Map Ref: 1C6

★★

GUEST HOUSE

The Trout Fly Guest House
8 Charlotte Street, Port Ellen, Isle of Islay, PA42 7DF
Tel:01496 302204   Fax:01496 300076

Centrally heated accommodation with TV and Tea/Coffee facilities. Ideal for Distillery tours, golf, walking, birdwatching, diving and fishing. Close to ferry terminal and airport.

5 rooms, Open Jan-Dec excl Xmas/New Year, B&B per person, single from £23.00, double from £23.00.

Killin, Perthshire   Map Ref: 1H2

★★

B&B

Ardlochay Lodge
Maragowan, Killin, Perthshire, FK21 8TN
Tel/Fax:01567 820962
Email:info@ardlochaylodge.co.uk
Web:www.ardlochaylodge.co.uk

Large modern house on the edge of the village of Killin offering warm Highland hospitality. Walkers and Cyclists especially welcome as well as weary travellers who will enjoy the picturesque village of Killin. Evening meals by arrangement.

3 rooms, all en-suite, Open Jan-Dec, B&B per person, single from £28.00, double from £25.00, BB & Eve.Meal from £34.00.

★★★

GUEST HOUSE

Drumfinn Guest House
Manse Road, Killin, Perthshire, FK21 8UY
Tel:01567 820900
Email:drumfinn@aol.com
Web:www.drumfinn.co.uk

A warm welcome assured in this country house set in the middle of the small Highland village of Killin. Large airy rooms, open fires, private parking.

5 rooms, some en-suite, Open All Year, B&B per person, single from £30.00, double/twin from £26.00.

★★★

GUEST HOUSE

Fairview House
Main Street, Killin, Perthshire, FK21 8UT
Tel:01567 820667
Email:info@fairview-killin.co.uk
Web:www.fairview-killin.co.uk

Family run guest house specialising in home cooking. Excellent touring centre, good walking and climbing area.

6 rooms, some en-suite, Open Jan-Dec excl Xmas/New Year, B&B per person, single from £25.00, double from £25.00.

Lochgilphead, Argyll   Map Ref: 1E4

★★★★

B&B

Corbiere
Achnabreac, Lochgilphead, Argyll, PA31 8SG
Tel:01546 602764

Detached family house in peaceful country location with lovely views across the surrounding farmlands. Ideal base for exploring historic Kilmartin Glen and the Kintyre Peninsula. Short drive to ferries for Inner Isles. Good walking with many forest tracks and the Crinan Canal tow path nearby for cyclists. No pets. Residents lounge with TV. No Smoking.

2 rooms, 1 double en-suite, 1 twin priv.facilities, Open Jan-Dec excl Xmas/New Year, Prices from £22.50 on request.

VAT is shown at 17.5%: changes in this rate may affect prices.   Key to symbols is on back flap.

by Lochgilphead, Argyll

Map Ref: 1E4

★★★

B&B

Somerled Bed & Breakfast
**Dunadd View, Bridgend, Kilmichael-Glassary,
by Lochgilphead, Argyll, PA31 8QA
Tel:01546 605226   Fax:01546 605229
Email:somerledbridgend@aol.com**

Somerled is a new country house within the village of Bridgend, set in Kilmartin Glen 5 miles from Lochgilphead on the A816. Within walking distance lies Dunadd Fort. We are close to many forest walks and cycle routes. The area is a haven for wildlife and birds and there are many lochs for fishing. We are approximately 2 hours from Glasgow. All bedrooms are ensuite and spacious. Two double and one twin.

3 rooms, all en-suite, Open Jan-Dec excl Xmas/New Year, B&B per person, single from £24.00, double from £22.00.

Luss, Argyll & Bute

Map Ref: 1G4

Shantron Farm

Mobile:
07768 378400

Shantron Farm, Luss, Alexandria G83 8RH
Telephone: 01389 850231 Fax: 01389 850231
e.mail: anne.shantron@fwi.co.uk
Web: www.stayatlochlomond.com/shantron

Enjoy a relaxing break in a spacious bungalow with outstanding views of Loch Lomond. Our 5,000-acre hill farm is the setting for Morag's croft in "Take the High Road" thirty minutes from Glasgow Airport. An ideal touring base and for hillwalking, fishing, watersports, golf. Large garden for guests' enjoyment.

★★★

B&B

Shantron Farm B&B
**Shantron Farm, Luss, Alexandria, G83 8RH
Tel/Fax:01389 850231
Email:anne.shantron@fwi.co.uk
Web:www.stayatlochlomond.com/shantron**

Cottage in elevated position with panoramic views over Loch Lomond to the Campsie Fells. Farm is used regularly for filming of 'High Road'. Real fire in the guests' lounge.

3 rooms, all en-suite, Open Mar-Oct, B&B per person, double from £22.00.

Bunessan, Isle of Mull, Argyll

Map Ref: 1C3

ARDNESS HOUSE

**BUNESSAN, ISLE OF MULL, ARGYLL PA67 6DU
TEL/FAX: 01681 700260
e.mail: ardness@supanet.com   Web: www.isleofmullholidays.com**
Ardness House is a family run Bed & Breakfast situated in a spectacular location 3 miles from ferries to Iona and Staffa. En-suite bedrooms are tastefully decorated. Perfect location for birdwatching, walking, exploring deserted sandy bays, observing the unique wildlife that roam free in their natural environment.

★★★

B&B

Ardness House
**Bunessan, Isle of Mull, Argyll, PA67 6DU
Tel/Fax:01681 700260
Email:ardness@supanet.com
Web:www.isleofmullholidays.com**

A well appointed modern bungalow with all bedrooms ensuite. Guests lounge with panoramic views of Loch Caol and dramatic cliffs beyond. Three and a half miles from Iona ferry.

3 rooms, all en-suite, Open Easter-Oct, B&B per person, double from £20.00.

Important: Prices stated are estimates and may be subject to amendments

by Craignure, Isle of Mull, Argyll

Map Ref: 1D2

B&B ★★★★

Inverlussa Bed & Breakfast
by Craignure, Isle of Mull, PA65 6BD
Tel:01680 812436 Fax:01680 812137

4 rooms, some en-suite, Open Apr-Oct, B&B per person, single from £23.00, double from £25.00.

Personally run modern house in idyllic setting. 6 miles/10 minutes from Craignure ferry. Ideal base for touring Isle of Mull.

Dervaig, Isle of Mull, Argyll

Map Ref: 1C1

B&B ★★★★

Inishkea
Dervaig, Isle of Mull, Argyll, PA75 6QW
Tel/Fax:01688 400296
Email:hcwood@compuserve.com
Web:www.inishkea.co.uk

3 rooms, all en-suite, Open Easter-Nov, B&B per person, double from £25.00.

Relax at Inishkea, a unique house with glorious views over loch and glen. Comfortable accommodation and breakfasts with vegetarian choices.

Kinlochspelve, Lochbuie, Isle of Mull, Argyll

Map Ref: 1D2

B&B ★★★★

The Barn
Barrachandroman, Lochbuie, Isle of Mull, PA62 6AA
Tel:01680 814220 Fax:01680 814247
Email:edwards@barrachandroman.co.uk
Web:www.barrachandroman.co.uk

2 rooms, some en-suite, Open Jan-Dec excl Xmas/New Year, B&B per person, single from £28.00, double from £28.00.

Luxuriously converted barn in secluded lochside location, both rooms with private facilities.

Pennyghael, Isle of Mull, Argyll

Map Ref: 1C2

SMALL HOTEL ★★★★

Pennyghael Hotel
Pennyghael, Isle of Mull, PA70 6HB
Tel:01681 704288 Fax:01681 704205
Email:enquiries@pennyghaelhotel.com
Web:www.pennyghaelhotel.com

6 rooms, all en-suite, Open Jan-Dec, B&B per person, single from £55.00, double from £55.00, BB & Eve.Meal from £80.00.

Relax in the peace and quiet of Pennyghael Hotel where we will use every endeavour to make your stay with us all that you would want it to be. The hotel can be used as a base for a family holiday, as a romantic hideaway far removed from the stresses and strains of modern life, as a centre for studying the amazingly diverse flora and fauna on the Ross of Mull and in the loch or just somewhere you want to be to explore all that this corner of Mull has to offer.

Salen, Aros, Isle of Mull, Argyll

Map Ref: 1D1

B&B ★★★

Callachally Farm
Salen, Aros, Isle of Mull, PA72 6JN
Tel/Fax:01680 300424
Email:macphail@tiscali.co.uk
Web:www.holidaysonmull.co.uk

2 rooms, Open Apr-Nov, B&B per person, single from £30.00, double £20.00-22.00.

Comfortable bungalow in peaceful location overlooking surrounding farmland to hills beyond. Short walk to coast and sea views. Ideal for touring, walking, wildlife and bird watching.

VAT is shown at 17.5%: changes in this rate may affect prices.

Key to symbols is on back flap.

Tobermory, Isle of Mull, Argyll   **Map Ref: 1C1**

Glengorm Castle

Tobermory, Isle of Mull, Argyll, PA75 6QE
Tel:01688 302321 Fax:01688 302738
Email:enquiries@glengormcastle.co.uk
Web:www.glengormcastle.co.uk

B&B

Spectacularly set, overlooking the wild Atlantic breakers to the Western
Isles beyond, this fairytale Baronial Castle offers a unique experience
never to be forgotten. Generous size rooms, log fires in season and a
charming hostess along with magnificent breakfasts offering the best of
Mull produce.

5 rooms, some en-suite, Open Jan-Dec excl Xmas/New Year, B&B per person,
double from £60.00.

Ptarmigan House

The Fairways, Tobermory, Isle of Mull PA75 6PS
Tel: 01688 302863 Fax: 01688 302913
e.mail: sue.fink@btopenworld.com
Web: www.bed-and-breakfast-tobermory.com

Ptarmigan is set in an acre of ground on the edge of
Tobermory Golf Course overlooking Tobermory Bay and the
Sound of Mull. Inside it is spacious, with modern interesting
furnishings and full of light and colour.
You can choose from 4 bedrooms, all ensuite, including
one with a balcony or one with a private patio. All are
comfortably furnished with large double/twin beds,
hospitality trays and television. Breakfast is served in
the conservatory which has stunning views over the
Sound of Mull. Dinner available.
Apart from the rooms we offer our guests the use of our
30' indoor heated swimming pool.

Ptarmigan House

The Fairways, Tobermory, Isle of Mull, PA75 6PS
Tel:01688 302863 Fax:01688 302913
Email:sue.fink@btopenworld.com
Web:www.bed-and-breakfast-tobermory.com

B&B

Recently built high quality house in elevated position above Tobermory
and with superb views. Excellent indoor swimming pool available to
guests, ample parking. Close to Tobermory Golf Club. German spoken.

4 rooms, all en-suite, Open Feb-Nov, B&B per person, double from £35.00.

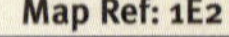

Oban, Argyll   **Map Ref: 1E2**

Aros Ard

Croft Road, Oban, Argyll, PA34 5JN
Tel:01631 565500
Email:maclean@arosard.freeserve.co.uk
Web:www.oban.org.uk/accommodation/arosard

B&B

Set up above the town this modern house offers two very spacious
bedrooms occupying the entire first floor. Both with picture windows with
beautiful views of Oban Bay. Each room is supplied with TV/video/mini-
fridge/tea and coffee tray and hairdryer and comfortable sofa and chairs.
Very friendly and hospitable hosts. Ample private parking.

2 rooms, all en-suite, Open Mar-Dec excl Xmas/New Year, B&B per person, single
from £46.00, double from £25.00.

Important: Prices stated are estimates and may be subject to amendments

Glengorm Castle
TOBERMORY, ISLE OF MULL

*Glengorm Castle is a fairytale Victorian castle with stunning views over the Atlantic Ocean and the Inner Hebrides.
The accommodation is spacious, whilst remaining very comfortable.
Please view our website for more information and photographs.*

GLENGORM CASTLE ✦ TOBERMORY ✦ ISLE OF MULL ✦ PA75 6QE
TEL: 01688 302321 FAX: 01688 302738
E.MAIL: enquiries@glengormcastle.co.uk
WEB: www.glengormcastle.co.uk
VisitScotland ★★★★ Bed & Breakfast
Photo courtesy of VisitScotland/Scottish Viewpoint

Oban, Argyll   Map Ref: 1E2

BRACKER

Polvinister Road, Oban, Argyll PA34 5TN
Telephone: 01631 564302 Fax: 01631 571167
e.mail: cmacdonald@connectfree.co.uk Web: www.bracker.co.uk

Modern bungalow situated in beautiful quiet residential area within walking distance of town (approx. 10-15 mins.) and the golf course. All bedrooms have private facilities, TV and tea/coffee-making. TV lounge, private parking. Non Smoking.

★★★

B&B

Bracker

Polvinister Road, Oban, Argyll, PA34 5TN
Tel:01631 564302   Fax:01631 571167
Email:cmacdonald@connectfree.co.uk
Web:www.bracker.co.uk

A warm welcome is assured at this modern family bungalow situated in a secluded residential area located a short distance from Oban town centre and all amenities. Private parking. Full en suite.

3 rooms, all en-suite, Open Mar-Oct, B&B per person, double from £20.00.

★★★★

GUEST HOUSE

Corriemar House

6 Corran Esplanade, Oban, Argyll, PA34 5AQ
Tel:01631 562476 Fax:01631 564339
Email:corriemar@tinyworld.co.uk
Web:www.corriemarhouse.co.uk

Situated on the seafront, this large Victorian family run Guest House is only 10 minutes walk along the prom to the town centre. Spectacular Oban sunsets looking from the lounge and seaview bedroom over to Kerrara with the hills of Mull beyond. Queen size deluxe rooms and four poster rooms available. One suite room with sea views.

14 rooms, 13 en-suite, 1 priv.facilities, Open Jan-Dec, B&B per person, double £30.00-48.00. Queen sized deluxe rooms and 4 poster room available.

★★★

B&B

Drumriggend

22 Drummore Road, Oban, Argyll, PA34 4JL
Tel:01631 563330   Fax:01631 564217

Detached house in quiet residential area. Situated on the south side of town about 1 mile (2kms) from the centre. All bedrooms comfortably furnished with ensuite facilities, TV's and tea-trays. Separate lounge available for guests' use. Ample private parking.

3 rooms, all en-suite, Open Jan-Dec excl Xmas/New Year, B&B per person, double £20.00-22.00.

★★★★

B&B

Dungrianach

Pulpit Hill, Oban, Argyll, PA34 4LU
Tel/Fax:01631 562840
Email:enquiries@dungrianach.com
Web:www.dungrianach.com

Secluded, in 4 acres of wooded garden on top of Pulpit Hill. Magnificent views over Oban Bay and the islands.

3 rooms, all en-suite, Open Easter-Sep, B&B per person, single from £45.00, double starting from £27.00 per night B&B.

Important: Prices stated are estimates and may be subject to amendments

GLENARA GUEST HOUSE

Rockfield Road, Oban, Argyll PA34 5DQ
Tel: 01631 563172 Fax: 01631 571125
email: glenara_oban@hotmail.com Web: www.glenara-oban.com

Centrally situated family run guest house. Excellent individually furnished en-suite rooms, doubles all kingsize, some with seaviews (see website). Enjoy breakfast of your choice, traditional or vegetarian. Explore Oban and surrounds by walking, car, bus, train or ferry and enjoy outstanding scenery. No smokers.

**GUEST
HOUSE**

Glenara Guest House
Rockfield Road, Oban, Argyll, PA34 5DQ
Tel:01631 563172   Fax:01631 571125
Email:glenara_oban@hotmail.com
Web:www.glenara-oban.com

Centrally situated family run guest house. Excellent individually furnished en-suite rooms (see website). Enjoy breakfast of your choice, traditional or vegetarian. Off-street car parking. Explore Oban and surrounds by walking. Ferry trips and outstanding scenery.

4 rooms, all en-suite, Open Jan-Dec, B&B per person, single from £35.00, double from £27.00.

**GUEST
HOUSE**

Greencourt Guest House
Benvoullin Road, Oban, Argyll, PA34 5EF
Tel:01631 563987
Email:relax@greencourt-oban.co.uk
Web:www.greencourt-oban.co.uk

Spacious family run property in quiet situation overlooking outdoor bowling green, a short stroll to town centre and adjacent to leisure centre. Attractive rooms, wholesome breakfasts, private parking. Ideal touring base.

6 rooms, most en-suite, Open Feb-Nov, B&B per person, single £24.00-33.00, double £24.00-3300.

B&B

Harlaw
Glenmore Road, Pulpit Hill, Oban, Argyll, PA34 4ND
Tel:01631 563295
Email:russell.harlaw@rdplus.net

Comfortable accommodation in quiet residential area within walking distance of all amenities.

2 rooms, Open Apr-Oct, B&B per person, double from £22.00. No dogs.

B&B

Hawthorn
Benderloch, Argyll, PA37 1QS
Tel:01631 720452
Email:june@hawthorncottages.com
Web:www.hawthorncottages.com

Warm welcome in peaceful setting 9 miles from Oban. Main ferry terminals for the islands. Three bedrooms furnished to a high standard with lots of little extras to make your holiday special. Restaurant adjacent. Home cooking a speciality. Special offers. 'AA' Listed.

4 rooms, some en-suite, Open Jan-Dec, B&B per person, single from £30.00, double from £22.50, BB & Eve.Meal from £35.00.

VAT is shown at 17.5%: changes in this rate may affect prices.

Key to symbols is on back flap.

Oban, Argyll   Map Ref: 1E2

Hawthornbank Guest House
Dalriach Road, Oban PA34 5JE
Tel/Fax: 01631 562041   e.mail: hawthornbank@aol.com
Web: www.SmoothHound.co.uk/hotels/hawthorn.html

Brian and Valerie welcome you to their tastefully refurbished Victorian villa. Immaculate, well-equipped, en-suite rooms. Two feature rooms: Regency with 4-poster and Victorian with brass bed. Beautiful views over Oban Bay. Close to sports centre. Five minutes walk to town centre. Private parking. Non-smoking.

GUEST HOUSE

Hawthornbank Guest House
Dalriach Road, Oban, Argyll, PA34 5JE
Tel/Fax:01631 562041
Email:hawthornbank@aol.com
Web:www.SmoothHound.co.uk/hotels/hawthorn.html

Brian and Valerie look forward to welcoming you to Hawthornbank, a tastefully refurbished Victorian villa set in a quiet location yet only a short stroll from the town centre. Comfortable well equipped rooms some with stunning views over Oban Bay. How can you resist?

7 en-suite rooms, 1 single with priv.fac. Open Jan-Dec excl Xmas, B&B per person, single from £25.00, double from £26.00.

Kilchrenan House
Corran Esplanade, Oban, Argyll PA34 5AQ
Tel: 01631 562663 Fax: 01631 562448
e.mail: info@kilchrenanhouse.co.uk
Web: www.kilchrenanhouse.co.uk

Spacious Victorian house in excellent seafront location with uninterrupted views over Oban Bay and the Islands beyond. The ideal setting for a peaceful break, Kilchrenan House offers a relaxing atmosphere combined with modern comforts. All ten bedrooms have been decorated to a high standard, and each has ensuite facilities, telephone, television, radio and hospitality trays. Most offer the delight of waking to a sea view....Read your book in the sunny bay window of the residents lounge and watch the boats from the dining room as you enjoy a tasty breakfast. Private car park.
We look forward to welcoming you. Open all year.

GUEST HOUSE

Kilchrenan House
Corran Esplanade, Oban, Argyll, PA34 5AQ
Tel:01631 562663 Fax:01631 562448
Email:info@kilchrenanhouse.co.uk
Web:www.kilchrenanhouse.co.uk

Assured high standard of service and comfort. Oban town centre and all amenities within five minutes walk along the esplanade. Sunny position on Oban's Esplanade - the ideal place to watch the glorious sunsets.

9 rooms, all en-suite, Open all year, B&B per person, single from £34.00, double from £34.00.

Important: Prices stated are estimates and may be subject to amendments

Map Ref: 1E2

THE OLD MANSE GUEST HOUSE

The Old Manse, Dalriach Road, Oban PA34 5JE
Tel: 01631 564 886
e.mail: oldmanse@obanguesthouse.co.uk   Web: www.obanguesthouse.co.uk

'Simply The Best'. 'Holiday Which' recommended guest house. Superior standard of comfort and hospitality. Stunning sea views. Beautiful gardens. Two minutes walk from town. Car park. Family suite and luxury rooms available. Off peak and special occasion breaks available.

★★★★

GUEST HOUSE

The Old Manse Guest House
Dalriach Road, Oban, Argyll, PA34 5JE
Tel:01631 564886
Email:oldmanse@obanguesthouse.co.uk
Web:www.obanguesthouse.co.uk

Magnificent views over Oban Bay and only minutes walk from the town centre.The Old Manse Guest House offers a superior standard of hospitality and comfort. Enjoy a freshly cooked breakfast from our varied menu. Private parking. Family ensuite available. Discounted 3, 5 and 7 day breaks. All major credit cards accepted.

6 rooms, Open Feb-Nov, B&B per person double from £26.00, family from £24.00, room only double from £52.00, family from £48.00.

Map Ref: 1E2

Braeside Guest House

Kilmore, By Oban, Argyll, Scotland PA34 4QR
Tel: 01631 770243 Fax: 01631 770343
e.mail: Braeside.Guesthouse@virgin.net
Web: www.braesideguesthouse.net

Braeside is a family run beautiful bungalow, overlooking the spectacular scenery of Loch Feochan. We are only a five minute drive from Oban. Jon and Cherry will welcome you, and serve wonderful home cooked evening meals and breakfasts, including vegetarian choice. Relax in the lounge with over 40 single malts or fine wines from the bar. We take great care and pride in offering excellent value, clean comfortable, well-furnished, en-suite rooms, in a completely non-smoking environment. Fishing, walking, golf, bird-watching and sailing are all nearby, together with Obans attractions and ferry boats to the Western Isles.

★★★

GUEST HOUSE

Braeside Guest House
Kilmore, by Oban, Argyll, PA34 4QR
Tel:01631 770243 Fax:01631 770343
Email:braeside.guesthouse@virgin.net
Web:www.braesideguesthouse.net

Quality licensed Guest House located 3 miles South of Oban. Rural setting with uninterrupted views of Loch Feochan and surrounding hills, private parking and pleasant gardens. All rooms are high standard, ensuite, ground level with full amenities. Fine cuisine using fresh produce. Choice of menu and good wine list. Ideal base for touring, walking, trips to Isles of Mull, Iona, Staffa, etc. No smoking or pets.   AA Four Diamond Award.

5 rooms, all en-suite, Open Jan-Dec, B&B per person, single from £21.00, double from £21.00, BB & Eve.Meal from £37.00.

VAT is shown at 17.5%: changes in this rate may affect prices.

Key to symbols is on back flap.

by Oban, Argyll

Map Ref: 1E2

★★★

HOTEL

Falls of Lora Hotel
Connel Ferry, by Oban, Argyll, PA37 1PB
Tel:01631 710483   Fax:01631 710694
Email:enquiries@fallsoflora.com
Web:www.fallsoflora.com

Oban 5 miles, only 2½ to 3 hours drive North-West of
Glasgow/Edinburgh. Overlooking Loch Etive, this fine owner run
Victorian Hotel has a modern extension. 30 rooms from special to
inexpensive family. The super cocktail bar has an open log fire and over
100 brands of whisky. There is an attractive and comfortable bistro for
evening meals - the menu is extensive and features local produce.

30 rooms, all en-suite, Open Feb-mid Dec, B&B per person, single from £39.50,
double from £23.50.

nr Oban, Argyll

Map Ref: 1E2

ROINEABHAL COUNTRY HOUSE

Kilchrenan, Taynuilt, Argyll PA35 1HD
Telephone: 01866 833207 Fax: 01866 833477
e.mail: maria@roineabhal.com Web: www.roineabhal.com

Luxury 4-star accommodation in the heart of Argyll. Set in own grounds.
Fishing, walking, 33 Monroes and easy access to the Western Isles.
An inspiration for artists and photographers alike. Glencoe, Oban,
Inveraray and Fort William nearby. Taste of Scotland.

★★★★

B&B

Roineabhal Country House
Kilchrenan, Taynuilt, Argyll, PA35 1HD
Tel:01866 833207   Fax:01866 833477
Email:maria@roineabhal.com
Web:www.roineabhal.com

Traditional country house, offering luxury accommodation. Centrally
situated within easy reach of Oban, Fort William and Inveraray. Dinner
by arrangement utilising local produce, organic meals also available.
Well behaved pets are welcome. Ensuring you of a warm West Highland
welcome from the whole family.

3 rooms, all en-suite, Open Jan-Dec excl Xmas, 2wks Oct, B&B per person, single
from £50.00, double from £37.50.

Port of Menteith, Stirlingshire

Map Ref: 1H3

★★★

B&B

Inchie Farm
Port of Menteith, Stirling, FK8 3JZ
Tel/Fax:01877 385233
Email:inchiefarm@ecosse.net

A warm welcome and friendly hospitality at this family farm situated on
the shore of Lake of Menteith in a quiet location. Traditional stone built
house. Home-made shortbread a speciality. Non smoking house.

2 rooms, some en-suite, Open Mar-Oct, B&B per person, single from £27.00,
double from £22.00.

Important: Prices stated are estimates and may be subject to amendments

Stirling

Map Ref: 2A4

★★★

B&B

Carseview
16 Ladysneuk Road, Cambuskenneth, Stirling FK9 5NF
Tel/Fax:01786 462235
Email:bandb@carseview.co.uk
Web:www.carseview.co.uk

Comfortable country home evolved from turn of the century stables. In small conservation village within 15-20 minutes walk of Stirling town centre. Home baked bread served at breakfast.

3 rooms, Open Jan-Dec, B&B per person, single from £20.00, double from £20.00.

★★★

GUEST HOUSE

Castlecraig Guest House
50 Causewayhead Road, Stirling, FK9 5EY
Tel:01786 475452
Email:ghmcivor@aol.com

Purpose-built accommodation adjacent to traditional stone semi-villa, only 5 minutes from Wallace Monument and University. Some ground floor rooms. Full fire certificate.

3 rooms, all en-suite, Open Jan-Dec excl Xmas/New Year, B&B per person, single from £35.00, double from £25.00.

★★★

B&B

Mrs Jennifer Dougall
14 Melville Terrace, Stirling, FK8 2NE
Tel/Fax:01786 475361
Email:mjdougall@hotmail.com

Georgian townhouse located near to city centre. Walking distance from town, railway and bus stations. Off street parking.

3 rooms, Open Jan-Dec excl Xmas/New Year, B&B per person, single from £25.00, double from £22.50.

Drum Farm

Carronbridge, Stirling, Stirlingshire FK6 5JL
Telephone and Fax: 01324 825518
e.mail: drumfarm@ndirect.co.uk   Web: www.ndirect.co.uk/~drumfarm

Beautiful 200 year-old farmhouse situated in unspoilt countryside with views overlooking Carron Dam, just 15 minutes from Stirling and the M9 and M80, where you can start your tours around this beautiful part of Scotland.

★★

B&B

Drum Farm
Carronbridge, Stirlingshire, FK6 5JL
Tel/Fax:01324 825518
Email:drumfarm@ndirect.co.uk
Web:www.ndirect.co.uk/~drumfarm

Beautiful farmhouse situated in unspoilt countryside with views overlooking Carron Dam. Just 15 minutes from Stirling and the M9 & M80 where you can start your tours around this beautiful part of Scotland.

2 rooms, some en-suite, Open Jan-Dec, B&B per person, single from £30.00, double £20.00-25.00, BB & Eve.Meal from £29.50-34.00.

Stirling
Map Ref: 2A4

GUEST HOUSE

Forth Guest House
23 Forth Place, Riverside, Stirling, FK8 1UD
Tel:01786 471020   Fax:01786 447220
Email:loudon@forthguesthouse.freeserve.co.uk
Web:www.forthguesthouse.freeserve.co.uk

Stirling's most conveniently situated guesthouse, 5 mins walk to town centre, bus and rail stations (200 metres). Private parking. Recommended by Which, Lonely Planet and Marco Polo tour guides.

3 rooms, all en-suite, Open Jan-Dec excl Xmas/New Year, B&B per person, single £20.00-40.00, double £19.00-23.00. Visa - Mastercard accepted.

B&B

Glenardoch House
Castle Road, Doune, Perthshire, FK16 6EA
Tel:01786 841489
Email:stay@glenardochhouse.com
Web:www.glenardochhouse.com

Quality traditional 18th century stone built house by historical Doune Castle. Set in its own riverside gardens, next to the old bridge. Peaceful location. Excellent base for exploring the Trossachs and Western Highlands.

2 rooms, all en-suite, Open May-Sep, B&B per person, single from £40.00, double from £27.50.

B&B

Laurinda B&B
66 Ochilmount, Ochilview, Bannockburn
Stirlingshire, FK7 8PJ
Tel:01786 815612

A warm welcome awaits you at this family home. Modern detached villa in residential area of Bannockburn. Ideal location for touring all main cities and tourist attractions. Parking area. Evening meal by arrangement.

2 rooms, 1 en-suite, 1 family room, Open Jan-Dec, B&B per person, single £23.00-24.00, double £21.00-23.00, BB & Eve.Meal from £31.00-32.00.

B&B

Sealladh Ard
Station Brae, Kippen, Stirlingshire, FK8 3DY
Tel:01786 870291
Email:ann@bandbstirling.com
Web:www.bandbstirling.com

Family home on the outskirts of conservation village within 5 mins walk of local hotels. Well laid out and interesting garden, full Scottish breakfast served with home made bread and preserves, sit back and enjoy the spectacular views across the valley.

3 rooms, some en-suite, Open Jan-Dec, B&B per person from £25.00-28.00.

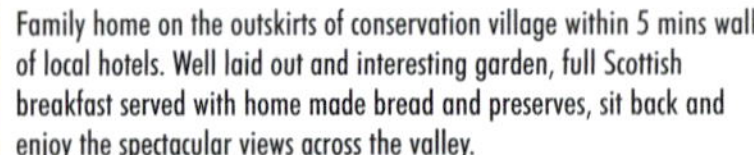

Strachur, Argyll
Map Ref: 1F3

SMALL HOTEL

The Creggans Inn
Strachur, Argyll, PA27 8BX
Tel:01369 860279   Fax:01369 860637
Email:info@creggans-inn.co.uk
Web:www.creggans-inn.co.uk

Country Hotel, steeped in history, with magnificent views of Loch Fyne. An excellent reputation for fine food. 20 miles from Dunoon or Inveraray and only an hour from Glasgow Airport, Creggans is renowned for its food, wine and quality of local produce. Our restaurant overlooking Loch Fyne offers guests the best view in Scotland. Good walking for all abilities.

14 rooms, all en-suite, Open Jan-Dec, B&B per person, single from £60.00, double from £60.00, BB & Eve.Meal from £85.00.

Important: Prices stated are estimates and may be subject to amendments

Tarbert, Loch Fyne, Argyll

Map Ref: 1E5

ARDGLASS

Ardglass, Garval Road, Tarbert, Argyll PA29 6TR
Tel: 01880 820884 Fax: 01880 820963 Mobile: 07899 875918
e.mail: nancyglentt100@hotmail.com

Modern bungalow overlooking Tarbert harbour and marina,
situated in quiet residential area. Off road parking.
10 mins walk to village centre for pubs, hotels, restaurants etc.
Early morning ferry passengers to Islay catered for.

★★★

B&B

Ardglass
Garval Road, Tarbert, Argyll, PA29 6TR
Tel:01880 820884/07899 875918 Fax:01880 820963
Email:nancyglentt100@hotmail.com

Modern bungalow overlooking Tarbert Harbour and Marina. Quiet
residential road on northside of harbour.

2 rooms, both with priv.facilities, Open Apr-Oct, B&B per person, single from
£20.00, double from £20.00.

Tillicoultry, Clackmannanshire

Map Ref: 2A3

Westbourne House

10 Dollar Road, Tillicoultry FK13 6PA
Tel: 01259 750314
e.mail: info@westbournehouse.co.uk
Web: www.westbournehouse.co.uk

Victorian mill owner's mansion set in wooded grounds beneath Ochil Hills. Warm, friendly
atmosphere. Delicious breakfasts. Log fires. Croquet lawn. TV/Radio, tea/coffee making facilities in
all rooms, one on ground floor. Centrally situated for Edinburgh, Glasgow, Perth, Stirling and
Trossachs – motorways fifteen minutes. Secure off-street parking. Single from £30. Double from £24.

★★★

B&B

Westbourne House
10 Dollar Road, Tillicoultry, FK13 6PA
Tel:01259 750314
Email:info@westbournehouse.co.uk
Web:www.westbournehouse.co.uk

Victorian mansion, full of character, 9 miles from Stirling and close to the
Sterling Mills 'Designer Outlet Village', nestling beneath the Ochil Hills.
Log fire. Secure off-road parking. E-mail facilities available.

3 rooms, some en-suite, Open Jan-Dec excl Xmas/New Year, B&B per person, single
from £30.00, double from £24.00.

★★★★

B&B

Wyvis Bed and Breakfast
70 Stirling Street, Tillicoultry, Clackmannanshire FK13 6EA
Tel:01259 751513
Email:wyvis@btopenworld.com
Web:www.wyvisbandbscotland.com

Cottage in conservation area overlooking the Ochil Hills and ideally
situated for hillwalking. Friendly atmosphere, home cooking and baking.
Evening meals by arrangement.

2 rooms, 1 double en-suite, 1 twin priv.facilities, Open Jan-Dec excl Xmas/New Year,
B&B per person, single £28.00-35.00.

VAT is shown at 17.5%: changes in this rate may affect prices.

Key to symbols is on back flap.

Welcome to Scotland

Perthshire, Angus & Dundee and the Kingdom of Fife

This is a good place for a break, with a little of everything within easy reach. Lose yourself among the forests of Perthshire, walk the hallowed turf of St Andrews, and marvel at the digital arts of Dundee.

The Old Course at St. Andrews.

Rich soils, scenes and tastes typify the Kingdom of Fife. Begin on the southeast coast among the former herring ports of the East Neuk. Whitewashed walls and hardy fishermen aplenty, Lower Largo provided Daniel Dafoe with inspiration for his novel, *Robinson Crusoe*. More a life than lifestyle, explore the 'old ways' at the Scottish Fisheries Museum in Anstruther.

The coastal road follows around to St. Andrews and the big daddy of golf courses. Yes, the royal golf club lives up to divine reputation, but don't overlook the 40 other golf courses peppering the Kingdom. Survey the majestic ruins of a Cathedral 'redecorated' by John Knox and the Reformation during the 16th century.

Follow the coastal road north of St. Andrews to encounter Dundee, the City of Discovery. Jute and jam were exports in bygone days, but art house and the avant-garde have revamped this industrial port. For a start, Dundee Contemporary Arts have inserted new multi-media facilities within the eroded shell of a former warehouse. The result?

Daring exhibitions that blend plastic arts, music, dance and cinema. Verdant Works, named Europe's Top Industrial Museum just a few years ago, weaves the story of Dundee through jute. And "Sensation" is a science centre for hands-on family capers.

Stay in the cultural quarter for good food. Try Howies, The Theatrecafe, Tapas and St Andrews Seafood restaurant. When dinner settles, join the throng of students pouring life into the bars, pubs and clubs. Quench a thirst for live music and affordable rounds at Drouthie Neebors. The Phoenix, Laings, Metro and Basement are also worth a look-in. To begin or end the

Perthshire, Angus & Dundee and the Kingdom of Fife

Water rafting down the River Tummel.

Perthshire, Angus & Dundee and the Kingdom of Fife

The lobster pots of St. Monans, an East Neuk fishing town.

night, swing by Fat Sam's, Mardi Gras or Sessions for some clubbing.

Escape the city limits – and most others - in Dunkeld. 'Nae Limits' organise a variety of hairy activities including Sphere Mania. Strap yourself into a giant 12ft inflatable sphere, point down the hill and relax… The region of Angus chooses to impress with miles of sandy beaches, the untainted beauty of five Glens, and over 2000 carved stones from the 5th century.

Perthshire has the fitting title of 'Big Tree Country', though everything seems epic. Deep forests, vast mountains, and broad rivers provide a playground for walking and adventure sports: white-water rafting, canyoning, cliff jumping, you name it. Even fishing has Olympic prowess – the River Tay holds the UK record for an Atlantic salmon weighing a hefty 64 pounds.

Brimming with specialist shops and cafes, Perth's considerable charm is bound in rich Georgian architecture. Just a stone's throw

away, Scone Palace marks the site where early kings were crowned. And if you crave the simple life, consider an Iron Age, Celtic loch-dwelling at the Crannog Centre, Kenmore.

Set deep within the mountains, Pitlochry is a Victorian spa town of natty streets and cheerful bustle. A short trip will take you to the lavish interiors of Blair Castle, or the dramatic river gorge carved by Bruar Falls. Once the visual appetite is sated, get along to the House of Bruar, an emporium of fine Scottish produce. Mmm…

Events

Perthshire, Angus & Dundee and the Kingdom of Fife

16-19 MARCH
STANZA 2006, St Andrews
Scotland's poetry festival.
www.stanzapoetry.org

18-28 MAY
PERTH FESTIVAL OF THE ARTS
Annual arts festival or originality
and playfulness.
Tel: 01738 475295
www.perthfestival.co.uk

13 AUGUST
PERTH HIGHLAND GAMES
Traditional Highland games with
cycling, running, solo piping,
Highland dancing, pipe bands,
tug o' war and heavyweight
events.
Tel: 01738 627782
www.highlandgames.org.uk

24-27 AUGUST
**BOWMORE BLAIR CASTLE
HORSE TRIALS, Blair Atholl**
International horse trials.
Tel: 01796 481207
www.blairhorsetrials.co.uk

1-3 SEPTEMBER
**DUNDEE FLOWER
AND FOOD FESTIVAL**
Scotland's premier flower and
food festival.
Tel: 01382 433815
www.dundeeflowerand
foodfestival.com

9 SEPTEMBER
RAF LEUCHARS AIR SHOW
Breathtaking displays of
precision flying.
Tel: 01334 839000
www.airshow.co.uk

29 SEPTEMBER - 4 OCTOBER
**BLAIRGOWRIE & EAST
PERTHSHIRE WALKING
FESTIVAL**
A four day festival of walking
and social events featuring
sections of the Cateran Trail,
Scotland's newest long distance
walk.
Tel: 01738 475255
www.perthshire.co.uk/walkingfest

28-29 OCTOBER
**GLENFIDDICH PIPING &
FIDDLING CHAMPIONSHIPS,
Blair Atholl**
International competitions
featuring piping on the 28th and
fiddling on the 29th.
Tel: 01698 573536
www.glenfiddich.com

23-30 NOVEMBER*
ST ANDREWS WEEK
A week of festivities culminating
in St Andrews Day.
Tel: 01334 472021
www.standrewsweek.co.uk

The Kingdom of Fife is a golfer's paradise.

** denotes provisional date, event
details are subject to change please
check before travelling*

Perthshire, Angus & Dundee and the Kingdom of Fife

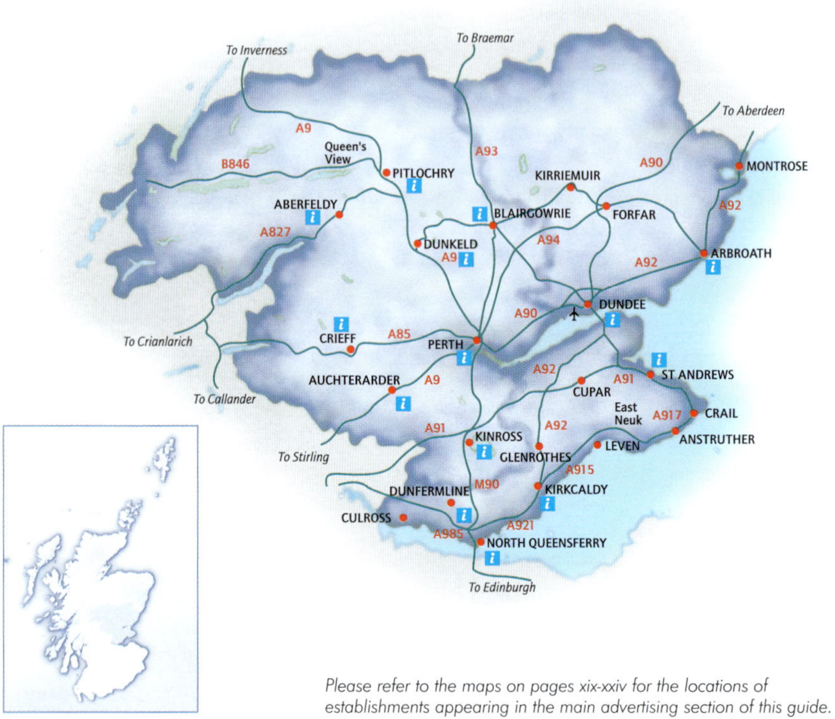

Please refer to the maps on pages xix-xxiv for the locations of establishments appearing in the main advertising section of this guide.

Finding out more...

For practical advice, ideas and information about exploring Scotland and to book your accommodation:

Tel: 0845 22 55 121*
or if calling from outside the UK: +44 (0) 1506 832121

Email: info@visitscotland.com
Web: www.visitscotland.com

* A £3 booking fee applies to telephone bookings of accommodation.

Tourist Information Centres

Perthshire, Angus & Dundee and the Kingdom of Fife

Angus & City of Dundee

Arbroath
Market Place
Tel: (01241) 872609
Jan – Dec

Brechin
Pictavia Centre, Haughmuir
Tel: (01356) 623050
Easter – Sep

Carnoustie
1b High Street
Tel: (01241) 852258
Easter – Sep

Dundee
21 Castle Street
Tel: (01382) 527527
Jan – Dec

Forfar
45 East High Street
Tel: (01307) 467876
Easter – Sep

Kirriemuir
Cumberland Close
Tel: (01575) 574097
Easter – Sep

Montrose
Bridge Street
Tel: (01674) 672000
Easter – Sep

Kingdom of Fife

Anstruther
Scottish Fisheries Museum
Tel: (01333) 311073
Apr – Oct

Crail
Crail Museum
and Heritage Centre
Marketgate
Tel: (01333) 450859
Apr – Oct

Dunfermline
1 High Street
Tel: (01383) 720999
Jan – Dec

Forth Bridges
Queensferry Lodge Hotel
St. Margaret's Head
Tel: (01383) 417759
Jan – Dec

Kirkcaldy
19 Whytescauseway
Tel: (01592) 267775
Jan – Dec

St Andrews
70 Market Street
Tel: (01334) 472021
Jan – Dec

Perthshire

Aberfeldy
The Square
Tel: (01887) 820276
Jan – Dec

Auchterarder
90 High Street
Tel: (01764) 663450
Jan – Dec

Blairgowrie
26 Wellmeadow
Tel: (01250) 872960
Jan – Dec

Crieff
Town Hall
High Street
Tel: (01764) 652578
Jan – Dec

Dunkeld
The Cross
Tel: (01350) 727688
Jan – Dec

Kinross
Heart of Scotland Visitor Centre
Junction 6, M90
Tel: (01577) 863680
Jan – Dec

Perth
Lower City Mills
West Mill Street
Tel: (01738) 450600
Jan – Dec

Pitlochry
22 Atholl Road
Tel: (01796) 472215/472751
Jan – Dec

Aberfeldy, Perthshire

Map Ref: 2A1

★★★

B&B

Ardtornish

Kenmore Street, Aberfeldy, Perthshire, PH15 2BL
Tel:01887 820629
Email:ardtornish@talk21.com

Traditional town house near centre of Aberfeldy. Ideal for touring and all outdoor pursuits. Private parking.

3 rooms, some en-suite, Open Jan-Dec excl Xmas/New Year, B&B per person, single from £22.00, double from £20.00.

★★★

B&B

Coshieville House

Coshieville, by Aberfeldy, Perthshire, PH15 2NE
Tel:01887 830319 Fax:01977 597369
Email:ian@coshieville.wanadoo.co.uk
Web:www.aberfeldybandb.com

Comfortable well appointed accommodation at this family home in the heart of rural Perthshire.

5 rooms, all en-suite, Open Jan-Dec, B&B per person, double from £22.00.

★★★

B&B

Tighnabruaich

Taybridge Terrace, Aberfeldy, PH15 2BS
Tel:01887 820456 Fax:01887 829254
Email:katesscott123@aol.com

A Victorian stone built house with fine views over the golf course to the hills. Sympathetically furnished retaining many original features, making a comfortable home from home. Off road parking.

3 rooms, Open Apr-Oct, B&B per person, single from £22.00, twin from £22.00 per night.

Tigh 'N Eilean

TAYBRIDGE DRIVE, ABERFELDY, PERTHSHIRE PH15 2BP
TEL/FAX: 01887 820109 MOBILE: 07889 472248 and 07753 637967
E.MAIL: info@tighneilean.com WEB: www.tighneilean.com

*Elegant Victorian house overlooking the River Tay beautifully decorated ensuite bedrooms one with jacuzzi. Wonderfully comfortable lounge with its open fire creates a warm and friendly atmosphere. Ideal centre for hill-walking, golf, fishing, pony-trekking and exploring beautiful Highland Perthshire. A warm and friendly welcome awaits you.
Recommended in Holiday 'Which' Magazine. One ground floor room.*

★★★★

B&B

Tigh'n Eilean Guest House

Taybridge Drive, Aberfeldy, Perthshire, PH15 2BP
Tel/Fax:01887 820109
Email:info@tighneilean.com
Web:www.tighneilean.com

Elegant Victorian house overlooking the river. Warm and comfortable, home cooking. One room with jacuzzi.

4 rooms, one ground floor bedroom available, all en-suite, Open Jan-Dec, B&B per person, single from £30.00, double from £25.00.

Important: Prices stated are estimates and may be subject to amendments

Glenfoot Bed & Breakfast

Earnview, Glenfoot, by Abernethy, Perthshire PH2 9LS
Tel: 01738 850353 email: anne.m@virgin.net

*Glenfoot is set at the foot of the Ochil Hills with wonderful views of the
Grampian and Sidlaw Hills, River Earn and Firth of Tay. Located on the
Perthshire/Fife border and only 45 minutes from St. Andrews. An ideal
base for golfing, fishing, cycling, walking and other rural pursuits.*

★★★

B&B

Glenfoot B&B
Earnview, Glenfoot, by Abernethy, Perthshire, PH2 9LS
Tel:01738 850353
Email:anne.m@virgin.net

2 rooms, with priv.facilities. Open Jan-Dec. B&B per person from £25.00-30.00.

Glenfoot set at the foot of the Ochil hills with wonderful views of the
Grampian and Sidlaw Hills, River Earn and Firth of Tay. Located on the
Perthshire/Fife border and only 45 minutes from St Andrews. An ideal
base for golfing, fishing, cycling, walking and other rural pursuits.

★★★

B&B

Invermay Cottage
Common Road, Kilrenny, Anstruther, Fife, KY10 3JQ
Tel:01333 312314
Email:jeremy-ruby@invermay.freeserve.co.uk
Web:www.invermaycottage.co.uk

2 rooms, Open Apr-Oct, B&B per person, single £25.00, double from £22.50.

Renovated 18th century cottage in peaceful location within walled
garden. 9 miles from St Andrews. Situated within the East Neuk, between
Crail and Anstruther.

The Spindrift

Pittenweem Road, Anstruther, Fife KY10 3DT
Tel/Fax: 01333 310573
e.mail: info@thespindrift.co.uk Web: www.thespindrift.co.uk

Set on the western edge of Anstruther, The Spindrift has established a
growing reputation for its unique brand of comfort, hospitality, freshly
prepared food and service. Convenient for golf, walking, bird watching or
exploring the picturesque and historic East Neuk.
Please contact Kenneth and Christine Lawson for reservations.

★★★★

**GUEST
HOUSE**

The Spindrift
Pittenweem Road, Anstruther, Fife, KY10 3DT
Tel/Fax:01333 310573
Email:info@thespindrift.co.uk
Web:www.thespindrift.co.uk

8 rooms, 7 en-suite, 1 priv.facilities, Open Jan-Dec, B&B per person, single from
£37.50, double from £27.50, BB & Eve.Meal from £45.00.

Stone built Victorian house with wealth of original features, set in fishing
village. Short walk from town centre. Ideal touring base. Non smoking.
Private parking. Evening meal by arrangement.

Anstruther, Fife
Map Ref: 2D3

B&B

Joyce and Tom Watson
8 Melville Terrace, Anstruther, Fife, KY10 3EW
Tel:01333 310453
Email:tomwatson@beeb.net

Victorian stone-built house near restaurants and harbour in picturesque East Neuk fishing village. Varied and interesting breakfast. Attractive garden with summer house where you can relax with your tea or coffee.

2 rooms, 1 en-suite, 1 priv.facilities, Open Apr-Oct, B&B per person, single from £30.00, double from £24.00.

Arbroath, Angus
Map Ref: 2D1

B&B

Mrs M Ferguson
20 Hillend Road, Arbroath, Angus, DD11 2AR
Tel:01241 873991
Email:macferg@btinternet.com

Spacious family house in quiet residential area within easy reach of all facilities in town. Off road parking. Gaelic and Spanish spoken. Non-smoking house. Hill walking and sea fishing can be arranged.

2 rooms, Open Apr-Sep, B&B per person, single from £25.00, double from £20.00.

Auchterarder, Perthshire
Map Ref: 2B3

B&B

Craigpark B&B
Townhead Wynd, Auchterarder, Perthshire, PH3 1JG
Tel/Fax:01764 662564
Email:mary@craigparkbb.wanadoo.co.uk

Detached bungalow in a quiet residential area of the town with fine views of the Ochil Hills. Both bedrooms have ensuite facilities etc. RcTV's, radios and hospitality trays. There is also a guest lounge that overlooks the garden.

2 rooms, all en-suite, Open Jan-Dec, B&B per person, single from £20.00, double from £20.00.

The Parsonage Guest House
111 High Street, Auchterarder, Perthshire, PH3 1AA
Tel/Fax:01764 662392
Web:www.visitscotland.com

Personally run guest house in the centre of Auchterarder. Convenient for golf courses. One room has ensuite facilities and all rooms have colour TV's and hospitality tray. Residents lounge.

4 rooms, some en-suite, Open Jan-Dec, B&B per person, single from £25.00, double £22.00-25.00.

B&B

Nether Coul
Auchterarder, Perthshire, PH3 1ET
Tel/Fax:01764 663119
Email:info@prestonpark.co.uk
Web:www.prestonpark.co.uk

Renovated stone cottage with large garden and stream, splendid southerly views to the Ochil Hills. Friendly relaxed atmosphere. Both rooms with private facilities. Ideal touring centre or stop over on the way North and South. A dozen golf courses within a short drive, including the world famous Gleneagles courses.

2 rooms, Open Jan-Dec excl Xmas/New Year, B&B per person, single from £21.00, double from £21.00.

B&B

Important: Prices stated are estimates and may be subject to amendments

Bankfoot, Perthshire

Map Ref: 2B2

★★★

B&B

Kayrene
Cairneyhill Road, Bankfoot, Perth, PH1 4AD
Tel/Fax:01738 787338

This modern bungalow is in an elevated position set back from the road. There is ample private parking. There are two bedrooms (both with en-suite shower rooms) and each room has a hospitality tray, a television and hair drier. There are over 30 golf courses within a half hours drive of Kayrene. Castles, lochs and beautiful scenery are all within easy day's drive. Bankfoot is 8 miles north of Perth on the A9.

2 rooms, all en-suite, Open Jan-Dec, B&B per person, double from £24.00.

Birnam, by Dunkeld, Perthshire

Map Ref: 2B1

★★★★

GUEST HOUSE

Birnam Wood House
Perth Road, Birnam by Dunkeld, Perthshire, PH8 0BH
Tel:01350 727782 Fax:01350 727196
Email:bob@birnamwoodhouse.co.uk
Web:www.birnamwoodhouse.co.uk

We are determined that your stay at our award winning guest house will be a delight, from the crisp white linen to the period furniture, everything is designed to help you unwind while enjoying the stunning Perthshire countryside.

4 rooms, some en-suite, Open Jan-Dec, B&B per person, single from £35.00, double from £25.00.

Blair Atholl, Perthshire

Map Ref: 4C12

★★★

GUEST HOUSE

The Firs
St Andrews Crescent, Blair Atholl, by Pitlochry PH18 5TA
Tel:01796 481256   Fax:01796 481661
Email:kirstie@firs-blairatholl.co.uk
Web:www.firs-blairatholl.co.uk

Friendly country home with half an acre of garden in a tranquil setting. Well situated in Highland Perthshire, close to Blair Castle and ideal as a base for either touring or a relaxing holiday.

4 rooms, all en-suite, Open Jan-Dec, B&B per person, single from £27.50, double from £22.50.

★★★

GUEST HOUSE

Ptarmigan House
The Terrace, Blair Atholl, Perthshire, PH18 5SZ
Tel/Fax:01796 481269
Email:lin@ptarmiganhouse.co.uk
Web:www.ptarmiganhouse.co.uk

Former Victorian shooting lodge in great setting, overlooking the hills and golf course. Not to be missed.

4 rooms, all en-suite, Open Jan-Dec excl Xmas, B&B per person, single from £35.00, double from £25.00.

VAT is shown at 17.5%: changes in this rate may affect prices.

Key to symbols is on back flap.

Blairgowrie, Perthshire   **Map Ref: 2B1**

★★★

B&B

Eildon Bank

118 Perth Road, Blairgowrie, Perthshire, PH10 6ED
Tel/Fax:01250 873648
Email:emurray@eildonbank.freeserve.co.uk

This comfortable family home is near to the town centre with its shops, hotels and variety of eating establishments. The bedrooms have either ensuite or private facilities, remote control TV's, hairdryers and hospitality trays. Good base for touring and enjoying the many outdoor activities that Perthshire has to offer. These include walking, skiing, golfing and fishing. Ample private parking.

3 rooms, some en-suite, Open Jan-Dec excl Xmas, B&B per person, double £19.00-22.00.

★★★

B&B

Garfield House B&B

Perth Road, Blairgowrie, Perthshire, PH10 6ED
Tel:01250 872999
Email:info@garfieldhouse.com
Web:www.garfieldhouse.com

Attractive detached Victorian house on main A93 with large off road parking and in walking distance of town centre. Ideal central base for touring, golfing etc.

4 rooms, some en-suite, Open Jan-Dec excl Xmas/New Year, B&B per person, single from £20.00, double from £20.00.

★★★★

B&B

Gilmore House

Perth Road, Blairgowrie, Perthshire, PH10 6EJ
Tel:01250 872791
Email:jill@gilmorehouse.co.uk
Web:www.gilmorehouse.co.uk

Comfortable bedrooms in this recently refurbished traditional stone built house on the outskirts of Blairgowrie. The three bedrooms are en suite, have colour TVs, radios, hair driers and hospitality trays. Gilmore House is ideally situated for ski-ing at Glenshee, the whisky and castle trails, fishing on the rivers Ericht and Tay. Plenty golf courses in the area. Private parking.

3 rooms, all en-suite, Open Jan-Dec excl Xmas/New Year, B&B per person, single from £27.00, double from £22.00.

★★★

B&B

Holmrigg Bed & Breakfast

Wester Essendy, Blairgowrie, Perthshire, PH10 6RD
Tel/Fax:01250 884309
Email:info@holmrigg.co.uk
Web:www.holmrigg-bnb.co.uk

A warm welcome awaits you in this modern bungalow (4 miles from Blairgowrie) which has wonderful views from the spacious lounge with its open fire. There are 4 ensuite bedrooms, one on the ground floor, the others (one with a 4 poster bed) on the first floor. Evening meals are available by prior arrangement. This is an ideal location for visiting many historic attractions and participating in many outdoor activities.

4 rooms, all en-suite, Open Mar-mid Dec, B&B per person, single £22.00-27.00, double £22.00-25.00, BB & Eve.Meal from £33.00-38.00.

Important: Prices stated are estimates and may be subject to amendments

Blairgowrie, Perthshire Map Ref: 2B1

IVYBANK GUEST HOUSE
*Boat Brae, Blairgowrie, Perthshire PH10 7BH
Tel/Fax: 01250 873 056
e.mail: ivybankguesthouse@btinternet.com
Web: www.ivybank-guest-house.co.uk
Ivybank offers a relaxed and friendly home from home atmosphere.
A non smoking guest house with a large car park and a
garage for motorbikes. Ivybank has two double rooms with
four poster beds, three twin rooms and a family room.
All ensuite except one twin which has private facilities.*

★★★★

**GUEST
HOUSE**

Ivybank Guest House

Boat Brae, Blairgowrie, Perthshire, PH10 7BH
Tel/Fax:01250 873056
Email:ivybankguesthouse@btinternet.com
Web:www.ivybank-guest-house.co.uk

Family run guest house where owners Chris and Marie-Celine provide a
relaxed and friendly atmosphere. There is ample off road parking and a
garage for motorbikes. Ivybank is an ideal base for the many attractions
that Perthshire has to offer, including Glamis and Blair Castle. Also
fishing for trout and salmon on the River Tay. In addition there are
places to walk and over 60 golf courses within an hour's drive, including
Gleneagles and St Andrews.

6 rooms, Open Jan-Dec, B&B per person twin/double £25.00-30.00, family room
£30.00. Children under 12 half price.

★★★

**GUEST
HOUSE**

The Laurels

Golf Course Road, Blairgowrie, Perthshire PH10 6LH
Tel/Fax:01250 874920
Email:laurels-blairgowrie@talk21.com
Web:http://member.visitscotland.com/laurelsguesthouse

Originally a farmhouse dating from 1873, set back from main road, on
outskirts of Blairgowrie with own large garden and ample parking.
Rosemount Golf Course is a short walk away with a selection of 20 golf
courses nearby. Ideal base for touring the beautiful Perthshire
countryside. Fishing, shooting, mountaineering, ski-ing, pony trekking all
in the local area.

6 rooms, some en-suite, Open mid Jan-mid Nov, B&B per person, single from
£22.00, double from £22.00, BB & Eve.Meal from £35.00.

**AWAITING
INSPECTION**

Royal Hotel

53 Allan Street, Blairgowrie, Perthshire, PH10 6AB
Tel:01250 872226 Fax:01250 875905
Email:visit@theroyalhotel.org.uk
Web:www.theroyalhotel.org.uk

27 rooms, all ensuite, Open Jan-Dec, B&B per person, single from £35.00, double
from £25.00.Room Only per night, single from £30.00, double from £40.00.

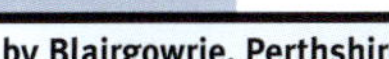

---

by Blairgowrie, Perthshire Map Ref: 2B1

★★★

B&B

Alcantara

Bamff View, New Alyth, Blairgowrie, Perthshire, PH11 8NG
Tel:01828 633304
Email:eejdavidson@aol.com

Modern detached bungalow with lovely open views, on outskirts of
village. 4.5 miles from Blairgowrie. Convenient for 3 golf courses. Ideal
for touring the glens. Private parking.

2 rooms, all en-suite, Open Mar-Nov, B&B per person, single from £25.00, double
from £20.00.

VAT is shown at 17.5%: changes in this rate may affect prices. | *Key to symbols is on back flap.*

by Blairgowrie, Perthshire

Map Ref: 2B1

B&B

Bankhead Bed & Breakfast
Clunie, Blairgowrie, Perthshire, PH10 6SG
Tel/Fax:01250 884281
Email:ian@ihwightman.freeserve.co.uk
Web:www.bankheadbnb.co.uk

Farmhouse on working family farm between Loch Marlee and Clunie. Central base for touring, local fishing, golfing and skiing, osprey spotting at local Lowes Nature Reserve. Traditional farmhouse cooking and baking.

2 rooms, all en-suite, Open Jan-Dec excl Xmas/New Year, B&B per person, single from £25.00, double from £22.00.

B&B

Ridgeway B&B
Wester Essendy, by Blairgowrie, Perthshire PH10 6RA
Tel:01250 884734   Fax:01250 884735
Email:Pam.Mathews@btinternet.com
Web:www.ridgewayb-b.co.uk

A warm welcome awaits. Detached bungalow with garden in peaceful country location. Views overlooking the spectacular scenery of Loch Marlee and surrounding farmland to the Grampian mountains. Only 3 miles from Blairgowrie. Ideal base for touring, hillwalking, golfing and fishing.

2 rooms, all en-suite, Open Jan-Dec, B&B per person, single from £28.00, double from £28.00.

Brechin, Angus

Map Ref: 4F12

B&B

Blibberhill Farmhouse
Blibberhill Farm, by Brechin, Angus, DD9 6TH
Tel/Fax:01307 830323
Email:wendysstewart@aol.com
Web:www.blibberhill.co.uk

Stone built farmhouse in peaceful situation on mixed working farm between Forfar and Brechin. Homemade preserves and home baking and cooking. No smoking. Children welcome.

3 rooms, all en-suite, Open Jan-Dec, B&B per person, single from £25.00, double from £22.50, BB & Eve.Meal from £35.00.

Burntisland, Fife

Map Ref: 2C4

B&B

Gruinard
148 Kinghorn Road, Burntisland, Fife, KY3 9JU
Tel:01592 873877
Email:gruinard@dircon.co.uk
Web:www.gruinardguesthouse.co.uk

Very well appointed traditional stone cottage (1904). Have breakfast in our conservatory overlooking the interesting and colourful garden. One room with extensive view across the Firth of Forth to the Edinburgh skyline. 30 minutes from Edinburgh and St Andrew's by car and easy access to Scotland's motorway system.

2 rooms, all en-suite, Open Mar-Nov, B&B per person, single from £35.00, double from £25.00.

Important: Prices stated are estimates and may be subject to amendments

Carnoustie, Angus — Map Ref: 2D2

THE OLD MANOR
PANBRIDE, CARNOUSTIE, ANGUS DD7 6JP
TEL: 01241 854804 FAX: 01241 855327
E.MAIL: STAY@OLDMANORCARNOUSTIE.COM
WEB: WWW.OLDMANORCARNOUSTIE.COM
Beautifully restored manse dating from 1765 overlooking the town of Carnoustie and coast of Fife. The large individually decorated en-suite bedrooms are complete with TV, tea, coffee and refreshments. Salmon fishing on the River South Esk and golf tee times on any of the local courses can be arranged.

★★★★

B&B

The Old Manor
Panbride, Carnoustie, DD7 6JP
Tel:01241 854804 Fax:01241 855327
Email:stay@oldmanorcarnoustie.com
Web:www.oldmanorcarnoustie.com

Spacious ensuite rooms in fully restored country house. Peaceful location close to Carnoustie. Convenient for golf, beaches and Angus glens. Non smoking house. Evening meals by arrangement using fresh local produce wherever possible.

5 rooms, some en-suite, Open Jan-Dec excl Xmas/New Year, B&B per person, single £35.00-45.00, double £27.50-35.00.

★★★★

B&B

Park House
12 Park Avenue, Carnoustie, Angus, DD7 7JA
Tel/Fax:01241 852101
Email:parkhouse@bbcarnoustie.fsnet.co.uk
Web:www.bbcarnoustie.fsnet.co.uk

A detached Victorian house in its own walled garden. Championship golf course and beach nearby. Private parking. Quiet location. Smoke free house.

4 rooms, some en-suite, Open Jan-Dec excl Xmas/New Year, B&B per person, single from £30.00, double from £30.00.

Coaltown of Wemyss, Fife — Map Ref: 2C3

★★★

B&B

Law View B&B
68 Millburn Avenue, Coaltown of Balgonie, Fife KY7 6HR
Tel:01592 774197
Email:bobpenn68@yahoo.co.uk
Web:www.stayinfife.co.uk

Bungalow accommodation in a purpose built two bedroomed extension. Comfortable ensuite rooms, modern breakfast area, private parking and attractive views of the local countryside. Situated in golfing country with up to 60 golf courses between St Andrews and Gleneagles. Charming harbour villages on the nearby Fife coast. Edinburgh 32 Miles, St Andrews 23, Perth 32, and Dundee 32 miles.

2 rooms, all ensuite, Open Jan-Dec, B&B per person, double £20.00-25.00.

Crail, Fife — Map Ref: 2D3

★★★

GUEST HOUSE

Caiplie House
53 High Street, Crail, Fife, KY10 3RA
Tel:01333 450564
Email:mail@caipliehouse.com
Web:www.caipliehouse.com

Very comfortable and friendly guest house renowned for its home cooking, with restricted table licence. On main street of fishing village near coastal path and picturesque harbour. Some rooms with sea views.

6 rooms, en-suite, Open Mar-Nov, B&B per person, single from £30.00, double from £25.00, BB & Eve.Meal from £35.00.

VAT is shown at 17.5%: changes in this rate may affect prices.

Key to symbols is on back flap.

Crail, Fife

Map Ref: 2D3

★★★

**GUEST
HOUSE**

The Honeypot Guest House & Tearoom
6 High Street South, Crail, Fife, KY10 3TD
Tel/Fax:01333 450935
Email:info@honeypotcrail.co.uk
Web:www.honeypotcrail.co.uk

The Honeypot is a traditional family run Guest House, providing clean comfortable accommodation in the picturesque fishing village of Crail; situated in the East Neuk of Fife ten miles from St Andrews. There are 25 Golf Courses/Links within 1 hours drive of Crail but the area is also popular with Walkers, Nature Lovers, Cyclists and Bird Watchers.

3 rooms, en-suite/priv.facilities, Open Jan-Dec, B&B per person £25.00 (Single supplement may apply).

Crieff, Perthshire

Map Ref: 2A2

★★★

B&B

The Carrick B & B
57 Burrell Street, Crieff, Perthshire, PH7 4GD
Tel:01764 656595
Email:Crieffcarricks@aol.com
Web:www.thecarrick.co.uk

Maxine & Mike welcome you to their home which is situated in picturesque Crieff within easy walking distance of the local shops and eating establishments, Crieff is ideally situated for walking, fishing, golfing and touring scenic Perthshire. All rooms have ensuite facilities, remote control TV's, CD radios, hairdryers and hospitality trays.

3 rooms. Open Jan-Dec. B&B per person, single from £23.00, double from £23.00.

★★★

B&B

Concraig Farm
Crieff, Perthshire, PH7 4HH
Tel:01764 653237 Fax:01764 650403
Email:scott@concraigfarm.fsnet.co.uk
Web:www.concraigfarm-holidays.com

Comfortable farmhouse with spacious rooms, including 1 en suite, peacefully situated just outside Crieff. Ideal location for golfing & touring.

3 rooms, some en-suite, Open Jan-Dec, B&B per person, single from £22.00, double from £18.00.

★★★

**GUEST
HOUSE**

Galvelbeg House
Perth Road, Crieff, Perthshire, PH7 3EQ
Tel:01764 655061 Fax:01764 650363
Email:mark@philp1984.fsnet.co.uk
Web:www.galvelbeghouse.co.uk

A warm welcome awaits you at this detached stonebuilt villa, conveniently situated near the town centre with all its amenities. A good base for touring, horseriding and golf, with many local courses. Ample car parking at the rear.

4 rooms en-suite, 1 private facilities, Open Jan-Dec, B&B per person, single from £25.00, double from £20.00.

Important: Prices stated are estimates and may be subject to amendments

Crieff, Perthshire | **Map Ref: 2A2**

KINGARTH

Perth Road, Crieff PH7 3EQ
Tel: 01764 652060 Fax: 01764 655302
e.mail: info@kingarthguesthouse.com
Web: www.kingarthguesthouse.com

Set in the heart of Scotland, in the bustling market town of Crieff, Kingarth is a comfortable and friendly guest house with 6 ensuite bedrooms, guest lounge and sunny conservatory. Surrounded by mature gardens and superb views over Strathearn to the Ochil Hills. Ample parking available on site.

★★★

**GUEST
HOUSE**

Kingarth
Perth Road, Crieff, Perthshire, PH7 3EQ
Tel:01764 652060 Fax:01764 655302
Email:info@kingarthguesthouse.com
Web:www.kingarthguesthouse.com
Set in the heart of Scotland, in the bustling town of Crieff, Kingarth is a homely Victorian guest house set in mature gardens, with stunning views overlooking the Strathearn Vale and Ochil Hills. The house has a relaxed, comfortable atmosphere with a cosy residents' lounge, sunny conservatory and dining room. The letting rooms are in the garden wing of the house, and are all ground floor, ensuite and non-smoking. There is ample parking.

6 rooms, all en-suite, Open Jan-Dec, B&B per person, single from £30.00-35.00, double from £25.00.

★★

**SMALL
HOTEL**

Leven House Hotel
Comrie Road, Crieff, PH7 4BA
Tel:01764 652529

Small family run hotel near town centre serving Scottish high teas. Ideally situated for touring and golf. Spacious car park.

10 rooms, Open Feb-Nov, B&B per person single from £25.00. double from £25.00.

MERLINDALE

Perth Road, Crieff PH7 3EQ Tel/Fax: 01764 655205
e.mail: merlin.dale@virgin.net Web: www.merlindale.co.uk
Merlindale is a luxurious Georgian house situated close to the town centre. All bedrooms are ensuite (2 with sunken bathrooms) and have tea/coffee making facilities. We have a jacuzzi available plus garden, ample parking and satellite television. We also have a Scottish library for the use of our guests. Cordon Bleu cooking is our speciality. A warm welcome awaits you in this non-smoking house.

★★★★

B&B

Merindale B&B
Perth Road, Crieff, Perthshire, PH7 3EQ
Tel/Fax:01764 655205
Email:merlin.dale@virgin.net
Web:www.merlindale.co.uk
John and Jackie provide a genuinely warm welcome at their comfortable family home with many touches of luxury. 6 languages spoken. By advance arrangement we offer a delicious four course dinner (Jackie is cordon bleu trained) and provide complimentary wine & liqueur. Extensive library with emphasis on Scotland. Jacuzzi bath. Relax and enjoy.

3 rooms, all en-suite, Open Feb-Dec excl Xmas/New Year, B&B per person, single from £45.00, double from £30.00.

VAT is shown at 17.5%: changes in this rate may affect prices. | *Key to symbols is on back flap.*

Crieff, Perthshire

Map Ref: 2A2

★★★

B&B

Somerton House
Turret Bank, Crieff, Perthshire, PH7 4JN
Tel:01764 652222 Mob:0789 999 6017
Email:enquiries@somertonhouse.net

3 rooms, all en-suite, Open Jan-Dec excl Xmas/New Year, B&B per person from £20.00.

Friendly bed and breakfast within 15 minutes walk of town centre. All rooms, including the family room, have a remote control TV, radio, hair dryer and a hospitality tray. Ideal touring base. Home of the Turretbank Cavalier King Charles spaniels.

Dundee, Angus

Map Ref: 2C2

★★★

B&B

Anlast Three Chimneys House
379 Arbroath Road, Dundee, DD4 7SQ
Tel:01382 456710
Email:angus.threechimneys@hotmail.co.uk
Web:www.visitscotland.com

3 rooms, some en-suite, Open Jan-Dec, B&B per person, single from £31.50.

A warm, friendly welcome awaits you at this attractive large detached villa on the east side of town, only 2 miles from city centre, near to busy bus route. All bedrooms have private shower/bath, colour TV, central heating and tea/coffee making facilties. A no smoking house, which has private parking, beautiful view and gardens.

ARDMOY
359 Arbroath Road, Dundee DD4 7SQ
TEL/FAX: 01382 453249
E-mail: ardmoy@btopenworld.com
Friendly welcome. Ample off-street parking. Near bus-stop for city centre. On tourist routes North- A92 to Carnoustie and Aberdeen. Near plenty Golf Courses and tourist attractions in Dundee.

★★★

B&B

Ardmoy B&B
359 Arbroath Road, Dundee, Angus, DD4 7SQ
Tel/Fax:01382 453249
Email:ardmoy@btopenworld.com

4 rooms, some en-suite, Open Jan-Dec, B&B per person, single from £20.00, double from £20.00, BB & Eve.Meal from £26.00.

Spacious stone built house in own garden on direct route to centre. Private parking. Close to Discovery and city centre. On tourist route A92 North to Carnoustie and Aberdeen. Evening meal by prior arrangement. En-suite rooms available.

★★★

B&B

Ashvilla
216 Arbroath Road, Dundee, Angus, DD4 7RZ
Tel/Fax:01382 450831
Email:ashvilla_guesthouse@talk21.com

3 rooms, some en-suite, Open Jan-Dec, B&B per person, single from £26.00, double £20.00-23.00.

Comfortable detached, stone-built house ideally situated on main route for both city centre and surrounding countryside. Private off-street parking, children welcome. Pets by arrangement. Guests and their children are welcome to relax in our spacious rear garden.

Important: Prices stated are estimates and may be subject to amendments

Dundee, Angus
Map Ref: 2C2

★★★

GUEST HOUSE

Errolbank Guest House
9 Dalgleish Road, Dundee, Angus, DD4 7JN
Tel/Fax:01382 462118

6 rooms, 5 en-suite, Open Jan-Dec excl Xmas/New Year, B&B per person, single from £26.00, double from £25.00.

Family run Victorian villa. All double/twin rooms en-suite. 2km east of Tay Bridge/city centre. Off main road near bus routes. No smoking throughout. Private parking.

Dunfermline, Fife
Map Ref: 2B4

★★★

B&B

Hopetoun Lodge
141 Halbeath Road, Dunfermline, Fife, KY11 4LA
Tel:01383 620906
Email:hopetounlodge@aol.com
Web:www.hopetounlodge.co.uk

3 rooms, 2 en-suite, Open Jan-Dec, B&B per person, single from £25.00, double from £24.00.

1920's bungalow with spacious rooms and Art Deco bathroom. Conveniently located for access to M90 and only 25 min by train from Edinburgh. Strictly non-smoking.

★★★

B&B

Roscobie Farmhouse B&B
Roscobie Farm, Dunfermline, Fife, KY12 0SG
Tel/Fax:01383 731571

2 rooms, some en-suite, Open Apr-Apr, B&B per person, single £20.00-25.00, double £20.00-25.00.

Traditional farmhouse, set on a 400 acre upland Beef and Sheep farm. Extensive rural views over Fife and southward to the Lothians. Ideal location for exploring central Scotland, only 3 miles from junction 4 on the M90 motorway.

Dunkeld, Perthshire
Map Ref: 2B1

★★★★

B&B

The Bridge Bed & Breakfast
10 Bridge Street, Dunkeld, Perthshire, PH8 0AH
Tel/Fax:01350 727068
Email:morans@thebridge-dunkeld.co.uk
Web:www.thebridge-dunkeld.co.uk

3 rooms, all en-suite, Open Jan-Dec, B&B per person, single £30.00-45.00, double/twin £28.00-35.00.

Welcome to the Bridge a beautiful restored Georgian home situated in the heart of historic Dunkeld. Ideally located for fishing, golf, cycling, walking, weddings, and enjoying the many attractions Perthshire has to offer. We will be happy to advise you. All rooms have RcTV's, hospitality trays and ensuite facilities. Please note that we are strictly non smoking.

★★★★

B&B

The Pend
5 Brae Street, Dunkeld, Perthshire, PH8 0BA
Tel:01350 727586 Fax:01350 727173
Email:molly@thepend.sol.co.uk
Web:www.thepend.com

3 rooms, Open Jan-Dec, B&B per person from £35.00, BB & Eve.Meal from £60.00. 50% discount for children aged 3-11 years.

Situated in the centre of Dunkeld, The Pend is a charming Georgian house full of character and retaining many original architectural features. Tastefully decorated and furnished using many fine antiques. Facilities include wash hand basin, shaver socket, hospitality tray, luxury bathrobe and colour television. Two large bathrooms.

VAT is shown at 17.5%: changes in this rate may affect prices.

Key to symbols is on back flap.

Forfar, Angus Map Ref: 2D1

Alton Bed and Breakfast

18 Wyllie Street, Forfar, Angus DD8 3DN
Tel: 01307 465193 e.mail: margaret@welcome2alton.com
web: www.welcome2alton.com

Ian and Margaret would like to wish you a warm Scottish welcome to their 19th Century Victorian house, which maintains many original and interesting features. These superior spacious rooms which are all en-suite have colour TV, radio, tea/coffee, trouser press/iron, hairdryer etc. Town centre 5 minutes walk. Easy access to A90. Further details and brochure on request.

B&B

Alton Bed and Breakfast

18 Wyllie Street, Forfar, Angus, DD8 3DN
Tel:01307 465193
Email:margaret@welcome2alton.com
Web:www.welcome2alton.com

Recommended by 'Which Holiday Magazine' 2003, Alton offers a superior quality of comfort and hospitality. This highly commended en-suite accommodation includes residents dining-room and lounge. The beautiful Victorian room furnishings boast a splendid 4 poster king-size bed. The extremely well maintained rooms have all necessary facilities, and pamper yourselves with the complimentary extras provided. Discounts on weekly bookings.

2 rooms, all en-suite, Open Jan-Dec excl Xmas/New Year, B&B per person, single from £28.00, double from £23.00.

B&B

Atholl Cottage B&B

2 Robertson Terrace, Forfar, Angus, DD8 3JN
Tel:01307 465755
Email:info@athollcottage.com
Web:www.athollcottage.com

Situated in a quiet residential area, yet only 5 minutes walk to town centre, a warm welcome assured here. Off road parking available. Open all year.

3 rooms, 2 en-suite, Open Jan-Dec, B&B per person, single from £29.00, double from £25.00.

Farmhouse Bed & Breakfast

WEST MAINS OF TURIN, FORFAR DD8 2TE
Telephone: 01307 830229 Fax: 01307 830229
e.mail: cjolly3@aol.com Web: www.turinfarmhouse.com

Family run stock farm has a panoramic view over Rescobie Loch. Warm welcome awaits you. Good home cooking and baking ensures guests have an enjoyable stay. Ideal area for golfing (20 mins from Carnoustie), hillwalking, horse-riding, visiting Castles, National Trust properties and gardens. Snooker for evening entertainment.

B&B

Farmhouse Bed & Breakfast

West Mains of Turin, Forfar, Angus, DD8 2TE
Tel/Fax:01307 830229
Email:cjolly3@aol.com
Web:www.turinfarmhouse.com

Farmhouse on working stock farm, 4 miles (6kms) east of Forfar. In elevated position with panoramic views southwards over Rescobie Loch. Historic houses and plenty of golf courses nearby.

3 rooms, en-suite + priv.facilities, Open Mar-Oct, B&B per person, single from £25.00, double from £23.00.

Important: Prices stated are estimates and may be subject to amendments

Forfar, Angus
Map Ref: 2D1

★★★

B&B

Whinney-Knowe
8 Dundee Street, Letham, Angus, DD8 2PQ
Tel:01307 818288
Email:whinneyknowe@btinternet.com
Web:www.whinneyknowe.co.uk

A warm Scottish welcome awaits you in our home situated in a friendly village. Hotel and pub five minutes walk. Golfing, fishing and scenic walks within a four mile radius. Good bus service to nearest towns. Own dining and TV lounge. Evening meals by prior arrangement.

3 rooms, some en-suite, Open Jan-Dec, B&B per person, single from £20.00, double from £18.00, BB & Eve.Meal from £30.00.

Forgandenny, Perthshire
Map Ref: 2B2

★★★★

B&B

Battledown Bed & Breakfast
Off Station Road, Forgandenny, Perthshire, PH2 9EL
Tel/Fax:01738 812471
Email:i.dunsire@btconnect.com
Web:www.battledownbb.co.uk

Quiet, comfortable cottage in rural village yet only seven miles from Perth. All 3 bedrooms are on the ground floor and all have en suite facilities, RcTVs, hair driers and hospitality trays. Good local eating establishments. Private parking. Ideal for all outdoor pursuits. No smoking.

3 rooms, all en-suite, Open Jan-Dec, B&B per person, single £30.00-35.00, double from £25.00-30.00.

Inverkeithing, Fife
Map Ref: 2B4

THE ROODS GUEST HOUSE
16 BANNERMAN AVE, INVERKEITHING KY11 1NG
Telephone/Fax: 01383 415049
e.mail: isobelmarley@hotmail.com   Web: www.theroods.com

Quietly situated yet only one minute from railway station. The Roods two ground floor bedrooms are attractively decorated and offer excellent facilities such as telephones and mini fridges ensuring guests want for nothing. The luxurious lounge leads onto a dining conservatory where guests can enjoy breakfast overlooking the garden.

★★★

B&B

The Roods Guest House
16 Bannerman Avenue, Inverkeithing, Fife, KY11 1NG
Tel:01383 415049
Email:isobelmarley@hotmail.com
Web:www.theroods.com

Quietly secluded family home. Close to rail station and M90. Well appointed bedrooms offering mini office and direct dial telephones. Evening meal by arrangement. Both rooms on ground floor.

2 rooms, all en-suite, Open Jan-Dec, B&B per person, single from £25.00, double from £25.00.

Kinross, Perthshire
Map Ref: 2B3

★★★★

B&B

Burnbank
79 Muirs, Kinross, Perthshire, KY13 8AZ
Tel:01577 861931
Email:bandb@burnbank-kinross.co.uk
Web:www.burnbank-kinross.co.uk

This delightful home, formerly a mill shop, is situated at the edge of town and surrounded by open farmland. Restful colours, quality fabrics and linen characterise the rooms. The comfortable ensuite bedrooms, including a ground floor double, are well equipped with TV, video, tea and coffee and have fine outlooks to the Lomond Hills. Fresh fruit and home baked bread add to the enjoyment of the delicious breakfast.

3 rooms, all en-suite, Open Jan-Dec, B&B per person, single from £35.00, double from £30.00.

VAT is shown at 17.5%: changes in this rate may affect prices. | *Key to symbols is on back flap.*

Mawcarse House

Milnathort, Kinross-shire KY13 9SJ
Tel/Fax: 01577 862220
e.mail: wsyoung@farmersweekly.net
Web: www.perthshires-best.co.uk

Set within five hundred acres of farmland which is centrally situated and easily accessible to Edinburgh, St Andrews, Perth and Glasgow. Traditional farmhouse with en-suites recently added. Many Golf Courses close by as is fishing, gliding, horseriding and cycling facilities. RSPB and walks also to hand.
Whisky trails and boat trips to Loch Leven Castle. Numerous excellent eating places with the new ferry terminal at Rosyth only a short drive away as is Edinburgh Airport.
A real Scottish breakfast served every morning with local produce used when available.

★★★★

B&B

Mawcarse House

Mawcarse Farm, Milnathort, Kinross-shire, KY13 9SJ
Tel/Fax:01577 862220
Email:wsyoung@farmersweekly.net
Web:www.perthshires-best.co.uk

Spacious and comfortable family farmhouse with fine open views. Peacefully situated, yet only minutes from M90. Next to designated country walk/cycle route. Golf, fishing, RSPB all nearby.

3 rooms, en-suite, Open Jan-Dec excl Xmas/New Year, B&B per person, single from £35.00, double from £30.00.

★★★★

B&B

A Haven Bed & Breakfast

288 High Street, Kirkcaldy, Fife, KY1 1LB
Tel/Fax:01592 267779
Email:gina@ahaven.co.uk
Web:www.ahaven.co.uk

Furnished to high standard, all rooms have en-suite facilities, hairdryer, widescreen TV, DVD player, free view satellite system and tea and coffee making facilities. Private parking to the rear. We are centrally situated, within walking distance of rail and bus stations, making this an ideal base for touring central Scotland and for business trips.

3 rooms, all ensuite. (1 dbl, 2 twns), Open Jan-Dec, B&B per person, single from £25.00, double from £22.00.

★★★

B&B

Annies'Lan

36 Bennochy Road, Kirkcaldy, Fife, KY2 5RB
Tel:01592 262231
Email:Lynmccuaig@aol.com

A traditional small B&B offering homely family-run accommodation. The two bedrooms are either ensuite or have private facilities, set in a quiet residential area with easy access to the Town centre.

2 rooms, some en-suite, Open Jan-Dec excl Xmas, B&B per person, single from £27.50, double from £22.50.

Important: Prices stated are estimates and may be subject to amendments

Kirkcaldy, Fife

Map Ref: 2C4

B&B ★★★★

North Hall
143 Victoria Road, Kirkcaldy, KY1 1DQ
Tel:01592 268864
Email:cairns@northhall.freeserve.co.uk
Web:www.northhall.co.uk

Former manse with original oak stairs and doors, open rear view over town and Firth of Forth Close to town centre. Ideal for touring Fife villages. Edinburgh 26 miles (42kms), 30minutes by train.

2 rooms, all en-suite, Open Jan-Dec excl Xmas/New Year, B&B per person, double from £25.00.

B&B ★★★

Scotties B&B
213 Nicol Street, Kirkcaldy, Fife, KY1 1PF
Tel:01592 268596
Email:bhscott43@msn.com/enquiries@scottiesbandb.co.uk
Web:www.scottiesbandb.co.uk

Comfortable personally run home, close to rail and bus station and within easy reach of High Street and other amenities. Off road private parking and all rooms and facilities on ground floor.

3 rooms, all en-suite, Open Jan-Dec excl Xmas/New Year, B&B per person, single from £28.00, double from £24.00.

Kirkmichael, Perthshire

Map Ref: 4D12

B&B ★★★★

Cruachan
Kirkmichael, Perthshire, PH10 7NZ
Tel:01250 881226
Email:vscotland@kirkmichael.net
Web:www.kirkmichael.net

Traditional Victorian country cottage overlooking River Ardle, quiet location close to village amenities. Rooms with ensuite & TVs. Personally run by Alan & Daphne we offer a varied a la carte dinner menu using fresh produce - WINNERS of the 1999 and 2001 Glenturret & Perthshire Tourist Board most enjoyable meal award. An ideal base for touring, with fishing, shooting, riding, walking & many visitor attractions nearby. Pets welcome.

3 rooms, some en-suite, Open Jan-Dec, B&B per person, single from £29.50, double from £24.50, BB & Eve.Meal from £36.50.

Kirriemuir, Angus

Map Ref: 2C1

B&B ★★

Crepto
1 Kinnordy Place, Kirriemuir, Angus, DD8 4JW
Tel:01575 572746
Email:davendjessma@easicom.com

A friendly welcome at this modern house in quiet cul-de-sac. Only 10 minutes walk from town centre. All rooms with TVs. Guests' lounge and tea-making facilities available. Ample private parking. Gateway to Angus glens.

3 rooms, Open Jan-Dec, B&B per person, single from £25.00, double from £25.00.

B&B ★★★★

Muirhouses Farm
Cortachy, Kirriemuir, Angus, DD8 4QG
Tel/Fax:01575 573128
Email:muirhousesfarm@farming.co.uk
Web:www.muirhousesfarm.co.uk

A warm welcome at this family B&B on a working farm set on the main route to Glens Prosen, Clova and Doll. Only 1 mile from Kirriemuir town centre and golf course.

3 rooms, 2 en-suite, 1 priv.facilities, closed Jan/Feb, B&B per person, single from £30.00, double from £25.00.

VAT is shown at 17.5%: changes in this rate may affect prices.

Key to symbols is on back flap.

Kirriemuir, Angus — Map Ref: 2C1

★★★★

B&B

Purgavie Farm
Lintrathen, by Kirriemuir, Angus, DD8 5HZ
Tel/Fax:01575 560213
Email:purgavie@aol.com
Web:www.purgavie.co.uk

A warm welcome in homely accommodation on our farm set in peaceful countryside with excellent views. All rooms have ensuite bathroom, TV and tea-making facilities. Good home cooking providing traditional Scottish Fayre. Fishing on Lintrathen Loch, pony trekking and hill-walking in Glen Isla. Glamis Castle 10 miles. Located 7 miles from Kirriemuir, follow the B951 to Glen Isla, farm signposted at roadside.

3 rooms, all en-suite, Open Jan-Dec, B&B per person, single from £27.00, double from £25.00, BB & Eve.Meal from £38.00.

Letham, Angus — Map Ref: 2D1

Woodville

Heathercroft, Guthrie Street, Letham, by Forfar, Angus DD8 2PS
Tel: 01307 818090 Mobile: 07765 387694

A warm welcome awaits you. Excellent food and accommodation. Bedrooms with wash-hand basin, tea facilities, TV. Two twin rooms are available. Letham is a village set in the middle of Angus. Excellent for touring Glens of Angus, Royal Deeside and Glamis. It is also near to new Pictavia Centre. Birdwatching, walks, fishing, golf, Pictish interest. Aberdeen, St Andrews, Edinburgh within easy reach. B&B from £22 pp twin/double. B&B from £24.00 pp single.

★★★

B&B

Woodville B&B
Heathercroft, Guthrie Street, Letham, by Forfar
Angus, DD8 2PS
Tel:01307 818090/07765 387694

A warm traditional Scottish welcome awaits in modern new house on the edge of the historic village of Letham. Ideal location for golf, fishing, walking, glens, castles (Glamis nearby) & birdwatching. Within easy distance of Dundee, Aberdeen, Edinburgh, Royal Deeside & St Andrews.

2 rooms, Open Jan-Dec, B&B per person, single from £24.00, double from £22.00.

nr Loch Leven, Fife — Map Ref: 2C3

NAVITIE HOUSE

Ballingry, Nr Loch Leven, Fife KY5 8LR
Tel: 01592 860295 Fax: 01592 869769
e.mail: navitie@aol.com
Web: http://navitiehouse.co.uk

This period mansion, set in four acres of ground, offers large rooms with ensuite facilities, home cooking, sauna and excellent views over the Forth Valley. Situated 4 miles off the M90 and only 30 minutes' drive from Edinburgh. Many golf courses within a short drive. B&B from £22 per night. Discounts for children.

★★

GUEST HOUSE

Navitie Guest House
nr Loch Leven, by Ballingry, Lochgelly, Fife KY5 8LR
Tel:01592 860295   Fax:01592 869769
Email:navitie@aol.com
Web:http://navitiehouse.co.uk

Detached 200-year-old house in its own grounds overlooking Ballingry village. Only 4 miles (6kms) from the Edinburgh to Perth motorway. Centrally located only 30/40 minutes drive from Edinburgh, Stirling, Perth and St Andrews. Evening meal by arrangement.

7 rooms, all en-suite, Open Jan-Dec, B&B per person, single from £25.00, double from £22.00, BB & Eve.Meal from £32.00.

Lundin Links, Fife

Map Ref: 2C3

★★★★

B&B

Sandilands B&B
20 Leven Road, Lundin Links, Leven, Fife, KY8 6AH
Tel/Fax:01333 329881
Email:sandilands@lundinlinks.wanadoo.co.uk
Web:www.sandilandsfife.co.uk

Victorian sandstone villa centrally located in the village of Lundin Links, gateway to the East Neuk of Fife. Several good hotels and pubs nearby. Largo Bay within walking distance. Fife coastal path provides excellent low-level walking. Prime golfing area. St Andrews 12 miles.

3 rooms, all en-suite, Open Jan-Dec, B&B per person, single from £30.00, double from £24.00.

Markinch, Fife

Map Ref: 2C3

★★★

B&B

Smythrum Farm
Markinch, Fife, KY7 6HB
Tel:01592 758372

Peaceful farmhouse adjacent to coaching route used by Mary Queen of Scots. Balgonie Castle, well known wedding venue, 0.5 mile (1km). Conveniently situated for Fife's famous golf courses and the scenic East Neuk of Fife. Edinburgh, Stirling, Perth and Dundee all in easy access for a day visit.

2 rooms, some en-suite, Open Mar-Nov, B&B per person, single from £20.00, double from £20.00.

Monifieth, by Dundee, Angus

Map Ref: 2D2

ASHLEA MANOR
2 Victoria Street, Monifieth, Dundee DD5 4HP
Tel: 01382 530015 Fax: 01382 528555
e.mail: enquiry@ashleamanor.co.uk
Web: www.ashleamanor.co.uk

Come and enjoy warm and welcoming hospitality in our large, elegant and comfortably appointed Victorian manor house with spacious and beautifully decorated rooms and pleasing lawns and garden. Our non-smoking home ensures all rooms are a pleasure to stay in with comfortable beds (kingsize/single) and pleasing surroundings.

★★★★

B&B

Ashlea Manor Guest House
2 Victoria Street, Monifieth, Dundee, DD5 4HP
Tel:01382 530015 Fax:01382 528555
Email:enquiry@ashleamanor.co.uk
Web:www.ashleamanor.co.uk

A detached Victorian mansion in a quiet area of Monifieth, which is well placed for touring the area, from St Andrews to Aberdeen. Many original features have been retained and refurbished to a high quality.

3 rooms (Doubles + Twin), en-suite or priv.bathrm. Open Jan-Dec. B&B per person, single from £30.00, double from £27.50. BB & Eve.Meal from £42.00.

Montrose, Angus

Map Ref: 4F12

★★★★

HOTEL

Best Western Links Hotel
Midlinks, Montrose, Angus, DD10 8RL
Tel:01674 671000 Fax:01674 672698
Email:reception@linkshotel.com
Web:www.bw-linkshotel.co.uk

A lovely hotel situated on the historic Midlinks. Within easy walking distance of the town centre, beaches and golf courses. Offering an all day 'Koffiehuis' with al-fresco terrace, a restaurant awarded with one AA Rosette and 25 individually designed bedrooms (some with balconies with views of the Midlinks). Enjoy excellent hospitality & a refreshing & relaxing stay.

25 rooms, all en-suite, Open Jan-Dec, B&B £29.00 per person per night sharing.

VAT is shown at 17.5%: changes in this rate may affect prices.

Key to symbols is on back flap.

Montrose, Angus   Map Ref: 4F12

Oaklands Guest House

10 Rossie Island Road, Montrose DD10 9NN
Tel/Fax: 01674 672018
e.mail: oaklands1@btopenworld.com
Web: www.nebsnow.com/oaklands

*Comfortable guest house within walking distance of town centre. Excellent breakfast
menu. All rooms ensuite with CTV. Off-street parking. Safe parking for
bicycles/motorcycles in locked garage. Golf links and beach nearby.
Children welcome. French and Dutch spoken.*

★★★

**GUEST
HOUSE**

Oaklands Guest House
10 Rossie Island Road, Montrose, DD10 9NN
Tel/Fax:01674 672018
Email:oaklands1@btopenworld.com
Web:http://www.nebsnow.com/oaklands

All rooms ensuite at this comfortable family house, within walking
distance of Montrose town centre. Parking. Secure parking for
motorcycles and bikes. Evening meals may be available. Please ask on
booking.

7 rooms, all en-suite, Open Jan-Dec, B&B per person, single from £25.00, double
from £22.00.

Perth   Map Ref: 2B2

★★★★

**GUEST
HOUSE**

Achnacarry Guest House
3 Pitcullen Crescent, Perth, PH2 7HT
Tel:01738 621421
Email:info@achnacarry.co.uk
Web:www.achnacarry.co.uk

Victorian dwelling house located a ten minute walk from city centre. We
offer warm hospitality in true Scottish tradition, in tastefully decorated
surroundings. En-suite rooms, including one on ground floor. Ample off
street parking. An ideal base for visiting the many attractions in the
area, and exploring the Central & Highland areas of Bonnie Scotland.
Golfers welcome, clubs available. See Website for seasonal offers.

4 rooms, all en-suite, Open Jan-Dec excl New Year, B&B per person, single £25.00-
30.00, double £22.50-27.50.

★★★★

**GUEST
HOUSE**

Ackinnoull Guest House
5 Pitcullen Crescent, Perth, PH2 7HT
Tel:01738 634165
Web:www.ackinnoull.com

Beautifully decorated Victorian semi-villa on the outskirts of town.
Private parking on premises. 'Perth in Bloom' winners, as picturesque
inside as out. Special rates for bookings of 3 days or more.

4 rooms, all en-suite, Open Jan-Dec, B&B per person, single from £25.00, double
from £20.00.

★★★

**GUEST
HOUSE**

Albert Villa Guest House
63 Dunkeld Road, Perth, PH1 5RP
Tel:01738 622730   Fax:01738 451182
Email:caroline@albertvilla.co.uk
Web:www.albertvilla.co.uk

Caroline and Alistair welcome you to their home which is situated near to
the Sports Centre and within walking distance of the city centre with its
variety of eating establishments to suit all tastes. Perth is an ideal base
for touring scenic Perthshire and enjoying the many outdoor activities
available in the area - fishing, golfing, walking to name but a few.

10 rooms, some en-suite, Open Jan-Dec, B&B per person, single from £22.00,
double from £27.00.

Important: Prices stated are estimates and may be subject to amendments

Perth

| Perth | Map Ref: 2B2 |

GUEST HOUSE ★★★★

Arisaig Guest House
4 Pitcullen Crescent, Perth, PH2 7HT
Tel:01738 628240 Fax:01738 638521
Email:mail@arisaigonline.co.uk
Web:www.arisaigonline.co.uk

Comfortable family run guest house, with off street parking. Close to city's many facilities. Local touring base. Ground floor bedroom.

5 rooms, all en-suite, Open Jan-Dec, B&B per person, single from £25.00-30.00, double £25.00, twin £27.50.

B&B ★★★

Beeches Guest House
2 Comely Bank, Perth, PH2 7HU
Tel:01738 624486 Fax:01738 643382
Email:enquiries@beeches-guest-house.co.uk
Web:www.beeches-guest-house.co.uk

Semi-detached villa, with ample car parking, conveniently situated on the A94 tourist route. Four of the bedrooms (including singles) have en suite facilities and all the rooms have a RC TV, hairdryer and hospitality tray. The guest's lounge has satellite TV and a video.

4 rooms, some en-suite, Open Jan-Dec, B&B per person, single from £22.00, double from £44.00 for 2 people.

GUEST HOUSE ★★★★

Beechgrove Guest House
Dundee Road, Perth, PH2 7AQ
Tel/Fax:01738 636147
Email:beechgroveg.h@sol.co.uk
Web:www.smoothhound.co.uk/hotels/beechgr

Listed building, former manse (Rectory) set in extensive grounds. Peaceful, yet only a few minutes walk from the city centre. Close to local attractions e.g. Scone Palace, Branklyn Gardens, Blackwatch Museum, new Perth Concert Mall just over bridge. Many award winning restaurants closeby. GlenTurret Tourism award winner. Non smoking establishment.

8 rooms, all en-suite, Open Jan-Dec, B&B per person, single from £35.00, double from £30.00.

GUEST HOUSE ★★★

Clunie Guest House
12 Pitcullen Crescent, Perth, PH2 7HT
Tel:01738 623625
Email:ann@clunieguesthouse.co.uk
Web:www.clunieguesthouse.co.uk

A warm welcome awaits you at Clunie Guest House which is situated on the A94 Coupar Angus road. There is easy access to the city centre with all its amenities including a variety of eating establishments. Alternatively, an evening meal can be provided if it is booked in advance. All rooms ensuite.

7 rooms, all en-suite, Open Jan-Dec, B&B per person, single from £25.00, double from £24.00, Room Only double from £40.00 , BB & Eve.Meal from £40.00.

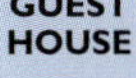

B&B ★★★

Comely Bank Cottage
19 Pitcullen Crescent, Perth, PH2 7HT
Tel:01738 631118 Fax:01738 571245
Email:comelybankcott@hotmail.com
Web:www.comelybankcottage.co.uk

Conveniently situated only ½ mile from city centre and all local amenities. All bedrooms are ensuite. An ideal base for touring Scotland. Friendly welcome assured.

3 rooms, all en-suite, Open Jan-Dec excl Xmas/New Year, B&B per person, single £25.00-30.00, double £20.00-25.00.

VAT is shown at 17.5%: changes in this rate may affect prices. | *Key to symbols is on back flap.*

Perth

Map Ref: 2B2

★★★

GUEST HOUSE

The Gables
24-26 Dunkeld Road, Perth, PH1 5RW
Tel:01738 624717
Email:gablesguesthouse@btconnect.com
Web:www.thegablesguesthouse.com

Stone built house on main road ½ mile (1km) north of Perth city centre. Close to sports centre, swimming pool and local golf course. Off road parking. Restricted hotel license.

7 rooms, some en-suite, Open Jan-Dec excl Xmas/New Year, B&B per person, single from £25.00, double from £25.00.

★★★

GUEST HOUSE

Pitcullen Guest House
17 Pitcullen Crescent, Perth, PH2 7HT
Tel:01738 626506
Email:pitcullen.guesthouse@virgin.net

Personally run and conveniently situated on A94 tourist route. Only 5 minutes from City Centre. Private parking. Ideal location for visits to Perth races or Scone Palace.

5 rooms, Open Jan-Dec, B&B per person, single from £22.00, double from £23.00, twin from £23.00, family from £60.00 per room.

★★★★

B&B

Westview Bed & Breakfast
49 Dunkeld Road, Perth, PH1 5RP
Tel:01738 627787 Tel/Fax:01738 447790
Email:angiewestview@aol.com

Welcoming Victorian villa with original features reflecting the Victorian theme throughout. Attractive rooms with private facilities and elegant touches including period sitting room and relaxing garden. An enjoyable trip back in time. Ample parking. Smoking area. Scottish High Teas served 5-7pm. Dinner served 7-8.30pm.

4 rooms, 3 en-suite, Open Jan-Dec, B&B per person, single from £25.00, double from £25.00, BB & Eve.Meal from £30.00.

by Perth

Map Ref: 2B2

★★★

B&B

Mrs Ann Guthrie
Newmill Farm, Stanley, Perth, PH1 4PS
Tel:01738 828281
Email:guthrienewmill@sol.co.uk
Web:www.newmillfarm.co.uk
Traditional farmhouse on 330 acre arable farm. Convenient for the A9, 6 miles (10kms) from Perth. Suitable for fishing, golfing and other outdoor pursuits. Secure parking and friendly atmosphere. Situated in an area known as 'The gateway to the Highlands', the farm is ideally placed for those seeking some of the best scenery in Western Europe. Local produce used.

3 rooms, all en-suite, Open Feb-Nov, B&B per person, single from £28.00, double from £22.00.

AWAITING INSPECTION

The Linn
3 Duchess Street, Stanley, Perth, PH1 4NF
Tel/Fax:01738 828293
Email:ettalundie@hotmail.com

3 rooms, 2 en-suite, 1 priv.facilities, Open Jan-Dec excl Xmas/New Year, B&B per person, double from £25.00 pppn.

by Perth

Map Ref: 2B2

★★★★

B&B

Ninewells Farmhouse
Woodriffe Road, Newburgh, Fife, KY14 6EY
Tel/Fax:01337 840307
Email:barbara@ninewellsfarm.co.uk
Web:www.ninewellsfarm.co.uk
Traditional farmhouse on operational arable/stock farm. Elevated position with glorious panoramic views over the Tay Valley towards the Perthshire hills. Convenient for Edinburgh, Perth and many golf courses. The lounge is a large conservatory type room with all round views. Visitors are welcomed with tea/coffee and homebaked biscuits or scones. Member of Scotland's Best.

3 rooms, en-suite and priv.facilities, Open Apr-Oct, B&B per person, single from £40.00, double from £25.00.

Pitlochry, Perthshire

Map Ref: 2A1

ASHBANK HOUSE

14 Tomcroy Terrace, Pitlochry, Perthshire PH16 5JA
Tel: 01796 472711
e.mail: ashbankhouse@btinternet.com Web: www.ashbankhouse.co.uk
Attractive detached Victorian villa with private parking. Set in beautiful scenery within easy reach of many attractions and activities. A short walk takes you into Pitlochry town centre or the village of Moulin. Comfortable ensuite B&B accommodation from £19.00 per night. A warm welcome awaits you from Helen and Bob Murr.

★★★

B&B

Ashbank House
14 Tomcroy Terrace, Pitlochry, Perthshire, PH16 5JA
Tel:01796 472711
Email:ashbankhouse@btinternet.com
Web:www.ashbankhouse.co.uk
A Victorian villa situated on the northern edge of Pitlochry. Within walking distance of town centre and nearby village of Moulin. Ideal base to explore scenic Perthshire and beyond. Off road parking, with secure storage and drying facilities available. Views over large woodland garden with stream, to a backdrop of surrounding mountains and hills. Tranquil and comfortable accommodation with a warm welcome guaranteed!

3 rooms, Open Jan-Dec, B&B per person from £19.00.

Balbeagan

Balnaguard, Pitlochry PH9 0PY
Tel: 01796 482627
e.mail: Paulscroft@aol.com Web: www.balbeagan.com
In tranquil Balnaguard between Pitlochry, Aberfeldy and Dunkeld, and with views into the Perthshire Hills, this is a friendly B&B which puts comfort and food quality above all. Traditionally produced bacon and sausage, Loch Fyne kippers, or platters of fresh fruits and cheeses. Vegetarians welcome. Taste it to believe it!

★★★★

B&B

Balbeagan
Balnaguard, Pitlochry, Perthshire, PH9 0PY
Tel:01796 482627
Email:paulscroft@aol.com
Web:www.balbeagan.com

Ann and Paul Croft wait to welcome you to Balbeagan, where you will be made to feel special. The en-suite rooms are comfortable and well equipped and Balbeagan will become your home during your stay.

3 rooms, all en-suite, Open Jan-Nov, B&B per person, single from £25.00, double from £25.00.

VAT is shown at 17.5%: changes in this rate may affect prices.

Key to symbols is on back flap.

Pitlochry, Perthshire

Map Ref: 2A1

★★★

B&B

Bridge House B&B
53 Atholl Road, Pitlochry, Perthshire, PH16 5BL
Tel:01796 474062
Email:fionabridgehouse@hotmail.co.uk

2 rooms, all en-suite, Open Jan-Dec excl Xmas/New Year, B&B per person, double from £22.00.

Comfortable family home with the dining room on the first floor overlooking Pitlochry town centre and the spacious bedrooms on the second floor with views of the hills to the west of the town. Easy access to the railway station (5 minutes walk) and close to the town's other amenities including a variety of eating establishments.

BUTTONBOSS LODGE
25 ATHOLL ROAD, PITLOCHRY, PERTHSHIRE PH16 5BX
Tel/Fax: 01796 472065 Evening Tel: 473000
e.mail: colin@buttonboss.fsnet.co.uk
web: www.buttonboss.pitlochry.co.uk/index.htm
Friendly and relaxed atmosphere guaranteed by Colin – P.G.A. golf professional, and Marleen – former KLM stewardess. This detached villa is centrally located. French, German and Dutch spoken. Ensuite bedrooms with TV and hospitality tray. Guest lounge with satellite TV. Ground floor rooms available. All rooms with thermostatic controlled central heating. Private parking. Garage for motorbikes and cycles. Prices from £18 B&B.

★★★

**GUEST
HOUSE**

Buttonboss Lodge
25 Atholl Road, Pitlochry, Perthshire, PH16 5BX
Tel:01796 472065/473000 eve Fax:01796 472065
Email:colin@buttonboss.fsnet.co.uk
Web:http://www.SmoothHound.co.uk/hotels/buttonbo.html

8 rooms, some en-suite, Open Jan-Dec, B&B per person, single from £18.00, double from £18.00.

Traditional Victorian house in centre of Pitlochry. Within walking distance of all facilities. Private parking. Nederlands, Deutsche and Francais spoken.

Important: Prices stated are estimates and may be subject to amendments

Carra Beag Guest House

**16 Toberargan Road, Pitlochry, Perthshire PH16 5HG
Tel/Fax: 01796 472835
e.mail: visitus@carrabeag.co.uk
Web: www.carrabeag.co.uk**

Carra Beag is a beautiful Victorian villa built in the 1870's as a family home. It still is a family home. These days Helen & Brian open the doors welcoming guests and travellers continuing the long tradition of Highland hospitality. Commanding an elevated position we enjoy magnificent views across the Tummel Valley to the hills beyond. We pride ourselves on offering excellent value, clean and comfortable rooms in a completely non-smoking environment. After parking your vehicle in our private car park, take a stroll through our award winning garden directly onto Pitlochry's main street, visit the famous theatre, or some of Pitlochry's many attractions, dine locally returning home to the open fire in our cosy guests lounge.

**GUEST
HOUSE**

Carra Beag Guest House

**16 Toberargan Road, Pitlochry, Perthshire PH16 5HG
Tel:01796 472835
Email:visitus@carrabeag.co.uk
Web:www.carrabeag.co.uk**

Whatever your pursuits a friendly enjoyable stay is assured at Carra Beag. Enjoy magnificent uninterrupted views of the surrounding hills or stroll through our garden directly to Pitlochry's main street. We offer full facilities for walkers and cyclists. Private car park, and value for money.

8 rooms, some en-suite, Open Jan-Dec, B&B per person, single from £17.00, double from £20.00.

Pitlochry, Perthshire   Map Ref: 2A1

Craigroyston House

2 Lower Oakfield, Pitlochry PH16 5HQ
Tel/Fax: 01796 472053
e.mail: reservations@craigroyston.co.uk
Web: www.craigroyston.co.uk

A Victorian country house set in own grounds with views of the surrounding hills. Centrally situated, there is direct pedestrian access to the town centre.

★ All rooms have private facilities, some with 4-posters and are equipped to a high standard.
★ Residents' lounge with real log fire.
★ Safe private parking.
★ Dining room with separate tables.
★ Colour TV, welcome tray, central heating.
★ Craigroyston is a non-smoking guest house.

Bed & Breakfast from £25.00 per person.

AA
SELECTED
♦♦♦♦

★★★★
**GUEST
HOUSE**

Craigroyston House
2 Lower Oakfield, Pitlochry, Perthshire, PH16 5HQ
Tel/Fax:01796 472053
Email:reservations@craigroyston.co.uk
Web:www.craigroyston.co.uk

Quietly situated in its own grounds with views of the surrounding hills. Offering safe off street parking and direct access to the town centre. The spacious bedrooms are well equipped with attention to detail and tastefully decorated with period furniture. Lounge with real log fire.

8 rooms, all en-suite, Open Jan-Dec, B&B per person, double from £25.00.

DALSHIAN HOUSE

OLD PERTH ROAD, PITLOCHRY, PERTHSHIRE PH16 5TD
Tel: 01796 472173
e.mail: dalshian@haworth7.fsnet.co.uk
Web: www.dalshian.com

Here is an atmosphere that is genuinely friendly, but not intrusive, in a finely furnished Georgian home set in beautiful gardens. Relax in this superb accommodation with the promise of waking to a wonderful cooked breakfast or our popular, imaginative alternatives. Special reduced rates for families, 2 nights or longer stays.

★★★
**GUEST
HOUSE**

Dalshian House
Old Perth Road, Pitlochry, PH16 5TD
Tel:01796 472173
Email:dalshian@haworth7.fsnet.co.uk
Web:www.dalshian.com

1.5 miles south of Pitlochry, Dalshian House is a fine, late 18th century home, accessed by a private drive and set in over an acre of woodland gardens. The spacious, individually appointed rooms, all upgraded with modern conveniences, still retain their original character of a former elegant age. You are assured of both good food and a genuinely warm welcome with the Haworth family. Dalshian is a non-smoking house.

7 rooms, all en-suite, Open Jan-Nov, B&B per person, single from £24.50, double from £24.50.

Important: Prices stated are estimates and may be subject to amendments

Pitlochry, Perthshire   Map Ref: 2A1

Derrybeg Guest House

18 Lower Oakfield, Pitlochry PH16 5DS ★★★★
Tel: 01796 472070 Fax: 01796 472070 GUEST HOUSE
e.mail: marion@derrybeg.fsnet.co.uk
Web: www.derrybeg.com

Both of DERRYBEG's adjoining buildings are set in a quiet location only a few minutes' walk from the town centre, enjoying magnificent views of the Vale of Atholl. The resident proprietors, Derek and Marion Stephenson, ensure only the finest hospitality, comfort, and good home cooking.
- All bedrooms with private facilities.
- Colour television and welcome tea/coffee tray in all bedrooms.
- Open all year for B&B or D,B&B. Unlicensed, but guests welcome to supply own table wine.
- Full central heating throughout.
- Comfortable lounge and dining room.
- Food Hygiene Excellent Award.
- Ample parking in the grounds.
- Leisure activities can easily be arranged, i.e. theatre bookings, golf, fishing, pony-trekking, etc.

Colour brochure/tariff and details of weekly reductions available on request.

★★★★

GUEST HOUSE

Derrybeg Guest House & Apartments
18 Lower Oakfield, Pitlochry, Perthshire, PH16 5DS
Tel/Fax:01796 472070
Email:marion@derrybeg.fsnet.co.uk
Web:www.derrybeg.com

Privately owned detached house, with large south facing garden, in quiet but central location. Elevated position with uninterrupted views across Tummel Valley and surrounding hill sides. Three annexe rooms. Ample off road parking. Four course evening meal available and guests welcome to supply their own table wine.

17 rooms, all en-suite, Open Jan-Nov, B&B per person, single from £21.00, double from £21.00, BB & Eve.Meal from £37.50.

DUNDARAVE HOUSE

Strathview Terrace, Pitlochry PH16 5AT Tel/Fax: 01796 473109
e.mail: dundarave.guesthouse@virgin.net
Web: www.SmoothHound.co.uk/hotels/dundarave.html

Dundarave Guest House, the ideal place for your overnight stay or longer. A relaxed atmosphere in this traditional home in a quiet location with stunning views, a short walk from the town. Ensuite facilities. A comfortable lounge. Non-smoking. Private parking. From £20 pppn.

AA SELECTED ◆◆◆◆ ★★★ GUEST HOUSE

★★★

GUEST HOUSE

Dundarave House
Strathview Terrace, Pitlochry, Perthshire PH16 5AT
Tel/Fax:01796 473109
Email:dundarave.guesthouse@virgin.net
Web:www.smoothhound.co.uk/hotels/dundarave.html

Victorian built, late nineteenth century by local craftsmen, and set in its own half acre of formal grounds. Dundarave is a house of great charm, character and atmosphere.

7 rooms, some en-suite, Open Jan-Dec, B&B per person, single from £20.00, double from £22.00, BB & Eve.Meal from £35.00.

VAT is shown at 17.5%: changes in this rate may affect prices.   **Key to symbols is on back flap.**

Pitlochry, Perthshire Map Ref: 2A1

EASTER DUNFALLANDY COUNTRY HOUSE B&B
PITLOCHRY, PERTHSHIRE PH16 5NA ★★★★ B&B
Tel: 01796 474128 Fax: 01796 474446
e.mail: sue@dunfallandy.co.uk Web: www.dunfallandy.co.uk

Quietly situated country house enjoying wonderful views just 1 mile from Pitlochry and within easy reach of the areas many attractions. All 3 bedrooms are ensuite. Decor and furnishing are high quality throughout. Afternoon tea on arrival and gourmet breakfast. **AA ♦♦♦♦♦**
Top 20 B&B "Which" Good B&B Guide.

★★★★

B&B

Easter Dunfallandy House
Logierait Road, Pitlochry, Perthshire, PH16 5NA
Tel:01796 474128 Fax:01796 474446
Email:sue@dunfallandy.co.uk
Web:www.dunfallandy.co.uk

A large Victorian country house retaining many original features and retaining its period charm. Ground floor room available. Situated in elevated position with panoramic views over the Vale of Atholl. 1.5 miles south of Pitlochry on quiet country road. Large country garden. Non-smoking house.

3 rooms, all en-suite, Open Jan-Dec excl Xmas, B&B per person, single £45.00-50.00, double £30.00-35.00.

FASGANEOIN COUNTRY HOUSE

Perth Road, Pitlochry PH16 5DJ
Tel: 01796 472387 Fax: 01796 474285
e.mail: sabrina@fasganeoin.freeserve.co.uk
Web: www.fasganeoincountryhouse.co.uk
A quiet country house full of Victorian charm standing in attractive grounds, overlooking the valley of the River Tummel. Close to the theatre, Dam and Salmon ladder. Licensed. Early evening meal served on request. We have been welcoming guests to "Fasganeoin" for over 38 years. Family run.

★★★

**GUEST
HOUSE**

Fasganeoin Country House
Perth Road, Pitlochry, PH16 5DJ
Tel:01796 472387 Fax:01796 474285
Email:sabrina@fasganeoin.freeserve.co.uk
Web:www.fasganeoincountryhouse.co.uk

A long established family run country house with the accent on traditional values of hospitality and service. Dating from the 1870s and set in spacious, secluded gardens, it stands on the edge of town, close to the theatre. Tasty theatre suppers are served between 5-7pm (last orders 6.45), bookings preferred.

8 rooms, 6 en-suite, 2 with priv.facilities, Open Apr-mid Oct, B&B per person, single from £28.00, en-suite double from £32.00, BB & Eve.Meal from £42.50.

★★★

B&B

Gardeners Cottage
Faskally, Pitlochry, Perthshire, PH16 5LA
Tel:01796 472450

Original gardeners cottage dating from mid 19th century. Adjoining Faskally wood and overlooking the Loch. Ground floor bedroom available.

3 rooms, some en-suite, Open Jan-Dec, B&B per person, double from £22.00.

Important: Prices stated are estimates and may be subject to amendments

Pitlochry, Perthshire

Map Ref: 2A1

★★★

B&B

Lavalette
**Manse Road, Moulin, Pitlochry, Perthshire
PH16 5EP
Tel/Fax:01796 472364
Email:barrypheonix@aol.com**

A warm welcome awaits you at 'Lavalette', a bungalow on the edge of the conservation village of Moulin which has its own hotel - a former staging post. Pitlochry town centre with its shops and a variety of eating establishments is within walking distance.

3 rooms, some en-suite, Open Mar-Oct, from £20.00.

Macdonald's Restaurant
& Guest House
**140 Atholl Road, Pitlochry PH16 5AG
Tel: 01796 472170   Fax: 01796 474460
e.mail: macdonalds.pitlochry@usa.net   Web: www.macdonalds-pitlochry.co.uk**
At the heart of Pitlochry Macdonald's Restaurant & Guest House has been welcoming visitors since 1959. Only minutes from Pitlochry Theatre and many other attractions. Our Guest House offers 10 ensuite bedrooms all with LCD televisions and private parking. Rates are £25 pppn B&B double occupancy and stays of 3 nights plus Sunday to Thursday at £20 pppn B&B. We look forward to making your visit to Pitlochry a special one. For the comfort of our guest we are a Non-Smoking house.

★★★

**GUEST
HOUSE**

Macdonald's Restaurant & Guest House
**140 Atholl Road, Pitlochry, Perthshire, PH16 5AG
Tel:01796 472170 Fax:01796 474460
Email:macdonalds.pitlochry@usa.net
Web:www.macdonalds-pitlochry.co.uk**

We have been welcoming guests since 1959. All rooms ensuite and have LCD televisions. Stay 3 nights or more Sunday-Thursday £20.00 pppn. Double occupancy required.

10 rooms, all en-suite. Open Jan-Dec, B&B per person, single £35.00, double £25.00.

★★★

B&B

Sunnybank B&B
**19 Lower Oakfield, Pitlochry, Perthshire, PH16 5DS
Tel:01796 473014
Email:thomas@tszeller.fsnet.co.uk
Web:www.sunnybank-web.co.uk**

Modern house in quiet but central location. Enjoys elevated position with view over the Tummel Valley and surrounding hills. Offers spacious and comfortable ensuite rooms, all non smoking. Access all day. Ample parking.

3 rooms, all en-suite, Open Jan-Dec, B&B per person, double £25.00-30.00.

★★★★

**GUEST
HOUSE**

Torrdarach House
**Golf Course Road, Pitlochry, Perthshire, PH16 5AU
Tel:01796 472136
Email:torrdarach@msn.com
Web:www.smoothhound.co.uk/hotels/torrdarach.html**

Listed Edwardian country house set in secluded gardens with gorgeous views over Tummel Valley. A highland burn, a family of red squirrels and a variety of wildlife all within its grounds. Located approximately 5 minutes walk from picturesque town centre and golf course. Douglas and June guarantee a friendly and relaxed atmosphere, hearty breakfasts and a fine selection of wines and malts.

7 rooms, some en-suite, Open Jan-Dec, B&B per person, single from £20.00, double from £20.00.

VAT is shown at 17.5%: changes in this rate may affect prices. | *Key to symbols is on back flap.*

Pitlochry, Perthshire   Map Ref: 2A1

WELLWOOD HOUSE

West Moulin Road, Pitlochry, Perthshire PH16 5EA
Tel: 01796 474288 Fax: 01796 474299
e.mail: bookings@wellwoodhouse.com
Web: www.wellwoodhouse.com

AA ♦♦♦♦

A warm welcome awaits at our stylishly refurbished, centrally situated licensed Scottish manor. Choose our tower ensuite bedroom and enjoy outstanding views down the Vale of Atholl, or an elegantly decorated standard, or family en-suite room at reasonable prices. Set in two acres, there is a delightful reed-bordered stream with wildlife.

★★★★

GUEST
HOUSE

Wellwood House
West Moulin Road, Pitlochry, Perthshire, PH16 5EA
Tel:01796 474288 Fax:01796 474299
Email:bookings@wellwoodhouse.com
Web:www.wellwoodhouse.com

Victorian manor with fine views over town yet only 200 yards to town centre. Ideal location for touring Perthshire.

8 rooms, some en-suite, B&B per person, single £33.00-43.00, double £24.00-33.00.

Wester Knockfarrie

Knockfarrie Road, Pitlochry PH16 5DN
Tel: 01796 472020
E-mail: sally.spaven@btopenworld.com

Victorian home quietly situated in woodlands only minutes walk from town centre. Beautiful views over Tummel Valley. Woodland walks, peaceful garden. Private parking. Individually designed bedrooms with ensuite facilities, TV and tea/coffee tray. A full Scottish breakfast is served in our elegant dining room. Contact Sally Spaven.

★★★★

B&B

Wester Knockfarrie
Knockfarrie Road, Pitlochry, Perthshire, PH16 5DN
Tel:01796 472020
Email:sally.spaven@btopenworld.com

Wester Knockfarrie, a Victorian home quietly situated in woodlands on the outskirts of Pitlochry, yet only a few minutes walk from the town. Beautiful views over the Tummel Valley and the hills beyond, a peaceful garden to relax in with woodland strolls and forest trails close by. Individually designed non smoking bedrooms with fully fitted ensuite facilities. A full Scottish breakfast is served in the elegant dining room. Private parking.

2 rooms, all en-suite, Open Mar-Oct, B&B per person, double from £25.00.

Important: Prices stated are estimates and may be subject to amendments

St Andrews, Fife

Map Ref: 2D2

B&B

Abbey Cottage
Abbey Walk, St Andrews, Fife, KY16 9LB
Tel:01334 473727
Email:coull@lineone.net
Web:www.abbeycottage.co.uk

Listed property dating from 18c with walled cottage garden. Close to centre of St. Andrews. Fantail doves and pet hens. Parking.

2 rooms, some en-suite, Open Jan-Dec, B&B per person, double from £24.00.

B&B

Anlaw House
21 Nelson Street, St Andrews, Fife, KY16 8AJ
Tel/Fax:01334 477994
Email:ann@anlawstandrews.co.uk
Web:www.anlawstandrews.co.uk

A warm welcome awaits you at this attractive and fully modernised detached family home within 5-minutes easy walking of the Town Centre, convenient for the many golf courses, University and the spendid local beaches, and offering the ideal base for exploring the 'Kingdom of Fife' and beyond.

3 rooms, Open Jan-Dec excl Xmas/New Year, B&B per person, single from £24.00, double from £24.00.

B&B

Barnhay Country Bed & Breakfast
Kinaldy Meadows, by St Andrews, Fife, KY16 8NA
Tel:01334 477791
Email:barnhay@btinternet.com

Barnhay is situated in a peaceful rural location just ten minutes drive from St Andrews. Well appointed and tastefully furnished en-suite rooms. Ideal location for touring, golfing, cycling or simply take time out to relax, refresh and recharge.

2 rooms, all en-suite, Open Jan-Dec, B&B per person, single from £36.00, double from £26.00, BB & Eve.Meal from £38.00-48.00.

B&B

Birchlea Bed & Breakfast
8 Horseleys Park, St Andrews, Fife, KY16 8RZ
Tel:01334 472698
Email:sheila@hartbnb.fsnet.co.uk

Birchlea is set in an extremely quiet residential area of St Andrews close to the Botanic Gardens and a ten minute walk from the bustling town centre. A fifteen minute walk will take you to the famous Old Course. Sheila invites guests to share her non-smoking family home with comfortable ground floor en-suite rooms. With ample safe parking you can leave the car and discover for yourself the delights St Andrews has to offer.

2 rooms, all en-suite, Open Jan-Dec excl Xmas/New Year, B&B per person, double from £27.50.

VAT is shown at 17.5%: changes in this rate may affect prices.

Key to symbols is on back flap.

St Andrews, Fife　　　　　　　　　　　　　　Map Ref: 2D2

Bramley House
10 Bonfield Road, Strathkinness, by St Andrews KY16 9RP
Tel/Fax:01334 850362
Email:heather@bramleyguesthouse.com
Web:www.bramleyguesthouse.com

Beautifully situated 2.5 miles west of St Andrews, this elegant country house is ideal for that special break away. The attractive bedrooms are spacious, well furnished and offer all the expected amenities. Your hostess, Heather McQueen, has a renowned reputation for her relaxed country house atmosphere, enjoyable home cooking and early bird golfing breakfast. Entry in 'Which' Best B&B.

3 rooms, all en-suite, Open Jan-Dec, B&B per person, double from £25.00.

B&B

Charlesworth House
9 Murray Place, St Andrews, KY16 9AP
Tel/Fax:01334 476528
Email:charlesworth@talk21.com
Web:www.charlesworthstandrews.co.uk

Victorian terraced, family-run guest house in the heart of St Andrews. A few minutes walk from the famous Old Course, beaches, historic buildings and shops. Non-smoking.

5 rooms, Open Jan-Dec, B&B per person, single from £30.00, double from £28.00.

GUEST HOUSE

Hawthorne House B&B
33 Main Street, Strathkinness, St Andrews, Fife KY16 9RY
Tel:01334 850855
Email:hawthornehouse@onetel.com
Web:www.thehawthornehouse.co.uk

Friendly family run bed and breakfast in attractive village only five minutes drive or approx 2.5 miles from the world famous 'Old Course' and the 'Old Grey Town' of St Andrews. Situated in a picturesque village. Free private parking. All rooms ensuite.

3 rooms, all en-suite, Open Jan-Dec, B&B per person, double from £20.00.

B&B

Hazelbank Hotel
28 The Scores, St Andrews, Fife, KY16 9AS
Tel/Fax:01334 472466
Email:michael@hazelbank.com
Web:www.hazelbank.com

Refurbished elegant Victorian townhouse. Overlooking St Andrews Bay and golf courses. 200 yards from the 1st tee on The Old Course. 3 minutes walk to University and historic town centre.

10 rooms, all en-suite, Open Jan-Dec excl Xmas/New Year, B&B per person, single from £54.50, double from £39.50.

SMALL HOTEL

Old Fishergate House
North Castle Street, St Andrews, Fife, KY16 9BG
Tel/Fax:01334 470874
Email:stay@oldfishergatehouse.co.uk
Web:www.oldfishergatehouse.co.uk

17th century town house in the oldest part of historic St Andrews, close to Castle, University, Byre Theatre and shops. 5 mins walk to the Old Course. Tastefully decorated retaining many original features.

2 rooms, both en-suite each with priv. sitting room, Open Jan-Dec excl Xmas/New Year, B&B per person, double from £40.00.

B&B

Important: Prices stated are estimates and may be subject to amendments

---

★★★★

GUEST HOUSE

The Old Station Country Guest House
Stravithie Bridge, St Andrews, KY16 8LR
Tel:01334 880505 Fax:01334 880622
Email:info@theoldstation.co.uk
Web:www.theoldstation.co.uk

Deluxe accommodation in converted Victorian railway station and train carriage, within 2 acres of peaceful gardens only 2 miles from St Andrews. Roaring log fire, candlelight, fresh flowers make this a luxury home from home.

8 rooms, Open Jan-Dec, B&B per person, single from £50.00, room only single from £50.00, double from £80.00, family from £110.00.

★★★★

B&B

The Paddock
Sunnyside, Strathkinness, by St. Andrews, Fife KY16 9XP
Tel:01334 850888   Fax:01334 850870
Email:thepaddock@btinternet.com
Web:www.thepadd.co.uk

Modern bungalow furnished to a high standard , in a semi-rural location on the edge of Strathkinness village, having open outlook to farmland to the rear. St Andrews is three miles away, with easy access to golf courses, beach , shops and cultural buildings. Craigtoun Country Park is within one and a half miles.

3 rooms, all en-suite, Open Feb-Nov, B&B per person, double from £27.00.

★★

B&B

St Nicholas Farmhouse
East Sands, St Andrews, Fife, KY16 8LD
Tel:01334 473090
Email:bill@pressegh.freeserve.co.uk

Traditional farmhouse set amidst modern housing on the eastern edge of St Andrews. East Sands beach is only about 400 metres away. Free Parking. Both rooms en-suite. Facilities for children, pets and non-smokers.

2 rooms, all en-suite, Open Jan-Dec, B&B per person, single from £28.00, double from £20.00.

Spinkieden
13 Cairnsden Gardens, St. Andrews KY16 8SQ
Tel/Fax: 01334 475303
e.mail: welcome@spinkieden.co.uk
Web: www.spinkieden.co.uk

The beautiful historic town of St. Andrews, the home of golf, is the perfect location to explore the East Neuk of Fife and well beyond. We offer you comfortable, friendly accommodation with central heating, TV/videos and tea/coffee facilities in all rooms to make your stay as enjoyable as possible.

★★★

B&B

Spinkieden
13 Cairnsden Gardens, St Andrews, Fife, KY16 8SQ
Tel/Fax:01334 475303
Email:welcome@spinkieden.co.uk
Web:www.spinkieden.co.uk

Be assured of a very warm welcome at this attractive bungalow where you'll find comfortable, ground floor accommodation with a home from home atmosphere. Situated in a quiet residential area. The town centre is only three minutes by car or easily accessible by a scenic stroll along the Lade Braes. Private Parking.

3 rooms, some en-suite, Open Mar-Nov, B&B per person, single from £30.00, double from £22.00.

VAT is shown at 17.5%: changes in this rate may affect prices.

Key to symbols is on back flap.

St Andrews, Fife · **Map Ref: 2D2**

SPINKSTOWN FARMHOUSE
St Andrews, Fife KY16 8PN
Tel/Fax: 01334 473475
e.mail: anne@spinkstown.com   Web: www.spinkstown.com
Two miles from St Andrews on A917 to Crail this bright uniquely designed farmhouse furnished to a high standard has spacious bedrooms, ensuite bathrooms (bath and shower) comfortable lounge dining room where substantial breakfast sets you up for the day. Historic St Andrews famous Old Course, fishing villages, National Trust properties nearby.

B&B

Spinkstown Farmhouse
St Andrews, Fife, KY16 8PN
Tel/Fax:01334 473475
Email:anne@spinkstown.com
Web:www.spinkstown.com

A warm welcome awaits at this uniquely designed farmhouse, only 2 miles (3km) east of St Andrews. Some rooms with sea views and surrounding countryside. Bright and spacious. Plenty free parking on site. Abundant wildlife in peaceful surroundings.

3 rooms, all en-suite, Open Jan-Dec excl Xmas/New Year, B&B per person, single from £30.00, double from £26.00.

B&B

Stravithie Castle
Stravithie, St Andrews, Fife, KY16 8LT
Tel:01334 880251   Fax:01334 880297

Bed & breakfast within 19c castle set in 30 acres of peaceful grounds, with nature walks, golf practice (9 holes), trout stream. St Andrews 3 miles (5kms). Come and experience the atmosphere of a fine old Scottish country estate. Large sitting room style bedrooms with own kitchen. Buffet breakfast.

3 rooms, all en-suite, Open May-Sep, B&B per person, single from £40.00, double from £38.00.

GUEST HOUSE

West Park House
5 St Marys Place, St Andrews, Fife, KY16 9UY
Tel:01334 475933   Fax:01334 476634
Email:rosemary@westparksta.freeserve.co.uk
Web:www.westpark-standrews.co.uk

Beautiful Listed Georgian house c1830 in heart of historic town. Close to Old Course and all amenities. Sandy beaches close by and within easy reach of the pretty East Neuk fishing villages (approx 10 miles).

4 rooms, 3 en-suite, Open Jan-Dec excl Xmas/New Year, B&B per person, single from £45.00, double from £30.00.

---

by St Andrews, Fife · **Map Ref: 2D2**

B&B

South House
Pitscottie Vale, Dura Den, Pitscottie, nr St Andrews, Fife, KY15 5TJ
Tel:01334 828784
Email:corriebrodie@aol.com
Web:www.pitscottievale.co.uk

South House is a peaceful country cottage set in ¾ acre of grounds in Dura Den beside the Ceres Burn. St Andrews, Cupar and East Neuk villages are all close by.

2 rooms, all en-suite, Open Jan-Dec excl Xmas/New Year, B&B per person, double from £25.00.

Important: Prices stated are estimates and may be subject to amendments

nr St Andrews, Fife

Map Ref: 2D2

Far-Reaches B&B

32 Pickford Crescent, Cellardyke, Anstruther, Fife, KY10 3AL
Tel/Fax:01333 310448
Email:accommodation@far-reaches.demon.co.uk

3 rooms, some en-suite, Open Mar-Oct, B&B per person, single from £34.00, double from £25.00.

Modern detached house in quiet residential area of a small fishing village. Excellent views across the Forth Estuary and the Isle of May. Warm welcome & homebaked bread. Plenty of off and on road parking.

St Fillans, Perthshire

Map Ref: 1H2

Earngrove Cottage

St Fillans, by Loch Earn, Perthshire, PH6 2ND
Tel:01764 685224
Email:ross@earngrovecottage.fsnet.co.uk
Web:www.earngrovecottage.fsnet.co.uk

2 twin rooms, Open Mar-Nov, B&B per person, double £18.00-20.00.

Traditional stone built c1846 cottage tastefully refurbished situated near Loch Earn amidst beautiful mountain scenery. Convenient for hillwalking, golfing, watersports, fishing, boat and bike hire.

Saline, by Dunfermline, Fife

Map Ref: 2B4

Kirklands House

Saline, Fife, KY12 9TS
Tel:01383 852737
Email:kirklands@kirklandshouseandgarden.co.uk
Web:www.kirklandshouseandgarden.co.uk

2 rooms (dbl/fam and twin), both en-suite, Open Jan-Dec, B&B per person, single from £30.00, double/family from £25.00, BB & Eve.Meal from £40.00.

We promise you a warm and friendly welcome to Kirklands, built in 1832 and set in two acres of stunning gardens and 20 acres of woodland. Secluded yet central for Edinburgh, Glasgow, Perth, Stirling, a perfect base to tour Scotland.

Tayport, Fife

Map Ref: 2D2

Forgans B&B

23 Castle Street, Tayport, Fife, DD6 9AE
Tel/Fax:01382 552682
Email:m.forgan@talk21.com

3 rooms, Open Jan-Dec, B&B per person, single from £26.00, sharing from £20.00.

Truly Scottish welcome awaits you here. Situated in centre of Tayport, just a short walk from picturesque harbour. Easy commuting to Dundee and St Andrews. Good bus service. Near to Dundee and Leuchars Railway Station. Many golf courses nearby. 1 hour drive from Edinburgh. Good home cooking. Full Scottish breakfast. Special diets catered for. Children free when sharing with adults.

VAT is shown at 17.5%: changes in this rate may affect prices.

Key to symbols is on back flap.

Welcome to Scotland

Aberdeen and Grampian Highlands – Scotland's Castle and Whisky Country

Sure, you'll find Scotland's crème de la crème of fortresses and single malts, but other prizes are for the taking. Aberdeen's nightlife, country towns favoured by the Royal family, and a dreamy coastline…

Balmoral Castle

Aberdeen is a city of tantalising possibilities. One mile is crammed with around 800 shops, the next mile leads to sandy beaches. Above the shopping glitterati of Union Street lies an old world resolutely cast in granite. The eclectic King's college and castellated Citadel at the Castlegate are just two of the architectural treasures to explore. Retrace the city's growth through fishing and offshore oil at the Maritime Museum, or admire the cream of Scottish painters housed in Aberdeen Art Gallery.

Turn to Martha's Bistro, La Bamba restaurant and The Moonfish Café for serious temptation in chilled surroundings. The mood lighting and chic décor continue in the style bars of Neo, Siberia and The Monkey House. Global flavours ensure that live music is never routine at The Lemon Tree, while Café Drummond regularly surprises with newcomers. And retreat to The Ministry, Babylon or The Priory for a dance odyssey.

Moving towards the Cairngorm Mountains, encounter a rich valley prized by the Royal Family. Queen Victoria gave Royal Deeside the thumbs up, acquiring Balmoral as the family's Highland estate. Open to the public in summer, Balmoral is part of the Victorian Heritage trail, encompassing Loch Muick, Crathie Church and Royal Lochnagar Distillery. Ballater, Braemar and other Deeside towns revel in fresh air, fine local foods and a wholesome spirit for adventure. It's a good thing too, because the Cairngorm Mountains are a frontier for mountain walkers who relish the grit of a Munro.

Heave! The clansmen 'Tug of War' competition at the Lonach Highland Games.

Aberdeen and Grampian Highlands – Scotland's Castle and Whisky Country

Sword dancing at the Ballater Highland Games.

Of course, you can't avoid the 350 odd castles in the area, but why would you? Each one has a distinct personality, from the imposing fortress walls of Kildrummy and Dunnottar, to the elegant furnishings of Crathes and Fyvie. Simply follow the signposted trail.

The other trail has become a pilgrimage for travellers throughout the world. Speyside has some sixty or so whisky distilleries within 15 square miles of barley fields and clear spring water. Follow the signposts marking the Malt Whisky trail to visit the famous seven: Benromach, Cardhu, Dallas Dhu (now a distillery museum), Glen Grant, Strathisla, the Glenlivet, and Glenfiddich. Learn how to spot the peat and oak tannins through a wee dram at the end of a distillery tour – or seven.

The narrow and meandering coastline shifts from sand dunes to dramatic cliffs, bonny fishing villages to rich ecosystems. Envy bottle-nosed dolphins leaping through the Moray Firth, or come face-to-beak with an octopus at the Macduff Marine Museum. Perhaps surfing? The waves of Balmedie beach are mesmerising, but then, you can have fun by doing nothing at all.

Events

Aberdeen and Grampian Highlands – Scotland's Castle and Whisky Country

7-12 MARCH
JAZZ ABERDEEN
An international jazz festival with a classy reputation.
Tel: 01224 619770
www.jazzaberdeen.com

27 APRIL-1 MAY
SPIRIT OF SPEYSIDE WHISKY FESTIVAL
A celebration of the "water of life" in whisky country. The festival blends whisky, music, food and fun into an irresistible cocktail with something for everyone.
Tel: 01343 542666
www.spiritofspeyside.com

20-26 MAY
BALLATER ROYAL DEESIDE WALKING WEEK
Annual week-long event on Deeside and the Grampians with 3 graded walks each day to suit all abilities.
Tel: 01339 755467
www.royal-deeside.org.uk

10 JUNE
TASTE OF GRAMPIAN, Inverurie
This food festival celebrates the richness and diversity of Grampians larder.
Tel: 0131 335 6200
www.tasteofgrampian.co.uk

8-9 JULY
SCOTTISH TRADITIONAL BOAT FESTIVAL, Portsoy
One of the largest rallies of traditional sailing craft in the UK plus a full programme of vents.
Tel: 01261 842894
www.scottishtraditionalboat festival.co.uk

2-12 AUGUST
ABERDEEN INTERNATIONAL YOUTH FESTIVAL
International multi arts festival featuring the best in youth talent.
Tel: 01224 213800
www.aiyf.org

26 AUGUST
LONACH GATHERING, Strathdon
Highland gathering including the march of the Lonach Highlanders.
Tel: 01975 651297
www.lonach.org

2 SEPTEMBER
BRAEMAR GATHERING
Grand finale of the Highland games calendar.
Tel: 01339 755377
www.braemargathering.org

28-29 OCTOBER
ARCHAEOLINK EVENTS, Oyne
Go back to the dawn of civilisation with ancient events at this Prehistory Park, including a Wickerman festival.
Tel: 01464 851500
www.archaeolink.co.uk

31 DECEMBER
STONEHAVEN FIREBALL FESTIVAL
Dramatic fireball 'swinging' New Year display.
Tel: 01569 764647
www.stonehavenfireballs.co.uk

** denotes provisional date, event details are subject to change please check before travelling*

The Still Room of Glenfiddich Distillery.

Aberdeen and Grampian Highlands – Scotland's Castle and Whisky Country

Please refer to the maps on pages xix-xxiv for the locations of establishments appearing in the main advertising section of this guide.

Finding out more...

For practical advice, ideas and information about exploring Scotland and to book your accommodation:

Tel: 0845 22 55 121*
or if calling from outside the UK: +44 (0) 1506 832121

Email: info@visitscotland.com
Web: www.visitscotland.com

* A £3 booking fee applies to telephone bookings of accommodation.

Tourist Information Centres

Aberdeen and Grampian Highlands – Scotland's Castle and Whisky Country

Aberdeen and Grampian

Aberdeen
23 Union Street
Tel: (01224) 288828
Jan – Dec

Alford
Railway Museum
Station Yard
Tel: (01975) 562052
Easter – Oct

Ballater
Albert Hall
Station Square
Tel: (01339) 755306
Jan – Dec

Banchory
Bridge Street
Tel: (01330) 822000
Easter – Oct

Banff
Collie Lodge
Tel: (01261) 812419
Easter – Oct

Braemar
The Mews
Tel: (01339) 741600
Jan – Dec

Crathie
Markethill Car Park
Tel: (01339) 742414
Easter-Oct

Dufftown
Clock Tower
The Square
Tel: (01340) 820501
Easter – Oct

Elgin
17 High Street
Tel: (01343) 542666/543388
Jan – Dec

Forres
116 High Street
Tel: (01309) 672938
Easter – Oct

Fraserburgh
3 Saltoun Square
Tel: (01346) 518315
Easter – Oct

Huntly
9a The Square
Tel: (01466) 792255
Easter – Oct

Inverurie
18 High Street
Tel: (01467) 625800
Jan – Dec

Stonehaven
66 Allardice Street
Tel: (01569) 762806
Easter – Oct

Tomintoul
The Square
Tel: (01807) 580285
Easter – Oct

Aberdeen   Map Ref: 4G10

Burnetts Guest House
**75 CONSTITUTION STREET, ABERDEEN AB24 5ET
TEL/FAX: 01224 647995   WEB: www.burnettsguesthouse.co.uk
EMAIL: diane.burnett@burnettsguesthouse.co.uk**

Diane Burnett welcomes you to Burnetts Guest House. Our newly refurbished accommodation is located in quiet area close to beach and city centre. We are a convenient base for cinema, funfair, theatre and restaurants. We provide a comfortable city centre guest house at reasonable prices and have a "no smoking" policy. A warm welcome awaits you. We will be happy to give you every assistance and hope you enjoy your stay with us.

★★★

**GUEST
HOUSE**

Burnett's Guest House
75 Constitution Street, Aberdeen, AB24 5ET
Tel/Fax: 01224 647995
Email:diane.burnett@burnettsguesthouse.co.uk
Web:www.burnettsguesthouse.co.uk

Terraced house in side street, close to RGU and 5 minutes walk to city centre. 10 minutes from bus and rail stations.

5 rooms, some ensuite. Open Jan-Dec. B&B per person, single standard from £25.00, double standard from £25.00, twin en-suite from £35.00, double en-suite from £35.00.

Cragganmore Guest House
63 SPRINGBANK TERRACE, FERRYHILL, ABERDEEN AB11 6JZ
Tel: 01224 572867 Fax: 01224 575002
e.mail: info@cragganmoreguesthouse.co.uk
Web: www.cragganmoreguesthouse.co.uk

Family run, friendly, tastefully decorated, comfortable accommodation in city centre. Convenient for bus/rail stations, Duthie Park Winter Garden, the beautiful river Dee, beach, carnival, swimming pools, shops, theatre and restaurants. Within 5 miles radius of 6 golf courses. Ideal base for touring the Highlands and whisky trails. Private parking.

**AWAITING
INSPECTION**

Cragganmore Guest House
63 Springbank Terrace, Ferryhill, Aberdeen
AB11 6JZ
Tel:01224 572867 Fax: 01224 575002
Email:info@cragganmoreguesthouse.co.uk
Web:www.cragganmoreguesthouse.co.uk

6 rooms, some en-suite, Open Jan-Dec excl Xmas/New Year, B&B per person, single from £33.00, double from £20.00.

★

**CAMPUS
ACCOMMODATION**

Crombie Johnston Hall
University of Aberdeen, Aberdeen, AB24 3TT
Tel:01224 273444 Fax:01224 276246
Email:accommodation@abdn.ac.uk
Web:www.abdn.ac.uk/confevents

Ensuite and standard student accommodation available during summer period. Accommodation is located in historic Old Aberdeen within easy reach of the city centre. Breakfast included.

375 rooms (some en-suite), Open mid Jun-mid Sep, B&B per person from £20.50.

FURAIN GUEST HOUSE

North Deeside Road, Peterculter, Aberdeen AB14 0QN
Telephone: 01224 732189 Fax: 01224 739070
e.mail: furain@btinternet.com

FURAIN GUEST HOUSE, on the A93, 8 miles west of
Aberdeen centre, close to several historic castles and
convenient for touring some of the most beautiful countryside
in the UK. We give a full Scottish breakfast with choice, special
diets catered for.

★★★

**GUEST
HOUSE**

Furain Guest House

92 North Deeside Road, Peterculter, Aberdeen, AB14 0QN
Tel:01224 732189   Fax:01224 739070
Email:furain@btinternet.com

Late Victorian house built of red granite. Family run. Convenient for
town, Royal Deeside and the Castle Trail. Private car parking. Dinner
available on Wednesday, Friday and Saturday.

8 rooms, all en-suite, Open Jan-Dec excl Xmas/New Year, B&B per person, single
from £33.00, double from £23.00.

★★

B&B

MacLeans B & B

8 Boyd Orr Avenue, Aberdeen, Grampian, AB12 5RG
Tel/Fax:01224 248726
Email:j.maclean@abdn.ac.uk
Web:www.ukcitydirectory.com

Family run B&B with conservatory dining area, set in quiet residential
area just south of the River Dee. Very handy for easy access to routes
going south. Off street parking.

2 rooms, all en-suite, Open Jan-Dec, B&B per person, ensuite single £27.00,
ensuite double/twin £24.00, single £25.00, double/twin £22.00. No family rooms.
Evening meals from £6.00.

★★★★

**GUEST
HOUSE**

Penny Meadow Private Hotel

189 Great Western Road, Aberdeen, AB10 6PS
Tel:01224 588037 Fax:01224 573639
Email:frances@pennymeadow.freeserve.co.uk

A high quality purpose built Guest House with all ensuite bedrooms and
off road parking. For the discerning visitor looking for a warm, friendly
atmosphere, comfortable accommodation and that little bit extra
attention to detail.

3 rooms, all en-suite, Open Jan-Dec, B&B per person, single from £34.00-46.00,
double from £25.00-35.00.

VAT is shown at 17.5%: changes in this rate may affect prices.

Key to symbols is on back flap.

Aberdeen

Map Ref: 4G10

St ELMO

64 HILTON DRIVE, ABERDEEN AB24 4NP
Tel: 01224 483065 e.mail: StElmoBandB@aol.com
Web: http://home.aol.com/StElmoBandB/

This comfortable, smoke-free, family accommodation with ensuite facilities is ideal for guests looking for a small quiet place to stay, yet on a city centre bus route, close to airport, university and hospital. CTV, courtesy tray, microwave and fridge facilities in bedrooms; full Scottish breakfast; special multinight rates; off-street parking available.

AWAITING INSPECTION

St Elmo

64 Hilton Drive, Aberdeen, AB24 4NP
Tel:01224 483065
Email:StElmoBandB@aol.com
Web:http://home.aol.com/StElmoBandB/

4 rooms, some en-suite, Open Jan-Dec, B&B per person, single £30.00-50.00, double £26.00-30.00.

Scottish Agricultural College

CRAIBSTONE ESTATE, BUCKSBURN, ABERDEEN AB21 9TR
Tel: 01224 711012 Fax: 01224 711298
e.mail: gwen.bruce@sac.co.uk Web: www.sac.ac.uk

Situated in quiet rural location within large woodland estate only 5 miles from Aberdeen and 5-minute drive from the airport. With leisure facilities, including 18-hole golf course, it is the ideal venue for touring the north east of Scotland or just relaxing. You're certainly guaranteed a warm welcome.

CAMPUS ACCOMMODATION

Scottish Agricultural College

Craibstone Estate, Bucksburn, Aberdeenshire AB21 9TR
Tel:01224 711012 Fax:01224 711298
Email:gwen.bruce@sac.co.uk
Web:www.sac.ac.uk

Halls of Residence, set in extensive country estate with new 18 hole golfcourse on outskirts of Aberdeen, with easy access to all amenities.

60 en-suite rooms. Open Jan-Dec. B&B per person, single from £25.00.

CAMPUS ACCOMMODATION

University of Aberdeen, King's Hall

College Bounds, Aberdeen, AB24 3TT
Tel:01224 273444 Fax:01224 276246
Email:accommodation@abdn.ac.uk
Web:www.abdn.ac.uk/confevents

Modern hotel style accommodation located in historic Old Aberdeen. Rooms are available year round, are all ensuite and include a TV, hairdryer, telephone and trouser press. Breakfast is also included within the Zeste restaurant. Guests at King's Hall have access to leisure facilities on the campus during their stay.

65 rooms, all en-suite, Open Jan-Dec excl Xmas/New Year, B&B per person, single from £42.00, twin from £59.00.

Important: Prices stated are estimates and may be subject to amendments

Aberdeen

Map Ref: 4G10

★★★

B&B

Viewfield B&B

Panmure Gardens, Potterton, Aberdeen, AB23 8UG
Tel:01358 742605

3 rooms, 1 double. 2 twin, Open Jan-Dec excl Xmas/New Year, B&B per person £20.00-25.00.

Family house situated in the quiet village of Potterton, yet just 6 miles from the centre of Aberdeen. Very convenient location for the Bridge of Don area, the airport and the Conference Centre. Also good base for exploring the North East corner of the region, with its golf, Coastal Trail and historic houses.

Aboyne, Aberdeenshire

Map Ref: 4F11

★★★★

B&B

Struan Hall

Ballater Road, Aboyne, Aberdeenshire, AB34 5HY
Tel/Fax:013398 87241
Email:struanhall@zetnet.co.uk
Web:www.struanhall.co.uk

3 rooms, all en-suite, Open Apr-Oct, B&B per person, single from £32.00, double from £32.00.

Peacefully situated in the two acres of mature gardens, this substantial family home has been sensitively restored to provide a traditional and very comfortable holiday base. Royal Deeside offers a vast range of outdoor and heritage attractions.

Alford, Aberdeenshire

Map Ref: 4F10

★★★

B&B

Bydand Bed & Breakfast

18 Balfour Road, Alford, Aberdeenshire, AB33 8NF
Tel:019755 63613

2 rooms, all en-suite, Open Jan-Dec, B&B per person, single from £22.00, double from £22.00.

A warm welcome in this family B&B set in quiet residential area yet only 5 minutes walk from village centre. Ideal location for Castle and Whisky trails. Plenty of outdoor activities within village including dry ski slope and 18 hole golf course.

Frog Marsh Bed & Breakfast

Mossat, Alford, Aberdeenshire AB33 8PL
Tel: 019755 71355 Fax: 019755 71366
e.mail: stay@frogmarsh.com Web: www.frogmarsh.com

Our lovingly restored home offers a mix between classic and contemporary styles. Close to Castle and whisky trails and the Cairngorm National Park. Choose between a double, twin or wonderful suite, ideal for spoiling that special person in your life. B&B or DB&B; Frog Marsh is the perfect choice.

★★★★

B&B

Frog Marsh Bed & Breakfast

Mossat, Alford, Aberdeenshire, AB33 8PL
Tel:01975 571355 Fax:01975 571366
Email:stay@frogmarsh.com
Web:www.frogmarsh.com

3 rooms, some en-suite, Open Jan-Dec excl New Year, B&B per person, single from £50.00, double from £30.00.

All rooms recently converted and finished with a contemporary feel. A luxurious double suite is ideal for couples getting away from it all. Ideally placed for Deeside, the Castle Trail and Aberdeen. Open all year round, it is perfectly placed for skiers and walkers.

VAT is shown at 17.5%: changes in this rate may affect prices.

Key to symbols is on back flap.

Glenernan Guest House

37 Braemar Road, Ballater, Aberdeenshire AB35 5RQ
Tel: 013397 53111 Fax: 013397 53288
e.mail: hutcheon@glenernanguesthouse.com
Web: www.glenernanguesthouse.com

Set in beautiful Ballater overlooking Craigendarrach Hill,
Glenernan is a comfortable, put your feet up kind of place. Seven
letting bedrooms, all with ensuite facilities, one is designed for less
able guests. Two are family rooms, three have twin beds and one
double. A warm welcome awaits. Your comfort is our priority.

★★★

**GUEST
HOUSE**

Glenernan Guest House

37 Braemar Road, Ballater, Aberdeenshire, AB35 5RQ
Tel:013397 53111 Fax:013397 53288
Email:hutcheon@glenernanguesthouse.com
Web:www.glenernanguesthouse.com

Modernised Victorian home offering a friendly welcome. En-suite
accommodation including less-abled facilities, hearty breakfasts and
private parking.

7 rooms, all en-suite, Open Jan-Dec excl Xmas, B&B per person, single from
£35.00, double from £25.00.

Inverdeen House B&B

*11 Bridge Square, Ballater,
Royal Deeside AB35 5QJ
Tel: 01339 755759 Fax: 01339 755993
e.mail: info@inverdeen.com
Web: www.inverdeen.com*

Beautifully restored 1820 Georgian townhouse with
excellent accommodation and delicious breakfasts. No
smoking. Situated next to River Dee and 6 miles from
Balmoral Castle. Decorated and furnished to a very
high standard. Fishing, golf, shooting arranged. B&B
from £25.00 per person per night. Recommended as
"Excellent" in the Rough Guide to Scotland. "The best
B&B we've ever stayed in." – The Fawcett Family.

★★★★

B&B

Inverdeen House

11 Bridge Square, Ballater, AB35 5QJ
Tel:013397 55759 Fax:013397 55993
Email:info@inverdeen.com
Web:www.inverdeen.com

We offer a splendid selection of great breakfasts featuring pancakes with
genuine Canadian maple syrup, Venison sausage and home-made jam.
Inverdeen House faces the A93 (at the Dee Bridge). There is easy access
to such attractions as hillwalking, mountain climbing, orienteering,
cycling, skiing, pony trekking, fishing, gliding, 4x4 driving, bird watching,
Archaeolink and the Whisky, Castle and Stone Circle trails.

3 rooms, some en-suite, Open Jan-Dec, B&B per person, single from £28.00,
double from £25.00.

Ballater, Aberdeenshire

Map Ref: 4E11

★★★

B&B

Langdale Bed and Breakfast
Hawthorn Place, Ballater, Aberdeenshire, AB35 5QH
Tel/Fax:013397 55500
Email:mrpenguin@eggconnect.net
Web:www.langdale.4t.com

A recently refurbished Victorian villa located in the centre of Ballater. Modern en suites with many original features retained. Off-street parking and secure storage for bikes available.

3 rooms, some en-suite, Open Jan-Dec excl Xmas/New Year, B&B per person, single from £28.00, double from £23.00.

Banchory, Aberdeenshire

Map Ref: 4F11

★★★★

B&B

Ardconnel
6 Kinneskie Road, Banchory, Aberdeenshire, AB31 5TA
Tel:01330 822478

Very comfortable modern bungalow in quiet spot overlooking local golf course. 3 minutes from town centre, and all amenities. Ground floor bedrooms, one with en suite, the other a private bathroom facility.

2 rooms, 1 en-suite, Open Mar-Oct, B&B per person, single from £30.00, double from £22.00.

★★★★

**GUEST
HOUSE**

Village Guest House
83 High Street, Banchory, Kincardineshire AB31 5PJ
Tel/Fax:01330 823307
Email:village@guest-house83.freeserve.co.uk
Web:www.guest-house83.freeserve.co.uk

Charming Victorian house in centre of Royal Deeside village. Warm Scottish welcome, finished with a taste of tartan. Stepped access from rear parking. Short stroll to village centre, restaurants and all amenities. Bus stop nearby.

4 rooms, 3 en-suite, 1 priv.bathroom, Open Jan-Dec, B&B per person, single £27.00-30.00, double £25.00-30.00.

---

by Banchory, Aberdeenshire

Map Ref: 4F11

★★★★

B&B

Dorena
Strachan, By Banchory, Kincardineshire, AB31 6NL
Tel/Fax:01330 822540

Modern bungalow on edge of quiet village, with views across the fields and woods. Private parking. Only 2.5 miles from Banchory. Excellent hospitality assured.

3 rooms, all en-suite, Open Jan-Dec excl Xmas/New Year, B&B per person, double from £24.00.

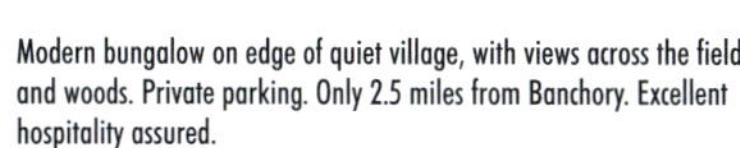

VAT is shown at 17.5%: changes in this rate may affect prices.

Key to symbols is on back flap.

Bryvard Guest House
Seafield Street, Banff AB45 1EB
Tel/Fax: 01261 818090
e.mail: bryvard@hotmail.com
Web: www.bryvardguesthouse.co.uk

An elegant Edwardian town house with friendly atmosphere which now incorporates our fully licensed restaurant from Thursdays to Saturdays (6pm-9pm). We offer a high standard of comfort with two lounges, all rooms have colour TV, hospitality trays etc. An ideal base location for golf, fishing and castle trail.

★★★★

B&B

Bryvard Guest House

Seafield Street, Banff, Aberdeenshire, AB45 1EB
Tel/Fax:01261 818090
Email:bryvard@hotmail.com
Web:www.bryvardguesthouse.co.uk

An elegant Edwardian Town House incorporating it's own licensed restaurant (Thur-Sat). Modernised to a high standard but retains character and style. Ideal base for touring this unspoilt hidden corner of Scotland.

4 rooms, some en-suite, Open Jan-Dec, B&B per person, single from £30.00, double from £27.50.

MORAYHILL
Bellevue Road, Banff AB45 1BJ
Tel: 01261 815956   Fax: 01261 818717
e.mail: morayhill@aol.com   Web: www.morayhill.co.uk

Situated in a residential area close to central amenities, this detached Victorian house offers a warm welcome. Close by are many golf courses including the highly rated Duff House Royal. The comfortable accommodation offers a relaxing lounge with log fire and a dining room overlooking the garden. Off road parking.

★★★★

B&B

Morayhill

Bellevue Road, Banff, Aberdeenshire, AB45 1BJ
Tel:01261 815956   Fax:01261 818717
Email:morayhill@aol.com
Web:www.morayhill.co.uk

Large Victorian house, centrally situated for town, golf, and fishing. Warm and friendly welcome assured. Private Parking. Many places of interest locally including Duff House and MacDuff Aquarium.

3 rooms, some en-suite, Open Jan-Dec, B&B per person, single from £29.00, double from £24.00.

★★★★

B&B

The Orchard B&B

Duff House, Banff, Aberdeenshire, AB45 3TA
Tel:01261 812146
Email:orchardbanff@aol.com
Web:www.orchardbanff.co.uk

Recently refurbished traditional house sitting in own grounds. Quiet location yet only 0.8 miles walk to town centre. On popular walk, near golf course, close proximity to River Deveron and within easy reach of Duff House. Many surrounding golf courses.

4 rooms, all en-suite, Open Feb-Nov, B&B per person, single from £25.00, double/twin from £25.00.

Important: Prices stated are estimates and may be subject to amendments

Braemar, Aberdeenshire

Map Ref: 4D11

GUEST HOUSE

Callater Lodge Guest House
9 Glenshee Road, Braemar, Aberdeenshire, AB35 5YQ
Tel:013397 41275   Fax:013397 41345
Email:laura2@hotel-braemar.co.uk
Web:www.hotel-braemar.co.uk

A warm welcome awaits you at this pleasant Victorian house in its own spacious grounds. Ideal centre for touring and walking. Close to village centre. 8 miles to Balmoral Castle and Glenshee Ski Centre. Take advantage of our snack menu and enjoy the benefits of our residents lounge.

6 rooms, all en-suite, Open Jan-Oct, B&B per person, single from £28.00, double from £26.00.

GUEST HOUSE

Clunie Lodge Guest House
Cluniebank Road, Braemar, Aberdeenshire, AB35 5ZP
Tel:013397 41330
Email:karen@clunielodge.com
Web:www.clunielodge.com

Victorian former manse house peacefully located close to village centre and short drive to golf course. Ideal base for walking, touring and golfing & ski-ing.

5 rooms with en-suite/private facilities, Open Jan-Dec, B&B per person, single from £26.00, double from £23.00.

SCHIEHALLION HOUSE
GLENSHEE ROAD, BRAEMAR, ABERDEENSHIRE AB35 5YQ
Tel: 013397 41679
e.mail: bookings@schiehallionhouse.com Web: www.schiehallionhouse.com
Combining mountain splendour with village charm, Schiehallion House lies in the very heart of the Scottish Highlands. Your hosts, Julie and Steve Heyes, welcome you with courteous, friendly and personal service. Why not make this your base to explore the delights of Royal Deeside, Private parking. Village centre 400 metres.

GUEST HOUSE

Schiehallion House
10 Glenshee Road, Braemar, Aberdeenshire, AB35 5YQ
Tel:013397 41679
Email:bookings@schiehallionhouse.com
Web:www.schiehallionhouse.com

Comfortable, tastefully decorated, Victorian house with attractive garden at gateway to Royal Deeside. Offering personal service and log fires. One ground floor annexe room. All nationalities welcome.

9 rooms, some en-suite, Open Jan-Oct, B&B per person, single from £25.00, double from £21.00.

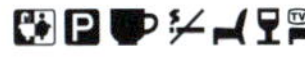

Dufftown, Banffshire

Map Ref: 4E9

B&B

Davaar Bed & Breakfast
Church Street, Dufftown, Keith, AB55 4AR
Tel/Fax:01340 820464
Email:davaar@cluniecameron.co.uk
Web:www.davaardufftown.co.uk

Comfortable and personally run accommodation. Close to Whisky and Castle Trails.

3 rooms, all en-suite, Open Jan-Dec excl Xmas/New Year, Room tariff from £22.50 per person.

VAT is shown at 17.5%: changes in this rate may affect prices.

Key to symbols is on back flap.

Dufftown, Banffshire — Map Ref: 4E9

B&B

Gowanbrae Guest House

19 Church Street, Dufftown, AB55 4AR
Tel/Fax:01340 821344
Email:bedbreakfast@gowanbrae-dufftown.co.uk
Web:www.gowanbrae-dufftown.co.uk

Family run bed & breakfast in small Speyside town. Ideal location for touring the whisky trail, touring and walking.

3 rooms, all en-suite, Open Jan-Dec excl Xmas/New Year, from £20.00 per person.

Elgin, Moray — Map Ref: 4D8

GUEST HOUSE

Colin & Wendy Clements

The Pines Guest House, East Road, Elgin, Moray IV30 1XG
Tel:01343 552495   Fax:01343 552495
Email:thepines@dsl.pipex.com
Web:www.thepinesguesthouse.com

Colin & Wendy Clements look forward to welcoming you to their home. Victorian elegance with modern comforts. Friendly atmosphere, freshly prepared food. Convenient for golf, fishing, Whisky and Castle Trails.

6 rooms, all en-suite, Open Jan-Dec, B&B per person, single from £35.00, double from £25.00.

B&B

Richmond

Moss Street, Elgin, Morayshire, IV30 1LT
Tel:01343 542561
Email:speybrewer@aol.com
Web:www.milford.co.uk/go/richmondelgin.html

Friendly, family home with garden close to railway station, town centre and all amenities. Ensuite rooms available.

3 rooms, some en-suite, Open Jan-Dec excl Xmas/New Year, £22.00-25.00.

by Elgin, Moray — Map Ref: 4D8

Parrandier, The Old Church of Urquhart

Meft Road, Urquhart, by Elgin, Moray IV30 8NH
Tel & Fax: 01343 843063
e.mail: parrandier@freeuk.com   Web: www.oldkirk.co.uk

Find your own little island of peace in this perpendicular Scottish Church surrounded by a sea of stormy farmland. Discover a distinctly DIFFERENT PLACE to explore secret Scotland. Relax in your spacious lounge in a real special atmosphere and enjoy good food and a taste of whisky. Guest lounges and open fire. Gardens for guest use.

B&B

The Old Church of Urquhart

Parrandier, Meft Road, Urquhart, by Elgin, Morayshire, IV30 8NH
Tel/Fax:01343 843063
Email:parrandier@freeuk.com
Web:www.oldkirk.co.uk

Perched on a hill top this beautiful rural setting offers uninterrupted views across surrounding farmland. Built in 1843 the church is recently converted into a unique family home. The character of the church has been retained encompassing arched windows and beamed ceilings. Guest lounges and fire. Dinner available.

3 rooms, some en-suite, Open Jan-Dec excl Xmas/Boxing Day, B&B per person, single from £34.00, double from £24.00, BB & Eve.Meal from £35.00.

Important: Prices stated are estimates and may be subject to amendments

nr Elgin, Moray

Map Ref: 4D8

Carsewell Farmhouse

★★

B&B

Alves, Nr Elgin, Morayshire, IV30 3UR
Tel:01343 850201

2 rooms, Open Apr-Oct, B&B per person, single from £20.00, double from £17.50.

Traditional stone-built farmhouse just off A96 in village of Alves, midway between Elgin & Forres. Short walk to local pub & restaurant. Bedrooms can be accessed by stair lift.

Findhorn, Moray

Map Ref: 4C7

Heath House

★★★★

B&B

Findhorn, Moray, IV36 3WN
Tel:01309 691082
Email:tandecowie@uwclub.net
Web:www.findhornaccommodation.com

3 rooms, some en-suite, Open Jan-Nov excl Xmas/New Year, B&B per person, single from £25.00, double from £23.00.

Modern bungalow in secluded cul-de-sac on outskirts of Findhorn close to beach. 4 miles (7km) to Forres. Walking, ornithology, various golf courses, the famous whisky trail and newly created walking trails.

Forres, Moray

Map Ref: 4C8

Caranrahd

★★★

B&B

19 Sanquhar Road, Forres, Moray, IV36 1DG
Tel:01309 672581
Email:jeancaranrahd@supanet.com

3 rooms, Open Jan-Dec excl Xmas/New Year, B&B per person, single from £25.00, double from £20.00.

Late Victorian stone built house within quiet residential area, yet close to all the facilities offered by the town of Forres. Traditional Scottish hospitality in a friendly family home. Excellent base for golf, touring and much more.

Milton of Grange Farmhouse B&B

★★★★

B&B

Milton of Grange, Forres, Moray, IV36 2TR
Tel/Fax:01309 676360
Email:hildamassie@aol.com
Web:www.forres-accommodation.co.uk

3 rooms, Open 15 Jan-15 Dec, B&B per person, single £25.00-40.00, double £25.00-30.00.

Beautifully appointed farmhouse on working farm, with all rooms ensuite. With Forres only 1 mile away, an ideal base for touring the whisky and castle trails or playing golf. Nearby is the historic village of Findhorn, popular with bird-watchers and boating enthusiasts. A warm welcome is assured here.

Morven

★★★

B&B

Caroline Street, Forres, Moray, IV36 1AN
Tel/Fax:01309 673788
Email:morven2@globalnet.co.uk
Web:www.golfgreenfees.com/morven/

2 ensuite, 1 standard room, Bed&Breakfast per person, ensuite twin £22.00, ensuite single £30.00, standard double £20.00, single £27.00.

Victorian house offering bed and breakfast in a warm friendly atmosphere, with all conveniences. Town centre location. En-suite bedrooms. Off-street parking. Ideal location for exploring the Whisky Trail, castles and Moray coast.

VAT is shown at 17.5%: changes in this rate may affect prices.

Key to symbols is on back flap.

Forres, Moray
Map Ref: 4C8

★★★★

B&B

Sherston House
Hillhead, Forres, Moray, IV36 0QT
Tel:01309 671087 Fax:01343 850535

3 rooms, all en-suite, Open Jan-Dec excl Xmas/New Year, B&B per person, single from £30.00, double from £25.00.

Traditional house with secluded garden grounds. Providing high quality accommodation and cuisine. Panoramic views across Findhorn Bay and the Moray Firth and wonderful parks and gardens nearby in Forres. Situated 1 mile East of Forres on A96.

★★★★

B&B

Springfield B&B
Croft Road, Forres, Moray, IV36 3JS
Tel:01309 676965   Fax:01309 673376
Email:catherinebain@tinyworld.co.uk
Web:www.springfieldb-b.co.uk

2 rooms, all en-suite, Open Jan-Dec, B&B per person, single from £30.00, double from £22.50.

Large, comfortable, modern home, set in own grounds. Short stroll to town centre, restaurants and all amenities. From Elgin on A96, left at roundabout first right (Findhorn Rd) first left to the bottom. From Inverness A96 over the first roundabout to next, take the right into Forres then as above.

---

by Forres, Moray
Map Ref: 4C8

★★★★

B&B

The Old Kirk
Dyke, By Forres, IV36 2TL
Tel:01309 641414 Fax:01309 641414
Email:oldkirk@gmx.net
Web:www.oldkirk.co.uk

3 rooms, some en-suite, Open Jan-Dec, B&B per person, single from £35.00, double from £25.00.

A warm welcome awaits you at this distinctly different Bed & Breakfast. This former Scottish church has been converted into a stylish family home with high quality standards. The Old Kirk is perfectly situated for exploring Moray tourist attractions as well as having a relaxing short break in the beautiful countryside. Choose your favourite breakfast variety from the delicious choice of our menu. Special breaks available.

---

by Fraserburgh, Aberdeenshire
Map Ref: 4G7

LONMAY OLD MANSE
Lonmay Old Manse, Lonmay, By Fraserburgh AB43 8UJ
Tel/Fax: 01346 532227
e.mail: info@lonmay.co.uk Web: www.lonmay.co.uk

A high quality Bed and Breakfast offering excellent accommodation and food whilst enjoying spectacular and uninterrupted views of open countryside. Situated between Fraserburgh and Peterhead, it is the perfect location to explore Aberdeenshire's sandy beaches and dramatic northeast coastline. Guests enjoy comfort and tranquility in an informal and friendly atmosphere.

★★★★

B&B

Lonmay Old Manse
by Fraserburgh, Aberdeenshire, AB43 8UJ
Tel:01346 532227
Email:info@lonmay.co.uk
Web:www.lonmay.co.uk

3 rooms, all en-suite, Open Jan-Dec, B&B per person, single from £35.00, double from £27.00, BB & Eve.Meal from £40.00.

A recently refurbished Manse with many traditional features. All rooms en suite and furnished with family antiques. Dinners served using local produce. Ideal for touring the North East coast.

Important: Prices stated are estimates and may be subject to amendments

nr Fraserburgh, Aberdeenshire — Map Ref: 4G7

B&B ★★★★

Rose Lodge
New Leeds, Peterhead, AB42 4HX
Tel:01346 531148
Email:lucinda@roselodge.fsworld.co.uk
Web:www.roselodge.fsworld.co.uk

A spacious detached modern home with all modern comforts. Ample off-road parking with landscaped gardens and open views. Well located on main Fraserburgh Road. Evening meals available on request.

2 rooms, 1 en-suite, 1 priv.facilities, Open Jan-Dec excl Xmas/New Year, B&B per person, single from £25.00, double from £21.00.

Fyvie, Aberdeenshire — Map Ref: 4G9

B&B ★★★★

Meikle Camaloun Bed & Breakfast
Meikle Camaloun, Fyvie, Turriff, Aberdeenshire, AB53 8JY
Tel/Fax:01651 891319
Email:w.wyness@btinternet.com

Large comfortable farmhouse, with inviting garden and superb views over rolling farmland. Ideal for Whisky and Castle Trails. Close to Fyvie Castle.

2 rooms, B&B per person double from £25.00. Room only double from £50.00.

Huntly, Aberdeenshire — Map Ref: 4F9

GUEST HOUSE ★★★

Greenmount Guest House
43 Gordon Street, Huntly, Aberdeenshire, AB54 8EQ
Tel:01466 792482
Email:greenmountguest@btconnect.com

c1854 town house with annexe. Friendly personal attention. Private parking. In town centre. On Castle and Whisky Trails, ideal touring base. Popular area for salmon and sea trout.

8 rooms, some en-suite, Open Jan-Dec excl Xmas/New Year, B&B per person, single from £18.00, double from £18.00.

B&B ★★★

Southview
Victoria Road, Huntly, Aberdeenshire, AB54 8AH
Tel:01466 792456

Detached Victorian house in quiet residential area close to town centre. Overlooking the bowling green. Good value accommodation, open all year. Excellent base for exploring this area, with its wide variety of attractions and activities.

4 rooms, Open Jan-Dec, B&B per person, single from £16.00, double from £16.00.

by Huntly, Aberdeenshire — Map Ref: 4F9

B&B ★★★

Haddoch Farmhouse Bed and Breakfast
Haddoch Farm, by Huntly, Aberdeenshire, AB54 4SL
Tel:01466 711217
Email:alice.morrison@tinyworld.co.uk

Mixed stock/arable farm near River Deveron, on B9022, 3 miles (5kms) from Huntly and 15 miles (24kms) from coast. Fine views of countryside. Home cooking. Ideal touring base for castle and Whisky Trail. A warm welcome awaits you.

3 rooms, Open Apr-Oct, B&B per person, single from £18.00, double from £17.00, BB & Eve.Meal from £28.00, booked in advance.

VAT is shown at 17.5%: changes in this rate may affect prices.

Key to symbols is on back flap.

by Inverurie, Aberdeenshire   Map Ref: 4G9

★★★

B&B

Broadsea (Mrs E Harper)
Burnhervie, Inverurie, Aberdeenshire, AB51 5LB
Tel:01467 681386 / 07792 083144 Fax:01467 681386
Email:Broadsea@aol.com

Accommodation of a high standard on this family farm of 200 acres.
Inverurie 5 miles. Aberdeen 20 miles. Bennachie is very close by. Ideally
situated for Archaeolink, Castle and Whisky Trails. Evening meal by
arrangement.

1 room, en-suite, Open Jan-Dec, B&B per person, double from £22.00, BB &
Eve.Meal from £34.00.

Keith, Banffshire   Map Ref: 4E8

★★★

**GUEST
HOUSE**

The Haughs
Keith, Moray, AB55 6QN
Tel/Fax:01542 882238
Email:jiwjackson@aol.com
Web:www.haughsfarmbedandbreakfast.net

Traditional farmhouse on 165 acre farm. Just off main road and near the
town. On Whisky Trail. Many local sports including golf available at
numerous courses.

3 rooms, all en-suite, Open Easter-Oct, B&B per person, single from £28.00-30.00,
double from £20.00.

Lossiemouth, Moray   Map Ref: 4D7

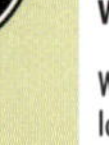

★★★

B&B

Carmania
45 St Gerardine's Road, Lossiemouth, Moray, IV31 6JX
Tel:01343 812276

Modern detached bungalow with large garden. In residential area on
south side of town centre. Within walking distance of beach, golf and
bowling.

2 rooms, 1 en-suite, Open Apr-Oct, B&B per person, double from £20.00.

Macduff, Aberdeenshire   Map Ref: 4F7

★★★

B&B

Monica & Martin's B&B
21 Gellymill Street, Macduff, Banffshire, AB44 1TN
Tel:01261 832336
Email:gellymill@aol.com
Web:www.members.aol.com/gellymill

Warm friendly atmosphere, in Georgian Town House, quiet convenient
location for shops, harbour aquarium, golf courses, perfectly situated for
exploring distilleries, castles, and Moray Firth Coast. Member of
Banffshire & Buchan Quality B & B Association.

3 rooms, some en-suite, Open Jan-Dec, B&B per person, single from £20.00,
double from £18.00.

Methlick, Aberdeenshire   Map Ref: 4G9

★★

B&B

Sunnybrae Farm
Gight, Methlick, Ellon, Aberdeenshire, AB41 7JA
Tel:01651 806456 Fax:01651 806456
Email:sunnybrae-farm@talk21.com

Comfortable accommodation on a working farm, in a quiet peaceful
location with superb views. Close to Castle and Whisky Trails. Dogs
welcome.

3 rooms, some en-suite, Open Jan-Dec, B&B per person, single from £22.00,
double from £22.00.

Oldmeldrum, Aberdeenshire · Map Ref: 4G9

CROMLET HILL

SOUTH ROAD, OLDMELDRUM, ABERDEENSHIRE AB51 0AB
Tel: 01651 872315 Fax: 01651 872164
e.mail: johnpage@cromlethill.co.uk Web: www.cromlethill.co.uk

A superb listed building overlooking *Bennachie* and the *Grampian Hills* beyond. Recently restored, the original features are retained inside and out and the house is furnished in sympathetic and luxurious style. Set in beautiful secluded gardens including a large Victorian conservatory. Private parking. Aberdeen city centre 30 minutes.

★★★★

B&B

Cromlet Hill Guest House
South Road, Oldmeldrum, Aberdeenshire, AB51 0AB
Tel:01651 872315   Fax:01651 872164
Email:johnpage@cromlethill.co.uk
Web:www.cromlethill.co.uk

Spacious, elegant, Listed Georgian mansion, in large secluded gardens within conservation area. Airport 20 minutes. On the castle trail and close to many well known National Trust properties. Including Fyvie Castle, Haddo House and Pitmedden Gardens.

3 rooms, all en-suite, Open Jan-Dec, B&B per person, single from £28.00, double from £24.00.

Peterhead, Aberdeenshire · Map Ref: 4H8

★★★

B&B

Greenbrae Farmhouse
Longside, By Peterhead, Aberdeenshire, AB42 4TX
Tel:01779 821051
Email:info@greenbraefarm.co.uk
Web:www.greenbraefarm.co.uk

19th century farmhouse that has been extended to provide three ground floor ensuite bedrooms. Ideal location for birdwatching, walking, exploring Aberdeen's castles or just relaxing. Ancestral Tourism Welcome Scheme.

3 rooms, all en-suite, Open Jan-Dec excl Xmas, B&B per person, single from £28.00, double from £25.00. Evening meal by arrangement.

by Peterhead, Aberdeenshire · Map Ref: 4H8

★★★

B&B

The Old Bank House
6 Abbey Street, Old Deer, Peterhead, Aberdeenshire AB42 5LN
Tel:01771 623463
Email:linda.rhind@btinternet.com
Web:www.btinternet.com/~gordonrhind

Originally village Bank, now comfortable family home, tastefully refurbished. In centre of quiet historic village, close to Aden Country Park. Non-smoking. Peterhead 9 miles. Evening meal on request.

2 rooms, all en-suite, Open Jan-Dec excl Xmas/New Year, B&B per person, single £25.00-30.00, double £23.00-24.00.

Portsoy, Banffshire · Map Ref: 4F7

★

SMALL HOTEL

The Boyne Hotel Portsoy
2 North High Street, Portsoy, Aberdeenshire AB45 2PA
Tel/Fax:01261 842242
Email:enquiries@boynehotel.co.uk
Web:www.boynehotel.co.uk

Refurbished 18c building on Square in seaside town, close to harbour and sandy seaside. Home cooking. Under personal supervision.

12 rooms, all en-suite, Open Jan-Dec, B&B per person, single £20.00-25.00, double £20.00-25.00, BB & Eve.Meal from £27.50-35.00.

VAT is shown at 17.5%: changes in this rate may affect prices.

Key to symbols is on back flap.

Stonehaven — Map Ref: 4G11

Ambleside B&B

Netherley, Stonehaven, Aberdeenshire, AB39 3RB
Tel:01569 731105
Email:helensbb@ambleside350.fslife.co.uk
Web:www.ambleside-bb.co.uk

Set in the heart of rural north-east 'Ambleside' offers views of the North Sea to the east and pine forests and heather clad hills to the west. Only 15 minutes drive from Aberdeen. An ideal location for working, shopping and sightseeing. All rooms en-suite.

3 rooms, all en-suite, Open Jan-Dec, B&B per person, single from £28.00, double from £22.50.

Dunnottar Mains Farmhouse B&B

Stonehaven, Kincardineshire, AB39 2TL
Tel/Fax:01569 762621
Email:dunnottar@ecosse.net

Traditional farmhouse welcome at this working farm, overlooking Dunnottar Castle on the coast.

2 rooms, 1 en-suite, 1 priv.facilities, Open Mar-Oct, B&B per person, single from £25.00, double from £24.00.

Tewel Farmhouse B&B

Tewel Farm, Stonehaven, South Aberdeenshire, AB39 3UU
Tel:01569 762306   Fax:01569 760386   Mobile:07815 167404
Email:tewelfarmhouse@btinternet.com

Traditional farmhouse in quiet location on the outskirts of Stonehaven. With lovely views of surrounding countryside, on Auchenblae Road.

2 rooms, all en-suite, Open Jan-Dec, B&B per person, single from £23.00, double from £20.00.

nr Stonehaven — Map Ref: 4G11

Ellington

Station Place, Johnshaven, DD10 0JD
Tel:0870 2252632
Email:ellington13@supanet.com
Web:www.ellingtonbandb.co.uk

Modern family home in old fishing village 28 miles south of Aberdeen. Ideally positioned to visit Glen Esk and 14th century Dunnottar Castle. Many well-known golf courses within easy range. Ground floor twin available. Small restaurant in village pub. Warm welcome assured.

2 rooms, all en-suite, Open Jan-Dec excl Xmas/New Year, B&B per person, single from £25.00, double from £22.00.

Tomintoul, Banffshire — Map Ref: 4D10

Findron Farm

Tomintoul, Ballindalloch, AB37 9ER
Tel:01807 580382
Email:elma.turner@btinternet.com
Web:www.findronfarmhouse.co.uk

Comfortable farmhouse on working farm offering a warm and friendly welcome, situated 1 mile (2 kms) from Tomintoul. 4 miles (7 km) from the Lecht ski-slopes. Ideal for touring, walking or just relaxing.

2 rooms, both en-suite, Open Jan-Dec excl Xmas, B&B per person, double from £20.00.

Important: Prices stated are estimates and may be subject to amendments

Welcome to Scotland

The Highlands and Skye

Once, the Highlands weren't just separated from the Lowlands by rugged mountains, but through a different language and culture too. Now you'll find their influence worldwide, from caber tossing in outback Australia, to the Highland songs of Nepalese Gurkhas.

Mountain bikes and adrenalin race at the Nevis Range, Fort William.

The Highlands continue to inspire people throughout the world. To some, the turbulent past is a role model for strength of character. For others, the epic wilderness denotes a simpler way of life. And some just like the whisky.

Inverness is dubbed 'capital of the Highlands' for a good reason: intense shopping, nightlife and activities are condensed into a city ideally situated to nearby wilderness. Fresh vegetables, leanest venison, seafood straight from the harbour and scotch beef are exemplified by the Highlands, including this city. The Mustard seed, Riva, Rocpool and Zanzibar are a few ideas for eating out. Hootenany offers live music of a Gaelic lilt; Bar Pivo and Barbazzas are softly lit style bars; and traditional pub fare is found at The Waterfront or picturesque Dores Inn. Johnny Foxes comes alive after dark, while Bakoo and Gs attract the clubbing crowd.

When Sunday arrives, unwind on the sandy beaches of Nairn.

A short drive from Inverness will take you to the seminal battlefield of Culloden, where Bonnie Prince and the Jacobites faced-off with the Duke of Cumberland. A real turning point, clan authority was undermined and the Highland Clearances followed. Pursue the trail of history through a series of stunning castles: Urquhart's ancient ruins are perched on Loch

The Highlands and Skye

A Highland cow.

The Highlands and Skye

Red deer in the wilderness.

Ness; Eilean Donan draws photographers to the west coast; and Dunrobin espouses French grandeur in the shire of Sutherland.

Craving some action? Described as the outdoor capital of the UK, Fort William's reputation is founded on The Nevis Range. A gondola effortlessly lifts you to 2150ft on the north face of Aonach Mor, catching views of the Great Glen and towering Ben Nevis. Mountain biking, climbing and skiing are first-rate experiences. Moving east, Aviemore is another action town noted for skiing on the Cairngorm Mountains, plus rollicking nightlife.

Of course, The Highlands are regarded as Europe's last great wilderness. The Cairngorm Mountain National Park, Glencoe, Ardnamurchan and Glen Affric are intimidating or liberating – from different points of view. Vast skies and Scotch pines are a backdrop to wildlife, from birds of prey and red deer to wildcats and red squirrels. Signposted walks can range from a sedate meander to the 73 miles of the Great Glen Way, stretching from Fort William to Inverness.

It's not all mountains, there are character-rich towns to explore: Dornoch with its cathedral and famous championship golf course, and the Glenmorangie Distillery of Tain are just two examples. Continue north to encounter the flat lands of the Flow Country in Caithness and Sutherland.

Soft accents, gentle manners and the craggy ridges of the Cuillin Hills have made the Isle of Skye a dream getaway. While climbers and campers stake the hills, a trip to Dunvegan Castle and the Aros Experience will reveal the island's startling history.

The Highlands and Skye

10-18 FEBRUARY
FORT WILLIAM FILM FESTIVAL
Delivers a world of celluloid through international film, lectures and activities.
www.mountainfilmfestival.co.uk

20 FEBRUARY-11 MARCH
INVERNESS MUSIC FESTIVAL
Instrumental and vocal performers compete in this major musical event.
Tel: 01463 716616

6-14 MAY
AVIEMORE WALKING FESTIVAL
A wide choice of guided walks from easy strolls in the forest floor to strenuous days out on the highest mountains, complimented by a full programme of entertainment.
www.aviemorewalking.com

13-21 MAY
CAITHNESS WALKING FESTIVAL
A variety of high and low level walks in the UK's most northerly county with superb wildlife watching and spectacular scenery.
Tel: 01847 851991
www.walkcaithness.com

20 MAY-4 JUNE
HIGHLAND WILD ENCOUNTERS, Caithness and Sutherland
An unrivalled opportunity to experience the wildlife of these unique islands through talks and walks.
Tel: 01847 821531
www.highlandwildencounters.com

3-4 JUNE*
MOUNTAIN BIKE WORLD CUP, Fort William
The world's best mountain bikers take part in the most gruelling mountain biking in the world.
Tel: 01397 705825
www.fortwilliamworldcup.co.uk

3-5 JUNE
GLEN AFFRIC WALKING FESTIVAL
Over 20 walks for all abilities centred around 2 National Nature Reserves and one bird reserve.
Tel: 01456 476363
www.glenaffric.info

JULY-SEPTEMBER
TALISKER SUMMER SESSIONS, Isle of Skye
Pubs and various venues jump with live bands and traditional melodies through summer months.
Tel: 01478 614003
www.skyemusic.org

2 SEPTEMBER
BEN NEVIS RACE, Fort William
Compete or just watch as the annual race up and down Britain's highest mountain unfolds.
www.bennevis.race.co.uk

** denotes provisional date, event details are subject to change please check before travelling.*

For seafood straight off the boat: Crannog Restaurant, Fort William.

The Highlands and Skye

Please refer to the maps on pages xix-xxiv for the locations of establishments appearing in the main advertising section of this guide.

Finding out more...

For practical advice, ideas and information about exploring Scotland and to book your accommodation:

Tel: 0845 22 55 121*
or if calling from outside the UK: +44 (0) 1506 832121

Email: info@visitscotland.com
Web: www.visitscotland.com

* A £3 booking fee applies to telephone bookings of accommodation.

Tourist Information Centres

The Highlands and Skye

The Highlands of Scotland

Aviemore
Grampian Road
Tel: (0845) 22 55 121
Jan – Dec

Daviot Wood
Picnic Area, A9
Tel: (0845) 22 55 121
Apr – Oct

Dornoch
The Square
Tel: (0845) 22 55 121
Jan – Dec

Drumnadrochit
The Car Park
Tel: (0845) 22 55 121
Easter – Oct

Dunvegan
2 Lochside
Tel: (0845) 22 55 121
Easter – Oct

Durness
Durine
Tel: (0845) 22 55 121
Easter – Oct

Fort Augustus
Car Park
Tel: (0845) 22 55 121
Apr – Oct

Fort William
Cameron Centre
Tel: (0845) 22 55 121
Jan – Dec

Grantown-on-Spey
54 High Street
Tel: (0845) 22 55 121
Jan – Dec

Inverness
Castle Wynd
Tel: (0845) 22 55 121
Jan – Dec

John O'Groats
County Road
Tel: (0845) 22 55 121
Apr – Oct

Kilchoan
Pier Road
Tel: (0845) 22 55 121
Apr – Oct

Lochinver
Kirk Lane
Tel: (0845) 22 55 121
Apr – Oct

Mallaig
Tel: (0845) 22 55 121
Apr – Oct. Oct-March (limited opening)

North Kessock
Picnic Site
Tel: (0845) 22 55 121
Apr – Sept

Portree
Bayfield House
Tel: (0845) 22 55 121
Jan – Dec

Strontian
Tel: (0845) 22 55 121
Apr – Oct

Thurso
Riverside
Tel: (0845) 22 55 121
Apr – Oct

Ullapool
Argylle Street
Tel: (0845) 22 55 121
Jan – Dec

THE HIGHLANDS AND SKYE

Ardgay, Sutherland — Map Ref: 4A6

★★

B&B

Corvost

Ardgay, Sutherland, IV24 3BP
Tel/Fax:01863 755317

Set in a beautiful and historical Highland Strath, this modern bungalow on working croft is homely and central for touring. Golfing, fishing, hillwalking and birdwatching all available in the area.

3 rooms, Open Jan-Dec excl Xmas/New Year, B&B per person, single from £16.00, double from £16.00.

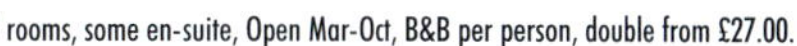

Arisaig, Inverness-shire — Map Ref: 3F11

★★★

B&B

Kilmartin Farm Guest House

Kinloid Farm, Arisaig, Inverness-shire, PH39 4NS
Tel:01687 450366   Fax:01687 450611
Email:gillies_alastair@yahoo.co.uk
Web:www.kinloid-arisaig.co.uk

B & B on working farm (0.5 miles) 1 km from Arisaig. Attractively sited on an elevated position commanding magnificent views overlooking the sea and the islands of Skye, Rhum and Eigg. 5 mins car journey to wonderful white sands. Golf course 3 miles.

3 rooms, some en-suite, Open Mar-Oct, B&B per person, double from £27.00.

Leven House Bed & Breakfast

★★★★

B&B

Leven House, Arisaig, Inverness-shire, PH39 4NR
Tel:01687 450238
Email:ejmacmillan@aol.com
Web:www.thelevenhouse.co.uk

Recently built modern, family home offering two comfortable ensuite bedrooms with TV's and tea-trays. Situated in peaceful setting just off the A830 Road to the Isles. Lovely beaches within a short stroll, ideal for relaxing break or as a base for walking, driving or sailing to the small isles of Eigg, Muck, Rhum. Scenic 9-hole golf-course only 6 miles.

2 rooms, all en-suite, Open Jan-Dec excl Xmas/New Year, B&B per person, single from £35.00, double from £23.00 pppn.

Aultbea, Ross-shire — Map Ref: 3F6

★★★★

GUEST HOUSE

Mellondale Guest House

47 Mellon Charles, Aultbea, Ross-shire, IV22 2JL
Tel/Fax:01445 731326
Email:mellondale@lineone.net
Web:www.mellondale.co.uk

Comfortable family guest house set in 4 acres, with open views of Loch Ewe. 9 miles (14.4 Kms) from Inverewe Gardens. All rooms have ensuite facilities and evening meals are available by arrangement. Plenty of walks close by including Slaggan, a village last inhabited in the 1930's, and the beach.

4 rooms, all en-suite, Open Feb-Nov, B&B per person, double from £25.00, BB & Eve.Meal from £41.00.

Tranquility

★★★

B&B

21 Mellon Charles, Aultbea, Ross-shire, IV22 2JN
Tel/Fax:01445 731241
Email:paulinephil2003@yahoo.com

Small comfortable family home overlooking Torridon Mountains, Loch Ewe and the Minch. Tea and biscuits on arrival. Home cooked evening meals available by arrangement. Private off-road parking. Ideal location for birdwatching and walking and close to Inverewe Gardens. Tranquility by name and by nature.

3 rooms, 2 en-suite, 1 priv bathroom, Open Jan-Dec excl Xmas/New Year, B&B per person, single from £22.00, double from £22.00.

VAT is shown at 17.5%: changes in this rate may affect prices.

Key to symbols is on back flap.

Aviemore, Inverness-shire   Map Ref: 4C10

CAIRN EILRIG

Mrs Mary Ferguson, Cairn Eilrig, Glenmore, Aviemore PH22 1QU
Telephone: 01479 861223 e.mail: mary@cairneilrig.fsnet.co.uk
Web: www.bedandbreakfast-aviemore-glenmore.com

Warm welcome in this small peaceful bed and breakfast situated in Glenmore Forest Park. Ideal base for exploring, walking, ski-ing, water sports, bird watching and relaxing. Tea/coffee and biscuits available in conservatory which provides panoramic views of the Cairngorms as do the bedrooms. Funicular Railway/Ski-lifts – two miles.

B&B

Cairn Eilrig
Glenmore, Aviemore, Inverness-shire, PH22 1QU
Tel:01479 861223
Email:mary@cairneilrig.fsnet.co.uk

2 rooms, Open Jan-Dec, B&B per person, single from £21.00, double from £21.00.

Cairn Eilrig is situated just behind Cairngorm Reindeer Centre, in Glenmore Forest Park with superb open views of the Cairngorms. Warm Highland hospitality guaranteed. Mountain railway and ski lifts 2 miles (3 kms).

GUEST HOUSE

Cairngorm Guest House
Grampian Road, Aviemore, Inverness-shire, PH22 1RP
Tel:01479 810630
Email:conns@lineone.net
Web:www.cairngormguesthouse.com

12 rooms, all en-suite, Open Jan-Dec, B&B per person, single from £30.00, double from £25.00.

Peter and Gail welcome you to our lovely Victorian House, 5 min walk from centre of Aviemore. Relax by the open fire in the guest lounge and enjoy home baking. Hearty breakfasts with vegetarian option. En-suite rooms some on ground floor. King sized beds with TV and VCR also available. Drying/storage facilities and private parking.

B&B

Carn Mhor
The Sheiling, Aviemore, Inverness-shire, PH22 1QD
Tel:01479 811004
Email:info@carnmhor.co.uk
Web:www.carnmhor.co.uk

5 rooms, some en-suite, Open Jan-Dec, B&B per person, single from £25.00, double from £22.00.

Modern centrally heated friendly B&B with some annex accommodation ideal for families or groups. Fields on two sides with views of the Cairngorms, quiet but not isolated.

B&B

Dunroamin Bed & Breakfast
Craig-Na-Gower Avenue, Aviemore, PH22 1RW
Tel:01479 810698
Email:lorrain.sheffield@virgin.net

3 rooms, all en-suite, Open Jan-Dec, B&B per person, single from £25.00, double from £22.00.

Family run bed and breakfast accommodation close to the centre of Aviemore. Many activities and attractions in the area, to keep the whole family occupied: walking, cycling, golf, play areas and much more.

Important: Prices stated are estimates and may be subject to amendments

Aviemore, Inverness-shire

Map Ref: 4C10

★★★

B&B

Eriskay

Craig-na-Gower Avenue, Aviemore, Inverness-shire PH22 1RW
Tel:01479 810717   Fax:01479 812015
Email:eriskay11@aol.com
Web:www.b-and-b-scotland.co.uk

3 rooms, Open Jan-Dec, B&B per person, single from £30.00, double £25.00-30.00.

Set in a quiet location close to Aviemore town centre, this modern family home offers the ideal base for exploring the magnificent scenery of the Spey valley and beyond. Evening meals available by prior arrangement.

LYNWILG HOUSE

Lynwilg, By Aviemore PH22 1PZ
Tel / Fax: 01479 811685
e.mail: marge@lynwilg.co.uk   Web: www.lynwilg.co.uk

Beautiful country house situated on the outskirts of Aviemore overlooking the Cairngorm mountains. Spacious, elegant rooms with log fires. Award winning food and hospitality. Home grown fruit, vegetables and herbs are used in our kitchen. A place to truly relax and enjoy. Prices from £30.00 - £35.00 p.p.

★★★★

GUEST HOUSE

Lynwilg House

Aviemore, Inverness-shire, PH22 1PZ
Tel:01479 811685
Email:marge@lynwilg.co.uk
Web:www.lynwilg.co.uk

3 rooms, all en-suite, Open Feb-end Oct, B&B per person, single £30.00-35.00, double £30.00-35.00, BB & Eve.Meal from £55.00.

1930's country house set in 4 acres of landscaped gardens overlooking the Cairngorms, approximately 1 mile (2kms) south of Aviemore. Evening meal available by prior arrangement.

★★★

GUEST HOUSE

Ravenscraig Guest House

Grampian Road, Aviemore, Inverness-shire, PH22 1RP
Tel:01479 810278   Fax:01479 810210
Email:info@aviemoreonline.com
Web:www.aviemoreonline.com

12 rooms, all en-suite, Open Jan-Dec, B&B per person, single from £22.00, double from £22.00.

Ravenscraig is centrally located in the village and an ideal base for touring the Highlands. Popular with birdwatchers, golfers, walkers & cyclists are our quiet ground floor garden rooms with their own front doors allowing easy access as well as privacy. We also offer family rooms, a comfortable guest lounge with local information, drying facilities, ski/golf locker, plentiful parking and legendary breakfasts!

VAT is shown at 17.5%: changes in this rate may affect prices.

Key to symbols is on back flap.

Aviemore, Inverness-shire — Map Ref: 4C10

VERMONT GUEST HOUSE
Grampian Road, Aviemore, Inverness-shire PH22 1RP
Tel: 01479 810470
email: info@vermontguesthouse.co.uk   Web: www.vermontguesthouse.co.uk
Located at the quiet end of Main Street. Ideal base to tour the Spey Valley. En-suite rooms with TVs and hospitality trays, full Scottish breakfast is served, vegetarians catered for when required. Five minutes walk to restaurants and hotels. Off road parking at rear of house. A warm and friendly greeting awaits you.

★★

GUEST HOUSE

Vermont Guest House

Grampian Road, Aviemore, PH22 1RP
Tel:01479 810470
Email:info@vermontguesthouse.co.uk
Web:www.vermontguesthouse.co.uk

Situated in centre of Aviemore, all bedrooms with some en suite facilities. Ideally placed for touring Spey Valley, and access to Cairngorm ski area.

6 rooms, some en-suite, Open Jan-Dec, B&B per person, double from £20.00.

Ballachulish, Argyll — Map Ref: 1F1

★★★★

GUEST HOUSE

Craiglinnhe House

Lettermore, Ballachulish, Argyll, PH49 4JD
Tel:01855 811270
Email:info@craiglinnhe.co.uk
Web:www.craiglinnhe.co.uk

Lochside Victorian villa amid spectacular mountain scenery offering period charm with modern comfort. Warm, friendly atmosphere, good food and wine. Ideal base for exploring the Western Highlands.

5 rooms, all en-suite, Open Feb-Dec, B&B per person, double from £28.00, BB & Eve.Meal from £45.50.

FERN VILLA GUEST HOUSE
Loanfern, Ballachulish, Argyll PH49 4JE
Telephone: 01855 811393 Fax: 01855 811727
e.mail: fernctg@aol.com Web: www.fernvilla.com
All rooms en-suite, comfortable guest lounge, Non Smoking. A warm drink welcomes you each time you return from your day's activity. Homemade natural Cooking of Scotland dinner menus using fresh local ingredients. **AA ◆◆◆◆**. **Perfect for the Great Outdoors** - walking, climbing, skiing, touring or just relaxing in beautiful surroundings. Short stay rates available.

★★★

GUEST HOUSE

Fern Villa Guest House

Loanfern, Ballachulish, PH49 4JE
Tel:01855 811393   Fax:01855 811727
Email:fernctg@aol.com
Web:www.fernvilla.com

A warm welcome awaits you in this fine Victorian granite built house in the lochside village amidst spectacular scenery. One mile from Glencoe, convenient for Fort William. Home baking and Natural Cook of Scotland features on our dinner menu. Table licence. The perfect base for walking, climbing or touring in the West Highlands. Private parking.

5 rooms, all en-suite, Open Jan-Dec, B&B per person, double from £25.00, BB & Eve.Meal from £39.00.

THE HIGHLANDS AND SKYE

Ballachulish, Argyll

Map Ref: 1F1

★★★

B&B

Parkview B&B

18 Park Road, Ballachulish, Argyll, PH49 4JS
Tel/Fax:01855 811560
Email:db.macaskill@talk21.com
Web:www.glencoe-parkview.co.uk

A traditional Highland welcome awaits you at this family run B&B, situated in the centre of Ballachulish village with views of Meall Mhor and The Pap of Glencoe. Ideal base for walkers and climbers in the Glencoe area. Fort William 14 miles to north. Glencoe 3 miles. In wet weather relax in our cosy TV lounge or read from our selection of local interest books. Drying facilities and parking available.

3 rooms, Open Jan-Dec excl Xmas/New Year. B&B per person, single from £20.00, double from £18.00.

Banavie, by Fort William, Inverness-shire

Map Ref: 3H12

★★★

B&B

Ronaval

Tomonie, Banavie, by Fort William, Inverness-shire, PH33 7LX
Tel:01397 772206

Quiet location 2.5 miles from town of Fort William with views overlooking Ben Nevis. Front and large rear garden. Ideal for travelling throughout the Highlands. All rooms on ground level. A warm Highland welcome awaits you here. Sorry no pets.

3 rooms, some en-suite, Open Feb-Dec excl Xmas/New Year, B&B per person, single from £20.00, double from £22.00.

Beauly, Inverness-shire

Map Ref: 4A8

★★★

B&B

Cruachan

Wester Balblair, Beauly, Inverness, IV4 7BQ
Tel:01463 782679 Fax:01463 783574
Email:isabella679@aol.com

Comfortable Bed & Breakfast in quiet location yet within easy reach of Beauly and its restaurants, shops and walks. 10 miles from Inverness. Convenient for Glen Affric and touring the Highlands.

3 rooms, 2 en-suite, 1 priv.facilities, Open Jan-Dec excl Xmas/New Year, B&B per person, single from £18.00-22.00, double from £18.00-22.00.

★★

B&B

Ellangowan

Croyard Road, Beauly, IV4 7DJ
Tel:01463 782273

Comfortable, centrally heated home near Priory. Ideal base for touring the Highlands of Scotland and Great Glen. A short walk to Beauly's shops, banks and restaurants. Off road parking.

3 rooms, some en-suite, Open Apr-Oct, B&B per person, single from £20.00, double from £16.00.

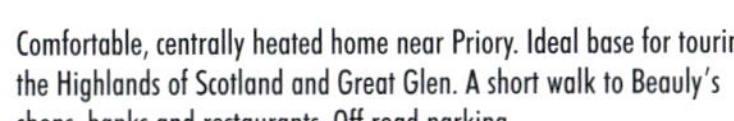

★★★

B&B

Rheindown Farm Holidays

Rheindown, Beauly, Inverness-shire, IV4 7AB
Tel:01463 782461
Email:mm.ritchie@btopenworld.com

Farmhouse on working farm, in elevated position overlooking Beauly and the Firth beyond. Farm walks.

2 rooms, Open Easter-Nov, B&B per person per night, double from £17.50.

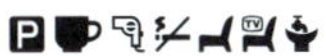

VAT is shown at 17.5%: changes in this rate may affect prices.

Key to symbols is on back flap.

by Beauly, Inverness-shire

Map Ref: 4A8

★★★

B&B

Broomhill

Kiltarlity, Beauly, Inverness-shire, IV4 7JH
Tel/Fax:01463 741447
Email:broomhill@cali.co.uk
Web:www.cali.co.uk/freeway/broomhill

Edwardian manse set in own grounds surrounded by open countryside 11 miles (18kms) from Inverness & 4 miles (6km) from Loch Ness. Large, warm comfortable rooms. Award-winning home cooking. Ideal touring base for the Highlands. Prices remain the same throughout the year.

2 rooms, Open Jan-Dec, B&B per person, single from £15.00, double from £15.00, BB & Eve.Meal from £24.00.

Boat of Garten, Inverness-shire

Map Ref: 4C10

★★★

GUEST HOUSE

Granlea House

Deshar Road, Boat of Garten, Inverness-shire PH24 3BN
Tel/Fax:01479 831601
Email:granlea.house@virgin.net
Web:http://freespace.virgin.net/granlea.house

Stone built Edwardian house, in village centre, close to Osprey reserve and golf course and Strathspey Steam Railway. Ideal touring base.

5 rooms, some en-suite, Open Jan-Dec excl Xmas, B&B per person, single from £21.00, double from £23.00.

Brora, Sutherland

Map Ref: 4C6

AR DACHAIDH

BADNELLAN, BRORA, SUTHERLAND KW9 6NQ
Tel/Fax: 01408 621658 e.mail: badnellan@madasafish.com

Traditional croft house in quiet crofting area. Ideal stop for touring the whole of the north. Ideal location for walking, birdwatching, golf, fishing, cycling, motorcycling or just sitting on the miles of quiet beaches. Home cooked meals a speciality. Treat yourself to a romantic stay in a four poster bed.

★★

B&B

Ar Dachaidh

Badnellan, Brora, Sutherland, KW9 6NQ
Tel/Fax:01408 621658
Email:badnellan@madasafish.com

Traditional 19c croft house, very quietly situated behind the village of Brora. Friendly welcome, home cooked evening meals, B&B certificate of excellence. Motorcycle friendly.

3 rooms, Open Mar-Nov, B&B per person, single from £19.00, double from £19.00, BB & Eve.Meal from £30.00.

Important: Prices stated are estimates and may be subject to amendments

Brora, Sutherland | Map Ref: 4C6

GLENAVERON

AA ◆◆◆◆◆

Golf Road, Brora, Sutherland KW9 6QS

Tel: 01408 621601

e.mail: glenaveron@hotmail.com   Web: www.glenaveron.co.uk

Glenaveron is a luxurious Edwardian house with extensive mature gardens. Only a short walk to Brora golf club and lovely beaches. A 25 minute drive to the Royal Dornoch golf club. An ideal base for touring The Northern Highlands and Orkney. All rooms are en-suite. Non smoking.

B&B

Glenaveron

Golf Road, Brora, Sutherland, KW9 6QS
Tel:01408 621601
Email:glenaveron@hotmail.com
Web:www.glenaveron.co.uk

Spacious stone built family home, set in mature gardens, in a peaceful area of Brora. A few minutes walk from the golf course; several others, including Royal Dornoch in the area. Other sporting and leisure facilities nearby, as are sandy beaches, historic sites, eating establishments. Excellent base for exploring the far north of Scotland; ideal stopover en route to Orkney.

3 rooms, all en-suite, Open Jan-Dec excl Xmas/New Year, B&B per person, single from £35.00, double from £30.00.

Carrbridge, Inverness-shire | Map Ref: 4C9

B&B

Birchwood

12 Rowan Park, Carrbridge, PH23 3BE
Tel/Fax:01479 841393
Email:normanwhitehall@lineone.net
Web:www.carrbridge.com/birchwood.htm

Modern bungalow in quiet Highland village, warm welcome assured. Ideal base for touring, bird watching, hillwalking and cycling. Entering Carrbridge from the south main street and across from the church is Carr Road. 500yds down Carr Road is Rowan Park. Birchwood is 6th. house on right.

2 rooms, all en-suite, Open Jan-Dec, B&B per person, single from £22.00, double from £22.00.

The Cairn Hotel

Main Road, Carrbridge, Inverness-shire, PH23 3AS
Tel:01479 841212   Fax:01479 841362
Email:info@cairnhotel.co.uk
Web:www.cairnhotel.co.uk

INN

Enjoy the country pub atmosphere, log fire, malt whiskies, real ales and affordable food in this family owned village centre hotel. Close to the historic bridge. A perfect base for touring the Cairngorms, Whisky Trail and Loch Ness.

7 rooms, most en-suite, Open Jan-Dec, B&B per person from £24.00.

Cromarty, Ross-shire | Map Ref: 4B7

Newfield

Newhall Bridge, Poyntzfield, by Dingwall, IV7 8LQ
Tel:01381 610325
Email:jean.munro@tesco.net
Web:www.newfield-bb.co.uk

B&B

Comfortable bed & breakfast in a traditional cottage set amidst peaceful farming country on the Black Isle. 18 miles from Inverness and 6 miles to Cromarty. An ideal location for touring the east, north and west coast of the Highlands. Udale Bay Bird Sanctuary 1 mile away. Dolphin trips available at Cromarty and Avoch.

1 family room en-suite, 1 double room priv.facilities, B&B per person from £23.00. Open Feb-Nov.

VAT is shown at 17.5%: changes in this rate may affect prices.

Key to symbols is on back flap.

nr Cromarty, Ross-shire

Map Ref: 4B7

B&B

Braelangwell House

Balbair, Ross-shire, IV7 8LT
Tel:01381 610353 Fax:01381 610467
Email:braelangwell@btinternet.com
Web:www.braelangwell.co.uk

Fine Georgian house dating from the late 18th Century, situated in 5 acres of garden and 50 acres of woodland. 7 miles from Cromarty. Convenient for road and air links from the south. Ideal base for exploring the northern Highlands.

3 rooms, Open Mar-Dec, B&B per person, single from £60.00, double from £40.00, room only single £60.00-80.00, double £80.00-100.00.

Culbokie, Black Isle

Map Ref: 4B7

AVERON HOUSE

Wester Toberchurn, Culbokie, Black Isle, Ross-shire IV7 8LS
Tel/Fax: 01349 877179
e.mail: averon.house@virgin.net
Web: www.smoothhound.co.uk/hotels/averonhouse.html

Averon is situated in its own extensive grounds overlooking the Cromarty Firth. Ground floor ensuite bedrooms with all amenities and lots of homely touches. Ideal base for touring the highlands, also for viewing the dolphins and seals. Perfect base for cyclists, walkers and birdwatchers. Own large parking bays. Non-Smoking.

B&B

Averon House

Wester Toberchurn, Culbokie, by Dingwall
Ross-shire, IV7 8LS
Tel/Fax:01349 877179
Email:averon.house@virgin.net
Web:www.smoothhound.co.uk/hotels/averonhouse.html

Set into the hillside above the Cromarty Firth, Averon House commands excellent views of the Firth and the hills and mountains beyond. Quiet peaceful location, yet within 5 mins of the A9, providing easy access to Inverness and for touring the Highlands.

3 rooms, all en-suite, Open Feb-Nov, B&B per person, double from £23.00.

Culloden Moor, Inverness-shire

Map Ref: 4B8

B&B

Bayview B&B

Westhill, Inverness, IV2 5BP
Tel/Fax:01463 790386
Email:bayview.guest@lineone.net

Quiet comfortable home in pleasant country surroundings with magnificent views over the Moray Firth. Evening meals can be provided with prior notification.

3 rooms, 2 en-suite, 1 priv.facilities, Open Mar-Oct, B&B per person, from £22.00.

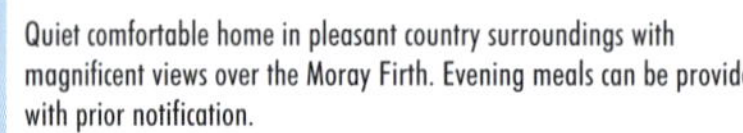

B&B

Westhill House

Westhill, Inverness, IV2 5BP
Tel:01463 793225
Email:j.honnor@bigfoot.com
Web:www.scotland-info.co.uk/westhill.htm

This modern family home offers a warm welcome, local knowledge and conversation with traditional bed & breakfast accommodation. Set in a beautiful garden within peaceful rural surroundings, it is one mile from Culloden Battlefield, 3 miles from Inverness city centre, 5 miles from the airport and within easy reach of Loch Ness and the Highlands.

3 rooms, some en-suite, Open Apr-Oct, B&B per person, single £23.00-£25.00, double £25.00, family £60.00-75.00.

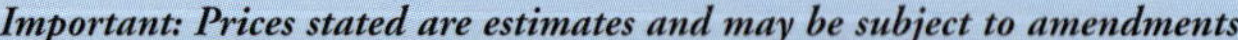

Important: Prices stated are estimates and may be subject to amendments

Dornie, by Kyle of Lochalsh, Ross-shire   Map Ref: 3G9

GUEST HOUSE

Eilean A-Cheo

Dornie, by Kyle of Lochalsh, Ross-shire, IV40 8DY
Tel:01599 555485
Email:stay@scothighland.com
Web:www.scothighland.com

Situated on a quiet side road just a few minutes walk from the picturesque Eilean Donan Castle and overlooking the loch. Easy access to the Isle of Skye, Plockton with its famous palm trees and the wonderful countryside round about. Excellent hospitality and a true Gaelic welcome.

5 rooms, some en-suite, Open Jan-Dec, B&B per person, single from £26.00, double from £18.00.

B&B

Fasgadale

2 Sallachy, Dornie, Kyle, Ross-shire, IV40 8DZ
Tel:01599 588238

Modern bungalow on working croft. An elevated position with views across Loch Long. Gaelic spoken.

2 rooms, Open Apr-Oct, B&B per person, double from £16.00.

B&B

Sealladh Mara

Dornie, Kyle of Lochalsh, Ross-shire, IV40 8EY
Tel:01599 555296   Fax:01599 555250

Modern family home, looking over Loch Duich and Eilean Donan Castle towards Kintail mountains. Handy for touring to Skye and Wester Ross. Ideal for walking.

3 rooms, 2 en-suite doubles, Open Jan-Dec, B&B per person, double £20.00-25.00.

Dornoch, Sutherland   Map Ref: 4B6

B&B

Corven B&B

Station Road, Embo, by Dornoch, Sutherland, IV25 3PR
Tel:01862 810128

Small detached bungalow with fine views across the Golspie/Helmsdale Rogart, Dornoch Bay/Lochfleet to hills beyond. Sandy beaches and golf courses nearby. Non-smoking throughout. All rooms on one level.

3 rooms, all en-suite, Open Mar-Oct, B&B per person, single from £30.00, double £20.00-24.00.

B&B

Hillview Bed and Breakfast

Evelix Road, Dornoch, Sutherland, IV25 3RD
Tel:01862 810151
Email:hillviewbb@talk21.com
Web:www.milford.co.uk/go/hillviewbb.html

Hillview is a double fronted bungalow situated in rural woodland setting. 3 mins from Dornoch, double and twin rooms with ensuite facilities and guest lounge. Private parking. Dornoch boasts breathtaking walks and views nearby. Award winning beach. Two golf courses one of which is a championship course.

2 rooms, (1double, 1 twin/family), both en-suite, Open Jan-Dec, B&B per person, single £24.00-35.00, double £22.00-28.00.

VAT is shown at 17.5%: changes in this rate may affect prices.   **Key to symbols is on back flap.**

Drumnadrochit, Inverness-shire   Map Ref: 4A9

★★★★

B&B

Kilmore Farmhouse
Drumnadrochit, IV53 6UF
Tel:01456 450524
Email:kilmorefarm@supanet.com

Modern farmhouse peacefully situated with splendid views of surrounding hills. Easy walking distance from Loch Ness through S.S.S.I. woodland.

3 rooms, all en-suite, Open Mar-Nov. Double from £22.00 per person.

★★★★

GUEST
HOUSE

Woodlands
East Lewiston, Drumnadrochit, Inverness-shire IV63 6UJ
Tel:01456 450356   Fax:01456 459343
Email:woodlands2004@btinternet.com
Web:www.woodlands-drumnadrochit.co.uk

Comfortable modern home, newly refurbished in peaceful location with panoramic views of the surrounding hills. Non smoking establishment for the comfort of our guests.

5 rooms, some en-suite, Open Jan-Dec excl Xmas, B&B per person, single from £30.00, double from £20.00.

Dunbeath, Caithness   Map Ref: 4D4

★★

B&B

Tormore Farm
Tormore, Dunbeath, Caithness, KW6 6EH
Tel:01593 731240

Warm Highland hospitality on this traditional working farm. Dinner available on request. One ground floor bedroom. Extensive sea view from the farm, clifftop walks, including varied bird species & especially puffins.

3 rooms, Open Jan-Dec, B&B per person, single from £18.00, double from £17.00, BB & Eve.Meal from £24.00.

Important: Prices stated are estimates and may be subject to amendments

Dundonnell, Ross-shire — Map Ref: 3G7

BADRALLACH D,B&B

Croft 9, Badrallach, Dundonnell, Ross-shire IV23 2QP
Tel: 01854 633281
e.mail: michael.stott2@virgin.net Web: www.badrallach.com
Dinner bed and breakfast in the old byre with peat stove, gas lighting and crisp linen sheets is truly special. The tranquil lochshore location on this working croft overlooking Anteallach is magnificent. You can walk, sleep, boat, fish, view orchids, otters, porpoises, golden eagles or just do nothing.

Badrallach D,B&B

Croft 9, Badrallach, Dundonnell, Ross-shire IV23 2QP
Tel:01854 633281
Email:michael.stott2@virgin.net
Web:www.badrallach.com

Traditional croft B&B in the Old Byre with peat stove, gas lighting, crisp linen sheets in a magnificent remote lochshore setting. Ullapool and Gairloch nearby.

1 room, en-suite, Open Jul-Aug (other times by appointment), B&B per person, single from £25.00, double from £25.00, BB & Eve.Meal from £50.00.

Durness, Sutherland — Map Ref: 4A3

Puffin Cottage

Durness, Sutherland, IV27 4PN
Tel/Fax:01971 511208
Email:puffincottage@aol.com
Web:www.puffincottage.com

A friendly welcome awaits you at this comfortable cottage. En-suite room has sea views. Close to the village, yet in a quiet location. Golf course and beaches only a short distance away. Smoo cave 2 miles away. Hillwalking, archaeology, bird and wildlife in abundance.

2 rooms, some en-suite, Open Apr-Sep, B&B per person, double from £18.00.

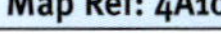

Fort Augustus, Inverness-shire — Map Ref: 4A10

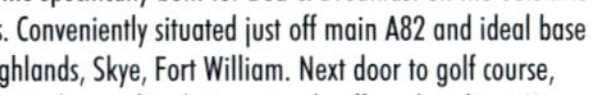

Carn A' Chuilinn, Anne Nicolson

Golf Course Road, Fort Augustus, Inverness-shire PH32 4BY
Tel/Fax:01320 366387
Email:info@carnachuilinn.com
Web:www.visitscotland.com

A new family home specifically built for Bed & Breakfast on the outskirts of Fort Augustus. Conveniently situated just off main A82 and ideal base for exploring Highlands, Skye, Fort William. Next door to golf course, trout fishery close to shores of Loch Ness. Ample off road parking. No smoking establishment.

3 rooms, all en-suite, Open Jan-Dec, B&B per person, single from £25.00, double from £23.00.

Cartref B&B

Fort William Road, Fort Augustus, Inverness-shire, PH32 4BH
Tel:01320 366255 Fax:01320 366782
Email:cartrefhouse@btinternet.com

Local stone built house situated in the village and with hotels and restaurants close by. Within walking distance of Loch Ness and Caledonian Canal. Ideal base for touring the Highlands and the Great Glen.

3 rooms, some en-suite, Open Mar-Nov, B&B per person, single from £25.00, double from £22.00.

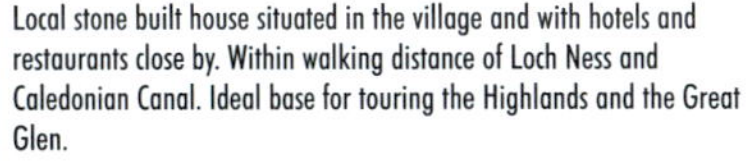

VAT is shown at 17.5%: changes in this rate may affect prices. | *Key to symbols is on back flap.*

Fort Augustus, Inverness-shire Map Ref: 4A10

★★★★

B&B

Sonas

Inverness Road, Fort Augustus, PH32 4DH
Tel/Fax:01320 366291
Web:www.nessaccom.co.uk/sonas

Comfortable modern house in elevated position on the northern edge of the village, with excellent views of surrounding hills. Attractive garden available for guests. Good parking.

3 rooms, all en-suite, Open Jan-Dec, B&B per person, single from £22.00, double from £20.00.

★★★

B&B

Thistle Dubh

Auchterawe Road, Fort Augustus, Inverness-shire, PH32 4BN
Tel:01320 366380
Email:thistledubh@supanet.com

Very comfortable rooms in large modern home set in peaceful surroundings on edge of natural woodlands. 10 minutes walk to village, shops, restaurants and canal side.

3 rooms, all en-suite, Open Jan-Dec, B&B per person, single from £20.00, double from £18.00.

AWAITING
INSPECTION

Tigh Na Mairi

Canalside, Fort Augustus, Inverness-shire PH32 4BA
Tel/Fax:01320 366766
Email:tighnamairi@yahoo.co.uk
Web:www.tighnamairi.co.uk

3 rooms, Open Jan-Dec excl Xmas/New Year, B&B per room, single from £22.50, double from £48.00, family from £65.00.

Important: Prices stated are estimates and may be subject to amendments

Fort William, Inverness-shire

Map Ref: 3H12

Alt-An Lodge

Achintore Road, Fort William PH33 6RN Tel: 01397 704546
e.mail: altanlodge@bushinternet.com
Quality accommodation enjoying superb location on the banks of Loch
Linnhe. Ensuite rooms with loch/mountain views. Private parking. All facilities
including hearty breakfast. Enjoy the picturesque 1 mile stroll to the town
centre along the loch side. Ideal base for mountain walks or touring.
£20.00 to £25.00
"A really nice place to stay".

★★★

B&B

Alt-An Lodge
Achintore Road, Fort William, Inverness-shire, PH33 6RN
Tel:01397 704546
Email:altanlodge@bushinternet.com

Enjoying a superb location on the banks of Loch Linnhe. En-suite rooms
with loch views. Private parking. Quality accommodation with hearty
breakfast. Town centre just a pleasant one-mile stroll along the loch side.

2 rooms en-suite, 1 room priv.facilities, Open Jan-Dec excl Xmas/New Year, B&B
per person, double from £20.00.

★★★

B&B

Ben Nevis View
Station Road, Corpach, by Fort William
Inverness-shire, PH33 7JH
Tel:01397 772131
Email:bennevisview@amserve.net
Web:www.bennevisview.co.uk

Modern house situated on the Road to The Isles near the beginning of
the Caledonian Canal. Only 3 miles from the centre of Fort William.
Beautiful view of Ben Nevis and surrounding hills. Ample private
parking. Local restaurants/pubs within walking distance. Comfortable
guests lounge with Sky TV.

2 rooms, all en-suite, Open Feb-Nov, B&B per person, double from £20.00-22.50.
Family room on application.

BLYTHEDALE

Seafield Gardens, Fort William, Inverness-shire PH33 6RJ
Tel: 01397 705523
Email: blythedalebandb@btinternet.com Web: www.blythedale.co.uk
Modern detached villa situated 1 mile from Fort William town centre.
Train and bus stations nearby. Set back from main A82 road in quiet
surroundings. Guests enjoy fine views of Loch Linnhe and Ardgour Hills.
Comfortable well equipped rooms, all ensuite. Colour TVs,
private car parking. Guests lounge. Open all year.

★★★★

B&B

Blythedale
Seafield Gardens, Fort William, Inverness-shire PH33 6RJ
Tel:01397 705523
Email:blythedalebandb@btinternet.com
Web:www.blythedale.co.uk

Blythedale is a modern detached villa situated approx 1 mile from Fort
William town centre. Set back and above the main A82 road in quiet
surroundings. Guests enjoy a fine view of Loch Linnhe, Loch Eil and the
Ardgour Hills. Full Scottish breakfast and a separate lounge for guests to
relax in.

3 rooms, all en-suite, Open Jan-Dec, B&B per person, single from £35.00, double
from £28.00.

VAT is shown at 17.5%: changes in this rate may affect prices.

Key to symbols is on back flap.

Corrieview

Corrieview, Lochyside
Fort William PH33 7NX
Tel: 01397 703608
e.mail: corrieview@hotmail.com

Traditional detached house in quiet residential area close to all amenities. All rooms with private facilities. Open views of Ben Nevis range and Mamore mountains. Well appointed and comfortable rooms and residents lounge. Ample private parking. Excellent base for touring the Highlands of Scotland.

★★★

B&B

Corrieview

Lochyside, Fort William, PH33 7NX
Tel:01397 703608
Email:corrieview@hotmail.com

Detached house in private grounds. 2 miles from Fort William town centre. Convenient for touring the Highlands, open views, close to Nevis Range, private parking, lockup for m.bikes.

3 rooms, some en-suite, Open Jan-Dec excl Xmas/New Year, B&B per person, double from £22.50.

Important: Prices stated are estimates and may be subject to amendments

"CROLINNHE"

"Crolinnhe", Grange Road, Fort William PH33 6JF
Tel: 01397 702709 Fax: 01397 700506
e.mail: crolinnhe@yahoo.com
Web: www.crolinnhe.co.uk

Spoil yourself with the elegance of Crolinnhe where this grand Victorian house stands proudly overlooking Loch Linnhe. Relax in the tastefully furnished rooms where the attention to detail is clearly visible. Start the day with a varied menu for breakfast in the charming dining room overlooking the loch and the hills beyond. Relax on cooler evenings by log fire with complementary sherry. The town of Fort William is only a 10 minute walk away where you may shop, take a boat trip on Loch Linnhe and more. Ben Nevis, Scotland's highest peak, invites you to a challenging but attainable climb.

Prices now from £50.00 - £65.00 per person per night B&B.

B&B

Crolinnhe
Grange Road, Fort William, PH33 6JF
Tel:01397 702709   Fax:01397 700506
Email:crolinnhe@yahoo.com
Web:www.crolinnhe.co.uk

Family run detached Victorian villa c1880, refurbished to a high standard. Friendly and welcoming atmosphere. Large colourful garden. Superb views. Short walk from town centre and all amenities.

3 rooms, all en-suite, Open Apr-Nov, B&B per person, double £50.00-65.00.

Glenlochy Guest House

Nevis Bridge, Fort William, Inverness-shire PH33 6LP
Tel: 01397 702909
e.mail: glenlochy1@aol.com Web: www.glenlochy.co.uk
Situated in own spacious grounds at entrance to Glen Nevis and end of West Highland Way yet easy walking distance to town. Glenlochy offers good value bed and breakfast accommodation in en-suite rooms. Recommended by "Which" Best B&B Guide. A warm welcome from our friendly staff.
Large private car park.

GUEST HOUSE

Glenlochy Guest House
Nevis Bridge, Fort William, Inverness-shire PH33 6LP
Tel:01397 702909
Email:glenlochy1@aol.com
Web:www.glenlochy.co.uk

Detached house with garden situated at Nevis Bridge, midway between Ben Nevis and the town centre. 0.5 miles (1km) to railway station. 2 annexe rooms.

10 rooms, some en-suite, Open Jan-Dec, B&B per person, single £20.00-50.00, double £20.00-35.00.

VAT is shown at 17.5%: changes in this rate may affect prices.   Key to symbols is on back flap.

Fort William, Inverness-shire

Map Ref: 3H12

★★

B&B

Keirlee

36 Grange Road, Fort William, Inverness-shire, PH33 6JF
Tel:01397 702803/07944 329499
Email:KeirLee@hotmail.com

Semi-detached house in a quiet street close to the centre of Fort William. Plenty to see and do in the area, an excellent base for exploring further afield.

2 rooms, Open Jan-Dec, B&B per person, twin/double from £18.00-22.00.

V

Lawriestone Guest House

Achintore Road, Fort William,
Inverness-shire PH33 6RQ
Tel/Fax: 01397 700777
e.mail: susan@lawriestone.co.uk
Web: www.lawriestone.co.uk

Treat yourself to a break in this beautifully maintained fully refurbished elegant Victorian townhouse built in 1885. Situated in its own grounds only 5 minutes walk from the town centre, this family run guest house offers a high standard of accommodation, a friendly Scottish welcome and excellent Scottish breakfasts. Fort William is an ideal touring base with Oban, Mallaig, Isle of Skye, Inverness and Speyside all within easy reach for a day's outing. Non-smoking. Private car park. Sorry no pets.

★★★★

B&B

Lawriestone Guest House

Achintore Road, Fort William, Inverness-shire PH33 6RQ
Tel/Fax:01397 700777
Email:susan@lawriestone.co.uk
Web:www.lawriestone.co.uk

A warm welcome awaits you at Lawriestone. Our main concern is your comfort and well being. The beautifully furnished rooms are all en-suite with colour TV and tea/coffee making etc. At breakfast a varied selection, including Scottish or vegetarian breakfasts, is available. Come and experience our hospitality and our beautiful location by Loch Linnhe and surrounding hills. Walking, fishing, golf, skiing etc are available locally.

4 rooms, all en-suite, Open Jan-Dec excl Xmas/New Year, B&B per person, double £27.50-40.00.

V

★★★

B&B

Leasona Bed & Breakfast

Torlundy, Fort William, PH33 6SW
Tel:01397 704661
Email:leasona@hotmail.com

Friendly, highland welcome awaits you in our modern family home. Situated in a beautiful Glen setting with outstanding views of Ben Nevis and Aonach Mor ski area. Only 2½ miles from Fort William town centre. Excellent base for hill-walking, skiing, pony trekking and touring. Private parking.

3 rooms, some en-suite, Open Jan-Dec excl Xmas/New Year, B&B per person, single £25.00, double £20.00-25.00.

C W V

Important: Prices stated are estimates and may be subject to amendments

Fort William, Inverness-shire

Map Ref: 3H12

GUEST HOUSE

Lochan Cottage Guest House

Lochyside, Fort William, Inverness-shire, PH33 7NX
Tel:01397 702695
Email:lochanco@btopenworld.com
Web:www.fortwilliam-guesthouse.co.uk

Lochan Cottage Guest House is situated in 1 acre of gardens with panoramic views of Ben Nevis, the highest mountain in Great Britian, and the ski slopes of Aonach Mor. Traditional Scottish, vegetarian or continental breakfast is served in the bright conservatory.

6 rooms, all en-suite, Open Jan-Dec excl Xmas, B&B per person, double from £25.00.

GUEST HOUSE

Mansefield Guest House

Corpach, Fort William, Inverness-shire, PH33 7LT
Tel:01397 772262
Email:mansefield@btopenworld.com
Web:www.fortwilliamaccommodation.com

This traditional Scottish guest house is situated on the 'Road to the Isles' and set in mature gardens with views of the surrounding mountains. We specialise in relaxation, comfort and home cuisine. Being small and select the ambience is special and attention personal and friendly. Sorry we are unable to accommodate children under 12 years of age.

6 rooms, all en-suite, Open Jan-Dec, B&B per person, single from £21.00, double from £21.00, BB & Eve.Meal from £34.00.

Mayfield
Bed and Breakfast

Mayfield, Happy Valley, Torlundy, Fort William PH33 6SN
Tel: 01397 703320 Fax: 01397 701926
e.mail: enquiry@torlundy.co.uk Web: www.torlundy.co.uk
A quiet place to stay in the shadow of Ben Nevis only 3 miles to Fort William. Ideal base for touring the Highlands. A warm welcome awaits you at Mayfield. We accept most major credit/debit cards.

B&B

Mayfield Bed & Breakfast

Happy Valley, Torlundy, Fort William, PH33 6SN
Tel:01397 703320 Fax:01397 701926
Email:enquiry@torlundy.co.uk
Web:www.torlundy.co.uk

A quiet place to stay in the shadow of Ben Nevis only 2 miles to Fort William. Convenient base for touring the Highlands. A warm welcome awaits you at Mayfield.

3 rooms, some en-suite, Open Jan-Dec, B&B per person, single from £25.00, double from £18.00.

VAT is shown at 17.5%: changes in this rate may affect prices.

Key to symbols is on back flap.

Fort William, Inverness-shire | Map Ref: 3H12

QUAICH COTTAGE

Upper Banavie, Fort William PH33 7PB
Tel: 01397 772799
e.mail: MacDonald@quaichcottage.fsnet.co.uk

Our modern detached home on an elevated rural site offers spacious accommodation and a warm friendly welcome. All rooms have uninterrupted views across the Great Glen and Caledonian Canal to Ben Nevis and ski area. The peaceful atmosphere will recharge the batteries. A Taste of Scotland restaurant close by.

★★★★

B&B

Quaich Cottage

Upper Banavie, Fort William, Inverness-shire PH33 7PB
Tel:01397 772799
Email:macdonald@quaichcottage.fsnet.co.uk
Web:www.visitscotland.com

Modern home nestling in the hills with spectacular views towards Ben Nevis and Nevis Range. Ideal base for those touring the West Highlands and for the outdoor enthusiast. All rooms ensuite. Ample parking. Wide choice for breakfast - both traditional and continental. Easy access to Caledonian Canal. Fort William 4 miles. Banavie 1.5 miles. Drying facilities available.

3 rooms, all en-suite, Open Jan-Dec, B&B per person, single from £25.00, double from £25.00.

★★★

B&B

Rhiw Goch

Banavie, Fort William, PH33 7LY
Tel/Fax:01397 772373
Email:kay@rhiwgoch.co.uk
Web:www.rhiwgoch.co.uk

Situated at the top of Neptune's Staircase, 3 miles from Fort William, our ensuite bedrooms have superb views overlooking the Caledonian Canal and beyond to Ben Nevis. We will happily share our knowledge of the area with you. Enjoy the outdoor activities on offer or simply take in the magnificent scenery. We also hire out mountain bikes and Canadian canoes.

3 rooms, all en-suite, Open Jan-Dec excl Xmas/New Year, B&B per person, twins £22.00-26.00.

★★★★

B&B

Seangan Croft

Banavie, Fort William, PH33 7PB
Tel:01397 773114
Email:seangan-chalets@fortwilliam59.freeserve.co.uk

Modern croft house within 5 miles of bustling Fort William, surrounded by open countryside, woodland, hills and moorland. Hours of relaxed hillwalking and a wealth of wildlife. Stroll along the nearby Caledonian Canal towpath or enjoy a leisurely meal in our Taste of Scotland restaurant.

3 rooms, all en-suite, Open Mar-Dec excl Xmas/New Year, B&B per person, single from £28.00-30.00, double from £25.00-28.00.

★★

B&B

Stobahn

Fassifern Road, Fort William, PH33 6BD
Tel/Fax:01397 702790
Email:boggi@supanet.com

Detached house, situated close to the town centre and just a few minutes walk from the High Street and the railway station.

4 rooms, some en-suite, Open Jan-Dec, B&B per person, single £18.00-28.00, double £18.00-28.00, BB & Eve.Meal from £40.00. No pets.

Important: Prices stated are estimates and may be subject to amendments

Fort William, Inverness-shire — Map Ref: 3H12

B&B ★

Taormina
Banavie, Fort William, PH33 7LY
Tel:01397 772217

4 rooms, Open Apr-Sep, B&B per person, single from £18.00, double from £18.00.

Taormina is in a quiet situation in Banavie Village close to Neptune's Staircase on the Caledonian Canal. Ben Nevis and Aonach Mor can be seen from the large garden. Banavie Scotrail station and bus halt are five minute's walk away. Several good hotels and pubs locally.

GUEST HOUSE ★★

Viewfield House
Alma Road, Fort William, Inverness-shire, PH33 6HD
Tel:01397 704763

4 rooms, 2 en-suite, 2 priv.facilities, Open all year, B&B per person, single/double £18.00-25.00.

Family house in elevated location set above Fort William yet within walking distance of town centre. Private parking available.

B&B ★★★★

Voringfoss B&B
5 Stirling Place, Fort William, Inverness-shire PH33 6UW
Tel:01397 704062
Email:info@voringfoss.co.uk
Web:www.voringfoss.co.uk

3 rooms, all en-suite, Open Jan-Dec, B&B per person, double from £25.00.

Highland hospitality at its best for those who prefer a quiet situation within one mile of the town centre. Landscaped garden affords panoramic views to surrounding hills. An ideal centre from which to explore the West Highlands. Special diets catered for.

---

by Fort William, Inverness-shire — Map Ref: 3H12

B&B ★★★★

Dailanna Guest House
Kinlocheil, Fort William, Inverness-shire PH33 7NP
Tel/Fax:01397 722253
Email:flo@dailanna.co.uk
Web:www.dailanna.co.uk

3 rooms, all en-suite, Open Apr-Oct, B&B per person, double £25.00-30.00.

Detached bungalow with large garden in elevated, peaceful position with fine views southwards over Loch Eil to the hills of Ardgour. Enjoy the colourful sunset skies from our spacious lounge. The Isle of Skye, Morvan and Moidart are all easily accessible along the 'Road to the Isles'.

---

nr Fort William, Inverness-shire — Map Ref: 3H12

B&B ★★★★

Springburn Farm House
Stronaba, Spean Bridge, Inverness-shire, PH34 4DX
Tel/Fax:01397 712707
Email:info@stronaba.co.uk
Web:www.stronaba.co.uk

3 rooms, all en-suite, Open Jan-Dec, B&B per person, single from £27.50, double from £22.50.

Family home in own grounds with panoramic views of Ben-Nevis and surrounding hills. Bedrooms with all facilities and comfortable lounge for relaxing after a days touring in the area. Why not spend the evening feeding the Highland Cows?

VAT is shown at 17.5%: changes in this rate may affect prices.

Key to symbols is on back flap.

Gairloch, Ross-shire   Map Ref: 3F7

HEATHERDALE

Charleston, Gairloch IV21 2AH

Tel/Fax: 01445 712388 e.mail: brochod1@aol.com

A warm welcome awaits at Heatherdale, situated on the outskirts of Gairloch, overlooking the harbour and bay beyond. Within easy walking distance of golf course and sandy beaches. Ideal base for hill-walking. All rooms en-suite facilities, some with seaview. Excellent eating out facilities nearby. Ample parking. Residents lounge with open fire.

B&B

Heatherdale

Charleston, Gairloch, Ross-shire, IV21 2AH
Tel/Fax:01445 712388
Email:BrochoD1@aol.com

Modern detached house on hill on outskirts of Gairloch and overlooking the harbour. Ideal base for a relaxing holiday. Ample space for parking. All bedrooms ensuite. A warm welcome assured.

3 rooms, all en-suite, Open Mar-Nov, B&B per person, double from £22.00.

B&B

Kerrysdale House

Gairloch, Rosshire, IV21 2AL
Tel/Fax:01445 712292
Email:mac.kerr@btinternet.com
Web:www.kerrysdalehouse.co.uk

18c farmhouse recently refurbished and tastefully decorated. Modern comforts in a peaceful setting. 1 mile (2kms) south of Gairloch.

3 rooms, some en-suite, Open Jan-Dec, B&B per person, single from £30.00, double from £26.00.

B&B

Mrs Maclean

Strathlene, 45 Strath, Lonmore, Gairloch, Ross-shire, IV21 2DB
Tel:01445 712170
Email:info@strathlene.com
Web:www.strathlene.com

Cosy bedrooms in this modern family home with views over Gairloch Bay to the Torridon Hills and Skye. No smoking house. Private parking. Tea tray and TV in bedrooms.

2 rooms, all en-suite, Open Mar-Nov, B&B per person, double from £20.00.

Important: Prices stated are estimates and may be subject to amendments

THE HIGHLANDS AND SKYE

Gairloch, Ross-shire

Map Ref: 3F7

NEWTON HOUSE, BED & BREAKFAST

Mihol Road, Strath, Gairloch, Scotland IV21 2BX
Tel: 01445 712007

Full of character, this 19th century Highland home has accommodation to hotel standards but with affordable B&B prices. This family run establishment is ideally situated in the centre of Gairloch. Within walking distance of excellent restaurants, shops, sandy beaches and outdoor activities.

B&B

Newton House Bed & Breakfast
Mihol Road, Strath, Gairloch, IV21 2BX
Tel:01445 712007

3 rooms, Open Jan-Dec, B&B per person single from £30.00, double from £25.00, family from £25.00.

19th Century Highland home, tastefully refurbished and extended. We offer comfortable en-suite accommodation, with cosy stove fire in breakfast area and central heating throughout. Newton House is centrally located within Gairloch, and only a few minutes walk from shops, hotels and restaurants.

Glencoe, Argyll

Map Ref: 1F1

GUEST HOUSE

Dunire Guest House
Glencoe, Argyll, PA39 4HS
Tel:01855 811305

5 en-suite rooms, Open Jan-Nov.

Modern bungalow in centre of Glencoe Village. Ideal base for touring, climbing and hill walking, in fact all outdoor pursuits. All bedrooms tastefully furnished with TV's, radio's and tea-making facilities. Cosy guests lounge. Ample private parking. Drying facilities for walkers.

SCORRYBREAC GUEST HOUSE

GLENCOE, ARGYLL PH49 4HT

Tel: 01855 811354 Fax: 01855 811024
e.mail: info@scorrybreac.co.uk
Web: www.scorrybreac.co.uk

Scorrybreac is a comfortable well-appointed guest house in beautiful woodland surroundings managed by the resident owners. We are a no-smoking establishment. It is an ideal base for exploring the Glencoe and Ben Nevis area or for a shorter stay on a more extended tour of the Highlands.

GUEST HOUSE

Scorrybreac Guest House
Glencoe, Argyll, PH49 4HT
Tel:01855 811354 Fax:01855 811024
Email:info@scorrybreac.co.uk
Web:www.scorrybreac.co.uk

6 rooms, some en-suite, Open Jan-Dec, B&B per person, single from £25.00, double from £20.00, BB & Eve.Meal from £34.00.

Scorrybreac sits on the edge of Glencoe village in an elevated forested location amidst some of the most dramatic scenery Scotland has to offer. The house has 6 well appointed bedrooms all with en-suite or private facilities. The lounge and dining room have excellent views across Loch Leven and to the mountains beyond, where guests talk enthusiastically to one another about their daily activities.

VAT is shown at 17.5%: changes in this rate may affect prices.

Key to symbols is on back flap.

Glencoe, Argyll
Map Ref: 1F1

★★★

GUEST HOUSE

Strathassynt Guest House
Loan Fern, Ballachulish, Argyll, PH49 4JB
Tel:01855 811261   Fax:01855 811914
Email:info@strathassynt.com
Web:www.strathassynt.com

Beautiful village location near Glencoe. All rooms are ensuite with TV/DVD and tea/coffee facilities. Drying room. Secure bike store. Access to leisure facilities including swimming, jacuzzi and sauna. Family room with discounts for children. Garden. Take an evening stroll beside the Loch or relax with a drink in our guest lounge. Always be assured of the warmest welcome. 10% discount for stays of 3 nights or longer.

6 rooms, all en-suite, Open Jan-Dec, B&B per person, single from £23.00, double from £18.00.

★★

B&B

Tigh Ard
Brecklet, Ballachulish, Argyll, PH49 4JG
Tel:01855 811328

Family home on edge of village, with magnificent views across Loch Leven to hills beyond. 12 miles (19 kms) from Fort William. Relax in our sun lounge and watch the sun set over the loch. All rooms with hospitality tray. Guests bathroom conveniently situated adjacent to the 2 bedrooms. Ample private parking.

2 rooms, Open Apr-Sep, B&B per person, double from £17.00.

Grantown-on-Spey, Moray
Map Ref: 4C9

An Cala Guest House
Woodlands Terrace, Grantown on Spey, Moray/Highlands PH26 3JU
Tel/Fax: 01479 873293
e.mail: ancala@globalnet.co.uk   Web: www.ancala.info

AA 5 Diamonds Rating. A lovely large Victorian House set in $1/2$ acre, overlooking woods yet within easy walking distance of Grantown centre. On-site parking. All rooms en suite, doubles are kingsize, including magnificent 4 poster bed bought from Castle Grant. We aim to make you feel relaxed and comfortable.

★★★★

GUEST HOUSE

An Cala Guest House
Woodlands Terrace, Grantown on Spey, Moray PH26 3JU
Tel/Fax:01479 873293
Email:ancala@globalnet.co.uk
Web:www.ancala.info

AA 5 diamond rating. A lovely large Victorian house set in ½ an acre with on-site parking, overlooking woods yet within easy walking distance of Grantown centre. Doubles are kingsize, including a magnificent mahogony 4 poster bed from Castle Grant; all rooms en-suite. We aim to make you feel welcome, relaxed and comfortable.

4 rooms, Open Jan-Dec, B&B per person single from £40.00, double from £26.00, family from £25.00. Room rate, single from £40.00, double from £52.00, triple from £75.00.

★★★★

GUEST HOUSE

Brooklynn
Grant Road, Grantown on Spey, PH26 3LA
Tel:01479 873113
Email:brooklynn@woodier.com
Web:www.woodier.com

A warm welcome and friendly personal service await you at Brooklynn. We use locally sourced or homegrown food wherever possible for our delicious dinners; sample a Speyside Malt and finally, sleep well in our comfortable individually decorated bedrooms. Enjoy our pretty gardens too.

7 rooms, some en-suite, Open Jan-Dec excl Xmas, B&B per person, single from £25.00, double from £25.00.

Important: Prices stated are estimates and may be subject to amendments

Grantown-on-Spey, Moray   Map Ref: 4C9

Dunallan House
Woodside Avenue, Grantown on Spey PH26 3JN
TEL/FAX: 01479 872140
E.MAIL: enquiries@dunallan.com   WEB: www.dunallan.com
Dunallan is a fine example of Victorian elegance. With pitched pine throughout and period fireplaces in the guest lounge and diningroom, this is an ideal and relaxing base for exploring the many places of local interest. All bedrooms are en-suite or private facility, and are tastefully furnished. Victorian room and Honeymoon suite available. Close to forest and river walks.
Prices: Dble/Twin £22 - £30

★★★★

GUEST HOUSE

Dunallan House
Woodside Avenue, Grantown-on-Spey, Moray, PH26 3JN
Tel/Fax:01479 872140
Email:enquiries@dunallan.com
Web:www.dunallan.com
Dunallan is a splendid example of Victorian elegance oozing with the charm of a bygone era. Original period fireplaces are in the residents lounge and dining room, giving extra warmth to cheer you on those cooler evenings. Elegant bedrooms, featuring Victorian Room and Honeymoon Suite with Victorian bathroom. We have a ground floor bedroom.

7 rooms, all en-suite, Open Jan-Dec, B&B per person, single £28.00-35.00, double £22.00-30.00.

FIRHALL GUEST HOUSE
Grant Road, Grantown-on-Spey, Morayshire PH26 3LD
Tel/Fax: 01479 873097
e.mail: info@firhall.com   Web: www.firhall.com
A warm friendly welcome awaits you at Firhall. Situated in the heart of the Highlands. Ideally placed for the Cairngorms National Park, malt whisky trail, historic castles, golf, fishing and the breathtaking local scenery. The town centre, golf course, forest trails and River Spey are just a short walk away.

★★★

GUEST HOUSE

Firhall Guest House
Grant Road, Grantown-on-Spey, Moray, PH26 3LD
Tel/Fax:01479 873097
Email:info@firhall.com
Web:www.firhall.com
Firhall is a fine example of Victorian elegance, retaining much of the original character of this period. Particular features include the beautifully preserved pitched pine woodwork, ornate cornices and marble fireplaces. Home cooking. Family run.

6 rooms, 3 en suite, Open Jan-Dec excl Xmas, B&B per person single from £18.00, double from £19.00, family from £18.00.

★★★

GUEST HOUSE

Rosegrove Guesthouse
Skye of Curr, Dulnain Bridge, Grantown on Spey
Inverness-shire, PH26 3PA
Tel/Fax:01479 851335
Email:info@rosegroveguesthouse.com
Web:www.rosegroveguesthouse.com
Traditional, family run guesthouse, home cooking. A short distance from Dulnain Bridge.

6 rooms, some en-suite, Open Jan-Dec, B&B per person, single from £18.00, double from £20.00, BB & Eve.Meal from £30.00.

ROSSMOR GUEST HOUSE
WOODLANDS TERRACE, GRANTOWN-ON-SPEY PH26 3JU
Tel/Fax: 01479 872201
e.mail: johnsteward.rossmor@lineone.net   Web: www.rossmor.co.uk
Splendid Victorian villa, with many original features, where a warm welcome with personal friendly service awaits you. Spacious and comfortable guest rooms, including a Four Poster Bed, all ensuite. A non-smoking house. Ideal location for touring the many distilleries, castles, Moray Firth coast, Cairngorms and RSPB reserves. **Proprietors: John & Julia Steward.**

★★★★

**GUEST
HOUSE**

Rossmor Guest House

Woodlands Terrace, Grantown on Spey, Moray PH26 3JU
Tel/Fax:01479 872201
Email:johnsteward.rossmor@lineone.net
Web:www.rossmor.co.uk

Spacious Victorian detached house with original features and large garden. A warm welcome. Parking. Panoramic views. No smoking throughout. Tudor style four poster bed, iron and trouser press facility available.

6 rooms, all en-suite, Open Jan-Dec, B&B per person, single from £26.00, double from £26.00.

★★★

B&B

Broomhill House

Navidale Road, Helmsdale, Sutherland, KW8 6JS
Tel/Fax:01431 821259
Email:asblance@aol.com
Web:www.Blancebroomhill.com

Victorian stone built house with turret. Magnificent panoramic view over Helmsdale to the sea. Local heritage centre and art gallery in the village. Harbour nearby. Ideal base for exploring the far north, or for stopping off en-route to Orkney. Golf, tennis, squash, indoor bowls, sea and river angling available nearby.

2 rooms, all en-suite, Open Feb-Dec, B&B per person, single from £25.00, double from £20.00, BB & Eve.Meal from £33.00.

FOREST LODGE
South Laggan, Invergarry, by Spean Bridge, Inverness-shire PH34 4EA
Tel: 01809 501219   Fax: 01809 501476
e.mail: info@flgh.co.uk   Web: www.flgh.co.uk

Staying one night or more, our comfortable home offers pleasant ensuite accommodation, relaxed surroundings and home cooking served with friendly attention. Forest Lodge is conveniently situated in the centre of the Great Glen and is ideal for touring or participating in outdoor pursuits.

**AWAITING
INSPECTION**

Forest Lodge

South Laggan, Invergarry, by Spean Bridge PH34 4EA
Tel:01809 501219   Fax:01809 501476
Email:info@flgh.co.uk
Web:www.flgh.co.uk

7 rooms, some en-suite, Open Jan-Dec excl Xmas/New Year, B&B per person, double from £23.00.

Important: Prices stated are estimates and may be subject to amendments

Invergordon, Ross-shire — Map Ref: 4B7

Craigaron

17 Saltburn, Invergordon, Ross-Shire IV18 0JX
Tel: 01349 853640 Fax: 01349 853619
e.mail: jobrown@craigaron.freeserve.co.uk Web: www.craigaron-invergordon.co.uk

Come and enjoy a warm welcome in sunny, seafront village adjoining Invergordon. Rest in warmth and comfort in bright, pleasant surroundings and breakfast with fantastic view. Excellent touring location whether walking or by bus, train, car, bicycle or motor cycle. Ground floor bedrooms, CH, CTV, Tea/Coffee tray.

★★
GUEST HOUSE

Craigaron
17 Saltburn, Invergordon, Ross & Cromarty IV18 0JX
Tel:01349 853640 Fax:01349 853619
Email:jobrown@craigaron.freeserve.co.uk
Web:www.craigaron-invergordon.co.uk

Sunny seafront cottage with warm, friendly welcome and a good breakfast. 20+ golf courses within 1 hr drive. Dolphins and other sea and birdlife. 49 cruise liner visits in '05, inc. QM2 and QE2. Perfect for walking, biking and all modes of transport.

3 twin rooms, (2 en-suite, 1 priv.shower), Open Jan-Dec excl Xmas/New Year, B&B per person from £25.00.

Invermoriston, Inverness-shire — Map Ref: 4A10

★★★★
B&B

Riverbank Lodge
Invermoriston, Inverness-shire, IV63 7YA
Tel:01320 351287
Email:riverbanklodge@supanet.com
Web:www.visitscotland.com

Set in an area of outstanding beauty in an acre of garden on the banks of the River Moriston near the shores of Loch Ness, this modern bungalow has three very comfortable, spacious, tastefully furnished en suite bedrooms. Double rooms have king-sized beds. Ideal location for walking, fishing, cycling and touring the Highlands. Restaurant, pub and shop nearby.

3 rooms, all en-suite, Open Mar-Oct, B&B per person, single from £25.00, double from £23.00.

Inverness — Map Ref: 4B8

★★★
GUEST HOUSE

Aberfeldy Lodge Guest House
11 Southside Road, Inverness, IV2 3BG
Tel:01463 231120 Fax:01463 234741
Email:class@algh.freeserve.co.uk
Web:www.SmoothHound.co.uk/hotels/aberfeld.html

Comfortable Guest House close to city centre. All rooms ensuite. Hearty breakfast, vegetarians catered for and children welcome. Private car park.

8 rooms, all en-suite, Open Jan-Dec.

★★★★
B&B

Advie Lodge
31 Crown Drive, Inverness, IV2 3QQ
Tel:01463 237247
Email:advielodge@fsmail.net

Traditional town house in quiet residential area of Inverness, offering ensuite rooms and private parking. Within walking distance of the town centre and River Ness.

3 rooms, some en-suite, Open Jan-Dec excl Xmas/New Year, B&B per person, £23.00-25.00, double/twin/single.

VAT is shown at 17.5%: changes in this rate may affect prices. | *Key to symbols is on back flap.*

Inverness	Map Ref: 4B8

Amulree

40 Fairfield Road, Inverness, IV3 5QD
Tel:01463 224822
Email:amulree@btinternet.com

Warm and friendly welcome in Victorian house within easy walking distance of town centre and all facilities. Close to Eden Court Theatre and the Aquadome.

3 rooms, some en-suite, Open Jan-Dec excl Xmas, B&B per person, single from £21.00, double from £22.00.

Aros

5 Abertarff Road, Inverness, IV2 3NW
Tel:01463 235674
Email:aros@5abertarff.fsnet.co.uk
Web:www.visit-inverness.com

Situated only 5 minutes walk from town centre, train and bus stations. A cheerful Highland welcome awaits you at this comfortable Victorian home. Ground floor room available.

3 rooms, all en-suite, Open Feb-Dec excl Xmas/New Year, B&B per person, double from £25.00.

Balcroydon

6 Broadstone Park, Inverness, IV2 3LA
Tel:01463 221506

Semi-detached house in quiet residential road, 5 minutes walk from town centre, bus and railway station. Off road parking.

3 rooms, some en-suite, Open Jan-Dec, B&B per person, single from £21.00, double from £20.00.

Bluebell House

31 Kenneth Street, Inverness, IV3 5DH
Tel:01463 238201
Email:info@bluebell-house.com
Web:www.bluebell-house.com

Four star comfort around four minutes walk from the city centre. Private car park.

3 rooms (ks.four poster, ks.double, ks.twin), all en-suite, Open Jan-Dec, B&B per person from £27.00-35.00.

Braehead

5 Crown Circus, Inverness, IV2 3NH
Tel:01463 224222
Email:ian.mackenzie@tinyworld.co.uk

Traditional stone built Victorian villa in residential area of Inverness with easy access to city centre and all amenities. Non-smoking.

2 rooms, some en-suite, Open Jan-Dec excl Xmas/New Year, B&B per person, double from £20.00.

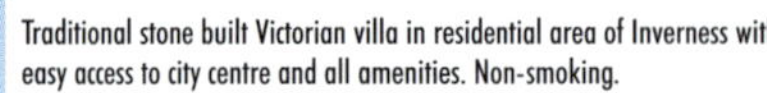

Important: Prices stated are estimates and may be subject to amendments

CLACH MHUILINN

7 HARRIS ROAD, INVERNESS IV2 3LS
TEL: 01463 237059   FAX: 01463 242092
E.MAIL: stay@ness.co.uk   WEB: www.ness.co.uk

Clach Mhuilinn, a 5 star B&B, has two delightful en-suite bedrooms, one double and one king/twin bedded suite with own sitting room. Every facility and many extra touches to enhance your stay. Delicious breakfasts served overlooking the beautiful garden. No smoking. Convenient for golf course, Loch Ness, Culloden, Cawdor Castle etc.

★★★★★

B&B

Clach Mhuilinn

7 Harris Road, Inverness, IV2 3LS
Tel:01463 237059   Fax:01463 242092
Email:stay@ness.co.uk
Web:www.ness.co.uk

Excellent, welcoming B&B hospitality, in modern detached home, in Inverness residential area. Two charming bedrooms: one double, one king twin suite, each with en-suite shower room, and many extra touches to make your stay special. Small friendly and welcoming. Delicious breakfast served overlooking colourful, mature gardens.

2 rooms, all en-suite (1Dbl, 1 Suite), Open Easter-Oct, B&B per person, double from £37.00-45.00.

★★★

GUEST HOUSE

Dalmore Guest House

101 Kenneth Street, Inverness, IV3 5QQ
Tel:01463 237224   Fax:01463 712249
Email:dalmoreguesthouse@tesco.net

Comfortable family run guest house close to the centre of Inverness and all facilities. Private parking. Ground floor room available. Credit cards accepted.

5 rooms, 4 en-suite, 1 priv.facilities, Open Jan-Dec, B&B per person, single from £25.00, double from £25.00.

FRASER HOUSE

49 Huntly Street, Inverness, Scotland IV3 5HS
Tel: 01463 716488   Fax: 01463 716488
e.mail: fraserlea@btopenworld.com   Web: www.fraserhouse.co.uk

Family owned & run Guest House superbly situated on the West Bank of River Ness in the heart of the Highland Capital. Bedrooms all ensuite overlooking the river. Just 5 minutes walk from City centre and main attractions. A warm welcome & big Scottish breakfast assured for all our visitors.

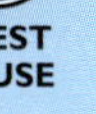

★★★

GUEST HOUSE

Fraser House

49 Huntly Street, Inverness, IV3 5HS
Tel/Fax:01463 716488
Email:fraserlea@btopenworld.com
Web:www.fraserhouse.co.uk

Fraser House built in 1821, a listed building, has been sympathetically refurbished to offer comfortable accommodation. All rooms are ensuite with river views. City centre & all amenities only 5 minutes walk.
AA ◆◆◆

5 rooms, all en-suite, Open Jan-Dec, B&B per person, single from £30.00, double from £25.00.

VAT is shown at 17.5%: changes in this rate may affect prices.

Key to symbols is on back flap.

Inverness   **Map Ref: 4B8**

★★★

B&B

Handa

56 Lochalsh Road, Inverness, IV3 8HW
Tel:01463 236530   Fax:01463 229575
Email:handaguesthouse@hotmail.co.uk
Web:www.handaguesthouse.co.uk

Family home in residential area with all rooms on ground floor. 15 minute walk to city centre and all amenities. Transport to/from Rail and Bus stations and airport available by prior arrangement.

4 rooms, Open Jan-Dec, B&B per person, single from £20.00-22.00, double from £20.00-22.00, BB & Eve.Meal from £30.00.

★★★★

B&B

Highfield House

62 Old Edinburgh Road, Inverness, IV2 3PG
Tel/Fax:01463 238892
Email:highfieldhouse62@talk21.com
Web:www.highfieldhouseinverness.co.uk

Warm friendly welcome in spacious detached house standing in its own grounds in a quiet residential area but only 0.5 miles (1km) from the city centre.

2 rooms, 1 en-suite, 1 priv.facilities, Open Feb-Nov, Rates per person, double from £26.00, single from £32.00.

AWAITING INSPECTION

J A Jamieson

The Linn, Inshes, Inverness, IV2 5BG
Tel:01463 231260
Email:alanjmsn@ail.com
Web:www.visitscotland.net

2 rooms, Open Apr-Nov, B&B per person, single £25.00-30.00, double £25.00-30.00.

★★★

GUEST HOUSE

Larchfield House

15 Ness Bank, Inverness, IV2 4SF
Tel:01463 233874   Fax:01463 711600
Email:info@larchfieldhouse.com
Web:www.larchfieldhouse.com

Peacefully situated on the banks of the River Ness and yet within five minutes pleasant walk to the city centre, rail and coach terminals. Larchfield House offers quality accommodation at a reasonable price. All rooms are fully ensuite and prices include a traditional cooked breakfast. All produce is sourced locally. Internet access is also available.

6 rooms, all en-suite, Open Jan-Dec excl Xmas/New Year, B&B per person, single from £30.00, double from £30.00.

★★★★

B&B

Lorne House

40 Crown Drive, Inverness, IV2 3QG
Tel:01463 236271

Victorian detached house in quiet residential area, close to town centre and railway station. Guest car parking. Ensuite facilities.

2 rooms, some en-suite, Open Jan-Dec excl Xmas/New Year, B&B per person, from £25.00-35.00.

Important: Prices stated are estimates and may be subject to amendments

Inverness

Map Ref: 4B8

B&B

Lynver

30 Southside Road, Inverness, IV2 3BG
Tel:01463 242906
Email:lynver@talk21.com
Web:www.lynver.co.uk

Extremely comfortable modern detached villa in quiet residential area within five minutes walk of city centre and easy strolling distance of a wide range of cafes, bars and restaurants, yet within easy access of all major road networks to and from Inverness. An excellent base for exploring the beauty of the Highlands. Private parking available on site.

4 rooms, all en-suite, Open Jan-Dec excl Xmas/New Year, B&B per person, single from £30.00, double from £22.50.

GUEST HOUSE

Malvern Guest House

54 Kenneth Street, Inverness, IV3 5PZ
Tel/Fax:01463 242251
Email:malvern.guesthouse@virgin.net

Victorian detached house in central location in Inverness. Off-street parking. All rooms are ensuite.

7 rooms, all en-suite, Open Jan-Dec, B&B per person, double from £20.00.

GUEST HOUSE

Parkhill Guest House

17 Ardconnel Street, Inverness, IV2 3EU
Tel/Fax:01463 223300
Email:cherryparkhill@hotmail.com
Web:www.parkhill-inverness.co.uk

Family run Guest House in quiet street; 2 minutes walk from city centre and within 5 minutes walk from bus and railway station.

7 rooms, Open Jan-Dec, B&B per person single from £20.00, double from £20.00, family from £20.00.

GUEST HOUSE

Strathmhor Guesthouse

99 Kenneth Street, Inverness, IV3 5QQ
Tel:01463 235397

Scottish hospitality in friendly family home. 10 minutes walk from town centre.

5 rooms, some en-suite, Open Jan-Dec, B&B per person, single £22.50-28.00, double £20.00-25.00, family.

VAT is shown at 17.5%: changes in this rate may affect prices.

Key to symbols is on back flap.

| Inverness | Map Ref: 4B8 |

Sunnyholm

12 MAYFIELD ROAD, INVERNESS IV2 4AE
Telephone: 01463 231336
e.mail: sunnyholm@aol.com
Web: www.invernessguesthouse.com

This well-appointed, traditionally built Scottish bungalow of the early 1930s is situated in a large, mature, secluded garden in a very pleasant, residential area and has ample private parking. It is within 6-7 minutes walking distance of the town centre, castle, Tourist Information Centre Office and other essential holiday amenities.

★★★

B&B

Sunnyholm
12 Mayfield Road, Inverness, IV2 4AE
Tel:01463 231336
Email:sunnyholm@aol.com
Web:www.invernessguesthouse.com

Bungalow situated in quiet residential area close to town centre and castle. All bedrooms ensuite and on ground floor. Private car park.

4 rooms, all en-suite, Open Jan-Dec, B&B per person, single from £30.00, double from £22.50.

★★★★

B&B

Taigh Na Teile
6 Island Bank Road, Inverness, Inverness-shire IV2 4SY
Tel:01463 222842 Fax:01463 713760
Email:jenny@islandbank.co.uk
Web:www.islandbank.co.uk

Bed and Breakfast in a comfortable home. Situated in a quiet location with views over River Ness yet only a short walk to town centre and all its amenities. Eden Court Theatre close by.

3 rooms, all en-suite, Open Jan-Dec excl Xmas/New Year, B&B per person, single £25.00-35.00, double £24.00-27.00.

★★★

B&B

Tamarue
70a Ballifeary Road, Inverness, Inverness-shire, IV3 5PF
Tel:01463 239724

Situated in quiet residential area, close to town centre, River Ness, golf course, Eden Court Theatre, Aquadome and Sports Centre. Off street parking.

3 rooms, some en-suite, Open Jan-Dec excl Xmas/New Year, B&B per person, double ensuite £18.00-25.00, double standard £18.00-22.00, twin £18.00-22.00.

| by Inverness | Map Ref: 4B8 |

★★★★

B&B

Easter Dalziel Farmhouse
Easter Dalziel Farm, Dalcross, Inverness, IV2 7JL
Tel/Fax:01667 462213
Email:wts@easterdalzielfarm.co.uk
Web:www.easterdalzielfarm.co.uk

Bob and Margaret invite you to stay in our Victorian farmhouse home with beautiful gardens on stock/arable farm. Panoramic views to open countryside, friendly atmosphere, log fire in lounge and home baking. Inverness 7 miles (11 kms). Culloden 5 miles (8 kms). Very central for touring Highlands.

3 rooms, Open Jan-Dec excl Xmas/New Year, B&B per person, double from £21.00.

Important: Prices stated are estimates and may be subject to amendments

John o'Groats, Caithness — Map Ref: 4E2

★★★

B&B

Bencorragh House
Upper Gills, Canisbay, by John O'Groats, Caithness KW1 4YD
Tel/Fax:01955 611449
Email:bartonsandy@hotmail.com
Web:www.bencorraghhouse.com

A working croft with Jacobs sheep, Highland cattle and Jersey cows, horses, chickens and other animals. Excellent outlook over the Pentland Firth towards the island of Stroma. Comfortable and spacious accommodation; a warm welcome and relaxing atmosphere. Excellent base for unwinding, while you explore this fascinating coastline and beyond. Convenient for visiting the Castle of Mey.

3 rooms, all en-suite, Open Mar-Nov, B&B per person, single from £30.00, double from £24.00, BB & Eve.Meal from £38.00.

★★

GUEST
HOUSE

Caber Feidh Guest House
John O'Groats, Wick, Caithness, KW1 4YR
Tel:01955 611219

Centrally situated in John O' Groats and 2 miles (3kms) from Duncansby Head. It is well situated for exploring the north east, including the north coast of Sutherland, the inland Flow Country, and more. Day trips to Orkney are a popular choice and the Castle of Mey 6 miles West.

14 rooms, some en-suite, Open Jan-Dec, B&B per person, single from £18.00, double from £17.00.

★★★

B&B

The Hawthorns
Mey, Thurso, Caithness, KW14 8XH
Tel:01847 851710
Email:hawthorns.scotland@btinternet.com
Web:www.thehawthornsbnb.co.uk

Spacious modern house, situated in the quiet village of Mey, on the north coast of Scotland. Open outlook towards Dunnet Head and across the Pentland Firth. Excellent base for exploring this fascinating corner of Scotland. Very close to John O'Groats and Gills Bay ferry.

5 rooms, all en-suite, Open Jan-Dec excl Xmas/New Year, B&B per person, single from £25.00, double from £22.00.

★★

B&B

Mill House
John O'Groats, Caithness, KW1 4YR
Tel:01955 611239

Traditional farmhouse, with all rooms on the ground floor; situated on working farm, 0.5 mile from John O' Groats and the Orkney passenger ferry, also from Gill Bay car ferry. Views over the Pentland Firth towards Stroma and Orkney. Duncansby Head, famous for its cliffs, Stacks and seabirds, is a short distance away. Much more to see and do in the area.

3 rooms, Open May-Oct, B&B per person, single £25.00-30.00, double £19.00-20.00.

Kincraig, by Kingussie, Inverness-shire — Map Ref: 4C10

★

B&B

Insh Hall Lodge
Kincraig, Inverness-shire, PH21 1NU
Tel:01540 651272   Fax:01540 651208
Email:office@lochinsh.com
Web:www.lochinsh.com

Ensuite accommodation with TV just 150m from the beach of scenic Loch Insh. Free watersports (set times) for guests staying 2 nights. Sauna, minigym. All meals taken in licensed Boathouse Restaurant overlooking the activities on the water. Watersports, Dry Ski Slope, Archery, Mountain Bikes, 3 Adventure Play Areas for Children. Dec-April downhill ski/snowboard packages.

22 rooms, all en-suite, Open Jan-Dec, B&B per person, single from £27.00, double from £22.00, BB & Eve.Meal from £37.25.

VAT is shown at 17.5%: changes in this rate may affect prices.

Key to symbols is on back flap.

Kincraig, by Kingussie, Inverness-shire
Map Ref: 4C10

GUEST HOUSE

Insh House Guesthouse
Kincraig, by Kingussie, Inverness-shire, PH21 1NU
Tel:01540 651377
Email:inshhouse@btinternet.com
Web:www.kincraig.com/inshhouse

Set in spacious grounds, this C listed Telford designed Manse, c1827, has all the original charm of a traditional Highland home. In good walking country, it is close to Glenfeshie & Loch Insh and equidistant from Kingussie & Aviemore. Birdwatching, watersports and skiing nearby.

5 rooms, all en-suite, Open Boxing Day-Oct, B&B per person single/double/twin £22.00-26.00.

Kingussie, Inverness-shire
Map Ref: 4B11

AWAITING INSPECTION

The Osprey Hotel
Ruthven Road, Kingussie, Inverness-shire, PH21 1EN
Tel/Fax:01540 661510
Email:aileen@ospreyhotel.co.uk
Web:www.ospreyhotel.co.uk

8 rooms, all en-suite, Open Jan-Dec, B&B per person, single from £27.00, double from £27.00, BB & Eve.Meal from £45.00.

B&B

St Helens
Ardbroilach Road, Kingussie, Inverness-shire PH21 1JX
Tel:01540 661430
Email:sthelens@talk21.com
Web:www.anotherworldminiatures.com/bandb.htm

Elegant stone built house c1895 in elevated position with large secluded gardens and excellent views over village and Cairngorm mountains beyond.

2 rooms, some en-suite, Open Jan-Dec, B&B per person, single from £30.00, double from £23.00.

Kinlochleven, Argyll
Map Ref: 3H12

B&B

Edencoille Guest House
Garbhien Road, Kinlochleven, Argyll, PH50 4SE
Tel/Fax:01855 831358
Email:edencoille@tiscali.co.uk
Web:www.kinlochlevenbedandbreakfast.co.uk

A warm, friendly welcome and excellent home cooking at our family-run B&B. Perfect base for touring, fishing, skiing, climbing, walking or just relaxing. We are situated opposite the Mamores, famous for their 12 Munroes which are within 5 mins walking distance from Edencoille.

5 rooms, some en-suite, Open Jan-Dec, B&B per person, single from £40.00, double £25.00-30.00, BB & Eve.Meal from £40.00-45.00.

GUEST HOUSE

Tigh-Na-Cheo Guest House
Garbhein Road, Kinlochleven, PH50 4SE
Tel/Fax:01855 831434
Web:www.tigh-na-cheo.co.uk

Under new management and newly refurbished. Tigh-Na-Cheo is in a village location with views of the Mamore Hills. Drying facilities and bike store. All rooms ensuite with baths, TV, hairdryer and tea/coffee making facilities.

9 rooms, Open All Year, B&B per person, single from £25.00, double from £25.00, BB & Eve.Meal from £35.00.

Important: Prices stated are estimates and may be subject to amendments

Kyle of Lochalsh, Ross-shire   Map Ref: 3F9

B&B ★

A'chomraich
Plockton Road, Kyle of Lochalsh, IV40 8DA
Tel:01599 534210

2 rooms, 1 dbl, 1 family. Open Apr-Oct, B&B per person, single from £18.00, double £17.00-18.00.

Warm welcome. Near all amenities. Peaceful. 10 mins walk from railway and bus station.

Laggan, by Newtonmore, Inverness-shire   Map Ref: 4B11

THE RUMBLIE

**THE RUMBLIE, GERGASK AVENUE, LAGGAN,
BY NEWTONMORE PH20 1AH
TEL: 01528 544766 FAX: 01528 544724
E.MAIL: mail@rumblie.com WEB: www.rumblie.com**

A friendly and relaxed highland home within the Cairngorms National Park, ideal for mountain biking and walking, cycle store, parking, drying room, and comfortable lounge with wood burning stove and lots of books. Dinner is available on request. No single supplement and special rates for longer stays.

B&B ★★★★

The Rumblie B&B
**Gergask Avenue, Laggan, by Newtonmore,
Inverness-shire, PH20 1AH
Tel:01528 544766 Fax:01528 544724
Email:mail@rumblie.com   Web:www.rumblie.com**

The Rumblie is located in the heart of Laggan, (Monarch of the Glen village of Glenbogle), ideally situated for exploring the Cairngorms National Park. All bedrooms are non-smoking, beautifully decorated,spacious with views, well equipped with king-size beds, colour TV, hospitality trays and adjustable central heating, all with en suite facilities. Private Parking. Breakfast menu available with vegetarian option & dinner available on request.

3 rooms, Open Dec-Oct, B&B per person, double from £23.50.

Lairg, Sutherland   Map Ref: 4A6

B&B ★★★

Ambleside
**Lochside, Lairg, Sutherland, IV27 4EG
Tel:01549 402130
Email:amblesidelairg@virgin.net**

3 rooms, all en-suite, all room ground floor, Open Jan-Dec, B&B per person, single from £25.00, double from £22.00.

Modern personally run bed and breakfast, comfortable and well furnished, centrally situated in quiet location with private parking. Evening meal available on request.

VAT is shown at 17.5%: changes in this rate may affect prices.   *Key to symbols is on back flap.*

Lairg, Sutherland — Map Ref: 4A6

PARK HOUSE
Station Road, Lairg, Sutherland IV27 4AU
Tel: 01549 402208 Fax: 01549 402693
e.mail: david-walker@park-house.freeserve.co.uk
Web: www.fishinscotland.net/parkhouse
Beautifully situated, overlooking Loch Shin in the Heart of Sutherland.
Edwardian Styled House. Tastefully furnished. Spacious en-suite rooms.
Dine in comfort enjoying Home Cooked, imaginative local produce.
Special Autumn, Winter and Spring breaks. Fishing, wild brown
trout/salmon, shooting and stalking, can be arranged.

★★★★

B&B

Park House
Station Road, Lairg, Sutherland, IV27 4AU
Tel:01549 402208   Fax:01549 402693
Email:david-walker@park-house.freeserve.co.uk
Web:www.fishinscotland.net/parkhouse

A warm welcome awaits you in this Victorian style house overlooking
Loch Shin. Friendly and relaxed atmosphere. Emphasis on home cooking.
Stalking, rough shooting, salmon and trout fishing available for guests
by arrangement.

3 rooms, all en-suite, Open Jan-Dec excl Xmas/New Year, B&B per person, single
£32.00-47.00, double £27.00-35.00.

Lochcarron, Ross-shire — Map Ref: 3G9

★★★

B&B

Castle Cottage
Main Street, Lochcarron, Ross-shire, IV54 8YB
Tel:01520 722564

Modernised detached house in village centre with fine views across Loch
Carron from all rooms. Castle Cottage is a good base for visiting Skye,
Eilean Donan Castle, Gairloch, Torridon and lots of walking and climbing
available in the area.

3 rooms, some en-suite, Open Jan-Dec excl Xmas/New Year, B&B per person, single
from £25.00, double from £20.00.

Lochinver, Sutherland — Map Ref: 3G5

★★★

**GUEST
HOUSE**

Ardglas Guest House
Lochinver, Sutherland, IV27 4LJ
Tel:01571 844257
Email:info@ardglas.co.uk
Web:www.ardglas.co.uk

Located in a popular fishing village, with spectacular views over harbour,
loch and mountains. Homely atmosphere with private parking. An ideal
location for walking, fishing, relaxing and touring the West Highlands.

8 rooms, Open all year, from £21.00 per person per night.

★★★★

B&B

Ardmore House
80 Torbreck, Lochinver, Sutherland, IV27 4JB
Tel:01571 844310

Mrs MacLeod offers warm, comfortable accommodation. Ardmore is an
ideal B&B to use as a base for touring the Northern Highlands. Many
excellent walks in the area and plenty of wildlife and sandy beaches.

2 rooms, Open Easter-Oct, B&B per person, double £20.00-22.00.

Important: Prices stated are estimates and may be subject to amendments

Map Ref: 3G5

DAVAR
LOCHINVER, SUTHERLAND IV27 4LJ
Tel: 01571 844501
e.mail: jean@davar36.fsnet.co.uk

A friendly welcome awaits you at Davar. In our well appointed purpose built house, with magnificent views of the mountains, harbour and bay. It is five minutes walk into the village.

B&B from £24 per person per night.

★★★★

B&B

Davar
Lochinver, Sutherland, IV27 4LJ
Tel:01571 844501
Email:jean@davar36.fsnet.co.uk
Web:www.davar_lochinver.co.uk

Modern family run house overlooking Lochinver Bay, with range of comfortable facilities. Private parking on site.

3 rooms, all en-suite, Open Apr-Nov, B&B per person, single from £30.00, double from £24.00.

★★★★

GUEST HOUSE

Polcraig Guest House
Lochinver, Sutherland, IV27 4LD
Tel/Fax:01571 844429
Email:cathelmac@aol.com
Web:www.smoothhound.co.uk/hotels/polcraig.html

A warm, friendly welcome awaits you here at Polcraig. Ideally situated in a quiet location with views across Lochinver Bay & Harbour. A short walk takes you to a choice of places for eating out. Your hosts Jean and Cathel will provide you with a hearty breakfast before you set out for your day. Explore the Highlands, taking in the spectacular views and an abundance of wildlife.

5 rooms, all en-suite, Open Jan-Dec, B&B per person, single from £25.00, double from £25.00.

VEYATIE

66 Baddidarrach, Lochinver, Sutherland IV27 4LP
Tel/Fax: 01571 844424
e.mail: veyatie-lochinver@tiscali.co.uk
Web: www.veyatie-scotland.co.uk

Relax in our very comfortable, modern bungalow set in a beautiful location. Panoramic views over Lochinver Bay to spectacular mountains beyond. This area is one of outstanding natural beauty. With woodland, coastal and hill walks, white sand beaches, abundant wildlife and our warm hospitality – altogether an unbeatable combination. B&B from £25 pppn double or twin.

★★★★

B&B

Veyatie
66 Baddidarrach, Lochinver, Sutherland, IV27 4LP
Tel/Fax:01571 844424
Email:veyatie-lochinver@tiscali.co.uk
Web:www.veyatie-scotland.co.uk

Spacious modern bungalow, with unique character, in peaceful, secluded location. Facing south, with magnificent views across Lochinver bay to spectacular mountains beyond. Ideally situated for bird watching, walking, fishing, or just relaxing break. Private parking on site.

3 rooms, some en-suite, Open Jan-Dec excl Xmas/New Year, B&B per person, single from £28.00, double from £25.00.

VAT is shown at 17.5%: changes in this rate may affect prices.

Key to symbols is on back flap.

FOYERS BAY HOUSE

Foyers, Loch Ness, Inverness IV2 6YB
Tel: 01456 486624 Fax: 01456 486337
e.mail: carol@foyersbay.co.uk Web: www.foyersbay.co.uk

Splendid Victorian villa overlooking Loch Ness. Lovely grounds adjoining famous falls of Foyers. Conservatory cafe-restaurant with breathtaking views of Loch Ness. Ideal base for touring the many historical and tourist attractions in this beautiful region. Also six self-catering units within grounds.

★★★

**GUEST
HOUSE**

Foyers Bay House

Lower Foyers, Inverness, IV2 6YB
Tel:01456 486624   Fax:01456 486337
Email:carol@foyersbay.co.uk
Web:www.foyersbay.co.uk

Set in its own 4 acres of wooded pine slopes, rhododendrons and apple orchard, Foyers Bay House offers 6 rooms all with ensuite facilities. Just 500 yards from the famous Falls of Foyers and situated just by Loch Ness, home of the famous monster.

6 rooms, all en-suite, Open Jan-Dec, B&B per person, single from £33.00, double from £27.00, BB & Eve.Meal from £37.00.

★★★

B&B

Anchorage

Gillies Park, Mallaig, Inverness-shire, PH41 4QU
Tel/Fax:01687 462454
Email:anchoragemallaig@btopenworld.com

Family run guest house centrally situated in Mallaig village and only a few minutes walk from ferry terminal and railway station. Two bedrooms with excellent views over harbour and bay. All bedrooms with TV's, tea-trays and ensuite bathrooms. Early breakfasts available for those catching first Skye ferry. Ideal base for walking, visiting the Small Isles and touring.

3 rooms, all en-suite, Open Jan-Dec excl Xmas/New Year, B&B per person, single from £20.00, double from £20.00.

★★★

B&B

Glencairn House

East Bay, Mallaig, Inverness-shire, PH41 4QG
Tel:01687 462359
Email:catherine@glencairn-house.co.uk
Web:www.glencairn-house.co.uk

Situated in a quiet area of the village, opposite the ferry terminal where you can go "Over the Sea to Skye". Views of the Inner Isles and Skye from your comfortable rooms.

2 rooms, Open Jan-Dec. B&B per person, double from £24.00, family from £30.00.

Muir of Ord, Ross-shire   Map Ref: 4A8

★★★

B&B

Dungrianach
Corrie Road, Muir of Ord, Ross-shire, IV6 7TN
Tel:01463 870316

Modern farmhouse with own garden, situated in secluded rural position,
1.5 miles (3kms) from Muir of Ord. Ideal location for touring Ross-shire.
14 miles from Inverness.

1 room, Open May-Oct, B&B per person single from £17.00, double from £17.00.

Nairn   Map Ref: 4C8

Ceolmara

Links Place, Nairn IV12 4NH
Tel: 01667 452495
e.mail: ceolmara15@aol.com
Web: www.ceolmara.co.uk

Traditional seaside cottage with panoramic views over the Moray Firth to the
Sutherland Hills beyond. 200yds from beach. Situated in the conservation area of the
fishertown. Warm hospitality, well appointed rooms and extensive breakfast menu.
Recommended by 'Which? Good B&B Guide 2005'. Member of Scotland's Best B&Bs.

★★★★

B&B

Ceolmara
Links Place, Nairn, IV12 4NH
Tel:01667 452495
Email:ceolmara15@aol.com
Web:www.ceolmara.co.uk
A warm Scottish welcome assured in this seaside cottage situated in the
fishertown conservation area with panoramic views over Moray Firth to the
Black Isle. A stones throw to the beach and close to Championship Golf
Courses. Welcome tray with home baking on arrival. Interesting breakfast
menu, vegetarian, vegan and gluten free diets catered for. A member of
Scotlands Best B&B's, recommended by Which? Good B&B Guide.

3 rooms, all en-suite, Open Mar-Oct, B&B per person, single £20.00-25.00, double
£20.00-25.00.

VAT is shown at 17.5%: changes in this rate may affect prices. | *Key to symbols is on back flap.*

Nethy Bridge, Inverness-shire | Map Ref: 4C10

★★★

B&B

Aspen Lodge

Nethybridge, Inverness-shire, PH25 3DA
Tel:01479 821042
Email:linda@aspenlodge.fsnet.co.uk
Web:www.nethybridge.com/aspenlodge.htm

A traditional stone built house set in the heart of this picturesque Highland village, which is an ideal base for touring Strathspey. A warm welcome, splendid breakfasts and well appointed rooms assure an enjoyable stay.

2 rooms, 1 double en-suite, 1 twin with priv.facilities, Open Jan-Dec excl Xmas/New Year, B&B per person, single from £28.00, double from £22.00.

North Kessock, Ross-shire | Map Ref: 4B8

★★★★

B&B

Craigiewood

North Kessock, Inverness, IV1 3XG
Tel/Fax:01463 731628
Email:minty@craigiewood.co.uk
Web:www.craigiewood.co.uk

Situated in superb countryside, Craigiewood is only 4 miles from Inverness on the Black Isle. The house is ideally situated for short trips to Inverness, Loch Ness, and the castles of Brodie and Cawdor. The famous Moray Firth dolphins are nearby. Craigiewood is an excellent starting point for journeys to Orkney or the West Coast. Inverewe Gardens, Loch Maree, Torridon and Skye are an easy day trip away. Come and spoil yourself!

2 rooms, all en-suite, Open Jan-Dec excl Xmas/New Year, B&B per person, single from £25.00, double from £28.00.

Plockton, Ross-shire | Map Ref: 3F9

★★★

B&B

Hill View Bed & Breakfast

2 Frithard Road, Plockton, Ross-shire, IV52 8TQ
Tel/Fax:01599 544226
Email:cameron06@freeserve.co.uk

Detached house, comfortable warm and quiet. Ideal for all ages. Situated near village and loch. Ground floor rooms.

3 rooms, en-suite, Open Jan-Dec, B&B per person, single from £25.00, double £18.00-22.00.

★★★

B&B

Janet Jones

Tomac's, Frithard Road, Plockton, Ross-shire, IV52 8TQ
Tel:01599 544321
Email:janet@tomacs.freeserve.co.uk

A warm welcome in very comfortable family home in quiet location in village of Plockton. Lovely views towards Applecross and Loch Carron to rear.

3 rooms, some en-suite, Open Jan-Dec excl Xmas/New Year, B&B per person, double £20.00-22.50.

★★★

B&B

Minvaugh

2 Railway Cottages, Plockton, Ross-shire, IV52 8TT
Tel:01599 544333

The warmest of Highland welcomes in traditional 100 year old cottage with elevated position and splendid views over Plockton. 5 minutes walk to village centre, shops, pubs and restaurants.

3 rooms, Open Jan-Dec excl Xmas/New Year, B&B per person, single from £18.00, double £17.00-18.00.

Important: Prices stated are estimates and may be subject to amendments

Plockton, Ross-shire   Map Ref: 3F9

SOLUIS GUEST HOUSE

Braeintra, by Achmore, Plockton, Lochalsh IV53 8UP
Tel: 01599 577219
e.mail: soluismuthuath@btopenworld.com
Web: www.highlandsaccommodation.co.uk
Situated in peaceful and scenic Strath Ascaig amid forestry and a
wide variety of flora and fauna. An ideal centre for exploring
Torridon, Skye, Glenelg and Kintail. Less than 25 minutes drive to
Plockton, Eilean Donan Castle, Stromeferry, Skye Bridge and Loch
Carron. Licensed Guest House.

★★

**GUEST
HOUSE**

Soluis Mu Thuath

Braeintra, by Achmore, Lochalsh, Ross-shire IV53 8UP
Tel:01599 577219
Email:soluismuthuath@btopenworld.com
Web:www.highlandsaccommodation.co.uk

Set amidst open countryside with views over surrounding mountains.
Excellent centre for North West of Scotland including Skye, Applecross
and Torridon. No smoking. Evening meal available. Suitable for disabled
accommodation.

5 rooms, all en-suite, Open Jan-Dec, B&B per person, single from £28.00, double
from £23.00, BB & Eve.Meal from £35.00.

Poolewe, Ross-shire   Map Ref: 3F7

★★★

B&B

Bruach Ard

7 Braes, Inverasdale, by Poolewe, Ross-shire, IV22 2LN
Tel:01445 781765
Email:dgeorge@globalnet.co.uk
Web:www.davidgeorge.co.uk

Spacious family home in elevated position with superb views over Loch
Ewe. 4 miles from Inverewe Garden.

3 rooms, Open Jan-Dec, B&B per person per night from £25.00.

Scourie, Sutherland   Map Ref: 3H4

★★★★

B&B

Scourie Lodge

Scourie, Sutherland, IV27 4TE
Tel/Fax:01971 502248
Email:scourielodge@aol.com

Beautifully situated on Scourie Bay on the west coast of Sutherland. Near
its picturesque harbour. Location for visiting the many local beauty spots.
The beautiful gardens can be accessed by guests at their leisure.

3 rooms, all en-suite, Open Mar-Nov, B&B per person, single from £45.00, double
from £30.00.

Breakish, Isle of Skye, Inverness-shire   Map Ref: 3F10

★★★

B&B

Ashfield

14 Upper Breakish, Isle of Skye, Inverness-shire, IV42 8PY
Tel:01471 822301

A warm Highland welcome in our very comfortable bungalow set in
croftland. Open views to Scalpay, Pabbay and the Applecross Mountains
on the Mainland. Gaelic spoken. Four miles from Skye bridge.

2 double rooms, 1 en-suite, 1 priv.bathroom, Open Easter-Oct, B&B per person
£20.00-23.00.

VAT is shown at 17.5%: changes in this rate may affect prices.   *Key to symbols is on back flap.*

Breakish, Isle of Skye, Inverness-shire

Map Ref: 3F10

★★★★

B&B

Tir Alainn Bed & Breakfast
8 Upper Breakish, Isle of Skye, IV42 8PY
Tel:01471 822366
Email:pam@davison2454.fsnet.co.uk
Web:www.visitskye.com

Modern bungalow with magnificent views to Cuillin and Torridon hills
and often enjoying splendid sunsets over the sea. Friendly welcome and
comfortable warm rooms.

3 rooms, some en-suite, Open Jan-Dec, B&B per person, single from £25.00,
double from £25.00, BB & Eve.Meal from £45.00.

Broadford, Isle of Skye, Inverness-shire

Map Ref: 3E10

★★★★

B&B

Birnam Guest House
Bayview Crescent, Broadford, Isle of Skye, IV49 9BD
Tel:01471 822417
Email:marionbirnam@hotmail.com
Web:www.isleofskye.net/birnam

A warm welcome assured at this family run B&B. In the village of
Broadford, only 7 miles from the Skye Bridge. This is ideal for touring
the area and visiting the Outer Hebrides.

2 rooms, Open Mar-Oct, B&B per person single from £25.00, double from 25.00.
Room only single from £30.00, double from 50.00.

LIME STONE COTTAGE

**KATHIE M McLOUGHLIN, 4 LIME PARK,
BROADFORD, SKYE IV49 9AE**

Tel: 01471 822142
e.mail: kathielimepark@btinternet.com
Web: www.limestonecottage.co.uk

*Welcome to Lime Stone Cottage. A charming turn of
the century crofters cottage originally built for
workers at the local lime kiln now fully restored
offering highest standards of modern comfort whilst
retaining all its original character. Add to this a truly
romantic atmosphere combined with panoramic
views over Broadford Bay and the mainland beyond.
Experience the real delight of a living fire in the
comfortable quiet surrounding of the sitting/dining
room or take the air in the floral garden and feel the
rolling sea breezes with scent of heather. All this
within easy walking distance of local amenities.*

★★★

B&B

Lime Stone Cottage
4 Lime Park, Broadford, Isle of Skye, IV49 9AE
Tel:01471 822142 Fax:01471 822142 (on demand)
Email:kathielimepark@btinternet.com
Web:www.limestonecottage.co.uk

Over the sea to Skye! & This 'old fashioned' bonny wee cottage offers a
rare blend of Romance, History, Panorama, Comfort & old-time
hospitality. Often quoted as a 'heart stopper'. The LimeStone Cottage is
so much more than just ordinary.

3 rooms, all en-suite, Open Jan-Dec, B&B per person, double from £30.00.

Map Ref: 3D9

Crossal House

Glen Drynoch, Isle of Skye, Inverness-shire IV47 8SP
Tel: 01478 640745 e.mail: andrea@richardson9031.freeserve.co.uk
Web: www.crossal.co.uk

Traditional Croft House set in a lovely scenic location with panoramic views of the Cuillin Mountains. Comfortable homely accommodation centrally situated as an ideal base for touring this magical island.

★★★

B&B

Crossal House

Glen Drynoch, Isle of Skye, Inverness-shire, IV47 8SP
Tel:01478 640745
Email:andrea@richardson9031.freeserve.co.uk
Web:www.crossal.co.uk

Set in lovely scenic location with panoramic views of the Cuillin Mountains, we offer comfortable homely accommodation in our traditional house. Crossal House is centrally located making it an ideal base for touring the Island, with Portree, the Island's capital, only 15 minutes drive and the Talisker Distillery, Skye's only producer of Malt Whisky, just 5 minutes away. The area is a paradise for walkers, climbers, bird watchers and photographers.

2 rooms, some en-suite, Open Jan-Dec, B&B per person, double from £24.00.

Map Ref: 3D9

Silverdale Guest House

Silverdale, 14 Skinidin, Dunvegan, Isle of Skye IV55 8ZS
Tel: 01470 521251
Web: www.silverdaleskye.com

Discover Skye from Silverdale and enjoy traditional Celtic hospitality, warm cosy rooms, stunning views, guest lounge with peat fire and fabulous local breakfasts. Ideal for romantic get-aways or walking, Silverdale is in one of the most beautiful and peaceful parts of Skye and you will leave feeling relaxed and refreshed. 3 Chimneys is 7 minutes walk away.

★★★★

B&B

Silverdale Guest House

14 Skinidin, Dunvegan, Isle of Skye, IV55 8ZS
Tel:01470 521251
Web:www.silverdaleskye.com

Beautiful Guesthouse, superb views of Loch Dunvegan, warm hospitality, furnished to a high standard. The 3 Chimneys Restaurant 7 min walk.

3 rooms, all en-suite, Open Feb-Dec, B&B per person, single from £40.00-45.00, double from £26.00-36.00 per night.

★★★

B&B

Uiginish Farmhouse

Uiginish Farm, Dunvegan, Isle of Skye
Inverness-shire, IV55 8ZR
Tel:01470 521431
Email:heather@uiginish.co.uk

Modern farmhouse on working farm. Scenic lochside location looking towards Dunvegan Castle. Quiet rural area only 4 miles from village with all its amenities.

3 rooms, all en-suite, Open May-Sep, B&B per person, single from £25.00, double from £22.00.

VAT is shown at 17.5%: changes in this rate may affect prices.

Key to symbols is on back flap.

Elgol, Isle of Skye, Inverness-shire — Map Ref: 3E10

★★★★

B&B

Rowan Cottage

9 Glasnakille, nr Elgol, Isle of Skye, IV49 9BQ
Tel/Fax:01471 866287
Email:ruth@rowancottage-skye.co.uk
Web:www.rowancottage-skye.co.uk

Traditional croft house with log fire. Magnificent views to Sleat and
Rhum. Very cosy, comfortable rooms, warm welcome, local seafood
dinners available in our licenced dining room by prior arrangement.

3 rooms, some en-suite, Open Mar-Oct, B&B per person, double £30.00-35.00,
BB & Eve.Meal from £55.00-60.00.

Glenhinnisdale, Isle of Skye, Inverness-shire — Map Ref: 3D8

★★★

B&B

Cnoc Preasach

2 Peinlich, Glenhinnisdale, by Portree
Isle of Skye, IV51 9UY
Tel:01470 542406

Comfortable Farmhouse on working croft in quiet elevated position
overlooking Glenhinnsdale. Excellent views down glen. 11 miles north of
Portree. 6 miles (9.6kms) from Uig Ferry. 100 acre croft. Home cooking.

3 rooms, Open Mar-Oct, B&B per person, double from £18.00.

Kyleakin, Isle of Skye, Inverness-shire — Map Ref: 3F10

Blairdhu House

Old Kyle Farm Road, Kyleakin, Isle of Skye IV41 8PR
Tel: 01599 534760 Fax: 01599 534623
e.mail: info@blairdhuhouse.co.uk Web: www.blairdhuhouse.co.uk

Blairdhu House is situated amidst beautiful scenery, offering
panoramic views, and is an ideal base for hillwalking and bird
watching. Just 5 minutes from the picturesque fishing village of
Kyleakin, and a 2 minute walk from the Skye Bridge.

★★★★

**GUEST
HOUSE**

Blairdhu House

Old Kyle Farm Road, Kyleakin, Isle of Skye IV41 8PR
Tel:01599 534760   Fax:01599 534623
Email:info@blairdhuhouse.co.uk
Web:www.blairdhuhouse.co.uk

A modern house within easy walking distance of the Skye Bridge. All
rooms ensuite and ample off-street parking. Make this your base on Skye
and all parts of the Island are within easy reach. Ideal for walkers,
climbers, photographers and birdwatchers. We have a comfortable
lounge with excellent views for those who just want to relax.

6 rooms, all en-suite, Open Jan-Dec excl Xmas/New Year, B&B per person, single
from £30.00, double from £25.00.

Important: Prices stated are estimates and may be subject to amendments

Kyleakin, Isle of Skye, Inverness-shire   Map Ref: 3F10

CORRAN GUEST HOUSE

KYLEAKIN, ISLE OF SKYE IV41 8PL

TEL: 01599 534859

E.MAIL: B&B@corranskye.co.uk   WEB: http://corranskye.co.uk

CORRAN OFFERS EXCELLENT BED & BREAKFAST ACCOMMODATION IN THE BEAUTIFUL FISHING VILLAGE OF KYLEAKIN. WITH SEA VIEWS AND WALKING DISTANCE TO ALL RESTAURANTS, BARS AND SHOPS. THERE ARE 4 BEDROOMS ALL WITH EN-SUITE FACILITIES, A SELECTION OF ROOMS HAVE SEA VIEWS AND ARE DECORATED TO A HIGH STANDARD. OUR BREAKFAST INCLUDES DISHES SUCH AS SMOKED SALMON AND KIPPERS. EXCELLENT BASE FOR EXPLORING SKYE.

★★★★

GUEST HOUSE

Corran Guest House
Kyleakin, Isle of Skye, IV41 8PL
Tel:01599 534859
Email:b&b@corranskye.co.uk
Web:www.corranskye.co.uk

Centrally located in the beautiful fishing village of Kyleakin, close to the sea and harbour. The house has been tastefully modernised and furnished to a high standard. A perfect base to tour the island.

4 rooms, Open Mar-Oct, B&B per person single from £25.00, double from £23.00, room only single from £30.00, double from £45.00.

Portree, Isle of Skye, Inverness-shire   Map Ref: 3E9

★★★★

GUEST HOUSE

Almondbank
Viewfield Road, Portree, Isle of Skye, IV51 9EU
Tel:01478 612696   Fax:01478 613114
Email:jansvans@aol.com

Modern house on the outskirts of Portree. Well appointed lounge and dining room with panoramic views of Portree Bay.

4 rooms, some en-suite, Open Jan-Dec, B&B per person, single from £30.00, double from £30.00.

Elizabeth Macdonald

25 Urquhart Place, Portree, Isle of Skye IV51 9HJ
Tel: 01478 612374
e.mail: elizabethmacdonald@talk21.com
Warm friendly accommodation. I mile from town centre.
An ideal base for exploring Skye.
Come and enjoy the best of hospitality.

★★★

B&B

Bed & Breakfast
25 Urquhart Place, Portree
Isle of Skye, Inverness-shire, IV51 9HJ
Tel:01478 612374
Email:elizabethmacdonald@talk21.com

Traditional Highland hospitality in friendly family home. 1 mile from town centre. Gaelic spoken.

3 rooms, some en-suite, Open Jan-Dec, B&B per person, single from £18.00, double from £15.00.

Portree, Isle of Skye, Inverness-shire   Map Ref: 3E9

★★★

B&B

Sandra Campbell B&B
9 Stormyhill Road, Portree, Isle of Skye, IV51 9DY
Tel/Fax:01478 613332
Email:sandra_campbell_b_b@yahoo.co.uk
Web:www.harbour-lodge.co.uk/BandB.html

A very warm welcome in our comfortable family home. 5 minutes walk from Portree village centre, open all year.

3 rooms, all en-suite, Open Jan-Dec.

★★★★

GUEST HOUSE

Corran House
Kensaleyre, Portree, Isle of Skye, Inverness-shire, IV51 9XE
Tel:01470 532311

In a small country village overlooking Loch Snizort, 8 miles (10kms) from Portree and from Uig ferry terminal. Extensive gardens with lovely views.

4 rooms, some en-suite, Open Jan-Dec, B&B per person, single £23.00-25.00, double £23.00-25.00.

Dalriada

Achachork, Portree, Isle of Skye IV5I 9HT
Tel: 01478 612397
e.mail: duncan.brown2@tesco.net

Situated just one and a half miles North of Portree, Dalriada is ideally suited for exploring the North and West of the Island. The guest lounge provides stunning views of Ben Tainavaig and the Cuillin Hills beyond. All rooms ensuite, TV and tea making facilities.
A warm welcome awaits you.

★★★

B&B

Dalriada
Achachork, Portree, Isle of Skye, IV51 9HT
Tel:01478 612397
Email:duncan.brown2@tesco.net

Spacious modern home in elevated position overlooking Portree and out to the Cullin Hills beyond. Convenient for visiting all Northern Skye attractions.

3 rooms, all ensuite, Open Jan-Dec excl Xmas/New Year, B&B per person £22.50 low season, £25.00 mid season, £27.50 high season.

★★★

B&B

Feochan
11 Fisherfield, Portree, Isle of Skye, IV51 9EU
Tel/Fax:01478 613508
Email:feochan@lineone.net
Web:www.feochan.co.uk

Family home with spendid views over Portree, a warm welcome and very comfortable rooms. Ideal base for touring the island and exploring the Cuillins and Trotternish Ridge.

3 rooms, all en-suite, Open Easter-Oct, B&B per person, double from £20.00.

Important: Prices stated are estimates and may be subject to amendments

Portree, Isle of Skye, Inverness-shire   Map Ref: 3E9

Grenitote

9 Martin Cresent, Portree, Isle of Skye IV51 9DW
Tel: 01478 612808
e.mail: e.a.matheson@amserve.net

Situated in quiet area, 5 minutes walk from centre of Portree. A favourite base for viewing the beautiful scenery throughout the Island. Comfortable ensuite rooms. Traditional breakfast served.

B&B

Grenitote
9 Martin Crescent, Portree
Isle of Skye, Inverness-shire, IV51 9DW
Tel:01478 612808
Email:e.a.matheson@amserve.net

A warm welcome and comfortable rooms in our friendly home in quiet residential area 5 minutes walk from Portree village centre. Gaelic spoken.

2 rooms, all en-suite, Open Jan-Dec, B&B per person, single £25.00-30.00, double £20.00-25.00.

Sleat, Isle of Skye, Inverness-shire   Map Ref: 3F10

TORAVAIG HOUSE HOTEL

Knock Bay, Sleat, Isle of Skye IV44 8RE
Tel: 01471 833231/01471 820200
e.mail: info@skyehotel.co.uk   Web: www.skyehotel.co.uk
"Scottish Island Hotel of the Year 2005" Winner (Hotel Review Scotland)
Charming 9 bedroom Country House Hotel, totally refurbished, beautifully decorated, personally run. Set in large garden, enjoying fine sea views. Parking, beautiful ensuite bedrooms, feature beds, Sky TV, direct dial telephones, and delightful restaurant. NEW – Hotel yacht trips daily. Real luxury . . . really affordable! B&B £59.50–£69.50 pppn

SMALL HOTEL

Toravaig House Hotel & Iona Restaurant
Knock Bay, Sleat, Isle of Skye, IV44 8RE
Tel:01471 833231/820200
Email:info@skyehotel.co.uk
Web:www.skyehotel.co.uk

Scottish Island Hotel of the Year 2005 - Toravaig is situated on the Sleat Peninsula. Personally-run by the owners Toravaig is enjoying a growing reputation for quality food and a high standard of accommodation and service. New for 2006 - daily yacht trips for residents.

9 rooms, all en-suite, Open Jan-Dec, B&B per person, single from £69.50, double from £59.50.

Struan, by Dunvegan, Isle of Skye, Inverness-shire   Map Ref: 3D9

B&B

Glenside
4 Lower Totarder, Struan, Isle of Skye, IV56 8FW
Tel:01470 572253

Traditional Highland hospitality on working 40 acre croft. Centrally situated for touring all areas of Skye.

2 rooms, some en-suite, Open Apr-Nov, B&B per person, double from £20.00-25.00.

Uig, Isle of Skye, Inverness-shire

Map Ref: 3D8

★★★

B&B

Mrs M MacLeod
11 Earlish, Uig, Isle of Skye, IV51 9XL
Tel:01470 542319

3 rooms, Open Mar-Nov, B&B per person, single from £17.50, double from £17.50.

Crofthouse on a working croft about 2 miles (3kms) from Uig Ferry Terminal. Complimentary tea and cakes served at 9pm. Emphasis on friendly welcome and a hearty breakfast. Quiet location.

Smithton, Inverness, Inverness-shire

Map Ref: 4D8

★★

B&B

Stonea
3a Resaurie, Smithton, by Inverness, IV2 7NH
Tel:01463 791714
Email:mbmansfield@uk2.net
Web:www.mansfieldhighlandholidays.com

3 rooms, some en-suite, Open Jan-Dec excl Xmas/New Year, B&B per person, single from £17.00, double from £17.00.

Modern house set in quiet residential area 4 miles (6kms) from Inverness with panoramic views across the Moray Firth. Warm and friendly stay assured. Non-smoking. Home-cooked evening meals by arrangement.

Spean Bridge, Inverness-shire

Map Ref: 3H12

★★★★

GUEST
HOUSE

Distant Hills Guest House
Roy Bridge Road, Spean Bridge, Inverness-shire PH34 4EU
Tel/Fax:01397 712452
Email:enquiry@distanthills.com
Web:www.distanthills.com

7 rooms, all en-suite, Open Jan-Dec excl Xmas, B&B per person, single from £35.00, double/twin from £26.00.

Comfortable modern bungalow set in large garden at edge of Spean Bridge. Friendly and personal attention. Excellent views of Aonach Mor, ideally situated for touring, skiing, walking and cycling. Evening meals by prior arrangement. Children and pets welcome.

★★★★

B&B

Riverside House
Invergloy, by Spean Bridge, Inverness-shire PH34 4DY
Tel:01397 712684
Email:enquiries@riversidelodge.org.uk
Web:www.riversidelodge.org.uk

1 room, en-suite, Open Jan-Dec excl Xmas/New Year, B&B p.p.night, single from £30.00, double from £30.00.

Comfortable Bed and Breakfast situated in a superb location. The house and extensive gardens front onto Loch Lochy where a gentle walk can be taken along the shores, or a longer walk through the grounds taking in the gorge walk. Or quite simply relax in the lounge which commands views of the gardens, the Loch and the hills beyond. An amazing collection of rhododendrons can be seen in the spring although anytime of the year the gardens can be enjoyed.

Important: Prices stated are estimates and may be subject to amendments

Strathpeffer, Ross-shire

Map Ref: 4A8

★★★★

B&B

Craigvar

The Square, Strathpeffer, Ross-shire, IV14 9DL
Tel/Fax:01997 421622
Email:craigvar@talk21.com
Web:www.craigvar.com

Beautifully situated overlooking The Square in this charming Victorian Spa Village. This distinctive house offers superb luxury facilities. It is a most comfortable, attractively furnished and restfully decorated house with good-sized rooms, all en-suite. Excellent parking, memorable breakfast menu, 4 poster beds and many personal touches.

3 rooms, all en-suite, Open Jan-Dec excl Xmas/New Year, B&B per person, single £30.00-37.00, double £28.00-32.00.

THE GARDEN HOUSE GUEST HOUSE

STRATHPEFFER, ROSS-SHIRE IV14 9BJ
Tel/Fax: 01997 421242
e.mail: garden.housedj@virgin.net
Web: gardenhouseguesthouse.co.uk

Set in the Victorian spa village of Strathpeffer it provides an ideal central touring base for Ross and Cromarty and other parts of the Northern Highlands. The guest house is located on the southwest side of the village surrounded by woodland and fields. The house is set well back from the main road through the village, about 250 metres from the village square. A lounge is available for guests at all times. Dinner is served each evening for guests wishing to sample home cooking. A table licence permits the sale of wine with meals.
NON-SMOKING ESTABLISHMENT

★★★

GUEST HOUSE

Garden House Guest House

Garden House Brae, Strathpeffer, Ross-shire IV14 9BJ
Tel/Fax:01997 421242
Email:garden.housedj@virgin.net
Web:www.gardenhouseguesthouse.co.uk

Friendly welcome at family run guest house in Spa village. Good walking country and touring base. 21 miles (32kms) from Inverness. Open March - October. Telephone/Fax bookings all year. Visa Mastercard and Switch accepted.

5 rooms, all en-suite, Open Mar-Oct, B&B per person, single from £35.00, double from £25.00, BB & Eve.Meal from £38.00.

Strathy Point, Sutherland

Map Ref: 4B3

★★★★

B&B

Sharvedda

Strathy Point, by Thurso, Sutherland, KW14 7RY
Tel:01641 541311
Email:patsy@sharvedda.co.uk
Web:www.sharvedda.co.uk

Modern family home with views to sea and open croft land. Evening meals available. Home baking. Lots of advice available on day trips and tours, both in the area and further afield, including Orkney. Wildlife, birdwatching, hillwalking and sandy beaches. Close to Castle Mey.

2 rooms, both en-suite, Open Jan-Dec excl Xmas/New Year, B&B per person, single £30.00-35.00, double/twin £26.00-28.00 pp, Dinner £20.00 per person.

Strontian, Argyll

Map Ref: 1E1

★★★

B&B

Struan

19 Anaheilt, Strontian, Acharacle, Argyll, PH36 4JA
Tel:01967 402057

A warm comfortable Highland welcome awaits you at 'Struan'. The B & B enjoys magnificent views of Ariundle Glen and Sgurr Dhomhnuill. Ariundle Nature Trail is within easy walking distance as is the compact village of Strontian set on the beautiful banks of Loch Sunart. Ideal base for walking, fishing and exploring the beautiful Ardnamurchan Peninsula.

3 rooms, all en-suite, Open Apr-Oct, B&B per person, single from £22.00, double from £22.00.

Tain, Ross-shire

Map Ref: 4B7

Morangie Bed & Breakfast
Morangie Road, Tain, Ross–shire IV19 1PY
Tel: 01862 893855
email: klbfiddles@aol.com

Morangie Bed and Breakfast offers you a warm, comfortable and homely atmosphere on your visit to the north of Scotland. The rooms are spacious and restful, one with a view over the Dornoch Firth, the other overlooking garden grounds. A good stopping place on your way to or from Orkney.

★★★

B&B

Morangie Bed & Breakfast

Morangie Road, Tain, Ross-shire, IV19 1PY
Tel:01862 893855
Email:klbfiddles@aol.com

Bed & Breakfast on northern outskirts of Tain, approximately 5 minutes walk to town centre. Totally non-smoking. Many excellent golf courses nearby. Views over Dornoch Firth.

2 rooms, all ensuite, Open Jan-Dec, B&B per person, single from £25.00, double from £20.00.

Talmine, Sutherland

Map Ref: 4A3

CLOISTERS
"Church Holme", Talmine (near Tongue), Sutherland IV27 4YP
Tel/Fax: 01847 601286 e.mail: reception@cloistertal.demon.co.uk
Web: www.cloistertal.demon.co.uk

Built in traditional style overlooking the beautiful Kyle of Tongue, "Cloisters" commands stunning sea views over inshore islands to the Orkneys beyond. Off the main tourist route it is an ideal base for exploration of Scotland's rugged north coast, mountains, rivers and lochs where wildlife abounds. *A photographers paradise.*

★★★★

B&B

Cloisters

Church Holme, Talmine, Sutherland, IV27 4YP
Tel/Fax:01847 601286
Email:reception@cloistertal.demon.co.uk
Web:www.cloistertal.demon.co.uk

Located four miles north of Tongue off the A838, Cloisters, built in traditional style alongside our home, a converted 19th century church offers superb B&B accommodation with stunning sea views. Enjoy birdwatching, fishing. Pack lunches are available and an excellent licensed restaurant is close by. Why not escape to the peace and tranquillity of Scotland's outback.

3 rooms, all en-suite, Open Jan-Dec excl Xmas/New Year, B&B per person, single from £27.50, double from £22.50.

Important: Prices stated are estimates and may be subject to amendments

| Thurso, Caithness | Map Ref: 4D3 |

B&B ★★★★

Annandale (Mrs D Thomson)
2 Rendel Govan Road, Thurso, Caithness, KW14 7EP
Tel:01847 893942 Mob:07733 167085
Email:thomson@annandale2.freeserve.co.uk

3 rooms with priv.facilities, 1 double, 2 twin, Open Jan-Dec excl Xmas/New Year, B&B per person, double from £22.50-23.00.

Comfortable B & B situated in quiet residential area. Ideal base for touring north coast and convenient for Orkney ferry.

Murray House
Mrs Angela Williamson, 1 Campbell Street, Thurso KW14 7HD
Tel:01847 895759
Email:angela@murrayhousebb.com
Web:www.murrayhousebb.com

B&B ★★★

5 rooms, all ensuite. Open Jan-Dec excl Xmas/New Year. B&B for all rooms £20.00-30.00.

Set in the centre of the town, a warm welcome and comfortable stay are assured in this refurbished 19c town house. Private parking. Ideal for visiting Dunnet Head, Britains most northerly point, John O'Groats and Orkney. Evening meals available by arrangement. Murray House has a table licence.

| by Thurso, Caithness | Map Ref: 4D3 |

THE SHEILING GUEST HOUSE
Melvich, By Thurso, Sutherland, KW14 7YJ
Tel/Fax: 01641 531256
e.mail: thesheiling@btinternet.com
Web: www.thesheiling.co.uk
Spectacular views! Fantastic breakfast in splendid dining room overlooking Melvich Bay. Guests return annually to very high standards in comfort, food and hospitality. Walking, golfing, fishing. Short drive to RSPB Forsinard, Orkney Ferry and Castle of Mey. Eat out nearby. AA 5 Diamond Golden Egg Award and 2003 AA Landlady of the Year Finalist. Good Breakfast Guide Award Winner. Contact Joan Campbell. From £32.00 B&B pppn.

B&B ★★★★★

The Sheiling
Melvich, Thurso, Caithness, KW14 7YJ
Tel/Fax:01641 531256
Email:thesheiling@btinternet.com
Web:www.thesheiling.co.uk

3 rooms, all en-suite, Open May-Sep, B&B per person, double from £32.00.

Peaceful and spacious accommodation in the village of Melvich, with spectacular views over the bay. Comfortable guest lounge. Extensive breakfast selection, fresh local produce homemade jams, preserves etc. Genuine Highland hospitality. 17 miles to Orkney ferry, 14 miles to Forsinard RSPB reserve. 30 miles to Castle of Mey, 17 miles to Thurso.

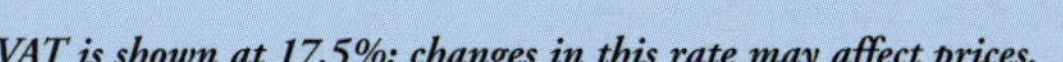

VAT is shown at 17.5%: changes in this rate may affect prices.

Key to symbols is on back flap.

by Thurso, Caithness
Map Ref: 4D3

Tigh-na-Clash Guest House

Mrs Joan Ritchie, Melvich, Thurso, Sutherland KW14 7YJ
Tel/Fax: 01641 531262
e.mail: joan@tighnaclash.co.uk   Web: www.tighnaclash.co.uk

We offer a high standard of accommodation in peaceful surroundings. Extensive breakfast menu, residents lounge, ample parking, friendly staff. Ideally situated for your tour of this most northerly part of Caithness and Sutherland from John O'Groats to Cape Wrath, RSPB Reserve at Forsinard, Flow Country and Orkney Islands. Wonderful scenery, birdwatching. The Queen Mother's Castle of Mey is now open to the public. Non smoking establishment. All ensuite.

★★★

GUEST HOUSE

Tigh-Na-Clash Guest House
Melvich, Sutherland, KW14 7YJ
Tel/Fax:01641 531262
Email:joan@tighnaclash.co.uk
Web:www.tighnaclash.co.uk

Personally run guest house in attractive garden. Five en-suite rooms. Single rooms available. Choice of eating establishments nearby. Situated on the edge of the village of Melvich. 16 miles from Thurso, and a short inland drive to the Flow Country. Beaches, birdwatching, walking, golf, fishing, all available in the area. The Queen Mother's Castle of Mey and Gardens are now open to the public Tues-Sun. April-October.

5 rooms, all en-suite, Open May-Sep, B&B per person, single from £26.50, double from £25.50.

Tongue, Sutherland
Map Ref: 4A3

★★★

B&B

Rhian Cottage Guest House
Tongue, Sutherland, IV27 4XJ
Tel:01847 611257
Email:info@rhiancottage.co.uk

Charming modernised croft cottage, 0.5 miles (1km) outside village. Dramatic views of Ben Loyal. Ideal base for fishing, bird watching, walking and touring. Annexe accommodation is available.

5 rooms, some en-suite, Open Jan-Dec, B&B per person, single from £35.00, double from £25.00.

Torridon, Ross-shire
Map Ref: 3G8

★★★

LODGE

Ben Damph Inn
Torridon, by Achnasheen, Wester Ross, IV22 2EY
Tel:01445 791242   Fax:01445 712253
Email:bendamph@lochtorridonhotel.com
Web:www.bendamph.lochtorridonhotel.com

Refurbished lodge accommodation in the midst of Torridon Mountains, with restaurant and bar.

12 rooms, all en-suite, Open Mar-Nov, from £35.00 pp.

Important: Prices stated are estimates and may be subject to amendments

Ullapool, Ross-shire

Map Ref: 3G6

★★★★

GUEST HOUSE

Ardvreck House
Morefield Brae, Ullapool, IV26 2TH
Tel:01854 612028 Fax:01854 613000
Email:ardvreck@btinternet.com
Web:www.smoothhound.co.uk/hotels/ardvreck.html

Guest house set amidst some of the best hillwalking country and breathtaking scenery in Scotland. Elevated country position overlooking Ullapool and Lochbroom. Spacious, well appointed rooms most with spectacular sea view, all with ensuite shower room, T.V and tea/coffee facility. Residents lounge available at all times. Local facilities include a leisure centre, swimming pool, sauna, golf course, fishing and museum.

10 rooms, all en-suite, Open Mar-Nov, B&B per person, single from £28.00, double from £28.00.

★★★

B&B

Broombank Bungalow
4 Castle Terrace, Ullapool, Ross-shire, IV26 2XD
Tel:01854 612247
Email:shirley.couper@tesco.net
Web:www.broombank.fsnet.co.uk

A warm welcome awaits in our modern, comfortable bungalow with open views to hills and down the loch to the Summer Isles. Quiet area but only five minutes walk to village centre.

3 rooms, all en-suite, Open Jan-Dec, B&B per person, double from £22.50.

★★★

B&B

Broomvale
26 Market Street, Ullapool, Ross-shire, IV26 2XE
Tel:01854 612559 Fax:01854 612654
Email:helenmac@ecosse.net

Comfortable accommodation in quiet location in fishing port of Ullapool. Excellent touring base, and handy for ferry to Stornoway.

2 rooms, 1 dbl en-suite, 1 twin priv.facilities, Open Mar-Nov, B&B per person, double £22.00-26.00.

★★★

B&B

Penny Browne
3 Castle Terrace, Ullapool, Wester Ross, IV26 2XD
Tel:01854 612409

Bed and Breakfast in family home, with ensuite available. Quiet residential location within walking distance of town amenities. House has views to Summer Isles. Vegetarian breakfast a speciality. Jams homemade. Plenty of parking on road and on private drive if asked.

3 rooms, some en-suite, Open Apr-Oct, B&B per person, single from £20.00, double £21.00-24.00.

VAT is shown at 17.5%: changes in this rate may affect prices. | *Key to symbols is on back flap.*

Ullapool, Ross-shire

Map Ref: 3G6

DROMNAN GUEST HOUSE

Mrs MacDonald, Garve Road, Ullapool IV26 2SX

Tel: 01854 612333

e-mail: info@dromnan.com   Web: www.dromnan.com

This modern family run guest house has everything you expect from a 4 star establishment with many more extras. A newly built conservatory has given guests the opportunity to enjoy stunning sea views from their breakfast table in relaxing and secluded surroundings. AA ◆◆◆◆◆

★★★★

GUEST HOUSE

Dromnan Guest House

Garve Road, Ullapool, Ross-shire, IV26 2SX

Tel:01854 612333

Email:info@dromnan.com

Web:www.dromnan.com

Modern family run guest house overlooking Lochbroom. Ideally situated, excellent facilities and stunning views. Sumptous buffet breakfasts served in our newly built conservatory. "All in All — First Class Accommodation" AA ◆◆◆◆◆

7 rooms, all en-suite, Open Jan-Dec, B&B per person, single £28.00-38.00, double £26.00-29.00.

★★★★

B&B

Mrs J Macrae

3 Vyner Place, Ullapool, Ross-shire, IV26 2XR

Tel/Fax:01854 612023

Email:jackie.macrae@virgin.net

Comfortable and modern accommodation in residential area of Ullapool. Close to golf course and leisure centre. Ideal base for touring Western Highlands.

2 rooms, some en-suite, Open Jan-Dec excl Xmas, B&B per person, single from £25.00, double £19.00-24.00.

★★★★

GUEST HOUSE

Point Cottage Guest House

22 West Shore Street, Ullapool, Ross-shire IV26 2UR

Tel:01854 612494

Email:macrae@pointcottage.co.uk

Web:www.pointcottage.co.uk

As featured in 'Holiday Which' a tastefully converted 18c fisherman's cottage where a warm welcome and a high level of local knowledge are assured. Marvellous lochside views to mountains beyond. Very quiet location but only 2 minutes walk to village centre. Vegetarian cooked breakfast available.

3 rooms, all en-suite, Open Feb-Nov, B&B per person, single £25.00-45.00, double £22.00-28.00.

| Ullapool, Ross-shire | Map Ref: 3G6 |

"TORRAN"

LOGGIE, LOCH BROOM, ULLAPOOL, ROSS-SHIRE IV23 2SG
TEL: 01854 655227 FAX: 01854 655344 MOBILE: 07753 854 281
E.MAIL: info@torranloggie.co.uk WEB: www.torranloggie.co.uk
A warm welcome awaits you at our family croft house peacefully situated overlooking the beautiful Loch Broom. Salmon farm and historic sites close by. This area is renowned for its beauty and you won't be disappointed. Very central for walking, several Munroe's within sight and easy reach. Come have a relaxing holiday at 'Torran'. Double room ensuite & twin room with private bathroom. Prices from £22.00.

★★★

B&B

Torran

Loggie, Lochbroom, Ullapool, Ross-shire, IV23 2SG
Tel:01854 655227 Fax:01854 655344
Email:info@torranloggie.co.uk
Web:www.torranloggie.co.uk

Family home on working croft in peaceful setting overlooking the beautiful Loch Broom. Enjoy a Scottish breakfast using our own free range eggs. Iron age brochs and salmon farm close by. A relaxing & peaceful holiday location.

2 rooms, Open Mar-Oct, B&B per person, double from £22.00-£27.00.

| nr Ullapool, Ross-shire | Map Ref: 3G6 |

★★★★

B&B

Braemore Square Country House

Braemore Square, Loch Broom, Wester Ross, IV23 2RX
Tel/Fax:01854 655357
Email:enquiries@braemoresquare.com
Web:www.braemoresquare.com

Braemore Square is set amongst 46 acres of croft and woodland beside the road to Ullapool, just a short walk from the famous Corrieshalloch Gorge and with fishing rights on the River Broom. Your experienced hosts Ed and Wendy Hughes guarantee a warm and friendly welcome.

3 rooms, some en-suite, Open Jan-Dec, B&B per person, double from £28.00.

VAT is shown at 17.5%: changes in this rate may affect prices.

Key to symbols is on back flap.

Wick, Caithness | **Map Ref: 4E3**

B&B

The Clachan
13 Randolph Place, South Road, Wick, Caithness KW1 5NJ
Tel:01955 605384
Email:enquiry@theclachan.co.uk
Web:www.theclachan.co.uk
Family run detached house dating back to 1938. Purpose built
accommodation to the back of the house, with all rooms ensuite,
ensuring a peaceful and relaxing stay. A wide variety of interests with
John O' Groats on the doorstep, where there are daily trips to Orkney in
the summer. Wick has many sites of historical interest. Meals available
within walking distance. Totally non-smoking house.

3 rooms, all ensuite, Open Jan-Dec, B&B per person, single from £30.00, double
from £22.00.

GUEST HOUSE

Wellington Guest House
41-43 High Street, Wick, Caithness, KW1 4BS
Tel:01955 603287
Email:ablett@philwick.fsnet.co.uk

Conveniently situated in the town centre opposite the Post Office. Private
off street parking. Plenty to do in the area - fishing, walking,
birdwatching, exploring the varied coastline of Caithness and much more.
Cycle storage available.

6 rooms, all en-suite, Open Jan-Dec excl Xmas/New Year, B&B per person, single
from £25.00, twin from £20.00 per person.

Welcome to Scotland

The Outer Islands: Outer Hebrides, Orkney, Shetland

Villages older than time. Accordians. Viking longships on fire. Standing stones. Cheese with bite. Birds. More birds. Holidays heat up under a midnight sun…

The Old Man of Hoy is a sea stack rising 449 feet off the Isle of Hoy, Orkney.

For a spot of meditation, seriously ponder the Outer Hebrides. Stretching for 130 miles, the islands indulge your thoughts - and fantasies – with oodles of quiet space. Sea kayaking along the coastline reveals inlets of seabirds and wildlife. Dreamy beaches await you on Harris, including Luskentyre and Scarista.

And the people? Charismatic, warm and Gaelic to their last breath. Pubs ignite with the toe-tapping lilt of poetry and fiddles embracing the Gaelic creed, 'ceud mile failte' - a hundred thousand welcomes. A rich source of island life, Stornoway is the main town of Lewis. Contact an operator to join a boat, trawl the Lewis coast and heave in a lobster creel. Catch up on 3000 years of prehistory in the Calanais Standing Stones, or 1000 years of croft domestics in the preserved Black House of Arnol.

Orkney has the mythical appeal of a Tolkien novel. Fiery sunsets, ancient ruins, lyrical and vibrant people. These islands defy backwater expectations with headline-grabbing festivals on the summer's bounty, music, even science.

Skara Brae is simply the best-preserved Stone Age village in Western Europe; farmsteads at Papa Westray predate the Pyramids, and some cheeky Vikings got to the Ring of Brodgar with graffiti - 900 years ago. Scuba divers are drawn to the ghostly depths of Scapa Flow where the German fleet was scuttled at the end of the First World War. Skip to the Second World War for a unique chapel built from scrap materials and the ingenuity of 500 Italian prisoners. And follow the scent of peat to Kirkwall, a frisky hub of Orkney life, especially under a

The Outer Islands:
Outer Hebrides, Orkney, Shetland

A group of kayakers take time out in the Outer Hebrides

Shetland's unmistakable fire festival, Up Helly Aa.

midnight sun. Don't overlook the jewellery shops opposite St. Magnus Cathedral; the smoky charm of Highland Park Distillery, or melting tang of Orkney cheese.

Shetland was a Viking playground, so plenty of axe waving and pathological tendencies here. Why don't you join in? A jolly good time is reserved for the world's biggest fire festival, Up Helly Aa. Held in January, a torchlit procession drags a Viking longboat through streets, sets it on fire, and retreats to the local halls for revelry. Old habits die hard in a land once home to the ancient Viking parliament of Althing and still influenced by Norse Udal law. The people have a gift for music, whether plucking the fiddle in a pub or wooing crowds, accordian style, at the October music festival.

Climb the stairs of Mousa Broch, an ancient stone tower guarding an island uninhabited for over 2000 years. The remains of 120 brochs inhabit the islands, and there are 100 or so islands to explore. And the wildlife is stunning. Puffins, arctic skuas and the rare phalaropes contribute to a bird haven, while some 1200 playful otters scour the island waters for dinner. Cue the Northern Lights, sigh, and enjoy the show…

Events

The Outer Islands: Outer Hebrides, Orkney, Shetland

OUTER HEBRIDES

19-23 JUNE
SEO SEINN
A Gaelic singing competition of lyrical beauty.
Tel: 01851 703088
www.visithebrides.com/seoseinn

MID JULY
HEBRIDEAN CELTIC FESTIVAL
Festival of Celtic music showcasing local and international talent.
Tel: 07001 878787
www.hebceltfest.com

LATE JULY
BARRA MUSIC FESTIVAL
Traditional live music festival in the beautiful setting of Barra.
Tel: 01871 810 579

Event details are subject to change please check before travelling.

ORKNEY

14-17 APRIL
ORKNEY DANCE FESTIVAL
Lively music and people will have you on the dance floor, learning new moves and old.
Tel: 01478 613104
www.orkneydancefestival.co.uk

25-28 MAY
ORKNEY FOLK FESTIVAL
Traditional music festival focused in the town of Stromness with events also staged in rural areas and smaller Islands.
Tel: 01856 851331
www.orkneyfolkfestival.com

16-21 JUNE
ST MAGNUS FESTIVAL
World-class performances and the magic of Orkney at midsummer combine to stage musical events, drama, dance, literature and the visual arts.
Tel: 01856 871445
www.stmagnusfestival.com

Event details are subject to change please check before travelling.

SHETLAND

31 JANUARY
UP HELLY AA
Viking fire festival.
Tel: 01595 693434
www.visitshetland.com

27 APRIL-30 APRIL
SHETLAND FOLK FESTIVAL
26th anniversary celebrations of this folk music festival featuring international musicians and home grown talent.
Tel: 01595 694757
www.shetlandfolkfestival.com

26 AUGUST-2 SEPTEMBER
NATWEST ISLAND GAMES XI
Lead with your feet, and your heart, in this remarkable corner of the world.
Tel: 01595 693434
www.visitshetland.com

Event details are subject to change please check before travelling.

The Outer Islands: Outer Hebrides, Orkney, Shetland

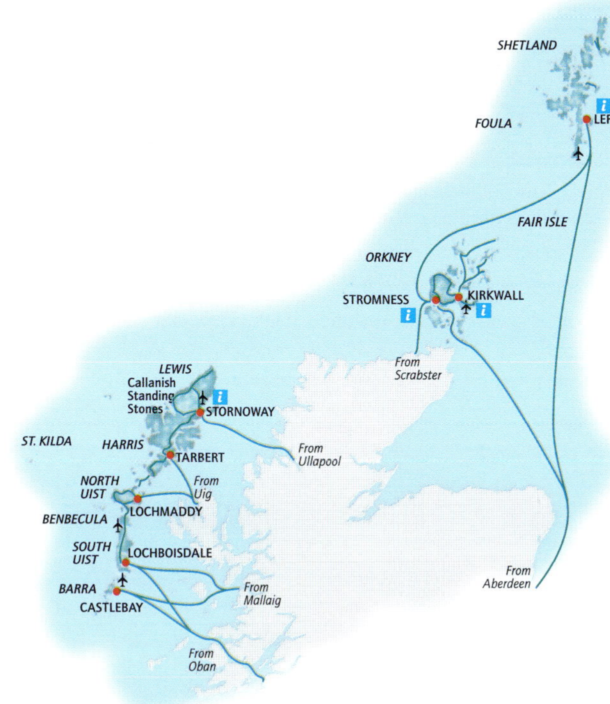

Please refer to the maps on pages xix-xxiv for the locations of establishments appearing in the main advertising section of this guide.

Finding out more...

For practical advice, ideas and information about exploring Scotland and to book your accommodation:

Tel: 0845 22 55 121*
or if calling from outside the UK: +44 (0) 1506 832121

Email: info@visitscotland.com
Web: www.visitscotland.com

* A £3 booking fee applies to telephone bookings of accommodation.

Tourist Information Centres

The Outer Islands: Outer Hebrides, Orkney, Shetland

Outer Hebrides

Castlebay
Main Street
Tel: (01871) 810336
Easter – Oct

Lochboisdale
Pier Road
Tel: (01878) 700286
Easter – Oct

Lochmaddy
Pier Road
Tel: (01876) 500321
Easter – Oct

Stornoway
26 Cromwell Street
Tel: (01851) 703088
Jan – Dec

Tarbert (Harris)
Pier Road
Tel: (01859) 502011
Jan – Dec

Orkney

Kirkwall
6 Broad Street
Tel: (01856) 872856
Jan – Dec

Stromness
Ferry Terminal Building
Tel: (01856) 850716
Jan – Dec

Shetland

Kirkwall
The Market Cross
Tel: (08701) 999440
Jan – Dec

OUTER ISLANDS

Northbay, Isle of Barra, Outer Hebrides

Map Ref: 3A11

★★★

B&B

Airds

244 Bruernish, Northbay, Isle of Barra
Tel:01871 890720
Email:airdsbarra@aol.com
Web:www.airdsbarra.co.uk

Airds Guest House is beautifully situated at the north end of the island. The house is a newly built, modern home away from home. There is a lounge and conservatory to sit and relax with stunning views.

3 rooms, all en-suite, Open Jan-Dec excl Xmas/New Year, B&B per person, double/twin £25.00.

Tarbert, Isle of Harris, Outer Hebrides

Map Ref: 3C6

★★★★

B&B

Hill Crest

Tarbert, Isle of Harris, HS3 3AH
Tel/Fax:01859 502119
Email:angusahillcrest@tiscali.co.uk

Modern croft in an elevated position overlooking West Loch Tarbert with fine views of mountains and islands. This is an excellent base for exploring all of Harris and Lewis. Miles of unspoilt beaches and an abundance of wildlife, with a variety of plantlife practically on our doorstep. Wonderful walking, country fishing trips and scenic cruises available. 1 mile from ferry terminal. Evening meal available by prior arrangement.

3 rooms, 2 en-suite, 1 priv.facilities, Open Jan-Dec, B&B per person, double from £24.00.

Back, Isle of Lewis, Outer Hebrides

Map Ref: 3E4

SEASIDE VILLA

Back, Isle of Lewis HS2 0LQ
Tel/Fax: 01851 820208   e.mail: seasidevilla22@talk21.com
Web: www.witb.co.uk/links/seasidevilla.htm

Peaceful location overlooking turquoise coloured sea and miles of unspoilt sandy beaches, glorious views across The Minch to the distant hills of Sutherland. Renowned for our home cooking, using local produce at all times. Vegetarians welcomed. Abundance of wildlife with seals being frequent visitors to our bay. Comfortable, superior accommodation.

★★★★

B&B

Seaside Villa

Back, Isle of Lewis, HS2 0LQ
Tel/Fax:01851 820208
Email:seasidevilla22@talk21.com
Web:www.witb.co.uk/links/seasidevilla.htm

Beautiful views overlooking picturesque bay with miles of unspoilt sandy beaches and Sutherland Hills in the distance. Home cooking and baking using all local fayre - vegetarians welcome. Special highland hospitality. 15 minutes drive from Stornoway.

3 rooms, 2 en-suite, Open Jan-Dec, B&B per person, single from £30.00, double from £22.50-25.00, BB & Eve. Meal from £37.50.

VAT is shown at 17.5%: changes in this rate may affect prices.

Key to symbols is on back flap.

Callanish, Isle of Lewis, Outer Hebrides — Map Ref: 3D4

ESHCOL GUEST HOUSE
21 Breasclete, Callanish, Isle of Lewis, Scotland HS2 9ED
Tel/Fax: 01851 621357
e.mail: neil@eshcol.com Web: www.eshcol.com

Well established guest house centrally situated for touring Lewis and Harris. Only two miles from the famous standing stones at Callanish. Your hosts, Neil and Isobel Macarthur run Eshcol with an emphasis on quality and attention to detail. Their menu's are created around the wonderful local produce available.

★★★★

GUEST HOUSE

Eshcol Guest House
Breasclete, Callanish, Isle of Lewis, HS2 9ED
Tel/Fax:01851 621357
Email:neil@eshcol.com
Web:www.eshcol.com

Modern detached house quietly situated in the crofting village of Breasclete, with an open outlook over Loch Roag towards the Uig hills. Good base to explore Lewis, or just to relax. Only 2 miles to the Callanish Standing Stones. All bedrooms non-smoking. Local produce used where possible in our highly recommended evening meals. B.Y.O.B.

3 rooms, 2 en-suite, 1 with priv.bath, Open Mar-Oct, B&B per person, single from £33.00, double from £33.00, BB & Eve.Meal from £55.00.

nr Stornoway, Isle of Lewis, Outer Hebrides — Map Ref: 3D4

★★★

B&B

Caladh
44 Gress, Isle of Lewis, Western Isles, HS2 0NB
Tel:01851 820743/07909 556584
Email:EVE@caladh.fsbusiness.co.uk
Web:http://caladhgress.mysite.freeserve.com

Modernised croft house situated in quiet crofting village, 9 miles north of Stornoway. Open outlook over Gress river and saltings, and to the nearby sandy beach. Good area for birdwatching trips. Resident talkative parrot provides free in-house entertainment. Room only rates avilable on request. Home cooked evening meals by special arrangement.

2 rooms, all en-suite, Open Jan-Dec, B&B per person, single from £22.00, double from £20.00, BB & Eve.Meal from £32.00. Room only £15.00 per person.

Birsay, Orkney — Map Ref: 5B11

★★★

B&B

Primrose Cottage
Birsay, Orkney, KW17 2NB
Tel/Fax:01856 721384
Email:i.clouston@talk21.com

In quiet location overlooking Marwick Bay, close to RSPB reserves. Ideal for bird watching, trout fishing and quiet cliff top walks. Local produce used whenever possible, fresh fish and shellfish. Reduced rates for longer stays.

3 rooms, some en-suite, Open Jan-Dec excl Xmas/New Year, B&B per person, single from £16.00, double from £20.00.

Kirkwall, Orkney — Map Ref: 5B12

★★

GUEST HOUSE

Sanderlay Guest House
2 Viewfield Drive, Kirkwall, Orkney, KW15 1RB
Tel:01856 875587   Fax:01856 876350
Email:enquiries@sanderlay.co.uk

Comfortable modern house in quiet residential area on outskirts of town. Some ensuite and 3 self-contained family units. Private parking available. Credit cards accepted. Ideal base for exploring the Orkney mainland or for visiting the North Isles.

7 rooms, some en-suite, Open Jan-Dec excl Xmas, New Year, B&B per person, single £20.00-26.00, double £18.00-24.00.

Important: Prices stated are estimates and may be subject to amendments

OUTER ISLANDS

Kirkwall, Orkney

Map Ref: 5B12

★★★

B&B

Shearwood

**Muddisdale Road, off Pickaquoy Road, Kirkwall
Orkney, KW15 1RR
Tel:01856 873494**

Bungalow situated in quiet residential area, 10 minutes walk from the town centre with own enclosed garden. New leisure centre nearby. Pick up with luggage from tourist board - available.

2 twin rooms, 1 en-suite, Open Jan-Dec, B&B per person, double £18.00-22.00.

Orphir, Orkney

Map Ref: 5B11

★★★

B&B

Scorralee

**Scorradale Road, Orphir, Orkney, KW17 2RF
Tel/Fax:01856 811268
Email:ebclouston@aol.com
Web:www.s-h-systems.co.uk/hotels/scorralee.html
or www.scorralee.com**

A warm welcome assured at this warm, comfortable, modern house on elevated site, looking out over Scapa Flow. Equal distance from Kirkwall and Stromness. Evening meals by arrangement.

3 rooms, all en-suite, Open Jan-Dec, B&B per person, single from £30.00, double/twin from £23.00.

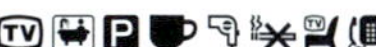

Rendall, Orkney

Map Ref: 5B11

★★★

B&B

Riff Farmhouse B&B

**1 Sinclair, Riff, Rendall, Orkney, KW17 2PB
Tel/Fax:01856 761541
Email:ida.sinclair@btopenworld.com
Web:www.orkney.co.uk/riff**

Riff Farm is situated 4 miles from Rousay Ferry close to the shore of Puldrite Bay with expansive views across to the Northern Isles. A warm Orcadian welcome assured.

3 rooms, all en-suite, Open Jan-Dec, B&B per person, double from £18.00, BB & Eve.Meal from £30.00.

St Margaret's Hope, Orkney

Map Ref: 4E1

**AWAITING
INSPECTION**

Roeberry House

**Sands of Wright Beach, St Margaret's Hope,
South Ronaldsay, Okney, KW17 2TW
Tel:01856 831228
Email:andrea.gillies@btconnect.com
Web:www.roeberry.co.uk**

2 rooms, Open Jan-Dec, B&B per person, single from £27.50, double from £27.50-35.00. Room only per night, single from £55.00, double from £55.00-70.00.

St Mary's Holm, Orkney

Map Ref: 5C11

★★★

LODGE

Commodore Chalets

**St Mary's, Holm, Orkney, KW17 2RU
Tel:01856 781319
Email:louise@commodorechalets.co.uk
Web:www.commodorechalets.co.uk**

Splendid views over St Marys Bay and the Churchill Barriers. 6 miles (10kms) from Kirkwall.

6 rooms, all en-suite, Open Jan-Dec, B&B per person, single from £20.00, double from £18.00.

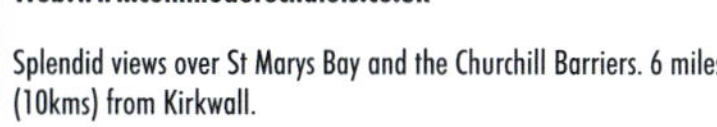

VAT is shown at 17.5%: changes in this rate may affect prices.

Key to symbols is on back flap.

Sandwick, Orkney

Map Ref: 5B11

B&B

Dencraigon B&B

Sandwick, Stromness, Orkney, KW16 3JB
Tel:01856 841647
Email:dencraigon@talk21.com

Bungalow on A967 overlooking Loch Harray, free fishing and boat available. 6 miles (10kms) from Stromness and 3 miles (5kms) from Skara Brae. Also close to Maes Howe, Standing Stones of Stenness, Ring of Brodgar. Visit St Magnus Cathedral in Kirkwall, go on over the Churchill Barriers, the Italian Chapel and beyond. Home baking always available.

3 rooms, Open Apr-Oct, B&B per person, single from £16.00, double from £16.00.

Stromness, Orkney

Map Ref: 5B12

B&B

Mrs Brown

Burnmouth, Cairston Road, Stromness, Orkney, KW16 3JS
Tel:01856 850186

Overlooking Stromness harbour and Scapa Flow. Comfortable accommodation comprising 2 rooms both with showers and washbasins. Skara Brae, Maes Howe, Standing Stones all nearby. Ideal as a base to tour mainland Orkney and outer islands.

2 rooms, all en-suite, Open Jan-Dec, B&B per person, single from £20.00, double from £20.00.

B&B

Ferry Bank

2 North End Road, Stromness, Orkney, KW16 3AG
Tel:01856 851250

Ferrybank is peacefully situated in a beautiful location in our garden grounds. Both bedrooms overlooking the Marina and Scapa Flow. Idyllic location for all amenities. Exceptional breakfast menu and many extras.

2 rooms, all en-suite, Open Jan-Dec excl Xmas/New Year, B&B per person £22.00-23.00 double.

45 JOHN STREET

Stromness, Orkney KW16 3AD

Tel: 01856 850949 e.mail: Glenpest@aol.com

Situated in the centre of Stromness this friendly, family run bed and breakfast is close to all amenities. 50 yards from ferry terminal and harbour. Stunning bedroom views overlooking Hoy Hills and Scapa Flow. Restaurants, bistro's and shops all within easy walking distance.
Open all year round.

B&B

45 John Street

Stromness, Orkney, KW16 3AD
Tel:01856 850949
Email:glenpest@aol.com

Situated very near to Stromness Ferry terminal - ideal as a base to tour Orkney and the Islands. See the varied bird and wildlife, archaeological sites, follow the Craft Trails, and experience Orkneys varied history.

2 rooms, Open Jan-Dec, B&B per person single from 22.00, double from £24.00, family from £24.00.

Stromness, Orkney

Map Ref: 5B12

★★★

B&B

Strowan Lodge

Stenness, Stromness, Orkney, KW16 3JX
Tel:01856 850521

1 single, 1 double, £25.00-35.00 per person per night. Dinner £12.50 each. Closed 1Oct-1Apr. Not suitable for children.

For the discerning guest who seeks quality of service in peaceful setting. Situated in the heart of neolithic Orkney overlooking Lochs Stenness and Harry. Large garden and parking area.

North Mainland, Shetland

Map Ref: 5F3

★★★★

B&B

Westayre B&B

Muckle Roe, Brae, Shetland, ZE2 9QW
Tel:01806 522368
Email:westayre@ukonline.co.uk
Web:www.westayre.shetland.co.uk

4 rooms, some en-suite, Open Mar-Nov, B&B per person, single from £24.00, double from £25.00, BB & Eve.Meal from £45.00.

A warm welcome awaits you at our 110 acre working croft on the picturesque island of Muckle Roe where we have been breeding sheep, pet lambs and ducks. Joined to the mainland by a small bridge and an ideal place for children. High standards of home cooking and baking. In the evening sit by the open peat fire and enjoy the view over Swarbacks Minn. Spectacular cliff scenery and clean, safe sandy beaches. Bird watching. Central for touring.

VAT is shown at 17.5%: changes in this rate may affect prices.

Key to symbols is on back flap.

VisitScotland, in conjunction with the English Tourism Council and Wales Tourist Board operates a national accessible scheme that identifies, acknowledges and promotes those accommodation establishments that meet the needs of visitors with disabilities.

The three categories of accessibility, drawn up in close consultation with specialist organisations concerned with the needs of people with disabilities are:

Category 1

Unassisted wheelchair access for residents

Category 2

Assisted wheelchair access for residents

Category 3

Access for residents with mobility difficulties

Category 1

ABERDEEN
Aberdeen Patio Hotel
Beach Boulevard
Aberdeen
Aberdeenshire
AB24 5EF
Tel: 01224 633339

Copthorne Hotel
122 Huntly Street
Aberdeen
AB10 1SU
Tel: 01224 630404

Crynoch
164 Bon-Accord Street
Aberdeen
Scotland
AB10 2TX
Tel: 01224 582743

Express by Holiday Inn
Chapel Street
Aberdeen
AB10 1SQ
Tel: 01224 623500

Kings Hall
University of Aberdeen
Aberdeen
AB24 3FX
Tel: 01224 272660

Thistle Aberdeen Airport Hotel
Argyll Road
Aberdeen
Aberdeenshire
AB21 0AF
Tel: 01224 640233

ABERNETHY
Gattaway Farm
Abernethy
Perthshire
PH2 9LQ
Tel: 01738 850746

ABINGTON
Days Inn
Welcome Break M74/A7
Abington
Lanarkshire
ML12 6RG
Tel: 01864 502782

ACHNASHEEN
Loch Torridon Hotel
Torridon
Achnasheen
Ross-shire
IV22 2EY
Tel: 01445 791242

ALEXANDRIA
De Vere Cameron House
Loch Lomond
Alexandria
Dunbartonshire
G83 8QZ
Tel: 01389 755565

ALTENS, ABERDEEN
Thistle Aberdeen Altens
Soutarhead Road
Altens, Aberdeen
Aberdeenshire
AB12 3LF
Tel: 01224 723101

AUCHENCAIRN,
BY CASTLE DOUGLAS
Balcary Bay Hotel
Auchencairn, By Castle Douglas
Kirkcudbrightshire
DG7 1QZ
Tel: 01556 640217

AUCHTERARDER
The Gleneagles Hotel
Auchterarder
Perthshire
PH3 1NF
Tel: 01764 662231

AULDEARN
Covenanters' Inn
High Street
Auldearn
Nairn
IV12 5TG
Tel: 01667 452456

BALLACHULISH
Isles of Glencoe Hotel &
Leisure Centre
Ballachulish
Argyll PH49 4HL
Tel: 01855 821582

BALLATER
Glenernan
37 Braemar Road
Ballater
Aberdeenshire
AB35 5RQ
Tel: 013397 53111

ISLE OF BARRA
Northbay House
Balnabodach
Isle of Barra
Outer Hebrides HS9 5UT
Tel: 01871 890255

BRAEMAR
The Invercauld Arms Hotel
Invercauld Road
Braemar
Aberdeenshire
AB35 5YR

BROUGHTON, BY BIGGAR
The Glenholm Centre
Broughton, by Biggar
Lanarkshire
ML12 6JF
Tel: 01899 830408

BROUGHTY FERRY, DUNDEE
The Fishermans Tavern Hotel
10-16 Fort Street
Broughty Ferry, Dundee
Angus
DD5 2AD
Tel: 01382 775941

BURNTISLAND
Kingswood Hotel
Kinghorn Road
Burntisland
Fife
KY3 9LL
Tel: 01592 872329

CARRADALE
Dunvalanree
Portrigh Bay
Carradale
Argyll
PA28 6SE
Tel: 01583 431226

CASTLE DOUGLAS
Douglas House B&B
63 Queen Street
Castle Douglas
Dumfries
DG7 1HS
Tel: 01556 503262

CLYDEBANK
Beardmore Hotel
Beardmore Street
Clydebank
Greater Glasgow
G81 4SA
Tel: 0141 951 6000

CONNEL, BY OBAN
Wide Mouthed Frog
Dunstaffnage Marina
Connel, by Oban
Argyll
PA37 1PX
Tel: 01631 567005

COYLTON
Finlayson Arms Hotel
24 Hillhead
Coylton
Ayrshire
KA6 6JT
Tel: 01292 570298

DAVIOT
The Lodge at Daviot Mains
Daviot
By Inverness
IV2 5ER
Tel: 01463 772215

DUNDEE
Days Inn Dundee
296a Strathmore Avenue
Dundee
DD3 6SP
Tel: 01382 826000

West Park Centre
319 Perth Road
Dundee
Angus
DD2 1NN
Tel: 01382 573050

DUNOON
Dhailling Lodge
155 Alexandra Parade
Dunoon
Argyll
PA23 8AW
Tel: 01369 701253

EDINBURGH
Ardgarth Guest House
1 St Mary's Place, Portobello
Edinburgh
EH15 2QF
Tel: 0131 669 3021

Best Western
Edinburgh City Hotel
79 Lauriston Place
Edinburgh
EH3 9HZ
Tel: 0131 622 7979

Brae Lodge Guest House
30 Liberton Brae
Edinburgh
Lothian
EH16 6AF
Tel: 0131 672 2876

Express By Holiday Inn
16-22 Picardy Place
Edinburgh
Lothian EH1 3JT
Tel: 0131 5582300

Jurys Inn Edinburgh
43 Jeffrey Street
Edinburgh
Lothian
EH1 1DH
Tel: 0131 200 3300

Melville Guest House
2 Duddingston Crescent
Edinburgh
Lothian
EH15 3AS
Tel: 0131 6697856

Novotel Edinburgh Centre
80 Lauriston Place
Edinburgh
Lothian
EH3 9DE
Tel: 0131 656 3500

Premier Travel Inn Metro
1 Morrison Link
Edinburgh
EH3 8DN
0870 238 3319

Ramada Mount Royal Hotel
53 Princes Street
Edinburgh
EH2 2DG
Tel: 0131 225 7161

Thistle Edinburgh
107 Leith Street
Edinburgh
EH1 3SW
Tel: 0141 3323311

**Toby Carvery &
Innkeepers Lodge**
114-116 St Johns Road
Edinburgh
EH12 8AX
Tel: 0131 334 8235

FALLS OF TRUIM
Crubenbeg House
Falls of Truim
By Newtonmore
PH20 1BE
Tel: 01540 673300

FINSTOWN
Lynwood
Maitland Place
Finstown
Orkney
KW17 2EQ
Tel: 01856 761786

FORGANDENNY
Battledown Bed & Breakfast
Off Station Road
Forgandenny
Perthshire
PH2 9EL
Tel: 01738 812471

FORT WILLIAM
Cuil-Na-Sithe
Lochyside
Fort William
Inverness-shire
PH33 7NX
Tel: 01397 702 267

GAILES
The Gailes Lodge
Marine Drive
Gailes
Irvine
KA11 5AE
Tel: 01294 204040

GLASGOW
Carlton George Hotel
44 West George Street
Glasgow
G2 1DH
Tel: 0141 353 6373

Glasgow Hilton
1 William Street
Glasgow
G3 8HT
Tel: 0141 204 5555

Glasgow Marriott
500 Argyle Street
Glasgow
G3 8RR
Tel: 0141 226 5577

Holiday Inn
161 West Nile Street
Glasgow
G1 2RL
Tel: 0141 352 8300

Holiday Inn Glasgow City West
Bothwell Street
Glasgow
G2 7EN
Tel: 0870 400 9032

Jurys Inn Glasgow
Jamaica Street
Glasgow
G1 4QE
Tel: 0141 334 8161

Tulip Inn Glasgow
80 Ballater Street
Glasgow
G5 0TW
Tel: 0141 429 4233

GREENOCK
Express by Holiday Inn
Cartsburn
Greenock PA15 4RT
Tel: 01475 786666

James Watt College
Waterfront Campus,
Customhouse Way
Greenock
Renfrewshire
PA15 1EN
Tel: 01475 731360

GRETNA
The Garden House Hotel
Sarkfoot Road
Gretna
Dumfriesshire
DG16 5EP
Tel: 01461 337621

GRETNA GREEN
Days Inn
Welcome Break Service Area,
M74
Gretna Green
Dumfriesshire
DG16 5HQ
Tel: 01461 337566

HADDINGTON
Maitlandfield House Hotel
24 Sidegate
Haddington
East Lothian
EH41 4BZ
Tel: 01620 826513

INVERALMOND, PERTH
Express by Holiday Inn
200 Dunkeld Road
Inveralmond, Perth
Perthshire
PH1 3AQ
Tel: 01738 636666

INVERGORDON
Delny House
Delny
Invergordon
Ross-shire
IV18 0NP
Tel: 01862 842678

INVERKIP
The Foresters
Station Road
Inverkip
Renfrewshire
PA16 0AY
Tel: 01475 521433

INVERNESS
Inverness Marriott
Culcabock Road
Inverness
Inverness-shire
IV2 3LP
Tel: 01463 237166

Silverwells Guest House
28 Ness Bank
Inverness
IV2 4SF
Tel: 01463 232113

IRVINE
Thistle Irvine
46 Annick Road
Irvine
Ayrshire
KA11 4LD
Tel: 0141 332 3311

KILMARNOCK
Park Hotel
Rugby Park
Kilmarnock
Ayrshire
KA1 2DP
Tel: 01563 545999

KINLOCHLEVEN
Tigh-Na-Cheo
Garbien Road
Kinlochleven
Argyll PH50 4SE
Tel: 01855 831434

KIRKWALL
Lav'rockha Guest House
Inganess Road
Kirkwall
Orkney KW15 1SP
Tel: 01856 876103

LAIRG
Lochview
Lochside
Lairg
Sutherland
IV27 4EH
Tel: 01549 402578

LERWICK
Shetland Hotel
Holmsgarth Road
Lerwick
Shetland
ZE1 0PW
Tel: 01595 695515

LEUCHARS, BY ST ANDREWS
Drumoig Hotel & Golf Resort
Drumoig
Leuchars, by St Andrews
Fife
KY16 0BE
Tel: 01382 541800

LEWIS
Western Isles Cross Inn
Cross Ness
Lewis, Western Isles
HS2 0SN
Tel: 01851 810152

LIVINGSTON
Ramada Jarvis Livingston
Almondview
Livingston
West Lothian EH54 6QB
Tel: 01506 431222

LOCHMABEN
The Crown Hotel
8 Bruce Street
Lochmaben
Dumfriesshire
DG11 1PD
Tel: 01387 811750

LOSSIEMOUTH
Ceilidh B&B
34 Clifton Road
Lossiemouth
Moray IV31 6DP
Tel: 01343 815848

MOFFAT
Lochhouse Farm Retreat Centre
Beattock
Moffat
Dumfries & Galloway
DG10 9SG
Tel: 01683 300451

MOTHERWELL
Express By Holiday Inn
Strathclyde Park M74 Jct 5
Motherwell
Lanarkshire ML1 3RB
Tel: 01698 858585

Motherwell College
Stewart Hall
Dalzell Drive
Motherwell
Lanarkshire
ML1 2DD
Tel: 01698 261890

NAIRN
Claymore House Hotel
45 Seabank Road
Nairn
Inverness-shire
IV12 4EY
Tel: 01667 453731

Windsor Hotel
16 Albert Street
Nairn
Inverness-shire
IV12 4HP
Tel: 01667 453108

PAISLEY
Express by Holiday Inn
Glasgow Airport
St Andrews Drive
Paisley PA3 2TJ
Tel: 0131 553 4422

Travelodge Glasgow Airport
Marchburn Drive
Paisley
Glasgow PA3 2AR
Tel: 0141 848 1359

PEEBLES
Cringletie House Hotel
Edinburgh Road
Peebles
Peeblesshire
EH45 8PL
Tel: 01721 725750

PETERHEAD
Invernettie Guest House
South Road
Peterhead
Aberdeenshire
AB42 0YX
Tel: 01779 473530

PITFODELS, ABERDEEN
Marcliffe at Pitfodels
North Deeside Road
Pitfodels, Aberdeen
AB15 9YA
Tel: 01224 861000

PITLOCHRY
Atholl Villa Guest House
29/31 Atholl Road
Pitlochry
Perthshire
PH16 5BX
Tel: 01796 473820

POINT
Dolly's B&B
33 Aignish
Point
Lewis, Western Isles
HS2 0PB
Tel: 01851 870755

PORTREE
Cuillin Hills Hotel
Portree
Isle of Skye
IV51 9QU
Tel: 01478 612003

Viewfield House Hotel
Portree
Isle of Skye
IV51 9EU
Tel: 01478 612217

PRESTWICK
Golf View Hotel
17 Links Road
Prestwick
Ayrshire
KA9 1QG
Tel: 01292 671234

ROTHESAY
The Boat House
15 Battery Place
Rothesay
Argyll & Bute
PA20 9DP
Tel: 01700 502696

SALEN
Ard Mhor House
Pier Road
Salen
Isle of Mull PA72 6JL
Tel: 01680 300255

SOUTH UIST
Crossroads
Stoneybridge
South Uist
Western Isles
HS8 5SD
Tel: 01870 620321

BY SPEAN BRIDGE
Old Pines Hotel and Restaurant
Gairlochy Road
By Spean Bridge
Inverness-shire
PH34 4EG
Tel: 01397 712324

ST ANDREWS
The Old Station, Country House
Stratvithie Bridge
St Andrews
Fife KY16 8LR
Tel: 01334 880505

ST BOSWELLS, MELROSE
Dryburgh Abbey Hotel
St Boswells, Melrose
Scottish Borders
TD6 0RQ
Tel: 01835 822261

STIRLING
Express by Holiday Inn -
Stirling
Springkerse Business Park
Stirling
Stirlingshire
FK7 7XH
Tel: 01786 449922

Stirling Management Centre
University of Stirling
Stirling
FK9 4LA
Tel: 01786 451666

STONEHOUSE
Thorndale Guest House
Manse Road
Stonehouse
Lanarkshire
ML9 3NX
Tel: 01698 791133

TOBERMORY
Highland Cottage
Breadalbane Street
Tobermory
Isle of Mull
PA75 6PD
Tel: 01688 302030

TURNBERRY
The Westin Turnberry Resort
Turnberry
Ayrshire
KA26 9LT
Tel: 01655 331000

WALLS
Burrastow House
Walls
Shetland
ZE2 9PD
Tel: 01595 809307

Category 2

ABBOTSINCH
Ramada Glasgow Airport
Marchburn Drive
Abbotsinch
Paisley
PA3 2SJ
Tel: 0141 8402200

ABERDEEN
Aberdeen Marriott Hotel
Riverview Drive
Farburn, Dyce
Aberdeenshire
AB21 7AZ
Tel: 0870 400 7291

Crombie Johnston
University of Aberdeen
Aberdeen
AB24 3TS
Tel: 01224 272660

ABERFELDY
Tomvale
Tom of Cluny
Aberfeldy
Perthshire PH15 2JT
Tel: 01887 820171

ABERFOYLE
Crannaig House
Trossachs Road
Aberfoyle
Stirlingshire
FK8 3SR
Tel: 01877 382276

BY ABERFOYLE
Forest Hills Hotel
Kinlochard
By Aberfoyle
Stirlingshire
FK8 3TL
Tel: 01877 387277

AVIEMORE
MacDonald Academy
Aviemore Highland Resort
Aviemore
Inverness-shire
PH22 1PF
Tel: 01479 810781

AYR
Horizon Hotel
Esplanade
Ayr
Ayrshire
KA7 1DT
Tel: 01292 264384

BY AYR
Alt-Na-Craig
Hollybush
By Ayr KA6 7EB
Tel: 01292 560555

AYRSHIRE
Glenapp Castle
Ballantrae
Ayrshire
KA26 0NZ
Tel: 01465 831212

BALLACHULISH
The Ballachulish Hotel
Ballachulish
Argyll
PH49 4JY
Tel: 01855 811606

BALTASOUND, UNST
The Baltasound Hotel
Baltasound, Unst
Shetland ZE2 9DS
Tel: 01957 711334

BLACK ISLE
Autumn Gold
Blablair
Black Isle
Ross & Cromarty
IV7 8LR
Tel: 01381 622315

BRIDGE OF ALLAN
The Queen's Hotel
24 Henderson Street
Bridge of Allan
Stirlingshire
FK9 4HP
Tel: 01786 833268

BRODICK
Auchrannie
Country House Hotel
Brodick
Isle of Arran
KA27 8BZ
Tel: 01770 302234

BRORA
Glenaveron
Golf Road
Brora
Sutherland
KW9 6QS
Tel: 01408 621 601

CARRUTHERSTOWN
Hetland Hall Hotel
Carrutherstown
Dumfriesshire
DG1 4JX
Tel: 01387 840201

CRIEFF
Comely Bank Guest House
32 Burrell Street
Crieff
Perthshire PH7 4DT
Tel: 01764 653409

Murraypark Hotel
Connaught Terrace
Crieff
Perthshire
PH7 3DJ
Tel: 01764 653731

CUMBERNAULD
Red Deer & Innkeeper's Lodge
1 Auchenkilns Park
Cumbernauld
North Lanarkshire
G68 9AZ
Tel: 01236 795 861

DRUMNADROCHIT
Clunebeg Lodge Guest House
Clunebeg Estate
Drumnadrochit
Inverness-shire
IV63 6US
Tel: 01456 450387

Woodlands
East Lewiston
Drumnadrochit
Inverness-shire
IV63 6UW
Tel: 01456 450356

DUNFERMLINE
Best Western
Keavil House Hotel
Crossford
Dunfermline
Fife KY12 8QW
Tel: 01383 736258

Garvock House Hotel
St John's Drive, Transy
Dunfermline
Fife KY12 7TU
Tel: 01383 621067

Rooms at 29 Bruce Street
29-35 Bruce Street
Dunfermline
Fife
KY12 7AG
Tel: 01383 840041

DYCE
Dyce Skean Dhu Hotel
Farburn Terrace
Dyce
Aberdeenshire
AB21 7DW
Tel: 01224 723101

Speedbird Inn
Argyll Road
Dyce, Aberdeen
Aberdeenshire
AB21 0AF
Tel: 01224 772884

EDINBURGH
Edinburgh First
Chancellor Court, Pollock Halls
18 Holyrood Park Road
Edinburgh
EH10 5AY
Tel: 0131 651 2011

EDINBURGH
Aalpha Laurels
320 Gilmerton Road
Edinburgh
Midlothian
EH17 7PR
Tel: 0131 666 2229

Caledonian Hilton Hotel
Princes Street
Edinburgh
EH1 2AB
Tel: 0131 222 8888

Edinburgh Marriott
111 Glasgow Road
Edinburgh
EH12 8NF
Tel: 0870 400 7293

Hilton Edinburgh Airport
Edinburgh International Airport
Edinburgh
EH28 8LL
Tel: 0131 519 4400

Hilton Edinburgh Grosvenor
7-21 Grosvenor Street
Edinburgh
EH12 5EF
Tel: 0131 226 6001

Holiday Inn Edinburgh
Corstorphine Road
Edinburgh
EH12 6UA
Tel: 0870 400 9026

Holiday Inn Edinburgh-North
107 Queensferry Road
Edinburgh
EH4 3HL
Tel: 0131-332-2442

Queen Margaret College
36 Clerwood Terrace
Edinburgh
EH12 8TS
Tel: 0131 317 3317/3314

FORT WILLIAM
Clan MacDuff Hotel
Achintore Road
Fort William
Inverness-shire
PH33 6RW
Tel: 01397 702341

GLASGOW
Bewleys Hotel Glasgow
110 Bath Street
Glasgow
G2 2EN
Tel: 0141 3530800

Campanile Glasgow
Tunnel Street
Glasgow
Scotland
G3 8HL
Tel: 0141 2877700

Glasgow Moat House
Congress Road
Glasgow
G3 8QT
Tel: 0141 306 9988

Ibis Hotel Glasgow
220 West Regent Street
Glasgow
G2 4DQ
Tel: 0141 225 6000

Wolfson Hall
Kelvin Campus, West Scotland
Science Park
Maryhill Road
Glasgow
G20 0TH
Tel: 0141 3303110

Milton Hotel & Spa, Glasgow
27 Washington Street
Glasgow
G3 8AZ
Tel: 0141 222 2929

Novotel Glasgow Centre
181 Pitt Street
Glasgow
G2 4DT
Tel: 0141 222 2775

Queen Margaret Hall
55 Bellshaugh Road
Glasgow
G12 0SQ
Tel: 0141 330 3110

The Millennium, Glasgow Hotel
George Square
Glasgow
G2 1DS
Tel: 0141 332 6711

GOREBRIDGE
Ivory House
14 Vogrie Road
Gorebridge
Midlothian
EH23 4HH
Tel: 01875 820755

GRANGEMOUTH
Leapark Hotel
130 Bo'ness Road
Grangemouth
Stirlingshire
FK3 9BX
Tel: 01324 486733

GRANTOWN-ON-SPEY
Muckrach Lodge Hotel
Dulnain Bridge
Grantown-on-spey
Moray PH26 3LY
Tel: 01479 851257

GRETNA
The Willows
Loanwath Road
Gretna
Dumfriesshire
DG16 5ES
Tel: 01461 337996

HAWICK
Whitchester Guest House
Hawick
Roxburghshire
TD9 7LN
Tel: 01450 377477

HOY
Stromabank
Hoy
Orkney
KW16 3PA
Tel: 01856 701494

INVERARAY
Loch Fyne Hotel
Newtown
Inveraray
Argyll PA32 8XJ
Tel: 0131 554 7173

INVERNESS
Ramada Jarvis Inverness
Church Street
Inverness
Inverness-shire
IV1 1DX
Tel: 01463 235181

ISLE OF MULL
Seilisdeir
Lochdon
Isle of Mull
PA64 6AP
Tel: 01680 812465

KELSO
Ingleston House
Abbey Row
Kelso
Roxburghshire
TD5 7HQ
Tel: 01573 225800/225315

KINGUSSIE
Arden House
Newtonmore Road
Kingussie
Inverness-shire
PH21 1HE
Tel: 01540 661369

KINLOCH RANNOCH
Dunalastair Hotel
The Square
Kinloch Rannoch
Perthshire
PH16 5PW
Tel: 01882 632323

KIRKMICHAEL, BLAIRGOWRIE
The Log Cabin Hotel
Glen Derby
Kirkmichael, Blairgowrie
Perthshire
PH10 7NA
Tel: 01250 881288

**KIRKPATRICK FLEMING,
BY LOCKERBIE**
The Mill
Grahamshill
Kirkpatrick Fleming,
by Lockerbie
Dumfriesshire
DG11 3BQ
Tel: 01461 800344

KIRKWALL
Eastbank House
East Road
Kirkwall
Orkney
KW15 1LX
Tel: 01856 870179

LEDAIG
Isle of Eriska Hotel
Ledaig
Argyll
PA37 1SD
Tel: 01631 720371

LOCHGILPHEAD
Empire Travel Lodge
Union Street
Lochgilphead
Argyll
PA31 8JS
Tel: 01546 602381

LOCKERBIE
Dryfesdale Country House Hotel
Dryfebridge
Lockerbie
Dumfriesshire
DG11 2SF
Tel: 01576 202427

MARKINCH, BY GLENROTHES
Balbirnie House Hotel
Balbirnie Park
Markinch, by Glenrothes
Fife
KY7 6NE
Tel: 01592 610066

MILLPORT
The Cathedral of the Isles
The College
Millport
Isle of Cumbrae
KA28 0HE
Tel: 01475 530353

MINARD
Minard Castle
Minard
Argyll
PA32 8YB
Tel: 01546 886272

MOTHERWELL
Moorings Hotel
114 Hamilton Road
Motherwell
Lanarkshire
ML1 3DG
Tel: 01698 258131

The Alona Hotel
Strathclyde Country Park
Motherwell
North Lanarkshire
ML1 3RT
Tel: 01698 333777

NETHYBRIDGE
Nethybridge Hotel
Nethybridge
Inverness-shire
PH25 3DP
Tel: 01479 821203

NEW LANARK
New Lanark Mill Hotel
New Lanark
Lanarkshire
ML11 9DB
Tel: 01555 667200

NORTH RONALDSAY
Observatory Guest House
North Ronaldsay
Orkney
KW17 2BE
Tel: 011857 633200

PEEBLES
Glentress Hotel
Innerleithen Road
Peebles
Peebles-shire
EH45 8NB
Tel: 01721 720100

PERTH
Huntingtower Hotel
Crieff Road
Perth
Perthshire
PH1 3JT
Tel: 01738 583771

PITLOCHRY
Cuil-an-Daraich
2 Cuil-an-Daraich, Logierait
Pitlochry
Perthshire
PH9 0LH
Tel: 01796 482750

PLOCKTON
Plockton Hotel
Harbour Street
Plockton
Ross-shire
IV52 8TN
Tel: 01599 544274

POLMONT
Inchyra Grange Hotel
Grange Road
Polmont
Stirlingshire
FK2 0YB
Tel: 01324 711911

PRESTWICK
Parkstone Hotel
Esplanade
Prestwick
Ayrshire
KA9 1QN
Tel: 01292 477286

ROY BRIDGE
The Stronlossit Inn
Roy Bridge
Inverness-shire
PH31 4AG
Tel: 0800 015 5321

SANQUHAR
Newark
Sanquhar
Dumfriesshire
DG4 6HN
Tel: 01659 50263

SCONE
Perth Airport Skylodge
Norwell Drive, Perth Airport
Scone
Perthshire PH2 6PL
Tel: 01738 555700

ST ANDREWS
Rufflets Country House Hotel
Strathkinness Low Road
St Andrews
Fife
KY16 9TX
Tel: 01334 472594

BY TAYNUILT
Roineabhal Country House
Kilchrenan
by Taynuilt
Argyll PA35 1HD
Tel: 01866 833207

THURSO
Weigh Inn Hotel
Burnside
Thurso
Caithness
KW14 7UG
Tel: 01847 893722

TROON
South Beach Hotel
South Beach
Troon
Ayrshire
KA10 6EG
Tel: 01292 312033

TUMMEL BRIDGE
Kynachan Loch Tummel Hotel
Tummel Bridge
Perthshire
PH16 5SB
Tel: 01389 713713

WESTHILL
Copperfield
Culloden Road
Westhill
Inverness
IV2 5BP
Tel: 01463 792251

WHITBURN
Hilcroft Hotel
East Main Street
Whitburn
West Lothian
EH47 0JU
Tel: 01501 740818

Category 3

ABERDEEN
Britannia Hotel
Malcolm Road
Aberdeen
Grampian
AB21 9LN
Tel: 01224 409988

Northern Hotel
1 Great Northern Road
Aberdeen
AB24 3PS
Tel: 01224 483342

ABERDOUR
Aberdour Hotel
38 High Street
Aberdour
Fife
KY3 0SW
Tel: 01383 860325

ABERFOYLE
Rob Roy Hotel
Aberfoyle
Stirlingshire
FK8 3UX
Tel: 01877 382245

ABERUTHVEN
Kilrymont
8 Loanfoot Park
Aberuthven
Perthshire PH3 1JF
Tel: 01764 662660

ABOYNE
Chesterton House
Formaston Park
Aboyne
Aberdeenshire AB34 5HF
Tel: 013398 86740

BY ACHMORE
Soluis Mu Thuath
Braeintra
by Achmore
Lochalsh
IV53 8UP
Tel: 01599 577219

ARDFERN,BY LOCHGILPHEAD
Galley of Lorne Inn
Main Street
Ardfern,by Lochgilphead
Argyll
PA31 8QN
Tel: 01852 500284

ARROCHAR
Village Inn
Main Street
Arrochar
Dunbartonshire
G83 7AX
Tel: 01301 702279

AUCHTERARDER
Greystanes
Western Road
Auchterarder
Perthshire PH3 1SS
Tel: 01764 664239

AVIEMORE
Ravenscraig Guest House
141 Grampian Road
Aviemore
Inverness-shire
PH22 1RP
Tel: 01479 810278

Waverley
35 Strathspey Avenue
Aviemore
Inverness-shire
PH22 1SN
Tel: 01479 811226

AVOCH
Inverleod
Toll Road
Avoch
Ross-shire
IV9 8PR
Tel: 01381 621595

AYR
Fairfield House Hotel
12 Fairfield Road
Ayr
Ayrshire
KA7 2AR
Tel: 01292 267461

Miller House
36 Miller Road
Ayr
Ayrshire KA7 2AY
Tel: 01292 282016

BY AYR
Enterkine Country House
Annbank
by Ayr
Ayrshire KA6 5AL
Tel: 01292 521608

BALLATER
Darroch Learg Hotel
Braemar Road
Ballater
Aberdeenshire
AB35 5UX
Tel: 01339 755443

Moorside Guest House
26 Braemar Road
Ballater
Aberdeenshire
AB35 5RL
Tel: 01339 755492

BALLOCH
Anchorage Guest House
31 Balloch Road
Balloch
Dunbartonshire
G83 8SS
Tel: 01389 753336

BELLOCHANTUY,
BY CAMPBELTOWN
Argyll Hotel
Bellochantuy,
by Campbeltown
Argyll
PA28 6QE
Tel: 01583 421212

BELLSHILL
Hilton Strathclyde
Pheonix Crescent
Bellshill
North Lanarkshire
ML4 3JQ
Tel: 01698 395500

BENDERLOCH, OBAN
Island Home
12 Pony Park, Letterwalton
Benderloch, Oban
Argyll
PA37 1SA
Tel: 01631 720078

BIGGAR
Cormiston Cottage
Cormiston Road
Biggar
Lanarkshire
ML12 6NS
Tel: 01899 220200

BISHOPTON
Mar Hall
Mar Estate
Bishopton
Renfrewshire
PA7 5PU
Tel: 0141 812 9999

BLACKFORD
Blackford Hotel
Moray Street
Blackford
Perthshire
PH4 1QF
Tel: 01764 682497

BLAIRGOWRIE
Holmrigg
Wester Essendy
Blairgowrie
Perthshire
PH10 6RD
Tel: 01250 884309

BRIDGE OF ALLAN
Lynedoch
7 Mayne Avenue
Bridge of Allan
Stirlingshire
FK9 4QU
Tel: 01786 832178

BRIDGE OF CALLY
Bridge of Cally Hotel
Bridge of Cally
Perthshire PH10 7JJ
Tel: 01250 886231

Glen Albyn
Bridge of Cally
Perthshire
PH10 7JL
Tel: 01250 886352

BROADFORD
Seaview
Main Street
Broadford
Isle of Skye
IV49 9AB
Tel: 01471 820308

BRODICK
Belvedere Guest House
Alma Road
Brodick
Isle of Arran
KA27 8AZ
Tel: 01770 302397

Strathwhillan House
Brodick
Isle of Arran
KA27 8BQ
Tel: 01770 302331

BUCKIE
The Bungalow
81 High Street
Buckie
Banffshire
AB56 1BB
Tel: 01542 832367

CALLANDER
Roman Camp Hotel
Main Street
Callander
Perthshire
FK17 8BG
Tel: 01877 330003

The Crags Hotel
101 Main Street
Callander
Perthshire
FK17 8BQ
Tel: 01877 330257

The Knowe
Ancaster Road
Callander
Perthshire
FK17 8EL
Tel: 01877 330076

The Old Rectory Guest House
Leny Road
Callander
Perthshire
FK17 8AL
Tel: 01877 339215

CANDERSIDE TOLL,
BY LARKHALL
Shawlands Hotel
Ayr Road
Canderside Toll, by Larkhall
Lanarkshire
ML9 2TZ
Tel: 01698 791111

COLDINGHAM
Dunlaverock
Coldingham Bay
Coldingham
Berwickshire
TD14 5PA
Tel: 01890 771450

COLVEND, DALBEATTIE
Clonyard House Hotel
Colvend, Dalbeattie
Kircudbrightshire
DG5 4QW
Tel: 01556 630372

COMRIE
Drumearn Cottage
The Ross
Comrie
Perthshire
PH6 2JU
Tel: 01764 670030

CONTIN
Hideaway
Craigdarroch Drive
Contin
Ross-shire
IV14 9EL
Tel: 01997 421127

COUPAR ANGUS
Red House Hotel
Station Road
Coupar Angus
Perthshire
PH13 9AL
Tel: 01828 628500

CRIEFF
Achray House Hotel
St Fillans
Crieff
Perthshire
PH6 2NF
Tel: 01764 685 231

Ardo Howe
31 Burrell Street
Crieff
Perthshire
PH7 4DT
Tel: 01764 652825

Crieff Hydro Hotel
Crieff
Perthshire
PH7 3LQ
Tel: 01764 655555

Fendoch Guest House
Sma' Glen
Crieff
Perthshire
PH7 3LW
Tel: 01764 653446

Tuchethill House
Dollerie
Crieff
Perthshire
PH7 3NX
Tel: 01764 653188

DALBEATTIE
Bellevue B&B
Port Road
Dalbeattie
DG5 4AZ
Tel: 01556 611833

DALMALLY
Glenorchy Lodge Hotel
Dalmally
Argyll
PA33 1AA
Tel: 018382 00312

DALRYMPLE
Kirkton Inn
1 Main Street
Dalrymple
Ayrshire
KA6 6DF
Tel: 01292 560241

DIRLETON
Station House
Station Road
Dirleton
North Berwick
EH39 5LR
Tel: 01620 890512

DORNOCH
Dornoch Castle Hotel
Castle Street
Dornoch
Sutherland
IV25 3SD
Tel: 01862 810216

DUFFTOWN
Braehead Villa
Braehead Terrace
Dufftown
Keith, Banffshire
AB55 4AN
Tel: 01340 320461

DUMFRIES
Hazeldean Guest House
4 Moffat Road
Dumfries DG1 1NJ
Tel: 01387 266178

Netherfield
Lochanhead
Dumfries
Dumfries & Galloway
DG2 8JE
Tel: 01387 730217

Torbay Lodge
31 Lovers Walk
Dumfries
DG1 1LR
Tel: 01387 253922

Wallamhill House
Kirkton
Dumfries
Dumfriesshire
DG1 1SL
Tel: 01387 248249

DUNBAR
Goldenstones Hotel
Queens Road
Dunbar
East Lothian
EH42 1LG
Tel: 01368 862356

DUNDEE
Hilton Dundee
Earl Grey Place
Dundee
Angus
DD1 4DE
Tel: 01382 229271

DUNFERMLINE
Clarke Cottage Guest House
139 Halbeath Road
Dunfermline
Fife
KY11 4LA
Tel: 01383 735935

Pitbauchlie House Hotel
Aberdour Road
Dunfermline
Fife
KY11 4PB
Tel: 01383 722282

DUNTOCHER
West Park Hotel
Great Western Road
Duntocher
Clydebank G81 6DB
Tel: 01389 872333

EDINBURGH
Abbey Lodge Hotel
137 Drum Street, Gilmerton
Edinburgh EH17 8RJ
Tel: 0131 6649548

Express By Holiday Inn
Britannia Way, Ocean Drive
Edinburgh
Lothian
EH6 6LA
Tel: 0131 5554422

Holland House
18 Holyrood Park Road
Edinburgh
EH16 5AY
Tel: 0131 651 2011

Holyrood Hotel
Holyrood Road
Edinburgh
EH8 6AE
Tel: 0131 550 4500

Hotel Ceilidh-Donia
14-16 Marchhall Crescent
Edinburgh
EH16 5HL
Tel: 0131 667 2743

International Guest House
37 Mayfield Gardens
Edinburgh
EH9 2BX
Tel: 0131 667 2511

Kelly's Guest House
3 Hillhouse Road
Edinburgh
Lothian
EH4 3QP
Tel: 0131 332 3894

Kings Manor Hotel
100 Milton Road East
Edinburgh
EH15 2NP
Tel: 0131 669 0444

Lindsay Guest House
108 Polwarth Terrace
Edinburgh
Midlothian
EH11 1NN
Tel: 0131 337 1580

Masson House
18 Holyrood Park Road
Edinburgh
EH16 5AY
Tel: 0131 651 2011

Roxburghe Hotel
38 Charlotte Square
Edinburgh
EH2 4HG
Tel: 0131 240 5500

Western Manor House Hotel
92 Corstorphine Road
Edinburgh
EH12 6JG
Tel: 0131 5387490

EDZELL
Kelvingrove
Dunlappie Road
Edzell
Angus
DD9 7UB
Tel: 01356 648316

ERSKINE
Erskine Bridge Hotel
Erskine
Renfrewshire
PA8 6AN

ESKBANK
Glenarch House
Melville Road
Eskbank
Dalkeith
EH22 3NJ
Tel: 0131 6631478

FINTRY
Culcreuch Castle
Culcreuch Castle Country Park
Fintry
Stirlingshire
G63 0LW
Tel: 01360 860555

FORT WILLIAM
Craig Nevis West
Belford Road
Fort William
Inverness-shire
PH33 6BU
Tel: 01397 702023

Lochan Cottage Guest House
Lochyside
Fort William
Inverness-shire
PH33 7NX
Tel: 01397 702695

BY FORT WILLIAM
The Inn at Ardgour
Ardgour
by Fort William
Inverness-shire
PH33 7AA
Tel: 01855 841225

GAIRLOCH
Dunedin
42 Strath
Gairloch
Ross-shire
IV21 2DB
Tel: 01445 712050

GALASHIELS
Ettrickvale
33 Abbotsford Road
Galashiels
Selkirkshire
TD1 3HW
Tel: 01896 755224

GLASGOW
The Knowes
32 Riddrie Knowes
Glasgow
G33 2QH
Tel: 0141 770 5213

GOUROCK
Spinnaker Hotel
121 Albert Road
Gourock
Renfrewshire
PA19 1BU
Tel: 01475 633107

GRANTOWN ON SPEY
Holmhill House
Woodside Avenue
Grantown on Spey
Morayshire
PH26 3JR
Tel: 01479 873977

Dunallan House
Woodside Avenue
Grantown-on-Spey
Moray
PH26 3JN
Tel: 01479 872140

Kinross Guest House
Woodside Avenue
Grantown-on-Spey
Moray
PH26 3JR
Tel: 01479 872042

GREENOCK
Tontine Hotel
6 Ardgowan Square
Greenock
Renfrewshire
PA16 8NG
Tel: 01475 723316

GRETNA
The Gables Hotel
1 Annan Road
Gretna
Dumfriesshire
DG16 5DQ
Tel: 01461 338300

GULBERWICK
Virdafjell
Shurton Brae
Gulberwick
Shetland ZE2 9TX
Tel: 01595 694336

ISLE OF HARRIS
Ardhasaig House
9 Ardhasaig
Isle of Harris
HS3 3AJ
Tel: 01859 502066

Carminish House
1 A Strond
Isle of Harris HS5 3UB
Tel: 01859 520400

HELENSBURGH
RSR Braeholm
31 East Montrose Street
Helensburgh
Argyll & Bute
G84 7HR
Tel: 01436 671880

HELMSDALE
Kindale House
5 Lilleshall Street
Helmsdale
Sutherland
KW8 6JF
Tel: 01431 821415

INVERGOWRIE, DUNDEE
Swallow Hotel
Kingsway West
Invergowrie, Dundee
Angus
DD2 5JT
Tel: 01382 641122

INVERNESS
Avalon Guest House
79 Glenurquhart Road
Inverness
Inverness-shire
IV3 5PB
Tel: 01463 239075

Drumossie Park Cottage
Drumossie Brae
Inverness
Inverness-shire
IV2 5BB
Tel: 01463 224127

Express by Holiday Inn
Stoneyfield
Inverness
IV2 7PA
Tel: 01463 732700

Glen Mhor Hotel
9-12 Ness Bank
Inverness
Inverness-shire
IV2 4SG
Tel: 01463 234308

INVERURIE
Strathburn Hotel
Burghmuir Drive
Inverurie
Aberdeenshire
AB51 4GY
Tel: 01467 624422

ISLE OF IONA
Finlay Ross (Iona) Ltd
Martyr's Bay
Isle of Iona
Argyll
PA76 6SP
Tel: 01505 704000

JEDBURGH
Allerton House
Oxnam Road
Jedburgh
Roxburghshire
TD8 6QQ
Tel: 01835 869633

Crailing Old School
Jedburgh
Roxburghshire
TD8 6TL
Tel: 01835 850382

KELSO
Craignethan House
Jedburgh Road
Kelso
Roxburghshire
TD5 8AZ
Tel: 01573 224818

Cross Keys Hotel
36-37 The Square
Kelso
Roxburghshire
TD5 7HL
Tel: 01573 223303

Edenmouth Farm
Kelso
Roxburghshire
TD5 7QB
Tel: 01890 830391

KILLIN
Breadalbane House
Main Street
Killin
Perthshire
FK21 8UT
Tel: 01567 820134

BY KILMARNOCK
Fenwick Hotel
Fenwick
by Kilmarnock
Ayrshire KA3 6AU
Tel: 01560 600 478

KINCLAVEN, BY STANLEY
Ballathie House Hotel
Kinclaven, by Stanley
Perthshire
PH1 4QN
Tel: 01250 883268

KINGUSSIE
The Hermitage Guest House
Spey Street
Kingussie
Inverness-shire
PH21 1HN
Tel: 01540 662137

KINTYRE
Hunting Lodge Hotel
Bellochantuy
Kintyre
Argyll PA28 6QE
Tel: 01583 421323

KIRKCALDY
Scotties B&B
213 Nicol Street
Kirkcaldy
Fife
KY1 1PF
Tel: 01592 268596

KIRKLISTON
Crannog
New Liston Road
Kirkliston
Edinburgh
EH29 9EA
Tel: 0131 333 4621

KYLE OF LOCHALSH
Isle of Raasay Hotel
Raasay
Kyle of Lochalsh
Ross-shire
IV40 8PB
Tel: 01478 660222

LAMLASH
Lilybank
Shore Road
Lamlash
Isle of Arran
KA27 8LS
Tel: 01770 600230

LERWICK
Glen Orchy Guest House
20 Knab Road
Lerwick
Shetland
ZE1 0AX
Tel: 01595 692031

LINLITHGOW
Arden House
Belsyde
Linlithgow
West Lothian
EH49 6QE
Tel: 01506 670172

LOANHEAD
Aaron Glen Guest House
7 Nivensknowe Road
Loanhead
Midlothian
EH20 9AU
Tel: 0131 440 1293

LOCH LOMOND
Culag Lochside Guest House
Luss
Loch Lomond
Argyll and Bute
G83 8PD
Tel: 01436 860248

LOCHMABEN
Ardbeg Cottage
19 Castle Street
Lochmaben
Dumfries-shire
DG11 1NY
Tel: 01387 811855

LOCKERBIE
Carik Cottage
Waterbeck
Lockerbie
Dumfriesshire
DG11 3EU
Tel: 01461 600 652

LUSS
Blairglas
Luss
Dunbartonshire
G83 8RG
Tel: 01389 850278

MELROSE
Easter Cottage
Lilliesleaf
Melrose
Roxburghshire
TD6 9JD
Tel: 01835 870281

MILTON
Milton Inn
Dumbarton Road
Milton
Dunbartonshire
G82 2DT
Tel: 01389 761401

MOFFAT
Black Bull Hotel
Churchgate
Moffat
Dumfriesshire
DG10 9EG
Tel: 01683 220206

MONIFIETH
Panmure Hotel
Tay Street
Monifieth
Angus
DD5 4AX
Tel: 01382 532911

MONTROSE
Best Western Links Hotel
Mid Links
Montrose
Angus
DD10 8RL
Tel: 01674 671000

MUIR-OF-ORD
Hillview Park
Muir-of-Ord
Ross-shire
IV6 7TU
Tel: 01463 870787

ISLE OF MULL
Birchgrove
Lochdon
Isle of Mull
PA64 4AP
Tel: 01680 812364

MUSSELBURGH
Carberry Conference Centre
Carberry Tower
Musselburgh
East Lothian
EH21 8PY
Tel: 0131 665 3135

NAIRN
Napier
60 Seabank Road
Nairn
IV12 4HA
Tel: 01667 453330

NEWTON STEWART
East Culkae Farm House
Sorbie
Newton Stewart
Wigtownshire
DG8 8AS
Tel: 01988 850214

NORTHBAY
Airds Guest House
244 Bruernish
Northbay
Isle of Barra
HS9 5UT
Tel: 01871 890720

ISLE OF NORTH UIST
Redburn House
Lochmaddy
Isle of North Uist
Western Isles
HS6 5AA
Tel: 0208 6927271

OBAN
The Caledonian Hotel
Station Square
Oban
Argyll PA34 5RT
Tel: 01631 563133

The Kimberley Hotel
Dalriach Road
Oban
Argyll
PA34 5EQ
Tel: 01631 571115

BY OBAN
Falls of Lora Hotel
Connel Ferry
by Oban
Argyll
PA37 1PB
Tel: 01631 710483

ORPHIR
Houton Bay Lodge
Houton Bay
Orphir
Orkney
KW17 2RD
Tel: 01856 811320

PAISLEY
Ardgowan Town House Hotel
94 Renfrew Road
Paisley
Renfrewshire
PA3 4BJ
Tel: 0141 889 4763

PERTH
Arisaig Guest House
4 Pitcullen Crescent
Perth
PH2 7HT
Tel: 01738 628240

Cherrybank Inn
210 Glasgow Road
Perth
PH2 0NA
Tel: 01738 624349

Petra's B&B
4 Albany Terrace
Perth
Perthshire
PH1 2BD
Tel: 01738 563050

Sunbank House Hotel
50 Dundee Road
Perth
Perthshire
PH2 7BA
Tel: 01738 624882

BY PETERHEAD
Greenbrae Farmhouse
Longside
By Peterhead
Aberdeenshire
AB42 4JX
Tel: 01779 821051

PIRNHALL, STIRLING
Barn Lodge
Croftside
Pirnhall, Stirling
Stirlingshire
FK7 8EX
Tel: 01786 813591

PITLOCHRY
Craigatin House & Courtyard
165 Atholl Road
Pitlochry
Perthshire
PH16 5QL
Tel: 01796 472478

Craigvrack Hotel
38 West Moulin Road
Pitlochry
Perthshire
PH16 5EQ
Tel: 01796 472399

Fishers Hotel
75-79 Atholl Road
Pitlochry
Perthshire
PH16 5BN
Tel: 0131 554 7173

Green Park Hotel
Clunie Bridge Road
Pitlochry
Perthshire
PH16 5JY
Tel: 01796 473248

The Poplars
27 Lower Oakfield
Pitlochry
Perthshire
PH16 5DS
Tel: 01796 472129

The Well House
11 Toberargan Road
Pitlochry
Perthshire PH16 5HG
Tel: 01796 472239

BY PITLOCHRY
East Haugh House Country Hotel & Restaurant
East Haugh
by Pitlochry
Perthshire PH16 5JS
Tel: 01796 473121

PORTPATRICK
Braefield Guest House
Braefield Road
Portpatrick
Wigtownshire DG9 8TA
Tel: 01776 810255

Portpatrick Hotel
Heugh Road
Portpatrick
Wigtownshire
DG9 8TQ
Tel: 01776 810333

The Fernhill Hotel
Heugh Road
Portpatrick
Wigtownshire
DG9 8TD
Tel: 01776 810220

SOUTH QUEENSFERRY
Priory Lodge
8 The Loan
South Queensferry
West Lothian
EH30 9NS
Tel: 0131 331 4345

SOUTH RONALDSAY
Taftshurie B&B
Grimness
South Ronaldsay
Orkney KW17 2IH
Tel: 01856 831323

SPEAN BRIDGE
Distant Hills Guest House
Roybridge Road
Spean Bridge
Inverness-shire
PH34 4EU
Tel: 01397 712452

The Heathers
Invergloy Halt
Spean Bridge
Inverness-shire PH34 4DY
Tel: 01397 712077

BY SPEAN BRIDGE
Dreamweavers
Mucomir
By Spean Bridge
Inverness-shire
PH34 4EQ
Tel: 01397 712 548

ST ANDREWS
Pitmilly West Lodge
Kingsbarns
St Andrews
Fife KY16 8QA
Tel: 01334 880581

STAFFIN
Gairloch View
3 Digg
Staffin
Isle of Skye
IV51 9LA
Tel: 01470 562718

STEIN, WATERNISH
Stein Inn
MacLeods Terrace
Stein, Waternish
Isle of Skye, Inverness-shire
IV55 8GA
Tel: 01470 592362

STIRLING
Cambria Guest House
141 Bannockburn Road
Stirling FK7 OEP
Tel: 01786 814603

BY STRANRAER
Corsewall Lighthouse Hotel
Kirkcolm
by Stranraer
Wigtownshire
DG9 0QG
Tel: 01776 853220

STRATHAVEN
Springvale Hotel
18 Lethame Road
Strathaven
Lanarkshire
ML10 6AD
Tel: 01357 521131

BY THURSO
Creag-Na-Mara
East Mey
by Thurso
Caithness
KW14 8XL
Tel: 01847 851850

Forss House Hotel
Forss
by Thurso
Caithness
KW14 7XY
Tel: 01847 861201

TOBERMORY
Tobermory House
Dervaig
Tobermory
Isle of Mull
PA75 6QW
Tel: 01688 400345

Tobermory Hotel
53 Main Street
Tobermory
Isle of Mull
PA75 6NT
Tel: 01688 302091

TROON
Piersland House Hotel
15 Craigend Road
Troon
Ayrshire
KA10 6HD
Tel: 01292 314747

ULLAPOOL
Dromnan Guest House
Garve Road
Ullapool
Ross-shire
IV26 2SX
Tel: 01854 612333

Directory of all VisitScotland Quality Assured Serviced Establishments

SOUTH OF SCOTLAND

Ayrshire and Arran, Dumfries & Galloway, Scottish Borders

ALLANTON, BY DUNS

Allanton Inn
Main Street, Allanton,
Scottish Borders, TD11 3JZ
Tel: 01890 818260
★★★ Inn

ANCRUM, BY JEDBURGH

Cheviot View
The Green, Ancrum, Jedburgh,
Roxburghshire, TD8 6XA
Tel: 01835 830563
★★★ Bed & Breakfast

ANNAN

East Upper Priestside
Cummentrees, Annan, Dumfries,
DG12 5PX
Tel: 01387 259219
★★ Bed & Breakfast

ARDROSSAN

Edenmore
47 Parkhouse Road, Ardrossan,
Ayrshire, KA22 8AN
Tel: 01294 462306
★★ Bed & Breakfast

BLACKWATERFOOT, ISLE OF ARRAN

The Greannan
Blackwaterfoot, Shiskine,
Isle of Arran, KA27 8HB
Tel: 01770 860200
★★★ Bed & Breakfast

Laighbent
Blackwaterfoot, Isle of Arran,
KA27 8HB
Tel: 01770 860405
★★★ Bed & Breakfast

Morvern
Blackwaterfoot, Isle of Arran,
KA27 8EU
Tel: 01770 860254
★★ Bed & Breakfast

BRODICK

Alltan
Knowe Road, Brodick,
Isle of Arran, KA27 8BY
Tel: 01770 302937
★★★★ Bed & Breakfast

Auchrannie Spa Resort
Brodick, Isle of Arran, KA27 8BZ
Tel: 01770 302234
★★★★ Lodge

Bay View
Brodick, Arran, KA27 8JU
Tel: 01770 302178
★★ Bed & Breakfast

Crovie
Corriegills, Brodick,
Isle of Arran, KA27 8BL
Tel: 01770 302193
★★★ Bed & Breakfast

Glencloy Farm Guest House
Glen Cloy Road, Brodick,
Isle of Arran, KA27 8DA
Tel: 01770 302351
★★★ Guest House

Glenn House
Brodick, Isle of Arran,
KA27 8DW
Tel: 01770 302 092
★★★ Bed & Breakfast

Ormidale Hotel
Brodick, Isle of Arran, KA27 8BY
Tel: 01770 302293
★★ Small Hotel

Rosaburn Lodge
Brodick, Isle of Arran, KA27 8DP
Tel: 01770 302383
★★★ Bed & Breakfast

Sunnyside
Kings Cross, Brodick,
Isle of Arran, KA27 8RG
Tel: 01770 700422
★★★ Bed & Breakfast

CORRIECRAVIE, ISLE OF ARRAN

Otterburn
Corriecravie, Isle of Arran,
KA27 8PD
Tel: 01770 870227
★★★★ Bed & Breakfast

LAMLASH, ISLE OF ARRAN

Brudair Bed and Breakfast
14 Moray Place, Lamlash, Arran,
KA27 8NH
Tel: 01770 600590
★★ Bed & Breakfast

The Shore
Mill Hill, Lamlash, Isle of Arran,
KA27 8JY
Tel: 01770 600764
★★★★ Bed & Breakfast

LOCHRANZA, ISLE OF ARRAN

Castlekirk
Lochranza, Isle of Arran,
KA27 8HL
Tel: 01770 830202
★★ Bed & Breakfast

PIRNMILL, ISLE OF ARRAN

Mill Cottage B&B
Pirnmill, Isle of Arran, KA27 7PP
Tel: 01770 850535
★★ Bed & Breakfast

SHISKINE, ISLE OF ARRAN

Croftlea
Shiskine, Isle of Arran,
KA27 8EW
Tel: 01770 860259
★★ Bed & Breakfast

WHITING BAY, ISLE OF ARRAN

Craigard
Shore Road, Whiting Bay,
Isle of Arran, KA27 8PZ
Tel: 01770 700378
★★★ Bed & Breakfast

Ellangowan
Middle Road, Whiting Bay,
Isle of Arran, KA27 8QH
Tel: 01770 700784
★★★ Bed & Breakfast

Mingulay
Middle Road, Whiting Bay,
Arran, North Ayrshire,
KA27 8QH
Tel: 01770 700346
★★★ Bed & Breakfast

AUCHENCAIRN, BY CASTLE DOUGLAS

Balcary Mews
Balcary Bay, Auchencairn, Castle
Douglas, Kirkcudbrightshire,
DG7 1QZ
Tel: 01556 640276
★★★★ Bed & Breakfast

Bluehill Farm
Auchencairn, By Castle Douglas,
Dumfries & Galloway, DG7 1QW
Tel: 01556 640228
★★★★ Bed & Breakfast

AUCHENCROW, BY EYEMOUTH

The Craw Inn
Auchencrow, Reston,
Berwickshire, TD14 5LS
Tel: 01890 761293
★★★ Inn

AYR

Afton House
17 Park Circus, Ayr, KA7 2DJ
Tel: 01292 611215
★★ Bed & Breakfast

Auld Ayr
11 Carrick Road, Ayr, Ayrshire,
KA7 2RA
Tel: 01292 283219
★★★ Bed & Breakfast

Belmont Guest House
15 Park Circus, Ayr, KA7 2DJ
Tel: 01292 265588
★★ Guest House

Canterholm Guest House
9 Racecourse Road, Ayr,
Ayrshire, KA7 2DG
Tel: 01292 880919
★★★ Bed & Breakfast

Chalmers
34 Carrick Road, Ayr, Ayrshire,
KA7 2RB
Tel: 01292 282841
★★★ Bed & Breakfast

Deanbank
44 Ashgrove Street, Ayr,
KA7 3BG
Tel: 01292 263745
★★★★ Bed & Breakfast

Deepdale
3 Carrick Road, Ayr, Ayrshire, KA7 2RA
Tel: 01292 265853
★★ Bed & Breakfast

Dunduff Farm
Dunure, Ayr, KA7 4LH
Tel: 01292 500225
★★★★ Bed & Breakfast

The Dunn Thing
13 Park Circus, Ayr, KA7 2DJ
Tel: 01292 284531
★★★ Bed & Breakfast

Failte
9 Prestwick Road, Ayr, Ayrshire, KA8 8LD
Tel: 01292 265282
★★★ Bed & Breakfast

Finlayson Arms Hotel
24 Hillhead, Coylton, Ayrshire, KA6 6JT
Tel: 01292 570298
★★ Inn

Garth Madryn
71 Maybole Road, Ayr, KA7 4TB
Tel: 01292 443346
★★★ Bed & Breakfast

Greenan Lodge
39 Dunure Road, Doonfoot, Ayr, Ayrshire, KA7 4HR
Tel: 01292 443939
★★★★ Bed & Breakfast

Greystones
4 Ashgrove Street, Ayr, Ayrshire, KA7 3AQ
Tel: 01292 266317
★★★ Bed & Breakfast

Heston
19 Castlehill Road, Ayr, Ayrshire, KA17 2HX
Tel: 01292 288188
★★★★ Bed & Breakfast

Iona
27 St Leonards Road, Ayr, KA7 2PS
Tel: 01292 269541
★★ Bed & Breakfast

Jacmar Guest House
23 Dalblair Road, Ayr, KA7 1UF
Tel: 01292 264798
★★★ Bed & Breakfast

Kensington House
37 Miller Road, Ayr, KA7 2AX
Tel: 01292 266301
★★★ Bed & Breakfast

Kilkerran Guest House
15 Prestwick Road, Ayr, KA8 8LD
Tel: 01292 266477
★★ Guest House

Leslie Anne Guest House
13 Castlehill Road, Ayr, Ayrshire, KA7 2HX
Tel: 01292 265648
★★★ Bed & Breakfast

Lochinver
32 Park Circus, Ayr, Ayrshire, KA7 2DL
Tel: 01292 265086
★★★ Bed & Breakfast

Nordek House
4 Bellevue Crescent, Ayr, Ayrshire, KA7 2DR
Tel: 01292 262289
★★★ Bed & Breakfast

No. 26 The Crescent
26 Bellevue Crescent, Ayr, Ayrshire, KA7 2DR
Tel: 01292 287329
★★★★ Bed & Breakfast

Perryston Farm
Dunure Road, Ayr, Ayrshire, KA7 4LD
Tel: 01292 441315
★★★ Bed & Breakfast

Shelldun
36 Arran Gardens, Barassie, Ayrshire, KA10 6TE
Tel: 01292 318323
★★★★ Bed & Breakfast

Sunnyside
26 Dunure Road, Ayr, Ayrshire, KA7 4HR
Tel: 01292 441234
★★★ Bed & Breakfast

Tramore Guest House
17 Eglinton Terrace, Ayr, Ayrshire, KA7 1JJ
Tel: 01292 266019
★★★ Bed & Breakfast

Woodall
Arran Terrace, Ayr, KA7 1JF
Tel: 01292 263183
★★ Bed & Breakfast

BY AYR

Fisherton Farm B&B
Dunure, Ayr, KA7 4LF
Tel: 01292 500223
★★★ Bed & Breakfast

BALLANTRAE

The Haven
75 Main Street, Ballantrae, Girvan, Ayrshire, KA26 0NA
Tel: 01465 831306
★★★ Bed & Breakfast

Mrs Georgina McKinley
Laggan Farm, Ballantrae, Ayrshire, KA26 0JZ
Tel: 01465 831402
★★★ Bed & Breakfast

BARRHILL, BY GIRVAN

Blair Farm
Barrhill, by Girvan, Ayrshire, KA26 0RD
Tel: 01465 821247
★★★★ Bed & Breakfast

BEITH

Farmhouse Bed & Breakfast
Shotts Farm, Beith, Ayrshire, KA15 1LB
Tel: 01505 502273
★★★ Bed & Breakfast

BLADNOCH, BY WIGTOWN

The Old Coach House
34 Bladnoch, Bladnoch, DG8 9AB
Tel: 01988 402316
★★★ Bed & Breakfast

BONCHESTER BRIDGE

Horse & Hound Inn
Bonchester Bridge, Roxburghshire, TD8 8JN
Tel: 01450 860645
★★★ Inn

BORGUE

Braefoot
Borgue, Kirkcudbright, DG6 4SH
★★ Bed & Breakfast

BOWDEN, BY MELROSE

Glenwhilt
Bowden, by Melrose, Roxburghshire, TD6 0SX
Tel: 01835 822408
★★★ Bed & Breakfast

CAIRNRYAN

The Homestead
Cairnryan, Wigtownshire, DG9 8QX
Tel: 01581 200203
★★★ Bed & Breakfast

CANONBIE

Four Oaks
Canonbie, Dumfriesshire, DG14 0TF
Tel: 01387 371329
★★★ Bed & Breakfast

North Lodge
Woodlees, Canonbie, Dumfriesshire, DG14 0TF
Tel: 013873 71409
★★★ Bed & Breakfast

CARSETHORN, BY DUMFRIES

The Old Shop
Carsethorn, Dumfriesshire, DG2 8DS
Tel: 01387 880799
★★★ Bed & Breakfast

CASTLE DOUGLAS

33 Abercromby Road
Castle Douglas, Kirkcudbrightshire, DG7 1BA
Tel: 01556 503103
★★ Bed & Breakfast

Albion House
49 Ernespie Road, Castle Douglas, Kirkcudbrightshire, DG7 1LD
Tel: 01556 502360
★★★★ Bed & Breakfast

Benmore
King Street, Castle Douglas, Kirkcudbrightshire, DG7 1LB
Tel: 01556 502693
★★★ Bed & Breakfast

The Craig
44 Abercromby Road, Castle Douglas, Kirkcudbrightshire, DG7 1BA
Tel: 01556 504840
★★★ Bed & Breakfast

Craigadam
Castle Douglas, Dumfries & Galloway, DG7 3HU
Tel: 01556 650233
★★★★ Bed & Breakfast

Croys
Bridge of Urr, Castle Douglas, Kirkcudbrightshire, DG7 3EX
Tel: 01556 650237
★★★★ Bed & Breakfast

Douglas House B&B
63 Queen Street, Castle Douglas, Dumfries, DG7 1HS
Tel: 01556 503262
★★★★ Bed & Breakfast

The Green House
Springholm, Castle Douglas, DG7 3LH
Tel: 01556 650144
★★★ Bed & Breakfast

Smithy House
The Buchan, Castle Douglas, Kirkcudbrightshire, DG7 1TH
Tel: 01556 503841
★★★★ Bed & Breakfast

Woodlea
37 Ernespie Road, Castle Douglas, Kirkcudbrightshire, DG7 1LD
Tel: 01556 502247
★★★ Bed & Breakfast

BY CASTLE DOUGLAS
Meiklewood Farmhouse
Ringford, Castle Douglas, Kirkcudbrightshire, DG7 2AL
Tel: 01557 820226
★★★ Bed & Breakfast

NR CASTLE DOUGLAS
Airds Farm
Crossmichael, Castle Douglas, Kirkcudbrightshire, DG7 3BG
Tel: 01556 670418
★★★ Guest House

CASTLE KENNEDY, BY STRANRAER
Plantings Inn
Castle Kennedy, Wigtownshire, DG9 8SQ
Tel: 01581 400633
★ Inn

CHIRNSIDE, BY DUNS
Naismiths Arms Hotel
Main Street, Chirnside, by Duns, Berwickshire, TD11 8UJ
Tel: 01890 818507
★★ Inn

The Waterloo Arms Hotel
Allanton Road, Chirnside, Berwickside, TD11 3XH
Tel: 01890 818034
★★★ Inn

COLDINGHAM
Dunlaverock House
Coldingham Bay, Berwickshire, TD15 5PA
Tel: 018907 71450
★★★ Guest House

Priory View
Eyemouth Road, Coldingham, Eyemouth, Berwickshire, TD14 5NH
Tel: 01890 771525
★★★ Bed & Breakfast

Rhovanian
Burn Hall, St Abbs Road, Coldingham, Berwickshire, TD14 5NR
Tel: 01890 771760
★★★ Bed & Breakfast

COLDSTREAM
Fernyrig Farm
Birgham, Coldstream, Berwickshire, TD12 4NB
Tel: 01890 830251
★★★ Bed & Breakfast

Haymount Guest House
Duns Road, Coldstream, TD12 4DP
★★★★ Bed & Breakfast

Nisbet House
Main Street, Leitholm, Coldstream, Berwickshire, TD12 4JL
Tel: 01890 840279
★★★★ Bed & Breakfast

The Steading
East Coldstream, Strathaven, Lanarkshire, ML10 6SU
Tel: 01357 522326
★★★ Bed & Breakfast

BY COLDSTREAM
Saint Foin
Birgham, Coldstream, Berwickshire, TD12 4ZH
Tel: 01890 830209
★★★ Bed & Breakfast

COLVEND
Wilmar B&B
Colvend, Dalbeattie, Kircudbrightshire, DG5 4QW
Tel: 01556 620648
★★ Bed & Breakfast

COYLTON, BY AYR
Coylton Arms Hotel
Low Coylton, Coylton, KA6 6LE
Tel: 01292 570149
★★ Inn

The Kyle Hotel
40-42 Main Street, Coylton, Ayrshire, KA6 6JW
Tel: 01292 570312
★★ Inn

Woodside Farmhouse
Dalrymple Road, Coylton, Ayrshire, KA6 6HQ
Tel: 01292 570254
★★★ Bed & Breakfast

CREETOWN
The Haven
23 Harbour Street, Creetown, Newton Stewart, Wigtownshire, DG8 7JJ
Tel: 01671 820546
★★ Bed & Breakfast

Marclaysean Guest House
51 St John's Street, Creetown, Wigtownshire, DG8 7JB
Tel: 01671 820319
★★ Bed & Breakfast

CROSSMICHAEL, BY CASTLE DOUGLAS
Deeside
42 Main Street, Crossmichael, by Castle Douglas, Kirkcudbrightshire, DG7 3AU
Tel: 01556 670239
★★★ Bed & Breakfast

MILLPORT, ISLE OF CUMBRAE
Cirmhor
35 West Bay, Millport, Isle of Cumbrae, KA28 0HA
Tel: 01475 530723
★★ Bed & Breakfast

Denmark Cottage
8 Ferry Road, Millport, Isle of Cumbrae, KA28
Tel: 01475 530958
★★★ Bed & Breakfast

DAILLY
Strathtalus
4 Brunston Wynd, Dailly, Ayrshire, KA26 9GA
Tel: 01465 811425
★★★★ Bed & Breakfast

DALBEATTIE
Bellevue B & B
Port Road, Dalbeattie, DG5 4AZ
Tel: 01556 611833
★★★★ Bed & Breakfast

East Daylesford B&B
Colvend, Dalbeattie, Kirkcudbrightshire, DG5 4QA
Tel: 01556 630483
★★★ Bed & Breakfast

13 Maxwell Park
Dalbeattie, Kirkcudbrightshire, DG5 4LR
Tel: 01556 610830
★★★★ Bed & Breakfast

Trewan
97 William Street, Dalbeattie, Kirkcudbrightshire, DG5 4EE
Tel: 01556 612337
★★★ Bed & Breakfast

DALRY

Langside Farm
By Dalry, Dalry, North Ayrshire, KA24 5JZ
Tel: 01294 834 402
★★★★ Bed & Breakfast

DALRY, BY CASTLE DOUGLAS

Clachan Inn
10 Main Street, Dalry, Near Castle Douglas, DG7 3UW
Tel: 01644 430241
★★★ Inn

The Lodgings
26 Main Street, St Johns Town of Dalry, Nr Castle Douglas, DG7 3UW
Tel: 01644 430023
★★★ Bed & Breakfast

DENHOLM

Auld Cross Keys Inn
Main Street, Denholm, Roxburghshire, TD9 8NU
Tel: 01450 870305
★★ Inn

DREM

Drem Farm House
Drem, North Berwick, East Lothian, EH39 5AP
Tel: 01620 850563
★★★★ Bed & Breakfast

DUMFRIES

Abarglen
7 Victoria Terrace, Dumfries, Dumfriesshire, DG1 1NL
Tel: 01387 252785
★★★ Bed & Breakfast

Brackenridge
67 New Abbey Road, Dumfries, DG2 2JY
★★★ Bed & Breakfast

Burnett House
4 Lovers Walk, Dumfries, Dumfries & Galloway, DG1 1LP
Tel: 01387 236164
★★★ Bed & Breakfast

The Cottage
17 Rotchell Road, Dumfries, Dumfriesshire, DG2 7SE
Tel: 01387 255615
★★ Bed & Breakfast

East Brae Cottage
Crocketford, Dumfries, Dumfriesshire, DG2 8QE
Tel: 01556 690296
★★★ Bed & Breakfast

Glenaldor House
5 Victoria Terrace, Dumfries, DG1 1NL
Tel: 01387 264248
★★★ Bed & Breakfast

Glencairn Villa
45 Rae Street, Dumfries, DG1 1JD
Tel: 01387 262467
★★ Bed & Breakfast

Glenure Bed and Breakfast
43 Moffat Road, Dumfries, Dumfries-shire, DG1 1NN
Tel: 01387 252373
★★★ Bed & Breakfast

The Haven
1 Kenmure Terrace, Dumfries, DG2 7QX
Tel: 01387 251281
★★★ Bed & Breakfast

Hawthorn Bank
45 Glebe Street, Dumfries, Dumfries & Galloway, DG1 2LZ
Tel: 01387 253845
★★★ Bed & Breakfast

Inverallochy
15 Lockerbie Road, Dumfries, Dumfriesshire, DG1 3AP
Tel: 01387 267298
★★★ Bed & Breakfast

Langlands Bed and Breakfast
8 Edinburgh Road, Dumfries, Dumfriesshire, DG1 1JQ
Tel: 01387 266549
★★★ Bed & Breakfast

Little Culmain (Bothy)
Crocketford Road, Near Milton, Dumfries, DG2 8QP
Tel: 01556 690 210
★★★ Bed & Breakfast

Low Kirkbride Farmhouse Bed&Breakfast
Low Kirkbride, Auldgirth, Dumfries, DG2 0SP
Tel: 01387 820258
★★★ Bed & Breakfast

Merlin
2 Kenmure Terrace, Dumfries, DG2 7QX
Tel: 01387 261002
★★★ Bed & Breakfast

Netherfield
Lochanhead, Dumfries, Dumfries & Galloway, DG2 8JE
Tel: 01387 730217
★★★ Bed & Breakfast

Nithcairn House
52 Annan Road, Dumfries, Dumfries and Galloway, DG1 3EQ
Tel: 01387 240082
★★★★ Bed & Breakfast

The Old Manse
1 North Laurieknowe Place, Dumfries, Dumfries & Galloway, DG2 7AL
Tel: 01387 269509
★★★ Bed & Breakfast

Rayola
19 Terregles Street, Dumfries, Dumfries-shire, DG2 9AA
Tel: 01387 250266
★★ Bed & Breakfast

Rivendell
105 Edinburgh Road, Dumfries, Dumfries-shire, DG1 1JX
Tel: 01387 252251
★★★★ Bed & Breakfast

Shambellie View
Wellgreen, Glencaple Road, Dumfries, DG1 4TD
Tel: 01387 69331
★★ Bed & Breakfast

Wallamhill House B&B
Kirkton, Dumfries, DG1 1SL
Tel: 01387 248249
★★★★ Bed & Breakfast

DUMFRIES BY

Branetrigg Farm
Torthorwald, Dumfriesshire, DG1 3QB
Tel: 01387 750650
★★★ Bed & Breakfast

Farmers Inn
Main Street, Clarencefield, Dumfriesshire, DG1 4NF
Tel: 01387 870675
★★ Inn

Locharthur House
Beeswing, by Dumfries, DG2 8JG
Tel: 01387 760235
★★★ Bed & Breakfast

Park Cottage
Kelton, by Dumfries, Dumfrisshire, DG1 4UA
Tel: 01387 770391
★★★ Bed & Breakfast

Smithy House
Torthorwald, by Dumfries, Dumfriesshire, DG1 3PT
Tel: 01387 750518
★ Bed & Breakfast

Southpark Country House
Quarry Road, Locharbriggs, Dumfries, DG1 1QG
Tel: 01387 711188
★★★ Bed & Breakfast

DUNS

Claymore Guest House
8 Langtongate, Duns, Berwickshire, TD11 3AE
Tel: 01361 883652
★★ Bed & Breakfast

Ravelaw Farmhouse
Ravelaw, Duns, Berwickshire, TD11 3NQ
Tel: 01890 870207
★★★★ Bed & Breakfast

DUNSCORE, BY DUMFRIES

George Hotel
Main Street, Dunscore, Dumfriesshire, DG2 0TB
Tel: 01387 820250
★★ Inn

EARLSTON

Harbur B&B
High Street, Earlston,
Berwickshire, TD4 6BS
Tel: 01896 848826
★★★ Bed & Breakfast

ECCLEFECHAN

Carlyle House
Main Street, Ecclefechan,
Lockerbie, Dumfriesshire,
DG11 3DG
Tel: 01576 300322
★ Bed & Breakfast

ETTRICK

Cross Keys Inn
Ettrickbridge, Selkirkshire,
TD7 5JN
Tel: 01750 52224
★★★ Inn

Roweburn
Ettrick, Selkirk, Selkirkshire,
TD7 5JD
Tel: 01750 62242
★★★ Bed & Breakfast

ETTRICK VALLEY

Tushielaw Inn
Ettrick Valley, Selkirkshire,
TD7 5HT
0750 62205
★★ Inn

EYEMOUTH

The Anchorage
Upper Houndlaw, Eyemouth,
Berwickshire, TD14 5BU
Tel: 01890 750307
★★★ Bed & Breakfast

Brown's B&B
1 Hallydown Cottages,
By Eyemouth, Berwickshire,
TD14 5PX
Tel: 01890 751242
★★★ Bed & Breakfast

Hillcrest
Coldingham Road, Eyemouth,
Berwickshire, TD14 5AN
Tel: 018907 50463
★★★ Bed & Breakfast

Mabula
53 Gillsland, Eyemouth,
Berwickshire, TD14 5JF
Tel: 01890 750307
★★★ Bed & Breakfast

BY EYEMOUTH

Redhall Cottage
Eyemouth, Berwickshire,
TD14 5SG
Tel: 01890 781488
★★★ Bed & Breakfast

Westwood House
Houndwood, By St Abbs,
Berwickshire, TD14 5TP
Tel: 01361 850333
★★★ Bed & Breakfast

FAIRLIE

Mon Abri
12 Main Road, Fairlie, Ayrshire,
KA29 0DP
Tel: 01475 568241
★★★ Bed & Breakfast

GALASHIELS

Dunriach
105 Melrose Road, Galashiels,
Selkirkshire, TD1 2BX
Tel: 01896 754146
★★ Bed & Breakfast

Ettrickvale
33 Abbotsford Road, Galashiels,
TD1 3HW
Tel: 01896 755224
★★★ Bed & Breakfast

Sunnybrae B&B
160 Magdala Terrace,
Galashiels, Selkirkshire,
TD1 2HZ
Tel: 01896 758 042
★★★ Bed & Breakfast

GATEHEAD, BY KILMARNOCK

Old Rome Farmhouse B & B
Gatehead, Kilmarnock, Ayrshire,
KA2 9AJ
Tel: 01563 850265
★★★ Bed & Breakfast

GATEHOUSE OF FLEET

Fleet Farmhouse
Gatehouse of Fleet, Castle
Douglas, Kirkcudbrightshire,
DG7 2BB
Tel: 01557 814205
★★★ Bed & Breakfast

High Auchenlarie Farmhouse
Gatehouse of Fleet,
Kirkcudbrightshire, DG7 2HB
Tel: 01557 840231
★★★ Bed & Breakfast

Tigh-an-Lios
High Street, Gatehouse of Fleet,
Kirkcudbright, DG7 2HS
Tel: 01557 814510
★★ Bed & Breakfast

GIRVAN

Ardwell Farm
Girvan, Ayrshire, KA26 0HP
Tel: 01465 713389
★★ Bed & Breakfast

Drumskeoch Farm
Pinwherry, Girvan, Ayrshire,
KA26 0QB
Tel: 01465 841172
★★★ Bed & Breakfast

Hawkhill Farm
Old Dailly, Girvan, Ayrshire,
KA26 9RD
Tel: 01465 871232
★★★★ Bed & Breakfast

GIRVAN BY

Glengennet Farm
Barr, Girvan, Ayrshire, KA26 9TY
Tel: 01465 861220
★★★★ Bed & Breakfast

GLASSERTON, BY WHITHORN

Craiglemine Cottage B&B
Glasserton, Near Whithorn,
Wigtownshire, DG8 8NE
Tel: 01988 500594
★★ Bed & Breakfast

GLENLUCE

Tha Butchach
New Luce, Newton Stewart,
Wigtownshire, DG8 0AW
Tel: 01581 600217
★★ Bed & Breakfast

GREENLAW, DUNS

Mansefield
35 East High Street, Greenlaw,
Berwickshire, TD10 6YF
Tel: 01361 810260
★★★★ Bed & Breakfast

GRETNA

166 Central Avenue
Gretna, Dumfriesshire,
DG16 5AF
Tel: 01461 337533
★★★ Bed & Breakfast

Thistlewood
Rigg, Gretna, Dumfriesshire,
DG16 5JQ
Tel: 01461 337810
★★★ Bed & Breakfast

The Willows
Loanwath Road, Gretna,
Dumfriesshire, DG16 5ES
Tel: 01461 337996
★★★ Bed & Breakfast

GRETNA GREEN

Barrasgate House
Millhill, Gretna Green,
DG16 5HU
Tel: 01461 337577
★★★ Bed & Breakfast

Craigarran
Main Street, Springfield, Gretna
Green, Dumfriesshire, DG16 5EH
Tel: 01461 337768
★★★ Bed & Breakfast

Days Inn
Welcome Break Service Area,
M74, Gretna Green,
Dumfriesshire, DG16 5HQ
0800 731 4466
★★ Lodge

HAWICK

Hopehill House
Wilton Crescent, Hawick,
Roxburghshire, TD9 7EH
Tel: 01450 375042
★★★ Bed & Breakfast

The Laurels
8 Princes Street, Hawick,
Roxburghshire, TD9 7AY
Tel: 01450 370002
★★ Bed & Breakfast

Oakwood House
Buccleuch Road, Hawick,
Roxburghshire, TD9 0EH
Tel: 01450 372814
★★★ Bed & Breakfast

Rosemount
84 Weensland Road, Hawick,
Roxburghshire, TD9 9PQ
Tel: 01450 375405
★★★ Bed & Breakfast

Scaurend Hoose
Roberton, Hawick,
Roxburghshire, TD9 7LX
Tel: 01450 880283
★★★ Bed & Breakfast

Wiltonburn Farm
Hawick, Scottish Borders,
TD9 7LL
Tel: 01450 372414
★★★ Bed & Breakfast

HAWICK BY
Cavers Garden Farm
Hawick, Roxburghshire, TD9 8LN
Tel: 01450 377222
★★★ Bed & Breakfast

Colterscleugh
Teviothead, Roxburghshire,
TD9 0LF
Tel: 01450 850 247
★★ Bed & Breakfast

HOLLYBUSH, BY AYR
Alt-Na-Craig
Hollybush, By Ayr, KA6 7EB
Tel: 01292 560555
★★★★ Bed & Breakfast

INNERLEITHEN
Corner House Hotel
1 Chapel Street, Innerleithen,
Peebles-shire, EH44 6HN
Tel: 01896 831181
★★★ Inn

Quair View
Traquair, Innerleithen,
Peeblesshire, EH44 6PL
Tel: 01896 830506
★★ Bed & Breakfast

The Old Schoolhouse
Traquair, Innerleithen,
Peeblesshire, EH44 6PL
Tel: 01896 830425
★★ Bed & Breakfast

St Ronans Hotel
High Street, Innerleithen,
Peeblesshire, EH44 6HF
Tel: 01896 830380
★ Inn

BY INNERLEITHEN
Traquair House
Innerleithen, Peeblesshire,
EH44 6PW
Tel: 01896 830323
★★★★ Bed & Breakfast

IRVINE
Mayfield Guest House
62 East Road, Irvine, Ayrshire,
KA12 0BS
Tel: 01294 279045
★★ Bed & Breakfast

ISLE OF WHITHORN
Dunbar House B&B
Tonderghie Road,
Isle of Whithorn, Wigtownshire,
DG8 8LQ
Tel: 01988 500336
★★ Bed & Breakfast

JEDBURGH
Edgerston Mill
Jedburgh, Roxburghshire,
TD8 6NF
Tel: 01835 840343
★★★ Bed & Breakfast

Fernlea
Allerton Place, Jedburgh,
Roxburghshire, TD8 6LG
Tel: 01835 862318
★★★★ Bed & Breakfast

Froylehurst
The Friars, Jedburgh,
Roxburghshire, TD8 6BN
Tel: 01835 862477
★★★★ Bed & Breakfast

Harden Vale
Ancrum, Jedburgh, TD8 6XH
Tel: 01835 830280
★★★ Bed & Breakfast

Hoolet's Nest
Mounthooly, Jedburgh, Borders,
TD8 6TJ
Tel: 01835 850 764
★★ Bed & Breakfast

Hundalee House
Jedburgh, Roxburghshire,
TD8 6PA
Tel: 01835 863011
★★★★ Bed & Breakfast

Kenmore Bank
Oxnam Road, Jedburgh,
Roxburghshire, TD8 6JJ
Tel: 01835 862369
★★★★ Bed & Breakfast

Palace Country House
Crailing, Jedburgh,
Roxburghshire, TD8 6TL
Tel: 01835 850225
★★★★ Bed & Breakfast

Reiver's Rest
91 Bongate, Jedburgh,
Roxburghshire, TD8 6DU
Tel: 01835 864977
★★★ Bed & Breakfast

Riverview
Newmill Farm, Jedburgh,
TD8 6TH
Tel: 01835 862145
★★★ Bed & Breakfast

The Royal Hotel
Cannongate, Jedburgh,
Roxburghshire, TD8 6AN
Tel: 01835 863152
★★ Inn

The School House
Edgerston, Jedburgh,
Roxburghshire, TD8 6PW
Tel: 01835 840627
★★★★★ Bed & Breakfast

The Spinney
Langlee, Jedburgh,
Roxburghshire, TD8 6PB
Tel: 01835 863525
★★★★ Bed & Breakfast

Willow Court
The Friars, Jedburgh,
Roxburghshire, TD8 6BN
Tel: 01835 863702
★★★ Guest House

Windyridge
39 Dounehill, Jedburgh,
Roxburghshire, TD8 6LJ
Tel: 01835 864404
★★★★ Bed & Breakfast

BY JEDBURGH
Ancrum Craig
Jedburgh, Roxburghshire,
TD8 6UN
Tel: 01835 830280
★★★★ Bed & Breakfast

Crailing Old School
Jedburgh, Roxburghshire,
TD8 6TL
Tel: 01835 850382
★★★★ Bed & Breakfast

KELSO
Abbeyside
The Knowes, Kelso,
Roxburghshire, TD5 7BH
Tel: 01573 223915
★★ Bed & Breakfast

The Bield
Hume, Kelso, Roxburghshire,
TD5 7TS
Tel: 01573 470349
★★★ Bed & Breakfast

Black Swan Hotel
7 Horsemarket, Kelso,
Roxburghshire, TD5 7HE
Tel: 01573 224563
★★ Inn

Brimham House
Girrick Farm, Kelso,
Scottish Borders, TD5 7SA
Tel: 01573 460647
★★★ Bed & Breakfast

Craignethan House
Jedburgh Road, Kelso,
Roxburghshire, TD5 8AZ
Tel: 01573 224818
★★★ Bed & Breakfast

Dispensary House
106 Roxburgh Street, Kelso,
Roxburghshire, TD5 7DY
Tel: 01573 228738
★★★★ Bed & Breakfast

Duncan House
Chalkheugh Terrace, Kelso,
Roxburghshire, TD5 7DX
Tel: 01573 225682
★★★ Bed & Breakfast

Edenbank House
Kelso, Scottish Borders,
TD5 7SX
Tel: 01573 226734
★★★★ Bed & Breakfast

Edenmouth Farm
Kelso, Roxburghshire, TD5 7QB
Tel: 01890 830391
★★★ Bed & Breakfast

Goldilands
Roxburgh Road, Heiton, Kelso,
Roxburghshire, TD5 8TP
Tel: 01573 450671
★★★ Bed & Breakfast

Highridgehall
Kelso, TD5 7QD
Tel: 01890 830605
★★ Bed & Breakfast

Mo Dhachaigh
11 Kings Croft, Kelso,
Roxburghshire, TD5 7NU
Tel: 01573 225480
★★★ Bed & Breakfast

BY KELSO
Crosshall Farm
Greenlaw, Duns, Berwickshire,
TD10 6UL
Tel: 0189084 0220
★★★★ Bed & Breakfast

Old School House
Birgham, Coldstream,
Berwickshire, TD12 4NF
Tel: 01890 830612
★★★ Bed & Breakfast

Whitehill Farm
Nenthorn, Kelso, Roxburghshire,
TD5 7RZ
Tel: 01573 470203
★★★★ Bed & Breakfast

KILMARNOCK
Heughmill
Craigie, Kilmarnock, Ayrshire,
KA1 5NQ
Tel: 01563 860389
★★★★ Bed & Breakfast

Tamarind Bed & Breakfast
24 Arran Avenue, Kilmarnock,
Ayrshire, KA3 1TP
Tel: 01563 571788
★★★ Bed & Breakfast

West Tannacrieff Bed & Breakfast
Fenwick, by Kilmarnock,
Ayrshire, KA3 6AZ
Tel: 01560 600258
★★★★ Bed & Breakfast

KILMAURS
Aulton Farm
Kilmaurs, Ayrshire, KA3 2PQ
Tel: 01563 538208
★★★ Bed & Breakfast

KILWINNING
Blairholme
45 Byres Road, Kilwinning,
KA13 6JU
Tel: 01294 552023
★★ Bed & Breakfast

High Smithstone Farm B&B
High Smithstone, Kilwinning,
Ayrshire, KA13 6PG
Tel: 01294 552361
★★★★ Bed & Breakfast

KIPPFORD, BY DALBEATTIE
Anchor Hotel
Main Street, Kippford,
Kirkcudbrightshire, DG5 4LN
Tel: 01556 620205
★ Inn

KIRKBEAN
Steamboat Inn
Carsethorn, Kirkbean, Dumfries,
DG2 8DS
Tel: 01387 880 631
★★★ Inn

KIRKCOLM
Blue Peter Hotel
23 Main Street, Kirkcolm,
Stranraer, Wigtownshire,
DG9 0NU
Tel: 01776 853221
★★ Bed & Breakfast

KIRKCUDBRIGHT
Anchorlee
95 St Mary Street,
Kirkcudbright,
Kirkcudbrightshire, DG6 4EL
Tel: 01557 330197
★★★ Bed & Breakfast

Baytree House
110 High Street, Kirkcudbright,
Dumfries & Galloway, DG6 4JQ
Tel: 01557 330824
★★★★ Bed & Breakfast

Benutium
2 Rossway Road, Kirkcudbright,
Kirkcudbrightshire, DG6 4BS
Tel: 01557 330788
★★★★ Bed & Breakfast

Craigie
17 Bourtree Avenue,
Kirkcudbright, Dumfries &
Galloway, DG6 4AU
Tel: 01557 330681
★★★★ Bed & Breakfast

1 Gordon Place
High Street, Kirkcudbright,
DG6 4LA
Tel: 01557 330472
★★★ Bed & Breakfast

The Green Gate
46 High Street, Kirkcudbright,
Dumfries & Galloway, DG6 4JX
Tel: 01557 331895
★★★★ Bed & Breakfast

14 High Street
Kirkcudbright, Dumfries &
Galloway, DG6 4SX
Tel: 01557 330766
★★★★ Bed & Breakfast

Millburn House
Millburn Street, Kirkcudbright,
Kirkcudbrightshire, DG6 4ED
Tel: 01557 339166
★★★ Bed & Breakfast

Number 3 B&B
3 High St, Kirkcudbright,
Dumfries & Galloway, DG6 4JZ
Tel: 01557 330881
★★★★ Bed & Breakfast

The Star Hotel
18 Main Street, Twynholm,
Kirkcudbright, Dumfries and
Galloway, DG6 4NT
Tel: 01557 860279
★★★ Inn

BY KIRKCUDBRIGHT
Boreland Of Borgue
Kirkcudbright,
Kirkcudbrightshire, DG6 4SX
Tel: 01557 860214
★★★ Bed & Breakfast

NR KIRKCUDBRIGHT
The Marks
Kirkcudbright,
Kirkcudbrightshire, DG6 4XR
Tel: 01557 30854
★★★ Bed & Breakfast

KIRKOSWALD
Shanter Hotel
47 Main Street, Kirkoswald,
Ayrshire, KA19 8HY
Tel: 01655 760653
★★ Inn

KIRK YETHOLM
The Border Hotel
The Green, Kirk Yetholm,
Scottish Borders, TD5 8PQ
Tel: 01573 420237
★★ Inn

Mill House B&B
Main Street, Kirk Yetholm,
Kelso, Roxburghshire, TD5 8PE
Tel: 01573 420604
★★★★ Bed & Breakfast

Valleydene B & B
High Street, Kirk Yetholm,
Roxburghshire, TD5 8PH
Tel: 01573 420286
★ Bed & Breakfast

LANGHOLM
Border House
28 High Street, Langholm,
Dumfriesshire, DG13 0JH
Tel: 013873 80376
★★★ Bed & Breakfast

Bush of Ewes Farmhouse
Ewes, Langholm, Dumfriesshire,
DG13 0HN
Tel: 013873 81241
★★★ Bed & Breakfast

Carnlea
16 Hillside Crescent, Langholm,
Dumfries-shire, DG13 0EE
Tel: 01387 380284
★★★ Bed & Breakfast

Wauchope Cottage
Wauchope Street, Langholm,
Dumfriesshire, DG13 0AY
Tel: 01387 380429
★★★ Bed & Breakfast

LARGS

Appin
172 Greenock Road, Largs,
Ayrshire, KA30 8SB
Tel: 01475 673075
★★★★ Bed & Breakfast

Belmont House
2 Broomfield Place, Largs,
Ayrshire, KA30 8DR
Tel: 01475 676264
★★★★ Bed & Breakfast

Broom Lodge
5 Broomfield Place, Largs,
Ayrshire, KA30 8DR
Tel: 01475 674290
★★★★ Bed & Breakfast

Glendarroch
24 Irvine Road, Largs, Ayrshire,
KA30 8HW
Tel: 01475 676305
★★★ Bed & Breakfast

Morvern Cottage
1 Boathouse Road, Largs,
Ayrshire, KA30 8PN
Tel: 01475 675718
★★★★ Bed & Breakfast

The Old Rectory
Aubery Crescent, Largs,
Ayrshire, KA30 8PR
Tel: 01475 674405
★★★ Bed & Breakfast

South Whittlieburn Farm
Brisbane Glen, Largs, Ayrshire,
KA30 8SN
Tel: 01475 675881
★★★★ Bed & Breakfast

St Leonard's Guest House
9 Irvine Road, Largs, Ayrshire,
KA30 8JP
Tel: 01475 673318
★★★★ Bed & Breakfast

Stonehaven Guest House
8 Netherpark Crescent, Largs,
Ayrshire, KA30 8QB
Tel: 01475 673319
★★★★ Bed & Breakfast

LAUDER

Black Bull Hotel
9 Market Place, Lauder,
Berwickshire, TD2 6SR
Tel: 01578 722 208
★★★ Inn

The Lodge, Carfraemill
Lauder, Berwickshire, TD2 6RA
Tel: 01578 750750
★★★★ Small Hotel

Thirlestane Farm
Lauder, Berwickshire, TD2 6SF
Tel: 01578 722216
★★★★ Bed & Breakfast

LOCHMABEN

Ardbeg Cottage
19 Castle Street, Lochmaben,
DG11 1NY
Tel: 01387 811855
★★★ Bed & Breakfast

The Crown Hotel
8 Bruce Street, Lochmaben,
Dumfriesshire, DG11 1PD
Tel: 01387 811750
★★ Inn

NR LOCHMABEN

Smallrigg Farm
Lochmaben, Lockerbie,
Dumfriesshire, DG11 1JH
Tel: 01387 810 462
★★★ Bed & Breakfast

LOCKERBIE

Claymore Lodge
2/4 Victoria Park, Victoria Road,
Lockerbie, DG11 2AX
Tel: 01576 202357
★★★ Bed & Breakfast

Holland Bush Garden Cottage
Holland Bush Cottage, Hightae,
Lockerbie, Dumfriesshire,
DG11 1JL
Tel: 01387 810294
★★★ Bed & Breakfast

Murrayfield
Lockerbie, Dumfriesshire,
DG11 2PJ
Tel: 01576 202258
★★★ Bed & Breakfast

Templeton
6 Victoria Road, Lockerbie,
Dumfries-shire, DG11 2BM
Tel: 01576 203201
★★★ Bed & Breakfast

BY LOCKERBIE

Carik Cottage
Waterbeck, Lockerbie,
Dumfriesshire, DG11 3EU
Tel: 01461 600652
★★★★ Bed & Breakfast

Castlehill Farm
Tundergarth, Lockerbie,
Dumfriesshire, DG11 2PX
Tel: 01576 710223
★★★ Bed & Breakfast

Corrie Lodge
Corrie Road, Lockerbie,
Dumfriesshire, DG16 2NG
Tel: 01576 710237
★★★ Bed & Breakfast

Nether Boreland
Boreland, Lockerbie,
Dumfriesshire, DG11 2LL
Tel: 01576 610248
★★★ Bed & Breakfast

MAUCHLINE

Ardwell Bed & Breakfast
103 Loudoun Street, Mauchline,
by Ayr, KA5 5BH
Tel: 01290 552987
★★★ Bed & Breakfast

Dykefield Farm
Mauchline, Ayrshire, KA5 6EY
Tel: 01290 553170
★ Bed & Breakfast

Treborane
Dykefield Farm, Mauchline,
Ayrshire, KA5 6EY
Tel: 01290 550328
★★ Bed & Breakfast

BY MAUCHLINE

Stair Inn
Stair, by Mauchline, Ayrshire,
KA5 5HW
Tel: 01292 591650
★★★ Inn

MELROSE

Braidwood Bed and Breakfast
Buccleuch Street, Melrose,
Roxburghshire, TD6 9LD
Tel: 01896 822488
★★★ Guest House

Collingwood
Waverley Road, Melrose,
Roxburghshire, TD6 9AA
Tel: 01896 822670
★★★★ Bed & Breakfast

Dunfermline House
Buccleuch Street, Melrose,
Roxburghshire, TD6 9LB
Tel: 01896 822411
★★★ Guest House

Easter Cottage
Lilliesleaf, Melrose,
Roxburghshire, TD6 9JD
Tel: 01835 870281
★★★★ Bed & Breakfast

Eildon House
Huntly Avenue, Melrose,
Roxburghshire, TD6 9SD
Tel: 01896 820196
★★★★ Bed & Breakfast

Fiorlin
Abbey Street, Melrose,
Roxburghshire, TD6 9PX
Tel: 01896 822984
★★★ Bed & Breakfast

The Gables
Darnick, Melrose,
Roxburghshire, TD6 9AL
Tel: 01896 822479
★★★ Bed & Breakfast

Kings Arms Hotel
High Street, Melrose,
Roxburghshire, TD6 9PB
Tel: 01896 822143
★★ Inn

No. 9
Townhead Way, Newstead,
Melrose, TD6 9BU
Tel: 01896 820435
★★★ Bed & Breakfast

Old Abbey School
Waverley Road, Melrose,
Roxburghshire, TD6 9SH
Tel: 01896 823432
★★★ Bed & Breakfast

Priory View
15 Priors Walk, Melrose,
Roxburghshire, TD6 9RB
Tel: 01896 822087
★★★ Bed & Breakfast

BY MELROSE

Fauhope House
Gattonside, Melrose,
Roxburghshire, TD6 9LU
Tel: 01896 823184
★★★★ Bed & Breakfast

MOFFAT

**Barnhill Springs
Country Guest House**
Moffat, Dumfries & Galloway,
DG10 9QS
Tel: 01683 220580
★★ Guest House

Blairdrummond House
School Lane, Moffat,
Dumfriesshire, DG10 9AX
Tel: 01683 221240
★★★★ Bed & Breakfast

Coxhill
Old Carlisle Road, Moffat,
Dumfriesshire, DG10 9QN
Tel: 01683 220471
★★★★ Bed & Breakfast

Craigie Lodge
Ballplay Road, Moffat,
Dumfriesshire, DG10 9JU
Tel: 01683 221769
★★★★ Bed & Breakfast

Dell-Mar
6 Beechgrove, Moffat, Dumfries
& Galloway, DG10 9RS
Tel: 01683 220260
★★★ Bed & Breakfast

Hartfell House
Hartfell Crescent, Moffat,
Dumfriesshire, DG10 9AL
Tel: 01683 220153
★★★ Guest House

Limetree House
Eastgate, Moffat, Dumfriesshire,
DG10 9AE
Tel: 01683 220001
★★★ Guest House

Lochhouse Farm Retreat Centre
Lochhouse Farm, Beattock,
Moffat, Dumfriesshire,
DG10 9SG
Tel: 01683 300451
★★ Bed & Breakfast

Morag
19 Old Carlisle Road, Moffat,
Dumfriesshire, DG10 9QJ
Tel: 01683 220690
★★★ Bed & Breakfast

Queensberry House
12 Beechgrove, Moffat,
Dumfriesshire, DG10 9RS
Tel: 01683 220538
★★★★ Bed & Breakfast

Seamore Guest House
Academy Road, Moffat,
Dumfriesshire, DG10 9HW
Tel: 01683 220404
★★★ Guest House

Seven Oaks Bed & Breakfast
School Lane, Moffat,
Dumfriesshire, DG10 9AX
Tel: 01683 220 584
★★★★ Bed & Breakfast

Stag Hotel
22 High Street, Moffat,
Dumfriesshire, DG10 9HL
Tel: 01683 220343
★★ Inn

Woodhead
Old Carlisle Road, Moffat,
Dumfriesshire, DG10 9LU
Tel: 01683 220225
★★★★ Bed & Breakfast

MONKTON, BY PRESTWICK

The Wee Hoosie
33 Main Street, Monkton, by
Prestwick, Ayrshire, KA9 2QJ
Tel: 01292 476026
★ Bed & Breakfast

MOREBATTLE

Templehall Hotel
Main Street, Morebattle, by
Kelso, Roxburghshire, TD5 8QQ
Tel: 01573 440249
★★ Inn

NEW ABBEY

Abbey Arms Hotel
1 The Square, New Abbey,
by Dumfries, Dumfriesshire,
DG2 8BX
Tel: 01387 850489
★★ Inn

NEWCASTLETON

Sorbietrees B&B
Newcastleton, Roxburghshire,
TD9 0TL
Tel: 01387 375 215
★★★ Bed & Breakfast

NEW CUMNOCK

Meikie Westland
New Cumnock, Ayrshire,
KA18 4NW
Tel: 01290 332327
★★★ Bed & Breakfast

NEW GALLOWAY

The Ken Bridge Hotel
Ayr Road, New Galloway,
Kirkcudbrightshire, DG7 3PR
Tel: 01644 420211
★★ Inn

NEWSTEAD, BY MELROSE

The Steading
Townhead Way, Newstead,
Melrose, TD6 9BU
Tel: 01896 820388
★★★ Bed & Breakfast

NEWTON STEWART

Benera Bed and Breakfast
Corsbie Road, Newton Stewart,
Wigtownshire, DG8 6JD
Tel: 01671 403443
★★★ Bed & Breakfast

Cairnholy Farmhouse
Carsluith, Newton Stewart,
DG8 7EA
Tel: 01557 840249
★★★ Bed & Breakfast

Cherrytrees
Fairway Drive, Newton Stewart,
Dumfries & Galloway, DG8 6PG
Tel: 01671 402502
★★★ Bed & Breakfast

Creebridge Lodge
Minnigaff, Newton Stewart,
Wigtownshire, DG8 6NR
Tel: 01671 402319
★★★ Bed & Breakfast

Flowerbank Guest House
Millcroft Road, Minnigaff,
Newton Stewart, DG8 6PJ
Tel: 01671 402629
★★★ Guest House

Kilwarlin
4 Corvisel Road, Newton
Stewart, Wigtownshire,
DG8 6LN
Tel: 01671 403047
★★★ Bed & Breakfast

BY NEWTON STEWART

**Auld Palnure House
Bed and Breakfast**
Auld Palnure House, Palnure,
Newton Stewart, Wigtownshire,
DG8 7RX
Tel: 01671 404224
★★ Bed & Breakfast

OCHILTREE

Laigh Tarbeg Farm
Ochiltree, Cumnock, Ayrshire,
KA18 2RL
Tel: 01290 700242
★★★ Bed & Breakfast

PEEBLES

Castlehill Knowe
Manor Valley, Peebles,
Peeblesshire, EH45 9JN
Tel: 01721 740218
★★★★ Bed & Breakfast

Dilkusha House
Chambers Terrace, Peebles,
Peeblesshire, EH45 9DZ
Tel: 01721 722888
★★★★ Bed & Breakfast

Drochil Castle B&B
by Romano Bridge, by Peebles,
EH46 7DD
Tel: 01721 752249
★★★★ Bed & Breakfast

Lyne Farmhouse
Lyne Farm, Peebles, EH45 8NR
Tel: 01721 740255
★★★ Bed & Breakfast

Rowanbrae
103 Northgate, Peebles,
Peeblesshire, EH45 8BU
Tel: 01721 721630
★★★★ Bed & Breakfast

Shalem
March Street, Peebles,
EH45 8EP
Tel: 01721 721047
★★★ Bed & Breakfast

Viewfield
1 Rosetta Road, Peebles,
Peebleshire, EH45 8JU
0721 721232
★★★ Bed & Breakfast

Whitestone House
Innerleithen Road, Peebles,
Peeblesshire, EH45 8B
Tel: 01721 720337
★★★ Bed & Breakfast

Whitie's
69 High Street, Peebles,
Scottish Borders, EH45 8AN
Tel: 01721 721605
★★★ Bed & Breakfast

Winkston Farmhouse Bed & Breakfast
Edinburgh Road, Peebles,
EH45 8PH
Tel: 01721 721264
★★★ Bed & Breakfast

Woodlands
Venlaw Farm Road, Peebles,
EH45 8QG
Tel: 01721 729882
★★★★ Bed & Breakfast

BY PEEBLES
Venlaw Farm
Peebles, EH45 8QG
★★★★ Bed & Breakfast

PORTPATRICK
Albony Guest House
4 Blair Terrace, Portpatrick,
DG9 8SY
Tel: 01776 810589
★★★ Bed & Breakfast

Ard Choille Guest House
1 Blair Terrace, Portpatrick,
Wigtownshire, DG9 8SY
Tel: 01776 810313
★★★ Bed & Breakfast

Muirheads Guest House
5 Blair Terrace, Portpatrick,
Wigtownshire, DG9 8SY
Tel: 01776 810522
★★★ Bed & Breakfast

PRESTWICK
Fionn Fraoch
64 Ayr Road, Prestwick,
Ayrshire, KA9 1RR
Tel: 01292 476838
★★★ Bed & Breakfast

Firhill
3 Seabank Road, Prestwick,
Ayrshire, KA9 1QS
Tel: 01292 478225
★★★ Bed & Breakfast

Knox
105 Ayr Road, Prestwick,
Ayrshire, KA9 1TN
Tel: 01292 78808
★★★ Bed & Breakfast

RESTON, BY EYEMOUTH
Fairlaw House
Fairlaw, Auchencrow, nr
Coldingham, Berwickshire,
TD14 5LN
Tel: 01890 761724
★★★★ Bed & Breakfast

ROCKCLIFFE, BY DALBEATTIE
The Cottage
1 Barcloy Road, Rockcliffe,
by Dalbeattie, Dumfrieshire,
DG5 4QL
Tel: 01556 630 460
★★★ Bed & Breakfast

Millbrae House
Rockcliffe, by Dalbeattie,
Dumfries and Galloway,
DG5 4QG
Tel: 01556 630217
★★★★ Bed & Breakfast

ST ABBS
Murrayfield
7 Murrayfield, St Abbs,
Berwickshire, TD14 5PP
Tel: 01890 771468
★★★ Bed & Breakfast

Springbank Cottage
The Harbour, St Abbs,
Berwickshire, TD14 5PW
Tel: 01890 771477
★★★ Bed & Breakfast

ST BOSWELLS
Mainhill
Charlesfield Road, St Boswells,
Roxburghshire, TD6 0HG
Tel: 01835 823788
★★★ Bed & Breakfast

SALTCOATS
Lochwood Farm
Saltcoats, Ayrshire, KA21 6NG
Tel: 01294 552529
★★★★ Bed & Breakfast

SANQUHAR
Newark
Sanquhar, Dumfriesshire,
DG4 6HN
Tel: 01659 50263
★★★ Bed & Breakfast

SELKIRK
Collingwood
The Green, Selkirk, Selkirkshire,
TD7 5AA
0750 20018
★★ Bed & Breakfast

Dinsburn
1 Shawpark Road, Selkirk,
TD7 4DS
Tel: 01750 20375
★★★ Bed & Breakfast

The Garden House
Whitmuir, Selkirkshire, TD7 4PZ
Tel: 01750 721 728
★★ Bed & Breakfast

Mrs J F Mackenzie
Ivy Bank, Hillside Terrace,
Selkirk, TD7 2LT
Tel: 01750 21470
★★ Bed & Breakfast

St Mary's House
Yarrow Feus, Selkirk, TD7 5NE
Tel: 01750 82287
★★★ Bed & Breakfast

Sunnybrae House
75 Tower Street, Selkirk,
Selkirkshire, TD7 4LS
0750 21156
★★★ Bed & Breakfast

SORBIE
East Culkae Farm House
Sorbie, Newton Stewart,
Wigtownshire, DG8 8AS
Tel: 01988 850214
★★★ Bed & Breakfast

SORN
The Sorn Inn
Main Street, Sorn, East Ayrshire,
KA5 6HU
Tel: 01290 551305
★★★★
Restaurant with Rooms

SOUTHWICK
Boreland of Southwick
Southwick, Dumfries, DG2 8AN
Tel: 01387 780225
★★★ Bed & Breakfast

SPRINGHOLM
Rangemhor
Springholm, Castle Douglas,
Dumfries and Galloway,
DG7 3LP
Tel: 01556 650296
★★ Bed & Breakfast

STEVENSTON
Ardeer Steading
Ardeer Mains Farm, Stevenston,
Ayrshire, KA20 3DD
Tel: 01294 465438
★★★ Bed & Breakfast

STRANRAER
Abonny House
10 Academy Street, Stranraer,
Wigtownshire, DG9 7DR
Tel: 01776 706313
★★★ Bed & Breakfast

Balyett House B&B
Cairnryan Road, Stranraer,
Wigtownshire, DG9 8QL
0776 703395
★★★ Bed & Breakfast

Barnhills Farm
Kirkcolm, Stranraer,
Wigtownshire, DG9 0QG
Tel: 01776 853236
★★★★ Bed & Breakfast

Crosshaven Guest House
Lewis Street, Stranraer,
Dumfries & Galloway, DG9 7AL
Tel: 01776 700598
★★★ Bed & Breakfast

Fernlea
Lewis Street, Stranraer,
Wigtownshire, DG9 7AQ
Tel: 01776 703037
★★★ Bed & Breakfast

Glenotter
Leswalt Road, Stranraer,
Wigtownshire, DG9 0EP
Tel: 01776 703199
★★★★ Bed & Breakfast

Kildonan
Lochview Road, Stranraer,
Wigtownshire, DG9 8HP
Tel: 01776 704186
★★★★ Bed & Breakfast

NR STRANRAER
East Challoch Farmhouse
Dunragit, Stranraer,
Wigtownshire, DG9 8PY
Tel: 01581 400391
★★★ Bed & Breakfast

TROON
Collenan House
38 Leven Road, Troon, Ayrshire,
KA10 7DX
Tel: 01292 313239
★ Bed & Breakfast

Copper Beech
116 Bentinck Drive, Troon,
Ayrshire, KA10 6JB
Tel: 01292 314100
★★★★ Bed & Breakfast

Fairway View
16 Harling Drive, Troon,
Ayrshire, KA10 6NF
Tel: 01292 312555
★★★ Bed & Breakfast

Fordell
43 Beach Road, Troon, Ayrshire,
KA10 6SU
Tel: 01292 313224
★★★ Bed & Breakfast

3 Lugar Place
Troon, Ayrshire, KA10 7EA
Tel: 01292 311909
★★★ Bed & Breakfast

Rosedale Guest House
9 Firth Road, Barassie, Ayrshire,
KA10 6TF
Tel: 01292 314371
★★★ Bed & Breakfast

Sandhill House
Southwood Road, Troon,
KA10 7EL
Tel: 01292 311801
★★★ Bed & Breakfast

Tigh Dearg
31 Victoria Drive, Troon,
Ayrshire, KA10 6JF
Tel: 01292 311552
★★ Bed & Breakfast

TURNBERRY
Fairways
Lodge Road, Turnberry, Ayrshire,
KA26 9LX
Tel: 01655 331522
★★★ Bed & Breakfast

Links Lodge
9 Maidens Road, Turnberry,
Ayrshire, KA26 9LS
Tel: 01655 331546
★★★★ Bed & Breakfast

TWYNHOLM
Kilkerran
Mansecroft, Twynholm,
Kirkcudbright,
Kirkcudbrightshire, DG6 4NY
Tel: 01557 860057
★★★ Bed & Breakfast

Linthorpe
14 Arden Road, Twynholm,
Dumfries and Galloway,
DG6 4PB
Tel: 01557 860662
★★★ Bed & Breakfast

Miefield Farm
Twynholm, Kirkcudbrightshire,
DG6 4PS
Tel: 01557 860254
★★ Bed & Breakfast

WALKERBURN
Hillside
Caberston Avenue, Walkerburn,
Peeblesshire, EH43 6BA
Tel: 01896 870439
★★★★ Bed & Breakfast

The Old Railway Station
Caberston Road, Walkerburn,
EH43 6DD
Tel: 01896 870544
★★ Bed & Breakfast

Tweedholm House
Walkerburn, Tweeddale,
EH43 6AN
Tel: 01896 870 266
★★ Bed & Breakfast

Windlestraw Lodge
Tweed Valley, Walkerburn,
Peeblesshire, EH43 6AA
Tel: 01896 870636
★★★★
Restaurant with Rooms

WEST LINTON
Gordon Arms Hotel
Dolphinton Road, West Linton,
Peeblesshire, EH46 7DR
Tel: 01968 660208
★★★ Inn

Jerviswood
Linton Bank Drive, West Linton,
Peeblesshire, EH46 7DT
Tel: 01968 660429
★★ Bed & Breakfast

The Meadows B&B
4 Robinsland Drive, West Linton,
Peeblesshire, FH46 7JD
Tel: 01968 661798
★★★ Bed & Breakfast

Rowallan
Mountain Cross, West Linton,
Peeblesshire,, EH46 7DF
Tel: 01968 660329
★★ Bed & Breakfast

WHITHORN
Craiglemine Tigh
Whithorn, Newton Stewart,
Wigtownshire, DG8 8NE
Tel: 01988 500490
★★★ Bed & Breakfast

Ravenstone House
Whithorn, Newton Stewart,
Wigtownshire, DG8 8DU
Tel: 01988 700756
★★★★ Bed & Breakfast

WHITSOME, BY DUNS
Ewart House
Main Street, Whitsome, By
Duns, Berwickshire, TD11 3NB
Tel: 01890 870271
★★★ Bed & Breakfast

WIGTOWN
Craigenlee
8 Bank Street, Wigtown,
Wigtownshire, DG8 9HP
Tel: 01988 402498
★★ Bed & Breakfast

Fordbank Country House Hotel
Potato Mill Road, Bladnoch,
Wigtown, DG8 9BT
Tel: 01988 402346
★ Inn

WINCHBURGH
Crannog
New Liston Road, Kirkliston,
Edinburgh, EH29 9EA
Tel: 0131 333 4621
★★★★ Bed & Breakfast

Niddry House B&B
Niddry Road, Winchburgh,
West Lothian, EH52 6PP
Tel: 01506 891816
★★ Bed & Breakfast

West End House
Winchburgh, West Lothian,
EH52 6TS
Tel: 01506 890528
★★ Bed & Breakfast

EDINBURGH AND LOTHIANS

ARMADALE, BY BATHGATE
Tarrareoch Farm
Station Road, Armadale,
West Lothian, EH48 3BJ
Tel: 01501 730404
★★★ Bed & Breakfast

ATHELSTANEFORD
Fidra House
Athelstaneford, East Lothian,
EH39 5BE
Tel: 01620 880777
★★★★★ Bed & Breakfast

BALERNO
Haughhead Farm
Balerno, Midlothian, EH14 7JH
Tel: 0131 4493875
★★ Bed & Breakfast

BATHGATE

Hillview
35 The Green, Bathgate,
West Lothian, EH48 4DA
Tel: 01506 654830
★★ Bed & Breakfast

BENTS, BY STONEYBURN

Eisenach
1 Cannop Crescent, Bents,
Nr Stoneyburn, West Lothian,
EH47 8EF
Tel: 01501 762659
★★★ Bed & Breakfast

BLACKBURN

Cruachan Bed & Breakfast
78 East Main Street, Blackburn,
West Lothian, EH47 7QS
Tel: 01506 655221
★★★ Bed & Breakfast

BONNYRIGG

1 Park Road
Bonnyrigg, Midlothian,
EH19 2AN
Tel: 0131 663 9183
★★ Bed & Breakfast

BROXBURN

Bankhead Farm
Dechmont, Broxburn,
West Lothian, EH52 6NB
Tel: 01506 811209
★★★★ Guest House

DALKEITH

The Guesthouse@Eskbank
Rathan, 45 Eskbank Road,
Eskbank, Dalkeith, EH22 3BH
Tel: 0131 663 3291
★★★ Guest House

Strathcairn
3 Eskview Grove, Dalkeith,
Midlothian, EH22 1JW
Tel: 0131 663 1208
★★★ Bed & Breakfast

Wester Cowden Farmhouse
Dalkeith, Midlothian, EH22 2QA
Tel: 0131 663 3052
★★★★ Bed & Breakfast

DIRLETON

Castle Inn
Main Road, Dirleton,
East Lothian, EH39 5EP
Tel: 01620 850221
★★ Inn

Station House
Station Road, Dirleton,
North Berwick, EH39 5LR
Tel: 01620 890512
★★★ Bed & Breakfast

DUNBAR

Rosedene
19A Belhaven Road, Dunbar,
East Lothian, EH42 1DD
Tel: 01368 862533
★★ Bed & Breakfast

Springfield Guest House
Belhaven Road, Dunbar,
East Lothian, EH42 1NH
Tel: 01368 862502
★★ Guest House

Woodside
13 North Street, Belhaven,
Dunbar, East Lothian, EH42 1NU
Tel: 01368 862384
★★★★ Bed & Breakfast

EAST CALDER

Ashcroft Farmhouse
East Calder, Nr Edinburgh,
EH53 0ET
Tel: 01506 881810
★★★★ Guest House

Overshiel Farm
East Calder, West Lothian,
EH53 0HT
Tel: 01506 880469
★★★ Bed & Breakfast

Whitecroft B&B
East Calder, West Lothian,
EH53 0ET
Tel: 01506 882494
★★★ Bed & Breakfast

EAST LINTON

Kippielaw Farmhouse
East Linton, East Lothian,
EH41 4PY
Tel: 01620 860368
★★★★ Bed & Breakfast

EDINBURGH

Aaron Guest House
16 Hartington Gardens,
Edinburgh, EH10 4LD
Tel: 0131 229 6459
★★★ Guest House

Abacus
7 Crawfurd Road, Newington,
Edinburgh, EH16 5PQ
Tel: 0131 667 2283
★★★ Bed & Breakfast

Abcorn Guest House
4 Mayfield Gardens, Edinburgh,
EH9 2BU
Tel: 0131 667 6548
★★★ Guest House

Abergowrie
41 Glasgow Road, Edinburgh,
EH12 8HW
Tel: 0131 334 5550
★★★ Bed & Breakfast

3A Clarence Street
Edinburgh, EH3 5AE
Tel: 0131 557 9368
★★ Bed & Breakfast

Addison House
43 Esslemont Road, Edinburgh,
Midlothian, EH16 5PY
Tel: 0131 667 1642
★★★★ Bed & Breakfast

Adria Hotel
11-12 Royal Terrace, Edinburgh,
EH7 5AB
Tel: 0131 556 7875
★★★ Guest House

46A Drumbrae South
Edinburgh, Lothian, EH12 8SZ
★★ Bed & Breakfast

Aeon-Kirklands Guest House
128 Old Dalkeith Road,
Edinburgh, EH16 4SD
Tel: 0131 664 2755
★★★ Guest House

Airport B&B
Park Lodge, Glasgow Road,
Ingliston, Edinburgh, Edinburgh,
EH28 8NB
Tel: 0131 335 3437
★ Bed & Breakfast

Mrs Linda J Allan
10 Baberton Mains Rise,
Edinburgh, EH14 3HG
Tel: 0131 442 3619
★★ Bed & Breakfast

Allt-nan-Craobh
28 Cammo Road, Edinburgh,
EH4 8AP
Tel: 0131 339 3613
★★★★ Bed & Breakfast

Almondhill Guest House
7 Almondhill Cottages,
Kirkliston, West Lothian,
EH29 9EQ
Tel: 0131 333 1570
★★★★ Bed & Breakfast

Almond House
52 Glasgow Road, Edinburgh,
Midlothian, EH12 8HN
Tel: 0131 467 4588
★★★ Bed & Breakfast

Arden Guest House
126 Old Dalkeith Road,
Edinburgh, EH16 4SD
Tel: 0131 664 3985
★★★ Guest House

Ardenlee Guest House
9 Eyre Place, Edinburgh,
EH3 5ES
Tel: 0131 556 2838
★★★ Guest House

9 Argyle Place
Edinburgh, Midlothian, EH9 1JL
Tel: 0131 6676861
★★ Bed & Breakfast

Arisaig
64 Glasgow Road, Corstorphine,
Edinburgh, EH12 8LN
Tel: 0131 334 2610
★★★★ Bed & Breakfast

Aros House
1 Salisbury House, Edinburgh,
EH9 1SL
Tel: 0131 667 1585
★★★ Bed & Breakfast

Ascot Garden
154 Glasgow Road, Edinburgh,
EH12 8LS
Tel: 0131 339 2092
★★★ Bed & Breakfast

Directory of all VisitScotland Quality Assured Serviced Establishments

Averon Guest House
44 Gilmore Place, Edinburgh, EH3 9NQ
Tel: 0131 229 9932
★ Guest House

Baberton Cottage
46 Gilmore Place, Edinburgh, Lothian, EH3 9NQ
★ Bed & Breakfast

Badjao B&B
21 Moat Place, Edinburgh, Midlothian, EH14 1PP
Tel: 0131 443 3170
★★ Bed & Breakfast

Baird, Lee, Ewing and Turner House
18 Holyrood Park Road, Edinburgh, EH16 5AY
★★ Campus

Bank Hotel
1 South Bridge, Edinburgh, Lothian, EH1 1LL
Tel: 0131 556 9043
★★ Inn

1B Barnton Grove
Edinburgh, EH4 6EQ
Tel: 0131 3398086
★★★★ Bed & Breakfast

Beresford Hotel
32 Coates Gardens, Edinburgh, EH12 5LE
Tel: 0131 337 0850
★★★ Guest House

Bield Bed & Breakfast
3 Orchard Brae West, Edinburgh, Midlothian, EH4 2EW
Tel: 0131 332 5119
★★★ Bed & Breakfast

Birch Tree House
419 Queensferry Road, Edinburgh, EH4 7NB
Tel: 0131 336 4790
★★★ Bed & Breakfast

Blacket Garden Flat
46c Blacket Place, Edinburgh, Midlothian, EH9 1RJ
Tel: 0131 668 1132
★★★ Bed & Breakfast

Blinkbonny House
23 Blinkbonny Gardens, Edinburgh, Lothian, EH4 3HG
Tel: 0131 467 1232
★★★ Bed & Breakfast

Blossom House
8 Minto Street, Edinburgh, EH9 1RG
Tel: 0131 667 5353
★ Guest House

Bonnington Guest House
202 Ferry Road, Edinburgh, EH6 4NW
Tel: 0131 554 7610
★★★★ Guest House

Borodale
7 Argyle Place, Edinburgh, EH9 1JU
Tel: 0131 667 5578
★★★ Bed & Breakfast

27 Braid Crescent
Edinburgh, EH10 6AX
Tel: 0131 447 5830
★★★ Bed & Breakfast

Mrs Karen Bridges
56 East Claremont Street, Edinburgh, EH7 4JR
Tel: 0131 478 4463
★★★★ Bed & Breakfast

Briggend Guest House
19 Old Dalkeith Road, Edinburgh, EH16 4TE
Tel: 0131 258 0810
★★★ Guest House

Brodies Guest House
22 East Claremont Street, Edinburgh, EH7 4JP
Tel: 0131 556 4032
★★★ Guest House

Bruntsfield Lodge
5 Bruntsfield Avenue, Edinburgh, Midlothian, EH10 4EL
Tel: 0131 4764240
★ Bed & Breakfast

Burns Guest House
67 Gilmore Place, Edinburgh, EH3 9NU
Tel: 0131 229 1669
★★★ Guest House

7 Cambridge Gardens
Edinburgh, Lothian, EH6 5DH
Tel: 0131 5546196
★★ Bed & Breakfast

Cannavan
3 Grigor Gardens, Edinburgh, Midlothian, EH4 2PA
Tel: 0131 3321723
★★★ Bed & Breakfast

Cannobie Lea
11 Western Terace, Edinburgh, EH12 5QF
Tel: 0131 337 7734
★★★ Bed & Breakfast

Caravel Guest House
30 London Street, Edinburgh, EH3 6NA
Tel: 0131 556 4444
★★ Guest House

Castle Park Guest House
75 Gilmore Place, Edinburgh, EH3 9NU
Tel: 0131 229 1215
★★ Guest House

Ceol-na-Mara
50 Paisley Crescent, Edinburgh, EH8 7JQ
Tel: 0131 661 6337
★★★ Bed & Breakfast

The Chaplins
13 Lansdowne Crescent, Edinburgh, EH12 5EH
Tel: 0131 4672983
★★★ Bed & Breakfast

Charleston House Guest House
38 Minto Street, Edinburgh, EH9 2BS
Tel: 0131 667 6589
★★★ Guest House

The Coaches
443 Queensferry Road, Edinburgh, Midlothian, EH4 7NB
★★★ Bed & Breakfast

Colquhoun
5 Marchhall Road, Edinburgh, EH16 5HR
Tel: 0131 6678481
★★★ Bed & Breakfast

The Conifers
56 Pilrig Street, Edinburgh, EH6 5AS
Tel: 0131 554 5162
★★★ Bed & Breakfast

Corner House
1 Greenbank Place, Edinburgh, EH10 6EW
Tel: 0131 447 1077
★★★ Bed & Breakfast

Craigmore Bed & Breakfast
20 Craigs Road, Edinburgh, EH12 8EL
Tel: 0131 339 4225
★★★★ Bed & Breakfast

Crannoch
467 Queensferry Road, Edinburgh, EH4 7ND
Tel: 0131 336 5688
★★★★ Bed & Breakfast

Crioch Guest House
23 East Hermitage Place, Leith Links, Edinburgh, EH6 8AD
Tel: 0131 554 5494
★★★ Guest House

Dalry Guest House
10 West End Place, Dalry Road, Haymarket, Edinburgh, EH11 2ED
Tel: 0131 3135536
Bed & Breakfast

5 Dean Park Crescent
Edinburgh, EH4 1DN
Tel: 0131 332 4620
★★★★ Bed & Breakfast

Mr & Mrs T Divine
116 Greenbank Crescent, Edinburgh, EH10 5SZ
Tel: 0131 447 9454
★ Bed & Breakfast

DonMarie
33 Silverknowes Crescent, Edinburgh, EH4 5JD
Tel: 0131 3365242
★★★ Bed & Breakfast

Doocote House
15 Moat Street, Edinburgh, EH14 1PE
Tel: 0131 443 5455
★★ Bed & Breakfast

Dovecot House
6 Dovecot Road, Edinburgh,
Midlothian, EH12 7LE
Tel: 0131 4677467
★★★★ Bed & Breakfast

Drumfin
35 Orchard Road South,
Edinburgh, Mid Lothian, EH4 3JA
Tel: 0131 3328209
★★★ Bed & Breakfast

38 Dublin Street
Edinburgh, Lothian, EH3 6NN
Tel: 0131 557 1789
★★★★ Bed & Breakfast

26 Duddingston Avenue
Edinburgh, EH15 1SQ
Tel: 0131 669 9689
★★ Bed & Breakfast

**Edinburgh City
Bed and Breakfast**
31 Grove Street, Edinburgh,
Midlothian, EH3 8AF
Tel: 0131 6220144
★ Bed & Breakfast

Edinburgh First
Chancellor Court, Pollock Halls,
18 Holyrood Park Road,
Edinburgh, EH10 5AY
Tel: 0131 651 2007
★★★ Campus

Ellesmere Guest House
11 Glengyle Terrace, Edinburgh,
EH3 9LN
Tel: 0131 229 4823
★★★★ Guest House

Elliston
5 Viewforth Terrace, Edinburgh,
EH10 4LH
Tel: 0131 229 6698
★★ Bed & Breakfast

Emerald Guest House
3 Drum Street, Gilmerton,
Edinburgh, EH17 8GG
Tel: 0131 664 5918
AWAITING INSPECTION

Falcon Crest Guest House
70 South Trinity Road,
Edinburgh, EH5 3NX,
Tel: 0131 552 5294
★ Guest House

Four Seasons Guest House
47 Minto Street, Newington,
Edinburgh, EH9 2BR
Tel: 0131 667 2963
★ Guest House

Frasers B&B
7 Bellevue Place, Edinburgh,
EH7 4BS
Tel: 0131 556 5123
★★★ Bed & Breakfast

Garonne House
21 West Mayfield, Edinburgh,
EH9 1TQ
Tel: 0131 668 2148
★★★★ Bed & Breakfast

Gifford House
103 Dalkeith Road, Edinburgh,
EH16 5AJ
Tel: 0131 667 4688
★★★★ Guest House

Gildun Guest House
9 Spence Street, Edinburgh,
EH16 5AG
Tel: 0131 667 1368
★★★★ Guest House

2 Gilmour Road
Edinburgh, EH16 5NF
Tel: 0131 667 4923
★★★ Bed & Breakfast

Glendevon
50 Glasgow Road, Edinburgh,
EH12 8HN
Tel: 011 539 0491
★★★ Bed & Breakfast

Glenfarrer House
36 Farrer Terrace, Edinburgh,
EH7 6SG
Tel: 0131 669 1265
★★ Bed & Breakfast

Glenturret
18 Downie Terrace, Edinburgh,
EH12 7AU
Tel: 0131 334 5434
★★★ Bed & Breakfast

Granville
1 Britwell Crescent, Edinburgh,
EH7 6PS
Tel: 0131 669 8426
★★★★ Bed & Breakfast

The Hedges
19 Hillside Crescent, Edinburgh,
EH7 5EB
Tel: 0131 558 1481
★★ Bed & Breakfast

Herald House Hotel
70 Grove Street, Edinburgh,
EH3 8AP
Tel: 0131 228 2323
★★ Hotel

Heriot-Watt University
Riccarton, Edinburgh, EH14 4AS
Tel: 0131 451 3669
★★ Campus

Holland House
18 Holyrood Park Road,
Edinburgh, EH16 5AY
Tel: 0131 651 2007
★★ Campus

Hopetoun
15 Mayfield Road, Edinburgh,
EH9 2NG
Tel: 0131 667 7691
★★★ Bed & Breakfast

37 Howe Street
Edinburgh, Midlothian, EH3 6TF
Tel: 0131 557 3487
★★ Bed & Breakfast

Ingleneuk
31 Drumbrae North, Edinburgh,
EH4 8AT
Tel: 0131 317 1743
★★★ Bed & Breakfast

International Guest House
37 Mayfield Gardens,
Edinburgh, EH9 2BX
Tel: 0131 667 2511
★★★★ Guest House

Jewel & Esk Valley College
24 Milton Road East, Edinburgh,
EH15 2PP
Tel: 0131 657 7292
★ Campus

12 Kilmaurs Road
Edinburgh, Lothian, EH16 5DA
Tel: 0131 667 5057
★★★ Bed & Breakfast

Kingswood
30 Arboretum Place, Inverleith,
Edinburgh, EH3 5NZ
Tel: 0131 332 7315
★★★ Bed & Breakfast

Lauriston Park
6 Lauriston Park, Edinburgh,
EH3 9JA
Tel: 0131 2285557
★★★ Bed & Breakfast

11-1 Learmonth Terrace
Edinburgh, Midlothian, EH4 1PG
Tel: 0131 3154035
★★★ Bed & Breakfast

17 Learmonth Terrace
Edinburgh, EH4 1PG
Tel: 0131 315 4088
★★★★ Bed & Breakfast

14 Lennel Avenue
Edinburgh, EH12 6DW
Tel: 0131 337 1979
★★★★ Bed & Breakfast

Lindenlea
6 St Marks Place, Portobello,
Edinburgh, EH15 2PY
Tel: 0131 669 6490
★★★ Bed & Breakfast

Mackenzie Guest House
2 East Hermitage Place,
Edinburgh, EH6 8AA
Tel: 0131 554 3763
★★★★ Guest House

McCrae's B & B
44 East Claremont Street,
Edinburgh, EH7 4JR
Tel: 0131 556 2610
★★★ Bed & Breakfast

Masson House
18 Holyrood Park Road,
Edinburgh, EH16 5AY
Tel: 0131 651 2007
★★ Campus

21 Mayfield Road
Newington, Edinburgh,
EH9 2NQ
Tel: 0131 667 8435
★★★ Bed & Breakfast

Md's B&B
20 Hillview, Queensferry Road,
Edinburgh, Midlothian, EH4 2AF
Tel: 0131 478 3228
★★★★ Bed & Breakfast

Meadowplace House
1 Meadowplace Road,
Edinburgh, EH12 7TZ
Tel: 0131 334 8459
★★ Bed & Breakfast

Directory of all VisitScotland Quality Assured Serviced Establishments

Meadows Festival Rooms
7 Hope Park Terrace, Edinburgh, Midlothian, EH8 9LZ
Tel: 0131 621 2141
★★★ Bed & Breakfast

17 Moat Street
Edinburgh, EH14 1PE
Tel: 0131 443 4902
★★ Bed & Breakfast

22 Murrayfield Gardens
Edinburgh, EH12 6DF
Tel: 0131 337 3569
★★★★ Bed & Breakfast

Newington Cottage
15 Blacket Place, Edinburgh, EH9 1RJ
Tel: 0131 6681935
★★★★★ Bed & Breakfast

Newington Lodge
222 Dalkeith Road, Edinburgh, EH16 5DT
Tel: 0131 667 0910
★★ Bed & Breakfast

Newmills Cottage
472 Lanark Road West, Balerno, Midlothian, EH14 5AE
Tel: 0131 449 4300
★★★★ Bed & Breakfast

No 45
45 Gilmour Road, Edinburgh, Midlothian, EH16 5NS
Tel: 0131 667 3536
★★★★ Bed & Breakfast

No 18
18 Danube Street, Edinburgh, EH4 1NT
★★★★ Bed & Breakfast

24 Northumberland Street
Edinburgh, EH3 6LS
Tel: 0131 556 8140
★★★★ Bed & Breakfast

Number 54
54 Orchard Drive, Edinburgh, EH4 2DZ
Tel: 0131 332 8810
★★★★ Bed & Breakfast

Catherine Parent B&B
5A Melgund Terrace, Edinburgh, Midlothian, EH7 4BU
Tel: 07773 915912
★★★ Bed & Breakfast

46 Pilrig Street
Edinburgh, Midlothian, EH6 5AL
Tel: 0131 554 6605
★★ Bed & Breakfast

Premier Travel Inn
1 Morrison Link, Edinburgh, EH3 8DN
0870 238 3319
★★★ Lodge

Priestville Guest House
10 Priestfield Road, Edinburgh, EH16 5HJ
Tel: 0131 667 2435
★★★ Guest House

Pringles Ingle
26 Morningside Park, Edinburgh, EH10 5HB
Tel: 0131 447 5847
★★★ Bed & Breakfast

Quaich Guest House
87 St John's Road, Edinburgh, EH12 6NN
Tel: 0131 334 4440
★★★ Bed & Breakfast

Queen Margaret College
36 Clerwood Terrace, Edinburgh, EH12 8TS
132
★ Campus

3 Randolph Crescent
Edinburgh, Midlothian, EH3 7TH
Tel: 0131 226
★★★ Bed & Breakfast

Redcraig Bed and Breakfast
Mid Calder, Livingston, EH53 0JT
Tel: 01506 884249
★★★ Bed & Breakfast

The Red House
1 Cluny Gardens, Edinburgh, EH10 6BE
Tel: 0131 2443727
★★★ Bed & Breakfast

The Residence
65 Colinton Road, Edinburgh, EH10 5EF
Tel: 0131 447 9118
★★★★ Bed & Breakfast

Rick's
55A Frederick Street, Edinburgh, EH2 1LH
Tel: 0131 6227800
★★★★
Restaurant with Rooms

Robert Bryson Hall
Riccarton, Edinburgh, Midlothian, EH14 4AS
Tel: 0131 451 3504
★★ Campus

St Margarets
13 Corstorphine High Street, Edinburgh, Midlothian, EH12 7SU
Tel: 0131 334 7317
★★★★ Bed & Breakfast

Sakura House
18 West Preston Street, Edinburgh, EH8 9PU
Tel: 0131 668 1204
★ Guest House

Salisbury Guest House
45 Salisbury Road, Edinburgh, EH16 5AA
Tel: 0131 667 1264
★★★ Guest House

Sandaig Guest House
5 East Hermitage Place, Leith Links, Edinburgh, EH6 8AA
Tel: 0131 554 7357
★★★★ Guest House

Sandeman House
33 Colinton Road, Edinburgh, EH10 5DR
Tel: 0131 447 8080
★★★★ Bed & Breakfast

2 Seton Place
Edinburgh, EH9 2JT
Tel: 0131 667 6430
★★★ Bed & Breakfast

Smiths' Guest House
77 Mayfield Road, Edinburgh, EH9 3AA
Tel: 0131 667 2524
★★★ Guest House

South Lodge
2A Dovecot Road, Edinburgh, EH12 7LG
Tel: 0131 334 4651
★★★ Bed & Breakfast

Spylaw Bank House
2 Spylaw Avenue, Edinburgh, Midlothian, EH13 0LR
Tel: 0131 441 5022
★★★★ Bed & Breakfast

Stewarts B&B
21 Hillview, Queensferry Road, Edinburgh, EH4 2AF
Tel: 0131 539 7033
★★★ Bed & Breakfast

St Mary's Music School
Coates Hall, 25 Grosvenor Crescent, Edinburgh, Lothian, EH12 5EL
Tel: 0131 538 7766
★★ Campus

Sure & Steadfast
76 Milton Road West, Edinburgh, EH15 1QY
Tel: 0131 657 1189
★★★ Bed & Breakfast

Tailors Hall Hotel
139 Cowgate, Edinburgh, Lothian, EH1 1JS
Tel: 0131 622 6801
★★ Inn

Tantallon Bed & Breakfast
17 Tantallon Place, Edinburgh, Lothian, EH9 1NZ
Tel: 0131 667 1708
★★★ Bed & Breakfast

Terringlen
65 Telford Road, Edinburgh, Midlothian, EH4 2AX
Tel: 0131 332 7273
★★★★ Bed & Breakfast

The Thistle Bed & Breakfast
111 Drum Street, Gilmerton, Edinburgh, EH17 8RJ
Tel: 0131 258 2511
★★ Bed & Breakfast

36 Upper Gray street
Edinburgh, Lothian, EH9 1SW
Tel: 0131 667 3565
★★★ Bed & Breakfast

The Victorian Townhouse
14 Eglinton Crescent, Edinburgh, Midlothian, EH12 5DD
Tel: 0131 337 7088
★★★★ Bed & Breakfast

Villa Nina Guest House
39 Leamington Terrace,
Edinburgh, EH10 4JS
Tel: 0131 229 2644
★★ Guest House

Violet Bank House
167 Lanark Road West,
Edinburgh, Midlothian,
EH14 5NZ
Tel: 0131 451 5103
★★★★★ Bed & Breakfast

The White House
4 Corbiehill Road, Edinburgh,
EH4 5EF
★★★ Bed & Breakfast

The Witchery by The Castle
Castlehill, The Royal Mile,
Edinburgh, Lothian, EH1 2NF
Tel: 0131 225 5613
★★★★★ Restaurant with
Rooms

FAULDHOUSE
East Badallan Farm
Fauldhouse, by Bathgate,
West Lothian, EH47 9AG
Tel: 01501 770251
★★★ Bed & Breakfast

GIFFORD
Goblin Ha' Hotel
Main Street, Gifford,
East Lothian, EH41 4QH
Tel: 01620 810244
★★ Inn

Rowan Park
Longnewton Farm, Gifford,
East Lothian, EH41 4JW
Tel: 01620 810327
★★★★ Bed & Breakfast

GULLANE
Faussetthill House
20 Main Street, Gullane,
East Lothian, EH31 2DR
Tel: 01620 842396
★★★★ Bed & Breakfast

Jadini Garden
Goose Green, Gullane,
East Lothian, EH31 2BA
Tel: 01620 843343
★★★ Bed & Breakfast

Kilmory
Marine Street, Gullane,
East Lothian, EH31 2AZ
Tel: 01620 842332
★★★ Bed & Breakfast

Saltcoats Farmhouse
Saltcoats Farm, Gullane,
EH31 2AG
Tel: 01620 842204
★★ Bed & Breakfast

HADDINGTON
Carfrae Farmhouse
near Garvald, Haddington,
East Lothian, EH41 4LP
Tel: 01620 830242
★★★★ Bed & Breakfast

Eaglescairnie Mains
by Gifford, Haddington,
East Lothian, EH41 4HN
Tel: 01620 810491
★★★★ Bed & Breakfast

East Mains Farmhouse
Samuelston, Haddington,
East Lothian, EH41 4HG
Tel: 01620 822208
★★★ Bed & Breakfast

Fieldfare B&B
Upper Bolton Farm, Haddington,
East Lothian, EH41 4HW
Tel: 01620 810346
★★ Bed & Breakfast

26 Letham Mains
Haddington, East Lothian,
EH41 4NW
Tel: 01620 822458
★★★ Bed & Breakfast

Orchard House
22 Letham Mains Holdings,
Haddington, East Lothian,
EH41 4HB
Tel: 01620 824898
★★★ Bed & Breakfast

LASSWADE
Carlethan House
Wadinburn Lane, Lasswade,
Midlothian, EH18 1HG
Tel: 0131 663 7047
★★★★ Bed & Breakfast

Droman House
Lasswade, Midlothian,
EH18 1HA
Tel: 0131 663 9239
★★ Bed & Breakfast

Gortonlee Farm
Lasswade, Midlothian, EH18 1EQ
Tel: 0131 440 2077
★ Bed & Breakfast

The Laird And Dog Hotel
5 High Street, Lasswade,
Midlothian, EH18 1NA
Tel: 0131 663 9219
★★ Inn

LINLITHGOW
Arden House
Belsyde, Linlithgow,
West Lothian, EH49 6QE
Tel: 01506 670 172
★★★★★ Bed & Breakfast

Aran House
Woodcockdale Farm, Lanark
Road, Linlithgow, West Lothian,
EH49 6QE
Tel: 01506 842088
★★ Guest House

Belsyde Farm
Lanark Road, Linlithgow,
West Lothian, EH49 6QE
Tel: 01506 842098
★★★★ Bed & Breakfast

Cauldburn House
Belsyde, Linlithgow,
West Lothian, EH49 6QE
Tel: 01506 846132
★★★★ Bed & Breakfast

Mrs Janet Gray
26 Cameron Knowe,
Philipstoun, Linlithgow,
EH49 6RL
Tel: 01506 834284
AWAIT INSPECTION

Rosebank
Blackness, Linlithgow,
EH49 7WL
Tel: 01506 834373
★★★ Bed & Breakfast

Strawberry Bank House
13 Avon Place, Strawberry Bank,
Linlithgow, West Lothian,
EH49 6BL
Tel: 01506 848372
★★★★ Bed & Breakfast

Thornton
Edinburgh Road, Linlithgow,
West Lothian, EH49 6AA
Tel: 01506 844693
★★★★ Bed & Breakfast

LONGNIDDRY
Canty Grove
1 Canty Grove, Longniddry,
East Lothian, EH32 0TB
Tel: 01875 853000
★★★ Bed & Breakfast

13 Glassel Park Road
Longniddry, East Lothian,
EH32 0NY
Tel: 01875 852333
★★★ Bed & Breakfast

MUSSELBURGH
Mrs Elizabeth Aitken
18 Woodside Gardens,
Musselburgh, East Lothian,
EH21 7LJ
Tel: 0131 665 3170
★★ Bed & Breakfast

8 Albert Terrace
Linkfield Road, Musselburgh,
East Lothian, EH21 7LR
Tel: 0131 665 3703
★★★ Bed & Breakfast

19 Bridge Street
Musselburgh, East Lothian,
EH21 6AA
Tel: 0131 665 6560
★★ Bed & Breakfast

Eildon
109 Newbigging, Musselburgh,
East Lothian, EH21 7AS
Tel: 0131 665 3981
★★★ Bed & Breakfast

Fairways
21 Linkfield Road, Musselburgh,
East Lothian, EH21 7LQ
Tel: 0131 665 5050
★★★ Bed & Breakfast

Windsor Park B&B
Musselburgh, East Lothian,
EH21 7QL
Tel: 0131 665 2194
★★★ Bed & Breakfast

NORTH BERWICK
The Folly
1 Station Hill, North Berwick,
East Lothian, EH39 4AN
Tel: 01620 895777
★★ Restaurant with Rooms

The Garden Flat B&B
10 York Road, North Berwick,
East Lothian, EH39 4LX
Tel: 01620 893544
★★★ Bed & Breakfast

The Glebe House
4 Law Road, North Berwick,
East Lothian, EH39 4PL
Tel: 01620 892608
★★★★ Bed & Breakfast

Glentruim
53 Dirleton Avenue, North
Berwick, East Lothian, EH39 4BL
Tel: 01620 890064
★★★★ Bed & Breakfast

Melbourne Mews B&B
43 Melbourne Place, North
Berwick, East Lothian, EH39 4JS
Tel: 01620 890895
★★★ Bed & Breakfast

Troon
Dirleton Road, North Berwick,
East Lothian, EH39 5DF
Tel: 01620 893555
★★★ Bed & Breakfast

The Wing
13 Marine Parade, North
Berwick, East Lothian, EH39 4LD
Tel: 01620 893162
★★★ Bed & Breakfast

BY PENICUIK
Patieshill Farm
Carlops,by Penicuik, Midlothian,
EH26 9ND
Tel: 01968 660551
★★★ Bed & Breakfast

Walltower
Howgate,by Penicuik,
Midlothian, EH26 8PY
Tel: 01968 674686
★★ Bed & Breakfast

PENICUIK
Braidwood Farm
Penicuik, Midlothian, EH26 9LP
Tel: 01968 679959
★★★ Bed & Breakfast

ROSLIN
Hunter Holiday Cottages B&B
Whitehill Estate, Rosewell,
Midlothian, EH24 9EF
Tel: 0131 448 0888
★★ Bed & Breakfast

The Steading
Slatebarns, Chapel Loan, Roslin,
Midlothian, EH25 9PU
Tel: 0131 4401608
★★★★ Bed & Breakfast

SOUTH QUEENSFERRY
Mr D & Mrs H Maclean
98 Provost Milne Grove, South
Queensferry, West Lothian,
EH30 9PL
Tel: 0131 331 1893
★★★ Bed & Breakfast

Priory Lodge
8 The Loan, South Queensferry,
West Lothian, EH30 9NS
Tel: 0131 331 4345
★★★★ Guest House

TRANENT
47 Carlaverock Avenue
Tranent, East Lothian,
EH33 2PW
Tel: 01875 614008
★★ Bed & Breakfast

Schiehallion
1 Edinburgh Road, Tranent,
East Lothian, EH33 1BA
Tel: 01875 611224
★★★★ Bed & Breakfast

UPHALL
Oatridge Hotel
2-4 Main Street, Uphall,
Broxburn, West Lothian,
EH52 5DA
Tel: 01506 856 465
★★ Inn

WEST CALDER
Limefield House
West Calder, West Lothian,
EH55 8QL
Tel: 01506 871237
★★ Bed & Breakfast

ABINGTON
Days Inn
Welcome Break M74/A7,
Abington, Lanarkshire,
ML12 6RG
Tel: 01864 502782
★★★ Lodge

AIRDRIE
Easter Glentore Farm
Slamannan Road, Greengairs,
Airdrie, Lanarkshire, ML6 7TJ
Tel: 01236 830243
★★★★ Bed & Breakfast

Laurel Inn
101 Main St, Chapelhall,by
Airdrie, Lanarkshire, ML6 8SB
Tel: 01236 763230
★★★ Inn

Rowan Lodge
23 Condorrat Road, Glenmavis,
Aridrie, Lanarkshire, ML6 0NS
Tel: 01236 753934
★★★ Bed & Breakfast

Shawlee Cottage
108 Luachope Street,
Chapelhall, Airdrie, Lanarkshire,
ML6 8SW
Tel: 01236 753774
★★★ Bed & Breakfast

BIGGAR
Cormiston Cottage
Cormiston Road, Biggar,
Lanarkshire, ML12 6NS
Tel: 01899 220200
★★★ Bed & Breakfast

Cuil Darach
7 Langvout Gate, Biggar, South
Lanarkshire, ML12 6UF
Tel: 01899 221259
★★★★ Bed & Breakfast

Dunsyre Mains Farm
Dunsyre, Lanarkshire, ML11 8NQ
Tel: 01899 810251
★★★ Bed & Breakfast

Elphinstone Hotel
145 High Street, Biggar,
Lanarkshire, ML12 6DL
Tel: 01899 220044
★ Inn

Hartree House
Station Road, Biggar,
Lanarkshire, ML12 6JJ
Tel: 01899 229108
★★★ Bed & Breakfast

High Meadows B&B
Meadowflats Road, Thankerton,
Biggar, Lanarkshire, ML12 6NF
Tel: 01899 308872
★★★ Bed & Breakfast

Lindsaylands House
Biggar, Lanarkshire, ML12 6NR
Tel: 01899 220033
★★★★ Bed & Breakfast

Walston House
Walston, by Biggar, South
Lanarkshire, ML11 8NF
Tel: 01899 810324
★★ Bed & Breakfast

BY BIGGAR
Walston Mansion Farmhouse
Walston, Carnwath, Lanarkshire,
ML11 8NF
Tel: 01899 810334
★★★ Bed & Breakfast

CALDERCRUIX
Craigpark House B&B
57 Airdrie Road, Caldercruix,
by Airdrie, Lanarks, ML6 8PA
Tel: 01236 843211
★★★ Bed & Breakfast

CHRYSTON, BY GLASGOW
Crowwood House Hotel
Cumbernauld Road, Muirhead,
Glasgow, G69 9BJ
Tel: 0141 779 3861
Lodge

CRAWFORD

Holmlands Country House
22 Carlisle Road, Crawford,
by Abington, Lanarkshire,
ML12 6TW
Tel: 01864 502753
★★★ Bed & Breakfast

CUMBERNAULD

Greenacres House
Palacerigg, Cumbernauld,
Lanarkshire, G67 3HU
Tel: 01236 724281
★★ Bed & Breakfast

Red Deer & Innkeeper's Lodge
1 Auchenkilns Park,
Cumbernauld, North
Lanarkshire, G68 9AZ
Tel: 01236 795861
★★★ Lodge

DOUGLAS

Kilchoman B&B
14 Addison Gardens, Douglas,
South Lanarkshire, ML11 0PW
07831 537702
★★★★ Bed & Breakfast

EAST KILBRIDE

2 Ashton Green
East Kilbride, South
Lanarkshire, G74 4LB
Tel: 01355 238 094
★★★ Bed & Breakfast

Creighton Grove
29 Brouster Hill, East Kilbride,
Lanarkshire, G74 1AJ
Tel: 01355 234998
★★ Bed & Breakfast

GIFFNOCK, GLASGOW

Giffnock Guest House
10 Forres Avenue, Giffnock,
G46 6LJ
Tel: 0141 638 5554
★★★ Bed & Breakfast

GLASGOW

Adelaides
209 Bath Street, Glasgow,
G2 4HZ
Tel: 0141 248 4970
★★ Guest House

Alison Guest House
26 Circus Drive, Glasgow,
G31 2JH
Tel: 0141 556 1431
★★ Guest House

Angus Hotel
966-970 Sauchiehall Street,
Glasgow, G3 7TH
Tel: 0141 357 515
★★★ Lodge

Belgrave Guest House
2 Belgrave Terrace, Hillhead,
Glasgow, G12 8JD
Tel: 0141 337 1850
★★ Guest House

Bewleys Hotel
110 Bath Street, Glasgow,
G2 2EN, Fax:0141 353 0900
Tel: 0845 234 5959
★★★ Hotel

Buchanan Hotel
185 Buchanan Street, Glasgow,
G1 2JY
Tel: 0141 332 7284
★ Hotel

Claremont House
2 Broompark Circus, Glasgow,
Lanarkshire, G31 2JE
Tel: 0141 554 7312
★★★ Bed & Breakfast

Craigielea House
35 Westercraigs, Glasgow,
G31 2HY
Tel: 0141 554 3446
★★ Bed & Breakfast

Douglas & Graham House
Jordanhill Campus,
76 Southbrae Drive, Glasgow,
G13 1PP
Tel: 0141 950 3508
★ Campus

East Rogerton Lodge
Markethill Road, East Kilbride,
G74 4NZ
Tel: 01355 263176
★★ Bed & Breakfast

The Georgian House
29 Buckingham Terrace, Great
Western Road, Hillhead,
Glasgow, G12 8ED
Tel: 0141 339 0008
★★ Guest House

The Guest Rooms at Matherton
5 Matherton Avenue,
Newtonmearns, Glasgow,
G77 5EY
Tel: 0141 639 8931
★★★ Bed & Breakfast

Park House
13 Victoria Park Gardens South,
Glasgow, G11 7BX
Tel: 0141 339 1559
★★★★ Bed & Breakfast

The Heritage Hotel
4-5 Alfred Terrace, Glasgow,
G12 8RF
Tel: 0141 339 6955
★★★ Guest House

Ivory Hotel
2 Camphill Avenue, Glasgow,
G41 3AY
Tel: 0141 636 0223
★★★ Restaurant with Rooms

The Knowes
32 Riddrie Knowes, Glasgow,
G33 2QH
Tel: 0141 770 5213
★★★ Bed & Breakfast

Lomond Hotel
6 Buckingham Terrace,
Great Western Road, Glasgow,
G12 8EB
Tel: 0141 339 2339
★★ Guest House

8 Marlborough Avenue
Glasgow, G11 7BW
Tel: 0141 334 5651
★ Bed & Breakfast

Meditation Centre
21 Clouston Street, Glasgow,
G20 8QR
Tel: 0141 946 4663
★ Bed & Breakfast

The Merchant Lodge
52 Virginia Street, Glasgow,
G1 1TY
Tel: 0141 552 2424
★★★ Lodge

Murray Hall
Collins Street, Glasgow, G4 0NG
★ Campus

The Old Schoolhouse
194 Renfrew Street, Glasgow,
Strathclyde, G3 6TX
Tel: 0141 332 7600
★★★ Lodge

The Piping Centre
30-34 McPhater Street,
Glasgow, G4 0HW
Tel: 0141 353 0220
★★★ Restaurant with Rooms

Queen Margaret Hall
55 Bellshaugh Road, Glasgow,
G12 0SQ
Tel: 0141 334 2192
★★ Campus

Rab Ha's
83 Hutcheson Street, Glasgow,
G1 1SH
Tel: 0141 5720400
★★★ Inn

25 Stamperland Avenue
Clarkston, Glasgow,
Renfrewshire, G76 8EX
Tel: 0141 644 2757
★★ Bed & Breakfast

University of Strathclyde
Residence and Catering
Services,, 50 Richmond Street,
Glasgow, G1 1XP
Tel: 0141 553 4148
★ Campus

The Townhouse Hotel
21 Royal Crescent, Glasgow,
G3 7SL
Tel: 0141 332 9009
★★ Lodge

Victoria Hall Limited
171 Kyle Street, Glasgow,
Strathclyde, G4 0JQ
Tel: 0141 3544100
★ Campus

The Victorian House Hotel
212 Renfrew Street, Glasgow,
G3 6TX
Tel: 0141 332 0129
★★★ Lodge

Wolfson Hall
Kelvin Campus,West Scotland
Science Park, Maryhill Road,
Glasgow, G20 0TH
Tel: 0141 3303773
★ Campus

GLASGOW, MILNGAVIE

Tambowie Farm
Milngavie, Glasgow, G62 7HD
Tel: 0141 956 1583
★★★ Bed & Breakfast

GOUROCK

Bed and Breakfast Castle Levan
Stirling Drive, Gourock,
Renfrewshire, PA19 1AH
Tel: 01475 659154
★★★ Bed & Breakfast

Berghaus
15 Turnberry Ave, Gourock,
Renfrewshire, PA19 1JA
Tel: 01475 634550
★★★ Bed & Breakfast

GREENOCK

Denholm Bed & Breakfast
22 Denholm Street, Greenock,
PA16 8RJ
Tel: 01475 781319
★★ Bed & Breakfast

Heather Bed and Breakfast
24 Denholm Street, Greenock,
Renfrewshire, PA16 8RJ
Tel: 01475 724002
★★ Bed & Breakfast

James Watt College
Waterfront Campus,
Customhouse Way, Greenock,
Renfrewshire, PA15 1EN
Tel: 01475 731360
★★ Campus

HAMILTON

Aaron House
1A Auchingramont Road,
Hamilton, ML3 6JP
Tel: 01698 428500
★★★ Bed & Breakfast

5A Auchingramont Road
Hamilton, South Lanarkshire,
ML3 6JP
Tel: 01698 285230
★★ Bed & Breakfast

Achill House
10A Auchingramont Road,
Hamilton, Lanarkshire, ML3 6JT
Tel: 01698 424923
★★★ Bed & Breakfast

Avonclyde
15 Smithycroft, Hamilton, South
Lanarkshire, ML3 7UL
Tel: 01698 422917
★★★ Bed & Breakfast

Reston House B&B
65A Clydesdale Street,
Hamilton, ML3 0DD
Tel: 01698 330614
★★★ Bed & Breakfast

HOWWOOD

Struparsaig
Bowfield Road, Howwood,
Renfrewshire, PA9 1BS
Tel: 01505 705 129
★★★ Bed & Breakfast

INVERKIP

The Foresters
Station Road, Inverkip,
Renfrewshire, PA16 0AY
Tel: 01475 521433
★★★ Bed & Breakfast

KILSYTH

Allanfauld Farm
Kilsyth, North Lanarkshire,
G65 9DF
Tel: 01236 822155
★★ Bed & Breakfast

Auchenrivoch Farm
Banton, Kilsyth, Stirlingshire,
G65 0QZ
Tel: 01236 822113
★ Bed & Breakfast

Twechar Farm B&B
Twechar Farm, Kilsyth, East
Dunbartonshire, G65 9LH
Tel: 01236 823 216
★★★ Bed & Breakfast

KIRKFIELDBANK

Clarkston Farm
Kirkfieldbank, Lanark, ML11 9UN
Tel: 01555 663751
★★★ Bed & Breakfast

KIRKINTILLOCH, GLASGOW

Mary Paterson
Bridgend Farm, Kirkintilloch,
East Dunbartonshire, G66 1RT
Tel: 0141 776 1607
★★ Bed & Breakfast

LANARK

Duneaton
159 Hyndford Road, Lanark,
Lanarkshire, ML11 9BG
Tel: 01555 665487
★★★ Bed & Breakfast

Jerviswood Mains Farm
Cleghorn, Lanark, ML11 7RL
Tel: 01555 663987
★★★★ Bed & Breakfast

Kirkfield Mains
Kirkfieldbank, Lanark, South
Lanarkshire, ML11 9UH
Tel: 01555 660094
★★★★ Bed & Breakfast

St Catherines B&B
1 Kenilworth Road, Lanark,
Lanarkshire, ML11 7BL
Tel: 01555 662295
★★★ Bed & Breakfast

Summerlea
32 Hyndford Road, Lanark,
South Lanarkshire, ML11 9AE
Tel: 01555 664 889
★★★ Bed & Breakfast

BY LANARK

Corehouse Farm
Lanark, ML11 9TQ
Tel: 01555 661377
★★★ Bed & Breakfast

LENNOXTOWN

Eilean
2 Whitefield Lodge, Service
Street, Lennoxtown, Glasgow,
G66 7JW
Tel: 01360 312123
★★★★ Bed & Breakfast

LESMAHAGOW

Dykecroft
Dykecroft Farm, Kirkmuirhill,
Lesmahagow, ML11 0JQ
Tel: 01555 892226
★★ Bed & Breakfast

LOCHWINNOCH

East Kerse Farm
Lochwinnoch, Renfrewshire,
PA12 4DU
Tel: 01505 502400
★★★★ Bed & Breakfast

East Lochhead
Country House & Cottages
Largs Road, Lochwinnoch,
PA12 4DX
Tel: 01505 842610
★★★★ Bed & Breakfast

The Hungry Monk
Largs Road, Lochwinnoch,
Renfrewshire, PA12 4JF
Tel: 01505 843848
★★★★ Inn

MILNGAVIE, GLASGOW

Auchenhowe Cottage B&B
9 Langbank Holdings,
Milngavie, Glasgow, G62 6EL
Tel: 0141 956 4003
★★★ Bed & Breakfast

93 Drumlin Drive
Milngavie, Glasgow, G62 6NF
Tel: 0141 956 1596
★★ Bed & Breakfast

High Craigton Farm
Stockmuir Road, Milngavie,
Glasgow, East Dunbartonshire,
G62 7HA
Tel: 0141 956 1384
★★ Bed & Breakfast

Laurel Bank
96 Strathblane Road,
Milngavie, Glasgow, G62 8HD
Tel: 0141 584 9400
★★★ Bed & Breakfast

MOTHERWELL

Express By Holiday Inn
Strathclyde Park M74 Jct 5,
Motherwell, Lanarkshire,
ML1 3RB
Tel: 01698 852375
★★★ Lodge

Motherwell College -
Stewart Halls of Residence
Dalzell Drive, Motherwell,
Lanarkshire, ML1 2DD
Tel: 01698 261890
★ Campus

OLD KILPATRICK

4 Mount Pleasant Drive
Old Kilpatrick, Dunbartonshire,
G60 5HJ
Tel: 01389 876903
★ Bed & Breakfast

PAISLEY

Abbey Hotel
Barrhead Road, Paisley,
Renfrewshire, PA2 7JF
Tel: 0141 889 4529
★★ Inn

Scotscraig House
18 Park Road, Paisley,
Renfrewshire, PA2 6JW
Tel: 0141 8842082
★★★★★ Bed & Breakfast

Travelodge Glasgow Airport
Marchburn Drive, Paisley,
Glasgow, PA3 2AR
Tel: 0141 848 1359
★★★ Lodge

STRATHAVEN

Avonlea
46 Millar Street, Glassford,
by Strathaven, Lanarkshire,
ML10 6TD
Tel: 01357 521748
★★★ Bed & Breakfast

The Sheiling
Lesmahagow Road, Strathaven,
Lanarkshire, ML10 6DA
Tel: 01357 520477
★★ Bed & Breakfast

WEST HIGHLANDS & ISLANDS, LOCH LOMOND, STIRLING AND TROSSACHS

ABERFOYLE

Balavulin
Loch Ard Road, Aberfoyle,
Stirlingshire, FK8 3TD
Tel: 01877 382771
★★★ Bed & Breakfast

The Barns of Shannochill
nr Aberfoyle, Stirlingshire,
FK8 3UZ
Tel: 01877 382878
★★★★ Bed & Breakfast

Corrie Glen
Manse Road, Aberfoyle,
Stirlingshire, FK8 3XF
Tel: 01877 382427
★★★ Bed & Breakfast

Creag-Ard House
Aberfoyle, Stirling, FK8 3TQ
Tel: 01877 382297
★★★★ Guest House

The Forth Inn
Main Street, Aberfoyle,
Perthshire, FK8 3UQ
Tel: 01877 382372
★★★ Inn

Inchrie Castle Inn
Duckray Road, Aberfoyle,
Perthshire, FK8 3XB
Tel: 01877 382347
★★★ Inn

ALEXANDRIA

Tigh Geal
Duncryne Road, Gartocharn,
Dunbartonshire, G83 8RY
Tel: 01389 830 633
★★★★ Bed & Breakfast

ALEXANDRIA, LOCH LOMOND

Sheildaig Farm
Upper Stoney Mollen Road,
Alexandria, G83 8QY
Tel: 01389 752459
★★★★ Bed & Breakfast

APPIN

Bealach House
Duror, Appin, Argyll, PA38 4BW
Tel: 01631 740298
★★★★ Bed & Breakfast

Lochside Cottage
Fasnacloich, by Appin, Argyll,
PA38 4BJ
Tel: 01631 730216
★★★★ Bed & Breakfast

ARDEN

Polnaberoch
Arden, By Luss, Dunbartonshire,
G83 8RQ
Tel: 01389 850615
★★★★ Bed & Breakfast

Waters Edge Cottage
Duck Bay, Arden, Loch Lomond,
Dunbartonshire, G83 8QZ
Tel: 01389 850629
★★★★ Bed & Breakfast

ARDFERN

Galley of Lorne Inn
Main Street, Ardfern, by
Lochgilphead, Argyll, PA31 8QN
Tel: 01852 500284
★★ Inn

**ARDRISHAIG,
BY LOCHGILPHEAD**

The Grey Gull Inn
Glenburn Road, Ardrishaig,
Argyll, PA30 8EU
Tel: 01546 606017
★★★ Inn

Moorings
17 Canal Basin, St Clair Way,
Ardrishaig, By Lochgilphead,
Argyll, PA30 8EW
Tel: 01546 600455
★★★ Bed & Breakfast

ARROCHAR

Argyll View
Main Street, Arrochar, Argyll,
G83 7AA
Tel: 01301 702932
★★★★ Bed & Breakfast

Ashfield House
Arrochar, Dunbartonshire,
G83 7AA
Tel: 01301 702287
★★★ Bed & Breakfast

Burnbrae
Shore Road, Arrochar,
Argyll & Bute, G83 7AG
Tel: 01301 702988
★★★★ Bed & Breakfast

Cruachan B&B
Shore Road, Arrochar, Argyll,
G83 7BB
Tel: 01301 702521
★★★ Bed & Breakfast

Dalkusha House
Arrochar, Loch Long, Argyll,
G83 7AA
Tel: 01301 702234
★★★★ Bed & Breakfast

Ferry Cottage
Ardmay, Arrochar, Argyll & Bute,
G83 7AH
Tel: 01301 702428
★★ Bed & Breakfast

Long Shadows
Succoth, Arrochar,
Dunbartonshire, G83 7AL
Tel: 01301 702546
★★★ Bed & Breakfast

The Roadmans Cottage
Glencroe, by Arrochar,
Dunbartonshire, G83 7AS
Tel: 01301 702557
★★ Bed & Breakfast

Village Inn
Main Street, Arrochar,
Dunbartonshire, G83 7AX
Tel: 01301 702279
★★★ Inn

BALLOCH

Aird House
1 Ben Lomond Walk, Balloch,
G83 8RJ
Tel: 01389 754464
★★★ Bed & Breakfast

Argyll Lodge
16 Luss Road, Balloch,
Alexandria, Dunbartonshire,
G83 0RH
Tel: 01389 759020
★★★ Bed & Breakfast

Arklet
11 Balloch Road, Balloch,
Dunbartonshire, G83 8SR
Tel: 01389 729442
★★★ Bed & Breakfast

The Balloch House
Balloch, Dunbartonshire,
G83 8LQ
Tel: 01389 752579
★★★ Inn

8 Balloch Road
Balloch, Dunbartonshire,
G83 8SR
Tel: 01389 750436
★★★ Bed & Breakfast

Carrochan Cottage
Arthurston Road, Jamestown,
Balloch, Dunbartonshire,
G83 8AU
Tel: 01389 757963
★★ Bed & Breakfast

Drumkinnon Cottage
Pier Road, Balloch,
Dunbartonshire, G83 8QX
Tel: 01389 759909
★★★ Bed & Breakfast

Dumbain Farm
Balloch, Dunbartonshire,
G83 8DS
Tel: 01389 752263
★★★ Bed & Breakfast

Fois is Sith
8 Gaitskell Avenue, Balloch,
Dunbartonshire, G83 0EL
Tel: 01389 605502
★★★ Bed & Breakfast

Glenfern
Balloch Road, Balloch, Loch
Lomond, Dunbartonshire,
G83 8SX
Tel: 01389 750098
★★★ Bed & Breakfast

Glyndale
6 Mackenzie Drive, Balloch,
Dunbartonshire, G83 8HL
Tel: 01389 758238
★★★ Bed & Breakfast

Kilchattan
5 Castle Avenue, Balloch,
G83 8HU
Tel: 01389 603618
★★★ Bed & Breakfast

Millhall
Old Luss Road, Balloch,
Dunbartonshire, G83 8QP
Tel: 01389 750451
★★★ Bed & Breakfast

Monday Cottage
29 Torrinch Drive, Balloch,
Dunbartonshire, G83 8JL
Tel: 01389 759932
★★★ Bed & Breakfast

Oakvale B&B
Drymen Road, Balloch,
Dunbartonshire, G83 8JY
Tel: 01389 751615
★★★ Bed & Breakfast

Station Cottages
Balloch Road, Balloch,
Dunbartonshire, G83 8SS
Tel: 01389 750759
★★★★ Bed & Breakfast

St Blanes
Drymen Road, Balloch,
Dunbartownshire, G83 8JY
Tel: 01389 729 661
★★★ Bed & Breakfast

Sunnyside B & B
35 Main street, Bonhill,
Dunbartonshire, G83 9JX
Tel: 01389 750282
★★ Bed & Breakfast

Tigh Mo Ghraidh
16 Endrick Drive, Balloch,
Dunbartonshire, G83 8HY
Tel: 01389 752312
★★★★ Bed & Breakfast

Tigh-Na-Roune
Mollanbowie Road, Balloch,
Dunbartonshire, G83 8EJ
Tel: 01389 755547
★★★★ Bed & Breakfast

Tir-Na-Og
Balloch Road, Balloch, Loch
Lomond, G83 8SR
Tel: 01389 604935
★★ Bed & Breakfast

Tullichewan Farm
Upper Stoneymollan Road,
Balloch, Loch Lomond, G83 8QY
Tel: 01389 711190
★★★★ Bed & Breakfast

Tullie Inn
Balloch Road, Balloch,
Dunbartonshire, G83 8SW
Tel: 01389 752052
★★ Inn

Uplands
27 Culloden Road, Balloch,
Inverness, IV2 7HQ
Tel: 01463 790339
★★★ Bed & Breakfast

Whitecraigs Cottage
Stirling Road, Ballagan,
Dunbartonshire, G83 8NA
Tel: 01389 757811
★★★ Bed & Breakfast

Willowdale
12 Old Luss Road, Balloch,
Dunbartonshire, G83 8QP
Tel: 01389 756481
★★★★ Bed & Breakfast

Woodvale B&B
Drymen Road, Balloch,
Dunbartonshire, G83 8HT
Tel: 01389 755771
★★★ Guest House

BY BALLOCH

Braeburn Cottage
Auchencarroch Farm, by
Balloch, Dunbartonshire,
G83 9LU
Tel: 01389 710998
★★★ Bed & Breakfast

BALMAHA

Conic View Cottage
Balmaha Road, Balmaha, by
Drymen, Stirlingshire, G63 0JQ
Tel: 01360 870297
★★★ Bed & Breakfast

Dunleen, Mrs K MacFadyen
Milton of Buchanan, Balmaha,
by Drymen, Glasgow, G63 0JE
Tel: 01360 870274
★★★★ Bed & Breakfast

Mar Achlais
Milton of Buchanan, Balmaha,
Stirlingshire, G63 0JE
Tel: 01360 870300
★★★ Bed & Breakfast

Oak Tree Inn
Balmaha, by Drymen,
Stirlingshire, G63 0JQ
Tel: 01360 870357
★★★ Inn

BALQUHIDDER

Calea Sona
Balquhidder, Perthshire,
FK19 8NY
Tel: 01877 384260
★★★★ Bed & Breakfast

BARRAPOL, ISLE OF BARRA

Heathbank Hotel
Bayherivagh, Isle of Barra,
HS9 5YQ
Tel: 01871 890266
★★★ Inn

BENDERLOCH, BY OBAN

An Struan
Benderloch, by Oban, Argyll,
PA37 1ST
Tel: 01631 720301
★★★★ Bed & Breakfast

Ardchoille
Benderloch, Argyll, PA37 1ST
Tel: 01631 720432
★★★ Bed & Breakfast

Barcaldine Castle
Ledaig, Oban, Argyll, PA37 1SA
Tel: 01631 720598
★★★★ Bed & Breakfast

Island Home
12 Pony Park, Letterwalton,
Benderloch, Oban, Argyll,
PA37 1SA
Tel: 01631 720078
★★★ Bed & Breakfast

Pine View
Benderloch, by Oban, Argyll,
PA37 1ST
Tel: 01631 720429
★★★ Bed & Breakfast

Rowantree Cottage B & B
Keil Farm, Benderloch, by Oban,
Argyll, PA37 1QP
Tel: 01631 720433
★★★ Bed & Breakfast

BLAIRLOGIE

Blairmains Farm
Blairlogie, Stirling, Stirlingshire,
FK9 5QA
Tel: 01259 761338
★★ Bed & Breakfast

BLAIRMORE, BY DUNOON

Duncreggan House
Blairmore, By Dunoon,
Argyllshire, PA23 9TG
Tel: 07973 129490
★★ Bed & Breakfast

BONAWE, BY OBAN

Blarcreen House
Ardchattan, By Oban, Argyll,
PA37 1RG
Tel: 01631 750272
★★★★ Bed & Breakfast

Directory of all VisitScotland Quality Assured Serviced Establishments

BO'NESS

Edenhill
7 Linlithgow Road, Bo'ness,
West Lothian, EH51 0NE
Tel: 01506 822417
★★★ Bed & Breakfast

48 Grange Terrace
Boness, West Lothian,
EH51 9DU
Tel: 01506 822784
★★★ Bed & Breakfast

NR BO'NESS

BONNYBRIDGE

Bandominie Farm
Walton Road, Bonnybridge,
Stirlingshire, FK4 2HP
Tel: 01324 840284
★★ Bed & Breakfast

BRIDGE OF ALLAN

Anam Cara
107 Henderson Street,
Bridge of Allan, Stirling,
FK9 4HH
Tel: 01786 832030
★★★ Bed & Breakfast

Kilronan House
15 Kenilworth Road,
Bridge of Allan, Stirling,
FK9 4DU
Tel: 01786 831 054
★★★ Bed & Breakfast

Lynedoch
7 Mayne Avenue,
Bridge of Allan, Stirlingshire,
FK9 4QU
Tel: 01786 832178
★★★ Bed & Breakfast

32 Pullar Avenue
Bridge of Allan, Stirling, FK9 4SJ
Tel: 01786 832780
★★★ Bed & Breakfast

The Tree House
4 Ferniebank Brae,
Bridge of Allan, Stirling, FK9 4PJ
Tel: 01786 832508
★★★ Bed & Breakfast

BRIDGE OF ORCHY

Bridge of Orchy Hotel
Bridge of Orchy, Argyll,
PA36 4AD
Tel: 01838 400208
★★★★ Inn

Inveroran Hotel
Inveroran, Bridge of Orchy,
Argyll, PA36 4AQ
Tel: 01838 400220
★★ Inn

BRIG O'TURK

BUCHLYVIE

Balochneck Country House
Buchlyvie, Stirling, Stirlingshire,
FK8 3PA
Tel: 01360 850216
★★★★★ Bed & Breakfast

Buchlyvie Bed and Breakfast
1 Station Road, Buchlyvie,
Stirlingshire, FK8 3NA
Tel: 01360 850580
★★ Bed & Breakfast

ASCOG, ISLE OF BUTE

Balmory Hall
Ascog, Isle of Bute, PA20 9LL
Tel: 01700 500669
★★★★★ Bed & Breakfast

NORTH BUTE

Glecknabae
North Bute, Isle of Bute,
PA20 0QX
Tel: 01700 505655
★★★★ Bed & Breakfast

ROTHESAY, ISLE OF BUTE

Craigewan
26 Auchnacloich Road,
Rothesay, Bute, PA20 0EB
Tel: 01700 504029
★★★ Bed & Breakfast

Cranford

Creek Drive, Port Banntyne,
Rothesay, PA20 0NU
Tel: 01700 504 688
★★ Bed & Breakfast

The Moorings
7 Mountstuart, Rothesay, Bute,
PA20 9DY
Tel: 01700 502277
★★★ Bed & Breakfast

CALLANDER

Ballachallan
Cambusmore, Callander,
Perthshire, FK17 8LJ
Tel: 01877 339190
★★★ Restaurant with Rooms

Bridgend Cottage
Kilmahog, Callander, Perthshire,
FK17 8HD
Tel: 01877 330385
★★★ Bed & Breakfast

Bridgend House Hotel
Bridgend, Callander, Perthshire,
FK17 8HH
Tel: 01877 330130
★★ Inn

Leighton House
162 Main Street, Callander,
Perthshire, FK17 8BG
Tel: 0877 330291
★★★ Bed & Breakfast

Lenymede B & B
Leny Road, Callander, Pethshire,
FK17 8AJ
Tel: 01877 330952
★★★★ Bed & Breakfast

Roslin Cottage
Stirling Road, Lagrannoch,
Callander, FK17 8LE
Tel: 01877 339787
★★★ Bed & Breakfast

Trean Farm
Leny Feus, Callander, Perthshire,
FK17 8AS
Tel: 01877 331160
★★★ Bed & Breakfast

CAMPBELTOWN

Braehead
Campbeltown, Argyll, PA28 6QW
Tel: 01586 553304
★★★★ Bed & Breakfast

Glen Mhairi
Craiggowan Road,
Campbeltown, Argyll, PA28 6HQ
Tel: 01586 552952
★★★ Bed & Breakfast

Oatfield House
Campeltown, Argyll, PA28 6PH
Tel: 01586 551551
★★ Bed & Breakfast

Redknowe
Witchburn Road, Campbeltown,
Argyll, PA28 6PD
Tel: 01586 550374
★★★ Bed & Breakfast

Sandiway
1 Fort Argyll Road,
Campbeltown, Argyll, PA28 6SN
Tel: 01586 552280
★★★ Bed & Breakfast

Springfield House
High Street, Campbeltown,
Argyll, PA28 6EL
Tel: 01586 552080
★★★ Bed & Breakfast

Directory of all VisitScotland Quality Assured Serviced Establishments

CARRADALE

Kiloran Guest House
Carradale, Argyll, PA28 6QG
Tel: 01583 431795
★★★ Bed & Breakfast

Mains Farm
Carradale, Argyll, PA28 6QG
Tel: 01583 431216
★★ Bed & Breakfast

CARRON BRIDGE

Carronbridge Hotel
Denny, Stirling, Stirlingshire,
FK6 5JG
Tel: 01324 823459
★ Inn

Lochend Farm
Carronbridge, Stirlingshire,
FK6 5JJ
Tel: 01324 822778
★★★★ Bed & Breakfast

CLACHAN, BY TARBERT

Dunultach
Clachan, by Tarbert, Argyll,
PA29 6XW
Tel: 01880 740650
★★★★ Bed & Breakfast

CLACKMANNAN

Tower House
10 Main Street, Clackmannan,
Clackmannanshire, FK10 4JA
Tel: 01259 213889
★★★ Bed & Breakfast

COLONSAY, ISLE OF

The Hannah's B&B
4 Uragaig, Isle of Colonsay,
Argyll, PA61 7YT
Tel: 01951 200150
★★★ Bed & Breakfast

Seaview
Isle of Colonsay, Argyll,
PA61 7YN
Tel: 01951 200315
★★★ Bed & Breakfast

CONNEL

Achnamara
Old Shore Road, Connel, Oban,
Argyll, PA37 1DT
Tel: 01631 710705
★★★ Bed & Breakfast

Ach-Na-Craig
Grosvenor Crescent, Connel,
Argyll, PA37 1PQ
Tel: 01631 710588
★★★ Bed & Breakfast

The Oyster Inn
Connel, by Oban, Argyll,
PA37 1PJ
Tel: 01631 710666
★★★ Inn

Rosebank
Connel, by Oban, Argyll,
PA37 1PA
Tel: 01631 710316
★ Bed & Breakfast

Scotholm
Connel, By Oban, Argyll,
PA37 1PG
Tel: 01631 710549
★★★★ Bed & Breakfast

Wide Mouthed Frog
Dunstaffnage Marina, Connel,
by Oban, Argyll, PA37 1PX
Tel: 01631 567005
★★★ Restaurant with Rooms

**CRAOBH HAVEN,
BY LOCHGILPHEAD**

Lunga
Craobh Haven, Argyll, PA31 8QR
Tel: 01852 500237
★★ Bed & Breakfast

CRIANLARICH

Ben More Lodge Hotel
Crianlarich, Perthshire,
FK20 8QP
Tel: 01838 300210
★★ Inn

Glen Bruar House
Main Street, Crianlarich,
Stirlingshire, FK20 8QR
Tel: 01838 300214
★★ Bed & Breakfast

Northumbria Guest House
Glenfalloch Road, Crianlarich,
Perthshire, FK20 8RJ
Tel: 01838 300253
★★★ Bed & Breakfast

Suie Lodge Hotel
Luib, Glen Dochart, Crianlarich,
Perthshire, FK20 8QT
Tel: 01567 820417
★★ Small Hotel

CRINAN, BY LOCHGILPHEAD

Bellanoch House
Bellanoch Yacht Basin, By
Lochgilphead, Argyll, PA31 8SN
Tel: 01546 830149
★★★★ Bed & Breakfast

DALMALLY

Craigroyston
Monument Hill, Dalmally, Argyll,
PA33 1AA
Tel: 01838 200234
★★★ Bed & Breakfast

Strathorchy
Dalmally, Argyll, PA33 1AE
Tel: 01838 200373
★★★ Bed & Breakfast

DENNY

Woodcockfaulds Farm
Thorney Dyke Road, by Denny,
Stirlingshire, FK6 6RH
Tel: 01786 811985
★★★ Bed & Breakfast

DOLLAR

Kennels Cottage
Dollar Beg, By Dollar, Clacks,
FK14 7PA
Tel: 01259 742476
★★★★ Bed & Breakfast

BY DOLLAR

Leys Farm
Muckhart, Dollar,
Clackmannanshire, FK14 7JL
Tel: 01259 781313
★★★ Bed & Breakfast

DOUNE

Inverardoch Mains Farm
Doune, Dunblane, Perthshire,
FK15 9NZ
Tel: 01786 841268
★★ Bed & Breakfast

DRYMEN

Ceardach
Gartness Road, Drymen,
Stirlingshire, G63 0BH
Tel: 01360 660596
★★ Bed & Breakfast

Easter Drumquhassle Farm
Gartness Road, Drymen,
Stirlingshire, G63 0DN
Tel: 01360 660893
★★★ Bed & Breakfast

Elmbank B&B
10 Stirling Road, Drymen,
Stirlingshire, G63 0BN
Tel: 01360 661016
AWAIT INSPECTION

Green Shadows
Buchanan Castle Estate,
Drymen, Stirlingshire, G63 0HX
Tel: 01360 660289
★★★ Bed & Breakfast

The Hawthorns
The Square, Drymen,
Stirlingshire, G63 0BH
Tel: 01360 660916
★★★ Bed & Breakfast

Hillview
The Square, Drymen,
Stirlingshire, G63 0BL
Tel: 01360 661000
Bed & Breakfast

Hoish Farm
Hoish, Balfron Station, Glasgow,
G63 0SQ
Tel: 01360 440313
★★★★ Bed & Breakfast

Lander Bed & Breakfast
17 Stirling Road, Drymen,
Stirlingshire, G63 0BW
Tel: 01360 660273
★ Bed & Breakfast

Overmains
Balamana Road, Drymen,
Stirlingshire, G63 0HY
Tel: 01360 660374
★★★★ Bed & Breakfast

BY DRYMEN

Croftburn Bed & Breakfast
Croftamie, by Drymen,
Stirlingshire, G63 0HA
Tel: 01360 660796
★★★ Bed & Breakfast

Loaninghead Farm
Balfron Station, Loch Lomond,
Glasgow, G63 0SE
Tel: 01360 440 432
★★★★ Bed & Breakfast

DUMBARTON

Kilmalid House
17 Glenpath, Dumbarton,
Dunbartonshire, G82 2QL
Tel: 01389 732030
★★ Bed & Breakfast

Milton Inn
Dumbarton Road, Milton,
Dunbartonshire, G82 2DT
Tel: 01389 761401
★★★ Inn

Positano
71 Glasgow Road, Dumbarton,
Dunbartonshire, G82 1RE
Tel: 01389 731943
★★★ Bed & Breakfast

Stelmast B&B
42 Stirling Road, Dumbarton,
G82 2PJ
Tel: 01389 604749
★★ Bed & Breakfast

DUNBLANE

Sheriffmuir Inn
Sheriffmuir, Dunblane,
Perthshire, FK15 0LN
Tel: 01786 823285
★★★ Restaurant with Rooms

DUNOON

Belmont House
2 Edward Street, Dunoon,
Argyll, PA23 7JF
Tel: 01369 701287
★★★★ Bed & Breakfast

Clyde View
Main Road, Sandbank, Argyll,
PA23 8PD
Tel: 01369 701638
★★★ Bed & Breakfast

Dunira
257 Marine Parade, Hunters
Quay, Dunoon, Argyll, PA23 8HN
Tel: 01369 702273
★★ Bed & Breakfast

Foxbank
Marine Parades, Hunters Uuay,
Dunoon, Argyll, PA23 8HJ
Tel: 01369 703858
★★ Bed & Breakfast

Northfield
70 Ardenslate Road, Kirn, Argyll,
PA23 8HY
Tel: 01369 705496
★★★ Bed & Breakfast

Riverside House
38 Victoria Parade, Dunoon,
Argyll, PA23 7HU
Tel: 01369 702105
★★★ Bed & Breakfast

Vaila
277 Argyll Street, Dunoon,
Argyll, PA23 7QY
Tel: 01369 707540
★★ Bed & Breakfast

FALKIRK

Arbuthnot House
Dorrator Road, Falkirk, FK1 4BN
Tel: 01324 634785
★★★★ Bed & Breakfast

Balgownie
95 Dorrator Road, Camelon,
Falkirk, FK1 4BL
Tel: 01324 639892
Bed & Breakfast

48 Cromwell Road
Falkirk, Stirlingshire, FK1 1SF
Tel: 01324 638227
★★★ Bed & Breakfast

Harlow Grange
Redding Road, Brightons,
Falkirk, Stirlingshire, FK2 0AA
Tel: 01324 410343
★★★ Bed & Breakfast

Wester Carmuirs Farm
Larbert, Stirlingshire, FK5 3NW
Tel: 01324 812459
★★★ Bed & Breakfast

GARELOCHHEAD

Mambeg Country Guest House
Mambeg, Garelochhead, Argyll
& Bute, G84 0EN
Tel: 01436 810136
★★★ Bed & Breakfast

GARTOCHARN

Ardoch Cottage
Main Street, Gartocharn,
Dunbartonshire, G83 8NE
Tel: 01389 830452
★★★★ Bed & Breakfast

The Hungry Monk
Main Street, Gartocharn,
Dunbartonshire, G83 8RX
Tel: 01389 830448
★★★ Inn

The Old School House
Gartocharn, Dunbartonshire,
G83 8SB
Tel: 01389 830373
★★★★ Bed & Breakfast

GIGHA, ISLE OF

Achamore House
Isle of Gigha, Argyll, PA41 7AD
Tel: 01583 505400
★★★★ Bed & Breakfast

GLENBARR

Arnicle House
Glenbarr, By Tarbert, Argyll,
PA29 6UZ
Tel: 01583 421208
★★★ Bed & Breakfast

GLENDARUEL

The Glendaruel Hotel
Clachan of Glendaruel, Argyll,
PA22 3AA
Tel: 01369 820274
★★ Inn

HELENSBURGH

Ashfield
38 William Street, Helensburgh,
Argyll, G84 8BJ
Tel: 01436 672259
★★★ Bed & Breakfast

Ava Lodge
44 Glasgow Street,
Helensburgh, Dunbartonshire,
G84 8YH
Tel: 01436 677751
★★★★ Bed & Breakfast

Balmillig
64B Colquhoun Street,
Helensburgh, Argyll, G84 9JP
Tel: 01436 674922
★★★★ Bed & Breakfast

Bluebell Cottage
107 West King Street,
Helensburgh, G84 8DQ
07890 861034
★★★ Bed & Breakfast

County Lodge
Old Luss Road, Craigendoran,
Helensburgh, Dunbartonshire,
G84 7BH
Tel: 01436 672034
★★ Lodge

Drumfork Farm
Helensburgh, Dunbartonshire,
G84 7JY
Tel: 01436 672329
★★★ Bed & Breakfast

Eastbank
10 Hanover Street, Helensburgh,
Argyll, G84 7AW
Tel: 01436 673665
★★★ Bed & Breakfast

Killin Cottage B&B
10 Lomond Street, Helensburgh,
Dunbartonshire, G84 7PN
Tel: 01436 673595
★★★ Bed & Breakfast

Larch View
10 Cumberland Avenue,
Helensburgh, Argyll and Bute,
G84 8QG
Tel: 01436 674078
★★★ Bed & Breakfast

Lethamhill
20 West Dhuhill Drive,
Helensburgh, Dunbartonshire,
G84 9AW
Tel: 01436 676016
★★★★ Bed & Breakfast

Longleat
39 East Argyle Street,
Helensburgh, Dunbartonshire,
G84 7EN
Tel: 01436 671041
★★★★ Bed & Breakfast

Directory of all VisitScotland Quality Assured Serviced Establishments

Maybank
185 East Clyde Street,
Helensburgh, Dunbartonshire,
G84 7AG
Tel: 01436 672865
★★★ Bed & Breakfast

Middledrift
85 James Street, Helensburgh,
Dunbartonshire, G84 9LE
Tel: 01436 674867
★★★ Bed & Breakfast

Ravenswood
32 Suffolk Street, Helensburgh,
Dunbartonshire, G84 9PA
Tel: 01436 672112
★★★ Bed & Breakfast

4 Redclyffe Gardens
Helensburgh, Dumbartonshire,
G84 9JJ
Tel: 01436 677688
★★★ Bed & Breakfast

RSR Braeholm
31 East Montrose Street,
Helensburgh, Argyll & Bute,
G84 7HR
Tel: 01436 671880
★★ Lodge

Shiloh Bed and Breakfast
201 East Clyde Street,
Helensburgh, Dunbartonshire,
G84 7AJ
Tel: 01436 671005
★★★ Bed & Breakfast

Sinclair House
91/93 Sinclair Street,
Helensburgh, Argyll & Bute,
G84 8TR
Tel: 0800 1646301
★★★★ Guest House

Westbank
122 West Clyde Street,
Helensburgh, Dunbartonshire,
G84 8ET
Tel: 01436 674816
★★★★ Bed & Breakfast

INVERARAY

10 Argyll Court
Inveraray, Argyll, PA32 8UT
Tel: 01499 302273
★★★ Bed & Breakfast

Arkland B&B
15 Arkland, Inveraray, Argyll,
PA32 8UD
Tel: 01499 302361
★★ Bed & Breakfast

Barn Park B&B
12 Barn Park, Inveraray, Argyll,
PA32 8UP
Tel: 01499 302483
★★ Bed & Breakfast

Breagha Lodge
The Avenue, Inveraray, Argyll,
PA32 8YX
Tel: 01499 302061
★★★ Bed & Breakfast

Claonairigh House
Bridge of Douglas, by Inverary,
Argyll, PA32 8XT
Tel: 01499 302160
★★★ Bed & Breakfast

Creag Dhubh
Inveraray, Argyll, PA32 8XT
Tel: 01499 302430
★★★ Bed & Breakfast

Goatfield Cottage B&B
Lower Goatfield Cottage,
Furnace, Inveraray, PA32 8XN
Tel: 01499 500615
★★ Bed & Breakfast

INVERBEG

The Inverbeg Inn
Luss, Loch Lomond, Argyll,
G83 8PD
Tel: 01436 860678
★★★ Inn

INVERSNAID

Corriearklet B&B
Inversnaid, Aberfoyle,
Stirlingshire, FK8 3TU
Tel: 01877 386208
★★ Bed & Breakfast

IONA, ISLE OF

Finlay Ross Ltd
Martyr's Bay, Isle of Iona, Argyll,
PA76 6SP
Tel: 01681 700357
★★ Bed & Breakfast

Kilona
Sithean, Isle of Iona, Argyll,
PA76 6SP
Tel: 01681 700362
★★ Bed & Breakfast

BOWMORE, ISLE OF ISLAY

The Harbour Inn and Restaurant
The Square, Bowmore, Isle of
Islay, Argyll, PA43 7JR
Tel: 01496 810330
★★★★ Inn

BRUICHLADDICH

Anchorage
Bruichladdich, Isle of Islay,
Argyll, PA49 7UN
Tel: 01496 850540
★★ Bed & Breakfast

GRUINART, BRIDGEND, ISLE OF ISLAY

The Farmhouse
Carnduncan, Gruinart,
Isle of Islay, PA44 7PS
Tel: 01496 850500
★★★ Bed & Breakfast

LAGAVULIN, BY PORT ELLEN, ISLE OF ISLAY

Tigh na Suil
Lagavulin, by Port Ellen,
Isle of Islay, Argyll, PA42 7DX
Tel: 01496 302483
★★★ Bed & Breakfast

PORT CHARLOTTE, ISLE OF ISLAY

The Monachs
Nerabus, Port Charlotte,
Isle of Islay, PA48 7WE
Tel: 01496 850049
★★★★★ Bed & Breakfast

PORT ELLEN, ISLE OF ISLAY

Caladh Sona
53 Frederick Crescent, Port
Ellen, Isle of Islay, PA42 7BD
Tel: 01496 302694
★★★ Bed & Breakfast

Glenmachrie Country House
Glenmachrie, Port Ellen, Isle of
Islay, Argyll, PA42 7AQ
Tel: 01496 302560
★★★★ Guest House

Kintra Farm
Kintra Beach, Port Ellen, Islay,
PA42 7AT
Tel: 01496 302051
★★★ Bed & Breakfast

The Oystercatcher
63 Frederick Crescent,
Port Ellen, Islay, PA42 7BD
Tel: 01496 300409
★★★ Bed & Breakfast

The Trout Fly Guest House
8 Charlotte Street, Port Ellen,
Isle of Islay, PA42 7DF
Tel: 01496 302204
★★ Guest House

ISLE OF ISLAY

Ballygrant Inn
Ballygrant, Isle of Islay, Argyll,
PA45 7QR
Tel: 01496 840277
★★ Inn

Burnside Lodge
Main Street, Port Wemyss,
Isle of Islay, PA47 7SR
Tel: 01496 860296
★★ Bed & Breakfast

Coultorsay House
Bruichladdich, Isle of Islay,
PA49 7UN
Tel: 01496 850298
★★★ Bed & Breakfast

KILBERRY, BY TARBERT

Kilberry Inn
Kilberry, by Tarbert, Argyll,
PA29 6YD
Tel: 01880 770223
★★★★ Restaurant with
Rooms

KILFINAN

Tregortha
Tighnabruaich, Argyll, PA21 2BD
Tel: 01700 811132
★★★ Bed & Breakfast

KILLIN

Ardlochay Lodge
Maragowan, Killin, Perthshire,
FK21 8TN
Tel: 01567 820962
★★ Bed & Breakfast

Drumfinn Guest House
Manse Road, Killin, Perthshire,
FK21 8UY
Tel: 01567 820900
★★★ Guest House

Fairview House
Main Street, Killin, Perthshire,
FK21 8UT
Tel: 01567 820667
★★★ Guest House

KILMELFORD, BY OBAN
Cnoc Na Ceardaich
Kilmelford, Oban, Argyll,
PA34 4XA
Tel: 01852 200348
★★★ Bed & Breakfast

KILMORE
Swallow Cottage
Musdale Road, Kilmore, Oban,
Argyll, PA34 4XX
Tel: 01631 770286
★★ Bed & Breakfast

KILMUN, BY DUNOON
The Cot House Hotel
by Sandbank, Kilmun, by
Dunoon, Argyll, PA23 8QS
Tel: 01369 840260
★★★ Inn

The Pier
Kilmun, Dunoon, Argyll,
PA23 8SB
Tel: 01369 840418
★ Restaurant with Rooms

St Munns Old Manse
Shore Road, Kilmun, Dunoon,
PA23 8SD
Tel: 01369 840311
★★★ Bed & Breakfast

LAURIESTON, BY FALKIRK
Oaklands
32 Polmont Road, Laurieston,
Falkirk, FK2 9QT
Tel: 01324 610671
★★★★ Bed & Breakfast

LOCH ECK, BY DUNOON
Coylet Inn
Loch Eck, by Dunoon, Argyll,
PA23 8SG
Tel: 01369 840426
★★★ Inn

LOCHGILPHEAD
The Argyll Hotel
69 Lochnell Street,
Lochgilphead, Argyll, PA31 8JN
Tel: 01546 602221
★★ Inn

Corbiere
Achnabreac, Lochgilphead,
Argyll, PA31 8SG
Tel: 01546 602764
★★★★ Bed & Breakfast

The Corran
Poltalloch Street, Lochgilphead,
Argyll, PA31 8LR
Tel: 01546 603866
★★★ Bed & Breakfast

Empire Travel Lodge
Union Street, Lochgilphead,
Argyll, PA31 8JS
Tel: 01546 602381
★★★ Lodge

Lochgair Hotel
Lochgair, by Lochgilphead,
Argyll, PA31 8SA
Tel: 01546 886333
★★★ Restaurant with Rooms

BY LOCHGILPHEAD
Somerled Bed & Breakfast
Dunadd View, Bridgend,
Kilmichael-Glassary, by
Lochgilphead, Argyll, PA31 8QA
Tel: 01546 605226
★★★ Bed & Breakfast

LUSS
Blairglas
Luss, Dunbartonshire, G83 8RG
Tel: 01389 850278
★★★ Bed & Breakfast

Burnside
2 Glenburn Cottages, School
Road, Luss, Argyle & Bute,
G83 8PA
Tel: 01436 860255
★★★ Bed & Breakfast

Doune of Glen Douglas Farm
Inverbeg, Luss, Loch Lomond,
G83 8PD
Tel: 01301 702312
★★★ Bed & Breakfast

Shantron Farm B&B
Shantron Farm, Luss,
Alexandria, G83 8RH
Tel: 01389 850231
★★★ Bed & Breakfast

BY LUSSY
The Corries
Inverbeg, Luss, Loch Lomond,
G83 8PD
Tel: 01436 860275
★★★ Bed & Breakfast

MADDISTON
Lismore House
Wester Bowhouse Farm,
Maddiston, Falkirk, Stirlingshire,
FK2 0BX
Tel: 01324 720929
★★★★ Bed & Breakfast

MINARD, BY INVERARAY
Minard Castle
Minard, Argyll, PA32 8YB
Tel: 01546 886272
★★★★ Bed & Breakfast

Oakbank
Minard, Inveraray, Argyll,
PA32 8YB
Tel: 01546 886305
★★★ Bed & Breakfast

AROS, ISLE OF MULL
Caorann
Aros Mains, Aros, Isle of Mull,
PA72 6JS
Tel: 01680 300355
★★★ Bed & Breakfast

BUNESSAN, ISLE OF MULL
Ardness House
Bunessan, Isle of Mull, Argyll,
PA67 6DU
Tel: 01681 700260
★★★ Bed & Breakfast

Ardtun House
Bunessan, Isle of Mull, Argyll,
PA67 6DG
Tel: 01681 700264
★★ Bed & Breakfast

Dunan
Bunessan, Isle of Mull,
PA67 6DH
Tel: 01681 700665
★★ Bed & Breakfast

Newcrofts
Bunessan, Isle of Mull, Argyll,
PA67 6DS
Tel: 01681 700471
★★★ Bed & Breakfast

Rhumhor
Bunessan, Isle of Mull, Argyll,
PA67 6DG
Tel: 01681 700275
★★★ Bed & Breakfast

Uisken Croft
Uisken, Bunessan, Isle of Mull,
Argyll, PA67 6DS
Tel: 01681 700307
★★★ Bed & Breakfast

CALGARY, ISLE OF MULL
Calgary Cottage
Calgary, Isle of Mull, Argyll,
PA75 6QT
Tel: 01688 400495
★★★ Bed & Breakfast

CRAIGNURE, ISLE OF MULL
Aon A Dha
Kirk Terrace, Craignure,
Isle of Mull, Argyll, PA65 6AZ
Tel: 01680 812318
★★ Bed & Breakfast

Clachan House
Lochdon, Craignure, Isle of Mull,
Argyll, PA64 6AP
Tel: 01680 812439
★★★ Bed & Breakfast

Craignure Inn
Craignure,, Isle of Mull,
PA65 6AY
Tel: 01680 812305
★★ Inn

Dee-Emm Bed & Breakfast
Druim Mhor, Craignure,
Isle of Mull, Argyll, PA65 6AY
1680812440
★★★ Bed & Breakfast

Linnhe View
Craignure, Isle of Mull, Argyll,
PA65 6AY
Tel: 01680 812369
★★★ Bed & Breakfast

Directory of all VisitScotland Quality Assured Serviced Establishments

BY CRAIGNURE, ISLE OF MULL

Inverlussa Bed & Breakfast
by Craignure, Isle of Mull,
PA65 6BD
Tel: 01680 812436
★★★★ Bed & Breakfast

DERVAIG, ISLE OF MULL

Ardbeg House
Dervaig, nr Tobermory,
Isle of Mull, PA75 6QJ
Tel: 01688 400254
★★★ Bed & Breakfast

Balmacara
Dervaig, Isle of Mull, PA75 6QN
Tel: 01688 400363
★★★★ Bed & Breakfast

Cuin Lodge
Dervaig, Isle of Mull, PA75 6QL
Tel: 01688 400346
★★★ Bed & Breakfast

Glen Bellart House
Dervaig, Isle of Mull, Argyll,
PA75 6QJ
Tel: 01688 400282
★★ Bed & Breakfast

Glenview
Dervaig, Isle of Mull, Argyll,
PA75 6QJ
Tel: 01688 400239
★★★★ Bed & Breakfast

Inishkea
Dervaig, Isle of Mull, Argyll,
PA75 6QW
Tel: 01688 400296
★★★★ Bed & Breakfast

FIONNPHORT, ISLE OF MULL

Abbey View
Fionnphort, Isle of Mull, Argyll,
PA66 6BL
Tel: 01681 700723
★★★ Bed & Breakfast

Caol-Ithe
Fionnphort, Isle of Mull, Argyll,
PA66 6BL
Tel: 01681 700375
★★★ Bed & Breakfast

Maolbhuidhe B&B
Maolbhuidhhe, Creich,
Fionnphort, Isle of Mull,
PA66 6BP
Tel: 01681 700718
★★★ Bed & Breakfast

Seaview
Fionnphort, Isle of Mull,
PA66 6BL
Tel: 01681 700235
★★★ Bed & Breakfast

GRULINE, ISLE OF MULL

Barn Cottage
Gruline, Isle of Mull, Argyll,
PA71 6HR
Tel: 01680 300451
★★★ Bed & Breakfast

Gruline Home Farm
Gruline, Nr Salen, Isle of Mull,
PA71 6HR
Tel: 01680 300581
★★★★★ Bed & Breakfast

Torlochan Farm
Gruline, Near Salen, Isle of Mull,
Argyll, PA71 6HR
Tel: 01680 300380
★★★ Bed & Breakfast

**KINLOCHSPELVE, LOCHBUIE,
ISLE OF MULL**

The Barn
Barrachandroman, Lochbuie,
Isle of Mull, PA62 6AA
Tel: 01680 814220
★★★★ Bed & Breakfast

LOCHBUIE, ISLE OF MULL

Laggan Farm
Lochbuie, Isle of Mull, Argyll,
PA62 6AA
Tel: 01680 814206
★★★ Bed & Breakfast

LOCHDON, ISLE OF MULL

Birchgrove
Lochdon, Isle of Mull, PA64 4AP
Tel: 01680 812 364
★★★ Bed & Breakfast

Seilisdeir
Lochdon, Isle of Mull, PA64 6AP
Tel: 01680 812465
★★★ Bed & Breakfast

PENNYGHAEL, ISLE OF MULL

Craig Rowan
Pennyghael, Isle of Mull, Argyll,
PA70 6HB
Tel: 01681 704230
★★★★ Bed & Breakfast

Pennyghael Hotel
Pennyghael, Isle of Mull,
PA70 6HB
Tel: 01681 704288
★★★★ Small Hotel

SALEN, AROS, ISLE OF MULL

Aros View
Salen, Isle of Mull, Argyll,
PA72 6JB
Tel: 01680 300372
★★★ Bed & Breakfast

Callachally Farm
Salen, Aros, Isle of Mull,
PA72 6JN
Tel: 01680 300424
★★★ Bed & Breakfast

Fascadail
Salen, Aros, Isle of Mull,
PA72 6JB
Tel: 01680 300444
★★★ Bed & Breakfast

Rivendell
Ardmore Road, Salen,
Isle of Mull, PA72 6JL
Tel: 01680 300219
★★★ Bed & Breakfast

Rock Cottage
Salen, Isle of Mull, Argyll,
PA72 6JB
Tel: 01680 300506
★★★ Bed & Breakfast

TOBERMORY, ISLE OF MULL

Achnadrish House
Achnadrish Estate,
by Tobermory, Isle of Mull,
PA75 6QF
Tel: 01688 400388
★★★★ Bed & Breakfast

Agata's Bed & Breakfast
Western Road, Tobermory,
Isle of Mull, PA75 6RA
Tel: 01688 302747
★★ Bed & Breakfast

Brockville
Raeric Road, Tobermory,
Isle of Mull, PA75 6RS
Tel: 01688 302741
★★★★ Bed & Breakfast

Copeland House
Viewmount Drive, Tobermory,
Isle of Mull, Argyll, PA75 6PZ
Tel: 01688 302049
★★★ Bed & Breakfast

Cuidhe Leathain
Breadalbane Street, Tobermory,
Isle of Mull, PA75 6PD
Tel: 01688 305204
★★★ Bed & Breakfast

Glengorm Castle
Tobermory, Isle of Mull, Argyll,
PA75 6QE
Tel: 01688 302321
★★★★ Bed & Breakfast

Lonan
Western Road, Tobermory,
Isle of Mull, Argyll, PA75 6RA
Tel: 01688 302082
★★★ Bed & Breakfast

Morvern
Rockfield Road, Tobermory,
Isle of Mull, Argyll, PA75 6PN
Tel: 01688 302804
★★★★ Bed & Breakfast

Oaklee
Erray Road, Tobermory,
Isle of Mull, PA75 6PS
Tel: 01688 302520
★★★★ Bed & Breakfast

Ptarmigan House
The Fairways, Tobermory,
Isle of Mull, PA75 6PS
Tel: 01688 302863
★★★★★ Bed & Breakfast

**Staffa Cottages
Bed & Breakfast**
Breadalbane Lane, Tobermory,
Argyll, PA75 6PL
Tel: 01688 302464
★ Bed & Breakfast

Strongarbh House
Strongarbh, Tobermory,
Isle of Mull, PA75 6PR
Tel: 01688 302730
★★★ Bed & Breakfast

Tobermory Holidays Ltd
Tobermory, Isle of Mull,
PA75 6QF
Tel: 01688 302301
★★★ Bed & Breakfast

11 West Street
Tobermory, Isle of Mull, Argyll,
PA75 6QZ
Tel: 01688 302560
★★★ Bed & Breakfast

TORLOISK, ULVA FERRY
The Old Mill
Achleck, Torloisk, Isle of Mull,
Argyll, PA74 6NH
Tel: 01688 500259
★★★ Bed & Breakfast

OBAN
Ardenlee
Pulpit Hill, Oban, Argyll,
PA34 4LX
Tel: 01631 564255
★★ Bed & Breakfast

Ard Struan
Croft Road, Oban, Argyll,
PA34 5JN
Tel: 01631 563689
★★★★ Bed & Breakfast

Ardura
Duncraggan Road, Oban, Argyll,
PA34 5DU
Tel: 01631 562380
★★★ Bed & Breakfast

Ariogan Farmhouse
Upper Soroba, Oban, Argyll,
PA34 4SD
Tel: 01631 563017
★★★ Bed & Breakfast

Aros Ard
Croft Road, Oban, Argyll,
PA34 5JN
Tel: 01631 565500
★★★★ Bed & Breakfast

Blair Villa South
Rockfield Road, Oban, Argyll,
PA34 5DQ
Tel: 01631 564813
★★★ Bed & Breakfast

Bracker
Polvinister Road, Oban, Argyll,
PA34 5TN
Tel: 01631 564302
★★★ Bed & Breakfast

Briarbank
Glencruitten Road, Oban, Argyll,
PA34 4DN
Tel: 01631 566549
★★★ Bed & Breakfast

Clohass
Connel Road, Oban, Argyll,
PA34 5TX
Tel: 01631 563647
★★★ Bed & Breakfast

The Coach House
Knipoch, By Oban, Argyll,
PA34 4QT
Tel: 01852 316106
★ Bed & Breakfast

Colmcille
Dunuaran Road, Oban, Argyll,
PA34 4NE
Tel: 01631 564329
★★★ Bed & Breakfast

Colryn
Rockfield Road, Oban, Argyll,
PA34 5DQ
Tel: 01631 565144
★★ Bed & Breakfast

Corriemar House
6 Corran Esplanade, Oban,
Argyll, PA34 5AQ
Tel: 01631 562476
★★★★ Guest House

Drumriggend
22 Drummore Road, Oban,
Argyll, PA34 4JL
Tel: 01631 563330
★★★ Bed & Breakfast

Dungrianach
Pulpit Hill, Oban, Argyll,
PA34 4LU
Tel: 01631 562840
★★★★ Bed & Breakfast

Eredine
Ardconnel Road, Oban, Argyll,
PA34 5DW
Tel: 01631 563917
★★★ Bed & Breakfast

Glenara Guest House
Rockfield Road, Oban, Argyll,
PA34 5DQ
Tel: 01631 563172
★★★★ Guest House

Glen Cottage
Longsdale Road, Oban, Argyll,
PA34 5JU
Tel: 01631 563420
★★★ Bed & Breakfast

Greencourt Guest House
Benvoullin Road, Oban, Argyll,
PA34 5EF
Tel: 01631 563987
★★★★ Guest House

Harlaw
Glenmore Road, Pulpit Hill,
Oban, Argyll, PA34 4ND
Tel: 01631 563295
★★★ Bed & Breakfast

Hawthorn
Benderloch, Argyll, PA37 1QS
Tel: 01631 720452
★★★★ Bed & Breakfast

Hawthornbank Guest House
Dalriach Road, Oban, Argyll,
PA34 5JE
Tel: 01631 562041
★★★★ Guest House

High Cliff Guest House
35 Glencruitten Road, Oban,
Argyll, PA34 4EW
Tel: 01631 565809
★★ Bed & Breakfast

Kilchrenan House
Corran Esplanade, Oban, Argyll,
PA34 5AQ
Tel: 01631 562663
★★★★ Guest House

Lagganbeg Guest House
Dunollie Road, Oban, PA34 5PH
Tel: 01631 563151
★★ Bed & Breakfast

Latheron
Longsdale Road, Oban, Argyll,
PA34 5JU
Tel: 01631 564974
★★★ Bed & Breakfast

Lochvoil House
Dunuaran Road, Oban, Argyll,
PA34 4NE
Tel: 01631 562645
★★★ Bed & Breakfast

Lower Soroba Farmhouse
Oban, Argyll, PA34 4LE
Tel: 01631 565349
★★★ Bed & Breakfast

The Nook B&B
Duncraggan Road, Oban, Argyll,
PA34 5DU
Tel: 01631 570955
★★ Bed & Breakfast

The Old Manse Guest House
Dalriach Road, Oban, Argyll,
PA34 5JE
Tel: 01631 564886
★★★★ Guest House

Rhumor
Drummore Road, Oban, Argyll,
PA34 4JL
Tel: 01631 563544
★★★ Bed & Breakfast

Sabden Brook
Ardconnel Hill, Oban, Argyll,
PA34 5DY
Tel: 01631 562649
★★★ Bed & Breakfast

Strumhor
Connel, Oban, Argyll, PA37 1PJ
Tel: 01631 710167
★★★ Bed & Breakfast

Torlin Guest House
Glencruitten Road, Oban, Argyll,
PA34 4EP
Tel: 01631 570432
★★★ Bed & Breakfast

Torr Buan House
Ulva Ferry, Isle of Mull, Argyll,
PA73 6LY
Tel: 01688 500121
★★★★ Bed & Breakfast

Woodside Hotel
Tweeddale Street, Oban, Argyll,
PA34 4DD
Tel: 01631 562184
★ Inn

BY OBAN

Braeside Guest House
Kilmore, by Oban, Argyll,
PA34 4QR
Tel: 01631 770243
★★★ Guest House

Falls of Lora Hotel
Connel Ferry, by Oban, Argyll,
PA37 1PB
Tel: 01631 710483
★★★ Hotel

NR OBAN

Roineabhal Country House
Kilchrenan, Taynuilt, Argyll,
PA35 1HD
Tel: 01866 833207
★★★★ Bed & Breakfast

PORT APPIN

Fasgadh Guest House
Port Appin, Argyll, PA38 4DE
Tel: 01631 730374
★★★ Bed & Breakfast

PORT OF MENTEITH

Collymoon Pendicle
Port of Menteith, Perthshire,
FK8 3JY
Tel: 01360 850222
★★★ Bed & Breakfast

Inchie Farm
Port of Menteith, Stirling,
FK8 3JZ
Tel: 01877 385233
★★★ Bed & Breakfast

RHU

Floral Cottage Guest House
Church Road, Rhu, Helensburgh,
G84 8RW
Tel: 01436 820687
★★★ Bed & Breakfast

Timber Cottage
Pier Road, Rhu, by Helensburgh,
Argyll and Bute, G84 8LH
Tel: 01436 820611
★★★ Bed & Breakfast

ROWARDENNAN

Anchorage Cottage
Rowardennan, nr Drymen,
Glasgow, G63 0AW
Tel: 01360 870394
★★★★ Bed & Breakfast

Coorie Doon
5 Forest Cottages,
Rowardennan, Glasgow,
G63 0AW
Tel: 01360 870320
★ Bed & Breakfast

SOUTHEND, BY CAMPBELTOWN

Ormsary Farm
Southend, by Campbeltown,
Argyll, PA28 6RN
Tel: 01856 830665
★★★ Bed & Breakfast

Pennyseorach Farm
Southend, By Campbeltown,
Argyll, PA28 6RF
Tel: 01586 830217
★★ Bed & Breakfast

STIRLING

Alberts
10 Hillfoots Road,
Causewayhead, Stirling,
Stirlingshire, FK9 5LF
Tel: 01786 478728
★★ Bed & Breakfast

Allerton
75 Newhouse, Stirling,
Stirlingshire, FK8 2AF
Tel: 01786 465677
★★★ Bed & Breakfast

Anderson House
8 Melville Terrace, Stirling,
Stirlingshire, FK8 2NE
★★★ Bed & Breakfast

Argyll House
26 Causewayhead Road,
Stirling, Stirlingshire, FK9 5EU
Tel: 01786 478864
★★★ Bed & Breakfast

Ashgrove
2 Park Avenue, Stirling, FK8 2LX
Tel: 01786 472640
★★★★★ Bed & Breakfast

Barn Lodge
Croftside, Pirnhall, Stirling,
Stirlingshire, FK7 8EX
Tel: 01786 813591
★★ Lodge

Barnsdale House
19 Barnsdale Road, St Ninians,
Stirling, FK7 0PT
Tel: 01786 461729
★★★ Bed & Breakfast

Broadford House
Ochtertyre, Stirling, FK9 4UN
Tel: 01786 464674
★★★ Bed & Breakfast

Carseview
16 Ladysneuk Road,
Cambuskenneth, Stirling,
FK9 5NF
Tel: 01786 462235
★★★ Bed & Breakfast

Castlecraig Guest House
50 Causewayhead Road,
Stirling, FK9 5EY
Tel: 01786 475452
★★★ Guest House

Craigard
40 Causewayhead Road,
Stirling, FK9 5EY
Tel: 01786 460540
★★★ Bed & Breakfast

Craigquarter Farm
Stirling, FK7 9QP
Tel: 01786 812668
★★★★ Bed & Breakfast

Mrs Jennifer Dougall
14 Melville Terrace, Stirling,
FK8 2NE
Tel: 01786 475361
★★★ Bed & Breakfast

Drum Farm
Carronbridge, Stirlingshire,
FK6 5JL
Tel: 01324 825518
★★ Bed & Breakfast

Firgrove
13 Clifford Road, Stirling,
Stirlingshire, FK8 2AQ
Tel: 01786 475805
★★★★ Bed & Breakfast

Forth Guest House
23 Forth Place, Riverside,
Stirling, FK8 1UD
Tel: 01786 471020
★★★★ Guest House

10 Gladstone Place
Stirling, Stirlingshire, FK8 2NN
Tel: 01786 472681
★★★★ Bed & Breakfast

9 Glebe Crescent
Stirling, Stirlingshire, FK8 2JB
Tel: 01786 473433
★★★ Bed & Breakfast

Glenardoch House
Castle Road, Doune, Perthshire,
FK16 6EA
Tel: 01786 841489
★★★★ Bed & Breakfast

Heatherdale
2 Dumyat Road, Stirling,
Stirlingshire, FK9 5HA
Tel: 01786 473574
★★★ Bed & Breakfast

Kerrann
110 Causewayhead Road,
Stirling, Stirlingshire, FK9 5HJ
Tel: 01786 462432
★★★ Bed & Breakfast

27 King Street
Stirling, Stirlingshire, FK8 1DN
Tel: 01786 471082
★★ Bed & Breakfast

Laurinda B&B
66 Ochilmount, Ochilview,
Bannockburn, Stirlingshire,
FK7 8PJ
Tel: 01786 815612
★★★ Bed & Breakfast

9 Maitland Crescent
St Ninians, Stirling, Stirlingshire,
FK7 0DN
Tel: 01786 474707
★★★ Bed & Breakfast

Neidpath B&B
24 Linden Avenue, Stirling,
FK7 7PQ
Tel: 01786 469017
★★★ Bed & Breakfast

The Old Tram House
42 Causeway Head Road,
Stirling, Stirlingshire, FK9 5EY
Tel: 01786 449774
★★★ Bed & Breakfast

5 Randolph Terrace
Stirling, FK7 9AA
Tel: 01786 472454
★★★ Bed & Breakfast

Sealladh Ard
Station Brae, Kippen,
Stirlingshire, FK8 3DY
Tel: 01786 870291
★★★★ Bed & Breakfast

Southfield
2 Melville Terrace, Stirling,
Stirlingshire, FK8 2ND
Tel: 01786 464872
★★★ Bed & Breakfast

14 Union Street
Stirling, Stirlingshire, FK8 1NY
Tel: 01786 461186
★★ Bed & Breakfast

West Plean House
Denny Road, Stirling, FK7 8HA
Tel: 01786 812208
★★★★ Bed & Breakfast

BY STIRLING
20 Manse Crescent
Stirling, Stirlingshire, FK7 9AJ
Tel: 01786 463264
★★★ Bed & Breakfast

STRACHUR
Barnacarry
Strathlachlan, Strachur, Argyll,
PA27 8BU
Tel: 01369 860212
★★ Bed & Breakfast

STRATHYRE
Airlie House
Main Street, Strathyre,
Callander, Perthshire, FK18 8NA
Tel: 01877 384247
★★★★ Bed & Breakfast

Ardoch Lodge
Strathyre, Perthshire, FK18 8NF
0877 384666
★★★★ Bed & Breakfast

TARBERT, LOCH FYNE
Ardglass
Garvel Road, Tarbert, Argyll,
PA29 6TR
Tel: 01880 820884
★★★ Bed & Breakfast

Dunivaig
Pier Road, Tarbert, Argyll,
PA29 6UG
Tel: 01880 820896
★★ Bed & Breakfast

Rhu House
Tarbert, Argyll, PA29 6YF
Tel: 01880 820231
★★★ Bed & Breakfast

Springside Bed & Breakfast
Pier Road, Tarbert, Loch Fyne,
Argyll, PA29 6UE
Tel: 01880 820413
★★ Bed & Breakfast

TARBET, BY ARROCHAR
Aye Servus
Tyneloan, Tarbet, Argyll & Bute,
G83 7DD
Tel: 01301 702819
★★★ Bed & Breakfast

33 Ballyhennan Crescent
Tarbet, by Arrochar,
Dunbartonshire, G83 8DA
Tel: 01301 702213
★★ Bed & Breakfast

Ballyhennan Old Toll House
Tarbet, Arrochar,
Dumbartonshire, G83 7DA
Tel: 01301 702203
★★★ Bed & Breakfast

Bon-Etive
Tarbet, by Arrochar,
Dunbartonshire, G83 7DF
Tel: 01301 702219
★★★ Bed & Breakfast

Lochview
Tarbet, by Arrochar,
Dunbartonshire, G83 7DD
Tel: 01301 702200
★★ Bed & Breakfast

Lomondbank House
Old Military Road, Tarbet,
By Arrochar, Argyll, G83 7DG
Tel: 01301 702258
★★★★ Bed & Breakfast

Lomond View
Tarbet, Arrochar, Argyll & Bute,
G83 7DG
Tel: 01301 702477
★★★★ Bed & Breakfast

Standish
3 Bemersyde Road, Tarbet,
Arrochar, G83 7DF
Tel: 01301 702815
★★ Bed & Breakfast

TAYNUILT
Cruailinn
Glenlonan Road, Taynuilt, Argyll,
PA35 1HY
Tel: 01866 822351
★★★ Bed & Breakfast

Gillean Brighde
Kilchrenan, Taynuilt, Argyll,
PA35 1HF
Tel: 01866 833286
★★★ Bed & Breakfast

TAYVALLICH
Little Keills
Tayvallich, Argyll, PA31 8PQ
Tel: 01546 870623
★★★★ Bed & Breakfast

THORNHILL
Easter Tarr Farmhouse
Thornhill, Stirlingshire, FK8 3LD
Tel: 01786 850225
★★★ Bed & Breakfast

The Granary
West Moss-side, Thornhill,
Stirlingshire, FK8 3QJ
Tel: 01786 850310
★★★★ Bed & Breakfast

Netherton Farmhouse
Thornhill, Stirling, Stirlingshire,
FK8 3QQ
Tel: 01786 850370
★★★★ Bed & Breakfast

TIGHNABRUAICH
Kames Hotel
Kames, Tighnabruaich, Argyll,
PA21 2AF
Tel: 01700 811489
★★★ Inn

Springbank
Tighnabruaich, Argyll & Bute,
PA21 2EJ
Tel: 01700 811611
★★★★ Bed & Breakfast

Tighnabruaich Hotel
Tighnabruaich, Argyll, PA21 2DX
Tel: 01700 811615
★★ Inn

TILLICOULTRY

TROSSACHS, BY CALLANDER
Frennich House
Brig O'Turk, Kilmahog,
Callander, Perthshire, FK17 8HT
Tel: 01877 376274
★★★★ Bed & Breakfast

TYNDRUM, BY CRIANLARICH
Glengarry House
Tyndrum, Perthshire, FK20 8RY
Tel: 01838 400224
★★★ Bed & Breakfast

WEST TARBERT
Struan House B&B
Harbour Street, Tarbert, Kintyre,
Argyll, PA29 6UD
Tel: 01880 820190
★★★ Bed & Breakfast

PERTHSHIRE, ANGUS AND DUNDEE AND THE KINGDOM OF FIFE

ABERDOUR
Peartree House
13A Shore Road, Aberdour, Fife,
KY3 0TR
Tel: 01383 860389
★★★ Bed & Breakfast

ABERFELDY

6 The Beeches
Kendore Road, Aberfeldy,
Perthshire, PH15 2BZ
Tel: 01887 829490

Directory of all VisitScotland Quality Assured Serviced Establishments

★★★★ Bed & Breakfast

Cedar House
30a Chapel Street, Aberfeldy,
Perthshire, PH15 2AS
Tel: 01887 820779
★★★ Bed & Breakfast

Coshieville House
Coshieville, by Aberfeldy,
Perthshire, PH15 2NE
Tel: 01887 830319
★★★ Bed & Breakfast

Guinach House
Urlar Road, Aberfeldy,
Perthshire, PH15 2ET
Tel: 01887 820251
★★★★ Bed & Breakfast

Lurgan Farm
Edradynate, Aberfeldy,
Perthshire, PH15 2JX
Tel: 01887 840451
★★ Bed & Breakfast

Mavisbank
Taybridge Drive, Aberfeldy,
Perthshire, PH15 2BP
Tel: 01887 820223
★★★ Bed & Breakfast

2 Rannoch Road
Aberfeldy, Perthshire, PH15 2BU
Tel: 01887 820770
★★★ Bed & Breakfast

Tighnabruaich
Taybridge Terrace, Aberfeldy,
PH15 2BS
Tel: 01887 820456
★★★ Bed & Breakfast

Tigh Na Sgoill
Weem, by Aberfeldy, Perthshire,
PH15 2LD
Tel: 01887 829043
★★★ Bed & Breakfast

Tigh'n Eilean Guest House
Taybridge Drive, Aberfeldy,
Perthshire, PH15 2BP
Tel: 01887 820109
★★★★ Bed & Breakfast

Tomvale
Tom of Cluny, Aberfeldy,
Perthshire, PH15 2JT
Tel: 01887 820171
★★★ Bed & Breakfast

BY ABERFELDY
Ailean Chraggan Hotel
Weem, by Aberfeldy, Perthshire,
PH15 2LD
Tel: 01887 820346
★★★ Inn

Farleyer Restaurant
Near Weem, Aberfeldy,
Perthshire, PH15 2JE
Tel: 01887 820332
★★★★
Restaurant with Rooms

ABERNETHY
Crees Inn
Main Street, Abernethy, Tayside,
PH2 9LA
Tel: 01738 850714
★★★ Inn

Gattaway Farm
Abernethy, Perthshire, PH2 9LQ
Tel: 01738 850746
★★★ Bed & Breakfast

Inverearn
Newburgh Road, Abernethy,
Perth, PH2 9JZ
Tel: 01738 850266
★★★ Bed & Breakfast

BY ABERNETHY
Easter Clunie Farmhouse
Newburgh, Fife, KY14 6EJ
Tel: 01337 840218
★★★ Bed & Breakfast

Glenfoot B&B
Earnview, Glenfoot, by
Abernethy, Perthshire,, PH2 9LS
Tel: 01738 850353
★★★ Bed & Breakfast

ABERUTHVEN
Kilrymont
8 Loanfoot Park, Aberuthven,
Perthshire, PH3 1JF
Tel: 01764 662660
★★★★ Bed & Breakfast

ALYTH
Old Stables
2 Losset Road, Alyth,
Perthshire, PH11 8BT
Tel: 01828 632547
★★★★ Bed & Breakfast

AMULREE
Amulree Country Hotel
Amulree, Dunkeld, Perthshire,
PH8 0EF
★★ Inn

ANSTRUTHER
The Bakehouse & The Granary
18/20 Shore Street, Anstruther,
Fife, KY10 3EA
Tel: 01333 312200
★★★ Restaurant with Rooms

Barnsmuir Farmhouse
Crail, Anstrither, Fife, KY10 3XB
Tel: 01333 450342
★★★ Bed & Breakfast

Beaumont Lodge
43 Pittenweem Road,
Anstruther, Fife, KY10 3DT
Tel: 01333 310315
★★★★ Bed & Breakfast

The Grange
45 Pittenweem Road,
Anstruther, Fife, KY10 3DT
Tel: 01333 310 842
★★★★ Bed & Breakfast

Invermay Cottage
Common Road, Kilrenny,
Anstruther, Fife, KY10 3JQ
Tel: 01333 312314
★★★ Bed & Breakfast

Laggan House
The Cooperage, Anstruther, Fife,
KY10 3AW
Tel: 01333 311170
★★★★ Bed & Breakfast

Mayview House
O'The Lands and Barony
O'Anstruther, Crail Road,
Anstruther, Fife, KY10 3EX
Tel: 0870 740 7826/
0468 945645 (mobile)
Bed & Breakfast

The Sheiling
32 Glenogil Gard, Anstruther,
Fife, KY10 3ET
Tel: 01333 310697
★★★ Bed & Breakfast

The Smugglers Inn
High Street, Anstruther, Fife,
KY10 3DQ
Tel: 01333 310506
★ Inn

Spalefield Lodge
Spalefield, Anstruther, Fife,
KY10 3LB
Tel: 01333 310036
★★★ Bed & Breakfast

The Spindrift
Pittenweem Road, Anstruther,
Fife, KY10 3DT
Tel: 01333 310573
★★★★ Guest House

Troustrie House
Crail, Anstruther, Fife, KY10 3XD
Tel: 01333 450130
★★★★ Bed & Breakfast

Joyce and Tom Watson
8 Melville Terrace, Anstruther,
Fife, KY10 3EW
Tel: 01333 310453
★★★ Bed & Breakfast

ARBROATH
Fairway View B&B
2 Fairway View, Letham Grange,
Arbroath, Tayside, DD11 4XE
Tel: 01241 890762
★★★ Bed & Breakfast

Mrs M Ferguson
20 Hillend Road, Arbroath,
Angus, DD11 2AR
Tel: 01241 873991
★★★ Bed & Breakfast

Glengarry
30 Nolt Loan Road, Arbroath,
Angus, DD11 2AL
Tel: 01241 870825
★★★ Bed & Breakfast

Inishowen Guest House
Dundee Road, Elliot, Arbroath,
DD11 2PE
Tel: 01241 871922
★★★ Bed & Breakfast

The Old Vicarage B & B
2 Seaton Road, Arbroath,
Angus, DD11 5DX
Tel: 01241 430475
★★★★ Bed & Breakfast

BY ARBROATH
Five Gables House
Elliot, by Arbroath, Angus,
DD11 2PE
Tel: 01241 871632
★★★ Bed & Breakfast

AUCHTERARDER

Alma House
Hunter Street, Auchterarder,
Perthshire, PH3 1PA
Tel: 01764 662894
★★★ Bed & Breakfast

Ashford House
59 High Street, Auchterarder,
Perthshire, PH3 1BN
Tel: 01764 663602
★★★ Bed & Breakfast

Craigpark B&B
Townhead Wynd, Auchterarder,
Perthshire, PH3 1JG
Tel: 01764 662564
★★★ Bed & Breakfast

Easterton Farm
Blackford, Auchterarder,
Perthshire, PH4 1RQ
Tel: 01764 682268
★★★ Bed & Breakfast

Greystanes
Western Road, Auchterarder,
Perthshire, PH3 1SS
Tel: 01764 664239
★★★★ Bed & Breakfast

6 High Street
Auchterarder, Perthshire,
PH3 1DF
Tel: 01764 662776
★★ Bed & Breakfast

Lang Toon
101 High Street, Auchterarder,
Perthshire, PH3 1BJ
Tel: 01764 662928
★★ Bed & Breakfast

Nether Coul
Auchterarder, Perthshire,
PH3 1ET
Tel: 01764 663119
★★★ Bed & Breakfast

The Parsonage Guest House
111 High Street, Auchterarder,
Perthshire, PH3 1AA
Tel: 01764 662392
★★★ Bed & Breakfast

Praslin
7 Abbey Park, Auchterarder,
Perthshire, PH3 1EN
Tel: 01764 660702
★★★ Bed & Breakfast

The Rowans
Ruthven Street, Auchterarder,
Perthshire, PH3 1BX
Tel: 01764 664577
★★★ Bed & Breakfast

Thistledhu
39 Townhead, Auchterarder,
Perthshire, PH3 1JG
Tel: 01764 622154
★★ Bed & Breakfast

BY AUCHTERARDER

Craiginver
1 Main Road,
Aberuthven,Auchterarder,
Perthshire, PH3 1HE
Tel: 01764 662411
★★★ Bed & Breakfast

Smiddy Haugh Hotel
Main Road, Aberuthven,
Perthshire, PH3 1HE
Tel: 01764 662013
★★ Inn

BALLINLUIG, BY PITLOCHRY

Ballinluig Inn
Ballinluig, By Pitlochry,
Perthshire, PH9 OLG
Tel: 01796 482242
★★ Inn

BALMULLO

Innemore Lodge
Pennyghael, Isle of Mull, Argyll,
PA70 6HD
Tel: 01681 704201
★ Bed & Breakfast

BANKFOOT

Forest Lodge
Forestry Place, Bankfoot,
Perthshire, PH1 4BN
Tel: 01738 787150
★★★ Bed & Breakfast

Kayrene
Cairneyhill Road, Bankfoot,
Perth, PH1 4AD
Tel: 01738 787338
★★★ Bed & Breakfast

BIRNAM, BY DUNKELD

Birnam Bank Cottage
Birnam Glen, Birnam, Dunkeld,
PH8 0BW
Tel: 01350 727628
★★ Bed & Breakfast

Birnam Wood House
Perth Road, Birnam by Dunkeld,
Perthshire, PH8 0BH
Tel: 01350 727782
★★★★ Guest House

BLAIR ATHOLL

The Firs
St Andrews Crescent, Blair
Atholl, by Pitlochry, PH18 5TA
Tel: 01796 481256
★★★ Guest House

Ptarmigan House
The Terrace, Blair Atholl,
Perthshire, PH18 5SZ
Tel: 01796 481269
★★★ Guest House

BLAIRGOWRIE

Drumellie Meadow
Wester Essendy, Blairgowrie,
Perthshire, PH10 6RD
Tel: 01250 884282
★★★★ Bed & Breakfast

EILDON BANK
118 Perth Road, Blairgowrie,
Perthshire, PH10 6ED
Tel: 01250 873648
★★★ Bed & Breakfast

Garfield House B&B
Perth Road, Blairgowrie,
Perthshire, PH10 6ED
Tel: 01250 872999
★★★ Bed & Breakfast

Gilmore House
Perth Road, Blairgowrie,
Perthshire, PH10 6EJ
Tel: 01250 872791
★★★★ Bed & Breakfast

Glenkilrie Bed and Breakfast
Blacklunans, Blairgowrie,
Perthshire, PH10 7LR
Tel: 01250 882241
★★★ Bed & Breakfast

Glenvar
High Street, Rattray,
Blairgowrie, PH10 7DG
Tel: 01250 875232
★★★ Bed & Breakfast

Heathpark House
Coupar Angus Road,
Blairgowrie, Perthshire,
PH10 6JT
Tel: 01250 870700
★★★★ Bed & Breakfast

Heathpark Lodge
Coupar Angus Road,
Blairgowrie, Perthshire,
PH10 6JT
Tel: 01250 874929
★★★ Bed & Breakfast

Holmrigg Bed & Breakfast
Wester Essendy, Blairgowrie,
Perthshire, PH10 6RD
Tel: 01250 884309
★★★ Bed & Breakfast

Ivybank Guest House
Boat Brae, Blairgowrie,
Perthshire, PH10 7BH
Tel: 01250 873056
★★★★ Guest House

The Laurels
Golf Course Road, Blairgowrie,
Perthshire, PH10 6LH
Tel: 01250 874920
★★★ Guest House

Royal Hotel
53 Allan Street, Blairgowrie,
Perthshire, PH10 6AB
Tel: 01250 872226
Awaiting Inspection

Shocarjen House
Balmoral Road, Blairgowrie,
Perthshire, PH10 7AF
Tel: 01250 870525
★★★★ Bed & Breakfast

BY BLAIRGOWRIE

Alcantara
Bamff View, New Alyth,
Blairgowrie, Perthshire,
PH11 8NG
Tel: 01828 633304
★★★ Bed & Breakfast

Bankhead Bed & Breakfast
Clunie, Blairgowrie, Perthshire,
PH10 6SG
Tel: 01250 884281
★★★ Bed & Breakfast

Lunanbrae
Wester Essendy, by Blairgowrie, Perthshire,, PH10 6RA
Tel: 01250 884224
★★★★ Bed & Breakfast

Ridgeway B&B
Wester Essendy, by Blairgowrie, Perthshire, PH10 6RA
Tel: 01250 884734
★★★ Bed & Breakfast

BLEBO CRAIGS
Upper Hillside
Blebo Craigs, by St Andrews, Fife, KY15 5UG
Tel: 01334 850252
★★★★ Bed & Breakfast

BRECHIN
Blibberhill Farmhouse
Blibberhill Farm, by Brechin, Angus, DD9 6TH
Tel: 01307 830323
★★★ Bed & Breakfast

Doniford
26 Airlie Street, Brechin, Angus, DD9 6JX
Tel: 01356 622361
★★★ Bed & Breakfast

Liscara
3A Castle Street, Brechin, Angus, DD9 6JW
Tel: 01356 625584
★★★★ Bed & Breakfast

BRECHIN BY
Brathinch Farm
by Brechin, Angus, DD9 7QZ
Tel: 01356 648292
★★★ Bed & Breakfast

BRIDGEND OF LINTRATHEN, BY KIRRIEMUIR
Lochside Lodge & Roundhouse Restaurant
Bridgend of Lintrathen, Kirriemuir, Angus, DD8 5JJ
Tel: 01575 560340
★★★★
Restaurant with Rooms

BRIDGE OF CALLY
Blackcraig Castle
Bridge of Cally, Perthshire, PH10 7PX
Tel: 01250 886251
★ Bed & Breakfast

Bridge of Cally Hotel
Bridge of Cally, Perthshire, PH10 7JJ
Tel: 01250 886231
★★★ Inn

Glen Albyn
Bridge of Cally, Perthshire, PH10 7JL
Tel: 01250 886352
★★★ Bed & Breakfast

BROUGHTY FERRY
Invergarth
79 Camphill Road, Broughty Ferry, Dundee, Tayside, DD5 2NA
Tel: 01382 736278
★★★ Bed & Breakfast

BURNTISLAND
The Beach House
Lochies Road, Burntisland, Fife, KY3 9JX
Tel: 01592 872 020
★★★ Bed & Breakfast

Gruinard
148 Kinghorn Road, Burntisland, Fife, KY3 9JU
Tel: 01592 873877
★★★★ Bed & Breakfast

Hersham Rhu B & B
48 Kirkcaldy Road, Burntisland, Fife, KY3 9EY
Tel: 01592 873329
★★★ Bed & Breakfast

CALVINE
The Struan Inn
Calvine, Perthshire, PH18 5UB
Tel: 01796 483208
★★ Inn

CARNOUSTIE
Airlie Bank
26 William Street, Carnoustie, Angus, DD7 6BW
Tel: 01241 859741
★★★ Bed & Breakfast

Lismore
21 Links Parade, Carnoustie, Angus, DD7 7JF
Tel: 01241 852378
★★★ Bed & Breakfast

Lum Cottage
43 Queen Street, Carnoustie, Angus, DD7 7AX
Tel: 01241 854245
★★★ Bed & Breakfast

Morven House
28 West Path, Carnoustie, Angus, DD7 7SN
Tel: 01241 852385
★★★★ Bed & Breakfast

The Old Manor
Panbride, Carnoustie, DD7 6JP
Tel: 01241 854804
★★★★ Bed & Breakfast

Park House
12 Park Avenue, Carnoustie, Angus, DD7 7JA
Tel: 01241 852101
★★★★ Bed & Breakfast

Roseneath
14 Church Street, Carnoustie, Angus, DD7 6DE
Tel: 01241 854872
★★★ Bed & Breakfast

CELLARDYKE, BY ANSTRUTHER
Kilrenny Mill Farmhouse
Cellardyke, Fife, KY10 3JW
Tel: 01333 311272
★★★★ Bed & Breakfast

CERES
Meldrums Hotel
56 Main Street, Ceres, Fife, KY15 5NA
Tel: 01334 828286
★★★ Inn

COALTOWN OF WEMYSS
Law View B&B
68 Millburn Avenue, Coaltown of Balgonie, Fife, KY7 6HR
Tel: 01592 774197
★★★ Bed & Breakfast

COLLINSBURGH
The Balcarres Arms Hotel
59 Main Street, Collinsburgh, Fife, KY9 1LS
Tel: 01333 340600
★★ Inn

COMRIE
Drumearn Cottage
The Ross, Comrie, Perthshire, PH6 2JU
Tel: 01764 670030
★★★★ Bed & Breakfast

Drummonie
Dalginross, Comrie, Perthshire, PH6 2HE
Tel: 01764 670271
★★★★ Bed & Breakfast

St Margaret's
Braco Road, Comrie, Perthshire, PH6 2HP
Tel: 01764 670413
★★★ Bed & Breakfast

CRAIL
Caiplie House
53 High Street, Crail, Fife, KY10 3RA
Tel: 01333 450564
★★★ Guest House

East Neuk Hotel
67 High Street, Crail, Fife, KY10 3RA
Tel: 01333 450 225
★★ Inn

The Honeypot Guest House & Tearoom
6 High Street South, Crail, Fife, KY10 3TD
Tel: 01333 450935
★★★ Guest House

Woodlands B&B
Balcomie Road, Crail, Fife, KY10 3TN
Tel: 01333 450147
★★ Bed & Breakfast

CRIEFF
The Carrick B & B
57 Burrell Street, Crieff, Perthshire,, PH7 4GD
Tel: 01764 656595
★★★ Bed & Breakfast

Concraig Farm
Crieff, Perthshire, PH7 4HH
Tel: 01764 653237
★★★ Bed & Breakfast

Galvelbeg House
Perth Road, Crieff, Perthshire,
PH7 3EQ
Tel: 01764 655061
★★★ Guest House

Galvelmore House
Galvelmore Street, Crieff,
Perthshire, PH7 4BY
Tel: 01764 655721
★★★ Bed & Breakfast

Glencairn B&B
Broich Terrace, Crieff,
Perthshire, PH7 3BD
Tel: 01764 655700
★★★ Bed & Breakfast

Kingarth
Perth Road, Crieff, Perthshire,
PH7 3EQ
Tel: 01764 652060
★★★ Guest House

Leven House Hotel
Comrie Road, Crieff, PH7 4BA
Tel: 01764 652529
★★ Small Hotel

Meadow Inn Hotel
38 Burrell Street, Crieff,
Perthshire, PH7 4DT
Tel: 01764 653261
★★ Inn

Merindale B&B
Perth Road, Crieff, Perthshire,
PH7 3EQ
Tel: 01764 655205
★★★★ Bed & Breakfast

Number 5
5 Duchlage Terrace, Crieff,
Perthshire, PH7 3AB
Tel: 01764 653516
★★★ Bed & Breakfast

The Rowans
New Fowlis, Crieff, Perthshire,
PH7 3NH
Tel: 01764 683720
★★★★ Bed & Breakfast

Somerton House
Turret Bank, Crieff, Perthshire,
PH7 4JN
Tel: 01764 652222
★★★ Bed & Breakfast

Tuchethill House
Dollerie, Crieff, Perthshire,
PH7 3NX
Tel: 01764 653188
★★★★ Bed & Breakfast

BY CRIEFF
Foulford Inn
Sma'Glen, by Crieff, Perthshire,
PH7 3LN
Tel: 01764 652407
★★ Inn

CUPAR
Anvil Cottage B&B
Radernie, By St Andrews, Fife,
KY15 5LN
Tel: 01334 840824
★★★★ Bed & Breakfast

Arisaig
Westfield Road, Cupar, Fife,
KY15 5AR
Tel: 01334 654529
★★★ Bed & Breakfast

Balderie of Carpow
Newburgh, Cupar, Fife,
KY14 6EN
Tel: 01738 850760
★★★★ Bed & Breakfast

Craigsview
3 Cairngreen, By Cupar, Fife,
KY15 5SY
Tel: 01334 657871
★★★ Bed & Breakfast

Fairway
Blebo Craigs, Cupar, Fife,
KY15 5UF
Tel: 01334 850371
★★★★ Bed & Breakfast

Mansfield
52 South Road, Cupar, Fife,
KY15 5JF
Tel: 01334 655120
★★★★ Bed & Breakfast

Osnaburgh
84 Main Street, Dairsie, Fife,
KY15 4SS
Tel: 01334 870603
★★★ Bed & Breakfast

The Shieling
4 East Road, Cupar, Fife,
KY15 4HQ
Tel: 01334 653268
★★★ Bed & Breakfast

Westfield House
Westfield Road, Cupar, Fife,
KY15 5TD
Tel: 01334 655699
★★★★★ Bed & Breakfast

BY CUPAR
The Peat Inn
By Cupar, Fife, KY15 5LH
Tel: 01334 840206
★★★★★
Restaurant with Rooms

DALGETY BAY
11 The Beeches
Dalgety Bay, Fife, KY11 9SN
Tel: 01383 822167
★★★★ Bed & Breakfast

The Coach House
1 Hopeward Mews, Dalgety Bay,
Fife, KY11 9TB
Tel: 01383 823584
★★★★ Bed & Breakfast

DUNDEE
Anlast Three Chimneys House
379 Arbroath Road, Dundee,
DD4 7SQ
Tel: 01382 456710
★★★ Bed & Breakfast

Ardmoy B&B
359 Arbroath Road, Dundee,
Angus, DD4 7SQ
Tel: 01382 453249
★★★ Bed & Breakfast

Ashvilla
216 Arbroath Road, Dundee,
Angus, DD4 7RZ
Tel: 01382 450831
★★★ Bed & Breakfast

Auchenean
177 Hamilton Street, Broughty
Ferry, Dundee, DD5 2RE
Tel: 01382 774782
★★★★ Bed & Breakfast

Balmuirfield House
Harestane Road, Dundee,
DD3 0NU
Tel: 01382 818444
★★★★ Bed & Breakfast

Brook House
86 Brook Street, Broughty Ferry,
Dundee, Tayside, DD5 1DQ
Tel: 01382 779166
★★★ Bed & Breakfast

Days Inn Dundee
296a Strathmore Avenue,
Dundee, DD3 6SP
Tel: 01382 826000
★★ Lodge

Errolbank Guest House
9 Dalgleish Road, Dundee,
Angus, DD4 7JN
Tel: 01382 462118
★★★ Guest House

Howies Restaurant
25 South Tay Street, Dundee,
DD1 3NR
Tel: 01382 200399
★★★ Restaurant with Rooms

Main Wing
Duntrune House, Duntrune,
Dundee, DD4 0PJ
Tel: 01382 350 239
★★★★ Bed & Breakfast

Nelson Guest House
8 Nelson Terrace, Dundee,
Angus, DD1 2PR
Tel: 01382 225354
★★★ Bed & Breakfast

West Park Centre
319 Perth Road, Dundee, Angus,
DD2 1NN
Tel: 01382 647177
★★★ Campus

BY DUNDEE
Viewlands
West Adamston, Muirhead,
Angus, DD2 5QX
Tel: 01382 580822
★★★ Bed & Breakfast

Directory of all VisitScotland Quality Assured Serviced Establishments

DUNFERMLINE

Bell House
23 Maitland Street,
Dunfermline, Fife, KY12 8HE
Tel: 01383 723701
★★★ Bed & Breakfast

Cameron House
4 Scobie Place, Dunfermline,
Fife, KY12 7RX
Tel: 01383 726540
★★ Bed & Breakfast

Carneil Farm
Carnock, Dunfermline, Fife,
KY12 9JJ
Tel: 01383 850285
★★★★ Bed & Breakfast

Hillview House
9 Aberdour Road, Dunfermline,
Fife, KY11 4PB
Tel: 01383 726278
★★★ Bed & Breakfast

Hopetoun Lodge
141 Halbeath Road,
Dunfermline, Fife, KY11 4LA
Tel: 01383 620906
★★★ Bed & Breakfast

The Learig
2A Victoria Street, Dunfermline,
Fife, KY12 0LW
Tel: 01383 729676
★★ Bed & Breakfast

Pitcairn House
82A Halbeath Road,
Dunfermline, Fife, KY12 7RS
Tel: 01383 732901
★★★ Bed & Breakfast

Roscobie Farmhouse B&B
Roscobie Farm, Dunfermline,
Fife, KY12 0SG
Tel: 01383 731571
★★★ Bed & Breakfast

**Scotland Peace Haven
Bed and Breakfast**
1 Bannoch Brae, Dunfermline,
Fife, KY12 7YF
Tel: 01383 726557
★★ Bed & Breakfast

Squirrel Lane Cottage
105 St Margaret Street,
Dunfermline, Fife, KY12 7PH
Tel: 01383 720522
★★★ Bed & Breakfast

BY DUNFERMLINE

Lochfitty Cottage
Lassodie, Kingseat,
Dunfermline, KY12 0SP
Tel: 01383 831081
★★ Bed & Breakfast

DUNKELD

The Bridge Bed & Breakfast
10 Bridge Street, Dunkeld,
Perthshire, PH8 0AH
Tel: 01350 727068
★★★★ Bed & Breakfast

Byways
Perth Road, Birnam,by Dunkeld,
Perthshire, PH8 0DH
Tel: 01350 727542
★★★ Bed & Breakfast

Hatton Grange
Lower Hatton, Dunkeld,
Perthshire, PH8 0ET
Tel: 01350 727137
★★★ Bed & Breakfast

The Pend
5 Brae Street, Dunkeld,
Perthshire, PH8 0BA
Tel: 01350 727586
★★★★ Bed & Breakfast

Tayburn House
Perth Road, Birnam,by Dunkeld,
Perthshire, PH8 0BQ
Tel: 01350 728822
★★★ Bed & Breakfast

Upper Hatton
Dunkeld, Perthshire, PH8 0ER
7762276693
★★★ Bed & Breakfast

DUNKELD BY

Letter Farm
Loch of the Lowes, Dunkeld,
Perthshire, PH8 0HH
Tel: 01350 724254
★★★★ Bed & Breakfast

DUNNING

Westburn House
Whitemoss Road, by Dunning,
Perthshire, PH2 0QY
Tel: 01738 730427
★★★★ Bed & Breakfast

EDZELL

Alexandra Lodge
Inveriscandye Road, Edzell,
Angus, DD9 7TN
Tel: 01356 648266
★★★ Bed & Breakfast

Doune Guest House
24 High Street, Edzell, Brechin,
Angus, DD9 7TA
Tel: 01356 648201
★★★ Bed & Breakfast

Kelvingrove
Dunlappie Road, Edzell, Angus,
DD9 7UB
Tel: 01356 648316
★★★ Bed & Breakfast

Kinnaber
Ramsay Street, Edzell, Angus,
DD9 7TT
Tel: 01356 648051
★★★★ Bed & Breakfast

Negara Bed & Breakfast
35 High Street, Edzell, Angus,
DD9 7TA
Tel: 01356 647463
★★★ Bed & Breakfast

North Esk Lodge
18A High Street, Edzell, Angus,
DD9 7TA
Tel: 01356 647409
★★★ Bed & Breakfast

FALKLAND

Covenanter Hotel
Falkland, Fife, KY7 7BU
Tel: 01337 857542/857224
★★ Inn

Ladywell House
Falkland, Fife, KY15 7DE
Tel: 01337 858414
★★★★ Bed & Breakfast

FEARNAN, BY KENMORE

Culdees
Boreland Farm, Fearnan,
Perthshire, PH15 2PG
Tel: 01887 830519
★★ Bed & Breakfast

FINAVON, BY FORFAR

Finavon Hotel
Finavon, by Forfar, Angus,
DD8 3QE
Tel: 01307 850267
★★★ Restaurant with Rooms

FORFAR

Alton Bed and Breakfast
18 Wyllie Street, Forfar, Angus,
DD8 3DN
Tel: 01307 465193
★★★ Bed & Breakfast

Atholl Cottage B&B
2 Robertson Terrace, Forfar,
Angus, DD8 3JN
Tel: 01307 465755
★★★ Bed & Breakfast

34 Canmore Street
Forfar, Angus, DD8 3HT
Tel: 01307 468285
★★★ Bed & Breakfast

Farmhouse Bed & Breakfast
West Mains of Turin, Forfar,
Angus, DD8 2TE
Tel: 01307 830229
★★★ Bed & Breakfast

Kalulu House
East Murthill, Tannadice, Forfar,
Angus, DD8 3SF
Tel: 01307 860205
★★★ Bed & Breakfast

Whinney-Knowe
8 Dundee Street, Letham,
Angus, DD8 2PQ
Tel: 01307 818288
★★★ Bed & Breakfast

BY FORFAR

Glencoul House
Justinhaugh,by Forfar, Angus,
DD8 3SF
Tel: 01307 860248
★★★ Bed & Breakfast

FORGANDENNY

Battledown Bed & Breakfast
Off Station Road, Forgandenny,
Perthshire, PH2 9EL
Tel: 01738 812471
★★★★ Bed & Breakfast

Craighall Farm
Forgandenny, Bridge of Earn,
Perthshire, PH2 9DF
Tel: 01738 812415
★★★ Bed & Breakfast

FORTINGALL
Kinnighallen Farm
Fortingall, Aberfeldy, Perthshire,
PH15 2LR
Tel: 01887 830619
★★ Bed & Breakfast

GLAMIS
Arndean
Linross, Glamis, Angus,
DD8 1QN
Tel: 01307 840535
★★★ Bed & Breakfast

Hatton of Ogilvy
Glamis, by Forfar, Angus,
DD8 1UH
Tel: 01307 840229
★★★★ Bed & Breakfast

GLENFARG
The Famous Bein Inn
Glenfarg, Perthshire, PH2 9PY
Tel: 01577 830216
★★ Inn

GLENLYON
Milton Lodge
Milton Eonan, Bridge of Balgie,
Glenlyon, Perthshire, PH15 2PT
Tel: 01887 866332
★★★ Bed & Breakfast

GLENROTHES
The Priory
East End, Star of Markinch,
By Glenrothes, Fife, KY7 6LQ
Tel: 01592 754 566
★★★★ Bed & Breakfast

GLENSHEE
Dalhenzean Lodge
Glenshee, Blairgowrie,
Perthshire, PH10 7QD
Tel: 01250 885217
★★★★ Bed & Breakfast

GRANDTULLY, PITLOCHRY
Oakbank House
Grandtully, by Aberfeldy,
Perthshire, PH15 2QZ
Tel: 01887 840265
★★★ Bed & Breakfast

**GUARDBRIDGE,
BY ST ANDREWS**
The Larches
7 River Terrace, Guardbridge,
Fife, KY16 0XA
Tel: 01334 838008
★★★★ Bed & Breakfast

GUILDTOWN, BY PERTH
The Millhouse
Newmiln, by Guildtown,
Perthshire, PH2 6AE
Tel: 01738 553248
★★★ Bed & Breakfast

Oakwood House
Myreside, Guildtown, Perth,
PH2 6DW
Tel: 01821 650800
★★★★ Bed & Breakfast

INVERKEILOR, BY ARBROATH
Ethie Castle
Inverkeilor, By Arbroath, Angus,
DD11 5SP
Tel: 01241 830434
★★★★ Bed & Breakfast

**Gordon's
Restaurant With Rooms**
Gordon's Restaurant, Main
Street, Inverkeilor, by Arbroath,
Angus, DD11 5RN
Tel: 01241 830364
★★★★
Restaurant with Rooms

INVERKEITHING
Elendil
10 Muckle Hill Park,
Inverkeithing, Fife, KY11 1BX
Tel: 01383 411367
★★★ Bed & Breakfast

The Roods Guest House
16 Bannerman Avenue,
Inverkeithing, Fife, KY11 1NG
Tel: 01383 415049
★★★ Bed & Breakfast

BY KENMORE
Ben Lawers Hotel
Lawers, Loch Tay, Perthshire,
PH15 2PA
Tel: 01567 820436
★★ Inn

KILRENNY, BY ANSTRUTHER
Calvine Cottage
Trade Street, Kilrenny,
Anstruther, Fife, KY10 3JG
Tel: 01333 311452
★★★ Bed & Breakfast

KINGSBARNS
Cambo House
Kingsbarns, St Andrews, Fife,
KY16 8QD
Tel: 01333 450313
★★★★ Bed & Breakfast

Kingsbarns Bed & Breakfast
3 Main Street, Kingsbarns, Fife,
KY16 8SL
Tel: 01334 880234
★★★ Bed & Breakfast

KINLOCH RANNOCH
The Gardens
Dunalastair, Kinloch Rannoch,
Perthshire, PH16 5PB
Tel: 01882 632434
★★★ Bed & Breakfast

KINROSS
Burnbank
79 Muirs, Kinross, Perthshire,
KY13 8AZ
Tel: 01577 861931
★★★★ Bed & Breakfast

The Grange
Scotlandwell, Kinross,
Kinross-shire, KY13 9JE
Tel: 01592 840220
★★★ Bed & Breakfast

Mawcarse House
Mawcarse Farm, Milnathort,
Kinross-shire, KY13 9SJ
Tel: 01577 862220
★★★★ Bed & Breakfast

St Serf's
35 The Muirs, Kinross,
Kinross-shire, KY13 8AS
Tel: 01577 862183
★★★ Bed & Breakfast

KIRKCALDY
A Haven Bed & Breakfast
288 High Street, Kirkcaldy, Fife,
KY1 1LB
Tel: 01592 267779
★★★★ Bed & Breakfast

Annies'Lan
36 Bennochy Road, Kirkcaldy,
Fife, KY2 5RB
Tel: 01592 262231
★★★ Bed & Breakfast

Cherrydene
44 Bennnochy Road, Kirkcaldy,
Fife, KY2 5RB
Tel: 01592 202147
★★★ Bed & Breakfast

Hollytree B&B
McIntosh Gardens, Kirkcaldy,
Fife, KY2 6RE
Tel: 01592 260026
★★★ Bed & Breakfast

H'uilie Beannachd
42 East Quality Street, Dysart,
Kirkcaldy, Fife, KY1 2TN
Tel: 01592 655455
★★ Bed & Breakfast

Invertiel B&B
19 Bennochy Road, Kirkcaldy,
Fife, KY2 5QJ
Tel: 01592 264849
★★★ Bed & Breakfast

North Hall
143 Victoria Road, Kirkcaldy,
KY1 1DQ
Tel: 01592 268864
★★★★ Bed & Breakfast

Scotties B&B
213 Nicol Street, Kirkcaldy, Fife,
KY1 1PF
Tel: 01592 268596
★★★ Bed & Breakfast

White Gates
91 Normand Road, Dysart, Fife,
KY1 2XR
Tel: 01592 655321
★★★ Bed & Breakfast

KIRKMICHAEL
Cruachan
Kirkmichael, Perthshire,
PH10 7NZ
Tel: 01250 881226
★★★★ Bed & Breakfast

KIRRIEMUIR

Beechie House
94 Glamis Road, Kirriemuir,
Angus, DD8 5DF
Tel: 01575 575227
★★★ Bed & Breakfast

Crepto
1 Kinnordy Place, Kirriemuir,
Angus, DD8 4JW
Tel: 01575 572746
★★ Bed & Breakfast

Falls of Holm
Lower Welton Farm,
By Kirriemuir, Angus, DD8 5HY
Tel: 01575 575867
★★★★ Bed & Breakfast

Muirhouses Farm
Cortachy, Kirriemuir, Angus,
DD8 4QG
Tel: 01575 573128
★★★★ Bed & Breakfast

Purgavie Farm
Lintrathen, by Kirriemuir, Angus,
DD8 5HZ
Tel: 01575 560213
★★★★ Bed & Breakfast

Strathisla
24 Court Hillock Gardens,
Kirriemuir, Angus, DD8 4JZ
Tel: 01575 572267
★★★ Bed & Breakfast

LESLIE

Greenhead of Arnot
Leslie, Glen Rothes, Fife,
KY6 3JQ
Tel: 01592 840459
★★★★ Bed & Breakfast

Teal Cottage B&B
1 Strathenry Farm, By Leslie,
Fife, KY6 3HY
Tel: 01592 621539
★★★ Bed & Breakfast

LETHAM

Woodville B&B
Heathercroft, Guthrie Street,
Letham, by Forfar, Angus,
DD8 2PS
Tel: 01307 818090
★★★ Bed & Breakfast

LEUCHARS

The White House
Leuchars Lodge, Leuchars, Fife,
KY16 0EY
Tel: 01334 838227
★★★★ Bed & Breakfast

BY LEUCHARS

Green Acres Lodge
Fordelhill, St Michaels,
by St Andrews, Fife, KY16 0BT
Tel: 01334 834985
★★★ Bed & Breakfast

St Michaels Inn
St Michaels, Leuchars,
by St Andrews, Fife, KY16 0DU
Tel: 01334 839220
★★★ Inn

Vicarsford Lodge
St Michaels, St Andrews, Fife,
KY16 0DT
Tel: 01334 834356
★★★ Bed & Breakfast

LEVEN

The Hamptons
6 Church Road, Leven, Fife,
KY8 4JE
Tel: 01333 300930
★★★★ Bed & Breakfast

Lorne House
Largo Road, Leven, Fife,
KY8 4TB
Tel: 01333 423255
★★★★ Bed & Breakfast

NR LOCH LEVEN

Navitie Guest House
nr Loch Leven, by Ballingry,
Lochgelly, Fife, KY5 8LR
Tel: 01592 860295
★★ Guest House

LUNDIN LINKS

Sandilands B&B
20 Leven Road, Lundin Links,
Leven, Fife, KY8 6AH
Tel: 01333 329881
★★★★ Bed & Breakfast

MARKINCH

Beechcroft Guesthouse
Balbirnie Street, Markinch, Fife,
KY7 6DA
Tel: 01592 611232
★★★★ Bed & Breakfast

Cruach Bed & Breakfast
Stobcross Road, Markinch, Fife,
KY7 6ED
Tel: 01592 751093
★★★ Bed & Breakfast

Gamekeeper's Cottage
Balbirnie Park, Markinch, Fife,
KY7 6NR
Tel: 01592 612742
★★★ Bed & Breakfast

Morven
Victoria Road, Markinch, Fife,
KY7 6AE
Tel: 01592 755692
★★★★ Bed & Breakfast

Smythrum Farm
Markinch, Fife, KY7 6HB
Tel: 01592 758372
★★★ Bed & Breakfast

Town House Hotel
1 High Street, Markinch, Fife,
KY7 6DQ
Tel: 01592 758459
★★★ Restaurant with Rooms

MONIFIETH, BY DUNDEE

Ashlea Manor Guest House
2 Victoria Street, Monifieth,
Dundee, DD5 4HP
Tel: 01382 530015
★★★★ Bed & Breakfast

MONTROSE

Best Western Links Hotel
Midlinks, Montrose, Angus,
DD10 8RL
Tel: 01674 671000
★★★★ Hotel

Fairfield
24 The Mall, Montrose, Angus,
DD10 8NW
Tel: 01674 676386
★★★ Bed & Breakfast

Lunan Lodge
Lunan, by Montrose, Angus,
DD10 9TG
Tel: 01241 830679
★★ Bed & Breakfast

36 The Mall
Montrose, Angus, DD10 8SS
Tel: 01674 673646
★★★★ Bed & Breakfast

Oaklands Guest House
10 Rossie Island Road,
Montrose, DD10 9NN
Tel: 01674 672018
★★★ Guest House

MUTHILL

Muthill Village Hotel
Willoughby Street, Muthill,
by Crieff, Perthshire, PH5 2AB
Tel: 01764 681451
★★★ Inn

NEWBURGH

Abbey Inn
High Street, Newburgh, Fife,
KY14 6EZ
Tel: 01337 840761
★★ Inn

NEWPORT-ON-TAY

Braemore
109b Tay Street, Newport-on-
Tay, Fife, DD6 8AR
Tel: 01382 542516
★★★★ Bed & Breakfast

NORTH QUEENSFERRY

Battery House
3 East Bay, North Queensferry,
Fife, KY11 1JX
07905 584089
★★★ Bed & Breakfast

PERTH

Achnacarry Guest House
3 Pitcullen Crescent, Perth,
PH2 7HT
Tel: 01738 621421
★★★★ Guest House

Ackinnoull Guest House
5 Pitcullen Crescent, Perth,
PH2 7HT
Tel: 01738 634165
★★★★ Guest House

Directory of all VisitScotland Quality Assured Serviced Establishments

Albert Villa Guest House
63 Dunkeld Road, Perth,
PH1 5RP
Tel: 01738 622730
★★★ Guest House

Arisaig Guest House
4 Pitcullen Crescent, Perth,
PH2 7HT
Tel: 01738 628240
★★★★ Guest House

Ballabeg Guest House
14 Keir Street, Bridgend,
Perthshire, PH2 7HJ
Tel: 01738 620434
★★★ Bed & Breakfast

Beeches Guest House
2 Comely Bank, Perth, PH2 7HU
Tel: 01738 624486
★★★ Bed & Breakfast

Beechgrove Guest House
Dundee Road, Perth, PH2 7AQ
Tel: 01738 636147
★★★★ Guest House

Cherrybank B&B
217 Glasgow Road, Perth,
Perthshire, PH2 0NB
Tel: 01738 451982
★★★★ Bed & Breakfast

Clunie Guest House
12 Pitcullen Crescent, Perth,
PH2 7HT
Tel: 01738 623625
★★★ Guest House

Comely Bank Cottage
19 Pitcullen Crescent, Perth,
PH2 7HT
Tel: 01738 631118
★★★ Bed & Breakfast

Dalvey
55 Dunkeld Road, Perth,
Perthshire, PH1 5RP
Tel: 01738 621714
★★★★ Bed & Breakfast

Express by Holiday Inn
200 Dunkeld Road,
Inveralmond, Perth, Perthshire,
PH1 3AQ
Tel: 01738 636666
★★★ Lodge

The Gables
24-26 Dunkeld Road, Perth,
PH1 5RW
Tel: 01738 624717
★★★ Guest House

Glendale Cottage
Drum, Perthshire, KY13 0PR
Tel: 01577 840664
★★★ Bed & Breakfast

Harbour Restaurant
Shore Road, Perth, Perthshire,
PH2 8BD
Tel: 01738 625788
★★ Lodge

Howards Inn & Restaurant
Marshall Way, Luncarty, Perth,
PH1 3UX
Tel: 01738 827777
★★★★
Restaurant with Rooms

Marshall House
6 Marshall Place, Perth,
PH2 8AH
0738 442886
★★★ Bed & Breakfast

Northlees Farm
Kingfauns, Perth, Perthshire,
PH2 7LJ
Tel: 01738 860852
★★ Bed & Breakfast

Over Kinfauns
Kinfauns, Perth, Perthshire,
PH2 7LD
Tel: 01738 860538
★★★★ Bed & Breakfast

Perth Airport Skylodge
Norwell Drive, Perth Airport,
Scone, Perthshire, PH2 6PL
Tel: 01738 555700
★★★ Lodge

Petra's B & B
4 Albany Terrace, Perth,
Perthshire, PH1 2BD
Tel: 01738 563050
★★★ Bed & Breakfast

Pitcullen Guest House
17 Pitcullen Crescent, Perth,
PH2 7HT
Tel: 01738 626506
★★★ Guest House

Rhodes Villa
75 Dunkeld Road, Perth,
Perthshire, PH1 5RP
Tel: 01738 628466
★★★ Bed & Breakfast

Taythorpe Guest House
Isla Road, Perth, Perthshire,
PH2 7HQ
Tel: 01738 447994
★★★★ Bed & Breakfast

Westview Bed & Breakfast
49 Dunkeld Road, Perth,
PH1 5RP
Tel: 01738 627787
★★★★ Bed & Breakfast

BY PERTH
Angler Inn
Main Road, Guildtown, Perth,
Perthshire, PH2 6BS
Tel: 01738 640329
★★★ Inn

The Bield
Pitcairngreen, Perth, Perthshire,
PH1 3LT
Tel: 01738 583606
★★★ Bed & Breakfast

Blackcraigs Farm
Balbeggie, by Perth, Perthshire,
PH2 7PJ
Tel: 01821 640254
★★★ Bed & Breakfast

Greenacres
Logiealmond, by Perth,
Perthshire, PH1 3TQ
Tel: 01738 880302
★★★ Bed & Breakfast

Mrs Ann Guthrie
Newmill Farm, Stanley, Perth,
PH1 4PS
Tel: 01738 828281
★★★ Bed & Breakfast

The Linn
3 Duchess Street, Stanley,
Perth, PH1 4NF
Tel: 01738 828293
★★★★ Bed & Breakfast

Ninewells Farmhouse
Woodriffe Road, Newburgh, Fife,
KY14 6EY
Tel: 01337 840307
★★★★ Bed & Breakfast

PITLOCHRY
Ardvane
8 Lower Oakfield, Pitlochry,
Perthshire, PH16 5DS
Tel: 01796 472683
★★★★ Bed & Breakfast

Ashbank House
14 Tomcroy Terrace, Pitlochry,
Perthshire,, PH16 5JA
Tel: 01796 472711
★★★ Bed & Breakfast

Balbeagan
Balnaguard, Pitlochry,
Perthshire, PH9 0PY
Tel: 01796 482627
★★★★ Bed & Breakfast

Beinn Bhracaigh
Knockard Road, Pitlochry,
Perthshire, PH16 5HJ
Tel: 01796 470355
★★★★ Bed & Breakfast

Bridge House B&B
53 Atholl Road, Pitlochry,
Perthshire, PH16 5BL
Tel: 01796 474062
★★★ Bed & Breakfast

Buttonboss Lodge
25 Atholl Road, Pitlochry,
Perthshire, PH16 5BX
Tel: 01796 472065
★★★ Guest House

Carra Beag Guest House
16 Toberargan Road, Pitlochry,
Perthshire, PH16 5HG
Tel: 01796 472835
★★★ Guest House

Craigroyston House
2 Lower Oakfield, Pitlochry,
Perthshire, PH16 5HQ
Tel: 01796 472053
★★★★ Guest House

Dalshian House
Old Perth Road, Pitlochry,
PH16 5TD
Tel: 01796 472173
★★★ Guest House

Derrybeg
Guest House & Apartments
18 Lower Oakfield, Pitlochry,
Perthshire, PH16 5DS
Tel: 01796 472070
★★★★ Guest House

Donavourd Farmhouse
Pitlochry, Perthshire, PH16 5JS
Tel: 01796 472254
★★★ Bed & Breakfast

Dundarave House
Strathview Terrace, Pitlochry, Perthshire, PH16 5AT
Tel: 01796 473109
★★★ Guest House

Easter Dunfallandy House
Logierait Road, Pitlochry, Perthshire, PH16 5NA
Tel: 01796 474128
★★★★ Bed & Breakfast

Farragon
Well Brae, Pitlochry, Perthshire, PH16 5HH
Tel: 01796 470051
★★★★ Bed & Breakfast

Fasganeoin Country House
Perth Road, Pitlochry, PH16 5DJ
Tel: 01796 472387
★★★ Guest House

Ferrymans Cottage
Port-Na-Craig, Pitlochry, Perthshire, PH16 5ND
Tel: 01796 473681
★★★★ Bed & Breakfast

Gardeners Cottage
Faskally, Pitlochry, Perthshire, PH16 5LA
Tel: 01796 472450
★★★ Bed & Breakfast

Grove Cottage
10 Lower Oakfield, Pitlochry, Perthshire, PH16 5DS
Tel: 01796 470108
★★★ Bed & Breakfast

The Highlands
Ferry Road, Pitlochry, Perthshire, PH16 5DD
Tel: 01796 474469
★★★ Bed & Breakfast

Kishorn
5 Lettoch Terrace, Pitlochry, Perthshire, PH16 5BA
Tel: 01796 472152
★★★ Bed & Breakfast

Lavalette
Manse Road, Moulin, Pitlochry, Perthshire, PH16 5EP
Tel: 01796 472364
★★★ Bed & Breakfast

Macdonald's Restaurant & Guest House
140 Atholl Road, Pitlochry, Perthshire, PH16 5AG
Tel: 01796 472170
★★★ Guest House

Moville
Kinnaird, Pitlochry, Perthshire, PH16 5JL
Tel: 01796 470100
★★★ Bed & Breakfast

Holtzhafen
5 Windsor Gardens, Pitlochry, Perthshire, PH16 5BE
Tel: 01796 473562
★★★ Bed & Breakfast

Silver Howe
Perth Road, Pitlochry, Perthshire, PH16 5LY
Tel: 01796 472181
★★★★ Bed & Breakfast

Sunnybank B&B
19 Lower Oakfield, Pitlochry, Perthshire, PH16 5DS
Tel: 01796 473014
★★★ Bed & Breakfast

Swallows Gait
4 Croftcroy, Croftinloan, Pitlochry, Perthshire, PH16 5TG
Tel: 01796 472071
★★★ Bed & Breakfast

Torrdarach House
Golf Course Road, Pitlochry, Perthshire, PH16 5AU
Tel: 01796 472136
★★★★ Guest House

Wellwood House
West Moulin Road, Pitlochry, Perthshire, PH16 5EA
Tel: 01796 474288
★★★★ Guest House

Wester Knockfarrie
Knockfarrie Road, Pitlochry, Perthshire, PH16 5DN
Tel: 01796 472020
★★★★ Bed & Breakfast

Woodburn House
Ferry Road, Pitlochry, Perthshire, PH16 5DE
Tel: 01796 473818
★★★ Bed & Breakfast

Woodshiel
23 West Moulin Road, Pitlochry, Perthshire, PH16 5EA
Tel: 01796 470358
★★★ Bed & Breakfast

PITTENWEEM

Marie Philp
4 St Abbs Crescent, Pittenweem, Fife, KY10 2LT
Tel: 01333 311964
★★★ Bed & Breakfast

Welch House
27 Viewforth Place, Pittenweem, Fife, KY10 2PZ
Tel: 01333 312289
★★★ Bed & Breakfast

ROSYTH

Backmarch House
54A Norval Place, Rosyth, Fife, KY11 2RJ
Tel: 01383 412997
★★★★ Bed & Breakfast

ST ANDREWS

Abbey Cottage
Abbey Walk, St Andrews, Fife, KY16 9LB
Tel: 01334 473727
★★ Bed & Breakfast

Abbotsview
31 Kinkell Terrace, St Andrews, Fife, KY16 8DS
Tel: 01334 472545
★★★ Bed & Breakfast

Acorn B & B
16 Priestden Road, St Andrews, Fife, KY16 8DJ
Tel: 01334 476009
★★★★ Bed & Breakfast

Anlaw House
21 Nelson Street, St Andrews, Fife, KY16 8AJ
Tel: 01334 477994
★★★ Bed & Breakfast

Arden House
2 Kilrymont Place, St Andrews, Fife, KY16 8DH
Tel: 01334 475478
★★★ Bed & Breakfast

Balrymonth B&B
6 Balrymonth Court, St Andrews, Fife, KY16 8XT
Tel: 01334 470855
★★★ Bed & Breakfast

Barnhay Country Bed & Breakfast
Kinaldy Meadows, by St Andrews, Fife, KY16 8NA
Tel: 01334 477791
★★★★ Bed & Breakfast

Birchlea Bed & Breakfast
8 Horseleys Park, St Andrews, Fife, KY16 8RZ
Tel: 01334 472698
★★★★ Bed & Breakfast

Bowmore
32 St Mary Street, St Andrews, Fife, KY16 8AZ
Tel: 01334 472875
★★★ Bed & Breakfast

Braeside House
25 Nelson Street, St Andrews, Fife, KY16 8AJ
Tel: 01334 473375
★★★★ Bed & Breakfast

Bramley House
10 Bonfield Road, Strathkinness, by St Andrews, KY16 9RP
Tel: 01334 850362
★★★★ Bed & Breakfast

Castlegate
32 East Scores, St Andrews, Fife, KY16
Tel: 01334 475579
★★★ Bed & Breakfast

Castlemount
The Scores, St Andrews, Fife, KY16 9AR
Tel: 01334 475579
★★★ Bed & Breakfast

Charlesworth House
9 Murray Place, St Andrews, KY16 9AP
Tel: 01334 476528
★★★ Guest House

30 Drumcarrow Road
St Andrews, Fife, KY16 8SE
Tel: 01334 472036
★★★ Bed & Breakfast

Ducks Crossing
5 Dempster Terrace, St Andrews, Fife, KY16 9QQ
Tel: 01334 477010
★★★ Bed & Breakfast

Fairnie House
10 Abbey Street, St Andrews, Fife, KY16 9LA
Tel: 01334 474094
★★★ Bed & Breakfast

1 Golf Place
1 Golf Place, St Andrews, Fife, KY16 9JA
Tel: 01334 472059
★★★ Inn

The Grange Inn
Grange Road, St Andrews, Fife, KY16 8LJ
Tel: 01334 472670
★★★ Restaurant with Rooms

Hawthorne House B&B
33 Main Street, Strathkinness, St Andrews, Fife, KY16 9RY
Tel: 01334 850855
★★★★ Bed & Breakfast

Hayston Farm
Balmullo, St Andrews, Fife, KY16 0AJ
Tel: 01334 870210
★★★ Bed & Breakfast

Hazelbank Hotel
28 The Scores, St Andrews, Fife, KY16 9AS
Tel: 01334 472466
★★★ Small Hotel

Hazlehead
16 Linsay Gardens, St Andrews, Fife, KY16 8XB
Tel: 01334 475677
★★★ Bed & Breakfast

Inn on North Street
127 North Street, St Andrews, Fife, KY16 9AG
Tel: 01334 473387
★★★ Inn

Kinburn guest house
5 Kinburn Place, Double Dykes Road, St Andrews, Fife, KY16 9DT
Tel: 01334 474711
★★★★ Bed & Breakfast

Kincaple Lodge
Kincaple, St Andrews, Fife, KY16 9SH
Tel: 01334 850 217
★★★★ Bed & Breakfast

Little Carron Cottage
St Andrews, Fife, KY16 8QN
Tel: 01334 474039
★★★★ Bed & Breakfast

Millhouse
2 Cauldside Farm Steading, St Andrews, Fife, KY16 9TY
Tel: 01334 850557
★★★★ Bed & Breakfast

25 North Street
St Andrews, Fife, KY16 9PW
Tel: 01334 477 453
★★★ Bed & Breakfast

Old Fishergate House
North Castle Street, St Andrews, Fife, KY16 9BG
Tel: 01334 470874
★★★★ Bed & Breakfast

Old Schoolhouse
Kingsmuir, St Andrews, Fife, KY16 8QQ
Tel: 01334 880777
★★★ Bed & Breakfast

The Old Station Country Guest House
Stratvithie Bridge, St Andrews, KY16 8LR
Tel: 01334 880505
★★★★ Guest House

The Paddock
Sunnyside, Strathkinness, by St. Andrews, Fife, KY16 9XP
Tel: 01334 850888
★★★★ Bed & Breakfast

The Pilmour Hotel
1 Pilmour Place, St Andrews, Fife, KY16 9HZ
Tel: 01334 473252
★★ Inn

Pitmilly West Lodge
Kingsbarns, St Andrews, Fife, KY16 8QA
Tel: 01334 880581
★★★★ Bed & Breakfast

11 Queens Gardens
St Andrews, Fife, KY16 9TA
Tel: 01334 478751
★★★ Bed & Breakfast

15 Queens Gardens
St Andrews, Fife, KY16 9TA
Tel: 01334 473081
★★★ Bed & Breakfast

18 Queens Terrace
St Andrews, Fife, KY16 9QF
Tel: 01334 478849
★★★★ Bed & Breakfast

St Nicholas Farmhouse
East Sands, St Andrews, Fife, KY16 8LD
Tel: 01334 473090
★★ Bed & Breakfast

Spinkieden
13 Cairnsden Gardens, St Andrews, Fife, KY16 8SQ
Tel: 01334 475303
★★★ Bed & Breakfast

Spinkstown Farmhouse
St Andrews, Fife, KY16 8PN
Tel: 01334 473475
★★★★ Bed & Breakfast

St Andrews B&B
Ladeddie Steading, by St Andrews, Fife, KY15 5TY
Tel: 01334 840514
★★★★ Bed & Breakfast

Stravithie Castle
Stravithie, St Andrews, Fife, KY16 8LT
Tel: 01334 880251
★★★ Bed & Breakfast

Tudor Inn
29 North Street, St Andrews, Fife, KY16 9AG
Tel: 01334 474906
★ Inn

Vardon House
22 Murray Park, St Andrews, Fife, KY16 9AW
Tel: 01334 475787
★★★ Bed & Breakfast

West Park House
5 St Marys Place, St Andrews, Fife, KY16 9UY
Tel: 0134 475933
★★★ Guest House

BY ST ANDREWS

Hillwood House
Cameron, St Andrews, Fife, KY16 8PD
Tel: 01334 840396
★★★ Bed & Breakfast

South House
Pitscottie Vale, Dura Den, Pitscottie, nr St Andrews, Fife, KY15 5TJ
Tel: 01334 828784
★★★ Bed & Breakfast

NR ST ANDREWS

Far-Reaches B&B
32 Pickford Crescent, Cellardyke, Anstruther, Fife, KY10 3AL
Tel: 01333 310448
★★★★ Bed & Breakfast

ST FILLANS

Achray Cottage
St Fillans, Perthshire, PH6 2NF
Tel: 01764 685383
★★★ Bed & Breakfast

Earngrove Cottage
St Fillans, by Loch Earn, Perthshire, PH6 2ND
Tel: 01764 685224
★★★ Bed & Breakfast

SALINE, BY DUNFERMLINE

Balnacraig B&B
Main Street, Saline, Fife, KY12 9TL
Tel: 01383 852568
★★★★ Bed & Breakfast

Kirklands House
Saline, Fife, KY12 9TS
Tel: 01383 852737
★★★★ Bed & Breakfast

The Saline Hotel
West Road, Saline, by Dunfermline, Fife, KY12 9UN
Tel: 01383 852798
★★ Inn

STANLEY

Glensanda House
Station Road, Stanley, Perth,
Perthshire, PH1 4NW
Tel: 01738 827016
★★★ Bed & Breakfast

Otterstones
Burnmouth Ferry, Stanley, Perth,
PH1 4QF
Tel: 01738 827 837
★★★ Bed & Breakfast

**STRATHKINNESS,
BY ST ANDREWS**

Longmuir
by Strathkinness, St Andrews,
Fife, KY16 9SL
Tel: 01334 850838
★★★ Bed & Breakfast

No 1 The Grove
High Road, Strathkinness,
By St Andrews, KY16 9XY
Tel: 01334 850 924
★★★★ Bed & Breakfast

Newton of Nydie Farmhouse
Strathkinness, KY16
Tel: 01334 850204
★★★ Bed & Breakfast

TAYPORT

Edenholme
10 Grey Street, Tayport, Fife,
DD6 9HW
Tel: 01382 552274
★★ Bed & Breakfast

Forgans B&B
23 Castle Street, Tayport, Fife,
DD6 9AE
Tel: 01382 552682
★★★ Bed & Breakfast

Kirkton Barns
Tayport, Fife, DD6 9PD
Tel: 01382 554402
★★★★ Bed & Breakfast

**WEST BALLOCHY,
BY MONTROSE**

Ballochy House
West Ballochy,by Montrose,
Angus, DD10 9LP
Tel: 01674 810207
★★★ Bed & Breakfast

WINDYGATES

Edenshead Stables
Main Street, Gateside, Fife,
KY14 7ST
Tel: 01337 868500
★★★★★ Bed & Breakfast

ABERDEEN AND GRAMPIAN HIGHLANDS – SCOTLAND'S CASTLE AND WHISKY COUNTRY

ABERDEEN

Aberdeen Nicoll's Guest House
63 Springbank Terrace, Ferryhill,
Aberdeen, AB11 6JZ
Tel: 01224 572867
AWAITING INSPECTION

Aldersyde Guest House
138 Bon Accord Street,
Aberdeen, AB11 6TX
Tel: 01224 580012
★★ Bed & Breakfast

Braeside Guest House
68 Bon-Accord Street,
Aberdeen, Scotland, AB11 6EL
Tel: 01224 571471
★★ Bed & Breakfast

Burnett's Guest House
75 Constitution Street,
Aberdeen, AB24 5ET
Tel: 01224 647995
★★★ Guest House

Butterywells Farm
Potterton, Aberdden,
Aberdeenshire, AB23 8UY
Tel: 01358 742673
★★★ Bed & Breakfast

Dunlaoire
430 King Street, Aberdeen,
AB24 3BS
Tel: 01224 634406/632169
★★★ Bed & Breakfast

Fairview
112 Fairview Circle, Aberdeen,
AB22 8YR
Tel: 01224 824622
★★★ Bed & Breakfast

Furain Guest House
92 North Deeside Road,
Peterculter, Aberdeen,
AB14 0QN
Tel: 01224 732189
★★★ Guest House

The Globe Inn
13-15 North Silver Street,
Aberdeen, AB10 1RJ
Tel: 01224 624258
★★★ Inn

**University of Aberdeen,
King's Hall**
College Bounds, Aberdeen,
AB24 3TT
Tel: 01224 273444
★★ Campus

20 Louisville Avenue
Aberdeen, AB10 6TX
Tel: 01224 319812
★★★ Bed & Breakfast

MacLeans B & B
8 Boyd Orr Avenue, Aberdeen,
Grampian, AB12 5RG
Tel: 01224 248726
★★ Bed & Breakfast

116 Osborne Place
Aberdeen, AB25 2DD
Tel: 01224 641651
★★ Bed & Breakfast

105 Osborne Place
Aberdeen, AB25 2DD
Tel: 01224 640780
★★★ Bed & Breakfast

Penny Meadow Private Hotel
189 Great Western Road,
Aberdeen, AB10 6PS
Tel: 01224 588037
★★★★ Guest House

St Elmo
64 Hilton Drive, Aberdeen,
AB24 4NP
Tel: 01224 483065
★★★★ Guest House

Scottish Agricultural College
Craibstone Estate, Bucksburn,
Aberdeenshire, AB21 9TR
Tel: 01224 711012
★★ Campus

St Magnus Court Hotel
22 Guild Street, Aberdeen,
AB11 6NF
Tel: 01224 589411
★★ Lodge

Crombie Johnston Hall
University of Aberdeen,
Aberdeen, AB24 3TT
Tel: 01224 273444
★ Campus

Viewfield B&B
Panmure Gardens, Potterton,
Aberdeen, AB23 8UG
Tel: 01358 742605
★★★ Bed & Breakfast

BY ABERDEEN

4 Brodiach Court
Westhill, Skene, Aberdeenshire,
AB32 6QY
Tel: 01224 742749
★★★★ Bed & Breakfast

3 Greystone Place
Newtonhill, Kincardineshire,
AB39 3UL
Tel: 01569 730391
★★★ Bed & Breakfast

ABERLOUR

The Auld Mill
Catherinebraes Farm, Elchies,
Aberlour, Banffshire, AB38 9SL
Tel: 01340 810888
★★★ Inn

Westburn
Milltown of Edinville, Aberlour,
Banff, AB38 9NB
Tel: 01340 871118
★★★ Bed & Breakfast

ABOYNE

Chesterton House
Formaston Park, Aboyne,
Aberdeenshire, AB34 5HF
Tel: 013398 86740
★★ Bed & Breakfast

Newton of Drumgesk
Dess, Aboyne, Aberdeenshire,
AB34 5BL
Tel: 01339 886203
★★ Bed & Breakfast

Struan Hall
Ballater Road, Aboyne,
Aberdeenshire, AB34 5HY
Tel: 013398 87241
★★★★★ Bed & Breakfast

ALFORD

Bydand Bed & Breakfast
18 Balfour Road, Alford,
Aberdeenshire, AB33 8NF
Tel: 019755 63613
★★★ Bed & Breakfast

Frog Marsh Bed & Breakfast
Mossat, Alford, Aberdeenshire,
AB33 8PL
Tel: 01975 571355
★★★★ Bed & Breakfast

ARCHIESTOWN

Archiestown Hotel
Archiestown, by Aberlour,
Moray, AB38 7QL
Tel: 01340 810218
★★★ Small Hotel

BALLATER

Celicall
3 Braemar Road, Ballater,
Aberdeenshire, AB35 5RL
Tel: 013397 55699
★★★ Bed & Breakfast

Craigard Lodge
Abergeldie Road, Ballater,
Aberdeenshire, AB35 5RP
★★★★ Bed & Breakfast

Eastbank
50 Albert Road, Ballater,
Aberdeenshire, AB35 5QU
Tel: 013397 55742
★★★ Bed & Breakfast

Glenernan Guest House
37 Braemar Road, Ballater,
Aberdeenshire, AB35 5RQ
Tel: 013397 53111
★★★ Guest House

The Green Inn
9 Victoria Road, Ballater,
Aberdeenshire, AB35 5QQ
Tel: 01339 755701
★★★★
Restaurant with Rooms

Inverdeen House
11 Bridge Square, Ballater,
AB35 5QJ
Tel: 013397 55759
★★★★ Bed & Breakfast

Langdale Bed and Breakfast
Hawthorn Place, Ballater,
Aberdeen-shire, AB35 5QH
Tel: 013397 55500
★★★ Bed & Breakfast

Monaltrie Lodge
Bridge Square, Ballater,
Aberdeenshire, AB35 5QJ
Tel: 013397 55296
★★★ Bed & Breakfast

Woodside
Old Line Road, Ballater,
Aberdeenshire, AB35 5UT
Tel: 01339 756351
★★★ Bed & Breakfast

BY BALLATER

Creag Meggan
Bridge of Gairn, Ballater,
Aberdeenshire, AB35 5UD
Tel: 013397 55767
★★ Bed & Breakfast

BALLINDALLOCH

Woodville
Ballindalloch, Banffshire,
AB37 9AD
Tel: 01807 500396
★★★ Bed & Breakfast

BANCHORY

Birchlea Cottage
Strachan, Banchory,
Aberdeenshire, AB31 6NL
Tel: 01330 824132
★★★ Bed & Breakfast

73 High Street
Banchory, Kincardinshire,
AB31 5TJ
Tel: 01330 824666
★★★ Bed & Breakfast

Lochton
Durris, Banchory,
Kincardineshire, AB31 6DB
Tel: 01330 844543
★★★ Bed & Breakfast

The Old West Manse
71 Station Road, Banchory,
Kincardineshire, AB31 5YD
Tel: 01330 822202
★★★★ Bed & Breakfast

Ardconnel
6 Kinneskie Road, Banchory,
Aberdeenshire, AB31 5TA
Tel: 01330 822478
★★★★ Bed & Breakfast

Village Guest House
83 High Street, Banchory,
Kincardineshire, AB31 5PJ
Tel: 01330 823307
★★★★ Guest House

BY BANCHORY

Dorena
Strachan, By Banchory,
Kincardineshire, AB31 6NL
Tel: 01330 822540
★★★★ Bed & Breakfast

Monthammock Farm
Durris, by Banchory,
Kincardineshire, AB31 6DX
Tel: 01330 811421
★★★ Bed & Breakfast

Struan
Echt, Westhill, Aberdeen,
Aberdeenshire, AB32 6UL
Tel: 01330 860799
★★★ Bed & Breakfast

Wester Durris Cottage
Kirkton of Durris, Banchory,
Kincardineshire, AB31 3BQ
Tel: 01330 844638
★★ Bed & Breakfast

BANFF

Bryden
Boyndie, Banff, Aberdeenshire,
AB45 2LD
Tel: 01261 861742
★★★★ Bed & Breakfast

Bryvard Guest House
Seafield Street, Banff,
Aberdeenshire, AB45 1EB
Tel: 01261 818090
★★★★ Bed & Breakfast

Durno House
Netherwood, Banff,
Aberdeenshire, AB45 3LQ
Tel: 01261 821203
★★★ Bed & Breakfast

Morayhill
Bellevue Road, Banff,
Aberdeenshire, AB45 1BJ
Tel: 01261 815956
★★★★ Bed & Breakfast

The Orchard B&B
Duff House, Banff,
Aberdeenshire, AB45 3TA
Tel: 01261 812146
★★★★ Bed & Breakfast

The Trinity and Alvah Manse
21 Castle Street, Banff,
Aberdeen-shire, AB45 1DH
Tel: 01261 812244
★★★ Bed & Breakfast

BRAEMAR

Callater Lodge Guest House
9 Glenshee Road, Braemar,
Aberdeenshire, AB35 5YQ
Tel: 013397 41275
★★★★ Guest House

Clunie Lodge Guest House
Cluniebank Road, Braemar,
Aberdeenshire, AB35 5ZP
Tel: 013397 41330
★★★ Guest House

Craiglea
Hillside Road, Braemar,
Aberdeenshire, AB35 5YU
Tel: 013397 41641
★★★ Bed & Breakfast

Dalmore House
Fife Brae, Braemar,
Aberdeenshire, AB35 5NS
Tel: 013397 41046
★★★ Bed & Breakfast

Schiehallion House
10 Glenshee Road, Braemar,
Aberdeenshire, AB35 5YQ
Tel: 013397 41679
★★★ Guest House

Wilderbank
Kindrochit Drive, Braemar,
Aberdeenshire, AB35 5YW
Tel: 013397 41651
★★ Bed & Breakfast

BUCKIE
Alexander House
Bed and Breakfast
26 Seaview Road, Buckie,
Banffshire, AB56 1RQ
Tel: 01542 835099
★★★★ Bed & Breakfast

The Bungalow
81 High Street, Buckie,
Banffshire, AB56 1BB
Tel: 01542 832367
★★★ Bed & Breakfast

Kintrae
39 East Church Street, Buckie,
Morayshire, AB56 1ES
Tel: 01542 839755
★★★★ Bed & Breakfast

Rosemount
62 East Church Street, Buckie,
Banffshire, AB56 1ER
Tel: 01542 833434
★★★★ Bed & Breakfast

BY BUCKIE
Glenelg
26 Richmond Terrace,
Portgordon, Buckie, Banffshire,
AB56 2RJ
Tel: 01542 833221
★★★★ Bed & Breakfast

BURGHEAD
Harbour Inn
59 Granary Street, Burghead,
Moray, IV30 5UA
Tel: 01343 835671
★★★ Inn

CATTERLINE
Upper Crawton
Catterline, By Stonehaven,
Kincardineshire, AB39 2TU
Tel: 01569 750243
★★★ Bed & Breakfast

CRAIGELLACHIE
Bridge View
Leslie Terrace, Craigellachie,
Banffshire, AB38 9SX
Tel: 01340 881376
★★★ Bed & Breakfast

CULLEN
Crannoch Hotel
12 Blantyre Street, Cullen,
Morayshire, AB56 4RQ
Tel: 01542 840210
★★★ Inn

DUFFTOWN
Braehead Villa
Braehead Terrace, Dufftown,
Keith, Banffshire, AB55 4AN
Tel: 01340 820461
★★★ Bed & Breakfast

Davaar Bed & Breakfast
Church Street, Dufftown, Keith,
AB55 4AR
Tel: 01340 820464
★★★ Bed & Breakfast

Gowanbrae Guest House
19 Church Street, Dufftown,
AB55 4AR
Tel: 01340 821344
★★★ Bed & Breakfast

Nashville
8A Balvenie Street, Dufftown,
Keith, Moray, AB55 4AB
Tel: 01340 820553
★★★ Bed & Breakfast

Old Road House
Buchrom, Dufftown, Keith,
AB55 4BN
Tel: 01340 871554
★★★ Bed & Breakfast

ELGIN
The Croft
10 Institution Road, Elgin,
Moray, IV30 1QX
Tel: 01343 546004
★★★★ Bed & Breakfast

Moray Bank Bed and Breakfast
21 Institution Road, Elgin,
Moray, IV30 1QT
Tel: 01343 547618
★★★★ Bed & Breakfast

Colin & Wendy Clements
The Pines Guest House, East
Road, Elgin, Moray, IV30 1XG
Tel: 01343 552495
★★★★ Guest House

Pluscarden House
Pluscarden, Elgin, Morayshire,
IV30 8TZ
Tel: 01343 890430
★★★ Bed & Breakfast

Richmond
Moss Street, Elgin, Morayshire,
IV30 1LT
Tel: 01343 542561
★★★ Bed & Breakfast

BY ELGIN
Burnside House
Duffus, Morayshire, IV30 5QS
Tel: 01343 835165
★★★★ Bed & Breakfast

The Old Church of Urquhart
Parrandier, Meft Road,
Urquhart, by Elgin, Morayshire,
IV30 8NH
Tel: 01343 843063
★★★★ Bed & Breakfast

NR ELGIN
Carsewell Farmhouse
Alves, Nr Elgin, Morayshire,
IV30 3UR
Tel: 01343 850201
★★ Bed & Breakfast

FINDHORN
Heath House
Findhorn, Moray, IV36 3WN
Tel: 01309 691082
★★★★ Bed & Breakfast

BY FOCHABERS
Castlehill Cottage
Blackdam, by Fochabers, Moray,
IV32 7LJ
Tel: 01343 820761
★★★ Bed & Breakfast

Castlehill Farm
Blackdam, Fochabers, Moray,
IV32 7LJ
Tel: 01343 820 351
★★★ Bed & Breakfast

FORDOUN
Cocketty Croft
Pitskelly, Fordoun,
Kincardineshire, AB30 1LB
Tel: 01561 320980
★★★ Bed & Breakfast

FORDYCE
Academy House
School Road, Fordyce,
Banffshire, AB45 2SJ
Tel: 01261 842743
★★★★★ Bed & Breakfast

FORRES
Caranrahd
19 Sanquhar Road, Forres,
Moray, IV36 1DG
Tel: 01309 672581
★★★ Bed & Breakfast

Mayfield Guest House
Victoria Road, Forres, Moray,
IV36 3BN
Tel: 01309 676931
★★★★ Bed & Breakfast

Milton of Grange
Farmhouse B&B
Milton of Grange, Forres, Moray,
IV36 2TR
Tel: 01309 676360
★★★★ Bed & Breakfast

Morven
Caroline Street, Forres, Moray,
IV36 1AN
Tel: 01309 673788
★★★ Bed & Breakfast

Sherston House
Hillhead, Forres, Moray,
IV36 0QT
Tel: 01309 671087
★★★★ Bed & Breakfast

Springfield B&B
Croft Road, Forres, Moray,
IV36 3JS
Tel: 01309 676965
★★★★ Bed & Breakfast

Uralla
Sanquhar Road, Forres, Moray,
IV36 0DG
Tel: 01309 672082
★★★★ Bed & Breakfast

BY FORRES

Invercairn House
Brodie, Forres, Morayshire,
IV36 2TD
Tel: 01309 641261
★★★ Bed & Breakfast

Moss-side Farm
Rafford, Forres, Moray, IV36 0SL
Tel: 01309 672954
★★★ Bed & Breakfast

The Old Kirk
Dyke, By Forres, IV36 2TL
Tel: 01309 641414
★★★★ Bed & Breakfast

BY FRASERBURGH

Lonmay Old Manse
by Fraserburgh, Aberdeenshire,
AB43 8UJ
Tel: 01346 532227
★★★★ Bed & Breakfast

NR FRASERBURGH

Rose Lodge
New Leeds, Peterhead,
AB42 4HX
Tel: 01346 531148
★★★★ Bed & Breakfast

FYVIE

**Meikle Camaloun
Bed & Breakfast**
Meikle Camaloun, Fyvie, Turriff,
Aberdeenshire, AB53 8JY
Tel: 01651 891319
★★★★ Bed & Breakfast

GARDENSTOWN

Palace Farm
Gamrie, by Macduff, Banffshire,
AB45 3HS
Tel: 01261 851261
★★★ Bed & Breakfast

GLENLIVET

Roadside Cottage
Tomnavoulin, Ballindalloch,
Banffshire, AB37 9JL
Tel: 01807 590486
★★★ Bed & Breakfast

HOPEMAN

Ardent House
43 Forsyth Street, Hopeman,
Moray, IV30 2SY
Tel: 01343 830694
★★★★ Bed & Breakfast

HUNTLY

Greenmount Guest House
43 Gordon Street, Huntly,
Aberdeenshire, AB54 8EQ
Tel: 01466 792482
★★★ Guest House

Hillview
Provost Street, Huntly,
Aberdeenshire, AB54 5BB
Tel: 01466 794870
★★★ Bed & Breakfast

New Marnoch
48 King Street, Huntly,
Aberdeenshire, AB54 8HP
Tel: 01466 792018
★★★★ Bed & Breakfast

Southview
Victoria Road, Huntly,
Aberdeenshire, AB54 8AH
Tel: 01466 792456
★★★ Bed & Breakfast

Strathlene
MacDonald Street, Huntly,
AB54 8EW
Tel: 01466 792664
★★★★ Bed & Breakfast

BY HUNTLY

Bandora
Yonder Bognie, Forgue,
By Huntly, Aberdeenshire,
AB54 6BR
Tel: 01466 730375
★★★ Bed & Breakfast

**Haddoch Farmhouse
Bed and Breakfast**
Haddoch Farm, by Huntly,
Aberdeenshire, AB54 4SL
Tel: 01466 711217
★★★ Bed & Breakfast

INSCH

The Steading
Old Westhall, Oyne, Insch,
Aberdeenshire, AB52 6QU
Tel: 01464 851641
★★★★ Bed & Breakfast

Troutbeck B&B
4 Riverside Drive, Old Rayne,
Insch,Aberdeenshire, AB52 6SF
Tel: 01464 851110
★★★★ Bed & Breakfast

INVERURIE

Dryburn House
Ordhead, Inverurie,
Aberdeenshire, AB51 7RL
Tel: 01330 833653
★★★★ Bed & Breakfast

Kingsgait
St Andrews Gardens, Inverurie,
Aberdeenshire, AB51 3XT
Tel: 01467 620431
★★★ Bed & Breakfast

BY INVERURIE

Broadsea (Mrs E Harper)
Burnhervie, Inverurie,
Aberdeenshire, AB51 5LB
Tel: 01467 681386
★★★ Bed & Breakfast

Fridayhill
Kinmuck, by Inverurie,
Aberdeenshire, AB51 0LY
Tel: 01651 882252
★★★★★ Bed & Breakfast

5 Kirkton Park
Chapel of Gairloch, Inverurie,
Aberdeenshire, AB51 5HF
Tel: 01467 681281
★★★ Bed & Breakfast

KEITH BY

Chapelhill Croft
Grange, Keith, Banffshire,
AB55 3LQ
Tel: 01542 870302
★★★ Bed & Breakfast

KEITH

The Haughs
Keith, Moray, AB55 6QN
Tel: 01542 882238
★★★ Guest House

LOSSIEMOUTH

Bri Heath
84 Queen Street, Lossiemouth,
Morayshire, IV31 6PY
Tel: 01343 814356
★★★ Bed & Breakfast

Carmania
45 St Gerardine's Road,
Lossiemouth, Moray, IV31 6JX
Tel: 01343 812276
★★★ Bed & Breakfast

Ceilidh B&B
34 Clifton Road, Lossiemouth,
Moray, IV31 6DP
Tel: 01343 815848
★★★ Bed & Breakfast

Lossiemouth House
33 Clifton Road, Lossiemouth,
Moray, IV31 6DP
Tel: 01343 813397
★★★ Bed & Breakfast

Mormond
Prospect Terrace, Lossiemouth,
Moray, IV31 6JS
Tel: 01343 813143
★★★★ Bed & Breakfast

Norland
Stotfield Road, Lossiemouth,
Moray, IV31 6QP
Tel: 01343 813570
★★★ Bed & Breakfast

LUMPHANAN

Mapleview
Lumphanan,by Banchory,
Kincardineshire, AB31 4RH
Tel: 013398 83481
★★★ Bed & Breakfast

LUMSDEN

Dunvegan
Main Street, Lumsden,
Aberdeenshire, AB54 4JN
Tel: 01464 861566
★★★ Bed & Breakfast

MACDUFF

Monica & Martin's B&B
21 Gellymill Street, Macduff,
Banffshire, AB44 1TN
Tel: 01261 832336
★★★ Bed & Breakfast

METHLICK

Sunnybrae Farm
Gight, Methlick, Ellon,
Aberdeenshire, AB41 7JA
Tel: 01651 806456
★★ Bed & Breakfast

MULBEN, BY KEITH

Gateside Farm
Mulben, by Keith, Banffshire,
AB55 6YX
★★★ Bed & Breakfast

NEWMACHAR

The School House
5 School Road, Newmachar,
Aberdeenshire, AB21 0WB
Tel: 01651 862970
★★★★ Bed & Breakfast

OLDMELDRUM

Cromlet Hill Guest House
South Road, Oldmeldrum,
Aberdeenshire, AB51 0AB
Tel: 01651 872315
★★★★ Bed & Breakfast

PETERHEAD

Durie House
Clola, Peterhead,
Aberdeenshire, AB42 5BE
Tel: 01771 622 823
★★★ Bed & Breakfast

Greenbrae Farmhouse
Longside, By Peterhead,
Aberdeenshire, AB42 4TX
Tel: 01779 821051
★★★ Bed & Breakfast

Pond View
Brucklay, Maud, Peterhead,
AB42 4QN
Tel: 01771 613 675
★★★★ Bed & Breakfast

BY PETERHEAD

The Old Bank House
6 Abbey Street, Old Deer,
Peterhead, Aberdeenshire,
AB42 5LN
Tel: 01771 623463
★★★ Bed & Breakfast

PORTSOY

The Boyne Hotel Portsoy
2 North High Street, Portsoy,
Aberdeenshire, AB45 2PA
Tel: 01261 842242
★★ Small Hotel

RHYNIE

Essie Croft
Rhynie, Nr Huntly,
Aberdeenshire, AB54 4HN
Tel: 01464 861120
★★★ Bed & Breakfast

ST CYRUS

Eskview Farm
Nether Warburton, St Cyrus,
Montrose, Angus, DD10 0AQ
Tel: 01674 830890
★★★ Bed & Breakfast

Woodston Fishing Station
St Cyrus, Montrose,
Kincardineshire, DD10 0DG
Tel: 01674 850226
★★★ Bed & Breakfast

STONEHAVEN

Ambleside B&B
Netherley, Stonehaven,
Aberdeenshire, AB39 3RB
Tel: 01569 731105
★★★ Bed & Breakfast

Beachgate House
Beachgate Lane, Stonehaven,
Kincardineshire, AB39 2BD
Tel: 01569 763155
★★★★ Bed & Breakfast

**Dunnottar Mains
Farmhouse B&B**
Stonehaven, Kincardineshire,
AB39 2TL
Tel: 01569 762621
★★★★ Bed & Breakfast

Glencairn
9 Dunnottar Avenue,
Stonehaven, Kincardineshire,
AB39 2JD
Tel: 01569 762612
★★★ Bed & Breakfast

Johnston Lodge
26 Ann Street, Stonehaven,
Aberdeenshire, AB39 2DA
Tel: 01569 763586
★★★ Bed & Breakfast

Norwood
48 Arduthie Road, Stonehaven,
Kincardineshire, AB39 2HU
Tel: 01569 762940
★★ Bed & Breakfast

Pitgaveny
Baird Street, Stonehaven,
Aberdeenshire, AB39 2SP
Tel: 01569 764719
★★★★ Bed & Breakfast

The Ship Inn
5 Shore Head, Stonehaven,
Aberdeen-Shire, AB39 2JY
Tel: 01569 762 617
★★ Inn

Station Hotel
Arduthie Road, Stonehaven,
Kincardineshire, AB39 2NE
Tel: 01569 762277
★★ Inn

Tewel Farmhouse B&B
Tewel Farm, Stonehaven, South
Aberdeenshire, AB39 3UU
Tel: 01569 762306
★★★ Bed & Breakfast

Woodburn
1 Carron Terrace, Stonehaven,
Kincardineshire, AB39 2HX
Tel: 01569 766779
★ Bed & Breakfast

NR STONEHAVEN

Ellington
Station Place, Johnshaven,
DD10 0JD
Tel: 0870 2252632
★★★★ Bed & Breakfast

STRATHDON

Auld Cummerton
Glen Nochty, Bellabeg,
Strathdon, AB36 8UP
Tel: 01975 651337
★★★★★ Bed & Breakfast

The Smiddy House
Glenkindie, Aberdeenshire,
AB33 8SS
Tel: 01975 641216
★★★ Bed & Breakfast

TARLAND

Kirklands of Cromar
Bridge Street, Tarland,
Aberdeenshire, AB34 4YN
Tel: 013398 81082
★★★ Bed & Breakfast

TOMINTOUL BY

Auchriachan Farmhouse
Mains of Auchriachan,
Tomintoul, Ballindalloch,
Banffshire, AB37 9EQ
Tel: 01807 580416
★★★ Bed & Breakfast

Croughly Farm
Tomintoul, Ballindalloch,
Banffshire, AB37 9EN
Tel: 01807 580476
★★★ Bed & Breakfast

TOMINTOUL

Findron Farm
Tomintoul, Ballindalloch,
AB37 9ER
Tel: 01807 580382
★★★★ Bed & Breakfast

TURRIFF

The Gables
Station Road, Turriff,
Aberdeen-shire, AB53 4ER
Tel: 01888 568715
★★★ Bed & Breakfast

THE HIGHLANDS AND SKYE

ACHMELVICH, BY LOCHINVER

Ardsaile
Achmelvich, Lochinver,
Sutherland, IV27 4SB
Tel: 01571 844363
★★★★ Bed & Breakfast

ACHMORE BY

Maple Lodge
Braeintra, Stromeferry,
Ross-shire, IV53 8UP
Tel: 01599 577276
★★★ Bed & Breakfast

ACHNASHEEN

Ferroch
Annat, Loch Torridon,
Auchnasheen, IV22 2EU
Tel: 01445 791451
★★★★ Bed & Breakfast

ALNESS

Marionville
82 Obsdale Park, Alness,
Ross-Shire, IV18 0TR
Tel: 01349 882667
★★★ Bed & Breakfast

Directory of all VisitScotland Quality Assured Serviced Establishments

APPLECROSS

Applecross Inn
Shore Street, Applecross,
Strathcarron, IV54 8LR
Tel: 01520 744262
★ Inn

ARDGAY

Corvost
Ardgay, Sutherland, IV24 3BP
Tel: 01863 755317
★★ Bed & Breakfast

Oriel Cottage
Ardgay, Sutherland, IV24 3BG
Tel: 01863 766460
★★ Bed & Breakfast

ARISAIG

Kilmartin Farm Guest House
Kinloid Farm, Arisaig,
Inverness-shire, PH39 4NS
Tel: 01687 450366
★★★ Bed & Breakfast

Leven House Bed & Breakfast
Leven House, Arisaig,
Inverness-shire, PH39 4NR
Tel: 01687 450238
★★★★ Bed & Breakfast

The Old Library Lodge
Main Street, Arisaig,
Inverness-shire, PH39 4NH
Tel: 01687 450651
★★★ Restaurant with Rooms

AULDEARN, BY NAIRN

Covenanters' Inn
High Street, Auldearn, Nairn,
IV12 5TG
Tel: 01667 452456
★★★ Inn

AULTBEA

Burnside
48 Mellon Charles, Aultbea,
Ross-shire, IV22 2JL
Tel: 01445 731270
★★★ Bed & Breakfast

Mellondale Guest House
47 Mellon Charles, Aultbea,
Ross-shire, IV22 2JL
Tel: 01445 731326
★★★★ Guest House

Tranquility
21 Mellon Charles, Aultbea,
Ross-shire, IV22 2JN
Tel: 01445 731241
★★★ Bed & Breakfast

AVIEMORE

Cairn Eilrig
Glenmore, Aviemore,
Inverness-shire, PH22 1QU
Tel: 01479 861223
★★★ Bed & Breakfast

Cairngorm Guest House
Grampian Road, Aviemore,
Inverness-shire, PH22 1RP
Tel: 01479 810630
★★★ Guest House

Carn Mhor
The Sheiling, Aviemore,
Inverness-shire, PH22 1QD
Tel: 01479 811004
★★★ Bed & Breakfast

Dunroamin Bed & Breakfast
Craig-Na-Gower Avenue,
Aviemore, PH22 1RW
Tel: 01479 810698
★★★ Bed & Breakfast

Eriskay
Craig-na-Gower Avenue,
Aviemore, Inverness-shire,
PH22 1RW
Tel: 01479 810717
★★★ Bed & Breakfast

Glenmore Lodge
Glenmore, Aviemore, PH22 1QU
★★ Campus

Junipers
5 Dellmhor, Aviemore,
Inverness-shire, PH22 1QW
Tel: 01479 810405
★★★ Bed & Breakfast

Lynwilg House
Aviemore, Inverness-shire,
PH22 1PZ
Tel: 01479 811685
★★★★ Guest House

MacDonald Academy
Aviemore Highland Resort,
Aviemore, Inverness-shire,
PH22 1PF
Tel: 01479 810781
★★★ Lodge

Ravenscraig Guest House
Grampian Road, Aviemore,
Inverness-shire, PH22 1RP
Tel: 01479 810278
★★★ Guest House

Vermont Guest House
Grampian Road, Aviemore,
PH22 1RP
Tel: 01479 810470
★★ Guest House

Waverley
35 Strathspey Avenue,
Aviemore, Inverness-shire,
PH22 1SN
Tel: 01479 811226
★★★ Bed & Breakfast

AVOCH, BY FORTROSE

Inverleod
Toll Road, Avoch, Ross-shire,
IV9 8PR
Tel: 01381 621595
★★★ Bed & Breakfast

BALBLAIR

Autumn Gold
Blablair, Black Isle,
Ross & Cromarty, IV7 8LR
Tel: 01381 622315
★★★★ Bed & Breakfast

BALLACHULISH

Ardno House
Lettermore, Ballachulish, Argyll,
PH49 4JD
★★★★ Bed & Breakfast

Craiglinnhe House
Lettermore, Ballachulish, Argyll,
PH49 4JD
Tel: 01855 811270
★★★★ Guest House

Cuildaff
West Laroch, Ballachulish,
Argyll, PH49 4JQ
Tel: 01855 811436
Bed & Breakfast

Fern Villa Guest House
Loanfern, Ballachulish,
PH49 4JE
Tel: 01855 811393
★★★ Guest House

Parkview B&B
18 Park Road, Ballachulish,
Argyll, PH49 4JS
Tel: 01855 811560
★★★ Bed & Breakfast

BALMACARA

Old Post Office House
Balmacara, by Kyle of Lochalsh,
Ross-shire, IV40 8DH
Tel: 01599 566772
★★ Bed & Breakfast

BANAVIE, BY FORT WILLIAM

Glenshian
Banavie, by Fort William,
Inverness-shire, PH33 7LX
Tel: 01397 772174
★★★★ Bed & Breakfast

Ronaval
Tomonie, Banavie,
by Fort William, Inverness-shire,
PH33 7LX
Tel: 01397 772206
★★★ Bed & Breakfast

Treetops
Badabrie, Banavie, Fort William,
PH33 7LX
Tel: 01397 772496
★★★ Bed & Breakfast

BEAULY

Croc End
Croyard Road, Beauly,
Inverness-shire, IV4 7DJ
Tel: 01463 782230
★★★ Bed & Breakfast

Cruachan
Wester Balblair, Beauly,
Inverness, IV4 7BQ
Tel: 01463 782679
★★★ Bed & Breakfast

Ellangowan
Croyard Road, Beauly, IV4 7DJ
Tel: 01463 782273
★★ Bed & Breakfast

Rheindown Farm Holidays
Rheindown, Beauly,
Inverness-shire, IV4 7AB
Tel: 01463 782461
★★★ Bed & Breakfast

BY BEAULY

Broomhill
Kiltarlity, Beauly,
Inverness-shire, IV4 7JH
Tel: 01463 741447
★★★ Bed & Breakfast

BETTYHILL

Farr Bay Inn
Bettyhill, By Thurso, Sutherland,
KW14 7SZ
Tel: 01641 521230
★★ Inn

BOAT OF GARTEN

The Boat House
Deishar Road, Boat of Garten,
Inverness-shire, PH24 3BN
Tel: 01479 831484
★★★ Bed & Breakfast

Granlea House
Deshar Road, Boat of Garten,
Inverness-shire, PH24 3BN
Tel: 01479 831601
★★★ Guest House

BRORA

Ar Dachaidh
Badnellan, Brora, Sutherland,
KW9 6NQ
Tel: 01408 621658
★★ Bed & Breakfast

Baldovie
Harbour Road, Brora,
Sutherland, KW9 6QF
Tel: 01408 621920
★★★ Bed & Breakfast

Glenaveron
Golf Road, Brora, Sutherland,
KW9 6QS
Tel: 01408 621601
★★★★ Bed & Breakfast

Rockpool Guest House
Rosslyn Street, Brora,
Sutherland, KW9 6NY
Tel: 01408 621505
★★★ Bed & Breakfast

Seaforth
Achrimsdale, Brora, Sutherland,
KW9 6LT
Tel: 01408 621793
★★★ Bed & Breakfast

Tigh Fada
18 Golf Road, Brora, Sutherland,
KW9 6QS
Tel: 01408 621332
★★★★ Bed & Breakfast

CANISBAY

Windybraes
Upper Gills, Canisbay,
Caithness, KW1 4YB
Tel: 01955 611386
★★★ Bed & Breakfast

CANNICH

Comar Lodge
Cannich, Bt Beauly,
Inverness-Shire, IV4 7NB
Tel: 01456 415251
★★ Bed & Breakfast

Kerrow House
Cannich, by Beauly,
Inverness-shire, IV4 7NA
Tel: 01456 415243
★★★ Bed & Breakfast

Westward
Cannich, By Beauly,
Inverness-shire, IV4 7LT
Tel: 01456 415708
★★ Bed & Breakfast

CARRBRIDGE

Birchwood
12 Rowan Park, Carrbridge,
PH23 3BE
Tel: 01479 841393
★★★ Bed & Breakfast

Caberfeidh Guest House
Station Road, Carrbridge,
Inverness-shire, PH23 3AN
Tel: 01479 841638
★★★ Bed & Breakfast

The Cairn Hotel
Main Road, Carrbridge,
Inverness-shire, PH23 3AS
Tel: 01479 841212
★★★ Inn

CAWDOR

Dallaschyle
Cawdor, By Nairn, Nairnshire,
IV12 5XS
Tel: 01667 493422
★★★ Bed & Breakfast

Newton of Budgate Farm
Cawdor, Nairnshire, IV12 5XS
Tel: 01667 404256
★★★ Bed & Breakfast

CONTIN

Hideaway
Craigdarroch Drive, Contin,
Ross-shire, IV14 9EL
Tel: 01997 421127
★★★★ Bed & Breakfast

CROMARTY

Newfield
Newhall Bridge, Poyntzfield,
by Dingwall, IV7 8LQ
Tel: 01381 610325
★★★★ Bed & Breakfast

NR CROMARTY

Braelangwell House
Balbair, Ross-shire, IV7 8LT
Tel: 01381 610353
★★★★★ Bed & Breakfast

CULBOKIE

Cam-mont House
No 2 Balloan, by Culbokie,
Ross-shire, IV7 8HU
Tel: 01349 877061
★★★★ Bed & Breakfast

Solus Or
Harmonology Centre, Findon
Hill, Culbokie, Black Isle,
Ross-shire, IV7 8JH
Tel: 01349 877828
★★★★ Bed & Breakfast

CULBOKIE, BLACK ISLE

Averon House
Wester Toberchurn, Culbokie,
by Dingwall, Ross-shire, IV7 8LS
Tel: 01349 877179
★★★★ Bed & Breakfast

CULLODEN MOOR

Bayview B&B
Westhill, Inverness, IV2 5BP
Tel: 01463 790386
★★★ Bed & Breakfast

Culdoich Farm
Culloden Moor, by Inverness,
Inverness-shire, IV1 2EP
Tel: 01463 790268
★★★ Bed & Breakfast

Leanach Farm
Culloden Moor, by Invernes,
Inverness-shire, IV1 2EJ
Tel: 01463 791027
★★★★ Bed & Breakfast

Strathmore
Viewhill Farm Road, Culloden
Moor, by Inverness,
Inverness-shire, IV1 2EA
Tel: 01463 791607
★★★ Bed & Breakfast

Westhill House
Westhill, Inverness, IV2 5BP
Tel: 01463 793225
★★ Bed & Breakfast

DALWHINNIE

Balsporran Cottages
Drumochter Pass, by
Dalwhinnie, Inverness-shire,
PH19 1AF
Tel: 01528 522389
★★★ Bed & Breakfast

DAVIOT

The Lodge at Daviot Mains
Daviot, By Inverness, IV2 5ER
Tel: 01463 772215
★★★★ Bed & Breakfast

DINGWALL

Fairfield House
Craig Road, Dingwall,
Ross-shire, IV15 9LF
Tel: 01349 864754
★★★★ Bed & Breakfast

Moydene
Craig Road, Dingwall,
Ross-shire, IV15 9LE
Tel: 01349 864965
★★★ Bed & Breakfast

DORES

Pottery House
Dores, Inverness, IV2 6TR
Tel: 01463 751267
★★★ Bed & Breakfast

**DORNIE,
BY KYLE OF LOCHALSH**

Castle View
Upper Ardelve, By Dornie,
Kyle of Lochalsh, Ross-shire,
IV40 8EY
Tel: 01599 555453
★★★ Bed & Breakfast

Eilean A-Cheo
Dornie, by Kyle of Lochalsh,
Ross-shire, IV40 8DY
Tel: 01599 555485
★★★ Bed & Breakfast

Fasgadale
2 Sallachy, Dornie, Kyle,
Ross-shire, IV40 8DZ
Tel: 01599 588238
★★★ Bed & Breakfast

Sealladh Mara
Dornie, Kyle of Lochalsh,
Ross-shire, IV40 8EY
Tel: 01599 555296
★★★ Bed & Breakfast

DORNOCH
Amalfi
River Street, Dornoch,
Sutherland, IV25 3LY
Tel: 01862 810015
★★★ Bed & Breakfast

Auchlea
Balnapolaig Muir, Dornoch,
Sutherland, IV25 3HY
Tel: 01862 811524
★★★ Bed & Breakfast

Corven B&B
Station Road, Embo, by
Dornoch, Sutherland, IV25 3PR
Tel: 01862 810128
★★ Bed & Breakfast

Crann Faibhile
The Mound, Dornoch,
Sutherland, IV25 3JF
Tel: 01408 634052
★★★ Bed & Breakfast

Hillview Bed and Breakfast
Evelix Road, Dornoch,
Sutherland, IV25 3RD
Tel: 01862 810151
★★★★ Bed & Breakfast

Tordarroch
Castle Street, Dornoch,
Sutherland, IV25 3SN
Tel: 01862 810855
★★★ Bed & Breakfast

The Trentham Hotel
The Poles, Dornoch, Sutherland,
IV25 3HZ
Tel: 01862 810551
★ Inn

DRUMNADROCHIT
Allanmore Farm
Drumnadrochit, Inverness-shire,
IV63 6XE
Tel: 01456 450247
★★★ Bed & Breakfast

Arden Lodge
East Lewiston, Drumnadrochit,
Inverness-shire, IV63 6UJ
Tel: 01456 450107
★★★★ Bed & Breakfast

Benleva Hotel
Drumnadrochit, Inverness-shire,
IV63 6UH
Tel: 01456 450080
★★ Inn

Bridgend House
The Green, Drumnadrochit,
Inverness-shire, IV63 6TX
Tel: 01456 450865
★★★★ Bed & Breakfast

Ferness Cottage
Lewiston, Drumnadrochit,
IV63 6UW
Tel: 01456 450564
★★★ Bed & Breakfast

Gillyflowers
East Lewiston, Drumnadrochit,
Inverness, IV63 6UJ
Tel: 01456 450641
★★★ Bed & Breakfast

Glenkirk
Drumnadrochit, Loch Ness,
IV63 6TZ
Tel: 01456 450802
★★★ Bed & Breakfast

Glen Rowan House
West Lewiston, Drumnadrochit,
Inverness-shire, IV63 6UW
Tel: 01456 450235
★★★ Bed & Breakfast

Kilmore Farmhouse
Drumnadrochit, IV53 6UF
Tel: 01456 450524
★★★★ Bed & Breakfast

Knowle B&B
136 Balmacaan Road,
Drumnadrochit, Inverness-shire,
IV63 6UP
Tel: 01456 450646
★★★ Bed & Breakfast

Maeshowe
Walled Garden, Balmacaan,
Drumnadrochit, Inverness-shire,
IV63 6UP
Tel: 01456 450 382
★★★★ Bed & Breakfast

Maily's Pool
Polmaily Farm, Drumnadrochit,
Inverness, IV63 6XT
Tel: 01456 450348
★★★ Bed & Breakfast

Woodlands
East Lewiston, Drumnadrochit,
Inverness-shire, IV63 6UJ
Tel: 01456 450356
★★★★ Guest House

DUIRINISH, BY PLOCKTON
Seann Bhruthach
Duirinish, by Plockton,
Ross-shire, IV40 8BE
Tel: 01599 544204
★★★ Bed & Breakfast

DUNBEATH
Tormore Farm
Tormore, Dunbeath, Caithness,
KW6 6EH
Tel: 01593 731240
★★ Bed & Breakfast

DUNDONNELL
Badrallach D,B&B
Croft 9, Badrallach, Dundonnell,
Ross-shire, IV23 2QP
Tel: 01854 633281
★★★★ Bed & Breakfast

4 Camusnagaul
Dundonnell, Ross-shire,
IV23 2QT
Tel: 01854 633237
★★★ Bed & Breakfast

DURNESS
Glengolly
Durine, Durness, by Lairg,
Sutherland, IV27 4PN
Tel: 01941 511255
★★★ Bed & Breakfast

Morven
Lerin, Durness, Sutherland,
IV27 4QB
Tel: 01971 511252
★★★ Bed & Breakfast

Puffin Cottage
Durness, Sutherland, IV27 4PN
Tel: 01971 511208
★★★ Bed & Breakfast

Smoo Cave Hotel
Durness, Sutherland, IV27 4QB
Tel: 01971 511227
★ Inn

Smoo Falls
Durness, by Lairg, Sutherland,
IV27 4QA
Tel: 01971 511228
★★★ Bed & Breakfast

FARR, BY INVERNESS
Dunlichity House
Tordarroch, Farr, by Inverness,
IV2 6XF
Tel: 01808 521442
★★★★ Bed & Breakfast

FORT AUGUSTUS
Cahirciveen
Canalside, Fort Augustus,
Inverness-shire, PH32 4BA
Tel: 01320 366202
★★ Bed & Breakfast

Carn A' Chuilinn, Anne Nicolson
Golf Course Road, Fort
Augustus, Inverness-shire,
PH32 4BY
Tel: 01320 366387
★★★★ Bed & Breakfast

Cartref B&B
Fort William Road, Fort
Augustus, Inverness-shire,
PH32 4BH
Tel: 01320 366255
★★★ Bed & Breakfast

Kettle House
Golf Course Road, Fort
Augustus, Inverness-shire,
PH32 4BY
Tel: 01320 366408
★★★ Bed & Breakfast

Lorien House
Station Road, Fort Augustus,
Inverness-shire, PH32 4AY
Tel: 01320 366736
★★★ Bed & Breakfast

Mavisburn
The Steadings, Auchterawe, Fort Augustus, Inverness-Shire, PH32 4BT
Tel: 01320 366479
★★★★ Bed & Breakfast

Sonas
Inverness Road, Fort Augustus, PH32 4DH
Tel: 01320 366291
★★★★ Bed & Breakfast

Thistle Dubh
Auchterawe Road, Fort Augustus, Inverness-shire, PH32 4BN
Tel: 01320 366380
★★★ Bed & Breakfast

Tigh Na Mairi
Canalside, Fort Augustus, Inverness-shire, PH32 4BA
Tel: 01320 366766
★★ Bed & Breakfast

FORTROSE

Hillhaven
Ordhill, Fortrose, Ross-shire, IV10 8RA
Tel: 01381 620826/
07719 889550
★★★ Bed & Breakfast

FORT WILLIAM

Achintee Farm Guest House
Achintee, Fort William, Inverness-shire, PH33 6TE
Tel: 01397 702240
★★★ Bed & Breakfast

81 Alma Road
Fort William, Inverness-shire, PH33 6HF
Tel: 01397 703757
★★ Bed & Breakfast

Alma View
Alma Road, Fort William, Inverness-shire, PH33 6HD
Tel: 01397 704115
★★★ Bed & Breakfast

Alt-An Lodge
Achintore Road, Fort William, Inverness-shire, PH33 6RN
Tel: 01397 704546
★★★ Bed & Breakfast

Ardblair
Fassifern Road, Fort William, Inverness-shire, PH33 6LJ
Tel: 01397 705832
★★★★ Bed & Breakfast

Ardmory
Victoria Road, Fort William, Inverness-shire, PH33 6BH
Tel: 01397 705943
★★★ Bed & Breakfast

Aros Ard
Seafield Gardens, Fort William, Inverness-shire, PH33 6RJ
Tel: 01397 704142
★★★★ Bed & Breakfast

Balcarres
Seafield Gardens, Fort William, Inverness-shire, PH33 6RJ
Tel: 01397 702377
★★★★ Bed & Breakfast

Ben Nevis View
Station Road, Corpach, by Fort William, Inverness-shire, PH33 7JH
Tel: 01397 772131
★★★ Bed & Breakfast

Blythedale
Seafield Gardens, Fort William, Inverness-shire, PH33 6RJ
Tel: 01397 705523
★★★★ Bed & Breakfast

Braemar
Lundy Gardens, Inverlochy, Fort William, Inverness-shire, PH33 6PD
Tel: 01397 705988
★★★★ Bed & Breakfast

Braeside House
Argyll Road, Fort William, Inverness-shire, PH33 6LF
Tel: 01397 705466
★★★ Bed & Breakfast

6 Caberfeidh
Fassifern Road, Fort William, Inverness-shire, PH33 6BE
Tel: 01397 703756
★★★ Bed & Breakfast

11 Castle Drive
Lochyside, Fort William, Inverness-shire, PH33 7NR
Tel: 01397 702659
★★★ Bed & Breakfast

Cloysta Cottage
Victoria Road, Fort William, Inverness-shire, PH33 6BH
Tel: 01397 706162
★★★ Bed & Breakfast

Corrieview
Lochyside, Fort William, PH33 7NX
Tel: 01397 703608
★★★ Bed & Breakfast

Crolinnhe
Grange Road, Fort William, PH33 6JF
Tel: 01397 702709
★★★★★ Bed & Breakfast

Cuil-Na-Sithe
Lochyside, Fort William, Inverness-shire, PH33 7NX
Tel: 01397 702267
★★★ Bed & Breakfast

Dalriada
71 Camaghael, Fort William, Inverness-shire, PH33 7NF
Tel: 01397 704048
★★★ Bed & Breakfast

Dorlin
Cameron Road, Fort William, Inverness-shire, PH33 6LG
Tel: 01397 701767
★★ Bed & Breakfast

22 Douglas Place
Fort William, Inverness-shire, PH33 6HL
Tel: 01397 702473
★★ Bed & Breakfast

Fernbank
5 Caberfeidh, Fassifern Road, Fort William, Inverness-shire, PH33 6BE
Tel: 01397 704341
★★★ Bed & Breakfast

Ferndale
Tomacharich, Torlundy, Fort William, Inverness-shire, PH33 6SP
Tel: 01397 703593
★★★ Bed & Breakfast

Garadh-Nan-Ros
24 Sutherland Avenue, Fort William, Inverness-shire, PH33 6JT
Tel: 01397 703861
★★★ Bed & Breakfast

Glengyle
Glen Nevis, Fort William, Inverness-shire, PH33 6PF
Tel: 01397 708622
★★★★ Bed & Breakfast

Glenlochy Guest House
Nevis Bridge, Fort William, Inverness-shire, PH33 6LP
Tel: 01397 702909
★★★ Guest House

Gowan Brae
Union Road, Fort William, Inverness-shire, PH33 6RB
Tel: 01397 704399
★★★ Bed & Breakfast

The Grange
Grange Road, Fort William, Inverness-shire, PH33 6JF
Tel: 01397 705516
★★★★★ Bed & Breakfast

24 Henderson Row
Fort William, Inverness-shire, PH33 6HT
Tel: 01397 702711
★★★ Bed & Breakfast

Huntingtower Lodge
Druimarbin, Fort William, Inverness-shire, PH33 6RP
Tel: 01397 700079
★★★★ Bed & Breakfast

Innishfree
Lochyside, Fort William, Inverness-shire, PH33 7NX
Tel: 01397 705471
★★★★ Bed & Breakfast

Keirlee
36 Grange Road, Fort William, Inverness-shire, PH33 6JF
Tel: 01397 702803
★★ Bed & Breakfast

Kintail
Seafield Gardens, Fort William, Inverness-shire, PH33 6RJ
Tel: 01397 701025
★★★★ Bed & Breakfast

Kismet Villa
Heathercroft, off Argyll Terrace, Fort William, Inverness-shire, PH33 6RE
Tel: 01397 703654
★★ Bed & Breakfast

Lawriestone Guest House
Achintore Road, Fort William, Inverness-shire, PH33 6RQ
Tel: 01397 700777
★★★★ Bed & Breakfast

Leasona Bed & Breakfast
Torlundy, Fort William, PH33 6SW
Tel: 01397 704661
★★★ Bed & Breakfast

Lochan Cottage Guest House
Lochyside, Fort William, Inverness-shire, PH33 7NX
Tel: 01397 702695
★★★★ Guest House

Mansefield Guest House
Corpach, Fort William, Inverness-shire, PH33 7LT
Tel: 01397 772262
★★★ Guest House

Mayfield Bed & Breakfast
Happy Valley, Torlundy, Fort William, PH33 6SN
Tel: 01397 703320
★★★★ Bed & Breakfast

Melantee
Achintore Road, Fort William, Inverness-shire, PH33 6RW
Tel: 01397 705329
★★ Bed & Breakfast

16 Melantee
Claggan, Fort William, Inverness-shire, PH33 6PL
Tel: 01397 703870
★★★ Bed & Breakfast

4 Perth Place
Fort William, Inverness-shire, PH33 6UL
Tel: 01397 706118
★★★ Bed & Breakfast

Quaich Cottage
Upper Banavie, Fort William, Inverness-shire, PH33 7PB
Tel: 01397 772799
★★★★ Bed & Breakfast

Rhiw Goch
Banavie, Fort William, PH33 7LY
Tel: 01397 772373
★★★ Bed & Breakfast

Ruaidheabhal
7 Seafield Gardens, Fort William, Inverness-shire, PH33 6RJ
Tel: 01397 703714
★★★ Bed & Breakfast

Rustic View
Lochyside, by Fort William, Inverness-shire, PH33 7NX
Tel: 01397 704709
★★★★ Bed & Breakfast

Seangan Croft
Banavie, Fort William, PH33 7PB
Tel: 01397 773114
★★★ Bed & Breakfast

St Anthonys
Argyll Road, Fort William, Inverness-shire, PH33 6LF
Tel: 01397 708496
★★ Bed & Breakfast

Stobahn
Fassifern Road, Fort William, PH33 6BD
Tel: 01397 702790
★★ Bed & Breakfast

Strathavon
Grange Road, Fort William, Inverness-shire, PH33 6JF
Tel: 01397 705033
★★★ Bed & Breakfast

Taormina
Banavie, Fort William, PH33 7LY
Tel: 01397 772217
★★ Bed & Breakfast

Thistle Cottage
Torlundy, Fort William, Inverness-shire, PH33 6SN
Tel: 01397 702428
★★★ Bed & Breakfast

Tigh Na Faigh
Achintore Road, Fort William, Inverness-shire, PH33 6RN
Tel: 01397 702079
★★★★ Bed & Breakfast

Torgulbin
Cameron Road, Fort William, Inverness-shire, PH33 6AJ
Tel: 01397 702220
★★★ Bed & Breakfast

Torlinnhe
Achintore Road, Fort William, Inverness-shire, PH33 6RN
Tel: 01397 702583
★★ Bed & Breakfast

Viewfield House
Alma Road, Fort William, Inverness-shire, PH33 6HD
Tel: 01397 704763
★★ Guest House

Voringfoss B&B
5 Stirling Place, Fort William, Inverness-shire, PH33 6UW
Tel: 01397 704062
★★★★ Bed & Breakfast

The Waterfront Lodge
An Aird, Fort William, Inverness-shire, PH33 6AN
Tel: 01397 703786
★★ Lodge

West Haven
Achintore Road, Fort William, Inverness-shire, PH33 6RW
Tel: 01397 705500
★★★★ Bed & Breakfast

BY FORT WILLIAM

Dailanna Guest House
Kinlocheil, Fort William, Inverness-shire, PH33 7NP
Tel: 01397 722253
★★★★ Bed & Breakfast

NR FORT WILLIAM

Springburn Farm House
Stronaba, Spean Bridge, Inverness-shire, PH34 4DX
Tel: 01397 712707
★★★★ Bed & Breakfast

FOYERS

Evergreen
Inverfarigaig, Inverness-shire, IV2 6XR
Tel: 01456 486717
★★★★ Bed & Breakfast

Intake House
Foyers, Inverness-shire, IV1 2YA
Tel: 01456 486258
★★★★ Bed & Breakfast

GAIRLOCH

Charleston House
Gairloch, Ross-shire, IV21 2AH
Tel: 01445 712497
★★★ Restaurant with Rooms

Dunedin
42 Strath, Gairloch, Ross-shire, IV21 2DB
Tel: 01445 712050
★★★ Bed & Breakfast

Heatherdale
Charleston, Gairloch, Ross-shire, IV21 2AH
Tel: 01445 712388
★★★★ Bed & Breakfast

Kerrysdale House
Gairloch, Rosshire, IV21 2AL
Tel: 01445 712292
★★★ Bed & Breakfast

Lochview
41 Lonemore, Gairloch, Ross-shire, IV21 2DB
Tel: 01445 712676
★★★ Bed & Breakfast

Mrs Maclean
Strathlene, 45 Strath, Lonmore, Gairloch,, Ross-shire, IV21 2DB
Tel: 01445 712170
★★★ Bed & Breakfast

Newton House Bed & Breakfast
Mihol Road, Strath, Gairloch, IV21 2BX
Tel: 01445 712007
★★★ Bed & Breakfast

Stratford House
Milhol Road, Strath, Gairloch, Ross-shire, IV21 2BX
Tel: 01445 712183
★★★ Bed & Breakfast

Tregurnow
57 Lonemore, Strath, Gairloch, Ross-Shire, IV21 2DB
Tel: 01445 712116
★★★★ Bed & Breakfast

GARVE

Birch Cottage
7 Station Road, Garve,
Ross-shire, IV23 2PS
Tel: 01997 414237
★★★ Bed & Breakfast

Hazelbrae House
Garve, Ross-shire, IV23 2PX
Tel: 01997 414382
★★★ Bed & Breakfast

GLENCOE

An Darag
Upper Carnoch, Glencoe, Argyll,
PH49 4HU
Tel: 01855 811643
★★★ Bed & Breakfast

Callart View B&B
Invercoe, Glencoe, Argyll,
PH49 4HP
Tel: 01855 811259
★★★ Bed & Breakfast

Dunire Guest House
Glencoe, Argyll, PA39 4HS
Tel: 01855 811305
★★★ Guest House

Gleann-Leac-Na-Muidhe
Glencoe, Argyll, PH49 4LA
Tel: 01855 811598
★★★★ Bed & Breakfast

Kings House Hotel
Glencoe, Argyll, PH49 4HY
Tel: 01855 851 259
★ Inn

Scorrybreac Guest House
Glencoe, Argyll, PH49 4HT
Tel: 01855 811354
★★★ Guest House

Strathassynt Guest House
Loan Fern, Ballachulish, Argyll,
PH49 4JB
Tel: 01855 811261
★★★ Guest House

Tigh Ard
Brecklet, Ballachulish, Argyll,
PH49 4JG
Tel: 01855 811328
★★ Bed & Breakfast

GLENELG

Galder
Glenelg, by Kyle of Lochalsh,
Inverness-shire, IV40 8JZ
Tel: 01599 522 287
★★★ Bed & Breakfast

GLENMORISTON

Burnside Guest House
Bhlaraidh, Glenmoriston,
Inverness-shire, IV63 7YH
Tel: 01320 351269
★★★ Bed & Breakfast

Ceannacroc Lodge
Glen Moriston, Inverness-shire,
IV63 7YN
Tel: 01320 340243
★★ Bed & Breakfast

Serendipity
Dalchreichart, Glenmoriston,
Inverness-shire, IV63 7YJ
Tel: 01320 340356
★★★ Bed & Breakfast

GLEN NEVIS, BY FORT WILLIAM

Glenfer
Glen Nevis, Fort William,
Inverness-shire, PH33 6PF
Tel: 01397 705848
★★★ Bed & Breakfast

**GLENSHIEL,
BY KYLE OF LOCHALSH**

Glomach House
Ault-Na-Chruinne, Glenshiel,
by Kyle of Lochalsh, Ross-shire,
IV40 8HN
Tel: 01599 511 222
★★★★ Bed & Breakfast

Mo-dhachaidh
Inverinate, Ross-shire, IV40 8HB
Tel: 01599 511351
★★★ Bed & Breakfast

GOLSPIE

Rhives House
Golspie, Sutherland, KW10 6SD
Tel: 01408 633285
★★★★ Bed & Breakfast

GRANTOWN-ON-SPEY

An Cala Guest House
Woodlands Terrace, Grantown
on Spey, Moray, PH26 3JU
Tel: 01479 873293
★★★★ Guest House

Bank House
1 The Square, Grantown-on-
Spey, Morayshire, PH26 3HG
Tel: 01479 873256
★★★★ Bed & Breakfast

Brooklynn
Grant Road, Grantown on Spey,
PH26 3LA
Tel: 01479 873113
★★★★ Guest House

Dunallan House
Woodside Avenue, Grantown-
on-Spey, Moray, PH26 3JN
Tel: 01479 872140
★★★★ Guest House

Firhall Guest House
Grant Road, Grantown-on-Spey,
Moray, PH26 3LD
Tel: 01479 873097
★★★ Guest House

Revoan
Seafield Avenue, Grantown-on-
Spey, Invernessshire, PH26 3JF
Tel: 01479 872 227
★★★★ Bed & Breakfast

Rosegrove Guesthouse
Skye of Curr, Dulnain Bridge,
Grantown on Spey,
Inverness-shire, PH26 3PA
Tel: 01479 851335
★★★ Guest House

Rossmor Guest House
Woodlands Terrace, Grantown
on Spey, Moray, PH26 3JU
Tel: 01479 872201
★★★★ Guest House

GRANTOWN-ON-SPEY BY

Haugh Hotel
Cromdale, Grantown-on-Spey,
PH26 3LW
Tel: 01479 872583
★★★ Inn

HELMSDALE

Broomhill House
Navidale Road, Helmsdale,
Sutherland, KW8 6JS
Tel: 01431 821259
★★★ Bed & Breakfast

Torbuie
Navidale, Helmsdale,
Sutherland, KW8 6JS
Tel: 01431 821424
★★★★ Bed & Breakfast

INSH

Greenfield Croft
Insh, by Kingussie,
Inverness-shire, PH21 1NT
Tel: 01540 661010
★★★ Bed & Breakfast

INVERGARRY

Forest Lodge
South Laggan, Invergarry,
by Spean Bridge, PH34 4EA
Tel: 01809 501219
★★★ Guest House

INVERGORDON

Craigaron
17 Saltburn, Invergordon,
Ross & Cromarty, IV18 0JX
Tel: 01349 853640
★★ Guest House

Delny House
Delny, Invergordon, Ross-shire,
IV18 0NP
Tel: 01862 842678
★★★★
Restaurant with Rooms

**INVERINATE,
BY KYLE OF LOCHALSH**

Sonas
Inverinate, By Kyle of Lochalsh,
IV40 8HB
Tel: 01599 511444
★★★ Bed & Breakfast

INVERMORISTON

Riverbank Lodge
Invermoriston, Inverness-shire,
IV63 7YA
Tel: 01320 351287
★★★★ Bed & Breakfast

Georgeston
Invermoriston, Inverness-shire, IV63 7YA
Tel: 01320 351264
★★★ Bed & Breakfast

Lann Dearg Studios
Lann Dearg, Dalcataig, Invermoriston, IV63 7YG
Tel: 01456 459083
★★★★ Bed & Breakfast

Tigh Na Bruach
Invermoriston, Inverness-shire, IV63 7YE
★★★★★ Bed & Breakfast

INVERNESS

Aberfeldy Lodge Guest House
11 Southside Road, Inverness, IV2 3BG
Tel: 01463 231120
★★★ Guest House

Advie Lodge
31 Crown Drive, Inverness, IV2 3QQ
Tel: 01463 237247
★★★★ Bed & Breakfast

Amulree
40 Fairfield Road, Inverness, IV3 5QD
Tel: 01463 224822
★★★ Bed & Breakfast

An Airidh
65 Fairfield Road, Inverness, IV3 5LH
Tel: 01463 240673
★★ Bed & Breakfast

Anchor and Chain
Coulmore Bay, North Kessock, Inverness-shire, IV1 3XB
Tel: 01463 731313
★★★ Restaurant with Rooms

Ardgowan Lodge Guest House
Wester Phoineas, By Beauly, Inverness-shire, IV4 7BA
Tel: 01463 741745
★★★★ Bed & Breakfast

Aros
5 Abertarff Road, Inverness, IV2 3NW
Tel: 01463 235674
★★★ Bed & Breakfast

Atherstone
42 Farifield Road, Inverness, IV3 5QD
Tel: 01463 240240
★★★ Bed & Breakfast

Balcroydon
6 Broadstone Park, Inverness, IV2 3LA
Tel: 01463 221506
★★ Bed & Breakfast

Balthangie B&B
Inverness, IV3 5PH
Tel: 01463 237637
★★★★ Bed & Breakfast

Benriach Guest House
18 Perceval Road, Inverness, Inverness-shire, IV3 5QE
Tel: 01463 241959
★★★ Bed & Breakfast

Bluebell House
31 Kenneth Street, Inverness, IV3 5DH
Tel: 01463 238201
★★★★ Bed & Breakfast

Braehead
5 Crown Circus, Inverness, IV2 3NH
Tel: 01463 224222
★★★ Bed & Breakfast

Bruar Cottage
11 Mayfield Road, Inverness, IV2 4AE
Tel: 01463 713949
★★ Bed & Breakfast

The Bungalow
21 Planefield Road, Inverness, IV3 5DL
Tel: 01463 237962
★★ Bed & Breakfast

Bunillidh
47 Montague Row, Inverness, IV3 5DX
Tel: 01463 225079
★★★ Bed & Breakfast

Cambeth Lodge
49 Fairfield Road, Inverness, IV3 5QP
Tel: 01463 231764
★★★ Bed & Breakfast

Cavell House
3 Moray Park, Island Bank Road, Inverness, IV2 4SX
Tel: 01463 232850
★★★ Bed & Breakfast

The Cherry Tree
9 Park Road, Inverness, Inverness-shire, IV3 5EP
Tel: 01463 233862
★★★ Bed & Breakfast

Clach Mhuilinn
7 Harris Road, Inverness, IV2 3LS
Tel: 01463 237059
★★★★★ Bed & Breakfast

Crathie
45 Old Edinburgh Road, Inverness, IV2 3PG
Tel: 01463 238259
★★★ Bed & Breakfast

21 Crown Drive
Inverness, IV2 3QF
Tel: 01463 232614
★★★ Bed & Breakfast

Culcabock House
3 Culcabock Road, Inverness, IV2 3XW
★★★★ Bed & Breakfast

Dalmore Guest House
101 Kenneth Street, Inverness, IV3 5QQ
Tel: 01463 237224
★★★ Guest House

Dionard
39 Old Edinburgh Road, Inverness, IV2 3HJ
Tel: 01463 233557
★★★★ Bed & Breakfast

Drumossie Park Cottage
Drumossie Brae, Inverness, Inverness-shire, IV2 5BB
Tel: 01463 224127
★★★★ Bed & Breakfast

Easter Muckovie Farm
Westhill, Inverness, Inverness-shire, IV1 2BN
Tel: 01463 791 556
★★★ Bed & Breakfast

Eiland View Bed & Breakfast
Woodside of Culloden, Westhill, Inverness, IV2 5BP
Tel: 01463 798900
★★★★ Bed & Breakfast

Express by Holiday Inn
Stoneyfield, Inverness, IV2 7PA
Tel: 01463 732700
★★★ Lodge

Fenton House
6 Crown Circus, Inverness, Inverness-shire, IV2 3NQ
Tel: 01463 223604
★★ Bed & Breakfast

Fraser House
49 Huntly Street, Inverness, IV3 5HS
Tel: 01463 716488
★★★ Guest House

Furan Cottage
100 Old Edinburgh Road, Inverness, IV2 3HT
Tel: 01463 712094
★★★ Bed & Breakfast

The Gatehouse
80 Old Edinburgh Road, Inverness, IV2 3PG
Tel: 01463 234590
★★★★ Bed & Breakfast

The Ghillies Lodge
16 Island Bank Road, Inverness, Inverness-shire, IV2 4QS
Tel: 01463 232137
★★★★ Bed & Breakfast

14 Glenburn Drive
Inverness, IV2 4ND
Tel: 01463 238832
★★★ Bed & Breakfast

Glendoune B&B
24 Perceval Road, Inverness, Inverness-shire, IV3 5QE
Tel: 01463 231493
★★★ Bed & Breakfast

Handa
56 Lochalsh Road, Inverness, IV3 8HW
Tel: 01463 236530
★★★ Bed & Breakfast

Heathmount Hotel
Kingsmills Road, Inverness,
IV2 3JV
Tel: 01463 235877
★★★ Inn

Heronwood
16A Island Bank Road,
Inverness, Inverness-shire,
IV2 4QS
Tel: 01463 243275
★★★ Bed & Breakfast

Highfield House
62 Old Edinburgh Road,
Inverness, IV2 3PG
Tel: 01463 238892
★★★★ Bed & Breakfast

Hornbeam
12A Lovat Road, Inverness,
Inverness-shire, IV2 3NT
Tel: 01463 225655
★★★ Bed & Breakfast

J A Jamieson
The Linn, Inshes, Inverness,
IV2 5BG
Tel: 01463 231260
Awaiting Inspection

The Kemps
64 Telford Street, Inverness,
IV3 5LE
Tel: 01463 285780
★★★ Bed & Breakfast

Kindeace
9 Lovat Road, Inverness,
Inverness-shire, IV2 3NT
Tel: 01463 241041
★★ Bed & Breakfast

Lakefield
21 Leys Drive, Inverness,
Inverness-shire, IV2 3JB
Tel: 01463 238352
★★★★ Bed & Breakfast

Larchfield House
15 Ness Bank, Inverness,
IV2 4SF
Tel: 01463 233874
★★★ Guest House

Lindores
20 Rangemore Road, Inverness,
Inverness-shire, IV3 5EA
Tel: 01463 235807
★★ Bed & Breakfast

Logan Cottage
43 Ballifeary Road, Inverness,
IV3 5PG
Tel: 01463 235514
★★★★ Bed & Breakfast

Lorne House
40 Crown Drive, Inverness,
IV2 3QG
Tel: 01463 236271
★★★★ Bed & Breakfast

Lyndon
50 Telford Street, Inverness,
IV3 5LE
Tel: 01463 232551
★★★★ Bed & Breakfast

Lynver
30 Southside Road, Inverness,
IV2 3BG
Tel: 01463 242906
★★★★ Bed & Breakfast

Lynwilg
5 Green Drive, Inverness,
IV2 4EX
Tel: 01463 232733
★ Bed & Breakfast

Malvern Guest House
54 Kenneth Street, Inverness,
IV3 5PZ
Tel: 01463 242251
★★★ Guest House

Melness
8 Old Edinburgh Road,
Inverness, IV2 3HF
Tel: 01463 220963
★★★★ Bed & Breakfast

Millwood House
36 Old Mill Road, Inverness,
Inverness-shire, IV2 3HR
Tel: 01463 237254
★★★★★ Bed & Breakfast

Parkhill Guest House
17 Ardconnel Street, Inverness,
IV2 3EU
Tel: 01463 223300
★★★ Guest House

Sealladh Sona
3 Whinpark, Canal Road,
Muirtown, Inverness,
Inverness-shire, IV3 8NQ
Tel: 01463 239209
★★★★ Bed & Breakfast

Strathmhor Guesthouse
99 Kenneth Street, Inverness,
IV3 5QQ
Tel: 01463 235397
★★★ Guest House

Summer Lee Guest House
33 Greig Street, Inverness,
Inverness-shire, IV3 5PX
Tel: 01463 225626
★★★ Bed & Breakfast

Sunnyholm
12 Mayfield Road, Inverness,
IV2 4AE
Tel: 01463 231336
★★★ Bed & Breakfast

Taigh Na Teile
6 Island Bank Road, Inverness,
Inverness-shire, IV2 4SY
Tel: 01463 222842
★★★★ Bed & Breakfast

Tamarue
70a Ballifeary Road, Inverness,
Inverness-shire, IV3 5PF
Tel: 01463 239724
★★★ Bed & Breakfast

Westerlea
Tower Brae South, Westhill,
Inverness, IV2 5BW
Tel: 01463 792890
★★★ Bed & Breakfast

Wimberley House
1 Wimberley Way, Inverness,
Inverness-shire, IV2 3XJ
Tel: 01463 224430
★★★★ Bed & Breakfast

Wychway
3 Haugh Road, Inverness,
IV2 4SD
Tel: 01463 239399
★★★ Bed & Breakfast

BY NVERNESS

Easter Dalziel Farmhouse
Easter Dalziel Farm, Dalcross,
Inverness, IV2 7JL
Tel: 01667 462213
★★★★ Bed & Breakfast

JOHN O'GROATS

Bencorragh House
Upper Gills, Canisbay, by John
O'Groats, Caithness, KW1 4YD
Tel: 01955 611449
★★★ Bed & Breakfast

Caber Feidh Guest House
John O'Groats, Wick, Caithness,
KW1 4YR
Tel: 01955 611219
★★ Guest House

Creag-Na-Mara
East Mey, by Thurso, Caithness,
KW14 8XL
Tel: 01847 851850
★★★ Bed & Breakfast

The Hawthorns
Mey, Thurso, Caithness,
KW14 8XH
Tel: 01847 851710
★★★ Bed & Breakfast

Mill House
John O'Groats, Caithness,
KW1 4YR
Tel: 01955 611239
★★ Bed & Breakfast

KEISS
Sinclair Bay Hotel
Keiss, Caithness, KW1 4UY
Tel: 01955 631233
★★ Inn

KILTARLITY
Cherry Trees
Kiltarlity, Inverness-shire,
IV4 7JQ
Tel: 01463 741368
★★★ Bed & Breakfast

KINCRAIG, BY KINGUSSIE
Insh Hall Lodge
Kincraig, Inverness-shire,
PH21 1NU
Tel: 01540 651272
★ Bed & Breakfast

Insh House Guesthouse
Kincraig, by Kingussie,
Inverness-shire, PH21 1NU
Tel: 01540 651377
★★★ Guest House

KINGUSSIE

Ardselma
The Crescent, Kingussie,
Inverness-shire, PH21 1JZ
Tel: 01540 661809
★★ Bed & Breakfast

The Auld Poor House
Kingussie, Inverness-shire,
PH21 1LS
Tel: 01540 661558
★★★★ Bed & Breakfast

The Cross
Tweed Mill Brae, Ardbroilach
Road, Kingussie, PH21 1LB
Tel: 01540 661166
★★★★
Restaurant with Rooms

Glengarry
East Terrace, Kingussie,
Inverness-shire, PH21 1JS
Tel: 01540 661386
★★★★ Bed & Breakfast

The Osprey Hotel
Ruthven Road, Kingussie,
Inverness-shire, PH21 1EN
Tel: 01540 661510
★★★ Small Hotel

Rowan House
Homewood, Newtonmore Road,
Kingussie, Inverness-shire,
PH21 1HD
Tel: 01540 662153
★★★★ Bed & Breakfast

Ruthven Farmhouse
Ruthven, Kingussie,
Inverness-shire, PH21 1NR
Tel: 01540 661226
★★★ Bed & Breakfast

St Helens
Ardbroilach Road, Kingussie,
Inverness-shire, PH21 1JX
Tel: 01540 661430
★★★★ Bed & Breakfast

Sonnhalde Guest House
East Terrace, Kingussie,
Inverness-shire, PH21 1JS
Tel: 015401 661 266
★★★ Bed & Breakfast

The Steadings at Ruthven
Ruthven, Kingussie,
Inverness-shire, PH21 1NR
Tel: 01540 662 328
★★★★ Bed & Breakfast

KINLOCHEWE

Hill Haven Bed and Breakfast
Kinlochewe, NR Achnasheen,
Ross-Shire, IV22 2PA
Tel: 01445 760204
★★★ Bed & Breakfast

Merlinwood
Kinlochewe, Achnasheen,
Ross-shire, IV22 2PA
Tel: 01445 760346
★★★ Bed & Breakfast

KINLOCHLEVEN

Edencoille Guest House
Garbhien Road, Kinlochleven,
Argyll, PH50 4SE
Tel: 01855 831358
★★★ Bed & Breakfast

Failte
6 Lovat Road, Kinlochleven,
Argyll, PH50 4RQ
Tel: 01855 831394
★★ Bed & Breakfast

Highland Getaway
28 Leven Road, Kinlochleven,
Argyll, PH50 4RP
Tel: 01855 831506
★★★ Restaurant with Rooms

Tigh-Na-Cheo Guest House
Garbhein Road, Kinlochleven,
PH50 4SE
Tel: 01855 831434
★★★ Guest House

KIRKHILL, BY INVERNESS

Old North Inn
Kirkhill, Inverness, IV5 7PX
Tel: 01463 831296
★★ Inn

KNOYDART

Doune Stone Lodges
Doune, Knoydart, Mallaig,
Inverness-shire, PH41 4PU
Tel: 01687 462667
★★★ Restaurant with Rooms

KYLE OF LOCHALSH

A'chomraich
Plockton Road, Kyle of Lochalsh,
IV40 8DA
Tel: 01599 534210
★ Bed & Breakfast

3 Lochalsh Road
Kyle of Lochalsh, Ross-shire,
IV40 8BP
Tel: 01599 534429
★★ Bed & Breakfast

The Old Schoolhouse
Erbusaig, Kyle, Ross-shire,
IV40 8BB
Tel: 01599 534369
★★★★ Bed & Breakfast

LAGGAN, BY NEWTONMORE

The Rumblie B&B
Gergask Avenue, Laggan, by
Newtonmore,, Inverness-shire,
PH20 1AH
Tel: 01528 544766
★★★★ Bed & Breakfast

LAIDE

Old Smiddy Guest House
Laide, Near Gairloch,
Ross-shire, IV22 2NB
Tel: 01445 731425
★★★★ Bed & Breakfast

The Sheiling
3 Achgarve, Laide, by
Achnasheen, Ross-shire,
IV22 2NS
Tel: 01445 731487
★★★★ Bed & Breakfast

LAIRG

Ambleside
Lochside, Lairg, Sutherland,
IV27 4EG
Tel: 01549 402130
★★★ Bed & Breakfast

Highland House
88 Lower Torroble, By Lairg,
Sutherland, IV27 4DH
Tel: 01549 402414
★★★★ Bed & Breakfast

Lochview
Lochside, Lairg, Sutherland,
IV27 4EH
Tel: 01549 402578
★★★★ Bed & Breakfast

Park House
Station Road, Lairg, Sutherland,
IV27 4AU
Tel: 01549 402208
★★★★ Bed & Breakfast

LEWISTON, DRUMANDROCHIT

Elmbank
Lewiston, Drumnadrochit,
Inverness-shire, IV63 6UW
Tel: 01456 450372
★★★ Bed & Breakfast

Linne Dhuinn
Lewiston, Drumnadrochit,
Inverness-shire, IV63 6UW
Tel: 01456 450244
★★★ Bed & Breakfast

LOCHCARRON

Castle Cottage
Main Street, Lochcarron,
Ross-shire, IV54 8YB
Tel: 01520 722564
★★★ Bed & Breakfast

Lethame
7 Kirkton Avenue, Lochcarron,
Ross-shire, IV54 8UE
Tel: 01520 722451
★★★ Bed & Breakfast

Lotta Dubh
Ardaneaskan, Lochcarron,
Ross-shire, IV54 8YL
Tel: 01520 722405
★★★ Bed & Breakfast

LOCHINVER

Ardglas Guest House
Lochinver, Sutherland, IV27 4LJ
Tel: 01571 844257
★★★ Guest House

Ardmore House
80 Torbreck, Lochinver,
Sutherland, IV27 4JB
Tel: 01571 844310
★★★★ Bed & Breakfast

Davar
Lochinver, Sutherland, IV27 4LJ
Tel: 01571 844501
★★★★ Bed & Breakfast

Polcraig Guest House
Lochinver, Sutherland, IV27 4LD
Tel: 01571 844429
★★★★ Guest House

Tigh Guithais
Lochinver, Sutherland, IV27 4LJ
Tel: 01571 844343
★★★ Bed & Breakfast

Veyatie
66 Baddidarrach, Lochinver, Sutherland, IV27 4LP
Tel: 01571 844424
★★★★ Bed & Breakfast

LOCH NESS

Foyers Bay House
Lower Foyers, Inverness, IV2 6YB
Tel: 01456 486624
★★★ Guest House

LYBSTER

The Croft House
Swiney, Lybster, Caithness, KW3 6BT
Tel: 01593 721342
★★★ Bed & Breakfast

BY MALLAIG

Faire-Nan-Eilean
Bracara, by Mallaig, Inverness-shire, PH40 4PE
Tel: 01687 462164
★★★ Bed & Breakfast

MALLAIG

Anchorage
Gillies Park, Mallaig, Inverness-shire, PH41 4QU
Tel: 01687 462454
★★★ Bed & Breakfast

Glencairn House
East Bay, Mallaig, Inverness-shire, PH41 4QG
Tel: 01687 462359
★★★ Bed & Breakfast

MELVICH

Tigh-Na-Clash Guest House
Melvich, Sutherland, KW14 7YJ
Tel: 01641 531262
★★★ Guest House

MORAR

Loch Morar House
Beoraid, Morar, by Mallaig, Inverness-shire, PH40 4PB
Tel: 01687 462 823
★★★ Bed & Breakfast

MUIR OF ORD

Dungrianach
Corrie Road, Muir of Ord, Ross-shire, IV6 7TN
Tel: 01463 870316
★★★ Bed & Breakfast

Hillview Park
Muir-of-Ord, Ross-shire, IV6 7TU
Tel: 01463 870787
★★★ Bed & Breakfast

Home Farm Bed and Breakfast
Highfield Mains, Muir of Ord, Ross-shire, IV6 7XN
Tel: 01463 871779
★★★ Bed & Breakfast

Shieldaig
Tore, Muir-of-Ord, Ross-shire, IV6 7RY
Tel: 01463 811410
★★★★ Bed & Breakfast

Wester Muckernich
Roadside, Killearan, Muir-of-Ord, IV6 7SA
Tel: 01349 861222
★★★★ Bed & Breakfast

MUNLOCHY

Kinneskie House
Balnakyle, Munlochy, Ross-shire, IV8 8PF
Tel: 01463 811779
★★★★ Bed & Breakfast

Munlochy Hotel
54 Millbank Road, Munlochy, Ross-shire, IV8 8NL
Tel: 01463 811494
★★ Inn

NAIRN

Brackla Farmhouse
Cawdor, Nairn, Inverness-shire, IV12 5QY
Tel: 01667 404223
★★★★ Bed & Breakfast

Ceolmara
Links Place, Nairn, IV12 4NH
Tel: 01667 452495
★★★★ Bed & Breakfast

Dalquillan
59 Park Street, Nairn, Nairnshire, IV12 4PP
Tel: 01667 451749
★★★ Bed & Breakfast

Drumblair
Lochloy Road, Nairn, Inverness-shire, IV12 5LF
Tel: 01667 456692
★★★ Bed & Breakfast

Glebe End
1 Glebe Road, Nairn, Inverness-shire, IV12 4ED
Tel: 01667 451659
★★★★ Bed & Breakfast

Inveran
Seabank Road, Nairn, Nairnshire, IV12 4HG
Tel: 01667 455666
★★★★ Bed & Breakfast

Napier
60 Seabank Road, Nairn, IV12 4HA
Tel: 01667 453 330
★★★★ Bed & Breakfast

Redburn
Queen Street, Nairn, Nairnshire, IV12 4AA
Tel: 01667 452238
★★★ Bed & Breakfast

NETHY BRIDGE

Aspen Lodge
Nethybridge, Inverness-shire, PH25 3DA
Tel: 01479 821042
★★★ Bed & Breakfast

Aultmore House
Nethy Bridge, Inverness-shire, PH25 3ED
Tel: 01479 821473
★★★★★ Bed & Breakfast

Juniper Cottage
Tulloch Road, Nethy Bridge, Inverness-shire, PH25 3DE
Tel: 01479 821456
★★★★ Bed & Breakfast

Tigh Na Fraoch
Nethybridge, Inverness-shire, PH25 3DA
Tel: 01479 821400
★★★ Bed & Breakfast

NORTH BALLACHULISH

Brudair
Kinlochleven Road, North Ballachulish, Argyll, PH33 6SB
Tel: 01855 821431
★★★ Bed & Breakfast

NORTH KESSOCK

Craigiewood
North Kessock, Inverness, IV1 3XG
Tel: 01463 731628
★★★★ Bed & Breakfast

Culbin
Drumsmittal, North Kessock, Inverness-shire, IV1 1XB
Tel: 01463 731455
★★★ Bed & Breakfast

Redfield Farm
North Kessock, Ross-shire, IV1 1XD
Tel: 01463 811228
★★★ Bed & Breakfast

Rose Cottage B&B
Kilmuir, North Kessock, Inverness, IV1 2ZG
Tel: 01463 731739
★★★ Bed & Breakfast

ONICH, BY FORT WILLIAM

Ceol-Na-Mara
North Ballachulish, Onich, Inverness-shire, PH33 6SA
Tel: 01855 821338
★★★ Bed & Breakfast

Nether Lochaber Hotel
South Corran, Onich, Inverness-shire, PH33 6SE
Tel: 01855 821235
★ Inn

Tom-na-Creige
Onich, Inverness-shire, PH33 6RY
Tel: 01855 821405
★★ Bed & Breakfast

PLOCKTON

Creag Liath
Achnandarach, Plockton, Ross-shire, IV52 8TY
Tel: 01599 544341
★★★★ Bed & Breakfast

Driseach
Plockton, Ross-shire, IV52 8TU
Tel: 01599 544362
★★★ Bed & Breakfast

Hill View Bed+Breakfast
2 Frithard Road, Plockton,
Ross-shire, IV52 8TQ
Tel: 01599 544226
★★★ Bed & Breakfast

Janet Jones
Tomac's, Frithard Road,
Plockton, Ross-shire,, IV52 8TQ
Tel: 01599 544321
★★★ Bed & Breakfast

Minvaugh
2 Railway Cottages, Plockton,
Ross-shire, IV52 8TT
Tel: 01599 544333
★★★ Bed & Breakfast

Plockton Inn
Plockton, Ross-shire, IV52 8TW
Tel: 01599 544222
★★★ Inn

Soluis Mu Thuath
Braeintra, by Achmore,
Lochalsh, Ross-shire, IV53 8UP
Tel: 01599 577219
★★ Guest House

POOLEWE
Bruach Ard
7 Braes, Inverasdale,
by Poolewe, Achnasheen,
Ross-shire, IV22 2LN
Tel: 01445 781765
★★★ Bed & Breakfast

RATAGAN
Grants at Craigellachie
Ratagan, Glenshiel, Ross-shire,
IV40 8HP
Tel: 01599 511331
★★★ Restaurant with Rooms

ROY BRIDGE
The Stronlossit Inn
Roy Bridge, Inverness-shire,
PH31 4AG
0800 015 5321
★★★ Inn

SCOURIE
Fasgadh
Scouriemore, By Lairg,
Sutherland, IV27 4TG
Tel: 01971 502402
★★★ Bed & Breakfast

Scourie Lodge
Scourie, Sutherland, IV27 4TE
Tel: 01971 502248
★★★★ Bed & Breakfast

ARDVASAR, SLEAT, ISLE OF SKYE
Homeleigh
3 Calgary, Ardvasar, Isle of Skye,
IV45 8RU
Tel: 01599 534011
★★★ Bed & Breakfast

BERNISDALE, BY PORTREE, ISLE OF SKYE
Lochview
45 Park, Bernsdale, Isle of Skye,
Inverness-shire, IV51 9NT
Tel: 01470 532 736
★★★★ Bed & Breakfast

BREAKISH, ISLE OF SKYE
Ashfield
14 Upper Breakish, Isle of Skye,
Inverness-shire, IV42 8PY
Tel: 01471 822301
★★★ Bed & Breakfast

Fernlea
11 Upper Breakish, near
Broadford, Isle of Skye,
IV42 8PY
Tel: 01471 822107
★★★ Bed & Breakfast

Ruisgarry
10 Upper Breakish, Breakish,
Isle of Skye, Inverness-shire,
IV42 8PY
Tel: 01471 822 850
★★★★ Bed & Breakfast

Tir Alainn Bed & Breakfast
8 Upper Breakish, Isle of Skye,
IV42 8PY
Tel: 01471 822366
★★★★ Bed & Breakfast

BROADFORD, ISLE OF SKYE
Benview
6 Black Park, Broadford,
Isle of Skye, IV49 9DE
Tel: 01471 822445
★★★★ Bed & Breakfast

Berabhaigh Bed & Breakfast
3 Lime Park, Broadford,
Isle of Skye, IV49 9AE
Tel: 01471 822372
★★★★ Bed & Breakfast

Birnam Guest House
Bayview Crescent, Broadford,
Isle of Skye,, IV49 9BD
Tel: 01471 822417
★★★★ Bed & Breakfast

Caberfeidh
1 Lower Harrapool, Broadford,
Isle of Skye, IV49 9AQ
Tel: 01471 822664
★★★ Bed & Breakfast

Clisham
Heaste Road, Broadford,
Isle of Skye, IV49 9AQ
Tel: 01471 822320
★★★★ Bed & Breakfast

Hillview
Black Park, Broadford, Isle of
Skye, Inverness-shire, IV49 9AE
Tel: 01471 822083
★★★★ Bed & Breakfast

Lime Stone Cottage
4 Lime Park, Broadford,
Isle of Skye, IV49 9AE
Tel: 01471 822142
★★★ Bed & Breakfast

Strathgorm
15 Upper Breakish, Broadford,
Isle of Skye, Inverness-shire,
IV42 8PY
Tel: 01471 822508
★★★★ Bed & Breakfast

Tigh A Croisean
4 Black Park, Broadford,
Isle of Skye, IV49 9AE
Tel: 01471 822338
★★★★ Bed & Breakfast

BY BROADFORD, ISLE OF SKYE
Hazelwood Cottage
Heaste, by Broadford, Isle of
Skye, Inverness-shire, IV49 9BN
Tel: 01471 822294
★★★ Bed & Breakfast

CARBOST, ISLE OF SKYE
Drynoch House
Drynoch, Carbost, Isle of Skye,
IV47 8SX
Tel: 01478 640441
★★★ Bed & Breakfast

Langal B&B
9 Carbostmor, Carbost,
Isle of Skye, IV47 8ST
Tel: 01478 640 409
★★★ Bed & Breakfast

BY CARBOST, ISLE OF SKYE
Crossal House
Drynoch, Isle of Skye,
Inverness-shire, IV47 8SP
Tel: 01478 640745
★★★ Bed & Breakfast

COLBOST, BY DUNVEGAN
Three Chimneys
Colbost, by Dunvegan,
Isle of Skye, IV55 8ZT
Tel: 01470 511258
★★★★★
Restaurant with Rooms

DUNVEGAN, ISLE OF SKYE
Ardmorn
Roskhill, Dunvegan,
Isle of Skye, IV55 8ZD
Tel: 01470 521354
★★★★ Bed & Breakfast

Sea View
3 Here Bost, Dunvegan, Isle of
Skye, Inverness-shire, IV55 8GZ
Tel: 01470 521705
★★★ Bed & Breakfast

Silverdale Guest House
14 Skinidin, Dunvegan,
Isle of Skye, IV55 8ZS
Tel: 01470 521251
★★★★ Bed & Breakfast

Uiginish Farmhouse
Uiginish Farm, Dunvegan, Isle of
Skye, Inverness-shire, IV55 8ZR
Tel: 01470 521431
★★★ Bed & Breakfast

ELGOL, ISLE OF SKYE

Rowan Cottage
9 Glasnakille, nr Elgol,
Isle of Skye, IV49 9BQ
Tel: 01471 866287
★★★★ Bed & Breakfast

GLENDALE, ISLE OF SKYE

Clach Ghlas
Lower Milovaig, Glendale,
Isle of Skye, IV55 8NR
Tel: 01470 511205
★★★★★ Bed & Breakfast

GLENHINNISDALE, ISLE OF SKYE

Cnoc Preasach
2 Peinlich, Glenhinnisdale,
by Portree, Isle of Skye,
IV51 9UY
Tel: 01470 542406
★★★ Bed & Breakfast

HARRAPOOL, BROADFORD, ISLE OF SKYE

Braigh A' Roid
Heaste Road, Harrapool,
Broadford, Inverness-shire,
IV49 9AQ
Tel: 01471 820221
★★★★ Bed & Breakfast

KILMUIR, ISLE OF SKYE

Kilmuir House
Kilmuir, Uig, Isle of Skye,
Inverness-shire, IV51 9UB
Tel: 01470 542262
★★★ Bed & Breakfast

KYLEAKIN, ISLE OF SKYE

Blairdhu House
Old Kyle Farm Road, Kyleakin,
Isle of Skye, IV41 8PR
Tel: 01599 534760
★★★★ Guest House

Corran Guest House
Kyleakin, Isle of Skye, IV41 8PL
Tel: 01599 534859
★★★★ Guest House

17 Kyleside
Kyleakin, Isle of Skye,
Inverness-shire, IV41 8PW
Tel: 01599 534197
★★★ Bed & Breakfast

Mo-Dhachaidh
Old Kyle Farm Road, Kyleakin,
Isle of Skye, IV41 8PR
Tel: 01599 534724
★★★★ Bed & Breakfast

Witchwood House
Kyleakin, Isle of Skye, IV41 9PL
Tel: 01599 530276
★★★ Bed & Breakfast

PORTNALONG, ISLE OF SKYE

The Seashell B+B
22 Fiscavaig, Isle of Skye,
IV47 8SN
Tel: 01478 640385
★★★★ Bed & Breakfast

PORTREE, ISLE OF SKYE

Almondbank
Viewfield Road, Portree,
Isle of Skye, IV51 9FU
Tel: 01478 612696
★★★★ Guest House

An Acarsaid
Viewfield Road, Portree,
Isle of Skye, IV51 9ES
Tel: 01478 612252
★★★ Bed & Breakfast

Bed & Breakfast
25 Urquhart Place, Portree,
Isle of Skye, Inverness-shire,
IV51 9HJ
Tel: 01478 612374
★★★ Bed & Breakfast

Sandra Campbell B&B
9 Stormyhill Road, Portree,
Isle of Skye, IV51 9DY
Tel: 01478 613332
★★★ Bed & Breakfast

Clynelish
Uigishadder, Portree,
Isle of Skye, IV51 9LN
Tel: 01470 532443
★★★ Bed & Breakfast

Corran House
Kensaleyre, Portree, Isle of
Skye, Inverness-shire, IV51 9XE
Tel: 01470 532311
★★★★ Guest House

Dalriada
Achachork, Portree, Isle of Skye,
IV51 9HT
Tel: 01478 612397
★★★ Bed & Breakfast

Drumorell
15 Fraser Crescent, Portree,
Isle of Skye, IV51 9DS
Tel: 01478 613058
★★★★ Bed & Breakfast

Easdale
Bridge Road, Portree,
Isle of Skye, IV51 9ER
Tel: 01478 613244
★★★ Bed & Breakfast

Eriskay
10 Achnacork, Portree,
Isle of Skye, IV51 9HT
Tel: 01478 611199
★★★ Bed & Breakfast

Feochan
11 Fisherfield, Portree,
Isle of Skye, IV51 9EU
Tel: 01478 613508
★★★ Bed & Breakfast

Foreland
Stormyhill Road, Portree,
Isle of Skye, IV51 9DT
Tel: 01478 612752
★★★ Bed & Breakfast

Furan B&B
26 Bernisdale, North Portree,
Isle of Skye, IV51 9NS
Tel: 01470 532771
★★★ Bed & Breakfast

Grenitote
9 Martin Crescent, Portree,
Isle of Skye, Inverness-shire,
IV51 9DW
Tel: 01478 612808
★★★ Bed & Breakfast

Heathfield
Achachork, Portree, Isle of Skye,
IV51 9HT
Tel: 01478 611125
★★★ Bed & Breakfast

Heronfield
Heron Place, Portree, Isle of
Skye, Inverness-shire, IV51 9GU
Tel: 01478 613050
★★★ Bed & Breakfast

Highfield
Viewfield Road, Portree, Isle of
Skye, Inverness-shire, IV51 9ES
Tel: 01478 612 781
★★★ Bed & Breakfast

Medina
Coolin Hills Gardens, Portree,
Isle of Skye, IV51 9NB
Tel: 01478 612821
★★★★ Bed & Breakfast

Sandgrounder Bed and Breakfast
13 Matheson Place, Portree,
Isle of Skye, IV51 9JA
Tel: 01478 612321
★★★ Bed & Breakfast

Sgiathan Mara
Hill Place, Portree, Isle of Skye,
IV51 9HS
Tel: 01478 612927
★★★ Bed & Breakfast

Stonefield
Oronsay Court, Portree,
Isle of Skye, IV51 9TL
Tel: 01478 611636
★★★ Bed & Breakfast

Torwood
1 Peiness, by Portree,
Isle of Skye, IV51 9LW
Tel: 01470 532479
★★★ Bed & Breakfast

Woodlands
Viewfield Road, Portree, Isle of
Skye, Inverness-shire, IV51 9EU
Tel: 01478 612980
★★★ Bed & Breakfast

BY PORTREE, ISLE OF SKYE

Croit Anna
28 Bernisdale, by Portree,
Isle of Skye, IV51 9NS
★★★ Bed & Breakfast

Cruinn Bheinn
4 Eyre, Snizort, Portree,
Isle of Skye, IV51 9XB
Tel: 01470 532459
★★★★ Bed & Breakfast

SCONSER, ISLE OF SKYE

Loch Aluinn B&B
7 Sconser, Kyle, Isle of Skye,
IV48 8TD
Tel: 01478 650288
★★★★ Bed & Breakfast

SLEAT, ISLE OF SKYE

6 Duisdale Beag
Isle Ornsay, Sleat, Isle of Skye,
Inverness-shire, IV43 8QU
Tel: 01471 833230
★★★ Bed & Breakfast

Toravaig House Hotel & Iona Restaurant
Knock Bay, Sleat, Isle of Skye,
IV44 8RE
Tel: 01471 833231
★★★★ Small Hotel

STAFFIN, ISLE OF SKYE

Gairloch View
3 Digg, Staffin, Isle of Skye,
IV51 9LA
Tel: 01470 562718
★★★ Bed & Breakfast

STRUAN, BY DUNVEGAN, ISLE OF SKYE

The Anchorage
9 Eabost West, Struan, Isle of
Skye, Inverness-shire, IV56 8FE
Tel: 01470 572206
★★★ Bed & Breakfast

Glenside
4 Lower Totarder, Struan,
Isle of Skye, IV56 8FW
Tel: 01470 572253
★★★ Bed & Breakfast

The Old Byre
Ose, Struan, Isle of Skye,
IV56 8FJ
Tel: 01470 572730
★★★ Bed & Breakfast

TREASLANE, ISLE OF SKYE

Hillcroft
2 Treaslane, by Portree,
Isle of Skye, IV51 9NX
Tel: 01470 582 304
★★★ Bed & Breakfast

UIG, ISLE OF SKYE

Ard-Na-Mara
11 Idrigill, Uig, Isle of Skye,
IV51 9XU
Tel: 01470 542281
★★★ Bed & Breakfast

Braigh-Uige
Uig, Isle of Skye, IV51 9YB
Tel: 01470 542228
★★★★ Bed & Breakfast

Cuil Lodge
Cuil, Uig, Isle of Skye, IV51 9YB
Tel: 01470 542216
★★★★ Bed & Breakfast

Ferry Inn Hotel
Uig, Isle of Skye, Inverness-
shire, IV51 9XP
Tel: 01478 611216
★★★ Inn

Harris Cottage
Uig, Isle of Skye,
Inverness-shire, IV51 9XU
Tel: 01470 542268
★ Bed & Breakfast

Laurel Bank
Uig, Portree, Isle of Skye,
IV51 9XP
Tel: 01470 542304
★★★ Bed & Breakfast

Mrs M MacLeod
11 Earlish, Uig, Isle of Skye,
IV51 9XL
Tel: 01470 542319
★★★ Bed & Breakfast

Orasay
14 Idrigill, Uig, Isle of Skye,
IV51 9XU
Tel: 01470 542316
★★★ Bed & Breakfast

Suainaval
3 Cradhiastadh, Uig,
Isle of Lewis, HS2 9JF
Tel: 01851 672386
★★★ Bed & Breakfast

SMITHTON, BY INVERNESS

Stonea
3a Resaurie, Smithton,
by Inverness, IV2 7NH
Tel: 01463 791714
★★ Bed & Breakfast

SPEAN BRIDGE

Achnabobane Farmhouse
Spean Bridge, Inverness-shire,
PH34 4EX
Tel: 01397 712919
★★★ Bed & Breakfast

Coinachan
Gairlochy Road
Spean Bridge, PH34 4EG
Tel: 01397 712 417
★★★ Bed & Breakfast

Distant Hills Guest House
Roy Bridge Road, Spean Bridge,
Inverness-shire, PH34 4EU
Tel: 01397 712452
★★★★ Guest House

Dreamweavers
Mucomir, By Spean Bridge,
Inverness-shire, PH34 4EQ
Tel: 01397 712548
★★★ Bed & Breakfast

Faegour House
Tirindrish, Spean Bridge,
Inverness-shire, PH34 4EU
Tel: 01397 712903
★★★★ Bed & Breakfast

Highbridge
Spean Bridge, Inverness-shire,
PH34 4EX
Tel: 01397 712493
★★★ Bed & Breakfast

Mahaar
Corriechoillie Road, Spean
Bridge, Inverness-shire,
PH34 4EP
Tel: 01397 712365
★★★ Bed & Breakfast

Marlaw
3 Lodge Gardens, Spean Bridge,
Inverness-shire, PH34 4EN
Tel: 01397 712603
★★★ Bed & Breakfast

Riverside
1 Lodge Gardens, Spean Bridge,
Inverness-shire, PH34 4EN
Tel: 01397 712702
★★★ Bed & Breakfast

Riverside House
Invergloy, by Spean Bridge,
Inverness-shire, PH34 4DY
Tel: 01397 712684
★★★★ Bed & Breakfast

Spean Lodge
Spean Bridge, Inverness-shire,
PH34 4EP
Tel: 01397 712004
★★★★ Bed & Breakfast

STRATHNAIRN

The Old Parsonage
Croachy, Strathnairn,
Inverness-shire, IV2 6UE
Tel: 01808 521441
★★★★ Bed & Breakfast

STRATHPEFFER

Birch Lodge
Strathpeffer, Ross-shire,
IV14 9BA
Tel: 01997 420118
★★★ Bed & Breakfast

Craigvar
The Square, Strathpeffer,
Ross-shire, IV14 9DL
Tel: 01997 421622
★★★★ Bed & Breakfast

Dunraven Lodge
Golf Course Road, Strathpeffer,
Ross-shire, IV14 9AS
Tel: 01997 421210
★★★★ Bed & Breakfast

Garden House Guest House
Garden House Brae,
Strathpeffer, Ross-shire,
IV14 9BJ
Tel: 01997 421242
★★★ Guest House

Linnmhor
Park Road, Strathpeffer,
Ross-shire, IV14 9BP
Tel: 01997 423357
★★★ Bed & Breakfast

White Lodge
The Square, Strathpeffer,
Ross-shire, IV14 9AL
Tel: 01997 421730
★★★★ Bed & Breakfast

STRATHY POINT

Sharvedda
Strathy Point, by Thurso,
Sutherland, KW14 7RY
Tel: 01641 541311
★★★★ Bed & Breakfast

STRONTIAN

Creag Ard House
5 Longrigg Road, Strontian,
Argyll, PH36 4HY
Tel: 01967 402012
★★★ Bed & Breakfast

Heatherbank
Upper Scotstown, Strontian,
Argyll, PH36 4JB
Tel: 01967 402201
★★★ Bed & Breakfast

Struan
19 Anaheilt, Strontian,
Acharacle, Argyll, PH36 4JA
Tel: 01967 402057
★★★ Bed & Breakfast

TAIN
Carringtons
Morangie Road, Tain,
Ross-shire, IV19 1PY
Tel: 01862 892635
★★★ Bed & Breakfast

Morangie Bed & Breakfast
Morangie Road, Tain,
Ross-shire, IV19 1PY
Tel: 01862 893855
★★★ Bed & Breakfast

TALMINE
Cloisters
Church Holme, Talmine,
Sutherland, IV27 4YP
Tel: 01847 601286
★★★★ Bed & Breakfast

THURSO
Annandale (Mrs D Thomson)
2 Rendel Govan Road, Thurso,
Caithness, KW14 7EP
Tel: 01847 893942
★★★★ Bed & Breakfast

9 Couper Street
Thurso, Caithness, KW14 8AR
Tel: 01847 894529
★★ Bed & Breakfast

1 Granville Crescent
Thurso, Caithness, KW14 7NP
Tel: 01847 892993
★★★★ Bed & Breakfast

Murray House
Mrs Angela Williamson,
1 Campbell Street, Thurso,
KW14 7HD
Tel: 01847 895759
★★★ Bed & Breakfast

3 Ravenshill Road
Thurso, Caithness, KW14 7PX
Tel: 01847 894801
★★ Bed & Breakfast

Seaview Farm
Hill of Forss, Thurso, Caithness,
KW14 7XQ
Tel: 01847 892315
★★ Bed & Breakfast

Skara
Dixonfield, Thurso, Caithness,
KW14 8YN
Tel: 01847 890062
★★★ Bed & Breakfast

Straven
Haimer, Thurso, Caithness,
KW14 8YN
Tel: 01847 893850
★★★ Bed & Breakfast

BY THURSO
The Sheiling
Melvich, Thurso, Caithness,
KW14 7YJ
Tel: 01641 531256
★★★★★ Bed & Breakfast

TOMACHARICH
Woodside
Tomacharich, Fort William,
Inverness-shire, PH33 6SP
Tel: 01397 705897
★★★ Bed & Breakfast

TONGUE
77 Dalcharn
Tongue, Lairg, Sutherland,
IV27 4XU
Tel: 01847 611251
★★ Bed & Breakfast

Rhian Cottage Guest House
Tongue, Sutherland, IV27 4XJ
Tel: 01847 611257
★★★ Bed & Breakfast

TORRIDON
Ben Damph Inn
Torridon, by Achnasheen,
Wester Ross, IV22 2EY
Tel: 01445 791242
★★★ Lodge

ULLAPOOL
Ardvreck House
Morefield Brae, Ullapool,
IV26 2TH
Tel: 01854 612028
★★★★ Guest House

Broombank Bungalow
4 Castle Terrace, Ullapool, Ross-shire, IV26 2XD
Tel: 01854 612247
★★★ Bed & Breakfast

Broomvale
26 Market Street, Ullapool,
Ross-shire, IV26 2XE
Tel: 01854 612559
★★★ Bed & Breakfast

Penny Browne
3 Castle Terrace, Ullapool,
Wester Ross, IV26 2XD
Tel: 01854 612409
★★★ Bed & Breakfast

Dromnan Guest House
Garve Road, Ullapool,
Ross-shire, IV26 2SX
Tel: 01854 612333
★★★★ Guest House

Essex Cottage
West Terrace, Ullapool,
Ross-shire, IV26 2UU
Tel: 01854 612663
★★ Bed & Breakfast

Hillview
1 Vyner Place, Ullapool,
Ross-shire, IV26 2XR
Tel: 01854 612700
★★★ Bed & Breakfast

Mrs J Macrae
3 Vyner Place, Ullapool,
Ross-shire, IV26 2XR
Tel: 01854 612023
★★★★ Bed & Breakfast

Oakworth
Riverside Terrace, Ullapool,
Ross-shire, IV26 2TE
Tel: 01854 612290
★★★ Bed & Breakfast

Point Cottage Guest House
22 West Shore Street, Ullapool,
Ross-shire, IV26 2UR
Tel: 01854 612494
★★★★ Guest House

Torran
Loggie, Lochbroom, Ullapool,
Ross-shire, IV23 2SG
Tel: 01854 655227
★★★ Bed & Breakfast

NR ULLAPOOL
Braemore Square Country House
Braemore Square, Loch Broom,
Wester Ross, IV23 2RX
Tel: 01854 655357
★★★★ Bed & Breakfast

WICK
Bayview
14 Port Dunbar, Wick, Caithness,
KW1 4JJ
Tel: 01955 604054
★★ Bed & Breakfast

Belhaven
13 Portdunbar, Wick, Caithness,
KW1 4JJ
Tel: 01955 603411
★★★ Bed & Breakfast

The Clachan
13 Randolph Place, South Road,
Wick, Caithness, KW1 5NJ
Tel: 01955 605384
★★★★ Bed & Breakfast

Seaview Guest House
14 Scalesburn, Wick, Caithness,
KW1 4JH
Tel: 01955 602735
★★★ Bed & Breakfast

Wellington Guest House
41-43 High Street, Wick,
Caithness, KW1 4BS
Tel: 01955 603287
★★★ Guest House

OUTER ISLANDS
Outer Hebrides, Orkney, Shetland

CASTLEBAY, ISLE OF BARRA
Faire Mhaoldonaich
Nask, Castlebay, Barra,
Western Isles, HS9 5XN
Tel: 01871 810441
★★★ Bed & Breakfast

Gearadhmor
123 Craigston, Castlebay,
Isle of Barra, HS9 5XS
Tel: 01871 810688
★★★ Bed & Breakfast

Ocean View
78 Borve, Castlebay,
Isle of Barra, HS9 5XR
Tel: 01871 810590
★★★ Bed & Breakfast

Orosay
170/2 Earsary, Castlebay,
Isle of Barra, HS9 5UR
Tel: 01871 810564
★★★ Bed & Breakfast

Ravenscroft
Nask, Castlebay, Barra,
Outer Hebrides, HS9 5YN
Tel: 08714 574
★★★ Bed & Breakfast

Tigh-Na-Mara
Castlebay, Isle of Barra,
HS9 5XD
Tel: 01871 810304
★★★ Bed & Breakfast

NORTHBAY, ISLE OF BARRA
Airds
244 Bruernish, Northbay,
Isle of Barra
Tel: 01871 890720
★★★ Bed & Breakfast

Aros Cottage
190 Buaile-nam-Bodach, North
Bay, Isle of Barra, HS9 5UT
Tel: 01871 890355
★★★ Bed & Breakfast

Northbay House
Balnabodach, Isle of Barra,
Outer Hebrides, HS9 5UT
Tel: 01871 890255
★★★★ Bed & Breakfast

BENBECULA, ISLE OF
Creag Liath
15 Griminish, Benbecula,
Western Isles, HS7 5QA
Tel: 01870 602992
★★★★ Bed & Breakfast

LINICLATE,
ISLE OF BENBECULA
Bainbhidh
9 Lionacleit, Benbecula,
Western Isles, HS7 5PY
Tel: 01870 602532
★★★ Bed & Breakfast

Hestimul
21 Liniclate, Benbecula,
South Uist, HS7 5PJ
Tel: 01870 602033
★★★★ Bed & Breakfast

CLUER, ISLE OF HARRIS
Mount Cameron
2 Cluer, Isle of Harris, HS3 3EP
Tel: 01859 530356
★★★★ Bed & Breakfast

KENDEBIG, BY TARBERT,
ISLE OF HARRIS
Langracleit
Kendebig, Tarbert, Harris,
Western Isles, HS3 3HQ
Tel: 01859 502413
★★★ Bed & Breakfast

KYLES HARRIS,
ISLE OF HARRIS
Dal-Na-Mara
Isle of Scalpay, Harris,
Western Isles, HS4 3XZ
Tel: 01859 540206
★★★ Bed & Breakfast

Dunvegan View
9 Cluer, Isle of Harris, HS3 3EP
Tel: 01859 530 294
★★★★ Bed & Breakfast

Hirta House
Isle of Scalpay, Harris,
Western Isles, HS4 3XZ
Tel: 01859 540394
★★★★ Bed & Breakfast

LEVERBURGH, ISLE OF HARRIS
3 Borrisdale
Leverburgh, Isle of Harris,
HS5 3UE
Tel: 01859 520201
★★★★ Bed & Breakfast

Sgeir na h - Iolaire
12 Strond, Leverburgh,
Isle of Harris, HS5 3UD
Tel: 01859 520 259
★★★ Bed & Breakfast

Sorrel Cottage
2 Glen, Leverburgh, Isle of
Harris, Western Isles, HS5 3TY
Tel: 01859 520319
★★ Bed & Breakfast

SCALPAY, ISLE OF
Bridgeside
Bayhead, Scalpay, Isle of Harris,
HS4 3XY
Tel: 01859 540 282
★★★★ Bed & Breakfast

New Haven
15 Scalpay, Isle of Harris,
Western Isles, HS4 3XZ
Tel: 01859 540325
★★★★ Bed & Breakfast

SEILEBOST, ISLE OF HARRIS
Beul-na-Mara Bed and
Breakfast
12 Seilebost, Isle of Harris,
Western Isles, HS3 3HP
Tel: 01859 550205
★★★★ Bed & Breakfast

14 Seilebost
Harris, Western Isles, HS3 3HP
Tel: 01859 550233
★★★★ Bed & Breakfast

STROND, ISLE OF HARRIS
Carminish House
1A Strond, Isle of Harris,
HS5 3UB
Tel: 01859 520400
★★★ Bed & Breakfast

TARBERT, ISLE OF HARRIS
Avalon
12 West Side, Tarbert, Harris,
Western Isles, HS3 3BG
Tel: 01859 502334
★★★★ Bed & Breakfast

Ceol Na Mara Guest House
7 Direclete, Tarbert, Isle of
Harris, HS3 3DP
Tel: 01859 502464
★★★★ Bed & Breakfast

Hill Crest
Tarbert, Isle of Harris, HS3 3AH
Tel: 01859 502119
★★★★ Bed & Breakfast

Skyeview
1 Scott Road, Tarbert,
Isle of Harris, HS3 3DL
Tel: 01859 502095
★★ Bed & Breakfast

ACHMORE
Ryancroft
10 Achmore, Isle of Lewis,
HS2 9DU
Tel: 01851 860334
★★ Bed & Breakfast

AIGNISH, POINT,
ISLE OF LEWIS
Ceol-Na-Mara
1a, Aignish, Isle of Lewis,
HS2 0PB
Tel: 01851 870339
★★★ Bed & Breakfast

Dolly's B & B
33 Aignish, Point, Lewis,
Western Isles, HS2 0PB
Tel: 01851 870755
★★★ Bed & Breakfast

BACK, ISLE OF LEWIS
Seaside Villa
Back, Isle of Lewis, HS2 0LQ
Tel: 01851 820208
★★★★ Bed & Breakfast

BALALLAN, ISLE OF LEWIS
40 Balallan
Stornoway, Isle of Lewis,
HS2 9PT
Tel: 01851 830326
★★★ Bed & Breakfast

Clearview
44 Balallan, Lochs, Isle of Lewis,
HS2 9PT
Tel: 01851 830472
★★★ Bed & Breakfast

BARVAS, ISLE OF LEWIS
Rockvilla
Barvas, Isle of Lewis, HS2 0QY
Tel: 01851 840286
★★★ Bed & Breakfast

BERNERA, ISLE OF LEWIS
Garymilis
Kirkibost, Bernera, Isle of Lewis,
Outer Hebrides, HS2 9LX
Tel: 01851 612341
★★★ Bed & Breakfast

Kelvindale
17 Tobson, Great Bernera,
HS2 9NA
Tel: 01851 612347
★★★ Bed & Breakfast

CALLANISH, ISLE OF LEWIS
27 Callanish
Callanish, Isle of Lewis, HS2 9DY
Tel: 01851 621392
★★★ Bed & Breakfast

Directory of all VisitScotland Quality Assured Serviced Establishments

CROSSBOST, ISLE OF LEWIS
Penuel
44 Crossbost, North Lochs,
Isle Of Lewis, HS2 9NP
Tel: 01851 860340
★★★ Bed & Breakfast

LAXDALE, ISLE OF LEWIS
Craigard
Newvalley, Stornoway,
Isle of Lewis, HS2 0DW
Tel: 01851 706174
★★★ Bed & Breakfast

16 Guershader
Laxdale, Isle of Lewis, HS2 0DS
Tel: 01851 703463
★★★ Bed & Breakfast

LEURBOST, ISLE OF LEWIS
Glen House
77 Leurbost, Lochs,
Isle of Lewis, HS2 9NU
Tel: 01851 860241
★★★ Bed & Breakfast

LOCHS, ISLE OF LEWIS
10 Laxay (Lacasaigh)
Lochs, Isle of Lewis,
Western Isles, HS2 9PJ
Tel: 01851 830432
★★ Bed & Breakfast

Lochs House
41 School Hill, Ranish, Lochs,
Isle of Lewis, HS2 9NW
Tel: 01851 860514
★★ Bed & Breakfast

MARVIG, ISLE OF LEWIS
Planasker Old School
Marvig, South Lochs,
Isle of Lewis, HS2 9QP
Tel: 01851 880476
★★★★ Bed & Breakfast

NEWMARKET, ISLE OF LEWIS
Lathamor
Bakers Road, Stornoway, Lewis,
Western Isles, HS2 0EA
Tel: 01851 706093
★★★ Bed & Breakfast

PORT OF NESS, ISLE OF LEWIS
The Cross Inn
Cross Ness, Lewis,
Western Isles, HS2 0SN
Tel: 01851 810152
★★★ Inn

Tom Gorm
40 Cross Skigersta Road, Port of
Ness, Isle of Lewis, HS2 0TQ
Tel: 01851 810661
★★★★ Bed & Breakfast

**SOUTH SHAWBOST,
ISLE OF LEWIS**
42 South Shawbost
Shawbost, Isle of Lewis,
HS2 9BS
Tel: 01851 710342
★★★ Bed & Breakfast

STORNOWAY, ISLE OF LEWIS
Ardmor
29 Urquhart Gardens,
Stornoway, Isle of Lewis,
HS1 2TX
Tel: 01851 702796
★★★ Bed & Breakfast

11 Columbia Place
Stornoway, Lewis, Western Isles,
HS1 2TN
Tel: 01851 704194
★★★ Bed & Breakfast

The Croft House
6A Perceval Road, Stornoway,
Isle of Lewis, HS1 2UG
Tel: 01851 701889
★★ Bed & Breakfast

Dunroamin
18 Plantation Road, Stornoway,
Isle of Lewis, HS1 2JS
Tel: 01851 704578
★★★ Bed & Breakfast

Fernlea
9 Matheson Road, Stornoway,
Isle of Lewis, HS1 2NQ
Tel: 01851 702125
★★★★ Bed & Breakfast

Gledfield
5 Balallan, Isle of Lewis,
Western Isles, HS2 9PN
Tel: 01851 830233
★★★ Bed & Breakfast

Heather View
55 North Galson, Isle of Lewis,
HS2 0SJ
Tel: 01851 850781
★★★ Bed & Breakfast

31 Jamieson Drive
Stornoway, Isle of Lewis,
HS1 2LE
Tel: 01851 704122
★★ Bed & Breakfast

Kildun
14 Goathill Road, Stornoway,
Isle of Lewis, Western Isles,
HS1 2NL
Tel: 01851 703247
★★★ Bed & Breakfast

26 Newton Street
Stornoway, Isle of Lewis,
HS1 2RE
Tel: 01851 702824
★★ Bed & Breakfast

Primrose Villa
31 Lewis Street, Stornoway,
Lewis, Western Isles, HS1 2JL
Tel: 01851 703387
★★ Bed & Breakfast

27 Springfield Road
Stornoway, Isle of Lewis,
HS1 2PS
Tel: 01851 703254
★★★ Bed & Breakfast

Sula Sgeir
6A Sand Street, Stornoway,
Isle of Lewis, HS1 2UE
Tel: 01851 705893
★★ Bed & Breakfast

Westwinds
34 Newton Street, Stornoway,
Lewis, Western Isles, HS1 2RW
Tel: 01851 703408
★★ Bed & Breakfast

**NR STORNOWAY,
ISLE OF LEWIS**

TIMSGARRY, ISLE OF LEWIS
Bonaventure
Aird Uig, Timsgarry,
Isle of Lewis, HS2 9JA
Tel: 01851 672474
★★ Restaurant with Rooms

TONG, ISLE OF LEWIS
Kearnaval
10 Tong, Isle of Lewis, HS2 0HS
Tel: 01851 702853
★★ Bed & Breakfast

BAYHEAD, NORTH UIST
Lapwings
Bayhead, Isle of North Uist,
HS6 5EB
Tel: 01876 510736
★★★★ Bed & Breakfast

Old Shop House
Bayhead, North Uist,
Western Isles, HS6 5DS
Tel: 01876 510395
★★★ Bed & Breakfast

CARINISH, NORTH UIST
Bonnie View
19 Carinish, North Uist,
Western Isles, HS6 5EJ
Tel: 01876 580211
★★★★ Bed & Breakfast

Carinish Inn
Carinish, Lochmaddy,
Isle of North Uist, HS6 5EJ
Tel: 01876 580673
★★★ Inn

GRIMSAY, NORTH UIST
Ardnastruban
Grimsay, North Uist, HS6 5HT
★★★★ Bed & Breakfast

Glendale
7 Kallin, Grimsay, N Uist,
Outer Hebrides, HS6 5HY
0870 602029
★★★★ Bed & Breakfast

Shivinish
Scotvein, Grimsay, North Uist,
HS6 5JA
Tel: 01870 602481
★★★ Bed & Breakfast

HOUGHARRY, NORTH UIST

Sgeir Ruadh
Hougharry, Lochmaddy, North Uist, Western Isles, HS6 5DL
Tel: 01876 510312
★★★ Bed & Breakfast

LOCHMADDY, NORTH UIST

The Old Courthouse
Lochmaddy, North Uist, HS6 5AE
Tel: 01876 500358
★★ Bed & Breakfast

Orisaigh
2 Ahmore, Lochmaddy, North Uist, HS6 5BW
Tel: 01876 560300
★★★ Bed & Breakfast

Redburn House
Lochmaddy, Isle of North Uist, Western Isles, HS6 5AA
Tel: 01876 500301
★★★ Bed & Breakfast

Rushlee House
Lochmaddy, North Uist, Western Isles, HS6 5AE
Tel: 01876 500274
★★★★ Bed & Breakfast

SOLLAS, NORTH UIST

Sheillaidh
8 Sollas, Lochmaddy, North Uist, HS6 5BS
Tel: 01876 560332
★★★ Bed & Breakfast

Struan House
Sollas, North Uist, Western Isles, HS6 5BX
Tel: 01876 560282
★★★★ Bed & Breakfast

BIRSAY, ORKNEY

Choin
Birsay, Orkney, KW17 2ND
Tel: 01856 721488
★★★★ Bed & Breakfast

Linkshouse
Birsay, Orkney, KW17 2LX
Tel: 01856 721221
★★★★ Bed & Breakfast

BURRAY, ORKNEY

Ankersted
Burray, Orkney, KW17 2SS
Tel: 01856 731217
★★★ Bed & Breakfast

Waaness
Burray, Orkney, KW17 2SX
Tel: 01856 731294
★★★★ Bed & Breakfast

FINSTOWN, ORKNEY

Linnadale
Heddle Road, Finstown, Orkney, KW17 2EG
Tel: 01856 761300
★★★★ Bed & Breakfast

Lynwood
Maitland Place, Finstown, Orkney, KW17 2EQ
Tel: 01856 761786
★★★ Bed & Breakfast

South Quatquoy
Firth, Finstown, Orkney, KW17 2ET
Tel: 01856 761335
★★★ Bed & Breakfast

HARRAY, ORKNEY

Holland House
Harray, Orkney, KW17 2LQ
Tel: 01856 771400
★★★★ Bed & Breakfast

Kenila
Harray, Kirkwall, Orkney, KW17 2LE
Tel: 01856 771431
★★★ Bed & Breakfast

Rickla
Harray, Orkney, KW17 2JT
Tel: 01856 761575
★★★★★ Bed & Breakfast

HOY, ORKNEY

Quoydale
Hoy, Stromness, Orkney, KW16 3NJ
Tel: 01856 791315
★★★ Bed & Breakfast

KIRKWALL, ORKNEY

Arundel
Inganis Road, Kirkwall, Orkney, KW15 1SP
Tel: 01856 873148
★★★★ Bed & Breakfast

Bellavista
Carness Road, Kirkwall, Orkney, KW15 1UE
Tel: 01856 872306
★★★ Bed & Breakfast

Bon Accord
New Scapa Road, Kirkwall, Orkney, KW15 1BT
Tel: 01856 873034
★★★ Bed & Breakfast

Brown's B&B, Heatherlea
Weyland Terrace, Kirkwall, Orkney Isles, KW15 1LS
Tel: 01856 873789
★★★ Bed & Breakfast

Crossford
Heathery Loan, St Ola, Kirkwall, Orkney, KW15 1SY
Tel: 01856 876142
★★★ Bed & Breakfast

Fairhaven
Ropewalk, Kirkwall, Orkney, KW15 1PX
Tel: 01856 874829
★★ Bed & Breakfast

Lerona
Cromwell Crescent, Kirkwall, Orkney, KW15 1LW
Tel: 01856 874538
★★★ Bed & Breakfast

1 Papdale Close
Kirkwall, Orkney, KW15 1QP
Tel: 01856 874201
★★★ Bed & Breakfast

Peter McKinlay B&B
13 Palace Road, Kirkwall, Orkney, KW15 1PA
Tel: 01856 872249
★★★ Bed & Breakfast

4 Seasons
Carness Road, Kirkwall, Orkney, KW15 1UE
Tel: 01856 875514
★★★★ Bed & Breakfast

ORPHIR, ORKNEY

Foin Haven
Germiston Road, Orphir, Stromness, Orkney, KW16 3HD
Tel: 01856 811249
★★★ Bed & Breakfast

Houton Bay Lodge
Houton Bay, Orphir, Scapa Flow, Orkney, KW17 2RD
Tel: 01856 811320
★★★★ Bed & Breakfast

The Noust
Orphir, Orkney, KW17 2RB
Tel: 01856 811348
★★★ Bed & Breakfast

Westrow Lodge
Orphir, Orkney, KW17 2RD
Tel: 01856 811360
★★★★ Bed & Breakfast

PAPA WESTRAY, ORKNEY

School Place
Papa Westray, Orkney, KW17 2BU
Tel: 01857 644268
★★ Bed & Breakfast

QUOYLOO, SANDWICK, ORKNEY

Hyval Farm B&B
North Dyke Road, Quoyloo, Orkney, KW16 3LS
Tel: 01856 841522
★★★ Bed & Breakfast

RENDALL, ORKNEY

Jorvik
Rendall, Orkney, KW17 2HF
Tel: 01856 751422
★★★★ Bed & Breakfast

Newark
Rendall, Orkney, KW17 2HF
Tel: 01856 751362
★★★ Bed & Breakfast

Directory of all VisitScotland Quality Assured Serviced Establishments

ROUSAY, ORKNEY

Taversoe Hotel
Frotoft, Rousay, Orkney,
KW17 2PT
Tel: 01856 821325
★★★ Inn

ST MARGARET'S HOPE, ORKNEY

The Creel Restaurant & Rooms
Front Road, St Margaret's Hope,
South Ronaldsay, Orkney,
KW17 2SL
Tel: 01856 831311
★★★★
Restaurant with Rooms

Roeberry House
Sounds of Wright Beach,
St Margaret's Hope,, South
Ronaldsay, Okney, KW17 2TW
Tel: 01856 831228
Awaiting Inspection

ST MARY'S HOLM, ORKNEY

Commodore Chalets
St Mary's, Holm, Orkney,
KW17 2RU
Tel: 01856 781319
★★ Lodge

ST OLA, ORKNEY

The Shambles
Foveran, St Ola, Orkney,
KW15 1SF
Tel: 01856 870 224
★★★★ Bed & Breakfast

SANDAY, ORKNEY

The Belsair
Kettletoft, Sanday, Orkney,
KW17 2BJ
Tel: 01857 600206
★★ Inn

Kettletoft Hotel
Sanday, Orkney, KW17 2BT
Tel: 01857 600217
★★ Inn

Ladybank
Sanday, Orkney, KW17 2BL
Tel: 01857 600339
★★★ Bed & Breakfast

SANDWICK, ORKNEY

Dencraigon B&B
Sandwick, Stromness, Orkney,
KW16 3JB
Tel: 01856 841647
★★★ Bed & Breakfast

Netherstove
Quoyloo, Sandwick, Orkney,
KW16 3LS
Tel: 01856 841625
★★★ Bed & Breakfast

SHAPINSAY, ORKNEY

Girnigoe
Shapinsay, Orkney, KW17 2EB
Tel: 01856 711256
★★★★ Bed & Breakfast

Harrolds Garth
Shapinsay, Orkney, KW17 2EA
Tel: 01856 711262
★★★★ Bed & Breakfast

Hilton Farmhouse
Shapinsay, Balfour, Orkney,
KW17 2EA
Tel: 01856 711239
★★★ Bed & Breakfast

SOUTH RONALDSAY, ORKNEY

Shoreside
South Ronaldsay, Orkney,
KW17 2TQ
Tel: 01856 831711
★★★★ Bed & Breakfast

Taftshurie B&B
Grimness, South Ronaldsay,
Orkney, KW17 2TH
Tel: 01856 831323
★★★ Bed & Breakfast

STENNESS, ORKNEY

Mill of Eyrland
Stenness, Orkney, KW16 3HA
Tel: 01856 850136
★★★★ Bed & Breakfast

Ramsquoy Farm
Stenness, Stromness, Orkney,
KW16 3EZ
Tel: 0185685 0316
★★★ Bed & Breakfast

STROMNESS, ORKNEY

Brettobreck Farm
Kirkbister, Stromness, Orkney,
KW16 3HU
Tel: 01856 850373
★★★ Bed & Breakfast

Mrs Brown
Burnmouth, Cairston Road,
Stromness, Orkney, KW16 3JS
Tel: 01856 850186
★★ Bed & Breakfast

Ferry Bank
2 North End Road, Stromness,
Orkney, KW16 3AG
Tel: 01856 851250
★★★★ Bed & Breakfast

Ferry Inn
John Street, Stromness, Orkney,
KW16 3AA
Tel: 01856 850280
★★ Inn

Ferry Inn Annex
15 John Street, Stromness,
Orkney, KW16 3AD
Tel: 01856 850 642
★★★ Inn

45 John Street
Stromness, Orkney, KW16 3AD
Tel: 01856 850949
★★ Bed & Breakfast

Lindisfarne
Stromness, Orkney, KW16 3LL
Tel: 01856 850 828
★★★ Bed & Breakfast

Olnadale
Innertown, Stromness, Orkney,
KW16 3JW
Tel: 01856 850418
★★★ Bed & Breakfast

Strowan Lodge
Stenness, Stromness, Orkney,
KW16 3JX
Tel: 01856 850521
★★★ Bed & Breakfast

Thira
Innertown, Stromness, Orkney,
KW16 3JP
Tel: 01856 851181
★★★★ Bed & Breakfast

WESTRAY, ORKNEY

Pierowall Hotel
Westray, Orkney, KW17 2BZ
Tel: 01857 677208
★★★ Inn

BRIDGE OF WALLS, SHETLAND

Pomona
Gruting, Bridge of Walls,
Shetland, ZE2 9NR
Tel: 01595 810438
★★ Bed & Breakfast

BURRAVOE, YELL, SHETLAND

Hillhead
Burravoe, Yell, Shetland,
ZE2 9BA
Tel: 01957722 274
★★★ Bed & Breakfast

CUNNINGSBURGH, SHETLAND

Windrush
Cunningsburgh, Shetland,
ZE2 9HE
Tel: 01950 477408
★★★ Bed & Breakfast

FETLAR, ISLE OF, SHETLAND

Gord Bed and Breakfast
Houbie, Fetlar, Shetland,
ZE2 9DJ
Tel: 01957 733227
★★★★ Bed & Breakfast

FOULA, ISLAND OF, SHETLAND

Leraback
Island of Foula, Shetland,
ZE2 9PN
Tel: 01595 753226
★ Bed & Breakfast

GULBERWICK, SHETLAND

Virdafjell
Shurton Brae, Gulberwick,
Shetland, ZE2 9TX
Tel: 01595 694336
★★★★ Bed & Breakfast

HILLSWICK, NORTH MAINLAND, SHETLAND

Almara
Upper Urafirth, Hillswick,
Shetland, ZE2 9RH
Tel: 01806 503261
★★★★ Bed & Breakfast

LERWICK, SHETLAND

Carradale Guest House
36 King Harald Street, Lerwick,
Shetland, ZE1 0EQ
Tel: 01595 692251
★★★ Bed & Breakfast

Cee Aa
133 North Road, Lerwick,
Shetland, ZE1 0PR
Tel: 01595 693362
★★★ Bed & Breakfast

Kumalang Guest House
89 St Olaf Street, Lerwick,
Shetland, ZE1 0ES
Tel: 01595 695731
★★★ Bed & Breakfast

Roseville Bed & Breakfast
95 King Harald Street, Lerwick,
Shetland, ZE1 0ER
Tel: 01595 697128
★★★ Bed & Breakfast

Seafield Farm
Lerwick, Shetland, ZE1 0RN
Tel: 01595 69853
★★★ Bed & Breakfast

Staneybrae B&B
Dunrossness, Shetland, ZE2 9JG
Tel: 01950 460734
★★★ Bed & Breakfast

NORTH MAINLAND, SHETLAND
Westayre B&B
Muckle Roe, Brae, Shetland,
ZE2 9QW
Tel: 01806 522368
★★★★ Bed & Breakfast

OUT SKERRIES, SHETLAND
Rocklea
Out Skerries, Shetland, ZE2 9AR
Tel: 01806 515228
★★★ Bed & Breakfast

SCALLOWAY, SHETLAND
Broch House B&B
Upper Scalloway, Scalloway,
Shetland, ZE1 0UP
Tel: 01595 880051
★★★ Bed & Breakfast

Windward
Port Arthur, Scalloway,
Shetland, ZE1 0UN
Tel: 01595 880769
★★★ Bed & Breakfast

SCOUSBURGH, SHETLAND
Setterbrae
Spiggie, Nr Scousburgh,
Shetland, ZE2 9JE
Tel: 01950 460468
★★★★ Bed & Breakfast

Wildrig
Scousburgh, Shetland, ZE2 9JE
Tel: 01950 460373
★★★ Bed & Breakfast

UNST, ISLAND OF, SHETLAND
Clingera Guest House
Baltasound, Unst, Shetland,
ZE2 9DT
Tel: 0195781 579
★★ Bed & Breakfast

Gerratoun
Haroldswick, Unst, Shetland,
ZE2 9EF
Tel: 01957 711323
★★ Bed & Breakfast

Prestegaard
Uyeasound, Unst, Shetland,
ZE2 9DL
Tel: 01957 755234
★★★ Bed & Breakfast

VIDLIN
Hamnavoe
Lunnaness, Vidlin, Shetland,
ZE2 9QF
Tel: 01806 577328
★★ Bed & Breakfast

Lunna House
Lunna, Vidlin, Shetland,
ZE2 9QF
Tel: 01806 577311
★★★ Bed & Breakfast

WALLS
Skeoverick
Bruna-Twatt, Walls, Shetland,
ZE2 9PJ
Tel: 01595 809349
★★★ Bed & Breakfast

WEST BURRAFIRTH, SHETLAND
Snaraness House
West Burrafirth, Bridge of Walls,
Shetland, ZE2 9NT
Tel: 01595 809375
★★★ Bed & Breakfast

WHITENESS, SHETLAND
The Westings Inn
The Westings, Wormadale,
Whiteness, Shetland, ZE2 9LJ
Tel: 01595 840242
★★★ Inn

GARRYHALLIE, SOUTH UIST
Clanranald
247/8 Garayhallie,
Lochboisdale, South Uist,
Western Isles, HS8 5SX
Tel: 01878 700 263
★★★★ Bed & Breakfast

The Shieling
238 Garryhallie, Lochboisdale,
South Uist, Western Isles,
HS8 5SX
Tel: 01878 700504
★★★★ Bed & Breakfast

GROGARRY, SOUTH UIST
Kinloch
Grogarry, Isle Of South Uist,
HS8 5RR
Tel: 01870 620316
★★★ Bed & Breakfast

Tigh an Droma
Drimore Farm, Grogarry, South
Uist, Western Isles, HS8 5RR
Tel: 01870 620292
★★★ Bed & Breakfast

KILPHEDAR, SOUTH UIST
Ard na Mara
Kilpheder, South Uist,
Western Isles, HS8 5TB
Tel: 01878 700452
★★★ Bed & Breakfast

KILPHEDER, SOUTH UIST
Bulard
289 Kilpheder, South Uist,
Western Isles, HS8 5TB
Tel: 01878 700425
★★★★ Bed & Breakfast

LOCHBOISDALE, SOUTH UIST
Kilchoan
445 Lochboisdale, South Uist,
Western Isles, HS8 5TN
Tel: 01878 700517
★★★ Bed & Breakfast

363 Leth Meadhanach
South Boisdale, South Uist,
Western Isles, HS8 5TE
Tel: 01878 700586
★★★ Bed & Breakfast

Lochside Cottage B & B
Lochboisdale, Isle of South Uist,
HS8 5TH
Tel: 01878 700472
★★★ Bed & Breakfast

3 Milton
3, Milton, Loch-Boisdale,
South Uist, HS8 5RY
Tel: 01878 7102254
★★★ Bed & Breakfast

MID YELL
Norwind
Mid Yell, Shetland
Tel: 01957 702312
★★★ Bed & Breakfast

POLLOCHAR, SOUTH UIST
Polochar Inn
Polachar, Kilbride, South Uist,
HS8 5TT
Tel: 01878 700215
★★★ Inn

SMERCLATE, SOUTH UIST
Kiaora
405 North Smerclate,
Lochboisdale, South Uist,
Western Isles, HS8 5TU
Tel: 01878 700382
★★★ Bed & Breakfast

SOUTH BOISDALE, SOUTH UIST
Braeview
3 Bornish, South Uist, HS8 5SA
Tel: 01878 710 227
★★★ Bed & Breakfast

STONEYBRIDGE, SOUTH UIST
Crossroads
Stoneybridge, South Uist,
Western Isles, HS8 5SD
Tel: 01870 620321
★★★ Bed & Breakfast

Taigh Morangie
198 Stoneybridge,
Isle of South Uist, HS8 5SD
Tel: 01870 620396
★★★ Bed & Breakfast

YELL, GUTCHER
Gutcher Post Office
Yell, Shetland, ZE2 9DF
Tel: 01957 744201
★★★ Bed & Breakfast

Index

By location